CULTURAL CLINICAL PSYCHOLOGY

THEORY, RESEARCH, AND PRACTICE

SHAHÉ S. KAZARIAN

DAVID R. EVANS

Editors

New York   Oxford • Oxford University Press   1998

Oxford University Press

Oxford   New York
Athens   Auckland   Bangkok   Bogota   Bombay   Buenos Aires
Calcutta   Cape Town   Dar es Salaam   Delhi   Florence   Hong Kong
Istanbul   Karachi   Kuala Lumpur   Madras   Madrid   Melbourne
Mexico City   Nairobi   Paris   Singapore   Taipei   Tokyo   Toronto   Warsaw

and associated companies in
Berlin   Ibadan

Copyright © 1998 by Oxford University Press, Inc.

Published by Oxford University Press, Inc.
198 Madison Avenue, New York, New York 10016

Oxford is a registered trademark of Oxford University Press

Library of Congress Cataloging-in-Publication Data
Cultural clinical psychology : theory, research, and practice / Shahé
    S. Kazarian and David R. Evans, editors.
      p.   cm.
    Includes bibliographical references and index.
    ISBN 0-19-510945-7; 0-19-510946-5 (pbk.)
    1. Cultural psychiatry.   2. Clinical psychology.   I. Kazarian.
Shahé S., 1945–   .   II. Evans, D. R. (David Richard), 1940–   .
RC455.4.E8C79   1997
616.89—dc21   96-40844

9 8 7 6 5 4 3 2 1
Printed in the United States of America
on acid-free paper

Preface

The purpose of this book is to describe cultural clinical psychology with a view toward providing a meaningful integration of the fields of clinical psychology and cross-cultural psychology. Two interrelated factors provided the impetus for undertaking this project. The first was the experience of the first author in an academic setting in which he designed a graduate course to familiarize students in a clinical psychology program with the role of culture in research, practice, and training in clinical psychology. Efforts to secure an appropriate textbook for the proposed course on the interface between clinical psychology and cross-cultural psychology were compromised by the dearth of comprehensive and conceptually integrated resources on the subject. Resources in clinical psychology, counseling psychology, and cross-cultural psychology were examined. There were several limitations to these resources. The content areas of these books were either too general or too specific. In addition, the available resources failed to provide comprehensive and, more important, integrative treatment of the subject matter of clinical psychology and cultural psychology. The availability of a conceptual model was deemed essential for theory-driven research and for clinical and ethical practice.

The second factor that inspired this project stemmed from our involvement in a variety of clinical settings in the health and mental health fields. We conducted formal and informal reviews and discussions of the cultural identity of clients in hospitals, community health centers, and private-practice settings and of the cultural appropriateness of the services rendered by mental health professionals in general and clinical psychologists in particular. Having confirmed that all of the various professionals and their students were seeing culturally diverse clients, we were of the opinion that more systematic and systemic education and training in the provision of culturally appropriate services are required due to the limited knowledge and familiarity of service providers with cross-cultural models of significant relevance for understanding psychopathology and its day-to-day management. We felt that an integration of clinical psychology and cross-cultural psychology was urgently required. We also felt that the availability of a resource in the form of a book on cultural clinical psychology, a hybrid of clinical and cross-cultural psychology, would be of benefit to clinical psychologists involved in teaching, research, and clinical practice.

An essential requirement for a book on the interface between clinical psychology and cross-cultural psychology is the advancement of a theoretical framework to guide research, training, and practice in cultural clinical psychology. The model will assist practitioners in case formulation, diagnosis, assessment, treatment, program planning, program evaluation, student training and supervision, and clinical research. The equal emphasis on both research and clinical practice is vital and consistent with the scientist-practitioner model of training employed with students in clinical psychology programs.

There were three important considerations in conceptualizing this book. First, it provides a new model, cultural clinical psychology, in which the fields of clinical psychology and cross-cultural psychology are integrated. Currently, there are no books which specifically deal with the topic of culture and clinical psychology. Books on the related topic of culture and health have generally been atheoretical and descriptive. While important, these resources have been based on observations rather than solid empirical studies, have tended to emphasize differences from mainstream cultures rather than similarities, and have provided the potential for generalizations and stereotyping of the cultural groups they have described.

Second, the chapters of this book provide comprehensive and critical reviews of the cultural aspects of theory, research, and practice in a broad range of areas of clinical psychology. The limited available resources on the interface between culture and clinical psychology have tended to focus on particular aspects of the practice (i.e., assessment or psychotherapy) to the neglect of the psychopathology domain of clinical psychology and of comprehensive coverage of the topic. In contrast, this book addresses theoretical, research, and practice issues in relation to the interface between clinical psychology and cultural psychology. In addition to providing an integrative overview of the two domains of psychology, cultural psychology and clinical psychology, the book addresses these domains in the context of major psychopathological conditions (anxiety disorders, eating disorders, depression, substance abuse, and schizophrenic disorders), health (pain and family violence), and special groups (children, refugees, and the Deaf). Of significant importance is the focus on the contribution that clinical psychologists have made in these areas. We have made a deliberate effort to allow our contributors the opportunity to highlight the achievements of clinical psychologists and the areas of expansion that are required.

We feel that a book on cultural clinical psychology is needed and timely. The matrimonial relationship between clinical psychology and cultural psychology is necessary in view of the worldwide phenomenon of pluralism. Sensitivity to culture is becoming a more pressing issue in view of global economic factors, political restructuring, a number of national and international trade agreements, and increased professional concern for cultural issues. These changes are providing fertile ground for intercultural interactions and conflicts. Needless to say, the evolving demographic, economic, social, political, and psychological conditions are providing a significant source of acculturative stress and health-related effects. Psychologists in general, and clinical psychologists in particular, have the responsibility and knowledge base to address such issues, to understand their psychosocial correlates, and to articulate strategies to deal with them effectively. Clinical psychologists also have the responsibility to advance sound research on the role of culture in psychopathology and to promote culturally appropriate clinical training and ethical practice. There continues to be a pressing concern on the part of various cultural groups for the availability of culturally appropriate services from clinical psychologists. Clinical psychologists have been at the forefront in research and training on the psychosocial correlates of health and mental health. Cultural clinical psychology requires a comparable advancement and recognition.

This book is designed for use with senior undergraduate- and graduate-level students in clinical psychology programs. It can be used as a textbook for courses on cultural clinical psychology or as a supplementary resource in other senior-level courses on clinical psychology. The book would be of interest and benefit to all those health practitioners and researchers interested in the cultural aspects of health and mental health. The ultimate aims are the advancement of scientific knowledge, the development of sound professional practice, the amelioration of human suffering, and the promotion of quality of life. It is our hope that this book will contribute to this cause.

London, Ontario S. S. K.
June 1997 D. R. E.

Contents

Contributors   xi

PART I.   Conceptual Framework

  I   Cultural Clinical Psychology   3
    SHAHÉ S. KAZARIAN & DAVID R. EVANS

  2   Acculturation and Health: Theory and Research   39
    J. W. BERRY

PART II.   Practice Issues

  3   Psychological Assessment of People in Diverse Cultures   61
    JAMES N. BUTCHER, ELAHE NEZAMI, & JOHN EXNER

  4   Cultural Aspects of Self-Disclosure and Psychotherapy   106
    SHAKÉ G. TOUKMANIAN & MELISSA C. BROUWERS

PART III.   Health and Mental Health Issues

  5   Culture and Anxiety Disorders   127
    IHSAN AL-ISSA & SHAHIN OUDJI

6   Cultural Aspects of Eating Disorders   152
INGRID C. FEDOROFF & TRACI MCFARLANE

7   Cultural Issues in the Management of Depression   177
AMY S. KAISER, RANDY KATZ, & BRIAN F. SHAW

8   Incorporating Culture into the Treatment of Alcohol Abuse
and Dependence   215
BRUCE BAXTER, RILEY E. HINSON, ANNE-MARIE WALL,
& SHERRY A. MCKEE

9   Cultural Aspects of Understanding People with Schizophrenic
Disorders   246
JEFFREY R. CARTER & RICHARD W. J. NEUFELD

10   Culture and Pain   267
GARY B. ROLLMAN

PART IV.   Groups of Special Interest

11   Culture and Child Psychopathology   289
BARRIE EVANS & BETTY KAMAN LEE

12   Cultural Aspects of Family Violence   316
SHAHÉ S. KAZARIAN & LEVONTY Z. KAZARIAN

13   Biopsychosocial Considerations in Refugee Mental Health   348
KATHY A. WINTER & MARTA Y. YOUNG

14   Cultural Aspects of Deafness   377
CATHY J. CHOVAZ

Index   401

Contributors

Ihsan Al-Issa, Department of Behavioral Sciences, American University of Beirut

Bruce Baxter, Department of Psychology, The University of Western Ontario

J. W. Berry, Psychology Department and School of Rehabilitation, Queen's University

Melissa Brouwers, Department of Psychology, The University of Western Ontario

James N. Butcher, Department of Psychology, University of Minnesota

Jeffrey R. Carter, Department of Psychology, The University of Western Ontario

Cathy J. Chovaz, Department of Psychology, The University of Western Ontario

Barrie Evans, Madame Vanier Children's Services and The University of Western Ontario

David R. Evans, Department of Psychology, The University of Western Ontario

John Exner, Rorschach Workshops, Asheville, North Carolina

Ingrid C. Fedoroff, Department of Psychology, University of Toronto

Riley E. Hinson, Department of Psychology, The University of Western Ontario

Amy S. Kaiser, Department of Psychology, The Toronto Hospital

Randy Katz, Department of Psychology, The Toronto Hospital

Levonty Z. Kazarian, London InterCommunity Health Centre, London, Ontario

Shahé S. Kazarian, Department of Psychology, The University of Western Ontario

Betty Kaman Lee, Department of Psychology, The University of Western Ontario

Traci McFarlane, Department of Psychology, University of Toronto

Sherry A. McKee, Department of Psychology, The University of Western Ontario

Richard W. J. Neufeld, Department of Psychology, The University of Western Ontario

Elahe Nezami, University of Southern California

Shahin Oudji, Department of Educational Psychology, University of Calgary

Gary B. Rollman, Department of Psychology, The University of Western Ontario

Brian F. Shaw, The Hospital for Sick Children, Toronto

Shaké G. Toukmanian, Department of Psychology, York University

Anne-Marie Wall, Department of Psychology, York University

Kathy A. Winter, Department of Psychology, The University of Western Ontario

Marta Y. Young, School of Psychology, University of Ottawa

PART I

CONCEPTUAL FRAMEWORK

1

Cultural Clinical Psychology

SHAHÉ S. KAZARIAN

DAVID R. EVANS

Since the founding of scientific psychology by Wilhelm Wundt at Leipzig in 1879, the contributions of the discipline to culture have been commendable. Psychology has advanced our understanding of behavior, alleviated human suffering, and improved our quality of life. This scientific and professional odyssey, however, has been replete with periods of transition, expansion, schism, growth, consolidation, and maturation. Currently, psychology is ranked fourth on the list of 50 top occupations, and a 64% increase in the membership of the American Psychological Association is anticipated by the year 2005 (Wiggins, 1994).

The focus of this chapter is on the interface between clinical psychology and the psychology of culture. In addition to providing a historical overview of clinical psychology and demonstrating the value its founders placed on the study of culture, we offer reasons for the relative neglect of the psychology of culture in modern clinical psychology. Finally, we propose cultural clinical psychology as a viable integration of culture in the science and practice of clinical psychology. We articulate the benefits of the marriage between cultural psychology and clinical psychology from the perspectives of responsiveness to societal needs and the further advancement of the discipline of psychology nationally and internationally.

CLINICAL PSYCHOLOGY: HISTORICAL OVERVIEW

Historical treatment of psychology has mostly been an American phenomenon (Woody & Robertson, 1988); however, Canadian psychology has begun to receive some attention as well (Wright & Myers, 1982; Dobson & Dobson, 1993). Needless to say, the history of clinical psychology has been closely associated with the discipline of psychology and has had its share of transitions, schism, growth, consolidation, conflict, and maturation. The major historical source of controversy, if not obsession, within clinical psychology has been the issue of whether the training of its members should be in the tradition of science or practice. It is instructive to reflect on the origin of clinical psychology in order to understand more fully the dynamic interplay between the two traditions in training clinical psychologists.

The birth of clinical psychology has been different from that of other professions. For example, psychiatry had its beginnings in clinical institutions (i.e., the asylums); hence, historically psychiatrists were practitioners first. A number of factors provided the impetus for psychiatry to shift its frontiers to university departments in medical schools. These factors included the disparagement of moral treatment due to inflated claims for its effectiveness, the importance of differentiating psychiatry from religion, and advances in 19th-century medicine (Reisman, 1991).

In contrast to psychiatry, the roots of clinical psychology were in academic departments (Hersch, 1969). The practitioner role for psychologists was proposed by Lightner Witmer (1867–1956), a psychologist at the University of Pennsylvania. He spoke of a new profession, which he christened "clinical psychology," in which psychological knowledge and skills would be used for the improvement of quality of life. Witmer founded the first child guidance clinic in the world in 1896. A brief sketch of the major historical developments in the field of clinical psychology since its inception is provided in Table 1.1.

The evolution of clinical psychology has been very much tied to a responsiveness to social, political, and economic forces (Kaswan, 1981; Strickland, 1988). Psychological testing and rehabilitation were major contributions in World War I and in the 1920s in both Canada and the United States. Canadian psychologists benefited from the success of their counterparts in the United States in that the American experience helped expand the role of Canadian psychologists from the laboratory to schools and clinics.

United States government support for the training of clinicians to care for large numbers of World War II veterans had the effect of accelerating the growth of clinical psychology in the United States (Shakow, 1969). Unlike the pre-World War II period, when many clinical psychology activities were with children, World War II provided and legitimized clinical psychology involvement in the assessment and diagnosis of, and psychotherapy with, adults. To ensure their acceptance and recognition, clinical psychologists embraced a training approach that required an empirical scientific base, high academic qualifications, and effective interventions. This scientist-practitioner model (Shakow, 1947) of training for clinical psychologists represented a major historical landmark for the emerging profession. Clinical psychologists were attaining Ph.D. degrees and being trained as both scientists and practitioners (Raimy, 1950).

Endorsement of the scientist-practitioner model (also known as the Boulder Model) and the evolution from the ivory tower to the real world have been a mixed blessing for clinical psychology. While they have provided responsiveness to many large-scale social issues confronting American society, they have also brought constraints and curtailments from both medicine (Hathaway, 1958) and academic psychology (Albee, 1970; Hersch, 1969). Hathaway (1958) reviewed historical approaches that had been taken to address identity issues confronting clinical

Table 1.1. Historical Landmarks in North American Clinical Psychology

1892	Foundation of American Psychological Association (APA)
1896	Foundation of first psychological clinic for handicapped children by Lightner Witmer
1904	Conceptualization of psychology both as a science and a profession
1917	Formation of the independent American Association of Clinical Psychology (AACP)
1919	Rejoining of AACP to APA
1937	Split of AACP from APA, joining of American Association of Applied Psychologists (AAAP)
1939	Foundation of Canadian Psychological Association (CPA)
1945	Division of Clinical Psychology (Division 12) within APA
1947	Establishment of APA committee for development of guidelines for graduate training in clinical psychology
1949	Boulder Conference mandating scientist-practitioner training
1950	Recommendation of doctoral degree for independent practice
1951	Establishment of APA Code of Professional Ethics
1961	First meeting of Psychonomic Science separatist group
1965	Proposal for professional model (Psy.D. programs) by Kenneth Clark
1965	Endorsement of scientist-practitioner model at Couchiching Conference (Canada)
1973	Endorsement of professional model at Vail Conference
1974	Establishment of the Association for the Advancement of Psychology of APA
1983	APA Accreditation Handbook
1984	CPA Accreditation Criteria
1986	Canadian Code of Ethics for Psychologists
1986	Canadian Register of Health Service Providers in Psychology
1989	CPA Practice Guidelines for Providers of Psychological Services
1992	APA Ethical Principles of Psychologists and Code of Conduct
1993	Guidelines for Providers of Psychological Services to Ethnic, Linguistic, and Culturally Diverse Populations
1994	National Conference on Professional Psychology, Mississauga, Canada

psychologists in relation to medicine and other professional bodies. His review included adoption of the doctorate as a professional degree, the teaching of mental testing exclusively to clinical psychology students, major emphasis on research, the creation of psychology department clinics, and the establishment of a clinical psychology subspecialty in psychology.

Despite the strong overall support for the Boulder Model, a number of prominent clinical psychologists pursued an alternate professional model of training so actively that a professional program was established for the first time by Gordon Derner at Adelphi in 1951 (Strickland, 1988). This professional training school provided for some a means of establishing clinical psychology as a profession independent of the constraints of both medicine and academic psychology (Hersch, 1969; Petersen, 1968). Hersch (1969) described the continued support for the creation of psychological service centers administered by psychologists and the establishment of Doctor of Psychology programs (proposed in 1965 by Kenneth Clark) in which greater focus could be placed on professional practice and less on academic training (e.g., elimination of the dissertation and language requirement). The rationale provided for an independent clinical psychology profession, maintenance of the integrity of the profession, and increased responsivity to the needs of the community (Hersch, 1969).

The groups identified for social responsibility by the emerging independent profession were the poor, the meagerly educated, and the mentally retarded (Hersch, 1969). The groups at the center of the "war on poverty" of the 1960s were reviewed by

Havinghurst (1970). He estimated that 15–20% of the American population at the time was socially disadvantaged. Of those, he identified 20 million as English-speaking Caucasians, 8 million as Negroes (his terminology), 2 million as Spanish Americans, 700,000 as Puerto Ricans, and 500,000 as American Indians. Interestingly, he also identified the Japanese and the Chinese as ethnic groups that serve to protect poverty by contributing more to the economic welfare of the host country (Havinghurst, 1970).

It should be noted that since Witmer's initiation of the clinical psychology training program, the introduction of the scientist-practitioner model, and the stamp of approval on the professional model of training at the Vail Conference (Korman, 1974), discussions concerning the training of clinical psychologists and efforts to reconcile the scientist-professional polarities have continued to be a dominant issue in the field. Akin to the identity problem of the parent discipline (Kimble, 1984), clinical psychology continued to experience periodic identity crises (Albee, 1970; Bickman, 1987; Fox, Kovacs, & Graham, 1985; Hathaway, 1958; Hersch, 1969; Korman, 1974; Petersen, 1968, 1976; Rie, 1976; Shakow, 1947, 1976, 1978; Strickland, 1985).

Despite the advent of the professional model of training, the scientist-practitioner model became firmly established by 1965 in the United States, received more than warm reception in Canada (Bernhardt, 1961; Webster, 1967), was well established as the preferred method of training in that country by 1975, and continues to be the dominant approach to the professional training of psychologists in North America (O'Sullivan & Quevillon, 1992; Pryzwanski & Wendt, 1987; Ritchie, Hogan, & Hogan, 1988). The centrality of the scientist-practitioner model in training clinical psychologists was reasserted at the Gainsville Conference in 1991 and the Mississauga Conference in Canada in 1994 (Belar & Perry, 1992; Dobson & King, 1995).

CLINICAL PSYCHOLOGY: DEFINITION

The image of clinical psychologists in North America has evolved over time. In the pre-World War I era, clinical psychologists were referred to as mental testers and abnormal psychologists (Hathaway, 1958), and clinical psychology was defined as the art and technology of dealing with human adjustment. The latter emphasis remained in the years between the wars.

The definition of clinical psychology continued to evolve after World War II. Doll (as cited in Ullman, 1947) defined clinical psychology as "the science and art of employing psychological principles, methods and procedures to promote the welfare of the individual person for the purposes of optimum social adjustment and expression" (p. 173). Shakow (1947) defined clinical psychology as seeking to "acquire systematic knowledge of human personality and to develop principles and methods by which it may use this knowledge to increase the mental well-being of the individual." Shakow (1947) also asserted that the preparation of clinical psychologists required the scientist-practitioner model of training and a combination of applied and theoretical knowledge in the three areas: diagnosis, therapy, and research.

Three decades later, Shakow (1976) also offered the following definition of clinical psychology:

Clinical psychology, a branch of psychology, is a body of knowledge growing out of both correlational and experimental techniques which are based on general, cryptic, psychobiological and psychosocial principles. The skills of assessment and therapy which derive from this knowledge can be used to help persons with behavior disabilities and mental disorders to achieve better adjustment and self-expression. (p. 559)

Half a decade later, the definition of clinical psychology was expanded (Fox, 1982; Fox, Barclay, & Rodgers, 1982) to include devotion "to enhancing the effectiveness of human behavior and human coping skills." Inclusion of general health issues in the scope of science and practice of clinical psychology provided the opportunity for clinical psychologists to use their scientific knowledge base to help people not only with mental and emotional problems but also people with physical health problems and unhealthy life styles (Fox, 1982). As will be discussed later, this new vision for clinical psychology led to the significant growth of its application to human welfare and provided the inspiration to explore new frontiers for application.

The scope of practice for psychologists in Ontario, Canada, reflects yet another potential expansion of the role of clinical psychologists into the domains of prevention and health promotion. The scope of practice reads in part "the prevention and treatment of behavioral and mental disorders and dysfunctions and the maintenance and enhancement of physical, intellectual, emotional, social and interpersonal functioning" (*Psychology Act,* 1991). The codification of such definitions of practice in law heralds an expanding role for clinical psychologists with a broader range of clients.

An alternate approach to defining clinical psychology involves comparison with other mental health professions. The most frequently posed public query in this regard involves the difference between psychologists and psychiatrists. Unfortunately, very few students in clinical psychology or psychiatry are well prepared to adequately cope with such a popular question. One consideration in responding to such a query relates to the differential training provided to clinical psychologists and psychiatrists (Kiesler, 1976). Psychiatrists undergo the 3- or 4-year standard medical school sequence plus a year of internship and a 3-year residency. The residency experience involves primarily patient assessment and treatment under supervision. Psychiatrists receive very little psychology in their medical training. Similarly, formal course work, while varied, tends to be minimal with regard to the theory and science of human behavior. For example, it is rare that resident psychiatrists receive formal exposure to scientific issues associated with normal and abnormal human behavior, advanced statistics, and research methodology. Clinical psychologists, on the other hand, become exposed to a broad study of the theory and science of human behavior for a period of 5 or more years, receive rather standardized and extensive coursework on research design and statistics, complete at least two extensive research projects, and, in addition to fairly extensive practicum work, undergo a year of internship training.

Clinical psychology celebrated its centennial in 1996. Within this short period, clinical psychology has shown tremendous growth in subspecialties, as well as diversity in theoretical and practice orientations (Garfield & Kurtz, 1976; Norcross & Prochaska, 1982; Woody & Robertson, 1988). Areas of subspecialty in clinical psychology include clinical child psychology, geropsychology, clinical neuropsychology, health psychology, and community psychology. In a study by Milan, Montgomery, and Rogers (1994), involving a 7% sample of registrants in the National Register of Health Service Providers in Psychology in 1981, 43% identified their primary theoretical orientation as Eclectic, 15% Psychoanalytic, 10% Interpersonal Relations, 9% Existential-Humanistic, 7% Behavioral, 5% Social Learning, 3% Systems Theory, 3% Rational Emotive-Cognitive, 2% Rogerian, 2% Gestalt, and 1% Reality. By 1989, only three significant changes in these data were observed: fewer selected Existential-Humanistic as their primary theoretical orientation (from 9% to 6%), more identified with Rational Emotive-Cognitive (from 3% to 7%) and Systems Theory (from 3% to 6%). Data from Canada are comparable to those of the United States.

Norcross and Prochaska (1982) reported the variety of activities of clinical psychologists. These included (in order of most time spent in activity) psychotherapy (34.7%), administration (13.4%), diagnosis and assessment (13.2%), teaching (12.0%), clinical supervision (8.5%), research (7.9%), consultation (7.5%), and other (2.9%). Similar results were reported by Watkins, Campbell, Nieberding & Hallmark (1995).

CLINICAL PSYCHOLOGY: CULTURAL NEGLIGENCE

Close examination of the history of psychology in North America supports the hypothesis that cultural issues were an integral part of the thinking of the founders. Among the 15 personality characteristics listed as a guide for recruitment of candidates for clinical psychology, Shakow (1947) included "breadth of cultural background." This requirement referred to exposure (via reading) to a wide range of psychological expression, whether in relation to individuals or cultures. It also implied training exposure to related disciplines, including influence of culture on personality (i.e., lectures on cultural anthropology's contribution to the understanding of personality). A foreign language course (French, German, or other languages) was recommended for inclusion in basic undergraduate training.

The cultural content of psychology was also on the minds of the founders of Canadian psychology. The first professor of abnormal psychology in Canada, J. W. Bridges, was an amateur anthropologist who imbued a cross-cultural orientation in his students (J. W. Berry, personal communication, July 1996). In his presidential address, the fifth president of the Canadian Psychological Association (CPA), Bernhardt (1947), advocated a scientist-practitioner model of training for psychology. "The psychologist is not deserting his laboratory, he is making the world his workshop," he commented (p. 60). Bernhardt (1947) was also explicit about the role of culture in psychological research. Of the list of 10 areas for collaborative research he provided, 3 were explicitly cultural or cross-cultural in nature. Item 2 referred to the need for research on "problems arising from the diversity of cultural grouping in Canada"; item 3 concerned "problems arising from Canada's relations with other nations, the United Nations, the British Empire, the United States, etc."; and item 4 dealt with problems of immigration and the relocation of groups. While these topics were not associated with Canadian clinical psychology, they nevertheless suggested the role and responsibility of the profession in addressing the practical consequences of intercultural contacts within the country and internationally. Cross-cultural psychologists in North America have remained faithful to the tradition of the founders with respect to the value of the study of culture in psychology. In contrast, culture has not occupied a central role in mainstream scientific or professional North American psychology.

Over the past 3 decades, North American psychology has been characterized mainly by the visual impairment of culture-blindness, as it has afforded culture negligible treatment in research and the development of theory. The lack of cultural content in North American psychological theory, research, practice, and training has been asserted consistently (Bernal, 1994a; Bernal & Castro, 1994; Betancourt & Lopez, 1993; Clark, 1987; Graham, 1992; Korchin, 1980; Segall, 1986; Suarez-Balcazar, Durlak, & Smith, 1994; Sue, 1983; Watts, 1992; Yutrzenka, 1995).

Clinical psychology in North America has not received a better overall rating than have North American psychology or other professional training programs in its treatment of culture (Allison, Crawford, Echemendia, Robinson, & Knapp, 1994; Bernal & Padilla, 1982; Quintana & Bernal, 1994). Despite the significant contributions that psychology in general and clinical psychology in particular have made over the years in advancing knowledge and promoting societal welfare, clinical psychology in North America has not assumed a leadership role in embracing the study of culture in psychological theory and research, nor has it responded in a socially responsible manner to the service needs of the pluralistic society of North America. There are a number of indicators to support the assertion that culture has not been adequately embraced in North American clinical psychology. These include the lack of adequate representation of students and faculty from various cultural groups in clinical psychology programs relative to their representation in the general population, the relative absence of cultural content in clinical psychology programs and resources, and inadequacies in meeting psychological service needs of people from diverse cultures.

Cultural Pluralism in North America

Examining cultural pluralism in psychology requires examining cultural pluralism in the general population. Valuable information on the cultural composition of populations is provided in government-sponsored census data, as well as non-government-sponsored surveys. Changes in use of indicators for culture have occurred in census surveys both in the United States and Canada, with race assuming a primary focus in the United States and ethnicity in Canada. Krotki and Reid (1994) listed 10 ethnocultural and language questions used in Canadian censuses since confederation: mother tongue, home language, official languages, place of birth, place of birth of parents, period or year of immigration, citizenship, ethnic origin, aboriginal status, and religion. In the 1996 Canada Census, as in 1951, the world's only official multicultural country allowed race to be a census focus along with ethnicity.

While providing for richness, census data present a number of definitional and methodological limitations (Ponterotto & Casas, 1991), resulting in underreporting or misreporting of certain cultural groups such as Hispanic and Native American populations. The use of nominal indicators of culture poses conceptual difficulties in classifying individuals into mutually exclusive categories or equating the indicators with cultural identity and acculturation. For example, an individual with an Armenian mother and a Russian-Jewish father who was born in Soviet Armenia (now the Republic of Armenia), was raised in England until the age of 18, acquired eight languages, and immigrated to Canada later in life poses a serious challenge to any census system!

Despite these limitations, the diversity of North American society is a reality, since both the United States and Canada are built on pluralistic societies. In addition, most North Americans can trace their origins back to an immigrant who was poor or persecuted and foreign to the prevailing North American culture.

Finally, nativism (i.e., "irrational and mean-spirited partiality toward native-born people and hostility toward immigrants") is as old as the American republic (Will, 1993, p. 7). Historically, Irish and Chinese immigrants on the East and West Coasts, respectively, have been greeted by religious and racial prejudice from other groups (Will, 1993). Xenophobia is as much a cultural issue as it is economic.

Karno and Edgerton (1969) estimated that 9% to 10% of the population of the United States in 1962–1963 was Mexican American. Based on the 1980 U.S. Census, 20% of the population in the United States was a minority population (Ponterotto & Casas, 1991). In the 1980s, about 9 million people immigrated to the United States legally and about 2 million illegally. By the year 2000, it is estimated that about 30% of the U.S. population (i.e., 81 million people) will constitute an ethnic minority population. Of these about 37.6 million will be African American, about 31.2 million Spanish, and 12.7 million Asians and other minority people (J. M. Jones, 1990). The minority population in California is already over 50%, and, according to population researchers, it is expected that by the year 2002, Hispanic Americans will constitute the majority culture in the most populous state in America.

The diversity in cultural groups in North America is also apparent in Canada. The 1991 Canada Census data indicated that over 40% of the Canadian population is of non-British and non-French culture. It should be realized that regional patterns may be different from those nationally. For example, whereas the ten fastest growing immigrant groups in Canada during 1987–1990 were from Hong Kong, Poland, India, the Philippines, the United Kingdom, Portugal, the Azores, Vietnam, South Korea, the United States, and Lebanon, the pattern for the city of London, a metropolitan community in southwestern Ontario, was Poland, Portugal, Vietnam/Cambodia, Britain, El Salvador, Hong Kong, Lebanon, the Union of Soviet Socialist Republics, and Hungary. Needless to say, examination of regional demographics is critical for research and service planning.

Cultural Pluralism in Clinical Psychology

Interest in the cultural composition of various groups of individuals in psychology programs relative to their representation in the general population dates back to the 1960s (Bayton, Roberts, & Williams, 1970; Ruiz, 1971). Despite this long tradition, comparisons across studies have been difficult because of differences in samples, variations in methodology and data reporting, and definitional inconsistency. It is of interest to note that biographical information about citizenship, race, and ethnic identification became part of the manpower data system for psychology in the United States in 1972 (Willette, 1972).

Findings reported from the American Psychological Association (APA) 1978 Human Resources Survey (Russo, Olmedo, Stapp & Fulcher, 1981) and from the 1987–

1988 Sex and Race/Ethnicity Data Survey (Ponterotto & Casas, 1991) on minority student representation in psychology are consistent with other studies (El-Khawas & Astin, 1972; Howard, Pion, Gottfredson, Flattau, Oskamp, Pfaffin, Bray, & Burstein, 1986; Jones, 1990; Suinn & Witt, 1982; VandenBos & Stapp, 1983). These results demonstrate a relative increase of minority representation over time but also show chronic underrepresentation for minority students. Ethnic minority representation specific to clinical psychology was not reported for the 1987/1988 survey. These data were available for the 1978 survey and showed a pattern of minority underrepresentation similar to that of psychology in general (Russo et al., 1981). African American doctoral students constituted 0.96% of all doctoral-level clinical psychology enrollments, Asian Americans 1.1%, Hispanic Americans 0.99%, Indigenous people 0.04%, and White individuals 96.2%. The comparable figures for MA-level students were 1.53%, 1.17%, 0.76%, 0.43% and 94.9%, respectively.

The Minority Retention Practices Survey (MRPS) completed for 32 of 34 member schools of the National Council of Schools for Professional Psychology (NCSPP) in the fall of 1988 showed that 10.2% of students were minorities and that 13.9% of all NCSPP member schools surveyed were minority faculty (McHolland, Lubin, & Forbes, 1990). Relative to their representation in the general population, minority psychologists in particular were underrepresented among doctoral psychologists. Kohout and Pion (1990) reported that, of the 56,400 doctoral psychologists in 1987, approximately 1300 were African Americans, 900 Asian Americans, 100 Indigenous people, and an estimated 1000 Hispanic American. Minority representation of Native American psychologists is of particular concern both from a role-modeling perspective and from the perspective of meeting the service needs of Native Americans (LaFromboise, 1988). According to the 1993 APA Directory Survey, 76.4% of APA members are White, 1.8% Hispanic, 1.6% Black, 1.2% Asian, 0.5% Native American, 0.1% Other, and 18.3% Not Specified (American Psychological Association [APA], 1993a).

Finally, Bernal and Castro (1994) examined minority representation in psychology across the years 1970–1990 and concluded that, since 1985, the percentages of minority students admitted into graduate programs have ranged between 10% and 11% and that the percentages for minority doctoral graduates and minority faculty have remained invariant.

All the information reviewed on cultural pluralism in psychology in general and on students and faculty in psychology programs in particular are based on data from the United States. Comparable Canadian studies are lacking. In an effort to fill this gap, we mailed survey questionnaires to the 12 directors of clinical psychology programs in the country. Only 3 responded to our survey. Nevertheless, the responses of these directors to items on student and faculty composition were suggestive of a cultural mix, for both students and faculty. The lack of representation from the Indigenous people among the student and faculty of these programs was noteworthy.

Cultural Diversity in the Clinical Population

The lack of the central role of culture has also been observed in the practice of clinical psychology. Dahlquist and Fay (1983) pointed out that since the 1960s there have been growing concerns over the failure of mental health professionals in general and counseling and clinical psychologists in particular to adequately meet the needs of the pluralistic society. Padilla, Ruiz, and Alvarez (1975) urged both the American Psychological Association and the American Psychiatric Association to assume leadership roles in the training of Spanish-speaking students in the mental health professions. Sue (1977) advocated focus on delivery of responsive services, while Korchin (1980) argued for commitment to training larger numbers of qualified minority psychologists. The need to focus on underrepresented groups was reaffirmed at the June 1987 National Conference on Graduate Education (Bickman, 1987).

There is no doubt that clinical and other psychologists from diverse cultures (including mainstream culture) are providing psychological services to diverse cultural groups, including individual clients, organizations, and government or community agencies. There is also no doubt that clinical services are being provided in a diversity of settings and for a diversity of psychological problems. These include private-practice settings, psychology department clinics, institutional settings (mental hospitals and general hospitals), community health and mental health centers, and universities.

Qualitative and quantitative research on the activities of clinical psychologists in diverse settings is sparse, even though such groups are served in public and private settings (Kazarian, Mazmanian, Sussman, & Persad, 1993; Snowden & Cheung, 1990). Consequently, little is known about the number of people from diverse cultures being seen by clinical psychologists in each setting and about the sociodemographic characteristics of the clients served. Sue (1977) reported psychologist involvement with minority patients from a variety of mental health community centers for the purpose of both intake and therapy. He provided the following percentages for intake involvement: Blacks (his terminology) 3.4%, Native Americans 6%, Asian Americans 2.1%, Chicanos 8.4%, and Whites 9.5%. The comparable figures for therapy involvement were 0.7%, 3.3%, 3.7%, 3.8%, and 7.0%, respectively.

Bernal and Padilla (1982) attempted to identify the minority groups being served in in-house and off-campus settings where students received their clinical training. The survey showed that minority clients were represented in the caseloads of staff in these settings, with African Americans (59% for in-house and 45% for off-campus) and Hispanic Americans (32% and 29%, respectively) providing the highest representations, followed by Native Americans (9% for both settings) and people of Asian/Pacific Islander background (4% for both settings). However, information about the extent of psychology involvement with these minority groups was not reported.

VandenBos and Stapp (1983) reported findings on the ethnicity of the clients served by APA-member health service providers from the 1982 APA Human Resources Survey. Separate data on clinical psychologists were not provided. Their results showed cultural diversity among both service providers and clients served. The five most frequently presenting problems of clients were anxiety and depression (87.1%), difficulties in social relationships (84.7%), marital strain (74.9%), and school difficulties (44.3%). Taube, Burns, and Kessler (1984) examined data from the National Medical Care Utilization and Expenditure Survey and reported on the office-based services provided by psychiatrists and psychologists. Their methodology was limited by its focus on race (White versus Other) as a function of visits but not of type of professional contact.

Data on the involvement of Canadian clinical psychology students and clinical psychologists are also lacking. In an effort to correct this omission, we surveyed accredited clinical internship programs in Canada. Of the 22 questionnaires mailed, 9 were returned (8 complete, 1 incomplete). Two of the settings could not provide information on the cultural composition of the clients served by psychology staff and interns, as their client record systems did not include such data. Information from the remaining settings indicated that cultural issues provided both central and tangential focus for psychologists and interns in serving their client populations. The mean percentages of client services (i.e., assessment, treatment, and consultation) by psychology staff and by interns for whom cultural issues were the central focus were 12.7 (range 0% to 40%) and 12.2 (range 0% to 30%), respectively. The comparable figures for those giving cultural issues as a tangential focus were 16.0 (range 1% to 30%) and 16.2 (range 2% to 35%). These results support psychology involvement in service delivery to culturally diverse groups. They also support the prevalence of cultural issues in the psychological service delivery process.

Despite the absence of systematic data, there is a recognition of the needs of people from diverse cultures for the services of clinical psychologists and of the current inability of psychologists to meet those needs (APA, 1993b). In fact, back in 1982, Bernal and Padilla pointed out the compelling need for preparing minority- and majority-culture clinical psychologists to provide psychological services to minority populations. In spite of this recognition, very little is known of clients who need the services of clinical psychologists and are not receiving them.

There are several major barriers to the utilization of the services of clinical psychologists by members of various cultural groups. As clinical psychologists, we have neither promoted ourselves adequately in culturally diverse groups nor have we established strong partnerships with the leaders of the culturally diverse communities. Financial barriers have also precluded people of various cultural groups from seeking the services of clinical psychologists. In Canada, the services of clinical psychologists are not covered by the national health insurance program, unlike medical and psychiatric services. This has resulted in people from various cultural groups receiving adequate medical but inadequate or sometimes inferior psychological care. Clinical psychologists from various cultural groups who specialize in serving diverse cultural groups have not been large enough in numbers to adequately meet the needs of their respective cultural communities. In addition, clinical psychologists have shown culture-blindness in their clinical practice and have treated all clients and families, irrespective of culture, the same way. A number of explanations can be offered for the culture-blindness, including conviction of the superiority of the Eurocentric approach to health care, belief in the universality of North American psychological constructs and interventions, and inadequacy in training. All these factors contribute to inappropriate service delivery, consumer dissatisfaction, and reluctance toward future psychological service utilization.

Finally, the definition of culturally appropriate service delivery has only recently received critical attention (Hays, 1996; Marin, 1993; Rogler, Malgady, Costantino, & Blumenthal, 1987; Zayas, Torres, Malcolm, & DesRosiers, 1996). It should be pointed out that cultural sensitivity is a necessary but not sufficient condition for culturally appropriate service delivery. Marin (1993) has been critical of the use of culturally hybrid interventions (e.g., translating pamphlets originally designed for mainstream culture into different languages or changing names of heroes in stories) in the name of cultural appropriateness. Such approaches do not define cultural appropriateness for two major reasons. First, their scientific effectiveness has not been demonstrated. Second, those providing these services to members of diverse cultures are unlikely to have received adequate and in-depth training in the theory and practice of cultural psychology. According to Marin (1993), cultural appropriateness in service delivery requires that interventions be based on the cultural values of the target culture, that the strategies of intervention be consistent with the attitudes, expectations and norms of the target culture, and that the components of the strategies reflect behavioral preferences and expectations of the members of the target culture.

Clinical Psychology Curricula and Resources

Examination of a typical APA-based curriculum for the training of clinical psychologists (see Table 1.2) supports the neglect of culture in the subject matter of graduate training in psychology. While these programs include Social Bases of Behavior as a substantive content area, the social psychology courses that the majority of, if not all, students take provide little in the way of cultural content (Bond, 1988).

Examination of resources used for the teaching of psychology and clinical psychology also support the relative lack of cultural content. A survey of textbooks commonly used in psychology and clinical psychology showed minimal coverage of cultural psychology. Jones (1990) reported that only 3% of the 3600 pages of six major introductory textbooks contained information relevant to culture, race, or ethnicity. In 1995, a random survey of the contents of clinical psychology books in the clinical and psychopathology sections of our university library, which accommodates a total of over one million references, revealed that inclusion of the topic of culture was the exception rather than the rule. In this particular unsystematic survey, the exceptions were a chapter by Dahlquist and Fay (1983) entitled "Cultural Issues in Psychotherapy" in *The Handbook of Clinical Psychology* (Walker, 1983), a chapter by Jenkins and Knox (1984) entitled "Minorities" in *The Clinical Psychology Handbook* (Hersen, Kazdin, & Bellack, 1983), and a chapter by MacCarthy (1988) entitled "Clinical Work with Ethnic Minorities" in *New Developments in Clinical Psychology* (Watts, 1988). The topic of culture hardly received mention in such popular textbooks on clinical psychology as Phares (1992) and Netzel, Bernstein, and Milich (1994).

Table 1.2. Curriculum for Training of Scientist-Practitioner Clinical Psychologists

Substantive Content Areas
  Biological, Cognitive-Affective, Social, and Individual Bases of Behavior
Scientific and Professional Ethics, and Standards of Practice
Research Training
  Natural and Laboratory Methodology
  Action Research Methodology
  Evaluation and Follow-up Studies
  Demonstration Projects
Development of Clinical Skills
  Individual Methods, Psychodiagnosis, Interventions
Internship (2000 hours)

Source: The Graduate Program in Clinical Psychology. (1996–1997). Department of Psychology, The University of Western Ontario, London, ON.

Culture as such was not even indexed in the fourth edition of the clinical psychology book by Phares (1992). More disheartening was the observation of the absence of culture in an edited book (Dobson & Dobson, 1993) purported to serve a documentary function for Canadian professional psychology. The authors of the chapter entitled "Counselling Psychology: Development, Identity and Issues" were completely oblivious to the issue of culture, a serious anomaly considering the leadership role of counseling psychology in training and service delivery to diverse cultures (Hills & Strozier, 1992; Speight, Thomas, Kennel, & Anderson, 1995; Sue, Bernier, Durran, Feinberg, Pederson, Smith, & Vasquez-Nuttall, 1982) and considering the image of Canada as the cradle of multiculturalism.

Clinical Psychology Programs

Concerns over the failure of clinical programs to prepare students for the task of caring for people from diverse cultures have been voiced since the 1960s (Dahlquist & Fay, 1983; Santiego-Negron, 1990). These concerns have been raised in a multiplicity of conferences on the training of psychologists, including those in Chicago (1965), Vail (1973), Austin (1975), Dulles (1978), Atlanta (1986), and Utah (1987) (Bickman, 1987; Hills & Strozier, 1992). Failure to adequately prepare psychologists for service provision to diverse cultural populations has been described as the "shirking of an ethical obligation" (Korman, 1974). Bernal and Padilla (1982) surveyed 106 accredited clinical psychology programs and, on the basis of responses from 76 programs, concluded that little was being done to prepare clinical psychologists to work with minority cultures. Sayette and Mayne (1990) surveyed the directors of all clinical Ph.D. and clinical Psy.D. programs fully accredited by the APA (N = 144). A summary of the research activities of the 115 schools that responded to the survey showed that only 10 schools representing 20 faculty members were involved in cross-cultural research and only 17 schools representing 32 faculty were conducting minority mental health research. Since the research categories listed were not mutually exclusive, the extent of overlap in these two classes of research is not known. The low priority of research on the interface between clinical psychology and culture in academic programs was evident by the failure of this topic to be included on the list of the 20 most popular areas summarized by Sayette and Mayne (1990). Information on the provision of minority and cross-cultural specialty clinics for clinical experience were more encouraging. A total of 34 schools were involved in such specialty clinics.

More recently, Hills and Strozier (1992) summarized results from surveys of training programs in professional psychology and concluded that endorsements of the need for inclusion of cultural issues in professional psychology training programs were inconsistent with the continued ethnocentric "White middle class" modus operandi of these programs. Allison et al. (1994) also showed that 34.4% of graduates from counseling and clinical programs felt dissatisfied with the supervision they had received in practicum and internship experiences involving service delivery to individuals from diverse cultures. Allison et al. (1994) also reported that few of these graduates felt competent in working with people from diverse cultures. In a study by Allison, Echemendia, Crawford, and Robinson (1996), it was found that practitioners who had seen more diverse clients during training tended to have a higher rate of diverse clients in their current case load.

Surveys of clinical programs in Canada are lacking. The survey responses we received from only three clinical programs indicated that, in general, specific courses on cultural issues were not available to undergraduate or graduate students but that some such content was provided in some courses. Results in relation to the importance of training students in cultural research and practice varied. On a 7-point rating scale (1 = not important at all, 7 = very important), ratings of 2, 4, and 6 were provided for research and ratings of 5, 4, and 6 for practice (assessment and treatment). The negligible focus of research on cultural issues in these programs was also supported by the reports on student and faculty involvement in cultural research. The data provided by the directors of the clinical programs indicated that student research in which cultural issues were either the central or a tangential focus was negligible (i.e., 5%). Similarly, clinical faculty research addressing cultural issues as a central or a tangential focus was slightly higher than that of students (range 5% to 10%) but lower than those of other faculty (range 10% to 20%). Our survey of the accredited Clinical Internship Programs in Canada confirmed the low priority psychologists or interns in these settings give to cultural research. Of the eight settings, only one indicated 10% involvement of psychologists in cultural research.

EXPLANATIONS FOR THE NEGLECT OF CULTURE

We offer several reasons rather than defensive rationalizations for the relative neglect of culture in North American clinical psychology research, practice, and training despite the historical emphasis on culture reviewed earlier.

Insulation and Preoccupation

A possible reason for the neglect of culture in clinical psychology and the failure to orient its activities to the broader needs of society pertains to insulation and preoccupation with internal and external threats. The academic world and the private-practice office may have insulated clinical psychologists from the realities of the outside world, thus rendering them oblivious to the social changes within their communities and the needs associated with these demographic and clinical transformations. The periodic cultural reality awareness campaigns of cultural psychologists may not have provided sufficient response-incompatibility to reciprocally inhibit mainstream habits of insulation. For example, clinical service delivery in the form of psychotherapy to the middle-class segment of society (Albee, 1970, 1987) has precluded responsivity to more serious societal problems such as racism (Albee, 1970) and needs of the diverse cultural segments of society (Padilla et al., 1975). Albee (1970) and Sue (1977) pointed to the focus of psychologists on the treatment of people with the YARVIS syndrome, that is, young, attractive, rich, verbal, intelligent, and successful (Schofield, 1964), to the neglect of people with HOUND that is, the homely, old, unattractive, nonverbal, and dumb) (Goldstein and Simonson, 1971). Today the word "homeless" could perhaps be substituted for the word "homely."

Preoccupation with internal and external threats and conflicts has precluded greater attention and resource allocation to the multiplicity of pressing societal needs. Schisms in the training of psychologists have been a major component of internal strife. The neglect of culture in psychology may have arisen from the inability of clinical psychologists interested in cultural issues to assert their needs in the science and practice of psychology. A variety of factors other than lack of effort (Bayton et al., 1970; Dong, Wong, Callao, Nishihara, and Chin, 1978; Stricker, Davis-Russell, Bourg, Duran, Hammond, McHolland, Polits, & Vaughn, 1990) may have contributed to ineffectiveness, including systemic barriers, complacency, minority status, and a lack of power base in academic and training programs. It is for these reasons that structural institutional change, social advocacy, and ongoing support for ethnic minority students, faculty, and practitioners have been recommended (McHolland et al., 1990).

External preoccupation, on the other hand, has involved efforts toward emancipation from the double-image of psychology and psychiatry and assertion of an independent profession. While on the whole, psychologists have successfully divorced themselves from being the "astrologers of mental health" (Weil, 1952), these achievements have been at a price. As McNeil (1959) so aptly stated: "The single most important cost of this diversion of our attention away from the consumers of psychology has yet to be reckoned" (p. 520).

Differences in Value Assumptions

A major culprit in the failure to embrace cultural psychology by North American psychology and clinical psychology has been the value assumptions associated with the dominant North American (Anglo American) paradigm (Ho, 1985; McHolland et al., 1990; Sue, 1983). Three such conflicting value assumptions are listed in Table 1.3.

The Western mainstream paradigm has followed the etic approach in research and training, in which the emphasis has been on "universals" and core human similarities. Cultural psychology, on the other hand, has focused on the emic approach with emphasis on culture-specificity and the influence of culture on human behavior. Consequently, the two groups have used different subject matter and associated terminology, as well as different scientific methodology (Clark, 1987; Sue, 1983). For example, cross-cultural comparisons and studies on the effect of culture on human adjustment have been central areas of research for cultural psychologists, whereas these issues have been considered of very little relevance to mainstream psychology at best and nuisance variables at worst (Clark, 1987).

Mainstream Western psychology has also valued a monoculturalistic ideology, partly due to belief in the superiority of the Anglo-Saxon culture and the inferiority of all other cultures. In this assimilation-oriented, unidirectional conceptualization of human behavior, Anglo conformity of indigenous culture and minority cultures is

Table 1.3. Value Assumptions of Mainstream Psychology and Cultural Psychology

Mainstream Psychology	Cultural Psychology
Etic approach	Emic approach
Monoculture	Cultural pluralism
Individualism	Collectivism

expected, and failure in detachment from the umbilical cord of the culture of origin is construed as a deep-seated defect in personality structure. Cultural psychology, on the other hand, has followed a cultural pluralistic model in which historical connectedness to culture of origin is valued and the reciprocal influences of cultures recognized. Consequently, the development of paradigms of adaptation and the effect of acculturation processes on health and mental health have been topics of focus in cultural psychology (Berry, 1990, 1994; Burnam, Hough, Karno, Escobar, & Telles, 1987; Rogler, Cortes, & Malgady, 1991; Triandis & Brislin, 1984) but of little significance to mainstream psychology.

Finally, mainstream Western psychology has followed the Judeo-Christian tradition of individualism in which self-reliance and the uniqueness, autonomy, freedom, and intrinsic worth of the individual have always been affirmed. In contrast to individualism, collectivism is based on the supreme guiding principle for social action, preservation, and enhancement of the well-being of the group (Ho, 1985; Kim, Triandis, Kagitcibasi, Choi, & Yoon, 1994). A collectivistic value system considers individual personality within the context of a cultural group and the economic and psychological benefits associated with group affiliation. These value assumptions produce incompatible approaches to the practice of clinical psychology. Practitioners and students in training in Anglo American clinical programs use psychotherapeutic interventions to promote individual self-containment, with little regard for the collectivistic culture of the recipient of these services. As Dana (1994) has observed, however, the self-concept of individuals from non-Western cultures is inclusionary of other persons, in addition to natural and spiritual forces. The role of culture in shaping and determining response to illness is illustrated in the case of a 24-year old Korean woman with leukemia who was also suspected to have depression. The client was seen by two clinicians, an American psychologist and an Asian physician (Nilchaikovit, Hill, & Holland, 1993). The two clinicians presented widely different perceptions of the client after the initial evaluation and recommended different approaches for treatment. In contrast to the physician's assessment that the client wanted continued involvement with family, the psychologist attributed the client's problem to family intrusiveness and prescribed *"parentectomy."* The discordance in case formulation and treatment was attributed to cultural differences in definition of self (Eastern centripetal-interdependent orientation versus Western centrifugal-independent orientation) and patterns of self-other interactions (Asian stress on interdependence, cohesion, and hierarchical mode of relations versus American stress on independence, differentiation, and an egalitarian mode of relations).

While differences in value assumptions have contributed significantly to the exclusion of cultural psychology from clinical psychology, creative attempts at synthesis have not been absent (Berry, 1994; Ho, 1985; Tyler, Susswell, & Williams-McCoy, 1985). For example, Tyler et al. (1985) have recommended a paradigmatic shift in Anglo American psychology in which culture, race, and ethnicity are incorporated into the definition of psychological constructs, concepts, and parameters.

Culture: Confused and Confusing

A third reason for the rejection of culture by clinical psychology has been the science of culture itself. In discussing psychological testing and assessment, Dana (1994) has commented that "cross-cultural psychology continues to occupy a state of limbo, with publication in a relatively small number of in-house or culture-specific journals or in 'fugitive' publication outlets with only limited general availability" (p. 352). While critics have acknowledged the contribution of cultural psychology in advancing greater understanding of human behavior, scholarly activity related to culture has also been compromised by the descriptive and atheoretical work on the topic, extensive use of specialized cross-cultural terminology, and conceptual and measurement problems (Betancourt & Lopez, 1993; Clark, 1987; Jahoda, 1980, 1984; Kalin & Berry, 1994; Ponterotto & Casas, 1991). Conceptual and methodological problems relate to the definition and understanding of culture from a psychological perspective; the measurement of the various psychologically relevant components of the construct; the interchangeable use of such terms as *culture, race, ethnicity, multicultural,* and *minority;* the confounding of culture with race, ethnicity, and social class; the use of umbrella terms for cultural groups (e.g., Hispanic); and the converting of "effect" (i.e., cultural variation in behavior) into "cause" (i.e., deification of culture).

Focus on ill-defined, unstable, categorical, static, exclusionary, and negative concepts has been detrimental to academic and social development. Minority and majority descriptors of social characters have fostered divisiveness, stereotypical attitudes, aggrandizement of majority members, pathologizing of minority groups, and a type of research that focuses on differences and ignores valuable similarities. In particular, the use of the term *minority* has damaged the psychological well-being of the recipients of the negative label. The association of culture in North America with minority culture has rendered all nonmainstream people permanent refugees, in addition to creating a Houdini-like illusion of culturelessness of majority culture. Needless to say, descriptors of social characters that constitute a composite portrait of cultures require a function that is conducive to personal growth, psychological well-being, and optimal quality of life.

CLINICAL PSYCHOLOGY: EFFORTS TOWARD RECONCILIATION

As pointed out earlier, psychology and clinical psychology have not been completely oblivious to cultural psychology. In addition to the healthy acknowledgement of the schism between mainstream psychology and cultural psychology, discussions have focused on barriers to integration, analysis of conceptual and methodological issues, and concrete approaches to bridging the gap between the two fields (Bayton et al., 1970; Isaac, 1985; McHolland et al., 1990; Sue, 1983). Factors that have provided the impetus for integration are listed in Table 1.4. It is worth noting that Anglo American "backlashes" in the form of denouncement of multiculturalism and assertion of the United States as an Anglo American nation and "immigrant-bashing" practices in Canada (e.g., British culture being destroyed by the existence of other cultures) are in vogue.

Increased Cultural Representation

The APA has assumed a leadership role in addressing the plight of "minority" representation in the discipline, including its establishment of committees (e.g., Committee

Table 1.4. Impetus for Interest in Cultural Psychology

Shift from melting-pot ideology to cultural pluralism
Social and ethical responsibility of psychology
Political and social presence of diverse cultural groups
Limitations of a purely biological model of human behavior
Scientific advances in cultural psychology
Global economic considerations
National and international intercultural contacts
Government emphasis through legislation and funding

on the Equality of Opportunity in Psychology in 1963, Division 45, the Society for the Psychological Study of Ethnic Minority Issues), its involvement in the Minority Fellowship Program, its development of guidelines for the provision of services to a culturally pluralistic society, its endorsement of cultural content in curricula, its development and refinement of accreditation guidelines, and its sponsoring of national conferences.

The history of the Minority Fellowship Program can be traced to 1974, when the National Institutes of Health awarded the American Psychological Association a grant for the doctoral training of "ethnic minority" students in psychology. Since the inception of the Minority Fellowship Program, more than 600 "ethnic minority" doctoral students in psychology have been supported, of whom more than 300 have earned doctoral degrees (Jones, 1990). Currently the program is supporting training of "minority" individuals in the neurosciences.

Organizations other than APA have also assumed a leadership role in advocating for increased cultural representation in psychology. The California School of Professional Psychology (CSPP) was founded to address the need for well-trained clinicians for the provision of mental health services to the community at large. The agenda developed at a retreat in 1986 called for a social-advocacy role and a shift in focus from private practice to social practice in order to address the needs of the underserved and those from diverse cultures (McHolland et al., 1990).

Similarly, the National Council of Schools of Professional Psychology (NCSPP; Batts, 1990) organized the 1988–1989 Puerto Rico conference to examine the role of cultural diversity in the education and training of professional psychologists. The activity was part of the continuing effort of the NCSPP to achieve cultural diversity in clinical psychology programs (Stricker, 1990). Attendees at the conference included representatives from 27 schools of professional psychology and the American Psychological Association.

No doubt these initiatives have contributed to increased representation of diverse cultures in psychology programs. Nevertheless, there continue to be perceptions of the existence of systemic barriers that create unequal opportunities for people from diverse cultures (Bernal, 1994a, 1994b). While not specific to psychology, a committee report from the University of Western Ontario recommended that recruitment of ethnic students be a priority of the university (Van Brenk, 1992). Opinions on the existence of systemic barriers and approaches to augment culturally diverse student representation in doctoral training programs have varied. In relation to recruitment, there have been three divergent suggestions: no action, affirmative action, and affirmative diversity. Affirmative action has received fierce opposition from some "mainstream" circles. Their reactions have ranged from charges of political correctness at best to reverse discrimination at worst. Those with irrational hostility towards affirmative action have seen it as "expiating the past sins" of clinical psychologists and "bestowing opportunities" on the unqualified segment of society.

There has not been consensus with regard to affirmative action even within the diverse cultural populations themselves. Affirmative diversity has been suggested as a viable alternative. J. M. Jones (1990) has defined affirmative diversity as "the affirmation of the fundamental value of human diversity in society, with the belief that enhancing diversity increases rather than diminishes quality." (p. 18). The objective of affirmative diversity is to provide student and faculty diversification to increase the relevance of psychology in general and clinical psychology in particular to culturally diverse populations.

The cultural diversity of North American society is unlikely to be ignored by clinical psychology, nor can academic settings and clinicians shrug off their responsibility for the multiplicity of issues associated with the science, practice, and training of clinical psychology in a pluralistic society. The profession has not as yet endorsed universal programs to systematically recruit individuals from various cultural groups, even though innovative approaches continue to evolve (Ponterotto, Burkard, Yoshida, Cancelli, Mendez, Wasilewski, & Sussman, 1995). The prevailing perceptions of the rise of the "white niggers" phenomenon and the negative sentiments of reverse discrimination associated with employment equity policies and legislation do not constitute rational condonation of the maintenance of unwritten exclusionary policies in "mainstream" institutions. An open dialogue on the issues and cultural partnerships are options available in democratic societies for addressing systemic barriers against citizens regardless of their cultural status.

Clinical psychology programs individually and clinical psychologists collectively require self-examination in relation to the relevance of cultural psychology to the communities they serve and the society at large. The success of clinical psychology in providing a culturally relevant psychology is likely to benefit not only the affected people but also the profession and the larger community.

Infusion of Culture in Clinical Psychology Curricula

The endorsement of the need to teach culture in psychology in the American Psychological Association (APA) report on education (McGovern, Furumoto, Halpern, Kimble, & McKeachie, 1991) has been consistent with efforts to promote the interface between culture and psychology. The impetus for psychology student exposure to cultural issues in psychological theory, research, practice, and training was the recognition of the changing demographics of the American nation and of its student population and of the social and ethical responsibility of the discipline to respond to these realities. Yutrzenka (1995) indicated that "the viability and integrity of psychology in general, and professional psychology training programs in particular, are related to psychology's willingness to face the challenge of diversity rather than to retreat from it" (p. 197). Betancourt and Lopez (1993) argued that the infusion of culture into mainstream psychology is likely to enhance the scientific and professional status of psychology, as more universal principles and theories will be advanced and assessment and treatment strategies more pertinent to a culturally pluralistic community will be developed.

Since the 1970s, psychology training programs have been increasingly incorporating cultural issues in their curricula. In addition to increased (albeit insufficient) cultural content in psychology resources, such as some abnormal psychology textbooks published in 1996 (e.g., Alloy, Acocella, & Bootzin, 1996; Carson, Butcher, & Mineka, 1996; Sarason & Sarason, 1996; Wilson, Nathan, O'Leary, & Clark, 1996), a variety of models have been considered in efforts to infuse culture into clinical psychology. The Separatist model advocates the establishment of a distinct ethnic psychology, a position strongly disfavored by psychologists (Korchin, 1980). The Culture-Sensitivity (or Ethnic-Minority) model provides development of specialty courses on cultural psychology or minority issues based on student and faculty interests and on the nature of the clinical groups represented in the community. While the Culture-Sensitivity model is an effective approach to raising cultural awareness in students enrolled in these specialty courses, it has the limitation that the courses offered are necessarily elective; students do not have to enroll in them (Kazarian, 1994). As pointed out by Jones (1990), they also promote ghettoization of ethnic minority faculty and students. The Integrative model, on the other hand, advocates the same basic psychology training with augmentation in the form of inclusion of several additional components. For example, Bernal and Padilla (1982) suggested augmentation by adding a multicultural philosophy to training. This philosophy included provision of a broad-based historical and cultural understanding of minority groups; increased theoretical knowledge and expertise in the scientific study of sociocultural factors; experience in the application of culturally appropriate primary, secondary, and tertiary prevention; and fluency in languages spoken by clients. The Integrative model thus advocates a multicultural focus in which ethnic-minority content is included in standard or core courses. In addition to integration of research findings on ethnic minority issues into psychology training programs, the Integrative model proposes cultural considerations in the diverse components of psychology training, including assessments, treatments, practice, and internships (Jones, 1990).

A final model represents a combined Culture-Sensitivity (Ethnic-Minority) and Integrative perspective. In this model, ethnic-minority issues are integrated into core curricula and specialty courses on ethnic-minority issues are offered (McHolland et al., 1990). This model is represented by the Ethnic Minority Institute (EMI) model program of the California School of Professional Psychology in Fresno (Bluestone, Stokes, & Kuba, 1996). The EMI provides special minority-issue education and training, including ethnic-minority proficiency. The latter incorporates the general clinical program as the basic training foundation and adds more specialized instruction and experiences in ethnic-minority issues in its courses (McHolland et al., 1990).

APA and CPA Accreditation Guidelines

A third indicator of efforts to strengthen the infusion of culture into the science, practice, and training of psychology is the gradual changes observed in accreditation standards and guidelines. The imperative for effective training of culturally competent professional psychologists was codified in Criterion II of the APA accreditation standard (APA, 1986). The rationale, meaning, scope, and implementation of this criterion was described more recently (APA Committee on Accreditation, 1991) and generated important debate within the profession (Altmaier, 1993; Clements & Rickard, 1993; Payton, 1993; Rickard & Clements, 1993). Criterion II requires consideration of social responsibility and respect for cultural and individual differences in the training of students and the operation of professional programs, consideration of social and personal diversity in program faculty and students, and consideration of knowledge and skills development relevant to human diversity. In the CPA accreditation criteria of 1989 (Canadian Psychological Association [CPA], 1989a), cultural content in the curriculum was not a requirement. It was only required that sensitivity to and respect for cultural and individual differences be reflected in the composition and operation of psychology programs. The 1994 CPA accreditation requirements for cultural inclusiveness are summarized in Table 1.5.

Ethical Principles, Codes of Conduct, and Professional Guidelines

A fourth major indicator of psychology's commitment to culture is the development of ethical principles, codes of conduct, and professional guidelines specific to cultural practices (American Association of State and Provincial Psychology Boards, 1991; APA, 1992, 1993b; CPA, 1989b, 1991, 1994; Kazarian, in press). Principle D of the APA Ethical Principles of Psychologists and Code of Conduct stipulates awareness of "cultural, individual, and role differences, including those due to age, gender, race, ethnicity, national origin, religion, sexual orientation, disability, language, and socioeconomic status" (APA, 1992, p. 1599). An essential requirement of the APA (1992) Ethics Code is awareness on the part of psychologists of "their own belief systems, values, needs, and limitations and the effect of these on their work" (Principle B, APA, 1992, p. 1599). As indicated by Dana (1994), the implication of this ethical principle is that all psychologists, irrespective of their "minority" or "mainstream" cultural status, are obligated to have an understanding of their own identity development.

In 1988, the Board of Ethnic Minority Affairs (BEMA) of the APA established a Task Force on the Delivery of Services to Ethnic Minority Populations. In recognition of the

Table 1.5. Clinical and Counseling Psychology Accreditation Criteria (CPA)

III.	Cultural and Individual Differences: social responsibility and respect for cultural and individual differences reflected in all phases of a program's operation, including faculty recruitment and promotion, student recruitment and evaluation, curriculum planning, and field training
IV.	Training Models and Curricula: demonstrated competence in the substantive content area of social bases of behavior (e.g., social psychology, cultural, ethnic, and group processes; sex roles; organizational and systems theory)
V.	Faculty: sensitivity and responsivity to culture and lifestyle issues; prohibition of systematic exclusion of candidates from consideration for hiring, promotion, retention, and granting of tenure on the basis of age, gender, ethnic, or racial background, lifestyle, religion, or physical handicap
VI.	Students: commitment, sensitivity, self-awareness, and tolerance of social justice, the welfare of others, and cultural and individual differences; prohibition of systematic exclusion on the basis of race, ethnic origin, sex, age, religion, or physical handicap

Source: Based on CPA (1994) Accreditation Criteria.

needs of ethnic, linguistic, and culturally diverse populations for psychological services, the Task Force developed guidelines for the provision of services to these groups (APA, 1993b). More specifically, the APA (1993b) articulated the knowledge and skills required for assessment and intervention in culturally diverse communities. The list of the abilities identified by the APA is provided in Table 1.6. The APA (1993b) also articulated nine guidelines for the provision of psychological services to ethnic, linguistic, and culturally diverse populations. These are summarized in Table 1.7.

CULTURAL CLINICAL PSYCHOLOGY

The reconciliation efforts described and the different models for interfacing culture with clinical psychology represent significant but insufficient directions in modern North American clinical psychology. Excepting few model efforts, most of the reform movements are perceived as "Band-Aid" approaches to profound deficiencies in the core system. Firm entrenchment of culture in the fabric of modern clinical psychology requires identification of culture as a third domain alongside the two historical domains of clinical psychology: science and practice.

We recommend retirement of such qualifiers as "minority" and "majority" and use of such terms as *diverse cultures, cultural groups, cultures of origin,* and *cultures of settlement.* We support retention of the terms *culture, ethnicity,* and *race* for psychological consideration, provided they are operationally defined and used in a socially responsible manner. We empathize with Segall's (1983) misgivings about the use of culture (add ethnicity and race) as an independent variable rather than focusing investigation on its components (e.g., cultural values). Finally, we recommend abandonment of the myopic approach to comparative cultural research, in which group difference is hailed as scientific discovery while "no group difference" is cast as scientific invalidity.

We define cultural clinical psychology as an attempt to acquire systematic knowledge of human behavior and to develop psychological principles and methods by which to use this knowledge to provide for culturally appropriate diagnostic, therapeutic, rehabilitation, prevention, research, and training functions and to promote the welfare and quality of life of people from all cultures within a particular society. The three related domains of the proposed field of cultural clinical psychology are presented in Table 1.8.

Table 1.6. Skills and Knowledge for Multicultural Assessment and Intervention

Recognizing cultural diversity

Understanding the role of culture, ethnicity, and race in the sociopolitical and economic development of ethnic and culturally diverse populations

Understanding the significant impact of socioeconomic and political factors on the psychosocial, political, and economic development of groups

Helping clients to understand/maintain/resolve their own sociocultural identification

Understanding the interaction of culture, gender, and sexual orientation on behavior and needs

Source: Based on APA (1993b).

Table 1.7. Guidelines for Ethnic, Linguistic, and Culturally Diverse Populations

1. Client education about processes of psychological interventions (e.g., goals and expectations)
2. Cognizance of relevant research and practice issues pertaining to populations served
3. Recognition of the significance of culture in understanding psychological processes
4. Respect for the roles of families, community structures, hierarchies, values, and beliefs within the client's culture
5. Respect for clients' religious and/or spiritual beliefs and values, including attributions and taboos
6. Interaction in the language requested by the client, or appropriate use of interpreters
7. Consideration of adverse social, environmental, and political factors in assessments and interventions
8. Attention to and elimination of biases, prejudices, and discriminatory practices
9. Documentation of culturally and sociopolitically relevant factors in clients' records

Source: Based on APA (1993b).

In this section we elaborate on the cultural domain of cultural clinical psychology, as the other two domains have already been described. We have defined the domain of culture in cultural clinical psychology in terms of the approach to culture, including cultural elements and cultural training (Brislin & Yoshida, 1994; Linton, 1945; Triandis, 1990), and cultural adaptation, in the form of acculturation and acculturative stress (Berry, 1990; Padilla, 1980).

Approach to Culture

The approach to culture entails identification of culture, its elements, and cultural training as essential to the science and practice of clinical psychology. A universal definition of culture is unavailable. Linton (1945) referred to culture as "the configuration of learned behavior and results of behavior whose component elements are shared and transmitted by the members of a particular society" (p. 32). He identified overt and covert aspects of culture. The overt aspect represented the concrete and the tangible (e.g., the material products of industry), whereas the covert aspect reflected the psychological phenomena of knowledge, attitudes, and values. Similarly, Triandis (1990) referred to culture as "the human-made part of the environment" (p. 36) and described two cultural elements: the objective (e.g., bridges) and the subjective (e.g., listed beliefs, attitudes, norms, roles, and values). LaFromboise, Coleman, and Gerton (1993) focused on a behavioral definition of culture and attributed behavior to the continuous interaction among cultural structure, individual cognitive and affective processes, biology, and the social environment. They also subscribed to Bandura's (1978, 1986) concept of reciprocal determinism, that is, behavior that influences and is influenced by a person's cognition and social milieu. Finally, they defined cultural competence as encompassing strong personal identity, knowledge of and facility with

Table 1.8. Cultural Clinical Psychology

Science	Practice	Culture
Research training	Substantive areas	Approach to culture
M.A. thesis	Practica	Cultural adaptation
Ph.D. thesis	Internship	

the beliefs and values of the particular culture, sensitivity to the affective processes of the culture, competence in the language of the culture, performance of socially sanctioned behavior, maintenance of social relations within the particular culture, and negotiation of the institutional structure of the particular culture. Inclusion of culture and its elements in the core curriculum, as well as research, diagnosis, and intervention, represents the centrality of cultural psychology in cultural clinical psychology.

It has been useful to conceptualize cultures on the basis of key characteristics, that is, dimensions of national culture, in much the same way that trait psychologists try to understand the personalities of individuals, and of the identification of dominant social characters within cultures as representing two poles of a continuum. A variety of cultural patterns or generalized traits of cultures have been identified, including masculinity versus femininity, individualism versus collectivism, looseness versus tightness, and separant versus participant cultures (Kim et al., 1994; Shoham, Ashkenasy, Rahav, Chard, Addi, & Addad, 1995; Triandis, 1990). In masculine cultures people primarily live to work, whereas in feminine cultures they work to live. Consequently, priorities for individuals from feminine cultures include quality of life, separateness of work from other life domains, close family relations, and nurturing. In contrast, individuals from masculine cultures tend to be achievement-oriented, with focus on progress, advancement, and "getting the job done."

Collectivist cultures are characterised by hierarchical structures and identification, loyalty, and dependence on in-groups. The selves of individuals from collectivistic cultures tend to be "appendages" of their in-groups rather than distinct entities (Triandis, 1990). Prime values for collectivistic individuals include family integrity, security, obedience, and conformity. In view of the emphasis on long-term relationships, individuals from collectivistic cultures are unlikely to "get into business" unless trust has been secured.

Individuals associated with tight cultures, in which societal norms are clear and imposed and deviation from such norms is met with punishment, tend to be anxious and insecure, to respond best to clearly articulated expectations, and to value predicability, certainty, and security. Finally, separant culture is characterized by an orientation toward action, plurality, reason, and object manipulation. In contrast, participant culture is characterized by an orientation toward resignation, unity, intuition, and self-manipulation (Shoham et al., 1995).

Longitudinal focus on the influence of cultural patterns and social characters on human development, encompassing the physical, psychological, social, and spiritual domains within the North American context, provides fertile investigative ground for cultural clinical psychology. In addition to its pragmatic value for the welfare of individuals, focus on cultural continua and social characters contributes to the elucidation of cultural processes that encompass conflicts and disharmonious relations which impact negatively on societal welfare in general and on certain groups in particular. For example, Shoham et al. (1995) have proposed that the separant-participant cultural continuum provides a useful explanatory model for the understanding of anti-Semitism and the Holocaust specifically. The application of their model to other contemporary and historical intercultural violence (e.g., the 1915 Armenian genocide) is instructive for intervention and prevention purposes.

Cultural training, adopted from intercultural training approaches (Brislin & Yoshida, 1994), also represents an essential ingredient of cultural clinical psychology. The primary rationale for cultural training is the inevitability of cultural contact in the academic and clinical settings, between students and faculty and between clinicians and clients. It is of value to know that cultural training programs have been developed for a variety of contexts, including universities and health care settings. Typically, these programs provide for 6 to 12 hours of exposure with modules that incorporate self-assessment exercises, case studies or critical incidents, and homework assignments (Brislin & Yoshida, 1994). Such programs facilitate discussion of issues that relate to cultural similarities and differences, as well as to professional effectiveness and personal competence in the context of culture.

The four components of cultural training, as identified by Brislin & Yoshida (1994), are listed in Table 1.9. The first component is Awareness of Culture. Awareness of Culture involves in-depth understanding of one's own culture and its influence on one's own behavior. This critical step leads to realization of the influence of one's own culture on one's thinking, emotions, and behavior. Knowledge of one's own culture is a prerequisite to understanding other cultures and is a requirement for residency training in psychiatry. In addition to supervised clinical experiences with clients from diverse cultures and socioeconomic backgrounds, the Accreditation Council for Graduate Medical Education (ACGME) requires didactic instruction about American culture and subculture (ACGME, 1993).

The second component of cultural training is Knowledge of Other Cultures. This involves awareness of the values, beliefs, norms, and behaviors of people from cultures other than one's own. Such awareness is likely to provide a blueprint for cultural appropriateness (cultural amenities) and minimization of errors of attribution.

The third component of cultural training is Coping With Other Cultures. This involves development of effective approaches to dealing with negative affective reactions to contact with diverse cultures, whether they involve students, colleagues, or clients. Two aspects of coping relate to acknowledgment of negative emotions (e.g., anger, frustration) toward people who are different, have different values, or simply behave differently and to tolerance and nonjudgmental attitudes.

The fourth component of cultural training is Culturally Appropriate Behaviors. This consists of supplementing cultural knowledge and understanding with engagement in culturally appropriate behaviors. Culture-bound behaviors include verbal and written communication, cultural protocol (e.g., how to greet individuals from diverse cultures, what type of gifts to give, and where to entertain), and nonverbal communication. In relation to the latter, it has been useful, for example, to conceptualize culture-based nonverbal behaviors in terms of contact cultures versus noncontact cul-

Table 1.9. Cultural Training Programs

Awareness of Own Culture
Knowledge of Other Cultures
Coping with Other Cultures
Culturally Appropriate Behaviors

Source: Adapted from Brislin & Yoshida (1994).

tures. In contact cultures much physical contact and touching is common. Similarly, the social distance for individuals from contact cultures is much smaller than those from noncontact cultures, such that individuals from the former may be breathing on the other person during social intercourse (Kazarian & Joseph, 1994).

Cultural Adaptation

Historically, cultural adaptation, in the form of mixed racial heritage or by virtue of living in two cultures, was deemed pathological and deserved such labels as "apple," "banana," and "Oreo." While these negative stereotypical references continue, there is increasing recognition of the viability and the protective value of cultural-adaptation processes. Park (1928) attributed the history and progress of humankind to the inter-face of cultures. He also indicated that the intermingling associated with migration and human movement produces the "cosmopile," an individual who is independent and wise. LaFromboise et al. (1993) reviewed the literature on the psychological impact of biculturalism and asserted that "a vital step in the development of an equal partnership for minorities in the academic, social, and economic life of the United States involves moving away from assumptions of the linear model of cultural acqui-sition" (p. 395).

Models of cultural adaptation and the psychological processes and consequences involved are important aspects of cultural clinical psychology. Five such conceptual frameworks are the Fusion model (i.e., the melting-pot theory), the Alternation model (i.e., social behavior that is appropriately applied in different social contexts), the Assimilation model (i.e, the ongoing process of absorption of a culture of origin into a dominant culture, with eventual loss of identification with culture of origin), the Acculturation model (i.e., the ongoing process of absorption of culture of origin into a culture of settlement, but with continued retention of culture of origin), and the Multicultural model (LaFromboise et al., 1993). The Multicultural model (Berry, 1984, 1990; Berry, Kim, Power, Young, & Bujaki, 1989) focuses on acculturative processes within a pluralistic society that involve individuals and groups. The accul-turative process refers to affective, cognitive, and behavioral changes in both the culture of origin and the culture of settlement due to coexistence. According to Berry and his colleagues, individuals and groups confront two main issues in cultural adap-tation: maintenance of the culture of origin and intercultural interaction. The four choices (outcomes) available to individuals and groups are *integration, assimilation, separation,* and *marginalization.* In integration, there is acceptance of both the culture of settlement and one's culture of origin. In assimilation, there is acceptance of the culture of settlement and simultaneous rejection of the culture of origin. In separation, there is acceptance of the culture of origin and rejection of the culture of settlement. In marginalization, there is rejection of both the culture of settlement and the culture of origin.

Important progress has been made in the advancement of cultural adaptation mod-els, the measurement of the acculturation construct, and the elucidation of the role of cultural adaptation in human adjustment (Berry et al., 1989; Kazarian, 1993; LaFrom-boise et al., 1993; Pachter & Weller, 1993). Research on acculturation processes, however, has primarily been cross-sectional. Their longitudinal investigation within the North American culture is long overdue. Nevertheless, cultural adaptation considerations are important, not only from the perspectives of research and measurement but also from the perspective of socially responsible and culturally appropriate training and practice in clinical psychology. Training and practice should include the role of cultural adaptation in classification, diagnosis, psychological assessment, service utilization, service delivery, and research on health. In addition to assessment, treatment, prevention, and research issues associated with refugee children and adults (Beiser, Dion, Gotowiec, Hyman, & Vu, 1995; Canadian Task Force on Mental Health Issues Affecting Immigrants and Refugees, 1988; Jaranson & Bamford, 1987; Kazarian & Joseph, 1994; Pernice, 1994; Williams & Berry, 1991), there are theoretical and practice considerations associated with the psychological assessment, treatment, and rehabilitation of people from various cultural groups. Psychological assessment issues include professional standards and ethics, cultural biases in content and standardization, selection of culturally appropriate tools, availability and translation of psychological tests, examiner variables, and the use of interpreters in the psychological assessment process (APA, 1985, 1992; Butcher, 1995; Dana, 1993, 1996; Jones & Thorne, 1987; Malgady, Rogler, & Costantino, 1987; Olmedo, 1981; Rogers, Flores, Ustad, & Sewell, 1995; Sattler, 1992; Schmidt & Hunter, 1974; Suzuki, Meller, & Ponterotto, 1996; Westermeyer, 1990).

Intervention considerations include professional standards and ethics, cultural beliefs about health and mental health and their etiology, conceptualization of client problems from the perspective of cultural adaptation, client-therapist cultural match, choice of therapy, the use of interpreters in therapy and the presence of third parties in the therapeutic process, treatment compliance and effectiveness, patterns of service utilization, and integration of culture of settlement health care and culture of origin approaches (APA, 1992, 1993b; Comas-Diaz & Griffith, 1988; Fernando & Kazarian, 1995; Hays, 1995; Nilchaikovit et al., 1993; Padilla et al., 1975; Ramirez, 1991; Rappaport & Rappaport, 1981; Rogler et al., 1987, 1991; Sue & Sue, 1975; Westermeyer, 1990). The realities of managed care, program management, and client-centered care (Kovner, 1995; Shortell & Kaluzny, 1994) provide additional challenges for culturally appropriate psychological service delivery.

CONCLUSIONS

Clinical psychology has the ethical and professional responsibility to be responsive to the needs of the pluralistic communities it serves. This includes the preparation of professionally and ethically competent clinical psychologists. Professional and ethical competence are consummated only with the infusion of culture into the science, practice, and training of clinical psychology. We have offered cultural clinical psychology as a viable approach to further facilitate this process.

Cultural clinical psychology is likely to become a reality when it is embraced by clinical psychology program directors, with support from departments of psychology and the larger psychological community. Needless to say, APA/CPA accreditation and the community at large are likely to play facilitative roles in promoting cultural clinical psychology as a dynamic training model for clinical psychology. Finally, the establishment of a journal of cultural clinical psychology to provide a forum for scholarly and professional activities will augment the viability and acceptance of the field. In embracing the scientific, professional, and cultural domains, both clinical psychology and psychology in general are likely to contribute to the development of partnerships in pluralistic communities and of a unified psychological theory and practice. The benefits of such a trilogy include universality, social responsibility, and quality of life. This direction in theory, research, and practice is all the more important as current and future technology allow a clinical psychologist in Canada to interact with a client in any country in the world over the Internet (Lloyd, Schlosser, & Stricker, 1996).

References

Accreditation Council for Graduate Medical Education. (1993). Special requirements for residency training in psychiatry. *Graduate Medical Education Directory, 1993–1994*. Chicago American Medical Association.

Albee, G. W. (1970). The uncertain future of clinical psychology. *American Psychologist, 25*, 1071–1080.

Albee, G. W. (1987). The uncertain direction of clinical psychology. In R. H. Dana and W. T. May (Eds.), *Internship training in professional psychology* (pp. 504–518). New York: Harper & Row.

Allison, K. W., Crawford, I., Echemendia, R., Robinson, L., & Knapp, D. (1994). Human diversity and professional competence: Training in clinical and counseling psychology revisited. *American Psychologist, 49*, 792–797.

Allison, K. W., Echemendia, R. J., Crawford, I., & Robinson, W. L. (1996). Predicting cultural competence: Implications for practice and training. *Professional Psychology: Research and Practice, 27*, 386–393.

Alloy, L. B., Acocella, J., & Bootzin, R. R. (1996). *Abnormal psychology: Current perspectives*. New York: McGraw-Hill.

Altmaier, E. M. (1993). Role of Criterion II in accreditation. *Professional Psychology: Research and Practice, 24*, 127–129.

American Association of State and Provincial Psychology Boards. (1991). *AASPPB code of conduct*. Montgomery, AL: Author.

American Psychological Association. (1985). *Standards for Educational and Psychological Testing*. Washington, DC: Author.

American Psychological Association. (1986). *Accreditation handbook*. Washington, DC: Author.

American Psychological Association. (1992). Ethical principles of psychologists and code of conduct. *American Psychologist, 47*, 1597–1611.

American Psychological Association. (1993a). *Profile of all APA members: 1993*. Washington, D.C.: Author.

American Psychological Association. (1993b). Guidelines for providers of psychological services to ethnic, linguistic, and culturally diverse populations. *American Psychologist, 48*, 45–48.

American Psychological Association Committee on Accreditation. (1991, Summer). The nature, scope, and implementation of Criterion II: Cultural and individual differences. *Capsule*, (pp.1–5).

Bandura, A. (1978). The self system in reciprocal determinism. *American Psychologist, 33*, 344–358.

Bandura, A. (1986). *Social foundations of thought and action: A social cognitive theory*. Englewood Cliffs, NJ: Prentice Hall.

Batts, V. A. (1990). An experiential workshop: Introduction to multiculturalism. In G. Stricker, E. Davis-Russell, E. Bourg, E. Duran, W. R. Hammond, J. McHolland, K. Polits, & B. E. Vaughn (Eds.), *Toward diversification in psychology education and training* (pp. 9–16). Washington, D.C: American Psychological Association.

Bayton, J. A., Roberts, S. O., & Williams, R. K. (1970). Minority groups and careers in psychology. *American Psychologist, 25,* 504–510.

Beiser, M., Dion, R., Gotowiec, A., Hyman, I., & Vu, N. (1995). Immigrant and refugee children in Canada. *Canadian Journal of Psychiatry, 40,* 67–72.

Belar, C. D., & Perry, N. W. (1992). National conference on scientist-practitioner education and training for the professional practice of psychology. *American Psychologist, 47,* 71–75.

Bernal, M. E. (1994a). Some issues and content missed by survey studies. *American Journal of Community Psychology, 22,* 799–801.

Bernal, M. E. (1994b). Integration of ethnic minorities into academic psychology: How it has been and what it could be. In E. J. Trickett, R. J. Watts, & D. Birman (Eds.), *Human diversity: Perspectives on people in context* (pp.404–423). San Francisco: Jossey-Bass.

Bernal, M. E., & Castro, F. G. (1994). Are clinical psychologists prepared for service and research with ethnic minorities? Report of a decade of progress. *American Psychologist, 49,* 797–805.

Bernal, M. E., & Padilla, A. M. (1982). Status of minority curricula and training in clinical psychology. *American Psychologist, 37,* 780–787.

Bernhardt, K. S. (1947). Canadian psychology–past, present, and future. *Canadian Journal of Psychology, 1,* 49–66.

Bernhardt, K. S. (Ed.). (1961). *Training for research in psychology.* Toronto, Ontario: University of Toronto Press.

Berry, J. W. (1984). Cultural relations in plural societies: Alternatives to segregation and their sociopsychological implications. In N. Miller & M. Brewer (Eds.), *Groups in contact* (p. 11–27). San Diego Academic Press.

Berry, J. W. (1990). Psychology of acculturation: Understanding individuals moving between cultures. In R. W. Brislin (Ed.), *Applied cross-cultural psychology* (pp. 232–252). Newbury Park, CA: Sage.

Berry, J. W. (1994). Cross-cultural health psychology. *The Canadian Health Psychologist, 2,* 37–41.

Berry, J. W., Kim, U., Power, S., Young, M., & Bujaki, M. (1989). Acculturation attitudes in plural societies. *Applied Psychology: An International Review, 38,* 185–206.

Betancourt, H., & Lopez, S. R. (1993). The study of culture, ethnicity, and race in American psychology. *American Psychologist, 48,* 629–637.

Bickman, L. (Ed.). (1987). Graduate Education in Psychology. *American Psychologist, 42,* 1041–1047.

Bluestone, H. H., Stokes, A., & Kuba, S. A. (1996). Toward an integrated program design: Evaluating the status of diversity training in a graduate school curriculum. *Professional Psychology: Research and Practice, 27,* 394–400.

Bond, M. (Ed.). (1988). *The cross-cultural challenge to social psychology.* Newbury Park, CA: Sage.

Brislin, R. W., & Yoshida, T. (Eds.). (1994). *Improving intercultural interactions: Modules for cross-cultural training programs.* Thousand Oaks, CA: Sage.

Burnam, M. A., Hough, R. L., Karno, M., Escobar, J. I., & Telles, C. A. (1987). Acculturation and lifetime prevalence of psychiatric disorders among Mexican Americans in Los Angeles. *Journal of Health and Social Behavior, 28,* 89–102.

Butcher, J. N. (Ed.). (1995). *Clinical personality assessment: Practical approaches.* New York: Oxford University Press.

Canadian Psychological Association. (1989a). *Accreditation criteria for professional psychology programs and internships and accreditation procedures.* Ottawa: Author.

Canadian Psychological Association. (1989b). *Practice guidelines for providers of psychological services.* Quebec: Author.

Canadian Psychological Association. (1991). *Canadian code of ethics for psychologists* (Rev. ed.). Quebec: Author.

Canadian Psychological Association. (1994). *Accreditation criteria for professional psychology programs and internships and accreditation procedures.* Ottawa: Author.

Canadian Task Force on Mental Health Issues Affecting Immigrants and Refugees. (1988). *After the door has been opened.* Ottawa: Health and Welfare Canada.

Carson, R. C., Butcher, J. N., & Mineka, S. (1996). *Abnormal psychology and modern life.* New York: Harper Collins.

Clark, L. A. (1987). Mutual relevance of mainstream and cross-cultural psychology. *Journal of Consulting and Clinical Psychology, 55,* 461–470.

Clements, C. B., & Rickard, H. C. (1993). Criterion II: A principle in search of guidelines. *Professional Psychology: Research and Practice, 24,* 133–134.

Comas-Diaz, L., & Griffith, E. E. H. (Eds.). (1988). *Clinical guidelines in cross-cultural mental health.* New York: Wiley.

Dahlquist, L. M., & Fay, A. S. (1983). Cultural issues in psychotherapy. In C. E. Walker (Ed.), *The handbook of clinical psychology: Theory, research and practice* (1219–1255). Homewood, IL: Dow-Jones Irwin.

Dana, R. H. (1993). *Multicultural assessment perspectives for professional psychology.* Needham Heights, MA: Allyn & Bacon.

Dana, R. H. (1994). Testing and assessment ethics for all persons: Beginning and agenda. *Professional Psychology: Research and Practice, 25,* 349–354.

Dana, R. H. (1996). Culturally competent assessment practice in the United States. *Journal of Personality Assessment, 66,* 472–487.

Dobson, K. S., & Dobson, D. J. G. (1993). *Professional psychology in Canada.* Toronto: Hogrefe & Huber.

Dobson, K. S., & King, M. C. (Eds.). (1995). *The Mississauga Conference on Professional Psychology: Final Report.* Ottawa: Canadian Psychological Association.

Dong, T., Wong, H., Callao, M., Nishihara, A., & Chin, R. (1978). Psychology in action: National Asian American psychology training conference. *American Psychologist, 33,* 691–693.

El-Khawas, E. H., & Astin, H. S. (1972). Current enrollment characteristics of graduate students in psychology. *American Psychologist, 27,* 457–461.

Fernando, M. L. D., & Kazarian, S. S. (1995). Patient education in the drug treatment of psychiatric disorders: Effect on compliance and outcome. *CNS Drugs, 3,* 291–304.

Fox, R. E. (1982). The need for a reorientation of clinical psychology. *American Psychologist, 37,* 1051–1057.

Fox, R. E., Barclay, A. G., & Rodgers, D. A. (1982). The foundations of professional psychology. *American Psychologist, 37,* 306–312.

Fox, R. E., Kovacs, A. L., & Graham, S. R. (1985). Proposals for a resolution in the preparation and regulation of professional psychologists. *American Psychologist, 40,* 1042–1050.

Garfield, S. L., & Kurtz, R. (1976). Clinical psychologists in the 1970s. *American Psychologist, 31,* 1–9.

Goldstein, A. P., & Simonson, N. (1971). Social psychological approaches to psychotherapy research. In A. Bergin & S. Garfield (Eds.), *Handbook of psychotherapy and behavior change* (154–195). New York: Wiley.

Graham, S. (1992). "Most of the subjects were white and middle class": Trends in published research on African-Americans in selected APA journals, 1970–1989. *American Psychologist, 47,* 629–639.

Hathaway, S. R. (1958). A study of human behavior: The clinical psychologist. *American Psychologist, 13,* 257–265.

Havinghurst, R. J. (1970). Minority subcultures and the law of effect. *American Psychologist, 25,* 313–322.

Hays, P. A. (1995). Multicultural applications of cognitive-behavioral therapy. *Professional Psychology: Research and Practice, 26,* 309–315.

Hays, P. A. (1996). Culturally responsive assessment with diverse older clients. *Professional Psychology: Research and Practice, 27,* 188–193.

Hersch, C. (1969). From mental health to social action: Clinical psychology in historical perspective. *American Psychologist, 24,* 909–916.

Hersen, M., Kazdin, A. E., & Bellack, A. S. (Eds.). (1983). *The clinical psychology handbook.* New York: Pergamon.

Hills, H. I., & Strozier, A. L. (1992). Multicultural training in APA-approved counseling psychology programs: A survey. *Professional Psychology: Research and Practice, 23,* 43–51.

Ho, D. Y. F. (1985). Cultural values and professional issues in clinical psychology: Implications from the Hong Kong experience. *American Psychologist, 40,* 1212–1218.

Howard, A., Pion, G. M., Gottfredson, G. D., Flattau, P. E., Oskamp, S., Pfaffin, S. M., Bray, D. W., & Burstein, A. G. (1986). The changing face of American psychology: A report from the committee on employment and human resources. *American Psychologist, 41,* 1311–1327.

Isaac, P. D. (1985). Recruitment of minority students into graduate programs in psychology. *American Psychologist, 40,* 472–474.

Jahoda, G. (1980). Theoretical and systematic approaches. In H. C. Triandis and W. W. Lambert (Eds.), *Handbook of cross-cultural psychology: Vol.1. Perspectives* (pp. 69–141). Boston: Allyn & Bacon.

Jahoda, G. (1984). Do we need a concept of culture? *Journal of Cross-Cultural Psychology, 15,* 139–151.

Jaranson, J. M., & Bamford, P. (1987). *Program models for mental health treatment of refugees.* St. Paul: University of Minnesota.

Jenkins, J. O., & Knox, K. (1983). Minorities. In M. Hersen, A. E. Kazdin, & A. S. Bellack (Eds.), *The clinical psychology handbook* (pp. 683–696). New York: Pergamon.

Jones, E. E., & Thorne, A. (1987). Rediscovery of the subject: Intercultural approaches to clinical assessment. *Journal of Consulting and Clinical Psychology, 55,* 488–495.

Jones, J. M. (1990). Who is training our ethnic minority psychologists, and are they doing it right? In G. Stricker, E. Davis-Russell, E. Bourg, E. Duran, W. R. Hammond, J. McHolland, K. Polits, & B. E. Vaughn (Eds.), *Toward ethnic diversification in psychology education and training* (pp. 17–34). Washington, DC: American Psychological Association.

Kalin, R., & Berry, J. W. (1994). Ethic and multicultural attitudes. In J. W. Berry & J. A. Laponce (Eds.), *Ethnicity and culture in Canada* (pp. 293–321). Toronto: University of Toronto Press.

Karno, M., & Edgerton, R. B. (1969). Perceptions of mental illness in a Mexican-American community. *Archives of General Psychiatry, 20,* 233–238.

Kaswan, J. (1981). Manifest and latent functions of psychological services. *American Psychologist, 36,* 290–299.

Kazarian, S. S. (1993). *Measurement of acculturation: A review.* Unpublished manuscript, The University of Western Ontario, London, Canada.

Kazarian, S. S. (1994). A graduate course on the role of culture in clinical psychology. *Health and Culture, 10,* 3–4.

Kazarian, S. S. (in press). Assessment and treatment of children and adults: Legal, professional standards and ethical considerations. In D. R. Evans (Ed.), *The law, standards of practice and ethics in the practice of psychology.* Toronto: Emond Montgomery.

Kazarian, S. S., & Joseph, L. W. (1994). Caring for refugees in a mental hospital. *Canadian Journal of Psychiatry, 29,* 189.

Kazarian, S. S., Mazmanian, D., Sussman, S. I., & Persad, E. (1993). Countries of origin of patients and professional staff in a mental hospital. *Canadian Journal of Psychiatry, 28,* 694.

Kendall, P. C., & Hammen, C. (1996). *Abnormal psychology.* Boston: Houghton Mifflin.

Kiesler, C. A. (1976). The training of psychiatrists and psychologists. *American Psychologist, 31,* 1–2.

Kim, U., Triandis, H. C., Kagitcibasi, G., Choi, S. G., & Yoon, G. (Eds.). (1994). *Individualism and collectivism: Theory, methods, and application.* Thousand Oaks, CA: Sage.

Kimble, G. A. (1984). Psychology's two cultures. *American Psychologist, 39,* 833–839.

Kohout, J., & Pion, G. (1990). Participation of ethnic minorities in psychology: Where do we stand today? In G. Stricker, E. Davis-Russell, E. Bourg, E. Duran, W. R. Hammond, J. McHolland, K. Polits, & B. E. Vaughn (Eds.), *Toward ethnic diversification in psychology education and training* (153–165). Washington, DC: American Psychological Association.

Korchin, S. J. (1980). Clinical psychology and minority problems. *American Psychologist, 35,* 262–269.

Korman, M. (1974). National conference on levels and patterns of professional training in psychology: The major themes. *American Psychologist, 29,* 441–449.

Kovner, A. R. (1995). *Jonas's health care delivery in the United States.* New York: Springer.

Krotki, K. J., & Reid, C. (1994). Demography of Canadian population by ethnic group. In J. W. Berry & J. A. Laponce (Eds.), *Ethnicity and culture in Canada: The research landscape* (pp. 17–59). Toronto: University of Toronto Press.

LaFromboise, T. D. (1988). American Indian mental health policy. *American Psychologist, 43,* 388–397.

LaFromboise, T., Coleman, H., & Gerton, J. (1993). Psychological impact of biculturalism: Evidence and theory. *Psychological Bulletin, 114,* 395–412.

Linton, R. (1945). *The cultural background of psychology.* New York: Appleton-Century.

Lloyd, M. G., Schlosser, B., & Stricker, G. (1996). The Forum. *Ethics and Behavior, 6,* 169–177.

MacCarthy, B. (1988). Clinical work with ethnic minorities. In F. N. Watts (Ed.), *New developments in clinical psychology* (pp. 122–139). New York: The British Psychological Society.

Malgady, R. G., Rogler, L. H., & Costantino, G. (1987). Ethnocultural and linguistic bias in mental health evaluation of Hispanics. *American Psychologist, 42,* 228–234.

Marin, G. (1993). Defining culturally appropriate community interventions: Hispanics as a case study. *Journal of Community Psychology, 21,* 149–161.

McGovern, T. V., Furumoto, L., Halpern, D. F., Kimble, G. A., & McKeachie, W. J. (1991). Liberal education, study in depth, and the arts and sciences major—psychology. *American Psychologist, 46,* 598–605.

McHolland, J., Lubin, M., & Forbes, W. (1990). Problems in minority recruitment and strategies for retention. In G. Stricker, E. Davis-Russell, E. Bourg, E. Duran, W. R. Hammond, J. McHolland, K. Polits, & B. E. Vaughn (Eds.), *Toward ethnic diversification in psychology education and training* (137–152). Washington, DC: American Psychological Association.

McNeil, E. B. (1959). The public image of psychology. *American Psychologist, 14,* 520–521.

Milan, M. A., Montgomery, R. W., & Rogers, E. C. (1994). Theoretical orientation revolution in clinical psychology: Fact or fiction? *Professional Psychology: Research and Practice, 25,* 398–402.

Netzel, M. T., Bernstein, D. A., & Milich, R. (1994). *Introduction to clinical psychology* (4th ed.). Englewood Cliffs, NJ: Prentice-Hall.

Nilchaikovit, T., Hill, J. M., & Holland, J. C. (1993). The effects of culture on illness behavior and medical care: Asian and American differences. *General Hospital Psychiatry, 15,* 41–50.

Norcross, J. C., & Prochaska, S. O. (1982). A national survey of clinical psychologists: Characteristics and activities. *Clinical Psychology, 35,* 1, 5–8.

Olmedo, E. L. (1981). Testing linguistic minorities. *American Psychologist, 36,* 1078–1085.

O'Sullivan, J. J., & Quevillon, R. P. (1992). 40 years later: Is the Boulder Model still alive? *American Psychologist, 47,* 67–70.

Pachter, L. M., & Weller, S. C. (1993). Acculturation and compliance with medical therapy. *Journal of Developmental and Behavioral Pediatrics, 14,* 163–168.

Padilla, A. M. (1980). Notes on the history of Hispanic psychology. *Hispanic Journal of Behavioral Science, 2,* 109–128.

Padilla, A. M., Ruiz, R. A., & Alvarez, R. (1975). Community mental health services for the Spanish speaking/surnamed population. *American Psychologist, 30,* 892–905.

Park, R. E. (1928). Human migration and the marginal man. *American Journal of Sociology, 5,* 881–893.

Payton, C. R. (1993). Review of APA accreditation Criterion II. *Professional Psychology: Research and Practice, 24,* 130–132.

Pernice, R. (1994). Methodological issues in research with refugees and immigrants. *Professional Psychology: Research and Practice, 25,* 207–213.

Peterson, D. R. (1968). The Doctor of Psychology program at the University of Illinois. *American Psychologist, 23,* 511–516.

Peterson, D. R. (1976). Need for the Doctor of Psychology degree in professional psychology. *American Psychologist, 21,* 792–798.

Phares, E. J. (1992). *Clinical Psychology: Concepts, methods, and profession.* Pacific Grove, CA: Brooks/Cole.

Ponterotto, J. G., & Casas, J. M. (1991). *Handbook of racial/ethnic minority counseling research.* Springfield, IL: Charles C. Thomas.

Ponterotto, J. G., Burkard, A., Yoshida, R. K., Cancelli, A. A., Mendez, G., Wasilewski, L., & Sussman, L. (1995). Prospective minority students' perceptions of application packets for professional psychology programs: A qualitative study. *Professional Psychology: Research and Practice, 26,* 196–204.

Pryzwanski, W. B., & Wendt, R. N. (1987). *Psychology as a profession: Foundations of practice.* New York: Pergamon Press.

Psychology Act, R.S.O. 1991, c. 38.

Quintana, S. M., & Bernal, M. E. (1994). Ethnic minority training in counseling psychology: Comparisons with clinical psychology and proposed standards. *Counseling Psychologist, 23,* 102–121.

Raimy, V. (Ed.). (1950). *Training in clinical psychology.* New York: Prentice-Hall.

Ramirez, M. (1991). *Psychotherapy and counseling with minorities: A cognitive approach to individual and cultural differences.* New York: Pergamon Press.

Rappaport, H., & Rappaport, M. (1981). The integration of scientific and traditional healing: A proposed model. *American Psychologist, 36,* 774–781.

Reisman, J. M. (1991). *A history of clinical psychology.* New York: Hemisphere.

Rickard, H. C., & Clements, C. S. (1993). Critique of APA accreditation Criterion II: Cultural and individual differences. *Professional Psychology: Research and Practice, 24,* 123–126.

Rie, H. E. (1976). Psychology, mental health and the public interest. *American Psychologist, 31,* 1–4.

Ritchie, P., Hogan, T. P., & Hogan, T. V. (Eds.). (1988). *Psychology in Canada: The state of the discipline, 1984.* Old Chelsea, Quebec: Canadian Psychological Association.

Rogers, R., Flores, J., Ustad, K., & Sewell, K. W. (1995). Initial validation of the Personality Assessment Inventory-Spanish version with clients from Mexican American communities. *Journal of Personality Assessment, 64,* 340–348.

Rogler, L. H., Cortes, D. E., & Malgady, R. G. (1991). Acculturation and mental health status among Hispanics: Consequence and new directions for research. *American Psychologist, 46,* 585–597.

Rogler, L. H., Malgady, R. G., Costantino, G., & Blumenthal, R. (1987). What do culturally sensitive mental health services mean? The case of Hispanics. *American Psychologist, 42,* 565–570.

Ruiz, R. A. (1971). Relative frequency of Americans with Spanish surnames in associations of psychology, psychiatry and sociology. *American Psychologist, 26,* 1022–1024.

Russo, N. F., Olmedo, E. L., Stape, J., & Fulcher, R. (1981). Women and minorities in psychology. *American Psychologist, 36,* 1315–1363.

Santiego-Negron, S. (1990). Institutional change and leadership: Challenges in education. In G. Stricker, E. Davis-Russell, E. Bourg, E. Duran, W. R. Hammond, J. McHolland, K. Polits, & B. E. Vaughn (Eds.), *Toward ethnic diversification in psychology education and training* (65–75). Washington, DC: American Psychological Association.

Sarason, I. G., & Sarason, B. R. (1996). *Abnormal psychology: The problem of maladaptive behavior.* Upper Saddle River, NJ: Prentice-Hall.

Sattler, J. M. (1992). *Assessment of children.* San Diego, CA: Author.

Sayette, M. A., & Mayne, T. J. (1990). Survey of current clinical and research trends in clinical psychology. *American Psychologist, 45,* 1263–1266.

Schmidt, F. L., & Hunter, J. E. (1974). Racial and ethnic bias in psychological tests: Divergent implications of two definitions of test bias. *American Psychologist, 29,* 1–8.

Schofield, W. (1964). *Psychotherapy: The purchase of friendship.* Englewood Cliffs, NJ: Prentice-Hall.

Segall, M. H. (1983). On the search for the independent variable in cross-cultural psychology. In S. H. Irvine & J. H. Berry (Eds.), *Human assessment and cultural factors* (pp. 127–137). New York: Plenum Press.

Segall, M. S. (1986). Culture and behavior: Psychology in global perspective. *Annual Review of Psychology, 37,* 523–564.

Shakow, D. (1947). Recommended graduate training program in clinical psychology. *American Psychologist, 2,* 539–558.

Shakow, D. (1969). *Clinical psychology as a science and profession: A 40 year odyssey.* Chicago: Aldine Press.

Shakow, D. (1976). What is clinical psychology? *American Psychologist, 29,* 553–560.

Shakow, D. (1978). Clinical psychology seen some 50 years later. *American Psychologist, 33,* 148–157.

Shoham, S. G., Ashkenasy, J. J. M., Rahav, G., Chard, F., Addi, A., & Addad, M. (1995). *Violence: An integrated multivariate study of human aggression.* Aldershot, England: Dartmouth.

Shortell, S. M., & Kaluzny, A. D. (1994). *Health care management: Organization design and behavior.* Albany, NY: Delmar.

Snowden, K. R., & Cheung, F. K. (1990). Use of inpatient mental health services by members of ethnic minority groups. *American Psychologist, 45,* 347–355.

Speight, S. L., Thomas, A. J., Kennel, R. G., & Anderson, M. E. (1995). Operationalizing multicultural training in doctoral programs and internships. *Professional Psychology: Research and Practice, 26,* 401–406.

Stricker, G. (1990). Keynote address: Minority issues in professional training. In G. Stricker,

E. Davis-Russell, E. Bourg, E. Duran, W. R. Hammond, J. McHolland, K. Polits, & B. E. Vaughn (Eds.), *Toward ethnic diversification in psychology education and training* (pp. 3–16). Washington, DC: American Psychological Association.

Stricker, G., Davis-Russell, E., Bourg, E., Duran, E., Hammond, W. R., McHolland, J., Polits, K., & Vaughn, B. E. (Eds.). (1990). *Toward ethnic diversification in psychology education and training.* Washington, DC: American Psychological Association.

Strickland, B. R. (1985). Over the Boulder(s) and through the Vail. *The Clinical Psychologist, 38,* 52–56.

Strickland, B. R. (1988). Clinical psychology comes of age. *American Psychologist, 43,* 104–107.

Suarez-Balcazar, Y., Durlak, J. A., & Smith, C. (1994). Multicultural training practices in community psychology programs. *American Journal of Community Psychology, 22,* 785–798.

Sue, S. (1977). Community mental health services to minority groups: Some optimism, some pessimism. *American Psychologist, 32,* 616–624.

Sue, S. (1983). Ethnic minority issues in psychology: A reexamination. *American Psychologist, 38,* 583–593.

Sue, S., & Sue, D. W. (1974). MMPI comparisons between Asian-American and non-Asian students utilizing a student health psychiatric clinic. *Journal of Counselling Psychology, 21,* 423–427.

Sue, D. W., Bernier, J. E., Durran, A., Feinberg, L., Pederson, P., Smith, E. J., & Vasquez-Nuttall, E. (1982). Position paper: Cross-cultural counselling competencies. *The Counseling Psychologist, 10,* 45–52.

Suinn, R. M., & Witt, J. C. (1982). Survey on the ethnic minority faculty recruitment and retention. *American Psychologist, 37,* 1239–1244.

Suzuki, L. A., Meller, P. J., & Ponterotto, J. G. (Eds.). (1996). *Handbook of multicultural assessment: Clinical, psychological and educational applications.* San Francisco: Jossey-Bass.

Taube, C. A., Burns, B. J., & Kessler, L. (1984). Patients of psychiatrists and psychologists in office-based practice: 1980. *American Psychologist, 39,* 1435–1447.

Triandis, H. C. (1990). Theoretical concepts that are applicable to the analysis of ethnocentrism. In R. W. Brislin (Ed.), *Applied cross-cultural psychology* (pp. 24–55). Newbury Park, CA: Sage.

Triandis, H. C., & Brislin, R. W. (1984). Cross-cultural psychology. *American Psychologist, 39,* 1006–1016.

Tyler, F. B., Susswell, D. R., & Williams-McCoy, J. (1985). Ethnic validity in psychotherapy. *Psychotherapy, 22,* 311–320.

Ullman, C. A. (1947). The training of clinical psychologists. *American Psychologist, 2,* 173–175.

Van Brenk, D. (1992, December 4). UWO urged to recruit more ethnic students. *London Free Press,* p. A1.

VandenBos, G. R., & Stapp, J. (1983). Service providers in psychology: Results of the 1982 APA human resources survey. *American Psychologist, 38,* 1330–1352.

Walker, C. E. (Ed.). (1983). *The handbook of clinical psychology: Theory, research, and practice.* Homewood, IL: Dow-Jones Irwin.

Watkins, C. E., Campbell, V. L., Nieberding, R., & Hallmark, R. (1995). Contemporary practice of psychological assessment by clinical psychologists. *Professional Psychology: Research and Practice, 26,* 54–60.

Watts, R. J. (1992). Elements of a psychology of human diversity. *Journal of Community Psychology, 20,* 116–131.

Watts, R. J. (1994). Graduate training for a diverse world. *American Journal of Community Psychology, 22,* 807–809.

Webster, E. C. (1967). *The Couchiching conference on professional psychology.* Montreal: McGill University, Industrial Relations Center.

Weil, R. (1952). The psychologist in a clinical setting. *Canadian Journal of Psychology, 6,* 131–140.

Westermeyer, J. (1990). Working with an interpreter in psychiatric assessment and treatment. *The Journal of Nervous and Mental Disease, 178,* 745–749.

Wiggins, J. G. (1994). Would you want your child to be a psychologist? *American Psychologist, 49,* 485–492.

Will, G. F. (1993, July 30). America's debate on immigration. *International Herald Tribune,* p. 7.

Willette, T. J. (1972). A manpower data system for psychology. *American Psychologist, 27,* 468–474.

Williams, C. L. & Berry, J. W. (1991). Primary prevention of acculturative stress among refugees: Application of psychological theory and practice. *American Psychologist, 46,* 632–641.

Wilson, G. T., Nathan, P. E., O'Leary, K. D., & Clark, L. A. (1996). *Abnormal psychology.* Needham Heights, MA: Allyn & Bacon.

Woody, R. H., & Robertson, M. (1988). Becoming a clinical psychologist. Madison, CT.: International Universities Press.

Wright, M. J., & Myers, C. R. (1982). *History of academic psychology in Canada.* Toronto: Hogrefe.

Yutrzenka, B. A. (1995). Making a case for training in ethnic and cultural diversity in increasing treatment efficacy. *Journal of Consulting and Clinical Psychology, 63,* 197–206.

Zayas, L. H., Torres, L. R., Malcolm, J., & DesRosiers, F. S. (1996). Clinicians' definitions of ethnically sensitive therapy. *Professional Psychology: Research and Practice, 27,* 78–82.

2

Acculturation and Health

Theory and Research

J. W. BERRY

This chapter presents a set of ideas and a selection of research findings that will allow clinicians to better understand and provide services to people of diverse cultural origins who now live together in plural societies. The orientation to these materials is provided from the perspective of cross-cultural psychology, whose central aim has been to demonstrate the influence of cultural factors on the development and display of individual human behavior. Many psychologists working in this field have concluded that there is now substantial evidence to document the outcome of this culture-behavior relationship: individuals generally act in ways that correspond to cultural influences and expectations (Berry, Poortinga, Segall, & Dasen, 1992).

If this is so, an important question concerns what happens to individuals who have developed in one cultural context when they attempt to live in a new cultural context. If culture is such a powerful shaper of behavior, do individuals just continue to act in the new setting as they did in the previous one, do they quickly and easily change their behavioral repertoire to be more appropriate in the new setting, or is there some more complex pattern of continuity and change in how people go about their lives in the new society? The answer provided by cross-cultural psychology is very clearly supportive of the last of these three alternatives (Berry, 1992).

How cross-cultural psychology arrived at this conclusion has involved a substantial amount of research over the past decades, which now has considerable potential for application in clinical psychology. In focusing on how people who have developed in one cultural context manage to adapt to new contexts that result from migration, researchers employ the concept of *acculturation* in two ways: first, to refer to the cultural changes resulting from these group encounters; second, the concept of *psychological acculturation* is used to refer to the psychological changes and eventual outcomes that occur as a result of individuals experiencing acculturation that is under way in their group.

CROSS-CULTURAL HEALTH PSYCHOLOGY

These two general themes (culture-behavior links across cultures and psychological adaptation to new cultures) are considered to be complementary and mutually informative aspects of the field of cross-cultural psychology. When applied to the specific area of health psychology, a new field of cross-cultural health psychology (Berry, 1994), which can be divided into two related domains, can be envisioned. The earlier, and more established, domain is the study of how cultural factors influence various aspects of health. This enterprise has taken place around the globe, driven by the need to understand individual and community health in the context of the indigenous cultures of the people being examined and served. The second, more recent and very active, domain is the study of the health of individuals and groups as they settle into and adapt to new cultural circumstances as a result of their migration and of their persistence over generations as ethnic groups. This enterprise has taken place in culturally plural societies where there is a need to understand and better serve an increasingly diverse population.

Cross-cultural Domain

The broad international and comparative work linking culture and health has been carried out by medical anthropology, transcultural psychiatry, and cross-cultural health psychology. Much of this work has resulted from the collaboration of medical, social, and behavioral scientists. The field is thus inherently an interdisciplinary one and is concerned with all aspects of health—physical, social, and psychological (see Dasen, Berry, & Sartorius, 1988; Landrine & Klonoff, 1992).

In this large and complex body of work, three theoretical orientations can be discerned: absolutism, relativism, and universalism (Berry et al., 1992). The *absolutist* position is one that assumes that human phenomena are basically the same (qualitatively) in all cultures: "honesty" is "honesty" and "depression" is "depression" no matter where one observes it. From the absolutist perspective, culture is thought to play little or no role in either the meaning or display of human characteristics. Assessments of such characteristics are made using standard instruments (perhaps with linguistic translation), and interpretations are made easily, without alternative culturally based views taken into account. It is essentially an *imposed etic* approach (Berry, 1989).

In sharp contrast, the *relativist* approach is rooted in anthropology and assumes that all human behavior is culturally patterned. It seeks to avoid ethnocentrism by trying to understand people "in their own terms." Explanations of human diversity are sought in the cultural context in which people have developed. Assessments are typically carried out employing the values and meanings that a cultural group gives to a phenomenon. Comparisons are judged to be problematic and ethnocentric and are thus virtually never made. This is the *emic* approach.

A third perspective, one that lies between the two positions, is that of *universalism*. Here it is assumed that basic human characteristics are common to all members of the species (i.e., constituting a set of biological givens) and that culture influences the development and display of them (i.e., culture plays different variations on these underlying themes). Assessments are based on the presumed underlying process, but measures are developed in culturally meaningful versions. Comparisons are made cautiously, employing a wide variety of methodological principles and safeguards. Interpretations of similarities and differences are attempted that take alternative culturally based meanings into account. This is the *derived etic* approach.

Perhaps the most comprehensive exposition of the way in which culture can influence health and disease was presented by Murphy (1982). He proposed that cultural factors can affect health in a number of ways, including its definition, recognition, symptomatology, prevalence, and response (by society or healer).

Numerous studies have shown that the very concepts of health and disease are defined differently across cultures; this basic link between culture and health was recognized early (see Polgar, 1962) and has continued up to the present time (see Helman, 1985, 1990, chap. 2). Indeed, the concept of health in international thought has recently undergone rapid change; witness the emphasis the World Health Organization (WHO) places on the existence of (positive) well-being rather than simply the absence of (negative) disease or disability. And while "disease" may be rooted in pathological biological process (common to all), "illness" is now widely recognized as a culturally influenced subjective experience of suffering and discomfort (Bishop, 1994).

Recognition of some condition either as healthy or as a disease is also linked to culture. Some activities, such as trance, are recognized as important curing (health-seeking) mechanisms in some cultures, but may be classified as psychiatric disorder in others (Ward, 1989). Similarly, the expression of a condition through the exhibition of various symptoms has also been linked to cultural norms. For example, it is claimed by many (e.g., Kirmayer, 1984; Kleinman, 1982) that psychological problems are expressed somatically in some cultures (e.g., Chinese; see Beinfield & Korngold, 1991) more than in other cultures.

Prevalence studies across cultures have produced very clear evidence that disease and disability are highly variable (Beardsley & Pedersen, 1996). From heart disease (Marmot et al., 1975) to cancer (Prener, Hojgaard-Nielson, Storm, & Hart Hansen, 1991) to schizophrenia (Murphy, 1982), cultural factors such as diets, substance abuse, and social relationships within the family all contribute to the prevalence of disease.

Ethnic Domain

When we focus on the health of culturally distinct groups and individuals who live in culturally plural societies, we are dealing with the ethnic domain. By "ethnic" we mean those phenomena that are *derived* from fully independent cultures; ethnic groups operate with an evolving culture that flows from their original heritage culture, in interaction with the culture of the larger (dominant) society.

While ethnic groups are not full-scale or independent cultural groups, it is a working belief of cross-cultural psychology that all the methodological, theoretical, and substantive lessons learned from working with cultural groups in the international enterprise should inform our work with ethnic groups. That is, we need to know both about their community health conceptions, values, practices, and institutions and about how these are distributed as health beliefs, attitudes, behaviors, and interpersonal relationships among individual members of the ethnic groups.

Put another way, we are not dealing with "minorities" that are simply deviant from some "mainstream," but with communities that deserve to have their health and health needs understood just as well as do any other cultural communities. In this sense, work on health in the ethnic domain does not differ in principle from work in the cultural domain. However, there is an important new element, that of contact and, possibly, conflict, between cultural groups. This is the case in a number of respects: first, the health phenomena of ethnic individuals may be quite different from those of the larger society, and may create misunderstanding, confusion, and conflict between the two groups; second, these conflicts may themselves generate health problems; and third, the health services of the larger society may not be sufficiently informed or sensitive to enable them to deal with either the health problems that are linked to the heritage of the ethnic group or those that have their roots in the conflict between the two groups in contact. Since the first of these issues is very similar to the discussion of the cultural domain, it will not be pursued further here. However, there is one important difference: when a health professional practicing in another country does not understand an individual's health needs, at least the individual may have recourse to an indigenous health system; when this lack of understanding occurs with respect to an ethnic individual who is living in a plural society, there may no longer be such an alternative health support service.

ACCULTURATION

With the overall field mapped out, we now turn to a consideration of the main theme of the chapter. The classical definition of acculturation was presented by Redfield, Linton, and Herskovits (1936, p. 149): "acculturation comprehends those phenomena which result when groups of individuals having different cultures come into continuous first-hand contact with subsequent changes in the original culture patterns of either or both groups." While *acculturation* is a neutral term in principle (that is, change may take place in either or both groups), in practice acculturation tends to induce more change in one of the groups (termed the *acculturating group* in this chapter) than in the other (Berry, 1990a).

A distinction has been made by Graves (1967) between acculturation as a collective or group-level phenomenon and psychological acculturation. In the former, acculturation is a change in the *culture* of the group; in the latter, acculturation is a change in the *psychology* of the individual. This distinction between levels is important for two reasons: first, in order to examine the systematic relationships between these two sets of variables; and second, because not all individuals participate to the same extent in the general acculturation being experienced by their group. While the general changes may be profound in the group, individuals are known to vary greatly in the degree to which they participate in these community changes (Berry, 1970; Furnham & Bochner, 1986).

Plural Societies

As a result of immigration and acculturation, many societies become *culturally plural*. That is, people of many cultural backgrounds come to live together in a diverse society. In many cases they form cultural groups that are not equal in power (numerical, economic, or political). These power differences have given rise to popular and social-science terms such as "mainstream," "minority," "ethnic group," and so forth. While recognizing the unequal influences and changes that exist during acculturation, I employ the term *cultural group* to refer to all groups and the terms *dominant* and *nondominant* to refer to their relative power where such a difference exists and is relevant to the discussion. This is an attempt to avoid a host of political and social assumptions that have distorted much of the work on psychological acculturation, in particular the assumption that "minorities" are inevitably (or should be in the process of) becoming part of the "mainstream" culture. While this does occur in many plural societies, it does not always occur, and in some cases it is resisted by either or both the dominant and nondominant cultural groups, resulting in the continuing cultural diversity of so many contemporary societies (Kymlicka, 1995; United Nations Educational, Scientific, & Cultural Organization [UNESCO], 1985).

Many kinds of cultural groups may exist in plural societies, and their variety is primarily due to three factors: voluntariness, mobility, and permanence. Some groups have entered into the acculturation process voluntarily (e.g., immigrants), while others experience acculturation without having sought it out (e.g., refugees, indigenous peoples). Other groups are in contact because they have migrated to a new location (e.g., immigrants and refugees), while others have had the new culture brought to them (e.g., indigenous peoples and "national minorities"). And, among those who have migrated, some are relatively permanently settled into the process (e.g., immigrants), while for others the situation is a temporary one (e.g., sojourners such as international students and guest workers or asylum-seekers who may eventually be deported).

Despite these variations in factors leading to acculturation, one of the conclusions that has been reached (Berry & Sam, 1996) is that the basic process of adaptation appears to be common to all these groups. What varies is the course, the level of difficulty, and to some extent the eventual outcome of acculturation; the three factors of voluntariness, mobility, and permanence, as well as others to be reviewed later, all contribute to this variation. Thus, while this chapter is mainly concerned with immigrants, many of the findings and conclusions have some degree of generalizability to other kinds of acculturating groups.

Acculturation Strategies

In all plural societies, cultural groups and their individual members, in both the dominant and nondominant situations, must deal with the issue of how to acculturate. Strategies with respect to two major issues are usually worked out by groups and individuals in their daily encounters with each other. These issues are cultural maintenance (to what extent are cultural identity and characteristics considered to be important, and their maintenance strived for); and contact and participation (to what extent should they become involved in other cultural groups, or remain primarily among themselves).

When these two underlying issues are considered simultaneously, a conceptual framework (Figure 2.1) is generated which posits four acculturation strategies. These two issues can be responded to on attitudinal dimensions, represented by bipolar

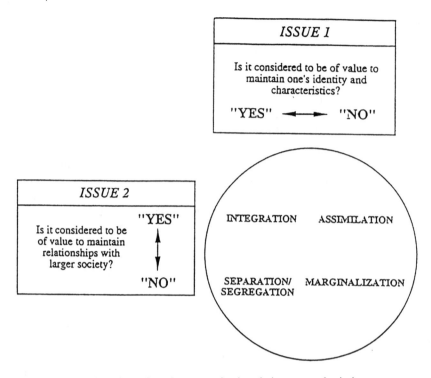

Figure 2.1 Varieties of acculturation strategies in relation to two basic issues

arrows. For purposes of presentation, generally positive or negative ("yes" or "no") responses to these issues intersect to define four acculturation strategies. These strategies carry different names, depending on which group (the dominant or nondominant) is being considered. From the point of view of nondominant groups, when individuals do not wish to maintain their cultural identity and seek daily interaction with other cultures, the *assimilation* strategy is defined. In contrast, when individuals place a value on holding onto their original culture and at the same time wish to avoid interaction with others, then the *separation* alternative is defined. When there is an interest in maintaining one's original culture while in daily interactions with other groups, *integration* is the option; here, there is some degree of cultural integrity maintained, while at the same time there is seeking to participate as an integral part of the larger social network. Finally, when there is little possibility or interest in cultural maintenance (often for reasons of enforced cultural loss) and little interest in having relations with others (often for reasons of exclusion or discrimination), then *marginalization* is defined.

The presentation above was based on the assumption that nondominant groups and their individual members have the freedom to choose how they want to acculturate. This, of course, is not always the case (Berry, 1974, 1990b). When the dominant group enforces certain forms of acculturation or constrains the choices of nondominant groups or individuals, then other terms need to be used. Most clearly, people may sometimes choose the separation option; but when it is required of them by the dominant society, the situation becomes one of *segregation*. Similarly, when people choose to assimilate, the notion of the *melting pot* may be appropriate; but when forced to do so, it becomes more like a *pressure cooker*. In the case of marginalization, people rarely choose such an option; rather, they usually become marginalized as a result of attempts at forced assimilation (pressure cooker) combined with forced exclusion (segregation); thus no other term seems to be required beyond the single notion of marginalization.

Integration can only be freely chosen and successfully pursued by nondominant groups when the dominant society is open and inclusive in their orientation toward cultural diversity (Berry, 1991). Thus, a mutual accommodation is required for integration to be attained, involving the acceptance by both groups of the right of all groups to live as culturally different peoples. This strategy requires nondominant groups to adopt the basic values of the larger society, while at the same time the dominant group must be prepared to adapt national institutions (e.g., education, health, labor) to better meet the needs of all groups now living together in the plural society.

Obviously, the integration strategy can only be pursued in societies that are explicitly multicultural, in which certain psychological preconditions are established (Berry & Kalin, 1995). These preconditions are: the widespread acceptance of the value to a society of cultural diversity (i.e., the presence of a positive "multicultural ideology"); relatively low levels of prejudice (i.e., minimal ethnocentrism, racism, and discrimination); positive mutual attitudes among cultural groups (i.e., no specific intergroup hatreds); and a sense of attachment to, or identification with, the larger society by all groups (Kalin & Berry, in press).

Acculturation Framework

The complex literature on acculturation has been the subject of numerous conceptual frameworks; these have attempted to systematize the process of acculturation and to illustrate the main factors that affect an individual's adaptation. In Figure 2.2, one such framework (Berry, 1992) is presented (see also Berry, 1976; Berry, Trimble, & Olmedo, 1986; Rogler, 1994).

On the left are group- or cultural-level phenomena, which are mainly situational variables; while to the right are individual- or psychological-level phenomena, which are predominantly person variables. Along the top are features that exist prior to acculturation taking place, while along the bottom are those that arise during the process of acculturation. Through the middle of the framework are the main group and psychological acculturation phenomena; these flow from left to right, beginning with the cultural groups in contact bringing about changes in many of their collective features (e.g., political, economic, social structures), then affecting the individual who is experiencing acculturation (resulting in a number of possible psychological experiences and changes), leading finally to a person's adaptation. The framework in Figure 2.2 combines both structural and process features: the central portion, flowing from group acculturation through individual acculturation to adaptation, is clearly a process that takes place over time; factors in the upper and lower levels that influence this process provide the broad structure in which acculturation takes place.

Contemporary reviews of the literature (Berry & Sam, 1996; Ward, 1996) show that this central flow is highly variable: the nature of a person's psychological accul-

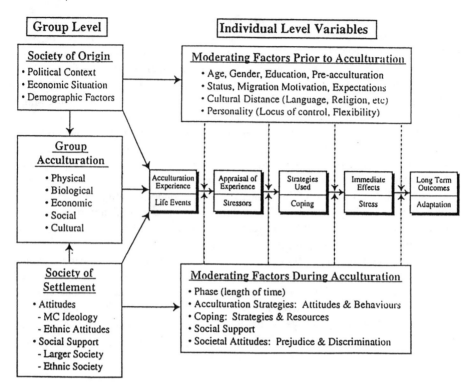

Figure 2.2 A framework for understanding acculturation and adaptation

turation and eventual adaptation depends on specific features of the group-level factors (on the left) and of the moderating influence (shown by the dotted lines) of individual factors that exist prior to, or arise during, acculturation (at the top and bottom).

It had been previously thought that acculturation inevitably brings social and psychological problems (Malzberg & Lee, 1956). However, such a negative and broad generalization no longer appears to be valid (Berry & Kim, 1988; Jayasuriya, Sang, & Fielding, 1992; Murphy, 1965; Westermeyer, 1986), with social and psychological outcomes now known to be highly variable. Three main points of view can be identified in acculturation research, each suggesting a different level of difficulty for the individual. The first is one that considers psychological changes to be rather easy to accomplish; this approach has been referred to variously as behavioral shifts by Berry (1980), "culture learning" by Brislin, Landis, & Brandt (1983), and "social skills acquisition" by Furnham and Bochner (1986). Here, psychological adaptations to acculturation are considered to be a matter of learning a new behavioral repertoire that is appropriate for the new cultural context. This also requires that some "culture shedding" (Berry, 1992) occur (the *un*learning of aspects of one's previous repertoire that are no longer appropriate); and it may be accompanied by some moderate "culture conflict" (where incompatible behaviors create difficulties for the individual).

In cases where greater conflict exists, then a second point of view is the appropriate one; here individuals may experience "culture shock" (Oberg, 1960) or "acculturative stress" (Berry, 1970; Berry, Kim, Minde, & Mok, 1987) if they cannot easily change their repertoire. While the culture-shock concept is older and has wide popular acceptance, I prefer the acculturative-stress conceptualization, for three reasons. One is that it is closely linked to psychological models of stress (e.g., Lazarus & Folkman, 1984) as a response to environmental stressors (which, in the present case, reside in the experience of acculturation), and thus has some theoretical foundation. The second is that "shock" suggests the presence of only negative experiences and outcomes of intercultural contact (cf. the "shell-shock" notion popular earlier as a psychological outcome of war experiences). However, during acculturation only moderate difficulties are usually experienced (such as some psychosomatic problems), since other psychological processes (such as problem appraisal and coping strategies) are usually available to the acculturating individual (Vega & Rumbaut, 1991). Third, the source of the problems that do arise is not cultural but intercultural, residing in the process of acculturation.

When major difficulties are experienced, then the "psychopathology" or "mental disease" perspective is most appropriate (Malzberg & Lee, 1956; Murphy, 1965; World Health Organization [WHO], 1991). Here, changes in the cultural context exceed the individual's capacity to cope because of the magnitude, speed or some other aspect of the change, leading to serious psychological disturbances, such as clinical depression and incapacitating anxiety (Berry & Kim, 1988; Jayasuriya et al., 1992).

With respect to the structuring of relationships, the framework in Figure 2.2 includes both mediating and moderating variables (Baron & Kenny, 1986); some variables may serve as both. For example, coping strategies serve as a mediator when they link stressors to the stress reaction, and as a moderator when they affect the degree of relationship between stressors and stress (Frese, 1986).

The main point of the framework is to show the key variables that should be attended to when carrying out studies of psychological acculturation. It is contended that any study that ignores any of these broad classes of variables will be incomplete and will be unable to comprehend individuals who are experiencing acculturation. For example, research that does not attend to the cultural and psychological characteristics that individuals bring to the process, merely characterizing them by name (e.g., as "Vietnamese", or "Somali", or, even less helpfully, as "minorities" or "immigrants"), cannot hope to understand their acculturation or adaptation. Similarly, research that ignores key features of the dominant society (such as their demography, immigration policies, and attitudes towards immigrants) is also incomplete. However, it is important to note that there is no single study that has incorporated or verified all aspects of the framework in Figure 2.2; it is a composite framework, assembling concepts and findings from numerous smaller-scale studies.

PHYSICAL HEALTH

Just as there are demonstrable links between physical health and its cultural context, so too there are relationships between physical health and changes in cultural context due to acculturation. In the process of migration, examination for and screening out of physical disease is a common practice (Siem & Bollini, 1992); this practice often results in better health status indicators for immigrants to a country than for those who are native-born. Moreover, most immigrants are also selected according to known correlates of good health (such as education, occupational status, and age). In a recent Canadian study, even when age-adjusted, Canadian-born individuals had a 7% higher prevalence of a variety of chronic diseases than did immigrants, but these differences were reduced the longer immigrants had lived in Canada (Statistics Canada, 1996).

Thus with increasing acculturation, health status "migrates" to the national norm. This phenomenon has been well established in the literature for over two decades (see Kliewer, 1992, for an overview). For example, coronary heart disease (age-standardized mortality rates) in immigrants changed substantially and variably following migration to Canada: it increased for Polish immigrants (whose rates were initially lower), but decreased for those from Australia and New Zealand (whose rates were initially higher). Data for immigrants from the 29 countries in the study show that all but 3 of the countries shifted their rates in the direction of the Canadian-born population.

In a second example (Lillenfeld, 1972), stomach and intestinal cancer rates of immigrants to the United States were examined. For stomach cancer, of the 14 samples included, 11 had higher rates in the countries of origin, and these shifted toward the U.S. norm following migration. For intestinal cancer, rates increased in samples from all 14 countries, 11 of which began with lower rates than in the United States.

It is not clear why these shifts in health status occur. One possibility is that health acculturates simply by increasingly resembling host-society norms over time. This could be due to exposure to widely shared risk factors in the physical environment (such as climate, pollution, pathogens) over which one has little choice. It could also be due to choosing to pursue assimilation (or possibly integration) as the way to acculturate; here one may be more exposed to cultural risk factors (such as diet, lifestyle, substance use) that are common in the society of settlement. It would be possible to support this linear "behavioral shift" interpretation if there were evidence for health status improving toward national norms, as well as declining. However, since the main evidence suggests a decline in health status, the "acculturative stress" or even "psychopathology" interpretations may also be supported. That is, the very process of acculturation may involve risk factors that can reduce one's health status. To the extent that stress has an effect on lowering resistance to disease, this is a plausible explanation. Such links to stress have been found for a variety of diseases among acculturating individuals, for example for hypertension (Cruz-Croke, 1987; Salmond, Prior, & Wessen, 1989) and diabetes (Hazuda, Haffner, Stern, & Eifler, 1988).

In addition to prevalence studies based on fairly objective diagnoses, there is also a literature on how individuals subjectively interpret physical symptoms. While most of this literature is in the broader cross-cultural domain (e.g., Angel & Thoits, 1987), one study has examined how migration and acculturation of Chinese peoples to Canada can affect interpretations of disease symptoms (Brown, 1996). In this study, a comparison was made between Chinese immigrants to Canada, Canadian-born Chinese, and Euro-Canadian samples. Significant differences on the Chinese Values Survey (Bond, 1991) confirmed the expected general cultural orientations of the three samples. Participants performed a card-sorting task using a set of 30 physical symptoms. Multidimensional scaling analyses revealed rather similar four-dimensional solutions of these symptom sorts, despite major differences in general between Chinese and Western medical systems, and despite significant Chinese value orientations. One interpretation of this similarity is that all three samples had a common experience of the Canadian health system; that is, cultural contact may have led to the acculturation of the two Chinese samples to Euro-Canadian views about health. Another possible interpretation is that there really is a fundamental underlying similarity in symptoms across cultures, with only an outer layer of cultural variation. A technique such as multidimensional scaling allows for a deeper examination below the cultural surface, possibly providing support for the universalist theoretical position.

PSYCHOLOGICAL HEALTH

Most research on psychological health in relation to acculturation has been guided by the acculturative-stress or psychopathology conceptualization. In the extreme case, researchers have systematically linked suicide to problems and difficulties of acculturation (Griffith, Syme, Kagan, Kato, Cohen, & Belsky 1989), using the acculturation framework outlined in Figures 2.1 and 2.2.

Within the acculturative-stress orientation, depression (due to cultural loss) and anxiety (due to uncertainty about how to live) are the problems most frequently found in a series of recent studies in Canada (e.g., Dona & Berry, 1994a; Kim & Berry, 1986; Sands & Berry, 1993; Zheng & Berry, 1991). In these studies, samples ranged widely (e.g., Central American, Korean, Greek, and Chinese immigrants), and a variety of assessment instruments and research procedures were used.

Perhaps the most consistent finding is that, as predicted, those who preferred and attained some degree of integration (as defined in Figure 2.1) experienced fewest problems. For example, in a study with Central American refugees in Toronto, individuals seeking integration had significantly lower psychological (and somatic) symptoms than those seeking to acculturate in other ways (Dona & Berry, 1994a). This pattern confirmed earlier findings with Korean immigrants in Toronto (Kim & Berry, 1986) and Chinese sojourners in Kingston (Zheng & Berry, 1991) and replicates results of a series of earlier studies with indigenous peoples in Canada (e.g., Berry, 1985; Berry, Wintrob, Sindell, & Mawhinney, 1982).

The mirror image of this relationship (i.e., high marginalization associated with poor psychological health) has also been found in these studies. In particular, among first- and second-generation Greek immigrants in Toronto (Sands & Berry, 1993), both a preference for marginalization (as an attitude) and a feeling of being marginalized, measured on a standard scale (Mann, 1958), were predictive of high acculturative stress. Moreover, these same two factors were significantly related to depression (on both the Beck and Zung scales). It is thus not only among first-generation immigrants themselves that problems associated with acculturation can be found; the second generation may also be at risk.

To pursue this particular aspect, a study was carried out in Montreal (Berry & Sabatier, 1996) among second-generation Greek, Haitian, Italian, and Vietnamese youth. In all four samples, a combined attachment to both the heritage and Canadian cultures (sometimes manifested in a hyphenated or bicultural ethnic identity, but sometimes by a preference for integration) was predictive of better self-image and self-esteem.

Beyond this research program in Canada, others acculturating elsewhere have evidenced this relationship between acculturation strategies and psychological well-being. Among South Asians in the United States (Krishnan & Berry, 1992), integration again predicted lower overall acculturative stress; separation predicted higher psychosomatic stress; and assimilation predicted higher psychological stress. In Norway, Berry and Sam (1996) found a consistent pattern of prediction for three outcome variables: assimilation and marginalization, as predicted, were associated significantly with global negative self-evaluation, depressive tendencies, and psychological and somatic symptoms.

Many other factors in the acculturation framework (Figure 2.2) have received research support (such as the roles of perception of discrimination, coping strategies, education, and cultural distance). The evidence is now clear: acculturation confronts individuals with new experiences, and some of these become stressors that challenge individuals and create conditions for lowered psychological health status. However, the outcome is highly variable, and depends upon numerous factors. The most important may well be the orientation that individuals have toward the acculturation process; those seeking to participate in the larger society from a position of valuing and retaining their heritage culture (i.e., integration, as defined in Figure 2.1) are better able to deal with acculturation.

From the psychopathology tradition of research, initial research with immigrants from Norway to the United States (Odegaard, 1932) found higher mental-hospital admission for schizophrenia among the Norwegian immigrants than among native-born Americans or Norwegian natives who did not migrate. He concluded that people who were predisposed to mental health problems were those who migrated. Subsequent studies in this area (Malzberg & Lee, 1956) also found that there is a higher incidence of hospital admission among immigrants than among native-born. Differences in admission rates between the two groups, however, become less when age and gender are controlled for.

More recent investigations have cast doubt on the association between migration and poor mental health. Burnam, Telles, Karno, Hough, and Escobar (1987), in a study of the prevalence of different psychiatric disorders among Mexican immigrants in Los Angeles, found that immigrants had a fewer risk factor for different disorders than their native-born peers. They attributed this difference to a stronger sense of self and coping ability among the Mexicans who migrated, a suggestion that is the opposite of that of Odegaard (1932). This conclusion is not an isolated one. Among Mexican-born immigrants in Los Angeles and U.S.-born Mexican Americans, Golding and Burnam (1990) found that immigrants had fewer depressive symptoms. In a study among Asian (mostly Indian and Pakistani) immigrants in the greater London area, Furnham and Sheikh (1993) found that female immigrants had higher levels of psychological symptomatology than their male counterparts. They found evidence linking social support to mental health, but no difference was noted between the first- and second-generation immigrants in their level of symptomatology.

In view of inconclusive evidence that immigrants have more psychopathology than native-born people (Burvill, 1984), especially when demographic and cultural factors that influence hospital admission are controlled for, Murphy (1977) suggested that instead of asking why migrants sometimes have higher rates of mental disorders, it might be better to ask under what circumstances they have higher rates; that is, we should seek to understand how the many variables involved in the process of migration interact to affect people's adaptation outcomes (Aronowitz, 1992).

More recently, studies with refugees have adopted the psychopathology perspective on the acculturation of forced migrants. Refugees face the greatest risks during the process of adaptation, according to three risk factors: they are involuntary, migratory, and in many cases temporary. In addition, they have likely experienced the most difficult preacculturation situations, including war, famine, deprivation, and humiliation (at the individual level), and massive exclusion or domination (at the group level).

At the present time, there are approximately 20 million refugees and asylum-seekers in the world. The vast majority (around 80%) are in Asia and Africa. While only a small proportion is eventually settled in Western countries, most of the research literature dealing with refugee adaptation has been done in the West, giving a very biased view of the refugee experience (Leopold & Harrell-Bond, 1994). Psychological knowledge about refugees in countries of first asylum and in camps is very limited, due to a number of factors. One is that the main refugee agency (United Nations High Commission for Refugees, UNHCR) was initially concerned only with the protection of refugees, not with their psychological well-being; mental health issues have not been a priority. A second reason is that psychological work in camps and first settlements is hazardous, and permission to do research or provide service is usually difficult to obtain. More comprehensive reviews of refugee mental health treatments can be found in books edited by Williams and Westermeyer (1986) and Holtzman and Bornemann (1990).

Perhaps the most important preacculturation factor identified in the refugee literature is that of traumatic stress, usually involving various forms of violence. Trauma has been defined as an event that an individual has experienced or witnessed "that involves actual or threatened death or injury, or threat to the physical integrity of others" (Friedman & Jaranson, 1994, p. 208). Some of these events are specifically related to the origin of one's refugee status (e.g., warfare, ethnic conflict, torture), while others may not be unique but have higher incidence among refugees (such as starvation and rape). Nevertheless, collectively they may constitute a set of "protracted, complex and catastrophic stressors" (Friedman & Jaranson, 1994, p. 209) that may give rise to *posttraumatic stress;* this is a syndrome involving intrusive recollections of the stressor events, which evoke panic, terror, grief, or despair and is manifested in daytime fantasies, traumatic nightmares, and psychotic reenactments ("flashbacks"). In addition there may be coping strategies that involve avoidance of stimuli that are similar to the original stressors, the avoidance of certain situations, and amnesia (Friedman & Jaranson, 1994). While there is some controversy concerning the definition and treatment of trauma, it is clear that such a set of stressors constitutes a risk to good psychological and sociocultural adaptation (Beiser et al., 1988) and that it may occur along with other serious problems (such as depression and substance abuse). This type of outcome clearly belongs to the psychopathology point of view on the psychological consequences of acculturation.

Some of the clearest evidence for the long-term negative consequences of traumatic stress come from a study in the United States by Chung and Kagawa-Singer (1993). Despite evidence of some short-term ability to cope with such experiences (e.g., Beiser et al., 1988; Rumbaut, 1991), these traumatic events appear to affect longer-term adaptation. In a large sample of Indochinese refugees (made up of sub-samples of Vietnamese, Cambodians, and Lao) in the Los Angeles area, the number of trauma events was a significant predictor of both depression and anxiety; this was true regardless of ethnicity or the number of years refugees had been settled.

Among risk factors arising during acculturation is the widely held view that all refugees are in need of constant control, monitoring, or support; this can well lead to a sense of dependency and to limits on the acquisition of the social skills necessary for good sociocultural adaptation (von Buchwald, 1994). Whether for positive (e.g., "assistance") or negative (e.g., "containment") motives, the outcome of such control can be the development of excessive dependency, involving a loss of a sense of personal control and self-confidence and eventually giving way to numbness and apathy. The psychological consequences of this dependency are similar to those of "learned helplessness" (Seligman, 1975), in which passivity takes over from more active coping strategies and may become a relatively permanent part of one's behavior (Dona & Berry, 1994b). The sociocultural consequences of this dependency and helplessness may be minimal participation in the daily activities of either society, including school, work, and community involvement (Rangaraj, 1988).

Despite these numerous risk factors, the research now available indicates that, like other acculturating people, many refugees eventually make successful adaptations. The most frequently researched group (Vietnamese) has provided much of the evidence for this conclusion. For example, a comprehensive longitudinal project (Beiser, 1994) included a representative group of "boat people" in Vancouver, interviewed in 1981, 1983, and 1992. After 10 years in Canada, unemployment rates were below the national average, educational attainment was at or above the national norms, and a variety of mental health indicators (anxiety, depression, and psychosomatic scales) revealed no heightened problems. Almost all had become Canadian citizens, and the vast majority indicated that they felt "at home" in their new country.

CONCLUSIONS

Research on acculturation and health, as sampled in this chapter, has provided some rather consistent and potentially applicable findings. This consistency is remarkable, since acculturation is one of the most complex areas of research in cross-cultural psychology. It is complex, in part, because the process involves more than one culture, in two distinct senses: acculturation phenomena result from contact between two or more cultures, and research on acculturation has to be comparative (like all cross-cultural psychology) in order to understand variations in psychological outcomes that are the result of cultural variations in the two groups in contact. This complexity has made the reviewing of the field both difficult and selective. The framing of the field (in Figures 2.1 and 2.2) was an attempt to provide a structure that could identify the main features of acculturation phenomena (the "skeleton") and into which illustrative studies could be inserted (bits of "flesh"). The questions naturally arise: to what extent are these findings generalizable to other cultures, and what research still needs to be accomplished in order to apply them?

The empirical studies available do seem to point to some consistent findings. First, psychological acculturation is influenced by numerous group-level factors in the society of origin and in the society of settlement: national immigration and acculturation policies, ideologies and attitudes in the dominant society, and social support. These population-level variables seem to be important in many studies, across many societies. However, their relative contributions will likely vary according to the specific acculturative context being considered. That is, they may be examples of a set of universal factors that operate everywhere, but whose specific influence will vary in relation to features of the particular cultures in contact.

Second, psychological acculturation is influenced by numerous individual-level factors. In particular, the integrationist or bicultural acculturation strategy appears to be a consistent predictor of more positive outcomes than do the three alternatives of assimilation, separation, or, especially, marginalization. The availability and success of such a dual-adaptation strategy, of course, depends on the willingness of the dominant society to allow it and the wish of coethnics to pursue it. Thus, there is an apparent interaction between population-level and individual-level factors in contributing to psychological adaptations. But even in societies that tend toward assimilation policies, there is evidence that immigrants and ethnocultural group members generally prefer integration, and, when they do integrate, they tend to make more positive adaptations. Whether such a finding is valid for all groups acculturating to all dominant societies is an important question for researchers, policymakers, and those involved in counseling or treating acculturating individuals.

Third, how are the personal outcomes of the acculturation process to be interpreted? Are they a matter of acquiring essential social skills (making some rather easy behavioral shifts), of coping with stressors in order to avoid acculturative stress, or of succumbing to problems so serious that psychopathology will result? In this chapter, there is evidence that all three conceptualizations are valid, but that they may constitute a sequence or hierarchy of outcomes. If sufficient behavioral shifts (involving new-culture learning and former-culture shedding) are demanded, but do not occur, stressors may appear in the daily intercultural encounters that require appraisal and coping in order to prevent acculturative stress. If these difficulties prove to be insurmountable, then psychopathologies may result. Because of the differing theoretical approaches taken by different researchers in their studies, such a conclusion has not been possible to draw from any one study. Large-scale longitudinal studies, carried out comparatively, in which all three conceptualizations are combined are required. In the meantime, it is possible to say on the basis of this review that most acculturating individuals make rather positive and healthy adaptations (i.e., there is not widespread psychopathology in evidence), but that the acculturative transition is not always an easy one (i.e., changing one's culture presents challenges that are not easy to meet). Immigration and acculturation are a risk, but risk is not destiny (Beiser et al., 1988).

Despite these general conclusions, the question of whether acculturation will improve or threaten one's health is still not clearly answered. While it is certain that changes will occur and that links between cultural context and health can be detected, much less certain is the direction and extent of changes to an individual's health. However, it should be clear that ignoring a person's cultural background and the cultural changes that occur with acculturation will undermine our ability to understand a person's physical and psychological health and will seriously limit our ability to serve those of diverse cultural backgrounds who come to live together in contemporary plural societies.

References

Angel, R., & Thoits, P. (1987). The impact of culture on the cognitive structure of illness. *Culture, Medicine and Psychiatry, 11,* 465–494.

Aronowitz, M. (1992). Adjustment of immigrant children as a function of parental attitudes to change. *International Migration Review, 26,* 86–110.

Baron, R. M., & Kenny, D. A. (1986). The moderator-mediator variable distinction in social psychological research: Conceptual, strategic and statistical considerations. *Journal of Personality and Social Psychology, 51,* 1173–1182.

Beardsley, L., & Pedersen, P. (1996). Health and culture-centered intervention. In J. W. Berry, M. H. Segall, & C. Kagitcibasi (Eds.), *Handbook of cross-cultural psychology; Vol. 3. Social behavior and applications* 413–448. Boston: Allyn & Bacon.

Beinfield, H., & Korngold, E. (1991). *Between heaven and earth: A guide to Chinese medicine.* New York: Ballantine Books.

Beiser, M. (1994). *Longitudinal study of Vietnamese refugee adaptation.* Toronto: Clarke Institute of Psychiatry.

Beiser, M., Barwick, C., Berry, J. W., Dacosta, G., Milne, W., Fantino, A. M. (1988). *Mental health issues affecting immigrants and refugees.* Ottawa, Ontario, Canada: Health and Welfare Canada.

Berry, J. W. (1970). Marginality, stress and ethnic identification in an acculturated Aboriginal community. *Journal of Cross-Cultural Psychology, 1,* 239–252.

Berry, J. W. (1974). Psychological aspects of cultural pluralism: Unity and identity reconsidered. *Topics in Culture Learning, 2,* 17–22.

Berry, J. W. (1976). *Human ecology and cognitive style: Comparative studies in cultural and psychological adaptation.* New York: Sage/Halsted.

Berry, J. W. (1980). Social and cultural change. In H. C. Triandis & R. Brislin (Eds.), *Handbook of cross-cultural psychology: Vol. 5, Social* (pp. 211–279). Boston: Allyn & Bacon.

Berry, J. W. (1985). Acculturation among circumpolar peoples: Implications for health status. *Arctic Medical Research, 40,* 21–27.

Berry, J. W. (1990a). Psychology of acculturation. In J. Berman (Ed.), *Nebraska Symposium on Motivation: vol. 37. Cross-cultural perspectives* (pp. 201–234). Lincoln: University of Nebraska Press.

Berry, J. W. (1990b). The role of psychology in ethnic studies. *Canadian Ethnic Studies, 22,* 8–21.

Berry, J. W. (1991). Understanding and managing multiculturalism. *Journal of Psychology and Developing Societies, 3,* 17–49.

Berry, J. W. (1992). Acculturation and adaptation in a new society. *International Migration, 30,* 69–85.

Berry, J. W. (1994, July). *Cross-cultural health psychology.* Keynote address presented to the International Congress of Applied Psychology, Madrid.

Berry, J. W., & Kalin, R. (1995). Multicultural and ethnic attitudes in Canada. *Canadian Journal of Behavioral Science, 27,* 301–320.

Berry, J. W., Kim, U., Minde, T., & Mok,. D. (1987). Comparative studies of acculturative stress. *International Migration Review, 21,* 491–511.

Berry, J. W., & Kim, U. (1988). Acculturation and mental health. In P. R. Dasen, J. W. Berry, & N. Sartorius (Eds.), *Health and cross-cultural psychology: Towards applications* (pp. 207–238). Newbury Park, CA: Sage.

Berry, J. W., Kim, U., Power, S., Young, M., & Bujaki, M. (1989). Acculturation attitudes in plural societies. *Applied Psychology: An International Review, 38,* 185–206.

Berry, J. W., Poortinga, Y. H., Segall, M. H., & Dasen, P. R. (1992). *Cross-cultural psychology: Research and applications.* New York: Cambridge University Press.

Berry, J. W., & Sabatier, C. (1996, August). *Acculturation and adaptation among second generation youth in Montreal.* Paper presented to the International Association for Cross-cultural Psychology, Montreal, Quebec, Canada.

Berry, J. W., & Sam, D. (1996). Acculturation and adaptation. In J. W. Berry, M. H. Segall, & C. Kagitcibasi (Eds.), *Handbook of cross-cultural psychology: Vol. 3. Social Behavior and Applications* (pp. 291–326). Boston: Allyn & Bacon.

Berry, J. W., Trimble, J., & Olmedo, E. (1986). The assessment of acculturation. In W. J. Lonner & J.W. Berry (Eds.), *Field methods in cross-cultural research* (291–324). Newbury Park, CA: Sage.

Berry, J. W., Wintrob, R. M., Sindell, P. S., & Mawhinney, T. A. (1982). Culture change and psychological adaptation. In R. Rath, H. Asthana, D. Sinha, & J. B. P. Sinha (Eds.), *Diversity and unity in cross-cultural psychology* (pp.157–170). Lisse, Netherlands: Swets & Zeitlinger.

Bishop, G. (1994). *Health psychology: Integrating mind and body.* Boston: Allyn & Bacon.

Bond, M. H. (1991). Chinese values and health: A cultural level examination. *Psychology and Health, 5,* 137–152.

Brislin, R., Landis, D., & Brandt, M. (1983). Conceptualizations of intercultural behavior and training. In D. Landis & R. Brislin (Eds.), *Handbook of intercultural training* (vol. 1, pp. 1–35). New York: Pergamon.

Brown, J. (1996). A comparison of lay illness representations among Euro-Canadians, Canadian-born Chinese and Chinese immigrants. Unpublished honors thesis, Queen's University, Kingston, Ontario, Canada.

Burnam, M. A., Telles, C. A., Karno, M., Hough, R. L., & Escobar, J. I. (1987). Measurement of acculturation in a community population of Mexican Americans. *Hispanic Journal of Behavioral Sciences, 9,* 105–130.

Burvill, P. W. (1984). Migration and mental disease. In J. E. Mezzich & C. E. Berganza (Eds.), *Culture and psychopathology* (pp. 243–256). New York: Columbia University Press.

Chung, R., & Kagawa-Singer, M. (1993). Predictors of psychological distress among Southeast Asian refugees. *Social Science and Medicine, 36,* 631–639.

Cruz-Croke, R. (1987). Correlation between the prevalence of hypertension and degree of acculturation. *Journal of Hypertension, 5,* 47–50.

Dasen, P. R., Berry, J. W., & Sartorius, N. (Eds.). (1988). *Health and cross-cultural psychology: Towards applications.* Newbury Park, CA: Sage.

Dona, G., & Berry, J. W. (1994a). Acculturation attitudes and acculturative stress of Central American refugees in Canada. *International Journal of Psychology, 29,* 57–70.

Dona, G., & Berry, J. W. (1994b). El estrés de acculturacion entre refugiados. In P. Campero & R. Redondo (Eds.), *Experiencias del Refugio Centroamericano* (pp. 47–52). San Crostobal de las Casas: Federacion Mundial de Salud Mental.

Frese, M. (1986). Coping as a moderator and mediator between stress at work and psychosomatic complaints. In M. H. Appley & R. Trumbull (Eds.), *Dynamics of stress* (pp. 183–206). New York: Plenum.

Friedman, M., & Jaranson, J. (1994). The applicability of the post-traumatic stress disorder concept to refugees. In A. Marsella , T. Bornemann, S. Ekblad, & J. Orley (Eds.). *Amidst peril and pain: The mental well-being of the world's refugees* (pp. 207–227). Washington, DC: American Psychological Association.

Furnham, A., & Bochner, S. (1986). *Culture shock: Psychological reactions to unfamiliar environments.* London: Methuen.

Furnham, A., & Shiekh, S. (1993). Gender, generation, and social support correlates of mental health in Asian immigrants. *International Journal of Social Psychiatry, 39,* 22–33.

Galding, J. M., & Burnam, M. A. (1990). Immigration, stress, and depressive symptoms in a

Mexican-American community. *The Journal of Nervous and Mental Disease, 178,* 161–171.

Graves, T. (1967). Psychological acculturation in a tri-ethnic community. *South-Western Journal of Anthropology, 23,* 337–350.

Griffith, E., Berry, J. W., Foulks, E., & Wintrob, R. (1989). *Suicide and ethnicity.* New York: Brunner/Mazel.

Hazuda, H. P., Haffner, S. N., Stern, M. P., & Eifler, C. W. (1988). Effects of acculturation and socioeconomic status on obesity and diabetes in Mexican Americans. *American Journal of Epidemiology, 128,* 1289–1301.

Helman, C. (1985). Psyche, soma and society: The social construction of psychosomatic disorders. *Culture, Medicine and Psychiatry, 9,* 1–26.

Helman, C. (1990). *Culture, health and illness.* London: Wright.

Holtzman, W., & Bornemann, T. (Eds.). (1990). *Mental health of immigrants and refugees.* Austin, TX: Hogg Foundation.

Jayasuriya, L., Sang, D., & Fielding, A. (1992). *Ethnicity, immigration and mental illness: A critical review of Australian research.* Canberra, Australia: Bureau of Immigration Research.

Kalin, R., & Berry, J. W. (in press). Ethnic and civic self-identity in Canada. *Canadian Ethnic Studies.*

Kim, U., and Berry, J. W. (1986). Predictors of acculturative stress: Korean immigrants in Toronto, Canada. In L. Ekstrand (Ed.), *Ethnic minorities and immigrants in a cross-cultural perspective* (pp. 159–170). Lisse, Netherlands: Swets & Zeitlinger.

Kirmayer, L. (1984). Culture, affect and somatization. *Transcultural Psychiatric Research Review, 21,* 158–159; 237–262.

Kleinman, A. (1982). Neurasthenia and depression: A study of somatization and culture in China. *Culture, Medicine and Psychiatry, 6,* 117–190.

Kliewer, E. (1992). Epidemiology of diseases among migrants. *International Migration, 30,* 141–165.

Krishnan, A., & Berry, J. W. (1992). Acculturative stress and acculturation attitudes among Indian immigrants to the United States. *Psychology and Developing Societies, 4,* 187–212.

Kymlicka, W. (1995). *Multicultural citizenship.* Oxford: Clarendon Press.

Landrine, H., & Klonoff, E. (1992). Culture and health-related schemas: A review and proposal for interdisciplinary integration. *Health Psychology, 11,* 267–276.

Lazarus, R. S,. & Folkman, S. (1984). *Stress, appraisal and coping.* New York: Springer.

Leopold, M., & Harrell-Bond, B. (1994). An overview of the world refugee crisis. In A. Marsella, T. Bornemann, S. Ekblad, & J. Orley (Eds.). *Amidst peril and pain: The mental well-being of the world's refugees* (pp. 17–31). Washington, DC: American Psychological Association.

Lillenfeld, A. M. (1972). *Cancer in the United States.* Cambridge: Harvard University Press.

Malzberg, B., & Lee, E. (1956). *Migration and mental disease.* New York: Social Science Research Council.

Mann, J. W. (1958). Group relations and the marginal man. *Human Relations, 11,* 77–92.

Marmot, M., Syme, S. L., Kagan, A., Kato, H., Cohen, J. B., & Belsky, J. (1975). Epidemiological studies of coronary heart disease and stroke in Japanese. *American Journal of Epidemiology, 102,* 514–525.

Murphy, H. B. M. (1965). Migration and the major mental disorders. In M. Kantor (Ed.). *Mobility and mental health* (pp. 221–249). Springfield, IL: Thomas.

Murphy, H. B. M. (1977). Migration, culture and mental health. *Psychological Medicine, 7,* 677–684.

Murphy, H. B. M. (1982). Culture and schizophrenia. In I. Al-Issa (Ed.), *Culture and psychopathology*. Baltimore: University Park Press.

Oberg, K. (1960). Culture shock: adjustment to new cultural environments. *Practical Anthropology, 7,* 177–182.

Odegaard, O. (1932). Emigration and insanity: A study of mental disease among the Norwegian-born population of Minnesota. *Acta Psychiatrica Scandinavica* (Suppl. 4), (p. 206).

Polgar, S. (1962). Health and human behavior: Areas of common interest to the social and medical sciences. *Current Anthropology, 2,* 159–205.

Prener, A., Hojgaard-Nielson, N., Storm, H., & Hart Hansen, J. P. (1991). Cancer in Greenland: 1953–1985. *Acta Pathologica, Microbiologica et Immunologica Scandinavia, 99* (Suppl. 20).

Rangaraj, A. (1988). The health status of refugees in South East Asia. In D. Miserez (Ed.). *Refugees: The trauma of exile* (pp. 39–44). Dordrecht, Netherlands: Nijhoff.

Redfield, R., Linton, R., & Herskovits, M. (1936). Memorandum on the study of acculturation. *American Anthropologist, 38,* 149–152.

Rogler, L. (1994). International migrations: A framework for directing research. *American Psychologist, 49,* 701–708.

Rumbaut, R. (1991). The agony of exile: A study of the migration and adaptation of Indochinese refugee adults and children. In F. Ahearn & J. Athey (Eds.), *Refugee children: Theory, research and services* (pp. 53–91). Baltimore: Johns Hopkins University Press.

Salmond, C. E., Prior, I. A., & Wessen, A. F. (1989). Blood pressure patterns and migration: A 14 year cohort study of adult Tokelauans. *American Journal of Epidemiology, 130,* 37–52.

Sands, E., & Berry, J. W. (1993). Acculturation and mental health among Greek-Canadians in Toronto. *Canadian Journal of Community Mental Health, 12,* 117–124.

Seligman, M. (1975). *Helplessness: On depression, development and death.* San Francisco: Freeman.

Siem, H., & Bollini, P. (Eds.). (1992). Migration and health in the 1990s [Special issue]. *International Migration, 30.*

Statistics Canada (1996, April 2). Immigrants healthier than Canadians. *Globe and Mail,* p. A8.

United Nations Educational, Scientific & Cultural Organization. (1985). *Cultural pluralism and cultural identity.* Paris: Author.

Vega, W., & Rumbaut, R. (1991). Ethnic minorities and mental health. *Annual Review of Sociology, 17,*

von Buchwald, U. (1994). Refugee dependency: Origins and consequences. In A. Marsella, T. Bornemann, S. Ekblad, & J. Orley (Eds.). *Amidst peril and pain: The mental well-being of the world's refugees* (pp. 229–237). Washington, DC: American Psychological Association.

Ward, C. (Ed.). (1989). *Altered states of consciousness and mental health.* London: Sage.

Ward, C. (1996). Acculturation. In D. Landis & R. Bhagat (Eds.), *Handbook of intercultural training* (2nd ed.). Newbury Park, CA: Sage.

Westermeyer, J. (1986). Migration and psychopathology. In C. L. Williams & J. Westermeyer (Eds.), *Refugee mental health in resettlement countries*. Washington, DC: Hemisphere.

Williams, C., & Westermeyer, J. (Eds.). (1986). *Refugee mental health in resettlement countries.* Washington, DC: Hemisphere.

World Health Organization (1991). *The mental health problems of migrants: Report from six European countries.* Geneva: Author.

Zheng, X., & Berry, J. W. (1991). Psychological adaptation of Chinese sojourners in Canada. *International Journal of Psychology, 26,* 451–470.

PART II

PRACTICE ISSUES

3

Psychological Assessment of People in Diverse Cultures

JAMES N. BUTCHER

ELAHE NEZAMI

JOHN EXNER

In clinical psychological practice today psychologists are often faced with the challenging task of assessing clients who come from diverse cultural backgrounds. Such assessments are often replete with difficulty and uncertainty and require special considerations to assure appropriate evaluation. For example, what special considerations will the clinician face in assessing the clients in the following problem situations?

A 36-year-old Cambodian refugee who cannot read or understand English has been referred for psychological evaluation and treatment for her profound depression and suicidal ideation.

A 34-year-old Cuban refugee who has been in the United States for only a few months and speaks little English was recently arrested for burglary and attempted murder. He is being evaluated in a pretrial forensic assessment.

In each of these situations, the practitioner faces the difficult task of making extremely important decisions and recommendations about individuals based on procedures and techniques developed in the United States, even though the clients are from extremely different cultures and backgrounds and only speak languages other than English, the language in which most of the frequently used assessment procedures were developed.

Clinicians who are asked to assess clients from different cultural backgrounds may be initially at a loss to know how to relate to the client, how to formulate the problem, and how to determine which (if any) psychological tests to use or which treatment strategies might be effective. It has become increasingly apparent that many psychologists must learn to adopt a broader cultural framework if they hope to serve people they may encounter in their practice.

THE CULTURAL PERSPECTIVE IN PSYCHOLOGY

In attempting to understand human behavior in a cultural context, one is immediately impressed by great commonality as well as differences between cultural groups. There are two general orientations with respect to defining our starting point in understanding people in different cultures: the *emic* and the *etic* views. The emic approach seeks to understand a given culture on its own terms without reference to other cultures or perspectives. This approach parallels the ideographic view of personality psychology, as described by Allport (1937). The etic approach is analogous to Allport's nomothetic view of science as a comparative strategy. This approach emphasizes universals and compares cultures along similar dimensions, seeking to determine whether data or theories developed in one culture are appropriate for another. For example, one might consider the applicability of diagnostic categories or the relative frequencies of certain disorders derived in one culture to different cultures. Both theoretic viewpoints are valid and essential, but each also has its limitations. Emic descriptions tend to yield rich information about a particular culture, but may not be readily translatable into data suitable for rigorous scientific comparisons. Etic approaches, on the other hand, though providing intercultural comparisons, may inappropriately impose the same categories of comparison across groups. The emic-etic problem is a pervasive one inherent in any comparison of cultural groups or cultures. There is no preferred strategy, and both approaches can be justified on the basis of particularity of data and goals of the study. Some researchers (e.g., Segall, 1986) have questioned whether any dichotomy really exists. In this chapter, we will follow an etic approach because the assessment procedures we will focus on involve normative comparisons.

Assumptions about the differences between cultural groups can lead us to make errors in evolving a culturally based mental health perspective. Moreover, assumptions about similarities in basic processes may lead to equally troublesome situations and may cause us, for example, to assume that subjects from different national or ethnic groups are similarly motivated. Different psychological factors may underlie behavior of people from different countries, and different social structures may allow or prevent the expression of some behavior. Therefore, comparing "behavior" in different cultural groups without giving enough weight to these potential sources of variance can result in misleading research or theoretical conclusions.

For our purposes in this chapter we will follow the definition of *culture* as involving: patterns of behavior acquired and transmitted by symbols or cognitions, that make up the aggregate achievement of human groups which are embodied in artifacts or materials passed on to others. The essential elements of culture consist of materials, traditional ideas, and values surviving within a group intergenerationally.

This chapter examines cultural factors that define or influence transnational or subcultural clinical assessment research or practice and issues or problems that apply to different cultural populations. (For a fuller exploration of subcultural psychological assessment issues, see articles by Gray-Little, 1995; Okazaki & Sue, 1995; Velasquez, 1995). The broad diffusion of psychological techniques and psychotechnology raises a number of issues, which are the focus of this chapter. We recognize that intercultural test adaptations are only beginning to evolve and that substantial research is required to assure that the test translations and adaptations are effective.

CHALLENGES OF CULTURAL PSYCHOLOGICAL ASSESSMENT

A number of challenging factors need to be considered in developing a cultural framework for clinical assessment, and a number of possible problems need to be resolved before appropriate assessments can be implemented. We will introduce these factors, and later in the chapter we will provide illustrations of how these problems can be resolved or at least substantially minimized in practical ways.

Subject Variables

Our initial point of attention involves examining the complicating factors in cultural assessment that relate to subject variables or those individual difference factors that might operate to defy assessment.

1. *Language limitations.* One of the first challenges faced by the psychologist in a cultural interaction involves the possibility, or actually the probability, of encountering an individual who does not speak one's native language. In order for the clinical interaction to proceed effectively, language factors need to be taken into consideration and appropriate translation implemented, for example, by working through translators (Egli, 1991). Language differences and their potential impact on intercultural test usage will be discussed more fully later.

2. *Cultural differences.* In addition to complications of language, there are also cultural factors that might enter into the clinical interaction. For example, individuals from cultures that are quite different from Western industrial civilization might have little experience or practice with some tasks such as paper-pencil inventories, computer-administered tasks, and so forth. Assuring the equivalence of processes and personality variables under study is a basic problem in the study of behavior across cultures. It is important to determine that variables operate the same way in all cultures under study. For example, if one is studying the personality variable of "assertiveness," it is important to evaluate whether the components and the meanings of the trait in each culture are generally equivalent. The clinical disorder of depression is manifested differently across cultures (Marsella, 1978) and comprises different characteristics (Butcher & Pancheri, 1976). Therefore, comparing "depressed" patients from different cultures might result in false generalizations across different cultural groups.

3. *Motivational differences.* Individuals from different cultural backgrounds might operate under different motivational sets than the ones the clinician-evaluator has adopted. For example, an individual from a different culture or background might view self-disclosure in a clinical situation as inappropriate and would therefore not openly or willingly participate in personality-assessment tasks.

4. *Definitions or perceptions of what is abnormal.* One basic task of the psychopathologist studying cultural factors is to develop working definitions of mental health and illness that will allow for the identification of abnormality in clients from different cultures. The distinction between normal and abnormal behavior is not easily drawn, even within one's own cultural group, and is more complex when standards applicable to many different societies must be established (Wittkower & Fried, 1959). Abnormality must be defined in social and behavioral terms, and thus it derives much

of its meaning from the context in which it occurs (Kennedy, 1973; Yap, 1951, 1967, 1969). Several different strategies for making determinations of abnormality have been advanced (Butcher, Narakiyo, & Bemis-Vitousek, 1992).

5. *Interpersonal expectations.* Different cultures impart somewhat different beliefs and attitudes about interpersonal interaction. For example, shyness in some countries might be considered a "value," whereas in other countries, such as the United States, it might be viewed as somewhat socially backward or, in the extreme, even pathological.

Procedural Variables

There are a number of relevant variables associated with the adoption of specific procedures for populations who differ from the standardized samples used in tests.

1. *Task appropriateness.* Is the task being required of the subjects culturally appropriate? The communication of psychological ideas or materials proves to be even more difficult than straight translation, since the psychological equivalence must be maintained. It is important that the appropriate psychological meanings be included in the stimulus materials and also reflected in the interpretation of results from different cultures.

2. *Form appropriateness.* Have the tasks involved in the procedure been adapted for the individual being assessed? For example, has there been an appropriate translation and adaptation of the test stimuli, such as the Vocabulary Subtest of the WAIS-R? In some cases the test norms might need to be modified or redeveloped in the target culture for the test to be applied.

3. *Psychological equivalence.* In order for psychological procedures to be effective in the target culture, the equivalence of the procedures needs to be demonstrated. As noted earlier, the constructs underlying the test must be considered equivalent in both cultures. Moreover, the means of assessing these constructs must be shown to be equivalent. Sound psychological tests and therapeutic techniques that have been developed in Western nations are becoming more widely applied in other countries as a result of the increased communication between countries and the great interchange between professionals from different countries.

Having briefly surveyed some of the general problems that face assessment psychologists in adapting procedures to different cultures, we now turn to a discussion of three major assessment approaches in wide use in clinical psychological assessment to provide examples of specific test translations or adaptations for differing cultural groups. Later we will illustrate these techniques with an actual cross-cultural clinical case in order to explore these techniques and how they can be adapted to different cultures.

ADAPTING PERSONALITY QUESTIONNAIRES TO OTHER CULTURES: THE MMPI-2

The most frequently used (Lubin, Larsen, & Matarazzo, 1984) and researched (Butcher & Rouse, 1996) psychological test in the United States is the Minnesota Multiphasic Personality Inventory (MMPI-2). Both the original MMPI and the revised form (MMPI-2) have been extensively adapted for international use (Butcher, 1985, 1996a; Butcher & Pancheri, 1976). In this section we will explore personality-scale adaptation to different cultures using the MMPI-2 as the model; however, many of the translation and adaptation procedures would also apply with other personality questionnaires.

Several problems are involved in the application of personality questionnaires in cultures that are different from the population on which the instrument was initially developed and standardized (Butcher, 1987). These problems need to be satisfactorily resolved before an instrument can be confidently applied in new cultures. As described earlier, the issues of task appropriateness, translation adequacy, and test validity must be addressed carefully in a test-adaptation project. Sound test adaptation cannot be done on a "safari" basis, that is, where a Western psychologist visits another country on a sabbatical and, while there, translates and administers a few tests. Effective personality-test adaptation requires the full participation of professionals from the target culture who are both competent in the procedures involved and are also living and working there.

The test adapter must ensure that the required task is relevant to the culture and that the likely responses to the items are equivalent to those in the standardization sample. Investigators must also be aware of possible cultural differences in response sets and must be prepared to evaluate and compensate for them (Lonner, 1985). For example, people who are unfamiliar with paper-pencil tests may simply acquiesce in responding to items out of politeness, perhaps to give socially desirable answers or to respond in a careless manner. Clinicians from test-oriented cultures may incorrectly assume that other cultures are equally comfortable with the standardized verbal, limited-option format of many Western measures (Draguns, 1984). Finally, the problem of illiteracy in some countries may preclude the use of written test materials. One practical solution to this problem is the use of a tape-recorded version of the test. Test materials and administrative formats need to be adapted or altered to make the test appropriate to the new culture. Test translation problems and issues of content equivalence have been described by numerous writers (Brislin, 1970, 1986; Brislin, Lonner, & Thorndike, 1973; Butcher, 1996b; Butcher & Pancheri, 1976; Flaherty et al., 1988, Marsella & Kameoka, 1989). In adapting test items, it is critical for the test developer to seek psychological equivalence of test items, not just a literal translation.

There are some generally accepted and sophisticated test-translation methods that have come to be adopted by test translators. Rigorous test-development standards provide safeguards against careless or shallow test-translation practices that were common 30 years ago. Test translation and adaptation today follows clear and substantial procedures, including such techniques as meticulous rendering of items into the target language; use of key informants to verify linguistic and social appropriateness; back-translation study of item translations; and the pretesting of the translation on a bilingual sample (Brislin, 1986; Draguns, 1984). An illustration of the procedures followed by many of the MMPI-2 test translators demonstrates the suggested process:

(a) Careful translation of items, usually by multiple translators who are bilingual, that is, who have more than 5 years of experience in both English and the target language.

    (b) Use of key informants to verify linguistic and social appropriateness of the items in a field evaluation. This might be particularly valuable in cases where items are difficult to translate or might have to be modified due to cultural differences.

    (c) Once the separate translations have been completed, it is usually desirable for the translation team to integrate the different renderings of items into an experimental form.

    (d) Back-translation study of the completed booklet. In this phase of the project, some items will not fare well in the back translation. These problem items need to be retranslated and again back translated until the desired form of the item is retained in the back translation.

    (e) Pretesting of the experimental translation on a bilingual sample. In this phase of the research, the translation team identifies a sample (about 50) of individuals who are fluent in both English and the target language. These individuals are administered the test in both languages (counterbalanced to eliminate order effects). The responses and scale scores can then be used to determine if the inventory is operating psychometrically in a comparable manner in both languages.

It is extremely important for the psychological-test adapter to show that test validity has been maintained in the target culture. In order for a translated or adapted test to be considered a valid indicator, it must be shown to measure the same constructs in the same ways in the new culture as it does in the culture of origin. Several ways have been developeded:

    (a) The initial validation method for adaptation of a test to another culture to ensure *content validity*. This initial procedure involves assuring that the content of the measures is relevant to the target culture.

    (b) The second approach to checking the validity of the measure in a new culture is to evaluate *factorial validity*. This procedure involves determining whether the items and scales maintain generally the same factors in the target population as in the population of origin (see Ben-Porath, 1990; Brislin et al., 1973; Butcher & Pancheri, 1976).

    (c) The most important validational effort is for *predictive validity*, which involves determining whether the scales actually predict the expected behavior in the target population (Han, 1996; Manos, 1981, 1985; Savasir & Erol, 1990). One initial validational approach involves a determination as to how much "transplant validity" a test might have in the target culture. In this situation the test is administered to a number of patients in the new country and interpreted according to the standard test interpretation procedures. The clinician determines the *test fit* of the interpretation and the description and predictions with known information about the cases. This clinical validation approach is a necessary but not sufficient means of cultural validation. This approach can be a valuable step in the adaptation process in that it might serve to guide the adapter toward specific changes in procedure or interpretations in the new culture. This method also provides the researcher with clear information as to how appropriate the test interpretations will be in the new culture. It is also necessary for the researcher/test adapter to demonstrate test validity in the new culture according to rigorous research methodology.

One question that needs to be addressed in any test adaptation is whether the original test norms will apply in the new culture or whether new specific norms will have to be developed. Many MMPI adaptation studies have involved the development of new norms for the target populations (Abe, Sumita, & Kuroda, 1963; Butcher &

Pancheri, 1976; Cheung, 1985; Clark, 1985; Manos, 1981, 1985; Pucheu & Rivera, 1976; Rissetti et al., 1979; Rissetti & Maltes, 1985). However, until the development of special norms for new populations, translators and indigenous clinicians can employ the U.S. norms as *itinerant norms* (Butcher & Garcia, 1978). Test translations should undergo a rigorous evaluation to determine if norms should be developed for the new populations. This normative research should be carried out with a normal, that is, a nonclinical, sample.

Translation of the MMPI-2

The MMPI was revised in 1989 after several years of research (Butcher, Dahlstrom, Graham, Tellegen, & Kaemmer, 1989). This revision of the MMPI was undertaken to improve the readability of items, to eliminate items that were objectionable or out of date, and to expand item coverage to address a broader range of clinical problems. New norms were developed that incorporated a broad-based nationally derived sample on nonclinical subjects. In addition, a new set of content scales was developed to provide a psychometric assessment of major clinical problem areas (Butcher, Graham, Williams, & Ben-Porath, 1990).

As the MMPI-2 began to be developed and adapted in different countries (Butcher, 1996b), one important side benefit of the MMPI-2 revision became very apparent. The work of test translators and international test publishers was much easier for several reasons. First, the item pool of the revised MMPI-2 did not contain the large number of awkward and inappropriate items that the original MMPI had contained. Therefore, the work of test translators was considerably easier, and fewer difficult items were encountered on translation projects. Second, the revised U.S. norms were more general and representative of the heterogeneous population of the United States. International normative researchers discovered that normal individuals in other countries usually scored quite close to the U.S. norms. Consequently, in some places, such as Norway and Iceland, the scores were so close to the American norms that new specific norms for those countries were seen as probably unnecessary. In other countries, for example, France, Belgium, Holland, and Mexico, the nationally derived norms that were produced were generally close to the American norms and within the standard error of measurement, yet separate norms were published in order to facilitate acceptance in the target country.

USE OF THE RORSCHACH ACROSS CULTURES

The use of the Rorschach across cultures has a lengthy and abundant history. Unlike self-report measures such as the MMPI or cognitive tests that involve a standardized presentation of verbal items, the Rorschach is not burdened by the language limitations that may occur when translation of the test stimuli is required. The 10 inkblots that comprise the stimulus figures of the test have no cultural specificity, and the basic instruction, "What might this be," does not appear to provoke any significant variation in performance when posed in various cultures.

In some instances the test has been used in emic studies, that is, to understand people from a culture without reference to other cultures. For example, DuBois

(1944) used Rorschach findings as part of a comprehensive study regarding the people of Alor. Similarly, Gladwin and Sarason (1953) used Rorschach data extensively in a detailed description of the people of Truk, and Abel (1944, 1948) and Hallowell (1945) became very well known for their Rorschach-based studies of Mormons and Native Americans. It has been obvious, however, that the Rorschach data included in these broad-brushed descriptions of various cultures must be approached very cautiously, mainly because the number of subjects from which data were collected is modest and not necessarily representative of a well-developed stratified random sampling.

A substantially larger number of publications have involved etic studies comparing findings from one culture to findings from one or several other cultures. For instance, Bleuler and Bleuler (1935) compared Moroccan and European data, whereas De Vos and Boyer (1988) have used the test to understand symbolic meaning in various cultures. In general, the bulk of etic publications concerning the Rorschach has focused mainly on issues of personality, abnormality, or cultural similarities and differences in score distributions (Exner, 1993; Fried, 1977; Sendin, 1995).

Rorschach Development and Method Variation

Although originally developed in Switzerland and published there in 1921, the Rorschach gained wide use throughout the world rather quickly. During the first few years after its publication, considerable interest about it and its use was evident in several European countries. In the late 1920s its use extended to North America, and by the mid-1930s numerous research reports and case studies concerning the test were published in American journals. By the mid-1940s publications about the test had become widespread in both Europe and North America, and clinical and research efforts involving the test were not uncommon in South America and several Asian countries, especially India and Japan.

Thus, since its inception the Rorschach has gained widespread use throughout the world; however, that does not necessarily mean that it has always been used in a standardized format. On the contrary, that has not been the case.

Hermann Rorschach died in the spring of 1922, only 8 months after his monograph was published. Thus, most of the work leading to the development of the test was left to others. Much of this occurred during the period from the mid-1930s to the mid-1950s, and, as one might have predicted, various approaches to its use evolved; however, they were not necessarily culture-specific. In the United States, five major Rorschach systems were developed during the 1940s and 1950s (Beck, 1944, 1945; Klopfer, Ainsworth, Klopfer, & Holt, 1954; Klopfer & Kelly, 1942; Piotrowski, 1957; Rappaport, Gill, & Schafer, 1946). In Europe, a sixth system was developed by Bohm (1948) and later, a seventh approach that was more culture-specific was developed in Japan by Kataguchi (1970).

At first glance, one might assume that the development of numerous approaches or systems for the test caused widespread differences to evolve in its use across cultures, but that is not true. With the exception of the Kataguchi approach, none of the systems or methodologies were developed in a cultural framework. The Beck System was developed empirically, while most of the others evolved from a conceptual or theoretical base. It is quite true that the different approaches did inhibit uniform standardization concerning the use of the test. Unfortunately, these various systems were marked by different criteria for some scorings, and, either because of scoring differences or conceptual differences, disagreements concerning the interpretation of findings often occurred. These differences have often made systematic comparisons across cultures difficult, but these differences have not been culture-specific because no single approach has been used in a uniform manner within any given culture.

For example, the Klopfer System, one of five approaches developed in the United States and used by nearly half of all American Rorschach users between 1935 and 1975, also became rather widely used in Europe during the late 1940s and 1950s. However, it competed in Europe with both the approach developed by Bohm and the method developed by Beck. Similarly, in Japan many Rorschach users tended to use the Klopfer method, beginning in the late 1940s; however, the Kataguchi approach gradually became widely respected there, and by the late 1970s many Japanese Rorschach users could be found using either the Klopfer, Beck, Rapaport, or Kataguchi methods. In other words, within a given culture, any of several different approaches to the test might be found.

Core Features of the Various Rorschach Systems

There is another important reason why the several approaches or systems of the Rorschach have not created the extensive differences in test interpretation or research findings that might be expected. This is because, in spite of conceptual and/or theoretical differences concerning the test, all of these systems, regardless of their origins, tend to retain the essentials of the method originally described by Rorschach in his monograph *Psychodiagnostik* (1921). This central core of elements probably has contributed greatly in maintaining a modicum of standardization in the use of the Rorschach test within and across the various cultures of the world. Thus, while differences among the approaches with regard to the tactics of administration and some criteria for scoring responses have created differences in interpretive hypotheses, the bulk of clinical findings derived from Rorschach data tend to be very similar.

This is probably best illustrated by the yield of the International Rorschach Society, formed in 1949 and consisting of member organizations and individual members from more than 30 countries throughout the world. Since 1949, the Society has held 14 International Rorschach Congresses. These have included the presentation of more than 2000 papers, most of which have been published in various peer review journals throughout the world, including *Rorschachiana,* the journal of the International Society. Overall, the Rorschach literature published since 1922 consists of between 8000 and 9000 books and articles, the authorship of which represents more than 30 countries. Findings, especially concerning personality description and/or psychopathology, have been strikingly similar.

Beginning in the mid-1970s the Comprehensive System (Exner, 1974, 1978, 1986, 1991, 1993; Exner & Weiner, 1982, 1994) has tended to become a standardized Rorschach method used in various countries throughout the world. The Comprehensive System has been translated into Danish, French, Italian, Japanese, Portuguese, Spanish, and Swedish, and most of the literature published since 1980 regarding Rorschach findings has used that methodology. Thus, whereas earlier findings were difficult to compare because of variations in Rorschach methodology, Rorschach findings published during the past 15 years are more easily contrasted because of the uniform methodology provided by the Comprehensive System.

Normative Data and Cultural Issues

The strength of Rorschach data is in its use to generate information regarding several personality features, such as basic coping styles; stress tolerance; capacities for control; abilities to handle emotions effectively; characteristics of thinking, information processing, reality testing, self-image and self-esteem; and perceptions of people. When data relating to these several features are compared across cultures, differences are very modest, because the distributions of Rorschach scores are surprisingly uniform regardless of which culture or country a sample of subjects may have been drawn from. For example, Exner (1993) examined the distributions of scores for 24 Rorschach variables[1] for subgroups drawn randomly from 293 adult nonpatient protocols collected from 12 different countries (Argentina = 15, Australia = 25, France = 37, India = 9, Italy = 16, Japan = 14, Malaysia = 22, Mexico = 60, Micronesia = 33, Philippines = 40, Switzerland = 8, and New Zealand = 14). Although none of the samples is large enough to make direct comparisons with the American nonpatient normative sample (N = 700), a format was used which involved several random combinations of the samples from four to six countries to create artificial comparison groups of between 95 and 125 subjects each. For instance, one combination consisted of the protocols from Argentina, Australia, France, Italy, and Japan (N = 107). Seven random combinations were created, and the resulting distributions for each of the 24 target variables were compared to the distributions from the American normative data. Thus, 168 comparisons were made, 7 for each of the 24 variables. No significant differences were noted in any of the 7 analyses for 18 of the 24 variables. Two of the remaining 6 variables (*EA* and *SumSh*) were significantly lower than the American sample in two of the seven artificially created distributions, and one *(Lambda)* was significantly higher than the American sample in the same two artificial distributions. The most important finding concerns the remaining 3 variables, Popular responses *(P)*, *X+%*, and *X−%*. The mean for *P* was significantly lower than the American sample in five of the seven artificial distributions; and the mean *X+%* was significantly lower and the mean *X−%* was significantly higher than the American sample in four of the seven artificial distributions.

The differences concerning Popular responses is not unexpected. Piotrowski (1957), following from Rorschach's original work, suggested that a listing of *P* should include only those defined as any answer that occurs at least once in every three protocols; that criterion is included in the Comprehensive System, leading to the identification of 13 Popular answers, at least one for each blot. Piotrowski suggested that cultural differences may have a more direct impact on Popular answers than on other kinds of Rorschach responses, and previous research has supported that notion. For example, Sendin (1995) has reported that only 10 of the 13 *P* derived from American data appear among the records of Spanish adult subjects. Likewise, Fried (1977) has noted that Finnish subjects offer a very different Popular answer to Card II than is typically found in other cultures throughout the world.

When the combined sample of protocols collected outside of the United States was studied for the presence or absence of Popular responses listed in the Comprehensive System, only 11 of the 13 P listed for the Comprehensive System occurred in at least 33% of the 293 records. The two that fall below the one-in-three criterion are the P for Cards II and IX, with percentages for those two cards being 31% and 24%, respectively. In fact, when the means for P are reviewed for the samples containing 25 or more records, all are lower than the mean of 6.89 reported for the American sample (Australia = 6.21, France = 5.84, Mexico = 5.93, Micronesia = 4.67, Philippines = 5.02).

The differences among the distributions for form quality ($X+$% and $X-$%) are possibly more important and less easily understood. It has been the focus of considerable attention in recent research across cultures (Mattlar et al., 1995; Mormont & Crollard, 1995; Pires, 1995; Sendin, 1995). It is not yet clear whether these differences exist because of shortcomings in the Form Quality Table or the manner in which the Form Quality Table is applied in selecting the appropriate scoring or whether they are representative of true cultural differences. It is an issue about which much collaborative cultural research continues and which, also, has prompted an expansion of the table itself (Exner, 1995).

Although the issues of Popular answers and appropriate form quality scoring remain as fertile points for investigation, the composite of data published regarding identification of serious pathologies from Rorschach data appears to be less compelling. Dozens of studies from various countries and cultures suggest that common features do exist in the Rorschach that accurately differentiate schizophrenia and the major affective disorders. One of the more recent of these is an extensive investigation concerning schizophrenia by Vives (1990), who compared Spanish and American schizophrenic subjects. Her findings are not unlike those from other countries, such as Brazil, France, India, Italy, Japan, Pakistan, Norway, and the United States.

In summary, as noted above, the distributions of scores related to various personality features, when derived either from nonpatient or patient samples, seem to be very similar across cultures. Obviously, there are some cultural differences that cannot be neglected, but, generally, they affect the overall interpretation of Rorschach test data in only minor ways. Although more systematic research concerning Rorschach applications across cultures is required, it seems unlikely at this time that new findings will have a significant impact on the major aspects of Rorschach interpretation as the test is employed across cultures. In other words, the validity of the substance of interpretation does appear to be reasonably uniform regardless of the culture from which the protocol is collected.

ASSESSMENT OF COGNITIVE FUNCTIONING IN DIFFERENT CULTURES

This century has witnessed the introduction and proliferation of formal intellectual assessment measures in clinical, academic, military, business, and vocational settings. Moreover, professionals have expanded the application beyond settings for which the tests were developed into diverse ethnic and cultural populations. Proponents of the use of standardized intelligence tests with individuals from culturally diverse back-grounds focus on the reported validity of such instruments to predict educational and occupational success (Hunter, Schmidt & Rauschenberger, 1984; Linn, 1982; Oak-land, 1983). They assert that the standardization of intelligence tests makes them objective and valid across cultures. Opponents of intelligence testing across cultures draw attention to cultural differences in the way intelligence is defined (Scarr, 1978). According to some theorists (Lave, 1977; Scribner & Cole, 1981), these differences necessarily affect our ability to objectively test intelligence across different cultures.

To gain a better understanding of true assessment of intelligence across different cultural groups, we begin with a general definition of our Western-based notion of intelligence and a historical overview of attempts to assess intelligence. Next, we offer a few examples of other cultures' concepts of intelligence, followed by a review of studies of intellectual assessment across cultures. Finally, we present a discussion of environmental influences on intelligence, a topic relevant to the cultural study of intelligence.

Defining Intelligence

Our fascination with the nature of intelligence has generated a remarkably extensive and diverse collection of research studies in the scientific literature. These efforts notwithstanding, to this day no single definition of intelligence has secured universal acceptance. A number of important theories of intelligence result from factor-analytic models and information-processing strategies. From the factor-analytic camp, Spear-man (1923) argued for a two-factor theory of intelligence, consisting of a general factor (g) and other specific factors. Among the information-processing theories is Sternberg's (1985) model, which asserts that intelligence comprises three compo-nents. Another strategy is Gardner's (1983) less conventional conception of intelli-gence, identifying "multiple intelligences" such as musical, bodily-kinesthetic, logical-mathematical, linguistic, spatial, interpersonal, and intrapersonal (Armour-Thomas, 1992).

Numerous theories of intelligence have resulted in a myriad of definitions. The great number of attempts in this century to define intelligence and the absence of consensus on the question confirm the complexity of the task. For example, in 1921, a formal symposium attended by the country's most prominent psychologists working together to produce an acceptable definition of intelligence resulted in even greater uncertainty about what intelligence is (Thorndike et al., 1921). However, it is some-what encouraging to note that the quest to define and effectively measure intelligence continues to result in refinement of theory and generation of important new research ideas. Contemporary research on intelligence is by no means stagnant. Some of this century's noteworthy attempts to define intelligence were summarized by Sattler (1988, p. 45) as follows:

> Binet & Simon (1916): ". . . judgement, otherwise called good sense, practical sense, initiative, the faculty of adapting one's self to circumstances. To judge well, to compre-hend well, to reason well, these are the essential activities of intelligence" (pp. 42–43).

> Spearman (1923): "everything intellectual can be reduced to some special case . . . of educing either relations or correlates" (p. 300);

Wechsler (1958): "The aggregate or global capacity of the individual to act purposefully, to think rationally and to deal effectively with his environment" (p. 7);

Gardner (1983): "a human intellectual competence must entail a set of skills of problem solving—enabling the individual to resolve genuine problems or difficulties that he or she encounters, and, when appropriate, to create an effective product—and must also entail the potential for finding or creating problems—thereby laying the groundwork for the acquisition of new knowledge" (pp. 60–61);

Sternberg (1986): "mental activity involved in purposive adaptation to, shaping of, and selection of real-world environments relevant to one's life" (p. 33).

The diversity in these definitions would seem to affirm Terman's (Thorndike et al., 1921) statement of caution of over 70 years ago regarding efforts to define intelligence. He noted,

> We must guard against defining intelligence solely in terms of ability to pass the tests of a given intelligence scale. It should go without saying that no existing scale is capable of adequately measuring the ability to deal with all possible kinds of material on all intelligence levels. (p. 131)

The lack of consensus regarding a Western-based definition and conception of intelligence has clearly influenced our ability to compare intellectual abilities across cultures.

Measuring Intelligence

Different models have been proposed to assess human intellectual ability. Irvine and Berry (1983) note three distinct models—traditional testing, Piagetian interviews, and information processing in a quasi-experimental setting—as the basis for assessment. Here our discussion is limited to the traditional instruments of intellectual assessment. We specifically focus on the models of Galton, Binet, and Wechsler.

Sir Francis Galton. England's Sir Francis Galton (Johnson et al., 1985) measured sensory discrimination as the prototype of intelligence. His strategy was based on the belief that our knowledge of the world depends on our senses (the emic approach). Therefore, according to Galton, measuring sensory abilities is an acceptable way to measure intelligence. Consistent with his hypothesis, Galton (1833) stated, "The only information that reaches us concerning outward events appears to pass through the avenues of our senses; and the more perceptive the senses are of differences, the larger is the field upon which our judgment and intelligence can act" (p. 27). Even though this strategy did not prove to be a valid way to measure intelligence (Johnson, McClearn, Yuen, Nagoshi, Ahern, & Cole, 1985), it was an important first step in the formal intellectual testing movement.

Alfred Binet. Later, in France, Alfred Binet was issued the challenge of developing a test to identify schoolchildren who required special educational assistance. Unlike Galton, Binet was a proponent of measuring more complex mental processes as a means to assessing intelligence. In 1905, in collaboration with Theodore Simon he developed the Binet-Simon Scale. A modification of this test was introduced by Lewis Terman of Stanford University in 1916. Since that time the test has gone through several revisions. The latest version, published in 1986, is a popular intellectual assessment with special capacity to identify mental retardation and giftedness, as well as providing important diagnostic information about learning disabilities.

David Wechsler. In the United States, David Wechsler's attempts to develop a global assessment of intellectual functioning resulted in the development of the Wechsler-Bellevue Intelligence Scale, Form I. This was followed by the development of three versions designed for preschool children (WPPSI, 1989), schoolchildren (WISC-III, 1991), and adults (WAIS-R, 1981). Wechsler's series of intellectual assessments are widely used in educational, clinical, and legal settings in the United States.

Cross Cultural Study of Intelligence

Berry, Poortinga, Dasen & Segall (1992) pointed out that "cross-cultural psychology is the study of similarities and differences in individual psychological functioning in various cultural and ethnic groups" (p. 1). There is increasing recognition that other cultures do not necessarily share our Western ideas of intelligence (Berry, 1984). However, this recognition has not resolved the historical quandary of the relationship between culture and intelligence (Ruzgis & Grigorenko, 1994). Different perspectives have been presented to help clarify this relationship. Berry (1974) presented one extreme perspective (an emic view), requiring that indigenous notions of cognitive abilities be the sole basis for the generation of a culturally valid assessment of intelligence. Accordingly, intellectual assessment tasks should be constructed for each culture based on its definition of intelligence, precluding the need for cross-cultural assessment. This argument is based on cross-cultural evidence amassed from studies in the first half of this century (Biesheuvel, 1943; Loram, 1917; Oliver, 1932, 1933).

At the other extreme (an etic approach), Eysenck (1982) asserted that intelligence is the same across otherwise diverse cultures. According to this view, cultural differences need not be taken into account when assessing intelligence.

Aside from these two extremes, a number of more moderate perspectives have been adopted. For example, one position draws attention to the adaptive properties of intelligence as the focal point in the study of cognitive functioning (Ceci, 1990; Charlesworth, 1976; Sternberg, 1985, 1988). According to Charlesworth (1976), people of all cultures strive for environmental adaptation. Hence, the role of culture is apparent in terms of what may or may not be adaptive in a particular cultural context. While the proponents of the adaptive theory of intelligence regard culture as an important element in defining intelligence, they do not necessarily advocate cultural relativity. Rather, they focus on what constitutes intellectual ability for all people (Berry, 1984). Theories of cross-cultural intelligence cover a wide range of beliefs from constancy (the etic approach) to complete relativity (the emic approach) of intelligence across cultures. These theories guide our efforts to study and measure intelligence.

If we believe that cultural variation is important in intellectual assessment, then it seems prudent to ascertain a particular culture's specific definition of intelligence. This step seems reasonable considering that our Western view of intelligence apparently does not possess international appeal. An example offered by Keats (1982) of the cultural discrepancies in defining intelligence is illuminating. He compared Eastern (Chinese) and Western (Australian) ideas of intelligence, concluding that while the former considers pragmatism, sense of responsibility, and social awareness as important aspects of intelligence, the latter places high value on problem-solving abilities, command of language, logic, and critical thinking. It is the latter notion of intelligence that appears more consistent with the achievement of individual goals. To achieve these ends, an intelligent person must have an ability to communicate effectively and to create positive impressions on others. Respect, conformity, and obedience, all characteristic of intelligent behavior in Eastern cultures which preserve social harmony, are not necessarily consistent with our Western conception of intelligence (Ruzgis & Grigorenko, 1994).

In a similar vein, Wober (1974) reported that among the Baganda people of Uganda, intelligence, or *obugezi,* is defined according to the capacity to ponder or consider. Deliberateness, slowness, and social accuracy are of great value. This is similar to the notion of intelligence, or *nzelu* (Serpel, 1982), held by the Chi-Chewa people of Zambia. Closer to home, the virtues of group contribution rather than individual accomplishments, as well as unrushed life styles, among Native Americans (Foerster & Little, 1974) are examples of how cultural differences impact on our conception of intelligence. Intelligence as defined in these cultures would likely be regarded as a liability in Western culture.

Cultural attitudes are undoubtedly important in nurturing, supporting, and reinforcing culturally appropriate, intelligent behavior (Light, 1983; Rogoff, 1990; Valsiner, 1989; Wertsch, 1979). This point is effectively articulated by Ferguson (1956), who observed that cultural factors determine what must be learned and at what age; consequently, different cultural environments lead to the development of different patterns of ability. In a similar vein, Kagitcibasi and Berry (1989) propose that while people have similar capacities for intellectual ability, different cultural environments can enhance or impede the development of these abilities. Recently, the influence of culture in prescribing "the rate and extent to which different cognitive processes develop" (Altarriba, 1993, p. 383) was confirmed in a collection of empirical studies by Altarriba (1993). Stated plainly, Berry (1986) holds the view that intelligence, as presently used in psychology, is culture-bound, ethnocentric, and excessively narrow. This view emphasizes cultural background as critical in the manifestation of intellectual functioning through its influence on our perception, our modes of interaction with others, and our problem-solving strategies (Gauvain, 1993). Accordingly, it is important for intellectual tests to measure abilities that represent relevant and culture-specific intellectual competencies (Berry, 1974; Smith, 1974). Consequently, the translation of Western intellectual assessments has not always attained popularity among cross-cultural researchers. The Wechsler series and Stanford-Binet tests have been translated and adapted for use in many countries across the world. However, the published literature on these instruments is often controversial. An example is the controversy surrounding the validity of the most popular and researched translation of the Wechsler Adult Intelligence Scale, Escala de Intelligencia Wechsler para Adultos, or EIWA (Kunce & de Vales, 1986; Lopez & Romero, 1988; Davis & Rodriguez, 1979).

We have known about the intricate relationship between intelligence and culture in intellectual assessment for many decades. We continue to seek an intelligence test that can be universally adopted, and the debate on how to accomplish this task persists. Berry (1986) suggests that a more "culturally-relevant, more comprehensive, and less ethnocentric conception of human cognitive functioning" is needed before we have intellectual assessments with the international appeal that personality assessments such as the MMPI and Rorschach enjoy.

Testing Across Cultures

Testing in different cultures is a politically and socially important topic for several reasons. Developing countries may need to incorporate intellectual assessment measures to assist them in educational employment and placement decisions because limited educational resources may demand that ability tests be used effectively to assist in prudent allocation of these resources. In addition, in the United States an increasing number of immigrants from non-Western cultures has introduced a special need for appropriate intellectual assessment. In Western cultures, cognitive functioning assessed through formal and standardized testing is a good indicator of educational success and potential for occupational success (Thompson, 1980). However, the validity of Western-based intellectual assessments in predicting future performance of immigrants' success within the dominant culture has yet to be established and remains an important issue.

An alternative to traditional intellectual assessment which may prove to be more culturally acceptable is a "culture-free" or culture-fair test. While it is commendable to develop tests that do not discriminate based on cultural backgrounds, it is important for these tests to demonstrate adequate validity in predicting educational and occupational success if they are to attain credibility.

Cultural Variation in IQ Scores

Studies comparing intellectual ability in individuals from Western cultures and people from developing countries suggest considerable discrepancy in favor of Western subjects (Berry, Poortinga, Segal, & Dasen, 1992; Irvine & Berry, 1983; Poortinga & Van Der Flier, 1988). Lynn (1982) compared the performance of Japanese children on the standardized Wechsler Intelligence Scale for Children with the performance of American children, for whom the test was developed. He reported that Japanese children scored significantly higher than American children. They also found that while IQs over 130 are rare in the United States, over 10% of Japanese scored in that range. Comparisons of mathematical abilities (an important component of formal intellectual assessment) of Asian, Western, and African children suggested superiority for Asians while African children scored lowest (Davis & Ginsburg, 1993; Orivel & Perrot, 1988; Stevenson, Lee, & Stigler, 1986). Are the lower or higher scores obtained by different cultures indicative of differences in innate intelligence or merely a reflection of cultural opportunities?

Cultural Variation in Intellectual Assessment

Language is important in all cultures. Consequently, if language is involved in any intellectual test, then an accurate translation must be secured. Given an accurate translation, appropriateness of item content must then be evaluated. Therefore, the same criteria for translation of objective personality tests applies to the intellectual assessments that include verbal components. However, other cultural variations can influence performance.

While time is crucial to our Western-based notion of intelligence, other cultures do not necessarily share our attitudes about the virtues of swift performance. Accordingly, intellectual assessment across cultures must be sensitive to this cultural difference.

Anastasi (1988) described four tests that she considered suitable for assessment across cultures (the Leiter International Performance Scale, the Culture Fair Intelligence Test by R. B. Cattell, the Raven Progressive Matrices, and Goodenough-Harris Drawing Test). Due to space limitations, only a brief description of the Raven Progressive Matrices (RPM) (Raven, Court, & Raven, 1986) is presented here; we will illustrate its use later in the chapter. The interested reader is referred to Anastasi (1988) for further discussion.

The Raven, one of the most popular intelligence tests for use with other cultures, was first introduced in 1938. It measures nonverbal cognitive ability by assessing the individual's competence in making visual comparisons and organizing spatial perceptions into systematically related wholes (Sattler, 1988). Items consist of matrices, or sets of designs, with missing parts. The subject is asked to select the missing part from a number of options. Three forms of the Raven are available, the Standard Progressive Matrices (SPM, 1983); the Colored Progressive Matrices (CPM, 1984), intended for younger children or mentally retarded individuals; and the Advanced Progressive Matrices (APM, 1962), for adolescents and adults in the above-average range of intellectual functioning. Acceptable reliability and validity have been established for the Raven tests (Raven et al., 1986).

While culture-fair tests eliminate problems associated with language and timing, comparing scores on such tests across cultures is not free from other problems. One problem lies in varying motivations or attitudes toward testing (Biesheuvel, 1952, 1972). Performance may also be affected by environmental variability.

The importance of environmental variability in testing is demonstrated in the test results of a group of very educated Chinese residents of New York on a presumably culture-fair and semistructured projective test (Abel, 1973). The examiner, who was not familiar with Chinese culture, maintained minimal contact with the subjects to ensure objectivity. However, the subjects perceived him as cold and distant. Their perception of the examiner played a role in affecting their responses. Another psychologist, interpreting the test results without benefit of knowledge of these circumstances, began his report, "These people are like a bunch of crazy mixed-up kids" (Abel, 1973, p. 18). Thus a lack of cultural understanding has the potential to negatively influence the subjects' performance, yielding invalid results and questionable interpretations.

Environmental Influences in Intelligence

Environmental influences constitute important factors in fostering or restricting intellectual growth (Sattler, 1988). For decades, socioeconomic status (SES), nutrition, health care, family environment, and educational opportunities have been studied as putative factors in intellectual development. One environmental factor with the power to negatively impact cognitive development is nourishment. Klein, Freeman, Kagen, Yarbrough, and Habicht (1972) suggested that cognitive development could be compromised by early malnutrition common to less affluent nations, a finding later confirmed by McShane and Berry (1988). According to McShane and Berry (1988) and Klein et al. (1972), malnutrition, poverty, and lack of adequate health care are environmental factors with potentially disabling effects on intellectual development. They assert that poor nutrition and sickness may translate into less energy being available to the child for learning. In addition, lack of economic stability may lead to frequent moves and changes of school, leading to interference in the learning process.

Another factor implicated in differences in cognitive abilities is differential opportunities for education (Goodnow, 1969). Specifically, familiarity gained through prior exposure to tasks approximating those on an intelligence test might enhance an individual's ability to score favorably. Differences in education across cultures might be manifest in varying degrees of familiarity with intelligence assessment tasks.

In sum, there are a number of potentially important factors (e.g., valuing or not valuing swift performance) that have the capacity to produce differences in test results. In addition, other cultural factors (e.g., prior exposure) may contribute to differential performance in culture-fair intellectual assessments. In conclusion, at present intellectual assessment across cultures using Western-based intelligence tests is at best limited. Accordingly, caution should be exercised in attributing differences in performance to varying levels of inherent ability.

Performance on intelligence tests is not determined purely by cognitive abilities. Rather, it is confounded by past experiences and accumulated knowledge. Each culture promotes values, experiences, and learning opportunities unique to that culture. This introduces a significant predicament in comparing intellectual abilities across cultures. Considering the prominent role of culture in the development and enhancement of intellectual abilities, the challenge for psychologists is to understand and measure intelligence with a genuine appreciation of the individual's cultural background. Gaining a better understanding of diverse cultures can ideally enrich our understanding of human cognitive ability and flexibility rather than posing an obstacle. Later in this chapter we provide the results of a cultural cognitive assessment using the Raven that provides information about the patient's intellectual functioning in the case example.

CULTURAL ASSESSMENT: A CASE ANALYSIS

The case study, based on a psychological evaluation of a 43-year-old Iranian computer-design specialist currently being seen in outpatient psychotherapy, will be presented as follows: First, we will provide a brief description of his biographical background and current psychological situation. Next, we will present information based on the three test evaluations, the MMPI-2, the Rorschach, and the Raven Progressive Matrices. Then we will present an integrated picture of the individual based on the psychological test battery.

Case Description

Mr. S. is a 43-year-old Iranian male who presently lives in the United States. He received his primary, secondary, and college educations in Iran. He attended graduate school for computer sciences in the United States before accepting a job with a computer manufacturing company. He has been employed as a computer design specialist in the United States for the past 10 years. He is fluent in both English and Farsi.

He was self-referred for individual psychotherapy because of his loneliness and because he has been experiencing interpersonal difficulties. His main problem has been his inability to form and maintain meaningful relationships. His underlying cravings and dependency needs were covered up by narcissistic attitudes, such as treating others as objects, denying his need for them, and sexualizing his heterosexual relationships to avoid intimacy. His narcissistic/grandiose defenses had also caused problems in finding and keeping jobs, and therefore he presently has serious financial problems. His suppressed/denied anger was also acted out indirectly, causing him legal problems such as traffic violations.

Later on in treatment, as his narcissistic defenses were worked through, he became depressed and recognized his longings for human contact. He became unemployed for a period of time and discontinued treatment temporarily. He presently is employed and has resumed therapy with another psychologist.

Diagnostic impressions:

Axis I.   Dysthymia
Axis II.   Narcissistic personality
Axis III.   Diabetes

Interpretation of the MMPI-2

In order to illustrate the utility of objective interpretation of the MMPI-2, even across cultural boundaries, we will provide a computer-based interpretation of the client's MMPI-2 responses. For this analysis, the client completed the Farsi version of the MMPI-2. His item responses were scanned with an optical scanner and then scored and interpreted by electronic computer, using the Minnesota Clinical Report provided by National Computer Systems. The computer-scored profiles are included in Figures 3.1, 3.2, and 3.3, and the narrative report based on his responses is shown in Figure 3.4.

Interpretation of the Rorschach

It is important to emphasize that the following interpretive hypotheses have been formulated in the context of somewhat limited nontest information that can often be very important to the clarification of postulates. It is known that the subject is a 43-year-old male whose occupation generally would place him in a middle-class socioeconomic level. He has apparently been divorced for quite some time, after a marriage that did not yield any children. Presumably, he has been in outpatient treatment for at least two years, and this evaluation was conducted at a time when he was forced to interrupt treatment due to financial problems.

General Overview   The data (refer to the appendix for the actual Rorschach protocol and Comprehensive System scoring summary) indicate that he prefers to use an ide-

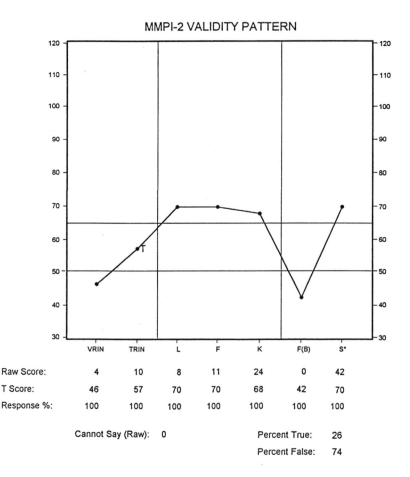

MMPI-2 VALIDITY PATTERN

	VRIN	TRIN	L	F	K	F(B)	S*
Raw Score:	4	10	8	11	24	0	42
T Score:	46	57	70	70	68	42	70
Response %:	100	100	100	100	100	100	100

Cannot Say (Raw):   0

Percent True: 26

Percent False: 74

*Experimental

Figure 3.1

ational style in most problem-solving or decision-making situations. In other words, he prefers to delay responses until he has given careful consideration to various alternative behaviors and their potential consequences. Typically, people with this sort of coping style prefer to avoid trial-and-error behaviors. However, there are several important issues that relate directly to the current effectiveness, or lack thereof, of this

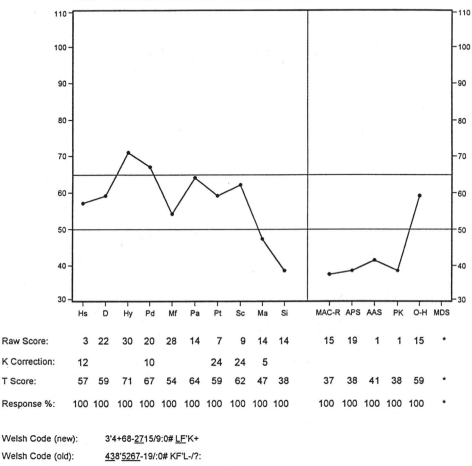

MMPI-2 BASIC AND SUPPLEMENTARY SCALES PROFILE

	Hs	D	Hy	Pd	Mf	Pa	Pt	Sc	Ma	Si		MAC-R	APS	AAS	PK	O-H	MDS
Raw Score:	3	22	30	20	28	14	7	9	14	14		15	19	1	1	15	*
K Correction:	12			10			24	24	5								
T Score:	57	59	71	67	54	64	59	62	47	38		37	38	41	38	59	*
Response %:	100	100	100	100	100	100	100	100	100	100		100	100	100	100	100	*

Welsh Code (new):	3'4+68-<u>27</u>15/9:0# <u>LF</u>'K+
Welsh Code (old):	<u>438</u>'<u>5267</u>-19/:0# KF'L-/?:
Profile Elevation:	60.80

*MDS scores are reported only for clients who indicate that they are married or separated.

Figure 3.2

coping style, the most important of which is that his thinking is often marked by very flawed logic or faulty judgment. It lacks clarity and seems much less mature than would be expected for one with his educational level.

In fact, the magnitude of his distorted and flawed thinking will often lead to very disorganized and/or inconsistent decision-making patterns that will be readily apparent to even the casual observer. It is possible that some Rorschach manifestations of

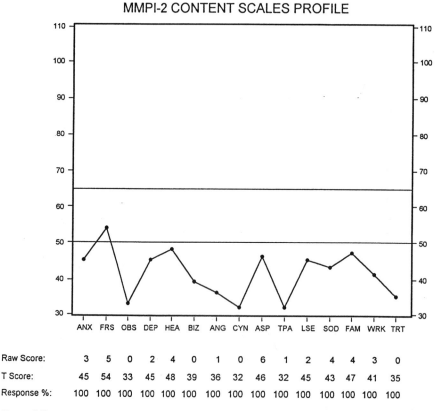

MMPI-2 CONTENT SCALES PROFILE

	ANX	FRS	OBS	DEP	HEA	BIZ	ANG	CYN	ASP	TPA	LSE	SOD	FAM	WRK	TRT
Raw Score:	3	5	0	2	4	0	1	0	6	1	2	4	4	3	0
T Score:	45	54	33	45	48	39	36	32	46	32	45	43	47	41	35
Response %:	100	100	100	100	100	100	100	100	100	100	100	100	100	100	100

Figure 3.3

flawed or immature thinking could be produced by a sense of futility that he is experiencing because of the changes in his treatment, but if that were true he would probably also exaggerate characteristics of distress in his MMPI performance. It does seem evident that he is currently experiencing some rather intense, situationally related stress experiences over which he has little or no control. Some of this stress appears to be related to a marked experience of emotional loss and may well relate directly to the changes in treatment status.

The current impact of this stress, whatever the cause, is of sufficient magnitude to disrupt his ordinarily adequate capacity for control, making him vulnerable to

PROFILE VALIDITY

The client has responded to the MMPI-2 items by claiming to be unrealistically virtuous. This test-taking attitude weakens the validity of the test and shows an unwillingness or inability on the part of the client to disclose personal information. Despite this extreme defensiveness, he has responded to items reflecting some unusual symptoms or beliefs. Many reasons may be found for this pattern of uncooperativeness: conscious distortion to present himself in a favorable light, lack of psychological sophistication, or rigid neurotic adjustment.

SYMPTOMATIC PATTERNS

Scales Hy and Pd were used as the prototype to develop this report. The client's MMPI-2 clinical scale profile suggests some problems with emotional control. He appears to be rather passive-aggressive and impulsive. He may overuse denial to control sexual or aggressive impulses and may have special difficulty controlling his anger.

He may also tend to be irritable or hostile, and he may occasionally have angry outbursts that cause him embarrassment or concern. Such individuals tend to believe that others are responsible for their difficulties. Although he appears to be moody and somewhat rebellious, his reactions are more likely to be passively resistant than actively aggressive. Under stress, he may have somatic complaints.

In addition, the following description is suggested by the content of the client's item responses. He appears to have very good social skills and tends to deny that he has any problems interacting with other people. He denies personal hostility or aggressiveness, and he is overly concerned and sensitive about what others think of him. He shows a tendency to reject authority and may have conflicts over rules.

PROFILE FREQUENCY

It is usually valuable in MMPI-2 clinical profile interpretation to consider the relative frequency of a given profile pattern in various settings. The client's MMPI-2 high-point clinical scale score (Hy) is found in 12.1% of the MMPI-2 normative sample of men. However, only 3.8% of the normative men have Hy as the peak score at or above a T score of 65, and only 2.3% have well-defined Hy spikes. This elevated MMPI-2 profile (3-4/4-3) is very rare in samples of normals, occurring in less than 1% of the MMPI-2 normative sample of men. His MMPI-2 high-point Hy score is found in 7.8% of the sample of military men (Butcher, Jeffrey, et al., 1990). But only 1.4% of the sample have this scale elevated at or over a T score of 65, and only 1% have well-defined Hy single-point codes at that elevation level. His MMPI-2 high-point Hy score is the second-highest peak score among men over the age of 40, occurring in 16.5% of a normative aging study (Butcher et al., 1991). But only 5% of the sample have this scale elevated at or over a T score of 65, and only 2.7% have well-defined Hy single-point peak scores at that level.

Figure 3.4

impulsiveness in thinking, manifestations of emotion, and disruption of his general pattern of behaviors. In effect, it has created more psychological complexity than is customary, resulting in a state of psychological overload. Consequently, the current clinical picture probably includes some report of irritating feelings, such as anxiety, apprehensiveness, periodic depression, and/or a marked reduction in motivation to fulfill everyday responsibilities.

PROFILE STABILITY

The relative scale elevation of his highest clinical scale scores suggests some lack of clarity in profile definition. Although his most elevated clinical scales are likely to be present in his profile pattern if he is retested at a later date, there could be some shifting of the most prominent scale elevations in the profile code. The difference between the profile type used to develop the present report and the next highest scale in the profile code was 3 points. So, for example, if the client is tested at a later date, his profile might involve more behavioral elements related to elevations on Pa. If so, then on retesting, externalization of blame, mistrust, and questioning the motives of others might become more prominent.

INTERPERSONAL RELATIONS

He tends to be rather sociable and outgoing, but his close relationships are superficial and somewhat rocky. He is not likely to accept much responsibility for these problems.

Quite outgoing and sociable, he has a strong need to be around others. He is gregarious and enjoys attention. Personality characteristics related to social introversion-extraversion tend to be stable over time. The client is typically outgoing, and his sociable behavior is not likely to change if he is retested at a later time. His personal relationships are likely to be somewhat superficial. He appears to be rather spontaneous and expressive and may seek attention from others, especially to gain social recognition.

DIAGNOSTIC CONSIDERATIONS

He has reported many personal problems and potentially maladaptive attitudes that need to be considered in any diagnostic formulation. Long-term personality maladjustment is likely to be central to his clinical picture.

TREATMENT CONSIDERATIONS

Individuals with this MMPI-2 clinical profile tend not to be very serious psychotherapy clients. They use denial a great deal and have little psychological insight, although they may make "therapist-pleasing" remarks. They tend not to seek psychological therapy on their own because they see no need to change their behavior. When they are pressured into treatment, they tend to be only marginally cooperative at best and to terminate treatment early. Individuals with this profile are often considered to be passive-aggressive in relationships. The manipulative behavior that many patients with this profile exhibit needs to be carefully evaluated before initiating treatment.

Figure 3.4 *(continued)*

Basic Personality Structure   As noted earlier, he is a very ideationally oriented person who prefers to think things through before taking action. Unfortunately, much of his thinking is strongly influenced by his rather conflicted sense of self. He is an extraordinarily self-centered person who tends to overestimate his own worth quite significantly. This narcissistic-like feature influences many of his decisions and also carries considerable weight in the manner in which he carries on interpersonal relationships. It also appears, however, that he is acutely aware of evidence suggesting that his own worth is really not as substantial as he has judged it to be in the past.

NOTE: This MMPI-2 interpretation can serve as a useful source of hypotheses about clients. This report is based on objectively derived scale indices and scale interpretations that have been developed in diverse groups of patients. The personality descriptions, inferences, and recommendations contained herein need to be verified by other sources of clinical information because individual clients may not fully match the prototype. The information in this report should most appropriately be used by a trained, qualified test interpreter. The information contained in this report should be considered confidential.

Figure 3.4 (*continued*)

This creates a conflict situation for him regarding his self-image and apparently has been one of several factors that has prompted an increase in his sense of negativism, so that now he tends to view the world as being less accepting and more hostile. This has provoked considerable anger within him, and this anger has great influence on his view of the world and his decisions about how to react to it.

His self-centeredness often contributes significantly to the development of motivation for status, and, if that recognition of status is achieved, self-centeredness is less likely to interfere with his overall adjustment. On the other hand, when he fails to obtain reassurance of his high self-value, this leads to negativism, and elaborate systems of defense are developed in an attempt to protect the integrity of his belief concerning his high personal worth. Consequently, rationalization, denial, and externalization occur, and he is especially prone to blame others and the external world for any difficulties in adjustment that he encounters.

Currently, he appears to be engaging in much more self-examining behavior than do most people. This seems to be related to the conflict that he is experiencing concerning his perceived self-image and includes a tendency to ruminate considerably about his less desirable features. This rumination often gives rise to very negative feelings and is possibly responsible for periodic episodes of depression.

His self-image obviously is based much more on imaginary than real experience. This contributes to a psychological situation in which there is less maturity and a greater number of distorted notions about the self than should be the case. Thus, while he has a very strong interest in people, he does not understand them very well. He is also a much more lonely person than might be expected for one of his age and apparent intellectual level. People such as this often tend to seek out relations with others, but also tend to use poor judgment in the manner in which they attempt to establish or maintain those relations. In effect, he is a socially isolated person who finds it quite difficult to sustain smooth or meaningful interpersonal relations.

He is not very flexible in the way he thinks about issues, and his values are quite well set. This has a considerable influence on the way in which he interacts with others. In fact, he tends to see interpersonal relationships as naturally marked by some aggressiveness and anticipates aggressive exchanges to occur routinely in his

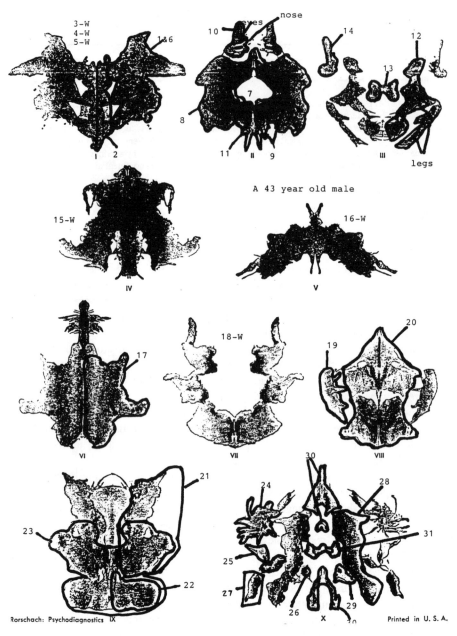

Figure 3A.1

own interpersonal world. At the same time, he tends to judge aggressiveness as a favorable characteristic and seems to anticipate that aggressive relationships will somehow be more rewarding and enduring than will nonaggressive relationships. Therefore, it is not unreasonable to speculate that some of his interpersonal relations have been and will continue to be marked by aggressiveness.

Even though he is an ideational person, he is also quite emotional, especially about his own values. Unfortunately, he is very lax about modulating or controlling his own emotional expressions. This is quite unusual for people of this age and apparent intellectual level, and frequently others will regard them as overly emotional, immature, or both. These more intense and less mature manifestations of his feelings tend to short-circuit other psychological operations and may be one of the factors currently responsible for his flawed judgment and distorted thinking. Obviously, his intense anger contributes to this, and many situations probably occur in which he is confused by his own feelings. His previously noted tendency to perceive aggressiveness as an acceptable form of interpersonal behavior, when combined with his considerable anger, may form a core from which asocial or even antisocial forms of behavior can evolve.

In spite of his perceived limitations in thinking and difficulties in emotional control, he is still able to process new information quite well, albeit conservatively. He works very hard to process new information adequately and also works hard to synthesize new information in a meaningful way. Unfortunately, his perceptions of reality are not very conventional. Thus, many of his behaviors will be formulated with less concern for social acceptability and more for the gratification of his own immediate needs. Although many of his behaviors may not be unacceptable, his strong individualistic orientation will often cause others to perceive him as being out of step with the environment, and because of this it is probable that he may experience frequent confrontations with authority figures. Actually, he is more likely to define things in a conventional manner and engage in socially expected behaviors when the cues of the situation are obvious and precisely defined.

Rorschach Summary   Overall, this seems to be an individual in considerable disarray. Although preferring an ideational approach to decision making, he is currently much more prone to impulsiveness and disorganization than should be the case, especially when the circumstances around him are marked by considerable ambiguity. He does not modulate his own emotional expressions very well, and thus they are prone to be much more intense than expected for one of his age; they are also probably marked by considerably more anger, negativism, and/or aggressiveness than should be the case. He seems to be struggling considerably with the issue of his own worth and has much difficulty relating to others. He is a very lonely man who wants desperately to be close to others but does not understand them well and does not understand how to create and maintain meaningful relationships.

There is some evidence in the data to suggest that he is psychologically similar in some ways to people who effect their own deaths, usually in a sense of extreme stress or frustration. While the likelihood of this seems remote when considered in the context of the history, it should not be taken lightly, and, assuming that he is able to continue treatment, his therapist might be cautioned to investigate this possibility more thoroughly.

Finally, his age, exquisite self-centeredness, and the overall complexity of his personality structure make the likelihood of significant therapeutic change unlikely. He is the type of person who needs close supports and structure in a therapeutic situation. Clear definitions of goals for treatment are very important to his future, and some cognitive-behavioral intervention methods designed to assist him in his interpersonal

```
CASE ILLUSTRATION ====== SEQUENCE OF SCORES ===============================

CARD NO LOC   #  DETERMINANT(S)    (2) CONTENT(S)    POP Z  SPECIAL SCORES
======= ======  =============      === ==========    === =  ==============
   I   1 Do    2  Mao              2   (H)
       2 Dd+  99  Mp.FVu               H,Cg           4.0
       3 WSo   1  Fo                   (Hd)           3.5
       4 W+    1  Ma-pu            2   H,(H)          4.0  FAB,COP
       5 Wo    1  FMao                 A              1.0
       6 Do    2  F-                   Ad

  II   7 DSo   5  Fo                   Sc
       8 D+    1  Ma.FTo           2   A            P 3.0  COP,FAB
       9 Ddv  99  ma.C                 Id
      10 D+    2  F-                   Hd,Id          3.0
      11 Do    3  Fu                   A

 III  12 D+    9  Mp.FDo               H,Cg,Ls      P 3.0
      13 Do    3  Fo                   A
      14 Do    2  FMpu                 A                   INC

  IV  15 W+    1  Ma.FT.FVo            (H),Cl       P 4.0  FAB

   V  16 W+    1  FMa.FDu              A,Ad           2.5  AG

  VI  17 DS/   4  ma.YF.FDu            Na             6.5

 VII  18 W+    1  Ma.FVu           2   Hd,Na        P 2.5

VIII  19 Do    1  FMao                 A            P
      20 D+    6  ma.CFo               Sc,Id          3.0  ALOG

  IX  21 DSo  12  FV.CFu               Ge                  ALOG
      22 D+    4  FY.CFo               (H),An         2.5
      23 Dd+  99  Ma.Fr-               H,Na,Hx        2.5  FAB

   X  24 Do    1  Fo                   A            P
      25 D+    7  FMa-                 A              4.0  AG,FAB
      26 Ddv  33  C                    Id
      27 DdS+ 99  FMau             2   A,Na           6.0
      28 Dv    9  YF-                  Ge
      29 Do    2  F-                   Cg
      30 DdS+ 99  mau                  Sc             6.0  DR,AG
      31 D+    6  Ma.FTo           2   A              4.0  COP,FAB

============================= SUMMARY OF APPROACH ==============================

     I :  D.Dd.WS.W.W.D              VI  :  DS
    II :  DS.D.Dd.D.D               VII  :  W
   III :  D.D.D                    VIII  :  D.D
    IV :  W                          IX  :  DS.D.Dd
     V :  W                           X  :  D.D.Dd.DdS.D.D.DdS.D
```

Figure 3A.2

interactions and the development of more appropriate modulation of his emotional expressions will be quite important to his future adjustment.

Cognitive Assessment: Raven Progressive Matrices

Mr. S. performed extremely well on the Raven Progressive Matrices (see Figure 3.5), producing a total score of 54 (he made only one mistake on the test). Unfortunately, the Iranian norms for the Raven do not include adults; therefore, we evaluated his score on the American norms. On the American norms his score places him above the 95th percentile of individuals taking the test.

```
CASE ILLUSTRATION ============ STRUCTURAL SUMMARY ==============================
```

LOCATION	DETERMINANTS		CONTENTS	S-CONSTELLATION
FEATURES	BLENDS	SINGLE		YES..FV+VF+V+FD>2
			H = 4, 0	YES..Col-Shd Bl>0
Zf = 18	M.FV	M = 2	(H) = 3, 1	YES..Ego<.31,>.44
ZSum = 65.0	M.FT	FM = 5	Hd = 2, 0	NO..MOR > 3
ZEst = 59.5	m.C	m = 1	(Hd) = 1, 0	YES..Zd > +- 3.5
	M.FD	FC = 0	Hx = 0, 1	YES..es > EA
W = 6	M.FT.FV	CF = 0	A =11, 0	YES..CF+C > FC
(Wv = 0)	FM.FD	C = 1	(A) = 0, 0	YES..X+% < .70
D = 19	m.YF.FD	Cn = 0	Ad = 1, 1	YES..S > 3
Dd = 6	M.FV	FC'= 0	(Ad) = 0, 0	NO..P < 3 or > 8
S = 6	m.CF	C'F= 0	An = 0, 1	NO..Pure H < 2
	FV.CF	C' = 0	Art = 0, 0	NO..R < 17
DQ	FY.CF	FT = 0	Ay = 0, 0	8.....TOTAL
.........(FQ-)	M.Fr	TF = 0	Bl = 0, 0	
+ = 15 (3)	M.FT	T = 0	Bt = 0, 0	SPECIAL SCORINGS
o = 12 (2)		FV = 0	Cg = 1, 2	Lv1 Lv2
v/+ = 1 (0)		VF = 0	Cl = 0, 1	DV = 0x1 0x2
v = 3 (1)		V = 0	Ex = 0, 0	INC = 1x2 0x4
		FY = 0	Fd = 0, 0	DR = 1x3 0x6
		YF = 1	Fi = 0, 0	FAB = 6x4 0x7
		Y = 0	Ge = 2, 0	ALOG = 2x5
		Fr = 0	Hh = 0, 0	CON = 0x7
		rF = 0	Ls = 0, 1	Raw Sum6 = 10
FORM QUALITY		FD = 0	Na = 1, 3	Wgtd Sum6 = 39
		F = 8	Sc = 3, 0	
FQx FQf MQual SQx			Sx = 0, 0	AB = 0 CP = 0
+ = 0 0 0 0			Xy = 0, 0	AG = 3 MOR = 0
o = 13 4 5 2			Id = 2, 2	CFB = 0 PER = 0
u = 10 1 3 4				COP = 3 PSV = 0
- = 6 3 1 0				
none= 2 -- 0 0		(2) = 6		

```
================== RATIOS, PERCENTAGES, AND DERIVATIONS ==================
```

R = 31	L = 0.35		FC:CF+C = 0: 5	COP = 3 AG = 3
			Pure C = 2	Food = 0
EB = 9: 6.0	EA = 15.0	EBPer= 1.5	SumC':WSumC= 0:6.0	Isolate/R =0.42
eb =10:10	es = 20	D = -1	Afr =0.72	H:(H)Hd(Hd)= 4: 7
	Adj es = 15	Adj D = 0	S = 6	(HHd):(AAd)= 5: 0
			Blends:R=13:31	H+A:Hd+Ad =19: 5
FM = 6 : C'= 0	T = 3		CP = 0	
m = 4 : V = 4	Y = 3			
		P = 6	Zf =18	3r+(2)/R=0.29
a:p = 16: 4	Sum6 = 10	X+% =0.42	Zd = +5.5	Fr+rF = 1
Ma:Mp = 7: 3	Lv2 = 0	F+% =0.50	W:D:Dd = 6:19: 6	FD = 3
2AB+Art+Ay= 0	WSum6 = 39	X-% =0.19	W:M = 6: 9	An+Xy = 1
M- = 1	Mnone = 0	S-% =0.00	DQ+ =15	MOR = 0
		Xu% =0.32	DQv = 3	

```
==========================================================================
SCZI = 2    DEPI = 4    CDI = 1    S-CON = 8*    HVI = No    OBS = No
==========================================================================
```

Figure 3A.2 (*continued*)

CASE SUMMARY

I. Identifying Information

The patient is a 43-year-old Iranian male who is divorced and currently is an unemployed computer-design specialist. The patient started therapy in 1991 and remained in therapy for a total of three and one-half years.

II. Presenting Problem

The patient was self-referred and sought therapy in order to resolve his interpersonal difficulties. He stated that he had no close friends, experienced friction with one

```
CASE ILLUSTRATION ============ CONSTELLATIONS TABLE=====================
SCZI (Schizophrenia Index):   Positive if 4 or more conditions are true

   YES   (X+% {0.42} < .61 and S-% {0.00} < .41)   or   (X+% {0.42} < .50)
   No    (X-% {0.19} > .29)
   No    (FQ- {6} >= FQu {10})   or   (FQ- {6} > FQo {13} + FQ+ {0}))
   No    (Sum Level 2 Sp. Sc. {0} > 1) and (FAB2 {0} > 0)
   YES   (Raw Sum of 6 Spec. Scores {10} > 6)   or
         (Weighted Sum of 6 Sp. Sc. {39} > 17)
   No    (M- {1} > 1)   or   (X-% {0.19} > .40)


DEPI (Depression Index):   Positive if 5 or more conditions are true

   YES   (FV+VF+V {4} > 0)   or   (FD {3} > 2)
   YES   (Col-Shd Blends {2} > 0)   or   (S {6} > 2)
   YES   (3r+(2)/R {0.29} > .45 and Fr+rF {1} = 0) or (3r+(2)/R {0.29} < .33)
   No    (Afr {0.72} < .46)   or   (Blends {13} < 4)
   No    (SumShading {10} > FM+m {10})   or   (SumC' {0} > 2)
   No    (MOR {0} > 2)   or   (2AB+(Art+Ay) {0} > 3)
   YES   (COP {3} < 2)   or   (Isolate/R {0.42} > .24)


CDI (Coping Deficit Index):   Positive if 4 or more conditions are true

   No    (EA {15.0} < 6)   or   (AdjD {0} < 0)
   No    (COP {3} < 2)   and   (AG {3} < 2)
   No    (Weighted Sum C {6.0} < 2.5) or (Afr {0.72} < .46)
   No    (Passive {4} > Active + 1 {17}) or (Pure H {4} < 2)
   YES   (Sum T {3} > 1) or (Isolate/R {0.42} > .24) or (Food {0} > 0)


HV (Hypervigilance Index):   Positive if condition (1) is true and
                             4 or more of conditions (2) to (8) are true
   No    (1) FT+TF+T {3} = 0
                                      YES   (5) H+(H)+Hd+(Hd) {11} > 6
   YES   (2) Zf {18} > 12             YES   (6) (H)+(A)+(Hd)+(Ad) {5} > 3
   YES   (3) Zd {5.5} > +3.5          YES   (7) H+A:Hd+Ad {19:5} < 4:1
   YES   (4) S {6} > 3                No    (8) Cg {3} > 3


OBS (Obsessive Style Index):
                                      YES   (3) Zd {5.5} > +3.0
   YES   (1) Dd {6} > 3               No    (4) Populars {6} > 7
   YES   (2) Zf {18} > 12             No    (5) FQ+ {0} > 1

Positive if 1 or more of the following are true:

   No   Conditions (1) to (5) are all true
   No   2 or more of conditions (1) to (4) are true and FQ+ {0} > 3
   No   3 or more of conditions (1) to (5) are true and X+% {0.42} > .89
   No   FQ+ {0} > 3   and   X+% {0.42} > .89
```

Figure 3A.2 (*continued*)

of his brothers, and could not sustain relationships with women for any length of time.

III. History of Present Illness

The patient stated that he had problems with his father, who verbally abused him, but he apparently was very close to his mother.

CASE ILLUSTRATION ====== SUMMARY OF RESPONSE CONTENTS ========================

Content		Number of Occurrences		Content		Number of Occurrences
H	WOMAN	3		*Ad	HEAD-BEAR	1
*H	MAN	1		An	WOMB	1
*(H)	BABY	2		Cg	SKIRT	1
(H)	ANGELS	2		*Cg	SHOE	1
(H)	GIANT	1		Cg	SHOES	1
*Hd	FACE	1		Cl	CLOUD	1
Hd	PEOPLE	1		*Ge	MAP	2
(Hd)	MASK	1		Ls	STONE	1
A	BIRD	3		Na	SEA	1
A	BEARS	1		Na	ICICLES	1
A	BEAR	1		Na	ROAD	1
A	BUTTERFLY	1		*Na	LAKE	1
A	SEAHORSE	1		Na	SHORE	1
A	TARANTULA	1		*Id	INK	2
*A	DINOSAUR	1		Id	LIPSTICK	1
*A	DUCK	1		Sc	PLANE	1
A	TURTLE	1		Sc	SPACESHIPS	1
A	MONKEYS	1		Sc	GLIDER	1
Ad	SNAIL	1				

* = Minus response

Figure 3A.2 (*continued*)

IV. Previous Illnesses

Psychiatric History   The patient had had brief short-term therapy before 1991. He denied a family history of psychiatric problems, but his brother was in treatment for low self-esteem and interpersonal difficulties. On one occasion he had to cancel his testing session because it was his brother's wedding day, and the brother had disappeared, leaving a note that he had changed his mind. The patient stated that he needed to take care of the situation.

Medical History   In 1992 he was diagnosed with diabetes, which has been controllable with diet alone. He has not had to receive insulin treatment at this point.

Substance Abuse History   Although he drinks socially, he denied a history of substance abuse.

V. Developmental and Social History

The patient is an Iranian and the fourth child in a family of six children. He has two older brothers, an older sister, and a younger brother and sister. Both his parents are deceased. His mother died when he was in his 20s, perhaps from diabetes. His father died in the 1980s from unknown causes. The patient described his relationship with his mother as very close; however, he had a very poor relationship with his father, characterized by a great deal of anger. The therapist noted that the client showed a large number of Oedipal themes and issues in his psychotherapy.

Answer Sheet for

RAVEN PROGRESSIVE MATRICES — 1938
Sets A, B, C, D, and E

Name ₃ *R . S .* ═══ .... Sex ...... *M* .... Age ....

School   .... Grade .... *B A* ......

Test Beg   ...~.~..~............Test Ended ... *7:40 P M* ....Total Time ....

A		B		C		D		E	
1 *4* ✓		1 *2* ✓		1 *8* ✓		1 *3* ✓		1 *7* ✓	
2 *5* ✓		2 *6* ✓		2 *2* ✓		2 *4* ✓		2 *6* ✓	
3 *1* ✓		3 *1* ✓		3 *3* ✓		3 *3* ✓		3 *8* ✓	
4 *2* ✓		4 *2* ✓		4 *8* ✓		4 *7* ✓		4 *2* ✓	
5 *6* ✓		5 *1* ✓		5 *7* ✓		5 *8* ✓		5 *1* ✓	
6 *3* ✓		6 *3* ✓		6 *4* ✓		6 *6* ✓		6 *5* ✓	
7 *6* ✓		7 *5* -		7 *5* ✓		7 *5* ✓		7 *1* ✓	
8 *2* ✓		8 *6* .		8 *1* -		8 *4* ✓		8 *6* ✓	
9 *1* ✓		9 *4*		9 *7* .		9 *1* ✓		9 *3*	
10 *3* ✓		10 *3*		10 *6* :		10 *2* ✓		10 *2* .	
11 *4* ✓		11 *4* .		11 *1* .		11 *2* ✗		11 *4* ✓	
12 *5* ✓		12 *5* .		12 *2* ✓		12 *6* ✓		12 *5* ✓	
11		*1*		*1:*		*10*		*1*	

Total Score ....*5 4*....Percentile ....

Published by The Psychological Corporation, 304 East 45th Street, New York 17, N. Y. under special arrangements
with H. K. Lewis and Company, Ltd., London, England.

Figure 3.5

VII. Mental Status

His therapist indicated that the patient is an intelligent individual who has had no cognitive impairment, no psychosis, and no suicidal ideation. His strong performance on the Raven Progressive Matrices supports the hypothesis that the client is functioning in the superior range of intellectual ability. On the day of testing he was well groomed and professionally dressed. He was oriented, and his speech was fluent and intelligible. No delusions were noted. Remote memory and immediate memory for recall was intact.

VIII. Patient's Goal for Treatment

The patient's goal for treatment was to find friends, establish meaningful relationships, start a family, and establish a stable financial status.

IX. Personality Dynamics

The patient has a long history of chronic relationship problems. He has general discontentment with his life due to relationship problems, possibly accompanied by mild depression. He is discontent with life, and his failures are overcompensated for and masked by narcissistic and grandiose attitudes. He has developed unrealistic idealized expectations that cause narcissistic injuries and underlying dependency conflicts, and some of his feelings of abandonment by his mother are acted out in his relationships with women. He appears to have a repetition compulsion in relationships with women.

The MMPI-2 and the Rorschach test interpretations are valuable in understanding Mr. S.'s personality dynamics. There is, moreover, considerable congruence between the MMPI-2 and the Rorschach interpretations. Each instrument also added uniquely to understanding the client's personality dynamics. Both the MMPI-2 and Rorschach point to considerable anger within the client. This anger appears to have much influence on his view of the world and his decisions about how to react to it. Both the MMPI-2 and Rorschach also describe his negativism and suggest an elaborate system of defenses that has been developed in an attempt to protect the integrity of his belief concerning his high personal worth. Consequently, rationalization, denial, and externalization occur, and he is especially prone to blame others and the external world for any difficulties in adjustment that he encounters. The MMPI-2 notes a clear tendency for him to become embroiled in authority conflicts. The client appears to have a strong individualistic orientation that often causes others to perceive him as being out of step with the environment, and because of this, it is likely that he may experience frequent confrontations with authority figures. Individuals with the personality patterns he shows may act out in immature and impulsive ways.

The MMPI-2 and Rorschach agree that Mr. S. is usually a very sociable and outgoing individual. The Rorschach suggests that he has a very strong interest in people and that he does not appear to understand them very well. He is also a much more lonely person than might be expected for one of his age and apparent intellectual level. People such as this often tend to seek out relations with others but also tend to use poor judgment in the manner by which they attempt to establish or maintain those relations. In effect, he is a socially isolated person who finds it quite difficult to sustain smooth or meaningful interpersonal relations. The client tends to see interpersonal relationships as naturally marked by some aggressiveness and anticipates aggressive exchanges to occur routinely in his own interpersonal world. At the same time, he tends to judge aggressiveness as a more favorable characteristic and seems to anticipate that aggressive relationships will somehow be more rewarding and enduring than will nonaggressive relationships. Therefore, it is not unreasonable to speculate that some of his interpersonal relations have been and will continue to be marked by aggressiveness. His MMPI-2 performance suggests that he becomes embroiled in interpersonal problems and frequently denies any responsibility for interpersonal turmoil.

The Rorschach suggests that he is very lax about modulating or controlling his own emotional expressions, resulting in flawed judgment and distorted thinking. This is quite unusual for people of this age and apparent intellectual level, and frequently others will regard them as overly emotional and/or less mature. Data on the MMPI-2 also suggest that the emotional control problems that he experiences are unusual and infrequent in the general population.

He is currently much more prone to impulsiveness and disorganization than should be the case, especially when the circumstances around him are marked by considerable ambiguity. He does not modulate his own emotional expressions very well, and thus they are prone to be much more intense than expected for one of his age; they are also probably marked by considerably more anger, negativism, and/or aggressiveness than should be the case.

The MMPI-2 interpretation and the hypotheses derived from the Rorschach raise the strong likelihood of there being significant long-term personality problems. Treatment prognosis is likely to be somewhat guarded, given that persistent personality-disordered elements are likely to exert an influence—producing a difficulty in bringing about behavioral change.

XI. Additional Information From the Test Information Feedback Session

Mr. S. was on time for the appointment. Consistent with previous sessions, he was very gregarious and willing to talk. The behavioral observations confirm the high and unrealistic standards that he sets for himself. Although he has been unemployed for the last month, he was talking about expanding his business. Later it was apparent that he is actually experiencing many financial problems. He was very pleased by his score on the intelligence test. He wanted to know how people in college did, and kept asking questions about how well he had done.

Sources of Stress   Mr. S. believes "not having accomplished in life" is a major source of stress for him. He also believes that tensions between himself and his brother are sources of stress. His brother is doing well financially and makes Mr. S. believe that what he has been doing in life has been wrong. According to the patient, he is experiencing financial problems at this time. In response to "what do you do when you are stressed?", he said "I walk back and forth in my apartment, yelling, banging on the wall and floor sometimes for 4 to 5 hours." He acknowledged that he hates ambiguity and that he does not function well when things are not clear. Ambiguity could be viewed as a potentially stressful element for Mr. S. to deal with.

Relationship Problems   Mr. S. was married for 1 year in 1980 to an American woman whom he married in order to get a visa. There were no problems with his marriage, but they separated anyway. He stated that it was hard on both of them. He was not clear about why they got divorced. His last serious relationship, with an Iranian woman, was a couple of years ago. Her parents returned to Iran because her business was not going well, so Mr. S. told her that it was best that she go back to Iran. (He was giving the impression of doing the right thing for others and being self-sacrificing.) He stated that he yearns for a family and a good relationship.

Family History Mr. S. indicated that in childhood his mother always set very high standards and expectations for him. At the same time, his father treated him as though he would not amount to anything in life. He said, "my dad kept saying I was going to goof up on things I tried to do and I did." He stated "and here was poor me at the middle of two extremes."

Thinking Processes He said, "I need, to have everything calculated and perfect, which becomes a problem for me. I keep thinking and thinking, which leads to an inability to make decisions."

CONCLUSIONS

In contemporary clinical psychology, psychologists are often faced with the challenging task of assessing clients who come from diverse cultural backgrounds. Assessments of individuals from different cultures can be difficult and uncertain. They require special considerations to ensure appropriate evaluation. Clinicians who are asked to assess clients from different cultural backgrounds may be initially at a loss to know how to relate to the client, how to formulate the problem, and how to determine which (if any) psychological tests to use or which treatment strategies might be effective. However, with careful and thoughtful effort, psychological assessment techniques might prove to be valuable in assessments of individuals from different cultures.

There are two general orientations to consider in any cross-cultural study with respect to defining our starting point in understanding people in different cultures: the emic and the etic views. The emic approach seeks to understand people on their own terms (that is, within their own culture) without reference to other cultures or perspectives. This approach parallels the ideographic view of psychology, as described by Allport (1937). The etic approach is analogous to Allport's nomothetic view of science as a comparative strategy and emphasizes universals by comparing individuals or cultures along similar dimensions, seeking to determine whether data or theories developed in one culture are appropriate for another.

A number of challenging factors must be considered in developing a cultural framework for clinical assessment, and a number of possible problems need to be resolved before appropriate assessments can be implemented. Some of the factors that require careful consideration are: language limitations, cultural differences, motivational differences, different conceptualizations of "what is abnormal," and different interpersonal expectations on the part of the client. There are a number of relevant variables associated with the adoption of specific procedures for populations different from the standardized samples used in tests. For example, the task being required of the subjects must be culturally appropriate; the responses required of the individual must be appropriate; and there must be demonstrated psychological equivalence of the procedures.

Three major clinical assessment approaches in wide use in clinical psychological assessment, the MMPI-2, the Rorschach, and the Raven, were described in detail in this chapter to provide examples of specific test applications in different cultures. Factors related to the interpretation of these procedures in cross-cultural assessment were discussed and limitations noted. The use of these procedures in an actual clinical case was included in this chapter as an illustration of their applicability with clients from diverse cultures and of how they can provide valuable information on clinical assessment across cultures.

Note

1. Variables studied include *R, Lambda, EA, es, adjes, SumSH, FM + m, SumC, WSumC, M, Zf, Sum6, WSum6, Afr, 3r + (2)/R, X + %, Xu%, X − %, P,* active movement, passive movement, Isolation Index, *S,* and Intellectualization Index.

References

Abe, M., Sumita, K., & Kuroda, M. (1963). *A manual of the MMPI, Japanese Standard Edition.* Kyoto, Japan: Sankyobo.

Abel, T. M. (1944). Responses of Negro and white Mormons to the Rorschach test. *American Journal of Mental Deficiency, 48,* 253–257.

Abel, T. M. (1948). The Rorschach test in the study of culture. *Rorschach Research Exchange and Journal of Projective Techniques, 12,* 2–15.

Abel, T. M. (1973). *Psychological testing in cultural contexts.* New Haven: United Printing.

Allport, G. W. (1937). *Personality: A psychological interpretation.* New York: Holt.

Altarriba, J. (Ed.) (1993). *Cognition and culture: A cross-cultural approach to cognitive psychology.* Amsterdam, Netherlands: Elsevier.

Anastasi, A. (1988). *Psychological testing.* New York: Macmillan.

Armour-Thomas, E. (1992). Intellectual assessment of children from culturally diverse backgrounds. *School Psychology Review, 21,* 552–565.

Beck, S. J. (1944). *Rorschach's test I: Basic processes.* New York: Grune & Stratton.

Beck, S. J. (1945). *Rorschach's test II: A variety of personality pictures.* New York: Grune & Stratton.

Ben-Porath, Y. S. (1990). Cross-cultural assessment of personality: The case for replicatory factor analysis. In J. N. Butcher & C. D. Spielberger (Eds.), *Recent advances in personality assessment* (pp. 27–48). Hillsdale, NJ: Erlbaum.

Berry, J. W. (1974). Radical cultural relativism and concept of intelligence. In J. Berry and P. Dasen (Eds.), *Culture and cognition: Readings in cross-cultural psychology* (225–229). London: Methuen.

Berry, J. W. (1984). Towards a universal psychology of cognitive competence. *International Journal of Psychology, 19,* 335–361.

Berry, J. W. (1986). A cross-cultural view of intelligence. In R. J. Sternberg and D. K. Detterman (Eds.), *What is intelligence?* (pp. 35–38). Norwood, NJ: Ablex.

Berry, J. W., Poortinga, Y., Segall, M. (1992). *Cross-cultural psychology: Research and application.* New York: Cambridge University Press.

Biesheuvel, S. (1943). *African intelligence.* Johannesburg: South African Institute of Race Relations.

Biesheuvel. S. (1952). The study of African ability, Part I: The intellectual potentialities of Africans. *African Studies, 11,* 45–57.

Biesheuvel. S. (1972). Adaptability: Its measurement and determinants. In L. J. Cronbach and P. J. D. Drenth (Eds.), *Mental tests and cultural adaptation* (pp. 47–62). The Hague: Mouton.

Binet, A., & Simon, T. (1916). *The development of intelligence in children* (E. S. Kit, Trans.). Baltimore: Williams & Wilkins.

Bleuler, E., & Bleuler, M. (1935) Rorschach's inkblot test and racial psychology. *Character and Personality, 4,* 94–114.

Bohm, E. (1948) *A textbook in Rorschach test diagnosis.* Bern, Switzerland: Verlag Han Huber.

Brislin, R. W. (1970). Back-translation for cross-cultural research. *Journal of Cross-Cultural Psychology, 1,* 185–216.

Brislin, R. W. (1986). The wording and translation of research instruments. In W. J. Lonner & J. W. Berry (Eds.), *Field methods in cross-cultural research* (pp. 137–164). Beverly Hills: Sage.

Brislin, R. W., Lonner, W. J., & Thorndike, R. (1973). *Cross-cultural research methods.* New York: Wiley.

Butcher, J. N. (1985). Perspectives on international MMPI use. In J. N. Butcher and C. D. Spielberger (Eds.), *Advances in personality assessment* (Vol. 4). Hillsdale, NJ: Erlbaum.

Butcher, J. N. (1987). Introduction to the special series. *Journal of Consulting and Clinical Psychology, 55,* 459–460.

Butcher, J. N. (1996a). *Handbook of international MMPI-2 research.* Minneapolis, MN: University of Minnesota Press.

Butcher, J. N. (1996b). *International adaptations of the MMPI-2: Research and clinical applications.* Minneapolis, MN: University of Minnesota Press.

Butcher, J. N., Dahlstrom, W. G., Graham, J. R., Tellegen, A. M., & Kaemmer, B. (1989). *MMPI-2: Manual for administration and scoring.* Minneapolis, MN: University of Minnesota Press.

Butcher, J. N., & Garcia, R. (1978). Cross-national application of psychological tests. *Personnel and Guidance, 56,* 472–475.

Butcher, J. N., Graham, J. R., Williams, C. L., & Ben-Porath, Y. S. (1990). *Development and use of the MMPI-2 content scales.* Minneapolis, MN: University of Minnesota Press.

Butcher, J. N., & Pancheri, P. (1976). *Handbook of cross-national MMPI research.* Minneapolis, MN: University of Minnesota Press.

Butcher, J. N. & Rouse, S. (1996). Personality: Individual differences and clinical assessment. *Annual Review of Psychology, 47,* 87–111.

Ceci, S. J. (1990). *On Intelligence—more or less: A bio-ecological treatise on intellectual development.* Englewood Cliffs, NJ: Prentice-Hall.

Charlesworth, W. (1976). Human intelligence as adaptation: An ecological approach. In L. Resnick (Ed.), *The nature of intelligence* (pp. 147–168). Hillsdale, NJ: Erlbaum.

Cheung, F. M. (1985). Cross-cultural considerations for the translation and adaptation of the Chinese MMPI in Hong Kong. In J. N. Butcher & C. D. Spielberger (Eds.), *Advances in personality assessment* (Vol. 4). Hillsdale, NJ: Erlbaum.

Clark, L. A. (1985). A consolidated version of the MMPI in Japan. In J. N. Butcher & C. D. Spielberger (Eds.), *Advances in personality assessment.* (Vol. 4). Hillsdale, NJ: Erlbaum.

Davis, J. C., & Ginsburg, H. P. (1993). Similarities and differences in the formal and informal mathematical cognition of African, American, and Asian children: The roles of schooling and social class. In J. Altarriba (Ed.), *Cognition and culture: A cross-cultural approach to psychology* (pp. 343–360). Amsterdam, Netherlands: Elsevier.

Davis, T. M., & Rodriguez, V. L. (1979). Comparison of WAIS and Escala de Inteligencia

Wechsler papa Adultos in an institutionalized Latin American psychiatric population. *Journal of Consulting and Clinical Psychology, 47,*181–182.

De Vos, G. A., & Boyer, B.L. (1988). *Symbolic analysis cross-culturally: The Rorschach test.* Berkeley, CA: University of California Press.

Draguns, J. G. (1984). Assessing mental health and disorder across cultures. In P. B. Pedersen, N. Sartorius, & A. J. Marsella (Eds.), *Mental health services: The cross-cultural context* (pp. 31–58). Beverly Hills: Sage.

DuBois, C. (1944). *The people of Alor.* Minneapolis, MN: University of Minnesota Press.

Egli, E. (1991). Bilingual workers. In J. Westermeyer, C. Williams, & A. Nguyen (Eds.), *Mental health services for refugees* (pp. 157–189). (DHHS Publication No. ADM 91–1824). Washington, D.C: U.S. Government Printing Office.

Exner, J. E. (1974). *The Rorschach: A comprehensive system: Vol. 1. Basic foundations.* New York: Wiley.

Exner, J. E. (1978). *The Rorschach: A comprehensive system: Vol. 2. Recent research and advanced interpretation.* New York: Wiley.

Exner, J. E. (1986). *The Rorschach: A comprehensive system: Vol. 1 Basic Foundations* (2nd Ed.). New York: Wiley.

Exner, J. E. (1991). *The Rorschach: A comprehensive system: Vol. 2. Interpretation* (2nd Ed.). New York: Wiley.

Exner, J. E. (1993). *The Rorschach: A comprehensive system: Vol. 1. Basic Foundations* (3rd Ed.). New York: Wiley.

Exner, J. E. (1995). *A Rorschach workbook for the comprehensive system.* Asheville, NC: Rorschach Workshops.

Exner, J. E., & Weiner, I. B. (1982). *The Rorschach: A comprehensive system: Vol. 3. Assessment of children and adolescence.* New York: Wiley.

Exner, J. E., & Weiner, I. B. (1994). *The Rorschach: A comprehensive system: Vol. 3. Assessment of children and adolescence* (2nd Ed.). New York: Wiley.

Eysenck, H. J. (1982). *A model for intelligence.* Berlin, Germany: Springer.

Ferguson, G. A. (1956). On transfer and the abilities of man. *Canadian Journal of Psychology, 10,* 121–131.

Flaherty, J. A., Gaviria, F. M., Pathak, D., Mitchell, T., Wintrob, R., Richman, J. A., & Birz, S. (1988). Developing instruments for cross-cultural psychiatric research. *Journal of Nervous and Mental Disease, 176,* 257–263.

Foerster, L. M., & Little, D. (1974). Open education and Native American values. *Educational Leadership, 32,* 41–45.

Fried, R. (1977 July). *Christmas elves on the Rorschach: A popular Finnish response and its cultural significance.* Paper presented at the 9th International Rorschach Congress of Rorschach and Projective Techniques, Fribourg, Switzerland.

Gardner, H. (1983). *Frames of mind: The theory of multiple intelligences.* New York: Basic Books.

Gauvian, M. (1993). Sociocultural processes in the development of thinking. In J. Altarriba (Ed.), *Cognition and culture: A cross-cultural approach to psychology* (pp. 299–316). Amsterdam, Netherlands: Elsevier.

Gladwin, T., & Sarason, S. B. (1953). *Truk: Man in paradise.* New York: Wenner-Gren Foundation.

Goodnow, J. (1969). Problems in research on culture and thought. In D. Elkind and J. Flavell (Eds.), *Studies in cognitive development: Essays in honor of Jean Piaget* (439–462). New York: Oxford University Press.

Gray-Little, B. (1995). The assessment of psychopathology in racial and ethnic minorities. In J. N. Butcher (Ed.), *Clinical personality assessment: Practical approaches* (pp. 140–157). New York: Oxford University Press.

Hallowell, A. I. (1945). "Popular" responses and cultural differences: An analysis based on a group of American Indian subjects. *Rorschach Research Exchange, 9,* 153–168.

Han, K. (1996). The Korean MMPI-2. In J. N. Butcher (Ed.), *(International adaptations of the MMPI-2: Research and clinical applications* (pp. 88–136). Minneapolis, MN: University of Minnesota Press.

Hunter, J. E., Schmidt, F. L., & Rauschenberger, J. (1984). Methodological, statistical and ethical issues in the study of bias in psychological tests. In C. R. Reynolds & R. T. Brown (Eds.), *Perspectives on bias in mental testing* (pp. 41–99). New York: Plenum Press.

Irvine, S. H., & Berry, J. W. (1983). *Human assessment and cultural factors.* New York: Plenum Press.

Johnson, R. C., McClearn, G. E., Yuen, S., Nagoshi, C. T., Ahern, F. M., & Cole, R. E. (1985). Galton's data a century later. *American Psychologist, 40,* 875–892.

Kagitcibasi, C., & Berry, J. W. (1989). Cross-cultural psychology: Current research and trends. *Annual Review of Psychology, 40,* 493–531.

Kataguchi, Y. (1970). *Psychpsy.* Tokyo: Kaneko Shobo.

Keats, D. M. (1982). Cultural bases of concepts of intelligence: A Chinese versus Australian comparison. *Proceedings of the Second Asian Workshop on Child and Adolescent Development,* Bangkok, Behavioral Science Research Institute, 67–75.

Kennedy, J. (1973). Cultural psychiatry. In J. Honigmann (Ed.), *Handbook of social and cultural anthropology* (1119–1198). Chicago: Rand-McNally.

Klein, R. E., Freeman, H. E., Kagen, J., Yarbrough, C., & Habicht, J. P. (1972). Is big smart? The relation of growth to cognition. *Journal of Health and Social Behavior, 13,* 219–225.

Klopfer, B., Ainsworth, M. D., Klopfer, W. G., & Holt, R. R. (1954). *Developments in the Rorschach technique. Vol. 1. Technique and theory.* Yonkers-on-Hudson, N.Y.: World Book.

Klopfer, B., & Kelly, D. (1942). *The Rorschach technique.* Yonkers-on-Hudson, NY: World Book.

Kunce, J. T., & De Vales, E. S. (1986). Cross-cultural factor analytic similarity of Wechsler intelligence scores for Mexican adults. *Journal of Clinical Psychology, 42,* 165–169.

Lave, J. (1977). Tailor-made experiments and evaluating the intellectual consequences of apprenticeship training. *The Quarterly Newsletter of the Institute for Comparative Human Development, 1,* 1–3.

Light, P. (1983). Social and cognitive development: A review of post-Piagetian research. In S. Meadows (Ed.), *Developing thinking* (67–88). New York: Methuen.

Linn, R. L. (1982). Admissions testing on trial. *American Psychologist, 37,* 279–291.

Lonner, W. J. (1985). Issues in testing and assessment in cross-cultural counseling. *The Counseling Psychologist, 13,* 599–614.

Lopez, S. C., & Romero, M. A. (1988). Assessing the intellectual functioning of Spanish-speaking adults: Comparisons of the EIWA and the WAIS. *Professional Psychology: Research and Practice, 19,* 263–270.

Loram, C. T. (1917). *The education of the South African native.* London: Longmans.

Lubin, B., Larsen, R. M. & Matarazzo, J. (1984). Patterns of psychological test usage in the United States 1936–1982. *American Psychologist, 39,* 451–454.

Lynn, R. (1982). IQ in Japan and the United States shows a growing disparity. *Nature, 297,* 222–223.

Mattlar, C. E., Carlsson, A., Forsander, C., Norrlund, L., Oist, A. S., & Alanen, E. (1995). *Rorschach content and structural summary features characteristic of adult Finns in cross cultural comparison. Proceedings of the 14th International congress of Rorschach and projective techniques,* 213–220.

Manos, N. (1981). *Translation and adaptation of the MMPI in Greece.* Paper presented at the International Conference on Personality Assessment, Honolulu, HI.

Manos, N. (1985). Adaptation of the MMPI in Greece: Translation, standardization, and cross-cultural comparisons. In J. N. Butcher & C. D. Spielberger (Eds.), *Advances in personality assessment* (Vol. 4) (pp. 159–208). Hillsdale, NJ: Erlbaum.

Marsella, A. J. (1978). Thoughts on cross-cultural studies on the epidemiology of depression. *Culture, Medicine, and Psychiatry, 2,* 343–357.

Marsella, A. J., & Kameoka, V. A. (1989). Ethnocultural issues in the assessment of psychopathology. In S. Wetzler (Ed.), *Measuring mental illness: Psychometric assessment for clinicians* (pp. 229–256). Washington, DC: American Psychiatric Press.

McShane, D., & Berry, J. W. (1988). Native North Americans: Indian and Inuit abilities. In S. H. Irvine and J. W. Berry (Eds.), *Human abilities in cultural context* (pp. 385–426) New York: Cambridge University Press.

Mormont, C. & Crollard, M. (1995). Recherches de norms Wallonnes. *Proceedings of the 14th International Congress of Rorschach and projective techniques,* 221–224.

Oakland, T. (1983). Joint use of adaptive behavior and IQ to predict achievement. *Journal of Consulting and Clinical Psychology, 51,* 298–301.

Okazaki, S., & Sue, S. (1995). Cultural considerations in psychological assessment of Asian-Americans. In J. N. Butcher (Ed.), *Clinical personality assessment: Practical approaches* (pp 107–119). New York: Oxford University Press.

Oliver, R. A. C. (1932). The comparison of the abilities of races with special reference to East Africa. *East African Medical Journal, 9,* 160–204.

Oliver, R. A. C. (1933). The adaptation of intelligence tests to tropical Africa, parts 1 & 2. *Overseas Education, 4,* 186-191, 8–13.

Orivel, F., & Perrot, J. (1988). *Les performances de l'enseignement primaire in Afrique Francophone.* Dijon, France: IREDU.

Piotrowski, Z. (1957). *Perceptanalysis.* New York: Macmillan.

Pires, A. A. (1995). O estudo normativo do teste de Rorschach na populacao Portugesa. *Proceedings of the 14th International congress of Rorschach and projective techniques,* 233–240.

Poortinga, Y. H., & Van Der Flier, H. (1988). The meaning of item bias in ability tests. In S. H. Irvine & J. W. Berry (Eds.), *Human assessment and cultural factors* pp. 166–183. New York: Cambridge University Press.

Pucheu, C., & Rivera, O. (1976). The development of a method of detecting psychological maladjustment in University students. In J.N. Butcher & P. Pancheri (Eds.), *Handbook of cross-national MMPI research* (pp. 218–330). Minneapolis, MN: University of Minnesota Press.

Rapaport, D., Gill, M., & Schafer, R. (1946). *Diagnostic psychological testing* (Vol. 1–2). Chicago: Yearbook Publishers.

Raven, J. C., Court, J. H., & Raven, J. (1986). *Manual for Raven's Progressive Matrices and Vocabulary Scales (Section 2-Colored Progressive Matrices).* London: Lewis.

Rissetti, F., Butcher, J. N., Agostini, J., Elgueta, M., Gaete, S., Margulies, T., Morlans, I., & Ruiz, R. (March 1979). *Translation and adaptation of the MMPI in Chile: Use in a university student health service.* Paper presented at the 14th Annual Symposium on Recent Developments in the Use of the MMPI. St. Petersburg, FL.

Rissetti, F. J., & Maltes, S. G. (1985). Use of the MMPI in Chile. In J. N. Butcher & C. D. Spielberger (Eds.), *Advances in personality assessment* (Vol. 4.) Hillsdale, NJ: Erlbaum.

Rogoff, B. (1990). *Apprenticeship in thinking.* New York: Oxford University Press.

Rorschach, H. (1921). *Psychodiagnostik.* Bern, Switzerland: Bircher.

Ruzgis, P., & Grigorenko, E. L. (1994). Cultural meaning systems, intelligence, and personality. In R. J. Sternberg & P. Ruzgis (Eds.), *Personality and Intelligence* (248–270). New York: Cambridge University Press.

Sattler, J. (1988). *Assessment of children.* San Diego: Author.

Savasir, I., & Erol, N. (1990). The Turkish MMPI: Translation, standardization, and validation. In J. N. Butcher & C. D. Spielberger (Eds.), *Advances in personality assessment* (Vol. 8) (49–62). Hillsdale, NJ: Erlbaum.

Scarr, S. (1978). From evolution to Larry P., or what shall we do about IQ test? *Intelligence, 2,* 325–342.

Scribner, S., & Cole, M. (1981). *The psychology of literacy.* Cambridge, MA: Harvard University Press.

Segall, M. H. (1986). Culture and behavior: Psychology in global perspective. *Annual Review of Psychology, 37,* 523–564.

Sendin, C. (1981). *Identification of Popular responses among Spanish adults.* 10th International Congress of Rorschach and Projective Techniques, Washington, D.C.

Sendin, C. (1995). Nonpatient transcultural comparison. *Proceedings of the 14th International Congress of Rorschach and projective techniques,* 207–212.

Serpel, R. (1982). Measures of perception, skills, and intelligence: The growth of a new perspective on children in a Third World country. In W. W. Hartup (Ed.), *Review of child development research* (Vol. 6) (pp. 392–440). Chicago: University of Chicago Press.

Smith, M. W. (1974). Alfred Binet's remarkable questions: a cross-national and cross-temporal analysis of the cultural biases built into the Stanford-Binet intelligence scale and other Binet tests. *Genetic Psychology Monographs, 89,* 307–334.

Spearman, C. E. (1923). *The nature of intelligence and the principles of cognition.* London: Macmillan.

Sternberg, R. J. (1985). *Beyond IQ: A triarchic theory of human intelligence.* New York: Cambridge University Press.

Sternberg, R. J. (1986). *Intelligence applied: Understanding and increasing your intellectual skills.* San Diego: Harcourt Brace Jovanovich.

Sternberg, R. J. (1988). *The triarchic mind.* New York: Viking Press.

Stevenson, H., Lee, H., & Stigler, J. (1986). Mathematics achievement of Chinese, Japanese, and American children. *Science, 231,* 693–699.

Thompson, W. (1980). Cross-cultural uses of biological data and perspectives. In H. C. Triandis & W. W. Lambert (Eds.), *Handbook of cross-cultural psychology* (pp. 205–252). Boston: Alyn & Bacon.

Thorndike, E. L., Terman, L. W., Freeman, F. M., Colvin, S. S., Pinter, R., Rumi, B., Pressey, S. L., Henmon, V. A. C., Peterson, J., Thurstone, L. L., Woodrow, E. H. Dearborn, W. F., & Haggerty, M. E. (1921). Intelligence and its measurement: A symposium. *Journal of Educational Psychology, 12,* 123–147, 195–216.

Valsiner, J. (1989). *Human development and culture.* Lexington, MA: Lexington Books.

Velasquez, R. (1995). Personality assessment of Hispanic clients. In J. N. Butcher (Ed.), *Clinical personality assessment: Practical approaches* (pp. 120–139). New York: Oxford University Press.

Vives, M. (1990). Estudio cuantitativo-cualitativo de la esquizofrenia de exacerbacion aguda. *Rorschachiana, 17,* 241–247.

Wechsler, D. (1958). *The measurement and appraisal of adult intelligence* (4th ed.). Baltimore: Williams & Wilkins.

Wertsch, J. V. (1979). From social interaction to higher psychological processes. *Human Development, 22,* 1–22.

Wittkower, E. D., & Fried, J. (1959). A cross-cultural approach to mental illness. *American Journal of Psychiatry, 116,* 423–428.

Wober, M. (1974). Towards an understanding of the Kiganda concept of intelligence. In J. W. Berry & P. R. Dasen (Eds.), *Culture and cognition* (pp. 260–280). London: Methuen.

Yap, P. M. (1951). Mental diseases peculiar to certain cultures: A survey of comparative psychiatry. *Journal of Mental Science, 97,* 313–327.

Yap, P. M. (1967). Classification of the culture-bound reactive syndromes. *Australian, New Zealand Journal of Psychiatry, 1,* 172–179.

Yap, P. M. (1969). The culture-bound reactive syndromes. In W. Caudill & T. Lin (Eds.), Mental Health Research in Asia and the Pacific (pp. 33–53). Honolulu, HI: East-West Center Press.

APPENDIX 3.1. RORSCHACH PROTOCOL AND COMPREHENSIVE SYSTEM STRUCTURAL SUMMARY

Case Illustration: 43-Year-Old Male

Card	Response	Inquiry
I	1 Angels	E: (Rpts S's Resp) S: It has wgs hre, ths is th head, th wgs r out as if it is flyg, thy r larger whn it flyg, thts wht maks it l thy r flyg
	2 A woman w her hands toward th sky	E: (Rpts S's Resp) S: Th womans waist is thin th hips r larger she is wearg a wmns clothg, ths is th skirt, u can c her legs frm bhind her skirt E: Behind her skirt? S: U can c thru it, it is a liter shade
	3 A mask which can b placed on a face, w places for th eyes so th person can c out	E: (Rpts S's Resp) S: It is a mask bec it can go on th face, both sides hav lik straps & it has two holes for eyes, it just ll a mask
	4 The W thg ll 2 angels flyg holdg a wm in the middl	E: (Rpts S's Resp) S: Th woman seems to b flyg w th angels, thy r bigger, the size & thy hav their wgs open, lik I said before, the wgs hav a smooth look, the edges r smooth
	5 Wgs, ll smthg flyg, l a bird	E: (Rpts S's Resp) S: The big wgs stretchd out & the body in the middl, it ll a bird
	6 A bear, th head of a bear	E: (Rpts S's Resp) S: A bear head, its coverd w hair E: Coverd w hair? S: It looks big & soft E: I'm still not sur I c the hair S: Well, its larg & full & it looks smooth, the outline gives tht effect a smooth look lik if a lot of hair were smoothd out
II	(This has color, it is a good thg its not bld)	
	7 It cb an airplane	E: (Rpts S's Resp) S: Th shap of it, th front prt is pointed
	8 A bear on each side, it ll thy r givg eo a hi five	E: (rpts S's Resp) S: Here r their bodies, the hair looks fluffy & their hands r here

Case Illustration: 43-Year-Old Male (*continued*)

Card	Response	Inquiry
		E: Th hair looks fluffy?
		S: The hair is drker c their hands r liter
	9 Ths red is ink drop tht has has nothg to do w the bears do with th rest	E: (Rpts S's Resp)
		S: It ll red ink tht is splashg th rest of th pict, the drops r round (pointing to all of th red spots on th black prt of th blot) & dwn here (D3) it ll it is splashg
	10 A girls fac w larg eyes nice nose	E: (Rpts S's Resp)
		S: Yes she has larg eyes, her face does is lik pretty, lik pretty girl
		E: Pretty girl
		S: Yes, I thk so
	11 Th red ink down here ll a bird too Idk wht knd of bird	E: (Rpts S's Resp)
		S: It has two wings & th wings r open & thy r large, lik wgs
III	12 A woman who has opend her legs & has put her hands on a stone (rock) she is wearg high heels, a side view	E: (rpts S's Resp)
		S: A wm bec of the shoes, lik a wm who has thin legs & curvature body she ll she has flexible body
		E: Flexible
		S: It ll she can reach fr her head to her th way her back & her legs stretchd apart, I cannot do such a thing, her body if flexible
	13 Th red in th midl is a bf	E: (Rpts S's Resp)
		S: I has the wgs & the body, it ll a bf
	14 Ths prt cb a seahorse	E: (Rpts S's Resp)
		S: A seahorse, it ll it is hangg bec it is in th watr lik floatg, th feet r up thr th head is down
		E: Floating?
		S: Th head is down th feet r high, it has th body & waist lik a seahorse & th shape of th head is lik one too
IV	15 Wow, it is a giant, a huge scary giant th head is small th body is huge, its body is covrd w hair & it has a thick tail as if it can use th tail as anothr leg, it is very strong as if it is comg or walking on th clouds	E: (Rpts S's Resp)
		S: Th size of th body & it is full of hair, a larg body, small head in comparison to th large body, which maks it dangerous, a small head can not control (or command) a large body (NOTE: th wording is lik a Persian sayg tht the physically strong who lack wisdom are dangerous)
		E: U said it is full if hair?
		S: Yes its size shows tht it has a lot of hair & th hair seems soft bec of the shade s of light & dark
		E: U said it is walkg on th clds?
		S: Yes, ths liter part here (D2) ll a cld bec of th diff in the shading, it is very light lik the

(*continued*)

Case Illustration: 43-Year-Old Male (*continued*)

Card	Response	Inquiry
		giant is walkg on th cloud, lik prt of th giant's feet are behind th cloud, lik u can c thru it a little
V	16 A bird tht has hunted a lamb & has caught it & is flying off w it, it is a bird w large wngs & an antennae	E: (Rpts S's Resp) S: It ll tht has antennae lik a snail, & it has very large wgs & feet, it ll it has caught a lamb, u can c the leg of the lamb extendg out from under the wg & it is carryg it off, u cannot c the rest of the lamb, it wb under the wgs
VI	<17 Sea, lik th waves in th sea th shores & th waves r comg toward it in th midl thr is a mtn & a road	E: (Rpts S's Resp) S: Th white arnd it is watr & th blk is land, th light lines shows tht th waves have left marks on th shore E: U said there is a mt & a road S: Th white & blck shadows sho tht at the middl, thr is mtn tht is highr land & here is the cntr is a line lik a road, it cb bec it is a strait line, lik smthg tht is man made
VII	18 Two peopl r lkg at eo & shoutg to eo, the W body is not drawn, just som of of thr lower body & it lik thr r icicles on their nose & chin & mouth	E: (Rpts S's Resp) S: Th way thr mouth is open maks it ll thy r shoutg it ll th chest & th abdomen r shown but not th legs E: U mentioned thy hav icicles on their nose chin & mouth S: Bec thes parts look sharp & also U can c thru thm bec thy look lighter
VIII	19 Very colorful, A bear climbing	E: (Rpts S's Resp) S: Th way th head & th body lks, it is lik a bear climbing, u can c the 4 legs
	20 Airplane thy hav colrd th wngs so it is a glider tht is towing ths orange thg behind it	E: (Rpts S's Resp) S: Th wgs r frm fabric bec it is colrd it is not solid material & th outline is not a strait line, so it must be a glider E: U said it is towing th orange thg? S: Yes, ths thg is atachd to th glider & th shap of it makes it ll th glider is towg it tht red thg behind it
IX	<21 A Map of a country, hre is a country & hre is anothr country & the white prt is water, there r mts in each country	E: (Rpts S's Resp) S: Yes it is an island divided, it has watr arnd it, frm a topographical stand point th darkr prt is mtns & as it gets it is more flat E: Im not sur tht I c th 2 countries as u do S: It is th map of th 2 country bec of th 2 diff colrs, threfore it is 2 countries
	<22 Now we come to th pink prt I thnk it ll a baby in th mothrs womb	E: (Rpts S's Resp) S: It is in th watr bec around it is a liter colr, it is pink but also diff colors of pink, u can c

Case Illustration: 43-Year-Old Male (*continued*)

Card	Response	Inquiry
		th forehead & mouth, lik still in the womb
	<23 Ths ll th daddy (D1) & a baby (D4) holdg th dad, thy r by a lake so u cld c thr reflectn in th watr	E: (Rpts S's Resp) S: Thy r vry close, th baby is holdg the dads beard & it seems lik th dad is enjoying it E: I'm not sur I c it rite, help me S: The baby is like before (Response 22) and the dad is here (D1), c the nose & beard & forehead & it is all reflected dwn here
X	24 A tarantula	E: (Rpts S's Resp) S: Bec it has a large numbr of legs lik one
	25 A dinosaur has caught a duck	E: (Rpts S's Resp) S: Th neck is long & its size compard to th legs & th body shows tht it is a dinosaur, & ths is a duck (D15) & it is tryg to get away, the way the body is stretched indicates tht it is tryg to get away
	26 A mark frm lipstick of a woman who has kissed hre	E: (Rpts S's Resp) S: Yes it ll lipstick bec of th red color, lik a mark left by a wm who kissed here
	27 A turtle tht is swimmg in the water	E: (Rpts S's Resp) S: Ths prt (D13) is shaped lik a turtle & the white prt arnd it is the water
	<28 Th pink ll map of an island w mtns on th side	E: (Rpts S's Resp) S: It is topographic, mtns r hre on the side bec of the drkr color & th liter colr is the flat land
	29 Ths yellow ll it is a high heel shoe	E: (Rpts S's Resp) S: Ths shape of it ll a high heel shoe
	30 3 spaceships, a mothr ship here (D11), a smalr spacshp folowg it (D3) & thn thr is anothr one, th guard shp (D10) th small one goes fastr one is mothr spacshp th second one the child space ship	E: (Rpts S's Resp) S: Bec of its size ths ll it is th mothr ship, th smallr one is th child shp, & the last one is going behind the othrs to guard thm, the mothr ship is slow & & child ship is faster & thyr being guarded from behind by the last ship, lik a formation for war
	v31 Two monkeys r givg eo five thy want to help eo so one goes frm one side to th othr thy want to go & have fun w eo (th word he used as fun has sexual connotation)	E: (Rpts S's Resp) S: Thy ll monkeys bec thy hav hair it lks soft & fluffy, thy hav two legs one is tryg to go to th othr side & th othr is tryg too thy r cooperatg w eo E: U said thy hav soft & fuffy hair? S: The shadg is diff, the diff colors ther mak it ll hair

4

Cultural Aspects of Self-Disclosure and Psychotherapy

SHAKÉ G. TOUKMANIAN

MELISSA C. BROUWERS

As Western societies become increasingly multicultural, there has been a growing recognition that the practice of Western-style psychotherapies may not necessarily be effective nor appropriate for the treatment of people from different cultures. Although these strategies differ considerably in terms of philosophy, view of human nature, conception of psychological dysfunctions, and therapeutic goals and techniques, the fact still remains that they are the product of a culture imbued with Western values and ideologies, and, as such, they share a common set of defining characteristics and assumptions.

One such feature inherent in most forms of psychotherapy is self-disclosure. Most therapists consider clients' willingness to talk openly about their difficulties a desirable characteristic. Yet there are observed individual and cultural differences among clients along this dimension. This leads us to believe that the level and extent to which clients are willing and/or able to talk about personal issues could be reflective of various factors (such as values, beliefs, views on interpersonal relationships, expectations, communication patterns, etc.) that have been identified in the literature as being relevant to the treatment and rehabilitation of individuals from diverse cultures. Thus, we will begin this chapter with a brief examination of self-disclosure from the vantage point of various Western conceptions of psychological health and well-being, with particular attention given to the assumptions on which they are based and their implications for psychotherapy practice. This will be followed by a discussion of both culture-specific and pancultural aspects of psychotherapy in light of some key concepts central to the psychodynamic, humanistic-existential and cognitive-behavioral approaches. In the final section, we will discuss the role of culture in psychotherapy practice and advance an experiential framework for psychotherapy training from a cross-cultural perspective.

SELF-DISCLOSURE

Cultural differences in disclosure tendencies have important implications for psychotherapy. Traditional North American psychotherapeutic treatment strategies typically adhere to a disclosure-dependent process and insight-oriented philosophy (Lee, 1988). D. W. Sue (1981) labels adoption of these principles as left-brain, an approach that endorses analytical, verbal, rational, and introspective states. A similar position has been taken by Schwartz (1990). He suggests that Western cultures adopt a "voice" approach (i.e., active confrontation) to solve problems and conflict. Adoption of this orientation in professional practice, however, may be inappropriate and of questionable clinical value for individuals from non-Western cultures.

As an example, several comparative descriptive studies on communication styles demonstrate significant differences in the extent to which members of Eastern cultures and members of Western cultures disclose (Ting-Toomey, 1991; True, 1990; Wheeless, Erickson, & Behrens, 1986). Although it is important to acknowledge that significant differences do exist between groups that comprise these broad categories (e.g., Mollica, Wyshak, & Lavelle, 1987), the general finding supports the belief that members of Western culture demonstrate greater disclosure tendencies than do members of Eastern culture. Other research has investigated and confirmed that, although differences in disclosure may reflect variations in language (Guttfreund, 1990), this greater reticence to disclose by members of Eastern culture does not appear to be linked to language capacity (e.g., restricted range of word choice), but rather to the restraint exercised by members of this group during the disclosure process (e.g., Mavreas & Bebbington, 1988).

This greater tendency for members of Eastern cultures relative to those of Western cultures, to conceal, carries over to specific patterns of interaction within the psychotherapeutic setting. For example, comparisons made between American and Japanese psychologists show that Japanese professionals are less likely to disclose a psychiatric diagnosis to a client, especially when the diagnosis yields disorders that have precarious or uncertain treatment and recovery prognosis (e.g., borderline personality disorder and schizophrenia; McDonald-Scott, Machizawa, & Satoh, 1992). This pattern has been explained in terms of the desire of professionals to protect patients from shame and misunderstandings, as well as their belief that such information is meaningless for treatment.

In order to account for this difference and to illustrate its importance in psychotherapeutic intervention, East-West cultural comparisons can be made along various dimensions. These dimensions include differences in definitions of mental health, differences in orientation styles to threatening information, and differences in value systems. In making these comparisons, the assumption of disclosure as a beneficial clinical process for all populations may be challenged.

The Definition of Mental Health

Mental health can be defined by various criteria, but two common features are (a) individuals' thoughts and psychological end states and (b) individuals' ability to cope with and respond to stressful situations (D. W. Sue, 1981; D. W. Sue & Sue, 1990).

However, analyses demonstrate cultural variability across these criteria. Western culture considers insight into, and understanding of, the self as a desirable and healthy end state (D. W. Sue, 1981). By approaching all aspects of the self and one's experiences, including the negative, one can gain a comprehensive understanding of personal attitudes, beliefs, and behaviors. Within other cultures, insight is not valued and is not a state to which individuals aspire (Brontzman & Butler, 1991). For example, Eastern cultures define a state of good mental health as successfully exercising one's will power, *avoiding* unpleasant thoughts, and addressing pleasant thoughts (Root, 1985; D. W. Sue, 1981). Thus, inhibition of negative or distressing thoughts is viewed by the Eastern community as a healthy, rather than an unhealthy, goal.

Not only specific desired psychological states but also specific behaviors and reactions to psychological distress must be considered when identifying markers of good mental health. Whereas in Eastern cultures, the inability to cope with a negative event or stressful period is viewed as an inherent weakness in an individual, such reactions are expected and therefore somewhat more accepted by individuals from Western cultures (Boehnlein, 1987; McDonald-Scott et al., 1992). Indeed, these differences may help explain the tendency for psychological problems to manifest and be presented as somatic symptoms, rather than emotional or cognitive symptoms, for individuals from Eastern cultures (Root, 1985; D. W. Sue & Zane, 1987). Physical ailments are acceptable, psychological ailments are not.

These contrasting perspectives have important implications for the disclosure process within a psychotherapeutic context. Disclosure of psychological distress requires an individual to focus on negative thoughts and emotions that are central to the self. Thus, Western culture that encourages insight-orientation, including insight to unpleasant and negative features, would support strategies such as disclosure that facilitate this process. In contrast, disclosure would be avoided in Eastern cultures, where such endeavors are discouraged.

Uncertainty Avoidance

Hofstede (1980, 1982) contends that differences exist in the extent to which people feel threatened by ambiguous situations and in the types of belief systems and institutions that are created to support an individual's approach to or avoidance of this ambiguity. This conceptualization of uncertainty avoidance is based on an affective or emotive perspective (i.e., that an individual's anxiety towards uncertainty determines the extent to which it is approached). Hofstede's findings from cross-cultural examinations of this variable indicate that people living in North America report less anxiety in uncertain situations than people living in Taiwan, Thailand, or Japan.

The uncertainty-avoidance dimension parallels the cognitive dimension of uncertainty orientation advanced by Sorrentino and his colleagues (e.g., Huber & Sorrentino, 1996; Sorrentino, Raynor, Zubek, & Short, 1990; Sorrentino & Short, 1986). The theory of uncertainty orientation differentiates between those who are motivated to resolve ambiguity about the self and the environment (uncertainty-oriented persons) and those who are motivated to maintain already existing schemata of the self and the environment (certainty-oriented persons) (Brouwers & Sorrentino, 1993; Sorrentino, Bobocel, Gitta, Olson, & Hewitt, 1988; Sorrentino & Hewitt, 1984). Unlike Hofstede's construct, however, differences due to uncertainty orientation are based on the information quality, rather than the affect quality, arising from the situation.

Confrontation of psychological distress through disclosure is a personally relevant endeavor. Disclosure often focuses attention onto the self as an object of evaluation. It may also require the integration of contrary thoughts and ideas as individuals work through the experience, with the outcome of such efforts often uncertain and unpredictable. A situation characterized by the culmination of these factors (i.e., a high-intensity trauma disclosure) supports the cognitive orientation style of the uncertainty-oriented person and opposes that of the certainty-oriented person. Therefore, whereas uncertainty-oriented persons would be most engaged by and approach the disclosure process, certainty-oriented persons would be most likely to avoid the process. Some preliminary investigations have documented that persons from Asiatic backgrounds are more likely to be certainty-oriented than uncertainty-oriented, whereas the reverse is true for persons from North American backgrounds (Brouwers, 1996). These results, in conjunction with Hofstede's findings, provide tentative evidence that disclosure may more readily adhere to the orientation styles of individuals from Western cultures.

Individualistic versus Collectivistic Values

Differences also emerge along the individualistic-collectivistic value orientation between Eastern and Western cultures (Hofstede, 1980, 1982; Ting-Toomey, 1991; Triandis, 1996). Western culture emphasizes the role of the individual, with little recognition of the link between individuals to their ancestors or progeny (Stewart, 1981). Indeed, D. W. Sue (1981) describes the Western community as adopting a primarily internal orientation; autonomy in decision making, control over one's choices and alternatives, and responsibility to the self are primary goals and considerations. This perspective is similar to Schwartz's (1990) contractual society, whose members are primarily self-directed (i.e, "I"-oriented) and self-stimulated and who endorse universal prosocial ideology. As a consequence of this orientation and the lack of interdependence among members of their families, individuals from Western cultures who are unable to cope on their own are inclined to seek assistance outside of the family during times of psychological crisis.

In contrast, members of Eastern cultures concentrate efforts toward the betterment and preservation of the family name, rather than the individual (Hofstede, 1980, 1982; Shon & Ja, 1982). Any behavior believed to corrupt or compromise a lineage results in serious sanctions against the offending members. To defend against a family's reputation being discredited, a strong link and interdependence among immediate and extended family members are sought and valued by members of Eastern culture. This interdependence, in fact, serves as the basis for an individual's personal identity and self-esteem, thereby encouraging a "we"-oriented self-concept (Boehnlein, 1987). The interdependence provides a large system that can be accessed to help solve problems and crises, while ensuring that the problems remain private within the boundaries of the family (Shon & Ja, 1982).

Thus differences along the individualistic-collectivistic continuum play a significant role in determining an individual's willingness to disclose. Disclosing psychological distress is a challenging process in that it may result in acknowledgment and display of vulnerable or unfavorable aspects of the self or family. Such an endeavor is likely to be particularly threatening and difficult for members of Eastern cultures, whose value systems run counter to acknowledging (to the self) and publicly announcing (to the therapist) these vulnerabilities. Indeed, relative to Western culture, the inability to cope with a negative event or stressful period is viewed by members of Eastern culture as an inherent weakness and disappointment (Boehnlein, 1987; McDonald-Scott et al., 1992), which may help explain the tendency for stress-related symptoms to manifest and be presented as somatic complaints in individuals from Eastern cultures (Root, 1985; Sue & Zane, 1987).

In conclusion, disclosure is a common feature of Western-style psychotherapeutic treatments, regardless of orientation. Differences found between members of Eastern and Western cultures on definitions of mental health, the orientation style toward uncertainty, and adoption of values along the individualistic-collectivistic continuum serve to illustrate, indeed challenge, the extent to which disclosure can be considered a suitable therapeutic strategy in the treatment of individuals from non-Western cultures. This issue will be considered further in the broader context of the role of culture in psychotherapy practice, dealt with in the final section of the chapter.

CULTURE AND PSYCHOTHERAPHY

Psychotherapy, as a formalized helping profession, is a Western phenomenon, originated and developed within the sociocultural context of Western Europe and North America. As such, all mainstream theories of psychotherapy may be seen as having evolved from a common "culture" or a "system of symbolic meanings" (Rohner, 1984) reflective of a "worldview" that is rooted in Western philosophical and ideological assumptions (e.g., Ibrahim, 1985; Ivey, Ivey & Simek-Morgan, 1993; D. W. Sue & Sue, 1990). In other words, these theories, and by implication the constructs on which they are based, may be seen as having been formulated from the vantage point of an ideational system that is characterized by certain beliefs, attitudes, and values, and hence by a certain outlook or a particular way of perceiving, thinking about, and making sense of the world. And to the extent that world views vary from one culture to the other, it is often argued that these theoretical frameworks may not necessarily be appropriate as guides for the treatment of clients from non-Western cultures (e.g., Kim & Berry, 1993; Triandis, 1996).

It should be recognized, however, that each culture, as an ideational system, is not a homogeneous or monolithic entity. Rather, as several authors have noted (e.g., Kessing, 1974; Parsons, 1973; Rohner, 1984), it is an aggregate of many subsystems of symbolic meanings that are associated with different subpopulations of a given society (e.g., men, women, minorities, ethnic groups, various professional and religious groups, etc.). It is crucial to keep in mind as well that there are significant intracultural variations in the degree to which the meanings (values, beliefs, standards, rules, conceptions) that define the culture of a given group are shared and/or maintained by each member of that community. Indeed, Rohner (1984) argues that, as ". . . no two individuals ever hold precisely identical meanings . . . with respect to any phenomenon . . ." (p. 121), it would be ecologically more valid to think of "culture" as a system of meanings wherein the meanings are more or less or "approximately" shared by most members of an identifiable group or segment of society.

The above conception of culture underscores the importance of individual differences within the broad parameters of a symbolic system common to a larger sociocultural collectivity. Implicit in this view is the recognition that "culture" does not determine behavior but is one of many interactive factors influencing an individual's own unique way of interpreting and experiencing events in everyday life situations. In this sense, when we speak of a person's "worldview" or the "worldview" reflected in a given theory of psychotherapy, we are essentially dealing with an individualized perspective or an outlook on how human beings function, wherein culture-specific meanings (beliefs and values) may play either a large or a relatively insignificant role in its formulation. Thus, before dismissing our current theories as inappropriate for cross-cultural psychotherapy, it would be useful first to identify what is culture-specific and what is transcultural in these orientations, and then see whether or not and in what way any one of these approaches could be adapted to accommodate the therapeutic needs of clients from different cultures. We begin, therefore, with a brief overview of the psychodynamic, cognitive-behavioral, and humanistic-existential orientations, the three most widely used approaches to psychotherapy practice.

Culture in Mainstream Theories of Psychotherapy

The *psychodynamic* framework entails a host of diverse theoretical orientations (e.g., Erikson, 1963; Hartmann, 1958; Kohut, 1971; Winnicott, 1988) which, to a greater or lesser degree, draw on Freud's psychoanalytic theory and approach to psychotherapy. Despite their conceptual differences, however, all share the fundamental belief that human behavior is determined, or at least governed to some extent, by unconscious motivational forces or processes that are not readily accessible to awareness. These forces are believed to originate from people's biological drives and/or memories of childhood experiences and past relationships with a caregiver or with other significant individuals in their lives. Furthermore, all psychodynamic theories maintain that these unconscious processes are played out throughout an individual's developmental history and are centrally involved in his/her daily behavior in the present. Consequently, all view psychological dysfunctions as expressions of underlying biological tensions, repressed memories of past conflictual experiences, and/or unresolved relational problems. All concur with the view that clients' disclosure of past and present experiences is a crucial element of psychotherapy. Finally, all agree that change occurs from within the client and that the main goal of psychotherapy is to help clients become aware of their unconscious processes and to develop an understanding of the relationship between their current problematic thoughts, feelings, and behavior and past issues in their developmental history.

The single most important theme underlying all *cognitive* and *cognitive-behavioral* psychotherapies (Beck, 1976; Beck & Weishaar, 1995; Ellis, 1962, 1994; Kelly, 1955; Meichenbaum, 1986), on the other hand, is the view that how one thinks about the world determines the way in which one feels and acts in the world. Although these orientations generally agree that cognitions, emotions, behavior, and the resultant consequences are functionally interrelated, their main concern is with people's cognitions and behavior. All share the view that psychological disorders are related to clients' inflexible, irrational, automatic, and/or faulty ways of thinking about themselves and the world, and all maintain that these maladaptive patterns are acquired through experience. Also common to these orientations is the view that psychotherapy is a learning process wherein clients learn to monitor their thoughts and actions and examine the misconceptions or faulty assumptions underlying their emotional and behavioral disturbances. All recognize that a collaborative working relationship between client and therapist is crucial to the therapeutic process, and all agree that psychotherapy has two main objectives: to help clients acquire new ways of thinking and behaving and to help them develop more effective ways of coping with problems through practice.

The *humanistic-existential* tradition in psychotherapy has two defining characteristics: a fundamental belief in the reality of human experience and an equally strong belief in human agency or in people's inherent capacity to choose, make decisions, act, and determine their own destiny (e.g., May, 1961; Perls, 1969; Rogers, 1942, 1961). According to these orientations, reality resides within the individual's phenomenology, or subjective experience of the world. Some, like Rogers, pay particular attention to the person's experience of self-in-relation-to-others-in-the-world, whereas others emphasize the person's experience of being-in-the-world, including the natural or the physical world. Rogers has a positive view of human nature: people are purposive, self-enhancing, goal-directed, and self-actualizing individuals. Others maintain a more negative and hopeless view of human existence. Despite their differences, however, all agree on the central importance of human awareness for "healthy" functioning. All share the view that psychological disturbances result from people's sense of alienation or, as Rogers suggests, from discrepancies between a person's view of self and his/her experience of self-in-relation-to-others. All operate from the basic premise that the experiential world of the client can be understood only from the vantage point of the client's internal frame of reference. All maintain that the main goal of psychotherapy is to help clients explore, discover, understand, and become aware of themselves in the world. Finally, all believe that the authenticity of the therapist in the therapeutic relationship and his/her active and empathic listening and acceptance of the client are critical to the psychotherapeutic change process.

Commonalities and Differences   It can be seen from the preceding overview that, even though all three theoretical frameworks have emerged from an ideational system commonly associated with Western "cultures", each has a unique worldview that draws on a different set of presuppositions, beliefs, values, and assumptions about human nature, behavior and experience. Each perspective represents a distinct configuration of different meaning components. Yet at the same time, each appears to be organized around a few core elements that are central also to all the others. We are inclined to believe, therefore, that whatever else this common core may be, it must consist of some shared meanings (values and beliefs) that give these conceptualizations their culture-specific character.

We contend that there are essentially two shared elements or organizing value orientations in traditional theories of psychotherapy and that these constitute the main sources of conceptual bias in cross-cultural psychotherapy practice. The first relates to the Western culture's fundamental belief in the primacy of the individual and the second, which may be subsumed under the first, to the assumption that human beings are internally directed and controlled. Both value orientations are recognized in the literature as being among the most pervasive features characterizing the Western ideational system (e.g., Katz, 1985; Pedersen, 1988; D. W. Sue & Sue, 1990; Triandis, 1996; Yamamoto & Kubota, 1983).

Specifically, when we look at the psychodynamic, cognitive-behavioral, and humanistic-existential approaches from the standpoint of how they are construed, it becomes apparent that the central organizing unit in each framework is the individual. We also see that, despite their sharp conceptual differences, all are formulated from the basic premise that problems reside within the individual, that change is an internal process, and that the responsibility for bringing about this change rests primarily with the individual. In other words, although contextual issues (environmental factors, life circumstances, etc.) are often considered important, typically these are either implicit or of secondary importance to the way in which these theories conceptualize the development and treatment of psychological dysfunctions. In short, it would seem that all three theoretical frameworks are formulated from the vantage point of an outlook that prizes individualism, self-reliance, and self-determination and emphasizes the importance of introspection, self-understanding, self-awareness, and self-initiated action as avenues for solving problems, resolving intra- and interpersonal conflicts, and attaining a healthier and more productive level of functioning. This individual-centered and internally focused orientation is in sharp contrast to that of non-Western cultures, wherein external processes, such as membership in family and community, group norms, collective needs, and collective self-definition are often of more importance (Triandis, 1996).

However, these therapeutic approaches are not as similar in value orientation as it would appear at first glance. As we noted earlier, each represents a different constellation of meaning components consisting of both shared and more or less shared beliefs and values. A clearer understanding of how these perspectives differ requires, therefore, that we use a well-articulated model that will allow us to examine the structure of values inherent in each approach more systematically, to compare the pattern of similarities and differences across the three theoretical frameworks, and to see which overall pattern is less culture-specific or more compatible with the value orientations of other cultures identified in the literature.

One approach to this type of analysis is the use of F. R. Kluckhohn and Stodtbeck's (1961) value-orientations model, which is recognized in the cross-cultural psychotherapy literature as one of the most useful frameworks for understanding worldview differences among individuals and groups within and across different cultures (e.g., Ho, 1987; Ibrahim, 1985; Pedersen, 1988; D. W. Sue & Sue, 1990). Derived from C. Kluckhohn's (1951, 1953, 1956) original work on cultural universals, this model maintains that differences in cultures may best be conceptualized and studied as variations in value orientations and outlook with respect to five universal themes or dimensions that are believed to be at the core of human experience. The authors specify these common themes and the ranges of variability in each to be as follows: human nature orientation (good, bad, neutral, or a mixture of good and bad), relational orientation (lineal, collateral, individualistic), people-nature orientation (subjugation to, harmony with, mastery over nature), activity orientation (being, being-in-becoming, doing), and time orientation (past, present, future). Our analysis of the values emphasized within the psychodynamic, cognitive-behavioral, and humanistic-existential frameworks in terms of these five experiential dimensions are presented in Table 4.1.

Table 4.1. Value Orientations of Three Mainstream Psychotherapeutic Frameworks

Dimensions	Psychodynamic	Cognitive-Behavioral	Humanistic-Existential
Human Nature	Negative Deterministic	Neutral/negative Deterministic; human agency implied	Positive Human beings are agency; they are self-enhancing and other-enhancing individuals
Human Relationships	Individualistic Focus on psychological processes within the individual	Individualistic Focus on the individual's cognitive processes and behavior	Individualistic Focus on the individual's experience of self and of self in-relation-to- others
People/Nature Relationships	No reference	No reference	Coexistence in harmony
Mode of Activity	Being Achieving intellectual awareness and understanding	Doing Action-oriented; learning new ways of thinking and behaving	Being-in-Becoming, self- actualization; increased spontaneity, personal growth and fulfillment
Orientation to Time	Past-Future	Past-Present-Future	Present-Future

Overall, it can be seen from this table that each conceptualization (worldview) has a different value structure, and, although there are some overlaps, the individualistic value orientation with respect to the relational dimension is the only element that is common to all three theoretical frameworks. It is also evident, however, that the values emphasized within the humanistic-existential perspective are considerably different from those identified in either of the other two orientations. Indeed, when we consult the literature, we find that most of these values seem to be compatible with the value preferences of many cultural groups in North America, whereas those portrayed in the psychodynamic and cognitive-behavioral frameworks appear to be closer to the value preferences of the Anglo American culture.

For example, the literature indicates that Asian Americans, Native Americans, and Hispanic Americans have a fundamental belief in the inherent goodness of people (e.g., D. W. Sue & Sue, 1990; Ho, 1987); that living in harmony and oneness with nature is basic to the philosophical outlook of individuals from Eastern and Native American cultures (e.g., Smith, 1981; D. W. Sue, 1981); that African Americans and Native Americans tend to be "here-and-now" or present-time oriented while Asian American and Hispanic populations have a past-present time focus (Ho, 1987; Smith, 1981; D. W. Sue, 1981); and that Native Americans and Hispanics prefer a being-in-becoming mode of activity that has as its goal the attainment of inner fulfillment through self-growth and development (e.g., Inclan, 1985; Lewis & Ho, 1985). In contrast, numerous writers have shown that, in addition to having an individualistic value orientation, middle-class White Americans generally (a) subscribe to a negative or neutral view of human nature with deterministic assumptions about human behavior and experience; (b) evaluate their worth in terms of what they can do or achieve through overt actions (such as the attainment of wealth and status); (c) believe in mastery and control over nature; and (d) place greater emphasis on the future than on the past or the present (e.g., Condon & Yousef, 1975; Ho, 1987; Inclan, 1985; Katz, 1985; F. Kluckhohn & Strodtbeck, 1961; Pedersen, 1988; Spence, 1985).

In short, it should be clear from the preceding discussion that the popular tendency to view all mainstream theories of psychotherapy as inappropriate for the treatment of clients from non-Western cultures is not necessarily warranted. This is not to say that there are no culture-specific elements inherent in these conceptualizations, because obviously there are, but to point out that significant variations in value orientation among these theories do exist and that the overall pattern of values reflected in the humanistic-existential perspective appears to be sufficiently flexible, or less entrenched in Western values, to make this approach a potentially more meaningful treatment modality for clients from different cultural backgrounds.

Cultural Factors in Psychotherapy Practice

There is a staggering number of publications on a variety of factors that are seen as potential sources of bias in cross-cultural psychotherapy practice. A detailed description of these factors is beyond the scope of this chapter. Suffice it to say, however, that the focus of much of this literature is on issues arising from value-system discrepancies between clients and therapists that impact the process of therapy and on various strategies and approaches for dealing with them (e.g., Brody, 1977; Dahlquist & Fay, 1983; D. W. Sue & Sue, 1990).

A number of these issues relate directly to what D. W. Sue and Sue (1990) call the "generic characteristics" inherent in the structure of traditional psychotherapy practice. For example, in most Western-style therapies, treatment is assumed to be individual-centered and unstructured, requiring that the flow of communication be from the client to the therapist. In addition, clients are expected to be objective and analytical in their approach to issues, play an active role in the treatment process, be verbally and emotionally expressive (that is, be able and willing to self-disclose and talk freely and openly about their thoughts and feelings), and seek long-term, as opposed to immediate or short-term, solutions for their problems (e.g., Dahlquist & Fay, 1983; D. W. Sue, 1981; D. W. Sue & Sue, 1990). As we noted earlier, these expectations are incompatible with the norms and patterns of social behavior found in many non-Western cultures (such as Eastern and Native American); and to the extent that they are, they can lead to breakdowns in communication, misinterpretations of clients' verbal and nonverbal behaviors, conflicts with respect to treatment goals, and confusion concerning the nature of therapeutic transactions and the overall process of therapy (e.g., D. W. Sue, 1981; Sue & Sue, 1977, 1990; Waxer, 1985).

However, cultural issues are not limited to the demand characteristics of the therapy situation. They also arise from discrepancies in clients' and therapists' value orientations along the lines suggested by F. R. Kluckhohn and Stodtbeck (1961), discussed earlier in this chapter. There is wide agreement in the literature that culturally different clients are at a disadvantage when working with therapists whose White, middle-class, Anglo values are in conflict with the beliefs and attitudes of their own cultural upbringing. For example, a therapist who fails to recognize that in most non-Western cultures family and group membership is more important for self-definition than individuality; who stresses separation from "parent and family of origin as a sign of psychological maturity and, therefore, as a goal of treatment" (Dahlquist & Fay, 1983, p. 1237); who overlooks situational or contextual factors and focuses instead on the client's internal processes as the locus of change for long-term personality development; and who believes that the client has the control and responsibility for what is happening in his or her life is likely to define problems and use interventions that are inconsistent with the client's way of perceiving and relating to the world. In other words, when treatment is guided by such assumptions, it often runs the risk of fostering misconstruals of issues and disjunctions in communication. This in turn creates an atmosphere wherein the client is likely to feel misunderstood and anxious, to lose trust in the therapist's credibility as a helper, and ultimately to become alienated and unable to benefit from therapy (e.g., Ivey et al., 1993; D. W. Sue, 1981; D. W. Sue & Sue, 1990; D. W. Sue & Zane, 1987; Szapocznik, Scopetta, de los Angeles Arnalde, & Kurtines, 1978).

A dominant perspective in the current literature is that cultural issues in psychotherapy may best be dealt with by providing therapists with cross-cultural training. Although the strategies vary, most authors agree that this kind of training must be directed at helping therapists (a) become aware of their clients' as well as their own cultural values, assumptions, and norms of social behavior so that they can be sensitive to existing differences in ways of thinking, feeling, and behaving; (b) know or learn about environmental conditions and factors that constitute sources of stress for clients from different minority groups; and (c) develop a wide repertory of intervention skills to enable them to communicate and interact with culturally diverse clients in an appropriate and effective manner (e.g., Pedersen, 1986; Root, Ho, & Sue, 1986; S. Sue, Akutsu, & Higashi, 1985; D. W. Sue, & Zane, 1987).

While we acknowledge that awareness, knowledge, and skill are essential components of cross-cultural training, we are inclined to believe that these elements are equally important in the training of all therapists. In order to be effective, all therapists must be aware of and responsive to the particular needs of their clients. They also must have adequate knowledge of the specific factors and circumstances surrounding their clients' difficulties and the skills with which to communicate with them appropriately and effectively. Thus, while awareness and knowledge of cultural issues are important, we believe that the difficulty in making psychotherapy therapeutic for culturally diverse clients resides mainly in the therapist's ability to translate his or her awareness and knowledge into actual practice (cf. D. W. Sue & Zane, 1987). This perspective will be the focus of our discussion in the section that follows.

A PERSPECTIVE ON CROSS-CULTURAL PSYCHOTHERAPY

There are many generic definitions of psychotherapy. D. W. Sue and Sue (1990) refer to it as "a process of interpersonal interaction and communication" and emphasize that each participant in this process "must be able to *send* and *receive* both *verbal* and *nonverbal* messages *accurately* and *appropriately*" (p. 30) in order for it to be productive. This description makes it clear that the success or failure of any psychotherapeutic endeavor is ultimately tied to the manner in which the client and therapist communicate and to the degree of mutual understanding developed between them. However, psychotherapy is more than a form of communication. It is also a helping relationship, which implies that it is a phenomenon occurring between two individuals or, stated in terms of this chapter, a dynamic encounter between two distinct views of the world. This perspective recognizes what we believe are the two most fundamental elements of psychotherapy practice, no matter what its form; namely, that each therapy participant is unique and that individual clients' and therapists' ways of construing and representing the world plays a crucial role in therapeutic transactions.

To elaborate, as we indicated earlier, the term "worldview" refers to a person's individualized "theory about the nature of things" (Ivey et al., 1993, p. 367) and their relationships in the world. In this sense, worldviews may be thought of as overarching cognitive frameworks consisting of different beliefs, presuppositions, and assumptions that influence and guide the way in which we perceive, evaluate, and interpret events in everyday life situations. Worldviews develop through experience and, therefore, are strongly influenced by a multiplicity of factors (physical/biological, social, economic, and cultural) that are specific to the particular conditions and circumstances of each person's developmental history (family upbringing, group affiliations, socioeconomic status, etc.). Thus, if we accept a broad definition of culture to include the system of meanings (values and beliefs) relevant to different subgroups (age, gender, ethnicity, etc.) within a community, then it can be argued that worldviews are embedded in a cultural context (Ibrahim, 1985), that culture is an integral part of people's everyday experiences, and that a person's distinctiveness as an individual can be attributed, at least in part, to cultural factors (Howard, 1991).

Furthermore, if we accept that the phenomenon of central importance in psychotherapy is not what is communicated but how this communication is interpreted by the client and therapist and that this process is filtered through the views that they each hold of the world, then it can also be argued that ". . . there is a multicultural dimension in every [psychotherapy] relationship" (Pedersen, 1985, p. 94). This perspective should not be taken to mean, however, that cultural issues do not require attention or that they are unimportant or irrelevant to psychotherapy practice. Quite the contrary. Our position, based on the arguments presented above, makes it clear that "culture" is an important and unavoidable component of psychotherapy, which must be recognized if we are to develop a fuller understanding of the therapy process and assist therapists to be effective in their therapeutic transactions with clients.

The foregoing also makes it clear that misconceptions and misunderstandings that lead to breakdowns in communication can and do occur in helping relationships, even when the helper and the "helpee" are from the "same culture". Indeed, such misunderstandings are inevitable when the client and therapist approach the therapeutic task from two different or incompatible life perspectives. In this sense, most issues typically seen as "barriers" to effective cross-cultural psychotherapy (that is, differences in communication patterns, individual versus group orientation, approaches to problem solving, self-disclosure, expressiveness, etc.) may also be considered relevant to therapeutic encounters in general, regardless of the "cultural" composition of the therapy dyad.

Take, for instance, the issue of self-disclosure. As we indicated earlier, the literature shows that members of Eastern cultures have a greater tendency to be less disclosing than members of Western cultures and that this tendency is related to differences in East-West cultural-value orientation. For example, Western cultures view introspection and insight as demonstrations of healthy psychological functioning, whereas Eastern cultures view healthy psychological states as the avoidance of negative thoughts (e.g., D. W. Sue & Sue, 1990). Members of Eastern cultures also appear to be reluctant to talk about negative experiences because revealing one's difficulties in coping would be indicative of human weakness (e.g., Boehnlein, 1987; McDonald-Scott, et al., 1992). The literature also shows that disclosure of vulnerable or undesirable aspects of the self or of one's family is threatening and aversive for members of Eastern cultures because they place greater value and rely more on a network of interdependence (e.g., Schwartz, 1990). Thus, a White, middle-class therapist who is unaware of these values and norms of social behavior is likely to be less sensitive to cultural factors that influence an Asian client's perceptions of the therapy situation and, consequently, more likely to misconstrue the client's in-therapy behaviors. Increased awareness could lead the therapist to understand that the client's reticence may be a reflection of the constraints of "culture" and to help him or her develop a more accepting therapeutic climate for the client.

Reluctance to self-disclose is not limited, however, to individuals from Eastern cultures. From time to time, most therapists encounter clients from different cultural backgrounds who are either unable or unwilling to talk openly about personal problems and difficulties coping with negative experiences. Consider, for example, a White, middle-class, North American therapist working with a client from a similar cultural background. In the context of Western "culture", where the norm is self-disclosure, the client's reluctance to self-disclose would be perceived as a major barrier to effective communication and would most likely be interpreted as "resistance" or as an indication of the client's "passive-aggressive" tendencies or simply that he/she is "not ready to talk about sensitive issues". However, admitting to having personal difficulties—to being a needy and dependent individual who is unable to rely on his/her resources for solving problems—would likely be inconsistent with the client's North American cultural upbringing, which places a high value on self-sufficiency, the ability to attain goals through one's own effort and autonomy (e.g., Pedersen, 1988). Thus, when the therapist fails to understand the client's reluctance toward self-disclosure in a cultural context (that is, as a reflection of the client's feelings of inadequacy and shame), he or she is likely to misconstrue the situation and use interventions that are likely to impede rather than enhance the therapy process.

In short, the findings of cross-cultural research are important to the extent that they provide useful information to the therapist about the broad parameters of the ideational system of a "community of individuals who see their world in a particular manner" (Howard, 1991, p. 190). This knowledge is important but not necessarily automatically transferable to making inferences and judgments about the behavior of individual members of that community. In the context of psychotherapy, where the focus is on the client and where being sensitive and responsive to individual differences is at the core of the work of the psychotherapist, these findings provide very little information regarding the client except for generalities. And when generalizations are not particularized for each client, they run the risk of becoming stereotypes.

How then can we assist psychotherapists and students of psychotherapy to be effective in their work with culturally diverse clients? Or more to the point, how can we help them gain an appreciation of broad cross-cultural issues without making them lose sight of the uniqueness of each client? One way of dealing with this issue is to separate the therapist from his/her method of therapy and then consider the personal/attitudinal and the conceptual/procedural aspects of psychotherapy practice in the context of training.

There is virtually a unanimous agreement among reviewers of the psychotherapy research literature (e.g., Lambert, DeJulio, & Stein, 1978; Orlinsky & Howard, 1986; Patterson, 1984) that the client/therapist relationship plays a central role in the process and outcome of therapy. The literature also indicates that, of the relationship factors studied, therapist empathy, warmth, and positive regard are good predictors of therapy outcome (e.g., Lambert, Christensen, & DeJulio, 1983) and that, although these factors constitute the core conditions of client-centered therapy, they are also central to most other therapeutic modalities (Lambert, 1983).

These observations make it clear that the therapist's manner of relating to the client is of greater importance as a factor in influencing treatment outcome than his/her particular theoretical orientation or approach to therapy. It can be argued, therefore, that training in psychotherapy requires an approach that focuses primarily on the personal/attitudinal component of trainee learning and only secondarily on the acquisition of specific therapeutic methods and techniques. Thus, training or learning to become a psychotherapist can be seen as a developmental process wherein the goal is to help trainees learn to develop an increased self-understanding and a broader perspective on issues related to their work as psychotherapists (Lawless, 1990; Toukmanian, 1996). The approach described below is not a formal model of training but a framework for understanding the necessary ingredients involved in the process of trainee learning from an experiential perspective.

Helping trainees (therapists) gain a meaningful understanding of their role as helpers revolves around a hierarchy of four attitudinal dimensions. These dimensions can be seen as the defining elements or the activities subsumed under Rogers' (1942, 1961) concept of empathic understanding. At the basic level, trainees need to recognize that in therapeutic encounters the primary medium or the vehicle through which help is given is the therapist. Help, however defined, comes through the involvement of the therapist as a person and as a trained professional. Therefore, at the most fundamental level, training must provide opportunities for the trainee to develop a degree of *self-understanding*. In other words, as therapists, we need to have an awareness of our needs, values, beliefs, and biases as human beings; we need to be aware of how our background and experiences play into our perceptions and interpretations of people, and we need to recognize that how we interact with our clients can make or fail to make psychotherapy a positive experience for them.

At the second level, therapists need to appreciate the fact that, as much as they are unique in their own views and perceptions of the world, so are their clients. This involves acknowledging that, regardless of apparent similarities between them (age, gender, sociocultural background), differences in interpretation of issues are inevitable and that this discrepancy in interpretation is greater when backgrounds are more divergent. Thus, while awareness and knowledge of different cultural values and norms of social behavior are important, we need to help therapists recognize the overriding importance of *listening* to each client's way of representing problematic experiences and to the meaning that such experiences have for them (Toukmanian, 1990). In other words, cross-cultural sensitivity requires that we develop habits of listening for ambiguities of meaning in clients' discourse and be willing and able to seek clarifications, because if we fail to do so, we run the risk of imposing our own assumptions and interpretations on what the client is saying and consequently of increasing the likelihood of creating misunderstandings and breakdowns in communication.

At the third level, therapists need to acknowledge and *accept* that there are different ways of interpreting "reality," but that no one way is superior to another. Learning to be accepting and respectful of clients, regardless of background, is fundamental to establishing a therapeutic relationship. Acceptance conveys the therapist's openness to diversity and commitment to the welfare of the client. As therapists, we need to appreciate the importance of this experience for the culturally different. This was demonstrated in a recent study by Phillion (1993), whose qualitative analyses of five Asian clients' accounts of their therapy experience revealed that experiencing *acceptance* (a feeling of being genuinely respected, understood and accepted as a person) was the single most important issue for them in therapy.

Finally, effective therapy also requires that therapists be able to *understand* the client from the vantage point of his/her unique worldview or experiential frame of reference. We must, therefore, help therapists recognize that how the client experiences a given situation is an important source of information, that these experiences are tied to his/her cultural upbringing within the context of family and community, and that an understanding of how contextual factors are playing into the client's perceptions and experiences of problems is crucial to the process of therapy. To simply know that the client's problematic experiences are related to "culture" is not sufficient. What is important is to understand the extent to which, and in what way, these factors are contributing to the difficulties experienced by the client. Consider, for example, the degree of conflict and stress encountered by the client during his/her process of acculturation (e.g., Berry, 1990; Berry, Poortinga, Segall, & Dasen, 1992). While a recognition of these difficulties is important, as therapists we must be able to go beyond what is communicated and understand how the client is interpreting his/her predicament of having to struggle to cope with such issues. Thus, training must provide therapists with opportunities to learn to be more differentiating and less rigid in their construals so that they can "see" other views and maximize their understanding of clients (Toukmanian, 1992, 1996). We also must help therapists to appreciate the fact that the effort to understand another human being is a slow and challenging process which is never complete; it requires attempting to "live in two quite different world views, both of which they must accept as meaningful and real" (Phillion, 1993, p. 29).

It is not possible to speak of training in psychotherapy without addressing the conceptual/procedural aspect of therapy practice. From a conceptual standpoint, there are now a number of approaches to multicultural counseling and psychotherapy that can be used for training cross-cultural therapists (e.g., Fukuyama, 1990; Ivey, et al., 1993; Locke, 1990). Although these approaches vary considerably in their conceptions of culture and the therapeutic methods that they advocate, they all stress the importance of helping therapists examine and understand their own as well as their clients' cultural beliefs, values, and attitudes as a way of enhancing their effectiveness as therapists. Our earlier analysis of the values emphasized in the three mainstream frameworks of psychotherapy suggested that the humanistic-existential perspective is sufficiently less entrenched in Western values to be worth considering as a possible treatment modality for clients across cultures. Our position on this issue is that approaches that focus on the phenomenology of the client (how the client construes self, the world, and self-in-relation-to-the-world) and emphasize the importance of understanding the client's subjective experience of events can provide an appropriate framework for cross-cultural psychotherapy. We contend that this framework has the flexibility to allow the use of various therapeutic interventions (family, group) and techniques (guided imagery, statements of paradoxical intention) as long as they meet the needs of the client and do not compromise the fundamental attitudes and the role of the therapist as a catalyst in the therapeutic change process. For as Howard (1991) states, "Empathic experiencing is perhaps the psychotherapist's greatest aid in escaping our inevitable limitations in understanding people from different cultures, races, belief systems, sexes, places, and times" (p. 196).

References

Beck, A. T. (1976). *Cognitive therapy and the emotional disorders.* New York: International Universities Press.

Beck, A. T., & Weishaar, M. E. (1995). Cognitive therapy. In R. J. Corsini & D. Wedding (Eds.), *Current psychotherapies* (5th ed, pp. 229–261). Itasca, IL: F. E. Peacock.

Berry, J. W. (1990). Psychology of acculturation: Understanding Individuals moving between cultures. In R. W. Brislin (Ed.), *Applied cross-cultural psychology* (pp. 232–253). Newbury Park, CA: Sage.

Berry, J. W., Poortinga,Y. H., Segall, M. H., & Dasen, P. R. (1992). *Cross-cultural psychology: Research & applications.* Cambridge, England: Cambridge University Press.

Boehnlein, J. K. (1987). Culture and society in posttraumatic stress disorder: Implications for psychotherapy. *American Journal of Psychotherapy, 41,* 519–530.

Brody, B. (1977). *Anthropological and cross-cultural themes in mental health: An annotated bibliography, 1925–1974.* Columbia, MO: University of Missouri Press.

Brontzman, G. L., & Butler, D. J. (1991). Cross-cultural issues in the disclosure of a terminal diagnosis: A case report. *The Journal of Family Practice, 32,* 426–427.

Brouwers, M. C. (1996). *Trauma disclosure: Differences as a function of personality and culture.* Unpublished raw data.

Brouwers, M. C., & Sorrentino, R. M. (1993). Uncertainty orientation and protection motivation theory: Individual differences in health compliance. *Journal of Personality and Social Psychology, 65,* 102–112.

Condon, J. C., & Yousef, F. (1975). *An introduction to intercultural communication.* New York: Bobbs-Merrill Co.

Dahlquist, Z. M., & Fay, A. S. (1983). Cultural issues in psychotherapy. In C. E. Walkes (Ed.), *Handbook of clinical psychology* (pp. 1219–1255). Homewood, IL: Dow-Jones Irwin.

Ellis, A. (1962). *Reason and emotion in psychotherapy.* New York: Lyle Stuart.

Ellis, A. (1994). Rational-emotive therapy. In J. K. Zeig & W. M. Munion (Eds.), *What is psychotherapy? Contemporary perspectives* (pp. 146–151). San Francisco: Jossey-Bass.

Erikson, E. (1963). *Childhood and society* (2nd ed.). New York: Norton.

Fukuyama, M. (1990). Taking a universal approach to multicultural counseling. *Counselor Education and Supervision, 30,* 6–17.

Guttfreund, D. G. (1990). Effects of language usage on the emotional experience of Spanish-English and English-Spanish bilinguals. *Journal of Consulting and Clinical Psychology, 58,* 604–607.

Hartmann, H. (1958). *Ego psychology and the problem of adaptation.* New York: International Universities Press.

Ho, M. K. (1987). *Family therapy with ethnic minorities.* Newbury Park, CA: Sage.

Hofstede, G. (1980). *Culture's consequences: Individual differences in work-related values.* Beverly Hills: Sage.

Hofstede, G. (1982). Dimensions of national cultures. In R. Rath, H. S. Asthana, D. Sinha, and J. B. H. Sinha (Eds.), *Diversity and unity in cross-cultural psychology* (pp.173–187). Lisse Netherlands: Swets and Zeitlinger.

Howard, G. S. (1991). A narrative approach to thinking, cross-cultural psychology, and psychotherapy. *American Psychologist, 46,* 187–197.

Huber, G. L., & Sorrentino, R. M. (1996). Uncertainty in interpersonal and intergroup relations. An individual-differences perspective. In R. M. Sorrentino & E. T. Higgins (Eds.), *The handbook of motivation and cognition: Foundations of social behavior,* (Vol. 3, pp. 591–619). New York: Guilford Press.

Ibrahim, F. A. (1985). Effective cross-cultural counseling and psychotherapy: A framework. *The Counseling Psychologist, 13,* 625–638.

Inclan, J. (1985). Variations in value orientations in mental health work with Puerto Ricans. *Psychotherapy, 22,* 324–334.

Ivey, A., Ivey, M. B., & Simek-Morgan, L. (1993). *Counseling and psychotherapy: A multicultural perspective.* Boston: Allyn & Bacon.

Katz, J. (1985). The sociopolitical nature of counseling. *The Counseling Psychologist, 13,* 615–624.

Kelly, G. (1955). *The psychology of personal constructs* (Vols. 1–2). New York: Norton.

Kessing, R. M. (1974). Theories of culture. *Annual Review of Anthropology, 3,* 73–97.

Kim, U. & Berry, J. W. (1993). *Indigenous psychologies.* Thousand Oaks, CA: Sage.

Kluckhohn, C. (1951). Values and value orientations in the theory of action. In T. Parsons & A. E. Shields (Eds.), *Toward a general theory of action* (pp. 388–433). Cambridge, MA: Harvard University Press.

Kluckhohn, C. (1953). Universal categories of culture. In A. L. Kroeber (Ed.), *Anthropology today* (pp. 507–523). Chicago, IL: University of Chicago Press.

Kluckhohn, C. (1956). Toward a comparison of value-emphases in different cultures. In L. D. White (Ed.), *The state of social sciences* (pp. 116–132). Chicago: University of Chicago Press.

Kluckhohn, F. R. & Stodtbeck, F. L. (1961). *Variations in value orientations.* Evanston, IL: Row, Peterson.

Kohut, H. (1971). *The analysis of the self.* New York: International Universities Press.

Lambert, M. (1983). Introduction to assessment of psychotherapy outcome: Historical perspective and current issues. In M. J. Lambert, E. R. Christensen, & S. S. DeJulio (Eds.), *The assessment of psychotherapy outcome* (pp. 3–32). New York: Wiley.

Lambert, M., Christenson, E., & DeJulio, S. S. (1983). *The assessment of psychotherapy outcome.* New York: Wiley.

Lambert, M., DeJulio, S. S., & Stein, D. M. (1978). Therapist interpersonal skills: Process, outcome, methodological considerations and recommendations for future research. *Psychological Bulletin, 85,* 467–489.

Lawless, D. (1990). *Interns' experience of learning psychotherapy: A process description.* Unpublished master's thesis, York University, North York, Ontario, Canada.

Lee, E. (1988). Cultural factors in working with Southeast Asian refugees. *Journal of Adolescence, 11,* 167–179.

Lewis, R. G., & Ho, M. K. (1985). Social work with Native Americans. *Social Work, 20,* 379–382.

Locke, D. (1990). Not so provincial view of multi-cultural counseling. *Counselor Education and Supervision, 30,* 18–25.

Mavreas, V. G., & Bebbington, P. E. (1988). Greeks, British Greek Cypriots and Londoners: A comparison study. *Psychological Medicine, 18,* 433–442.

May, R. (1961). *Existential psychology.* New York: Random House.

McDonald-Scott, P., Machizawa, S., & Satoh, H. (1992). *Psychological Medicine, 22,* 147–157.

Meichenbaum, D. (1986). Cognitive behavior modification. In F. H. Kanfer & A. P. Goldstein (Eds.), *Helping people change: A textbook of methods* (pp. 346–380). New York: Pergamon Press.

Mollica, R. F., Wyshak, G., & Lavelle, J. (1987). The psychosocial impact of war trauma and torture on Southeast Asian refugees. *American Journal of Psychiatry, 144,* 1567–1572.

Orlinsky, D., & Howard, K. (1986). Process and outcome in psychotherapy. In S. L. Garfield & A. E. Bergin (Eds.), *Handbook of psychotherapy and behavior change* (pp. 311–384). New York: Wiley.

Parsons, T. (1973). Culture and social system revisited. In L. Schneider & C. Bonjean (Eds.), *The idea of culture in the social sciences* (pp. 33–46). London: Cambridge University Press.

Patterson, C. H. (1984). Empathy, warmth, and genuineness in psychotherapy: A review of reviews, *Psychotherapy, 21,* 431–438.

Pedersen, P. B. (1988). *A handbook for developing a multicultural awareness.* Alexandria, VA: American Association for Counseling and Development.

Perls, F. (1969). *Gestalt therapy verbatim.* Moab, UT: Real People Press.

Phillion, R. N. (1993). *Experiencing acceptance: A qualitative analysis of the cross-cultural client's experience of psychotherapy.* Unpublished master's thesis, York University, North York, Ontario, Canada.

Rogers, C. (1942). *Counseling and psychotherapy.* Boston: Houghton-Mifflin.

Rogers, C. (1961). *On becoming a person.* Boston: Houghton-Mifflin.

Rohner, P. P. (1984). Toward a conception of culture for cross-cultural psychology. *Journal of Cross-Cultural Psychology, 15,* 111–138.

Root, M. P. (1985). Guidelines for facilitating therapy with Asian American clients. *Psychotherapy, 22,* 349–356.

Root, M., Ho, C., & Sue, S. (1986). Issues in the training of counselors for Asian Americans. In H. P. Lefley & P. B. Pedersen (Eds.), *Cross-cultural training for mental health professionals* (pp. 199–209). Springfield, IL: Charles C. Thomas.

Schwartz, S. (1990). Individualism-collectivism:Critique and proposed refinements. *Journal of Cross-Cultural Psychology, 21,* 139–157.

Shon, S. P., & Ja, D. Y. (1982). Asian families. In M. McGoldrick, J. K. Pearce, & J. Giordano (Eds.), *Ethnicity and family therapy* (pp. 208–228). New York: Guilford Press.

Smith, E. (1981). Cultural and historical perspectives in counseling American Indians. In D. Sue (Ed.), *Counseling the culturally different: Theory, research and practice* (pp. 141–185). New York: Wiley.

Sorrentino, R. M., Bobocel, D. R., Gitta, M. Z., Olson, J. M., & Hewitt, E. C. (1988). Uncertainty orientation and persuasion: Individual differences in the effects of personal relevance on social judgements. *Journal of Personality and Social Psychology, 55,* 357–371.

Sorrentino, R. M., & Hewitt, E. C. (1984). The uncertainty-reducing properties of achievement tasks revisited. *Journal of Personality and Social Psychology, 47,* 884–899.

Sorrentino, R. M., Raynor, J. O., Zubek, J. M., & Short, J.C. (1990). Personality functioning and change: Information and affective influences on cognitive, moral, and social development. In E. T. Higgins & R. M. Sorrentino (Eds.), *The handbook of motivation and cognition: Foundations of social behavior* (Vol. 2, pp. 193–288). New York: Guilford Press.

Sorrentino, R. M., & Short, J. C. (1986). Uncertainty orientation, motivation and cognition. In R. M. Sorrentino & E. T. Higgins (Eds.), *The handbook of motivation and cognition: Foundations of social behavior* (pp. 379–403). New York: Guilford Press.

Spence, J. J. (1985). Achievement American style. *American Psychologist, 40,* 1285–1295.

Stewart, E. C. (1981). Cultural sensitivities in counseling. In P. B. Pederson, J. G. Draguns, W. J. Lonner, & H. E. Trimble (Eds), *Counseling across cultures: Revised and expanded edition* (pp. 61–86). University of Hawaii: East-West Center.

Sue, D. W. (1981). *Counselling the culturally different.* New York: Wiley.

Sue, D. W., & Sue, S. (1990). *Counselling the culturally different* (2nd ed.) New York: Wiley.

Sue, D. W., & Zane, N. (1987). The role of culture and cultural techniques in psychotherapy. *American Psychologist, 42,* 37–45.

Sue, S., Akutsu, P. D., & Higashi, C. (1985). Training issues in conducting therapy with ethnic minority group clients. In P. B. Pedersen (Ed.), *Handbook on cross-cultural counseling and therapy* (pp. 275–280). Westpoint, CT: Greenwood Press.

Szapocznik, J., Scopetta, M., de los Angeles Arnalde, M., & Kurtines, W. (1978). Cuban value structure: Treatment implications. *Journal of Consulting and Clinical Psychology, 46,* 961–970.

Ting-Toomey, S. (1991). Intimacy expressions in three cultures: France, Japan, and the United States. *International Journal of Intercultural Relations, 15,* 29–46.

Toukmanian, S. G. (1990). A schema-based information processing perspective on client change in experiential psychotherapy. In G. Lietaer, J. Rombauts, & R. Van Balen (Eds.), *Client-centered and experiential psychotherapy in the nineties* (pp. 326–390). Leuven, Belgium: Leuven University Press.

Toukmanian, S. G. (1992). Studying the client's perceptual processes and their outcomes in psychotherapy. In S. G. Toukmanian & D. L. Rennie (Eds.), *Psychotherapy process research: Paradigmatic and narrative approaches* (pp. 77–107). Newbury Park, CA: Sage.

Toukmanian, S. G. (1996). Clients' perceptual processing: An integration of research and practice. In W. Dryden (Ed.), *Research in counseling and psychotherapy: Practical applications* (pp. 184–210). London: Sage.

Triandis, H. C. (1996). The psychological measurement of cultural syndromes. *American Psychologist, 51,* 402–415.

True, R. H. (1990). Psychotherapeutic issues with Asian American women. *Sex Roles, 22,* 477–486.

Waxer, P. (1985). Nonverbal aspects of intercultural counseling: Interpersonal issues. In R. J. Samuda & A. Wolfgang (Eds.), *Intercultural counseling and assessment: Global perspectives* (pp. 49–66). Toronto, Ontario, Canada: Hogrefe.

Wheeless, L. R., Erickson, K. V., & Behrens, J.S. (1986). Cultural differences in disclosiveness as a function of locus of control. *Communication Monographs, 53,* 36–46.

Winnicott, D. (1988). *Human nature.* New York: Schocken.

Yamamoto, J., & Kubota, M. (1983). The Japanese American family. In J. Yamamoto, A. Romero, & A. Morales (Eds.), *The psychosocial development of minority group children.* New York: Brunner/Mazel.

PART III

HEALTH AND MENTAL HEALTH ISSUES

5

Culture and Anxiety Disorders

IHSAN AL-ISSA

SHAHIN OUDJI

Anxiety is a household word in the Western world. It is claimed that anxiety has existed throughout human history and across cultures (Good & Kleinman, 1985; McReynolds, 1975). Indeed, the 20th century is considered the age of anxiety (Auden, 1946; May, 1977), a recognition of a link between anxiety and contemporary sociocultural conditions. Although it is recognized that the latter part of the 20th century had moved into an age of melancholy (Hagnell, Lanke, Rosman, & Oyesjo, 1982), this chapter clearly shows that the rates of anxiety remain unabated during this century. Yet the concept of anxiety is notorious in its ambiguity (Jablensky, 1985; Lewis, 1980), and both its meaning and contents tend to vary across nations. Lewis (1980) pointed out that in most European languages there are many words and idiomatic expressions describing psychological and bodily states that represent different facets of the anxiety experience. For example, although the words *anxiety* in English, *anxiété* in French, and *ansiedad* in Spanish are derived from the Latin word *anxietas,* they do not cover the same linguistic space. Therefore the classification and phenomenology of anxiety is expected to be influenced by the lexicology of the language in which it is used. Lewis (1980) has shown that semantic differences may affect the reliability of the concept of anxiety across nations. In a World Health Organization (WHO) study of psychiatric diagnosis, the agreement of leading psychiatrists from 30 countries on neuroses was found to be extremely low (World Health Organization, 1970). In a case that would have conformed fully both to the *ICD-10 (International Classification of Diseases—10th Revision)* description of an anxiety state and the *DSM-IV (Diagnostic and Statistical Manual—4th Edition)* criteria of generalized anxiety disorder, only 9 out of 21 psychiatrists made a diagnosis of "anxiety neurosis."

In the study of anxiety across cultures, there is also the problem of the differentiation between anxiety as a normal response, as a symptom, or as a syndrome. It has been suggested that normal anxiety helps in defending against a wide variety of threats and is necessary for optimal performance (Marks & Nesse, 1994; Mueller, 1992). Similar to depressive mood, which may have the function of insuring the cohesiveness of the group (Averill, 1968), anxiety may be adaptive in some cultures by rallying the family and the community around the individual and help to relieve his or her stress (Guarnaccia, De La Cancela, & Carrillo, 1989). The suggestion by Seligman (1971) of a biological preparedness to fear objects or situations that were dangerous to the human species in the past received some support in Western and non-Western cultures (de Silva, 1988; de Silva, Rachman, & Seligman, 1972; Zaffropoulon & McPherson, 1986). Although physiological reactions underlying anxiety appear to be universal, culture may define the situations that arouse anxiety and determine how it is expressed and reacted to by the individual and his or her group.

The cross-cultural study of anxiety is complicated by the overlap between different anxiety disorders themselves or between these disorders and depression (Breslau, 1985; Racagni & Smeraldi, 1987; Weissman, Myers, & Harding, 1978). People with generalized anxiety, for example, are more likely to suffer from at least one other *DSM-IV* disorder, especially panic disorder or major depression (Blazer, Hughes, George, Swartz, & Boyer, 1991). In the early cross-cultural studies, anxiety disorders were not differentiated but were subsumed under neurosis (Linton, 1956) with psychoanalytical implications reflecting *DSM-I* (American Psychiatric Association, 1952).

Bearing in mind a multiplicity of problems in reviewing studies on culture and anxiety, we deal with the following topics in this chapter: (1) intercultural and cross-cultural epidemiology of anxiety disorders; (2) culture-specific anxiety reactions; (3) the cross-cultural measurement of anxiety by psychological inventories; and (4) the treatment of anxiety in the culturally different.

THE EPIDEMIOLOGY OF ANXIETY DISORDERS

African Americans, Hispanics, and Whites

Early epidemiological studies were community surveys of anxiety states without specified diagnostic criteria. Before *DSM-III,* there was no standardized criteria available on which to base diagnosis, and the criteria used varied considerably from one study to another. In an early review by Marks and Lader (1973) of five population studies in the United States, United Kingdom, and Sweden done between 1943 and 1966, the rates reported for anxiety states were between 2.0% and 4.7% for current prevalence. In a more recent review, Weissman (1985) added other community studies to the Marks and Lader list (Canada, France, United Kingdom, Switzerland, Norway, Sweden, Denmark, Finland, and the United States). The rates were similar to those reported by Lader and Marks, even though the time periods and the diagnostic methods used were varied. In these studies, the rates of anxiety states in women tended to be higher than in men.

In an early community study in the United States, a relationship between gender, social class, ethnicity, and anxiety was found. In a survey of urban and rural residents of northern Florida in the late 1960s, using an anxiety scale containing 12 items, Warheit, Bell, Schwab, and Buhl (1986) reported that 14.6% of the sample had significant symptoms of anxiety. African Americans, females, the elderly, people at the lowest socioeconomic level, and the separated, widowed, and divorced had the highest scores. The larger the number of these associated factors, the greater the likelihood of high scores on the anxiety scale. A national survey in 1979 using a symptom checklist (Uhlenhuth, Balter, Mellinger, Cisin, & Clinthorne, 1983) indicated that Generalized Anxiety Disorder was the most common disorder (6.4%, 1 year prevalence), followed by phobias other than agoraphobia (2.3/100) and agoraphobia/panic (1.2%). The rates of anxiety disorders were higher in women than in men.

With improved reliability of psychiatric diagnoses by the use of structured diagnostic interviews and specified criteria, more reliable information about the epidemiology of anxiety disorders became available. The first application of the new structured diagnostic interview techniques came in a pilot survey of persons living in the New Haven, Connecticut, area in 1975–1976 (Weissman, Myers, & Harding, 1978). Using the Schedule for Affective Disorders and Schizophrenia—Lifetime Version (SAD-L), the current rate for anxiety disorders was 4.3%, a finding quite similar to the rate of anxiety states reviewed by Marks and Lader (1973). The rate of generalized anxiety disorder was 2.5%, slightly more common in middle- and younger-aged women, African Americans, persons not currently married, and those in the lower socioeconomic classes. It was also found that only about a quarter of persons with any current anxiety disorder had received treatment for an emotional disorder in the past year. However, the use of health facilities for nonpsychiatric reasons was higher among persons with anxiety disorders than those with other psychiatric disorders or with no psychiatric disorder.

One of the most extensive epidemiological studies with large samples of African Americans, Hispanics, and Whites is the epidemiologic catchment area (ECA) study (Robins & Regier, 1991). The Diagnostic Interview Schedule (DIS), which was devised to match the criteria of *DSM-III,* was used in this study. The combined data, with or without exclusion of panic or major depression, revealed that generalized anxiety disorder was significantly more prevalent among females than males, as well as among lower income groups. African Americans had significantly higher rates than Whites only when panic and depression were excluded. Hispanics obtained the lowest rate of generalized anxiety. There was no consistent difference in rates of panic disorder between Whites, African Americans, and Hispanics, although African Americans and Hispanics had lower lifetime prevalence rates than Whites. Females had about twice the rate of panic disorder as males throughout all ethnic groups. The rates of phobias (agoraphobia, simple phobia, and social phobia) were more prevalent in females than in males, and in African Americans than in Whites and Hispanics. For women, there was no relation between educational level and either panic or phobia. Similarly, for men, there was no regular relationship between panic and educational level, except that there was a tendency for men with lower education to have higher rates of phobia.

The National Comorbidity Survey (Kessler et al., 1994) did not confirm all the ECA findings of higher rate of anxiety disorders in African Americans. While it was consistent with the ECA finding that African Americans and Whites have similar prevalence of panic disorder, it was inconsistent with ECA findings that African

Americans have significantly higher lifetime prevalence of simple phobia and agoraphobia. Differences in these results may be due to a sampling bias of the ECA study, with overrepresentation of lower income, elderly, and female African American participants (Neal & Turner, 1991).

Asian Americans

Although Asian Americans (Chinese, Japanese, Vietnamese, and other southeast Asians) were not included in the ECA study, a few other studies indicate that they tend to be more anxious than White Americans (Uba, 1994) and Canadians (Lin & Endler, 1993). For example, Sue and Kirk (1973) found that Chinese American and Japanese American male college students and Chinese American female college students were more anxious than other students. Many factors were suggested to explain the high anxiety among Asian Americans. One factor is that Asian Americans experience more ambiguity in nonfamilial social relationships than White Americans do. Difficulty with the English language that foreign-born Asian Americans have may also contribute to increased anxiety. It is also possible that Asian Americans who feel uncomfortable in new social situations come from conservative, traditional families who emphasize rigid ways of behavior (D. W. Sue & Kirk, 1973). They may experience more conflicts during interpersonal interaction and attribute it to their own behavior because of their concern that they are not behaving appropriately. Moreover, biculturality may create conflict and stress for Asian Americans. One study cited by Huang and Ying (1989) showed that the more Chinese was spoken between immigrant Chinese parents and their fifth- and sixth-grade sons, the more anxious the boys were; and the more favorable the attitude of parents toward Chinese culture, the lower was the self-esteem of the sons. Minority-group status may also be a major source of anxiety as a result of stigmatization, stereotyping, and racial rejection (Uba, 1994). In the conclusion of a study comparing Chinese with White American students on anxiety, Lin and Endler (1993) pointed out situational and linguistic factors as a source of anxiety for the Chinese:

> The results of the present study support findings previously reported in the literature, suggesting that Chinese immigrants in North America may be especially vulnerable to higher levels of anxiety (Chataway & Berry, 1989; Sue & Morishima, 1982). Of particular note here was the finding that Chinese students were prone to feeling more anxious in ambiguous situations or daily routines than were the Caucasians, a finding which supports the notion that daily life hassles are significantly associated with anxiety (Kuo & Tsai, 1986). Chinese North Americans are consequently more likely to feel threatened in a given situation in a relatively unfamiliar culture, regardless of the objective reality of that situation. Moreover, having to confront, on a daily basis, new and possibly frightening situations, only serves to further increase their anxiety for routine, daily life situations. . . . The level of English fluency also appeared to play an important role. As English proficiency was found to be the single most powerful covariate in predicting the results of the present research, these findings confirmed what previous researchers have noted (Chataway & Berry, 1989; Padilla, Wagatsuma, & Lindholm, 1984; Sung, 1985): That because Chinese immigrants feel inadequate in their level of English proficiency, their adjustment to living in a new country may be hindered by feelings of inadequacy and, thus, anxiety. (p. 17)

Non-Western and Communal Societies

Does a simple non-Western and a communal style of living protect people against anxiety? An early study by Kidson and Jones (1968) among Australian natives found no case of anxiety. A later study by Jones (1972) among the same group reported only one case of "free-floating" anxiety in an individual. Small samples, limited period of observation, and the definition of anxiety by the researcher, which ignored its atypical expressions, might have contributed to the low rates of anxiety found by some of these early studies. Unlike studies of native Australians, an extensive study by Hallowell (1970) revealed a variety of fears and anxieties among the Berens River Indians in Canada. In particular, Hallowell discussed the relationship between some of the characteristic fears experienced by these people and their traditional system of beliefs. The Berens River Indians believe that animals have souls, and the approach of a wild animal to their camp is an ill omen and a sign that somebody is trying to bewitch them, a situation in which the animal is a malevolent agent of the sorcerer. Despite this general attitude toward animals, their affective response to them is not uniform. Wolves and bears do not arouse their fears, but toads and frogs are a source of fear even though they are among the most harmless animals in their environment. Fear of toads and frogs is fostered by the belief that monster species inhabit the country. Toads are not simply "loathsome creatures" to these Indians, but are associated with evil forces and with certain parts of the animal being used in malevolent magic. Similar to agoraphobia in the West, Hallowell (1970) described a case of:

> an Indian who could go nowhere unaccompanied by one or more companions. When alone he would always keep within sight of human habitations or people. This was the rule even when he had to urinate or defecate. If he had to relieve himself at night his wife would always get up and go with him. He rationalized his anxiety by saying that he once dreamed that a jackfish would swallow him, if this creature found him alone. (Hallowell, 1970, p. 474)

Unlike traditional Berens River Indians, the Hutterites have a way of life which is much more similar to the larger American society. However, J. W. Eaton and Weil (1970) suggested that their communal living style may provide them with immunity against anxiety. They found that in a population of 8,542, anxiety states tended to be very rare. Eaton and Weil reported that

> Six patients showed enough general anxiety about specific problems to justify the diagnosis of *anxiety reaction*. Most of these cases also had vague neurasthenic complaints. We did not observe many symptoms typical of free-floating anxiety. This may explain the general impression that Hutterite colonies are populated by relaxed, well-adjusted, and mentally healthy individuals. It could be expected that free-floating anxiety would be rare in a culture where the individual has many close interpersonal relationships and is generally given a great deal of social and psychological support by his family and his community. A Hutterite usually knows how others will react to something he does. There is little of the deep uncertainty in social relations which is experienced by many people living in a metropolis with widely differing cultural expectations. (p. 452)

Population surveys carried out by psychiatrists in many non-Western countries (see review by Good & Kleinman, 1985; Murphy, 1982) seem to support the universality of anxiety. Anxiety was studied in the 1960s and 1970s as a part of neuroses in urban and/or rural settings in Ethiopia, Iran, and India, with rates ranging between 1% and 3%. More recently, a study in Lesotho, South Africa, reported that panic disorder and generalized anxiety disorder were equal or more prevalent among natives than in the United States (Hollifield, Katon, Spain, & Pule, 1990).

In a landmark study, the Cornell-Aro Mental Health Project, the rates of anxiety were found to be extremely high in Nigeria as compared with Nova Scotia, Canada (D. C. Leighton, Harding, Macklin, MacMillan, & Leighton, 1963; A. H. Leighton, Lambo, Hughes, Leighton, Murphy, & Macklin, 1966). In Nigeria, 36% of urban and 27% of rural residents had symptoms of anxiety, with 19% and 16%, respectively, significantly impaired. In the Sterling County of Nova Scotia, 13% of urban and 10% of rural residents manifested these symptoms, with 38% and 32%, respectively, significantly impaired. That Nigerians had significantly less impairment than Canadians may be the result of differences in the nature of the work situation (e.g., less complexity, competition, or aggression in Nigeria) and could reflect the transcultural inequivalence of the concept of impairment cross-culturally.

In evaluating these epidemiological data, the question of cultural differences in the definition of anxiety may pose serious problems. For example, apprehension and worry about unknown factors is part of the Western definition of anxiety. In contrast, anxiety in non-Western societies is culturally conditioned to specific sociocultural events, such as maintenance of a large family, procreation, and witchcraft (see culture-specific syndromes, this chapter). Furthermore, in many non-Western societies, anxiety reactions tend to be associated with cultural beliefs that are shared by the whole group rather than being an individual phenomenon.

The Epidemiology and Phenomenology of Obsessive-Compulsive Disorder

Obsessive-compulsive disorder (OCD) was traditionally considered uncommon, with poor prognosis. The *DSM-III* (American Psychiatric Association, 1980), for example, reported that "the disorder is apparently rare in the general population." Based on clinical data, Nemiah (1984) estimated the rate of OCD in the general population at 0.05%. Later, large-scale studies such as the ECA study (Karno & Golding, 1991) indicated that the lifetime prevalence was about 2.5%, which was significantly higher than previous estimates. The rates among ethnic groups reported in the ECA study indicated that OCD is highest among Whites and lowest among Hispanics, with African American rates in between. Females tended to have higher rates than males in all ethnic groups, particularly those between the ages of 18 and 44. OCD is also more prevalent among the underemployed than the fully employed, and among those on welfare than those who are self-supporting. The high comorbidity of OCD with affective disorder and other anxiety disorders found in the ECA study confirmed previous findings in the West (Rasmussen & Tsuang, 1984, 1986), as well as in non-Western countries such as Benin (Bertschy & Ahyi, 1991), Egypt (Okasha, Saad, Khalil, El Dawia, & Yehia, 1994), Saudi Arabia (Mahgoub & Abdel-Hafeiz, 1991), and many other nations (Weissman, et al., 1994).

Obsessive-compulsive disorder was also considered rare in certain communities in the West and non-Western cultures. It is assumed that OCD is masked by rigid and ritualistic behavior. J. W. Eaton and Weil (1970), for example, described OCD among the Hutterites:

> It was our impression that neurotic Hutterites react to most stresses with signs of depression rather than with anxiety symptoms or obsessive or paranoid tendencies as neurotic patients often do in the American culture. This rareness of obsessive and compulsive behavior may have something to do with the relative rigidity of the Hutterite culture. Persons who would seem to be compulsive in a loosely structured social system would be more normal in a Hutterite colony, where life is highly regulated by tradition. The Hutterite culture provides such persons with socially approved outlets for compulsiveness. They need only to be orthodox! Some Hutterites were regarded by their community as fanatical in their orthodoxy, but in no case seen by our staff did the psychiatrist think that a diagnosis of compulsive neurotic reaction would be justified. (p. 452)

Other cross-cultural examples of OCD that are believed to be masked by religious rituals came from Islamic countries and India. One culture-specific obsessive-compulsive syndrome among practicing Muslims is *waswās,* which literally refers to whispered promptings of the devil (Pfeiffer, 1982). It relates to ritual cleanliness and to doubt about the validity of the ritual procedures during prayer. The faithful suffering from *waswās* find it hard to terminate the ablution because they are afraid that they are not yet clean enough to carry out their prayer in the acceptable manner. Starting the prayer immediately after the ablution ritual, the faithful will repeat the introductory invocations, as well as the raising of the arms, more times than is called for because they are distracted from focusing on God. Finally, at the end of the prayer, the faithful may have doubts about whether they might perhaps have forgotten some words, and so they will start all over again from the beginning. This syndrome, however, is not considered an illness that requires treatment; it is simply a temptation of the devil that distracts the faithful from carrying out their daily religious duties. The meticulousness of the victim in religious matters deserves respect rather than ridicule by the community. Another example from India is purity mania (Suci Bhay), which is based on Hinduism (Chakraborty & Banerji, 1975). A typical example of purity mania is an elderly woman who always carries a bottle of Ganges water under her arm, which she uses to dispense "purity" by sprinkling water around her.

Cross-national studies indicate that the rates of OCD are quite similar among Western and non-Western countries. Recently, Staley and Wand (1995) reviewed nine studies of clinical reports from China, Hong Kong, Japan, and India showing that the prevalence rate for OCD among psychiatric inpatients ranged from 0.1% (Hong Kong) to 2.4% (Japan). They also reported cross-cultural epidemiological surveys from four non-Western and seven European countries. Two surveys using the Present State Examination (PSE) reported current prevalence for OCD of 2.4% in Uganda (Orley & Wing, 1979) and 2.7% in Athens, Greece (Mavreas & Bebbington, 1988). Using a structured interview based on *DSM-III* criteria, a study in Florence, Italy, found a current prevalence of 0.6%. Two other surveys of 6-month prevalence using DIS in Puerto Rico (Canino et al., 1987) and in Germany (Wittchen, Essay, Von Zerssen, Kreig and Zandig, 1992) found a rate of 1.8% in both countries. The lifetime prevalence rates of OCD varied from 0.3% in rural Taiwan (Compton, et al., 1991) to 3.2% in Puerto Rico (Canino et al., 1987). A recent cross-national study (Weissman, et al., 1994) using the DIS in the United States, Canada, Puerto Rico, Germany, Taiwan, Korea, and New Zealand found that lifetime prevalence rates for OCD ranged from 1.9% to 2.5%, with the exception of a low rate of 0.7% for Taiwan. Since these prevalence rates were standardized to the age and gender distribution of the United States ECA household sample and based on the same interview procedure, the cross-cultural similarity of the rate of OCD between the United States and other nations is impressive.

One of the earliest studies of the contents of OCD was carried out in India by Akhtar, Wig, Varma, Pershad, & Verma (1975). As a result of interviews with 82 obsessive-compulsive patients, they identified five forms of obsessions and two forms of compulsions. Obsessive doubts were the most frequent (75%), followed by obsessive thinking (34%), obsessive fears (26%), obsessive impulses (17%), and obsessive images (7%). They also found two forms of compulsion: yielding, in which compulsive urges forced action on 61% of patients, and controlling, where diverting action had the function of allowing 6% of the patients to control a compulsive urge without giving in to it. Similarly, yielding compulsions, which consist mainly of cleaning and checking, are also found to be the predominant forms of compulsions among Western patients (Rachman & Hodgson, 1980).

In a more recent study in Saudi Arabia, Mahgoub and Abdel-Hafeiz (1991) found that compulsions, doubts, thoughts, impulses, fears, and images, in descending order, were the most frequent forms of OCD. Body-washing and fear of contamination related to religious themes were frequent among patients. In a study in Egypt, Okasha, et al. (1994) found that the most common obsessive symptoms were related to religious themes and contamination (60% each), while rituals (68%) were the most common compulsions. Religious and sexual themes were the most prevalent among patients. In another study in Qatar, obsessive thoughts of harming oneself or others were attributed to impulses induced by the devil among female patients (El-Islam, 1994). These religious themes seem to be more frequent among Muslim OCD patients than among Hindu patients studied by Akhtar et al. (1975) and are almost absent among Western patients.

CULTURE-SPECIFIC ANXIETY REACTIONS

A culture-specific anxiety reaction is a behavior that does not fit within the Western classification system because cultural factors may contribute differentially to its etiology, symptoms, interpretation, and treatment. However, these reactions show some similarity to anxiety disorders known in the West. The following are some examples of culture-specific anxiety reactions.

The Brain-Fag syndrome

This syndrome was first described by Prince (1960) in a clinic in Nigeria and confirmed in other parts of Africa (Collignon & Gueye, 1995; Minde, 1974). The syndrome is characterized by somatic symptoms such as pain in the back of the neck, frontal headache, burning sensations over the scalp (as if pepper has been rubbed into it), a burning sensation in the center of the head (like a piece of red hot iron), and waves passing over the scalp. The cognitive symptoms consist of difficulty in attention and thinking, inability to grasp what one reads, and complete amnesia of what one has just studied. Affective symptoms are not usually mentioned by patients. Patients with the brain-fag syndrome were students at secondary schools or universities. As the symptoms were precipitated during an intense study period, patients attributed it to "fatigue of the brain" due to excessive "brainwork;" hence it was labeled "brain-fag" by Prince (1960).

The brain-fag syndrome involves an intense fear of failure. Education is at a premium in Africa and is the road to wealth and prestige. In addition to fecundity, education is a major cultural value, which is regarded as a family affair. A student becomes the center of attention, and the burden of family expectations and prestige rests upon his or her shoulders. More recently, Prince (1981) suggested "the forbidden knowledge theory" to explain the brain-fag syndrome. He pointed out that by attending Western schools or reading Western books, students see themselves as betraying their ancestors. For example, patients reported that they dreamed of ancestors beating them, a common dream in the Nigerian culture when the person is not conforming with customs or is failing to follow the wishes of ancestors. These patients tended to come from the least Westernized families, and thus find acculturation more arduous.

Shinkeishitsu

Shinkeishitsu represents a group of anxiety disorders in Japan (Russell, 1989). These disorders are of three types: (1) ordinary neurasthenia, with symptoms such as poor concentration and memory impairment in addition to hypochondriacal symptoms and fatigue; (2) anxiety state, which is characterized by palpitations, anxiety, and panic; and (3) obsessive phobic state, or Taijinkyofusho (TKS), which is the most prevalent type of these anxiety disorders. TKS is characterized by anxiety about offending others by blushing, emitting offensive odors or being flatulent, staring inappropriately, presenting improper facial expressions, or having physical deformity (Takahashi, 1989).

TKS is usually compared with agoraphobia in the West (Good & Kleinman, 1985; Murphy, 1982). Agoraphobia affects mainly women, while TKS is equal in both sexes. The former is associated with panic attacks and fear of fainting, while the latter is associated with feelings of shame and fear of harming others. The common feature of both is the desire to stay at home. TKS also shares with social phobia a concern with being publicly observed and the avoidance of social situations. However, in social phobia the patients are anxious about embarrassing themselves, while in TKS they are worried about offending or embarrassing others (Kleinnecht, Dinnel, Tanouye, & Lonner, 1994). Prince (1991) pointed out that, in contrast to the egocentric social phobias in the West such as stage fright, where individuals fear they will not live up to the expectation of their audience, social phobic reactions in Japan are altruistic and involve concern about not offending others. TKS seems to represent "Japanese normative values that positively sanction allocentric, or other-oriented behavior, the denial of self, and the importance of harmonious interpersonal relations" (Russell, 1989, p. 398).

Koro (Chinese Shuk yang)

This syndrome has its origin in Chinese medicine. *Yang* refers to the male principle (yin is the female principle), as well as to the male genitals. *Shuk* denotes withdrawal and dwindling. *Shuk yang* is the withdrawal of the male principle of life, expressed by the retraction of the penis into the body, causing death. It is manifested as an overwhelming acute anxiety related to sexual functioning and sexual organs, characterized by heart palpitations and outbursts of sweating and vertigo, accompanied by an intense fear of death (Pfeiffer, 1982). In the Chinese communal society, *Koro* may be conceptualized as a cry to rally the immediate and extended family or even the whole community. This intense anxiety can be reduced if the family and the community show concern and support for the patient (Tan, 1980).

Ataque de nervios

This syndrome, characterized by uncontrollable shouting, crying, trembling, heat in the chest rising into the head, and verbal or physical aggression, is a sudden transient state which is prevalent among Latin Americans from the Caribbean and other Hispanic groups. It usually occurs following a stressful life event relating to the family (death, separation or divorce, conflict with spouse or children). *Ataque* closely fits with the *DSM-IV* description of panic attack, except that its association with a precipitating event distinguishes it from panic disorder (Barron, 1994). Another culture-specific expression of anxiety among Hispanics is *nervios*. Headache, insomnia, lack of appetite, depression, fear, anger, trembling, disorientation, and other symptoms of *nervios* are socially acceptable expressions of being out of control. These symptoms are precipitated by various life events such as disrupted family relationships (Low, 1981). Guarnaccia and Farias (1988) have shown that the social meaning of nervios among Salvadorian refugees in the United States included family and work issues, fears for relatives left in El Salvador, and social commentary on racism and problems of adjustment to life in the United States.

Kayak-angst

This syndrome is an acute panic state which develops among the Inuit. When the hunters sit immobile for hours waiting for the seals to surface, they experience vertigo, feel dazed, and experience spatial disorientation, such as the loss of awareness of the horizontal position of the boat, an experience which is extremely frightening. Pfeiffer (1982) pointed out that

> In panic-stricken anguish and with violent vegetative reaction, they can become so helpless that they have to be guided to land by their companions. The disturbance often takes a progressive course, so that a large number of victims are unable to continue in the kayak hunt (p. 204).

Like agoraphobia, the anxiety is relieved in kayak-angst when the subject is reached by others and brought into a situation where other people are around.

THE CROSS-CULTURAL MEASUREMENT OF ANXIETY BY PSYCHOLOGICAL INVENTORIES

One of the early studies of cross-cultural anxiety using psychological inventories was reported by Cattell and Scheier (1961). Using the IPAT Anxiety Scale, they found significant differences in anxiety level among six cultural groups of college students. American students had the lowest level of anxiety, followed by the British, Italians, and French, with the Indians and the Polish obtaining the highest scores. National differences were explained in terms of standard of living and the relative political freedom in these countries. Two other studies by Tsujioka and Cattell (1965) and Cattell and Warburton (1961) compared students in the United States with Japanese and British students, respectively. It was found that Americans were less anxious than Japanese, with the British showing the lowest level of anxiety.

The State-Trait Anxiety Inventory (STAI)

Spielberger (1966, 1972) discussed the measurement of anxiety and elaborated on the concepts of state and trait anxiety originally introduced by Cattell and Scheier (1961). He also developed short reliable and valid scales to measure state and trait anxiety in adults (Spielberger, Gorsuch, & Lushene, 1970) and children (Spielberger, 1973). In the first volume of *Cross-cultural anxiety*, edited by Spielberger and Diaz-Guerrero (1976), the authors discussed the adaptation of the STAI and the problems arising from its use in cross-cultural research. Instead of following a procedure of literal translation of the items and 'back translation' into the original language, which is usually emphasized in cross-cultural approaches, they recommended either adapting the original items or constructing new items, particularly in the translation of idiomatic expressions. In the same volume they reported the construction and validation of the Spanish, Portuguese, French, Hindi, and Turkish forms of the STAI, as well as the development of the Spanish Children's Form. The development and validation of the Russian, Hungarian, and Kiswahili forms of the STAI were reported in the second volume of the same series by Spielberger and Diaz-Guerrero (1983). They also reported that the adapted forms of the State-Trait Anxiety Inventory for Children (STAIC) (Spielberger, 1973) were available for use with German, Greek, Portuguese, Spanish, and Turkish populations. The adaptation of the Spielberger measures of anxiety for research in different cultures was considered supportive evidence of the universality of the anxiety phenomenon.

In the first volume of Spielberger and Diaz-Guerrero (1976), Endler and Magnusso compared Canadian and Swedish students on A-trait and A-state. They argued that the relationship between A-trait and A-state is influenced by the nature of the evocative situations in the context of possible person-by-situation interactions. They mentioned that in some situations one aspect of A-state, such as an autonomic and physiological response, may be aroused rather than others, such as avoidance responses, suggesting a multidimensionality of A-trait. In comparing Canadian and Swedish samples, Endler and Magnusson (1976) used two self-report trait anxiety inventories (a revised form of the SS-R Inventory of General Trait Anxiousness, and the A-trait scale of the Spielberger State-Trait Anxiety Inventory), as well as two self-report measures of state anxiety (the Behavioral Reaction Questionnaire and the A-State scale of the Spielberger State-Trait Anxiety Inventory). The results of the factor analysis showed considerable similarities between the two cultures. The trait anxiety situation scales yielded two main factors for both the Swedish and the Canadian male and female samples: interpersonal ego threat and physical danger, suggesting two types of anxiety (shame anxiety and harm anxiety). Analysis of the state anxiety measures yielded at least three factors for both the Swedish and Canadian subjects, with similar factor structure for both samples. Yet the patterning with respect to specific item loadings was different for the two groups. With respect to cultural differences, Swedish subjects reported more physical danger and ambiguous (novel) trait anxiety and less general trait anxiety than Canadian males and females combined. Overall, considering the similarities between the two cultures, it is not surprising that Endler and Magnusson concluded that "there is a remarkable similarity between Swedish and Canadian college students with respect to anxiety reactions in different kinds of situations" (p. 169). However, because of the selective nature of the samples, it is difficult to generalize these results to the whole population in Canada or Sweden.

More recently, Endler (1983) developed the original Endler and Magnusson ideas into an interactional model in which he emphasized the situational context in the assessment of trait anxiety. He pointed out that the particular cultural context influences both the situations that evoke anxiety and the way in which the individual experiences are perceived and interpreted. In order to test this model cross-culturally, Endler, Lobel, Parker, and Schmitz (1991) used the Endler Multidimensional Anxiety Scales (EMAS) (Endler, Edwards, & Vitelli, 1990), consisting of self-report measures of state and trait anxiety and based on Endler's interactional model. Factor analyses of the EMAS-state items with samples of Canadian and American college students and normal adults have yielded two separate factors, cognitive worry and autonomic emotional factors. The EMAS-trait measure assesses the predisposition to experience anxiety in four different types of threatening situations: social evaluation, physical danger, ambiguous situations, and daily routines. Endler et al. (1991) studied the psychometric adequacy of the EMAS and its generalizability for use with American, Canadian, German, and Israeli undergraduate students. It was found that Israelis scored significantly lower than the other three groups on trait anxiety. According to the authors, "the Israelis normally live amidst higher tension than young adults from the other three cultures and may have to adapt to this tension by developing a cognitive schema that helps them to cope with these stresses" (p. 269). A factor analysis of subscale scores indicated that the EMAS assesses separate state and trait dimensions. With the exception of the Israeli sample, factor analysis of the EMAS-State items supports the distinction between cognitive-worry and autonomic-emotional state anxiety. The lack of empirical support for these two components of state anxiety in the Israeli subjects is explained by the low scores on the EMAS-State, and hence the failure to differentiate the two components.

Test Anxiety

Test anxiety is defined by Schwarzer, van der Ploeg, and Spielberger (1982)

as a situation-specific personality trait that contains a cognitive component, called "worry", and an affective arousal-related component, called "emotionality". Research on test anxiety has focussed on perceptions of achievement situations as threats to the self. In essence, test anxiety refers to individual difference in the disposition to experience feelings of apprehension and worry cognitions in academic environments where the performance of students is under scrutiny. (p. 4)

One of the early studies of test anxiety was reported by Diaz-Guerrero (1976), who compared Mexican and American school children using the Test Anxiety Scale for Children (TASC) developed by Sarason, Davidson, Lighthall, Waite, and Ruebush (1960). Items that make up a lie scale and a defensiveness scale were also added to TASC. Subjects consisted of a total of 392, half Mexican and half American, from first, fourth and seventh grades. These school children were equated for sex, socio-economic level, and school grade at the time they were initially tested. The overall results for the groups revealed higher scores for Mexican than American children on all three scales. The difference between the two groups was the largest on TASC and relatively smaller on the Defensiveness Scale. Regardless of culture, subjects from the lower socioeconomic class scored higher on the test anxiety scale than those from the upper socioeconomic level. However, there were no differences on the lie and defensiveness scales as a function of socioeconomic level. Similarly, girls scored higher on TASC in both cultures. Most recent cross-cultural research on test anxiety used the Test Anxiety Inventory (TAI) developed by Spielberger (1980). Between 1982 and 1992, H. M. van der Ploeg, R. Schwarzer, and C. D. Spielberger edited six volumes (K. A. Hagtvet and T. B. Johnson edited the seventh volume) entitled *Advances in test anxiety research,* reporting data dealing mainly with TAI across cultures. The TAI was translated into almost all European languages, many southeast Asian languages, Hindi, and Arabic. The volumes reported studies on the psychometric characteristics of the TAI showing high reliability and validity. The two factors of emotionality and worry were reported in many cultures. Studies reveal that in most non-Western countries such as Arab countries, Korea, Mexico, and Turkey, test anxiety scores of students on the TAI tended to be significantly higher than those obtained in Western countries. There was almost consistent evidence that girls score higher than boys on the TAI (e.g., Schwarzer & Kim, 1984). Richmond, Rodrigo, and Lusiardo (1989) found social-class differences in test anxiety in Uruguay, supporting previous research data from other cultures (Boyce, 1974; Gunthley & Sinha, 1983; Ziv & Luz, 1973).

Concluding Remarks

The major aim of cross-cultural studies of anxiety has been to establish the universality of the concept of anxiety and its structure. We concur with the conclusion of an early review of culture and anxiety (Good & Kleinman, 1985) that the evidence indicates that:

anxiety and disorders of anxiety are universally present in human societies. It makes equally clear that the phenomenology of such disorders, the meaningful forms through which distress is articulated and constituted as social reality, varies in quite significant ways across cultures. (p. 298)

In this vein, psychologists and psychiatrists have translated personality inventories, symptom checklists, and interview schedules from English into different languages with the prospect of investigating the universality of anxiety. The specific aim of these studies was to find out whether the same dimensions of anxiety and similar structure occurred cross-culturally; in this way the prevalence of anxiety could be compared across cultures. A major question that may be raised is whether anxiety as reflected by the translated instruments from English is conceptually equivalent across cultures. In the first volume of *Cross-cultural anxiety,* Spielberger and Sharma (1976) warned translators of the Spielberger State-Trait Anxiety Inventory by pointing out nuances of meaning of some words in English, for example, feeling comfortable versus feeling at ease, or the overlap between the words *worry, tense,* and *jittery.* These words may not have an equivalence in other languages. Moreover, when an inventory is modified and adapted to the new culture, the meaning of the total score of anxiety in the new version may not mean the same thing as those from the original version. Thus, while comparison of certain variables within a culture (e.g., gender or social class differences) may be valid, anxiety scores across cultures may not be the same. For example, significantly high scores on the Spielberger TAI by Arab, Korean, or Turkish students as compared with Americans may reflect the use of different measures of anxiety rather than true cultural differences in anxiety levels.

In order to overcome the problem of equivalence of translated tests, scores from bilingual subjects were compared on the translated and the original English versions of the test. Similar scores on the two tests by bilinguals was reported as evidence of cross-cultural validity of the tests (e.g., Bergeron, 1983). However, similar scores on an inventory or symptom checklist may not overcome cultural bias reflected in the weight of individual items in each culture and their contribution to the total score. Inkeles (1983), for example, found in a cross-national study that although the average response to a symptom checklist is quite similar between Indian, Chilean, Israeli, and Nigerian subjects, the frequency of reporting particular symptoms varied significantly from one country to another. For example, "trouble sleeping" and "nervousness" were reported more frequently in India, while "heart beating," "shortness of breath" and "disturbing dream" were most emphasized by Nigerians. "Shortness of breath" was the least frequently reported in both India and Israel. Thus, the type of symptoms included in the measurement of anxiety and their frequency in a population may increase or decrease the mean scores on the measurement instrument, depending on the cultural background.

Samples used by psychologists to assess the psychometric characteristics of State-Trait Anxiety or Test Anxiety in other cultures were random samples of "normal" students, and results may not be generalized to the whole population. We still do not know how patients diagnosed with anxiety disorders or students seeking help for anxiety disorders react to anxiety inventories.

The seven volumes of *Advances in test anxiety research* referred to earlier in this review reported impressive evidence of the universality of emotionality and worry as dimensions of the Spielberger TAI, but one wonders whether the same factors would be obtained if the investigators had measured the full range of culture-specific idioms of anxiety in different cultures. Worry, for example, is an important part of the cognitive dimension of anxiety, but the subjects of worry may vary from one culture to another. Early clinical observations of anxiety states in Nigeria (Collis, 1966) indicated that most patients' worries were culturally conditioned concerns with procreation and maintaining a large family, leading to anxieties associated with sterility, impotence, or death of a child or a spouse. In contrast, they do not worry about their work or complain about difficulty in concentration, loss of interest, and poor memory usually seen in Western patients (cf. Borkovec, Shadick, & Hopkins, 1991). Collis (1966) also found that although nightmares are associated with anxiety in Nigeria, their contents are different; they tend to be stylized in the form of visitations from ancestors.

A valid cross-cultural model of anxiety should be emically conceived and constructed in different cultures. Investigations reviewed by Good and Kleinman (1985) and Murphy (1982) in Senegal (Beiser, Benfari, Collomb, & Ravel, 1976; Beiser, Ravel, Collomb, & Egelhoff, 1972; Benfari, Beiser, Leighton, & Mertens, 1972) and in India (Carstairs & Kapur, 1976) have developed their anxiety measurement instruments by exploring clinical and anthropological findings concerning native illness lexicons to form the basis of their investigation. For instance, the Beiser team's measure of anxiety was based on interviews with native healers and discussions with persons who were identified by informers as suffering from "illnesses of the spirit." Similarly, Carstairs and Kapur (1976) developed a Psychiatric Interview Schedule based on local expressions of distress, such as spirit possession and preoccupation with sexual inadequacy. Carstairs and Kapur (1976) also measured dysfunction on the basis of local norms. More recently, Okasha and Ashour (1981) made many changes in the items of the Present State Examination (PSE) to conform with local expression of anxiety in Egypt (e.g., items related to possession, witchcraft, sexual inadequacy, and praying were added to the PSE). Future research on anxiety across cultures should start with local idioms of distress as the basis for the measurement of anxiety, rather than with symptoms of Western patients (Ebigo, 1982). Clinical psychology and psychiatry are predominantly etically oriented, and early research endeavors in the 1970s to define anxiety emically have not yet been emulated in the study and measurement of anxiety across cultures.

TREATMENT OF ANXIETY IN THE CULTURALLY DIFFERENT

Little attention has been given to ethnic response to behavioral and organic treatment of anxiety disorders. However, some recent evidence suggests that sociocultural factors play a major role in both the diagnosis and treatment of ethnic groups in the United States. Although it has been suggested that the basic symptoms of anxiety are similar among ethnic groups in the United States (Friedman, Paradis, & Hatch, 1994), how these symptoms are expressed may result in the misdiagnosis of non-White patients. For example, Friedman et al. (1994) pointed out that certain expressions of anxiety (e.g., "someone is doing roots on me") among African-Americans are often considered as signs of psychosis rather than culturally appropriate symptoms of anxiety. Similarly, Williams and Chambless (1994) reported that African Americans present an atypical picture of panic disorder with agoraphobia. While agoraphobics in general are almost always frightened by their panic sensation, several of the African Americans expressed more than the usual distress about their symptoms, describing them in a misleading language such as "getting mental, going crazy, feeling really paranoid." However, further exploration by Williams and Chambless revealed that these patients were simply describing the fear that accompanies the panic attack.

An example of a symptom not described in *DSM-IV* (American Psychiatric Association, 1994) criteria for panic disorder but related to such a diagnosis among African Americans is isolated sleep paralysis (ISP). Sleep paralysis is a state of consciousness occurring while one is falling asleep or awakening. It lasts from several seconds to a few minutes and is characterized by inability to move. Vivid hallucinations (hypnopompic and hypnagogic) often occur with the feeling of acute danger. Once the paralysis passes, the subject sits up with a start and experiences symptoms of panic, such as tachycardia, hyperventilation, and fear. Sleep paralysis is usually associated with narcolepsy, but when it occurs in the absence of narcolepsy, it is referred to as ISP (Bell & Jenkins, 1994). ISP is more common among African Americans and tends to be associated with panic disorder (Bell, Hildreth, Jenkins, & Carter, 1988). It is so common among African Americans that it is incorporated into their folklore and described as "Being ridden by the witch or haint" or "grabbed or held by the spider." Hallucinations accompanying ISP may be described as visitations from a dead loved one, increasing the probability of misdiagnosis of panic disorder (Lewis-Hall, 1994).

Misdiagnosis of African Americans has resulted in higher rates of unnecessary hospitalization and the prescription of antipsychotic drugs (Friedman et al., 1994; Williams & Chambless, 1994). Since antipsychotic medication can worsen the symptoms of agoraphobic clients (Klein & Fink, 1962) African American patients seem more likely to be inappropriately medicalized.

Behavior therapy

In vivo exposure tends to help African Americans with agoraphobia (Williams & Chambless, 1994), yet the progress clients make in treatment seems to be influenced by race. A study by Williams and Chambless (1994) found that African Americans tended to report the same change as Whites in their ability to go to places alone, in their anxiety during the behavioral avoidance test, and in phobia severity. However, African Americans improved less on the frequency of panic attacks, a result obtained previously by Friedman and Paradis (1991). Williams and Chambless (1994) suggested that socioeconomic status may in part account for the disparity between Whites and African American patients. The daily life of an individual living in the poor inner city, with more crime and general danger, is more stressful than that of his or her suburban counterpart. Although socioeconomic status indicators such as educational and occupational level of the household were controlled in the study by Williams and Chambless (1994), the characteristics of the community in which the patients lived was not considered. A disproportionate number of African American clients lived and worked in the inner-city areas of Washington, D.C., while most White clients lived either in the suburbs or in the relatively safe areas of the city.

Another issue relates directly to prejudice, which interferes with treatment outcome. African Americans face daily incidents of discrimination. How discrimination may interfere with the behavioral treatment of agoraphobia is illustrated in the case of an African American woman during *in vivo* exposure to a shopping mall. As she and the therapist approached the shopping mall, she refused to continue the therapy session. The therapist thought that the problem was related to anticipatory anxiety, and he encouraged her not to be anxious, "but think of it as a chance to confront and overcome the fear." The dialogue between the client and the therapist that ensued is instructive:

Client:	No, you don't understand. I don't have any money with me. I can't buy anything.
Therapist:	That's OK. You can window shop. A lot of people do that. For some people, it's a cheap way to have a good time.
Client:	That's OK for you. White people can go into a store and just browse. But if a black person does it, the store security people will watch her like a hawk. If I don't act like I'm really buying something, they'll think I'm stealing. (Williams & Chambless, 1994, p. 159)

The process of exposure is clearly made more difficult when the fear of a panic attack is aggravated by encountering racism during actual exposure sessions. Williams and Chambless (1994) found that African American clients routinely encountered reactions of prejudice and discrimination during their treatment sessions and when carrying out exposure sessions on their own in grocery stores, restaurants, and department stores. The high level of stressors in African American life

> creates a state of arousal that impedes habituation during exposure and makes it more difficult to achieve the self-discipline to carry out practice sessions and to stick with an anxiety-inducing form of treatment. Not only do our African American clients encounter racism on a daily basis, but their lives seem to contain more major stress and minor hassles than the lives of our white clients. (Williams & Chambless, 1994, p. 159)

Another factor that might contribute to difficulties in therapy is a mismatch between therapist and client, since therapist-client racial differences may influence the outcome of therapy. Shared racial identity may be important in the perception of caring and involvement. Williams and Chambless (1990) found a positive correlation between the agoraphobic clients' perceptions of their therapists' caring and involvement on the one hand and improvement in the exposure treatment on the other.

Friedman et al. (1994) found that treatment with African American patients had a more successful outcome when the extended family was included. Referral of clients to different social services and providing instructions in child-management skills was also found to be helpful. Many African American patients who were single and unemployed benefited from this addition to standard cognitive-behavioral therapy and psychopharmacological treatment. Friedman et al. (1994) concluded that:

> cognitive-behavioral and psychopharmacological approaches have been validated in research with White, middle class and often highly educated patients. These approaches can be successfully applied to people from other ethnic, racial, or socioeconomic backgrounds. It appears, however, that treatment protocols may be more successful if they are adapted to fit the particular needs of each population. (p. 144)

Uba (1994) pointed out that in the treatment of ethnic minorities, a distinction should be made between social anxiety and intergroup anxiety. Intergroup anxiety stems from contact with outgroup members and anticipation of negative consequences (Stephan and Stephan, 1985). In responding to psychological inventories, scores of ethnic groups (e.g., Asian Americans) may be raised because of intergroup anxiety (Uba, 1994). It was found that the more ethnic minorities in the United States were acculturated, the less they experienced group anxiety (Bowler, Rauch, & Schwarzer, 1985). Intergroup anxiety as measured by physiological responses was positively associated with the degree of prejudice of White subjects toward minorities (Al-Issa, 1997; Dijker, 1987; Vidulich & Krevanick, 1966). Systematic desensitization is found useful in reducing prejudice (Sappington, 1976) and may be effective in dealing with intergroup anxiety.

Drug therapy

In recent years, there has been a growing area of study involving differential interethnic pharmacological responses to various psychotropic drugs. Different ethnic groups showed varied responsiveness to beta blockers, such as the treatment for hypertension that is less effective in African Americans than in Whites (Moser & Lunn, 1981). It is suggested that Asian Americans may be more sensitive to the effects of various psychotropics, including anxiolytics, than Whites (Kumana, Lauder, Chan, Ko, & Lin, 1987; Murphy, 1969; Rosenblat & Tang, 1987). Results of these studies showed that the mean dosages of benzodiazepines received by Asians were about one half to two thirds of those prescribed for their White counterparts. It is suggested that African Americans may respond more rapidly than Whites to tricyclic antidepressants. Fleishaker and Phillips (1989) compared African Americans and Whites on adinazolam, a benzodiazepine, and found that African Americans showed both larger metabolic capacity and a stronger drug effect due to higher plasma levels of the active metabolite n-demethyl adinazolam. Ethnic differences in the pharmacological treatment of anxiety disorders are reviewed in more detail by Hollander and Cohen (1994) and Lesser, Lin, and Poland (1994).

CONCLUSIONS

Epidemiological data suggest that anxiety disorders are universal. However, the meaning of the concept of anxiety and of its manifestations seems to vary from one culture to another. This poses validity problems in the measurement or diagnosis of anxiety across cultures. Test anxiety and state-trait anxiety inventories have been translated into many languages, but problems related to linguistic and metric equivalence still remain unresolved. It is suggested that the transcultural measurement of anxiety should follow an emic approach that takes into consideration the idioms of distress of particular cultures. This would avoid problems related to equivalence in the application of anxiety inventories in specific cultural settings.

Behavioral-cognitive principles seem to be universal. However, the therapeutic application of these principles requires some adaptation to clients from different ethnic groups and other cultures. Problems brought into the therapeutic situation by ethnic groups and clients from other cultures tend to be direct and concrete and perhaps more related to economical, racial, and political issues. Therapy has to deal with the immediate problems of the clients that may be the source of their psychological maladjustment. An important growing area of research involves ethnic differences in reaction to drug therapy for anxiety disorders.

References

Akhtar, S., Wig, N. N., Varma, V. K., Pershad, D., & Verma, S. K. (1975). A phenomenological analysis of symptoms in obsessive-compulsive neurosis. *British Journal of Psychiatry, 127,* 342–348.

Al-Issa, I. (1997). The psychology of prejudice and discrimination. In I. Al-Issa & M. Tousignont (Eds.), *Ethnicity, immigration and psychopathology* (17–32). New York: Plenum.

American Psychiatric Association. (1952). *Diagnostic and statistical manual of mental disorders.* Washington, DC: Author.

American Psychiatric Association. (1980). *Diagnostic and statistical manual of mental disorders* (3rd ed.). Washington, DC: Author.

Auden, W. H. (1946). *The age of anxiety.* New York: Random House.

Averill, G. R. (1968). Grief: Its nature and significance. *Psychological Bulletin, 70,* 721–748.

Barron, D. L. (1994). *DSM-IV:* Making it culturally relevant. In S. Friedman (Ed.), *Anxiety disorders in African-Americans* (pp. 15–39). New York: Springer.

Beiser, M., Benfari, R. C., Collomb, H., & Ravel, J. (1976). Measuring psychoneurotic behavior in cross-cultural surveys. *Journal of Nervous and Mental Disease, 163,* 10–23.

Beiser, M., Ravel, J., Collomb, H., & Egelhoff, C. (1972). Assessing psychiatric disorder among the Serer of Senegal. *Journal of Nervous and Mental Disease, 154,* 141–151.

Bell, C. C., Hildreth, C. J., Jenkins, E. J., & Carter, C. (1988). The relationship of isolated sleep paralysis and panic disorder to hypertension. *Journal of the National Medical Association, 80,* 289–294.

Bell, C. C., & Jenkins, E. J. (1994). Isolated sleep paralysis and anxiety disorders. In S. Friedman (Ed.). *Anxiety disorders in African-Americans* (pp. 117–127). New York: Springer.

Benfari, R. C., Beiser, M., Leighton, A. H., & Mertens, C. (1972). Some dimensions of psychoneurotic behavior in an urban sample. *Journal of Nervous and Mental Disease, 155,* 77–90.

Bergeron, J. (1983). State-trait anxiety in French-English bilinguals: Cross-cultural considerations. In C. D. Spielberger & R. Diaz-Guerrero (Eds.), *Cross-cultural anxiety* (Vol. 2, pp. 157–176). Washington, DC: Hemisphere.

Bertschy, G., & Ahyi, R. G. (1991). Obsessive-compulsive disorder in Benin: Five case reports. *Psychopathology, 24,* 398–401.

Blazer, D. G., Hughes, D., George, L. K., Swartz, M., & Boyer, R. (1991). Generalized anxiety disorder. In L. N. Robins & D. A. Regier (Eds.), *Psychiatric disorders in America: The epidemiologic catchment area study* (180–203). New York: The Free Press.

Borkovec, T. D., Shadick, R. N., & Hopkins, M. (1991). The nature of normal and pathological worry. In R. M. Rapee & D. H. Barlow (Eds.), *Chronic anxiety: Generalized anxiety disorder and mixed anxiety-depression* (pp. 29–51). New York: Guilford Press.

Bowler, R., Rauch, S., & Schwarzer, R. (1985). Anxiety in multiethnic high schools. In H. M. van der Ploeg, R. Schwarzer, & C. D. Spielberger (Eds.), *Test anxiety research* (Vol. 4, pp. 183–201). Lisse Netherlands: Swets & Zeitlinger.

Boyce, M. W. (1974). Student teacher misconceptions of manifestations of anxiety in children from different socioeconomic ethnicity background. *Australian and New Zealand Journal of Sociology, 10,* 138–139.

Breslau, N. (1985). Depressive symptoms, major depression and generalized anxiety. A comparison of self-reports on the CES-D and results from diagnostic interviews. *Psychiatry Research, 15,* 219–229.

Canino, G. J., Bird, H. R., Shrout, P. E., Rubio-Stipec, M., Bravo, M., Martinez, R., Sesman, M., & Guevara, L. M. (1978). The prevalence of specific psychiatric disorders in Puerto Rico. *Archives of General Psychiatry, 44,* 727–735.

Carstairs, G. M., & Kapur, R. L. (1976). *The Great Universe of Kota: Stress, change and mental disorder in an Indian village.* Berkeley, CA: University of California Press.

Cattell, R. B., & Scheier, I. H. (1961). *The meaning and measurement of neuroticism and anxiety.* New York: Ronald Press.

Cattell, R. B., & Warburton, F. W. (1961). A cross cultural comparison of patterns of extroversion and anxiety. *British Journal of Psychology, 52,* 3–15.

Chakraborty, A., & Banerji, G. (1975). Ritual: A culture-specific neurosis, and obsessional states in Bengali culture. *Indian Journal of Psychiatry, 17,* 211–216.

Chataway, C. J., & Berry, J. W. (1989). Acculturation experiences, appraisal, coping and adaptation: A comparison of Hong Kong Chinese, French, and English students in Canada. *Canadian Journal of Behavioral Science, 21,* 295–309.

Collignon, R., & Gueye, M. (1995). The interface between culture and mental illness in French-speaking West Africa. In I. Al-Issa (Ed.), *Culture and mental illness: An international perspective* (93–112). Madison, WI: International Universities Press.

Collis, R. I. M. (1966). Physical health and psychiatric disorder in Nigeria. *Transactions of the American Philosophical Society, 56,* 1–45.

Compton, W. M., Helzer, J. E., Hwu, H., Hey, E., McEvoy, L., Tipp, J. E., & Spitznagel, E. L. (1991). New methods in cross-cultural psychiatry: Psychiatric illness in Taiwan and the United States. *American Journal of Psychiatry, 148,* 1697–1704.

de Silva, P. (1988). Phobias and preparedness: Replication and extension. *Behaviour Research and Therapy, 26,* 97–98.

de Silva, P., Rachman, S., & Seligman, M. E. P. (1972). Prepared phobias and obsessions: Therapeutic outcome. *Behaviour Research and Therapy, 15,* 65–77.

Diaz-Guerrero, R. (1976). Test anxiety and general anxiety in Mexican and American school children. In C. D. Spielberger & R. Diaz-Guerrero (Eds.), *Cross-cultural anxiety* (Vol. 1, pp. 135–142). Washington: Hemisphere.

Dijker, A. J. M. (1987). Emotional reactions to ethnic minorities. *European Journal of Social Psychology, 17,* 305–325.

Eaton, J. W., & Weil, R. J. (1970). The mental health of the Hutterites. In I. Al-Issa & W. Dennis (Eds.), *Cross-cultural studies of behavior* (445–454). New York: Holt, Rinehart & Winston.

Ebigo, P. O. (1982). Development of a culture specific (Nigeria) screening scale of somatic complaints indicating psychiatric disturbance. *Culture, Medicine and Psychiatry, 6,* 29–43.

El-Islam, M. F. (1994). Cultural aspects of morbid fear in Qatari women. *Social Psychiatry and Psychiatric Epidemiology, 29,* 137–140.

Endler, N. S. (1983). Interactionism: A personality model, but not yet a theory. In M. M. Page (Ed.), *Nebraska Symposium on Motivation—1982: Personality—Current theory and research* (pp. 155–200). Lincoln: University of Nebraska Press.

Endler, N. S., Edwards, J. M., & Vitelli, R. (1990). *Endler Multidimensional Anxiety Scales: Manual.* Los Angeles, CA: Western Psychological Services.

Endler, N. S., Lobel, T., Parker, J. D. A., & Schmitz, P. (1991). Multidimensionality of state and trait anxiety: A cross-cultural study comparing American, Canadian, Israeli and German young adults. *Anxiety Research, 3,* 257–272.

Fleishaker, J. C., & Phillips, J. P. (1989). Adinazolam pharmacokinetics and behavioral effects following administration of 20–60 mg oral doses of its mesylate salt in healthy volunteers. *Psychopharmacology, 99,* 34–39.

Friedman, S., & Paradis, C. (1991). African-American patients with panic disorder and agoraphobia. *Journal of Anxiety Disorders, 5,* 35–41.

Friedman, S., Paradis, C. M., & Hatch, M. L. (1994). Issues of misdiagnosis in panic disorder with agoraphobia. In S. Friedman (Ed.), *Anxiety disorders in African-Americans* (pp. 128–146). New York: Springer.

Good, B. J., & Kleinman, A. M. (1985). Culture and anxiety: Cross-cultural evidence for the patterning of anxiety disorders. In A. H. Tuma & J. D. Maser (Eds.), *Anxiety and the anxiety disorders* (297–323). Hillsdale, NJ: Erlbaum.

Guarnaccia, P. J., De La Cancela, V., & Carrillo, E. (1989). The multiple meanings of *ataques de nervios* in the Latino community. *Medical Anthropology, 11,* 47–62.

Guarnaccia, P. J., & Farias, P. (1988). The social meaning of nervios: A case study of the central American woman. *Social Science and Medicine, 26,* 1223–1231.

Gunthley, R., & Sinha, P. C. (1983). Socioeconomic status as a determinant of anxiety, adjustment and affiliation in teenagers. *Indian Psychological Review, 24,* 1–6.

Hagnell, O., Lanke, J., Rosman, B., & Oyesjo, L. (1982). Are we entering an age of melancholy? *Psychological Medicine, 12,* 279–289.

Hallowell, A. I. (1970). Fear and anxiety as cultural and individual variables in a primitive society. In I. Al-Issa & W. Dennis (Eds.), *Cross-cultural studies of behavior* (pp. 467–475). New York: Holt, Rinehart & Winston.

Hollander, E., & Cohen, L. J. (1994). Obsessive-compulsive disorder. In S. Friedman (Ed.), *Anxiety disorders in African-Americans* (pp. 185–202). New York: Springer.

Hollifield, M., Katon, W., Spain, D., & Pule, L. (1990). Anxiety and depression in a village in Lesotho, Africa: A comparison with the United States. *British Journal of Psychiatry, 156,* 343–350.

Huang, L. N., & Ying, Y. W. (1989). Chinese American children and adolescents. In J. T. Gibbs, L. N. Huang and associates (Eds.), *Children of color: Psychological interventions with minority children* (pp. 30–66). San Francisco: Jossey-Bass.

Inkeles, A. (1983). *Exploring individual modernity.* New York: Columbia University Press.

Jablensky, A. (1985). Approaches to definition and classification of anxiety and related disorders in European psychiatry. In A. H. Tuma & J. D. Maser (Eds.), *Anxiety and the anxiety disorders* (pp. 735–773). Hillside, NJ: Erlbaum.

Jones, I. H. (1972). Psychiatric disorders among aborigines of the Australian Western Desert. *Social Science and Medicine, 6,* 263–267.

Karno, M., & Golding, J. M. (1991). Obsessive-compulsive disorder. In L. N. Robins & D. A. Regier (Eds.), *Psychiatric disorders in America: The epidemiologic catchment area study* (pp. 204–219). New York: The Free Press.

Kessler, R. C., McGonangle, K. A., Zhao, S., Nelson, C. B., Hughes, M. Eshelman, S., Wittchen, H., & Kendler, K. S. (1994). Life time and 12 month prevalence of *DSM-III-R* psychiatric disorders in the United States: Results from a national comorbidity survey. *Archives of General Psychiatry, 51,* 8–20.

Kidson, M. A., & Jones, I. H. (1968). Psychiatric disorders among aborigines of the Australian Western Desert. *Archives of General Psychiatry, 19,* 413–417.

Klein, D. F., & Fink, M. (1962). Behavioral reaction patterns with phenothiazines. *Archives of General Psychiatry, 7,* 449–459.

Kleinnecht, R. A., Dinnel, D. L., Tanouye, W. S., & Lonner, W. J. (1994). Cultural variation in social anxiety: A study of Taijen Kyofush. *The Behavior Therapist, 17,* 175–178.

Kumana, C. R., Lauder, I. J., Chan, M., Ko, W., & Lin, H. J. (1987). Differences in diazepam pharmacokinetics in Chinese and White Caucasians: Relation to body lipid store. *European Journal of Clinical Pharmacology, 32,* 211–215.

Kuo, W. H., & Tsai, Y. M. (1986). Social networking, hardiness and immigrant's mental health. *Journal of Health and Social Behavior, 27,* 133–149.

Leighton, A. H., Lambo, T. A., Hughes, C. A., Leighton, D. C., Murphy, J. M., & Macklin, D. B. (1966). *Psychiatric disorder among the Yoruba.* Ithaca, NY: Cornell University Press.

Leighton, D. C., Harding, J. S., Macklin, D. B., MacMillan, A. M., & Leighton, A. H. (1963). *The character of danger: Psychiatric symptoms in selected communities.* New York: Basic Books.

Lesser, I., Lin, K. M., & Poland, R. (1994). Ethnic difference in response to psychotropic drugs. In S. Friedman (Ed.), *Anxiety disorders in African-Americans* (pp. 203–231). New York: Springer.

Lewis, A. (1980). Problems presented by the ambiguous word 'anxiety' as used in psychopathology. In G. D. Burrows & B. Davies (Eds.), *Handbook of studies on anxiety* (pp. 1–15). Amsterdam: Elsevier/North Holland Biomedical Press.

Lewis-Hall, F. C. (1994). The use of *DSM* in the diagnosis of panic disorder and obsessive-compulsive disorder. In S. Friedman (Ed.), *Anxiety disorders in African-Americans* (pp. 102–116). New York: Springer.

Lin, M. C., & Endler, N. S. (1993). *State and trait anxiety: A cross-cultural comparison of Chinese and Caucasian students in a Canadian sample* (Res. Rep. No. 210). North York, Ontario, Canada: York University, Department of Psychology.

Linton, R. (1956). *Culture and mental disorders.* Springfield, IL: C. C.Thomas.

Low, S. M. (1981). The meaning of nervios: A sociocultural analysis of symptom presentation in San Jose, Costa Rica. *Culture, Medicine and Psychiatry, 5,* 25–48.

Mahgoub, O. M., & Abdel-Hafeiz, H. B. (1991). Pattern of obsessive-compulsive disorder in Eastern Saudi Arabia. *British Journal of Psychiatry, 158,* 840–842.

Marks, I. M., & Lader, M. (1973). Anxiety states (anxiety neurosis): A review. *Journal of Nervous and Mental Disease, 156,* 3–18.

Marks, I. M., & Nesse, R. M. (1994). Fear and fitness: An evolutionary analysis of anxiety disorders. *Ethology and Sociobiology, 15,* 247–261.

Mavreas, V. G., & Bebbington, P. E. (1988). Greeks, British Greek Cypriots and Londoners: A comparison of morbidity. *Psychological Medicine, 18,* 433–442.

May, R. (1977). *The meaning of anxiety.* New York: Ronald Press.

McReynolds, P. (1975). Changing conceptions of anxiety: A historical review and a proposed integration. In I. G. Sarason & C. D. Spielberger (Eds.), *Stress and anxiety* (Vol. 2, pp. 3–26). Washington, DC: Hemisphere.

Minde, K. K. (1974). Study problems in Uganda secondary school students: A controlled evaluation. *British Journal of Psychiatry, 125,* 131–137.

Moser, M., & Lunn, J. (1981). Comparative effects of pendolol and hydrochlorothiazide in black hypertensive patients. *Angiology, 32,* 561–566.

Mueller, J. H. (1992). Anxiety and performance. In A. P. Smith & D. M. Jones (Eds.), *Handbook of human performance* (Vol. 3, pp. 127–160). New York: Academic Press.

Murphy, H. B. M. (1969). Ethnic variations in drug responses. *Transcultural Psychiatric Research Review, 6,* 6–23.

Murphy, H. B. M. (1982). *Comparative psychiatry: The international and intercultural distribution of mental illness.* Berlin, Germany: Springer.

Neal, A. M., & Turner, S. M. (1991). Anxiety disorders research with African Americans: Current status. *Psychological Bulletin, 109,* 400–410.

Nemiah, J. C. (1984). Obsessive compulsive disorder. In H. I. Kaplan & B. J. Sadock (Eds.), *Comprehensive textbook of psychiatry* (4th ed., pp. 904–917). Baltimore: Williams & Wilkins.

Okasha, A., & Ashour, A. (1981). Psycho-demographic study of anxiety in Egypt: The PSE in its Arabic version. *British Journal of Psychiatry, 139,* 70–73.

Okasha, A., Saad, A., Khalil, A.H., El Dawla, A. S., & Yehia, N. (1994). Phenomenology of obsessive-compulsive disorder: A transcultural study. *Comprehensive Psychiatry, 35,* 191–197.

Orley, J., & Wing, J. K. (1979). Psychiatric disorders in two African villages. *Archives of General Psychiatry, 36,* 513–520.

Padilla, A. M., Wagatsuma, Y., & Lindholm, K. J. (1984). Acculturation and personality as predictors of stress in Japanese and Japanese-Americans. *Journal of Social Psychology, 125,* 295–305.

Pfeiffer, W. (1982). Culture-bound syndromes. In I. Al-Issa (Ed.), *Culture and psychopathology* (pp. 201–218). Baltimore: University Park Press.

Prince, R. (1981). Some transcultural aspects of adolescent affective disorder: The example of the brain-fag syndrome. *Transcultural Psychiatric Research Review, 18,* 53–54.

Prince, R. (1991). Transcultural psychiatry's contribution to international classification systems: The example of social phobias. *Transcultural Psychiatric Research Review, 28,* 124–132.

Prince, R. H. (1960). The "brain-fag" syndrome in Nigerian students. *Journal of Mental Science, 106,* 559–570.

Racagni, G., & Smeraldi, E. (Eds.) (1987). *Anxious depression: Assessment and treatment.* New York: Raven Press.

Rachman, S. J., & Hodgson, R. J. (1980). *Obsessions and compulsions.* Englewood Cliffs, NJ: Prentice-Hall.

Rasmussen, S. A., & Tsuang, M. T. (1984). Epidemiology of obsessive-compulsive disorder: A review. *Journal of Clinical Psychiatry, 45,* 450–457.

Rasmussen, S. A., & Tsuang, M. T. (1986). Epidemiology and clinical features of obsessive-compulsive disorder. In M. A. Jenike, L. Baer, & W. Minichiello (Eds.), *Obsessive compulsive disorders* (pp. 23–44). Littleton, MA: PSG.

Richmond, B. O., Rodrigo, C., & Lusiardo, M. (1989). Measuring anxiety among children in Uruguay. In R. Schwarzer, H. M. van der Ploeg, & C. D. Spielberger (Eds.), *Advances in test anxiety* (Vol. 6, pp. 215–221). Amsterdam/Lisse: Smets & Zeitlinger.

Robins, L. N., & Regier, D. A. (1991). *Psychiatric disorders in America. The Epidemiologic catchment area study.* New York: The Free Press.

Rosenblat, R., & Tang, S. W. (1987). Do oriental psychiatric patients receive different dosages of psychotropic medication when compared with occidentals? *Canadian Journal of Psychiatry, 32,* 270–274.

Russell, J. G. (1989). Anxiety disorders in Japan: A review of the Japanese literature on Shinkeishitsu and Taijinkyofusho. *Culture, Medicine and Psychiatry, 13,* 391–403.

Sappington, A. A. (1976). Effects of desensitization of prejudiced whites to blacks upon subjects' stereotypes of blacks. *Perceptual and Motor Skills, 43,* 938.

Sarason, S. B., Davidson, K. S., Lighthall, F. F., Waite, R. R., & Ruebush, I. G. (1960). *Anxiety in elementary school children.* New York: Wiley.

Schwarzer, C., & Kim, M. J. (1984). Adaptation of the Korean form of the Test Anxiety Inventory: A research note. In H. M. van der Ploeg, R. Schwarzer, & C. S. Spielberger (Eds.), *Advances in test anxiety research* (Vol. 3, pp. 277–282). Lisse Netherlands: Swets & Zeitlinger.

Schwarzer, R., van der Ploeg, H. M., & Spielberger, C. D. (1982). Text anxiety: An overview of theory and research. In R. Schwarzer, H. M. van der Ploeg, & C. D. Spielberger (Eds.), *Advances in test anxiety research* (Vol. 1, pp. 3–9). Lisse Netherlands: Swets & Zeitlinger.

Seligman, M. E. P. (1971). Phobias and preparedness. *Behavior Therapy, 2,* 307–320.

Spielberger, C. D. (1966). Theory and research in anxiety. In C. D. Spielberger (Ed.), *Anxiety and behavior* (pp. 3–20). New York: Academic Press.

Spielberger, C. D. (1972). Anxiety as an emotional state. In C. D. Spielberger (Ed.), *Anxiety: Current trends in theory and research* (pp. 481–493). New York: Academic Press.

Spielberger, C. D. (1973). *Manual for the State-Trait Anxiety Inventory for Children.* Palo Alto, CA: Consulting Psychologists Press.

Spielberger, C. D. (1980). *Test Anxiety Inventory, preliminary professional manual for the Test Anxiety Inventory ("Test Attitude Inventory") TAI.* Palo Alto, CA: Consulting Psychologists Press.

Spielberger, C. D., & Diaz-Guerrero, R. (Eds.). (1976). *Cross-cultural anxiety* (Vol. 1). New York: Wiley.

Spielberger, C. D., & Diaz-Guerrero, R. (Eds.). (1983). *Cross-cultural anxiety* (Vol. 2). Washington, DC: Hemisphere.

Spielberger, C. D., & Sharma, S. (1976). Cross-cultural measurement of anxiety. In C. D. Spielberger & R. Diaz-Guerrero (Eds.), *Cross-cultural anxiety* (Vol. 1, pp. 13–25). New York: Wiley.

Spielberger, C. D., Gorsuch, R. L., & Lushene, R. G. (1970). *Manual for the State-Trait Anxiety Inventory.* Palo Alto, CA: Consulting Psychologists Press.

Staley, D., & Wand, R. R. (1995). Obsessive-compulsive disorder: A review of the cross-cultural epidemiological literature. *Transcultural Psychiatric Research Review, 32,* 103–136.

Stephan, W. G., & Stephan, C. W. (1985). Intergroup anxiety. *Journal of Social Issues, 41,* 157–175.

Sue, D. W., & Kirk, B. C. (1973). Differential characteristics of Japanese-American and Chinese-American college students. *Journal of Counseling Psychology, 20,* 142–148.

Sue, S., & Morishima, J. K. (1982). *The mental health of Asian Americans.* San Francisco, CA: Jossey-Bass.

Sung, B. L. (1985). Bicultural conflicts in Chinese immigrant children. *Journal of Comparative Family Studies, 16,* 255–269.

Takahashi, T. (1989). Social phobia syndrome in Japan. *Comprehensive Psychiatry, 30,* 45–52.

Tan, E. (1980). Transcultural aspects of anxiety. In G. D. Burrows & B. Davies (Eds.), *Handbook of studies on anxiety* (pp. 133–144). Amsterdam: Elsevier/North Holland Biomedical Press.

Tsujioka, B., & Cattell, R. (1965). A cross-cultural comparison of the second stratum questionnaire personality factor structures—anxiety and extroversion—in America and Japan. *Journal of Social Psychology, 65,* 205–219.

Uba, L. (1994). *Asian Americans: Personality patterns, identity and mental health.* New York: Guilford Press.

Uhlenhuth, E. G., Balter, M. B., Mellinger, G. D., Cisin, I. H, & Clinthorne, J. (1983). Symptom checklist syndromes in the general population: Correlations with psychotherapeutic drug use. *Archives of General Psychiatry, 40,* 1167–1173.

Vidulich, R. N., & Krevanick, F. W. (1966). Racial attitudes and emotional response to visual representation of the Negro. *Journal of Social Psychology, 68,* 82–93.

Warheit, G. J., Bell, R. A., Schwab, J. J., & Buhl, J. M. (1986). An epidemiologic assessment of mental health problems in the southeastern United States. In M. M. Weissman, J. K. Myers, & C. E. Ross (Eds.), *Community surveys of psychiatric disorders* (pp. 191–208). New Brunswick, NJ: Rutgers University Press.

Weissman, M. M. (1985). The epidemiology of anxiety disorders. In A. H. Tuma & J. D. Maser (Eds.), *Anxiety and the anxiety disorders* (pp. 275–296). Hillsdale, NJ: Erlbaum.

Weissman, M. M., Bland, R. C., Canino, G. J., Greenwald, S., Hwu, H., Lee, C. K., Newman, S. C., Oakley-Browne, M. A., Rubio-Stipel, M., Wickreamaratne, P. J., Wittchen, H., & Hey, E. (1994). The cross national epidemiology of obsessive compulsive disorder. *Journal of Clinical Psychiatry, 55* (Suppl.), 5–10.

Weissman, M. M., Myers, J. K., & Harding, P. S. (1978). Psychiatric disorders in a U.S. urban community. *American Journal of Psychiatry, 135,* 459–462.

Williams, K. E., & Chambless, D. (1994). The results of exposure-based treatment in agoraphobia. In S. Friedman (Ed.), *Anxiety disorders in African-Americans* (pp. 149–165). New York: Springer.

Williams, K. E., & Chambless, D. L. (1990). The relationship between therapist characteristics and outcome in vivo exposure treatment of agoraphobia. *Behavior Therapy, 21,* 111–116.

Wittchen, H., Essau, C. A., Von Zerssen, D., Kreig, J., & Zandig, M. (1992). Lifetime and six-month prevalence of mental disorders in the Munich follow-up study. *European Archives of Psychiatry and Clinical Neuroscience, 241,* 247–258.

World Health Organization. (1970, December). *Report of the Sixth WHO Seminar on Psychiatric Diagnosis and Classification and Statistics* (WHO Document MH71.7). Geneva, Switzerland: Author.

Zafiropoulon, M., & McPherson, F. M. (1986). Preparedness and severity and outcome of clinical phobias. *Behavioral Research and Therapy, 24,* 221–222.

Ziv, A., & Luz, M. (1973). Manifest anxiety in children of different economic levels. *Human Development, 16,* 224–232.

6

Cultural Aspects of Eating Disorders

INGRID C. FEDOROFF

TRACI MCFARLANE

In the past 30 years eating disorders have become widespread in Western societies. Anorexia nervosa is characterized by an intense fear of gaining weight that results in marked food restriction and a refusal to maintain a normal body weight (American Psychiatric Association [APA], 1994). Eating pathology is also recognized in normal and overweight individuals who engage in chaotic eating patterns. Bulimia nervosa is identified in these individuals by recurrent episodes of binge eating, followed by inappropriate compensatory behavior aimed at preventing weight gain. These behaviors include but are not limited to vomiting, fasting, excessive exercise, and misuse of laxatives, diuretics, and enemas. An essential feature of both anorexia and bulimia nervosa is a disturbance in the perception of personal body shape and weight (APA, 1994).

According to the American Psychiatric Association *Diagnostic and Statistical Manual of Mental Disorders* (*DSM-IV,* APA, 1994), eating disorders appear to be far more prevalent in industrialized societies. This may be related to the overabundance of food, but it is also likely to be influenced by societal norms that link attractiveness to being thin (APA, 1994). Indeed, the popular and scientific assumption is that the preoccupation with thinness and dieting rampant in Western societies is directly implicated in the etiology and expression of eating disorders (King, 1993; Striegel-Moore, Silberstein, & Rodin, 1986). However, it is well established that eating disorders are multidetermined and that culture is only one of many factors that contribute to the development of eating disorders (Garner & Garfinkel, 1980; Johnson, Steinberg, & Lewis, 1988). Furthermore, cultural factors can only be understood as they interact with the psychology and biology of the vulnerable individual. It has been stated that a culture cannot cause a disorder (Garner, Garfinkel, & Olmsted,

1983). With this caveat in place, the following chapter examines the cultural aspects of eating disorders.

PREOCCUPATION WITH THINNESS

Body weight and shape have traditionally been important indicators of attractiveness for women. Recently, low body weight and a lean shape have become the major factors for determining women's beauty and desirability in modern Western society (Hesse-Biber, Downey, & Clayton-Matthews, 1987). Historically, excess body weight was a sign of affluence, indicating that the person had ample resources. However, in current prosperous Western societies it is thinness that has become a status symbol for women. The association of body weight and social class seems to be much stronger for women than men, and it appears that slimmer physiques reflect upward mobility and fatter figures reflect downward mobility. It has been demonstrated that the pressure to remain thin in Western countries increases with socioeconomic status (SES) and overall wealth of the country (Goldblatt, Moore, & Stunkard, 1965; Moore, Stunkard, & Srole, 1962; Silverstone, Gordon, & Stunkard, 1969).

In addition, research has shown that fat is generally degraded and stigmatized in the Western world. For example, when asked to rank-order various categories of people as potential marital partners, American students reported preferring to marry an embezzler, cocaine user, shoplifter, and blind person before they would marry an obese person (Venes, Krupka, & Gerard, 1982). Obese children are rated by other children and adults as less successful, motivated, and intelligent than normal weight children. At later ages, beginning with adolescence, females are more targeted and affected by this prejudicial attitude (Tiggemann & Rothblum, 1988; Wooley & Wooley, 1979).

Since the 1960s, the ideal female body size has been getting smaller and less rounded. One study used *Playboy* magazine centerfolds and Miss America contestants to represent the Western ideal of feminine beauty. Changes over a 20-year period (i.e., 1959 to 1978) were examined within each group, revealing that the ideal shape for women has become progressively slimmer. Interestingly, while there were no differences in weight between Miss America contestants and winners until 1970, after that year winners' weights were consistently less than the average weight of all contestants (Garner, Garfinkel, Schwartz, & Thompson, 1980). An update to this study found that Miss America contestants continued to show a decrease in their weight from 1979 to 1988 (Wiseman, Gray, Mosimann, & Ahrens, 1992). Coupled with the fact that the actual weight and size of the female population has been increasing over this same time period (presumably due to better nutrition), this shrinking body ideal has put increasing pressure on Western women to become ever thinner. This obsession with thinness is so widespread that a moderate degree of body dissatisfaction is now normative among Western women (Rodin, Silberstein, & Striegel-Moore, 1985). Studies of college women indicate that they would like to have a smaller body shape than they currently possess, and the physique they choose as ideal is thinner than the one that men consider most attractive (Fallon & Rozin, 1985).

It is generally assumed that the female preference for ultraslim bodies is influenced by the media's glorification and proliferation of the thin female body ideal.

Women are confronted with an onslaught of messages from the media indicating that beauty, success, happiness, and self-worth are all predicated on achieving a slender body shape. The number of diet and exercise advertisements has been growing steadily for the last 30 years (Snow & Harris, 1986; Wiseman et al., 1992). Between 1960 and 1980, the number of diet articles in women's magazines increased dramatically (Garner et al., 1980), and there are now magazines devoted entirely to advice on dieting and reshaping the body. One study found that women's magazines contained 10.5 times more advertisements and articles promoting weight loss than a comparable sample of men's magazines (Andersen & DiDomenico, 1992). Interestingly, this figure corresponds to the sex ratio for eating disorders.

These images of unrealistically thin or toned women illustrate the myth that it is possible for all women to reshape their bodies. This myth produces feelings of failure and frustration in women who are confronted with images they are unable to attain. One study shows that Western women report feeling more depression, stress, guilt, shame, insecurity, and body dissatisfaction when they are exposed to thin models than when they see average-sized models or no models at all (Stice & Shaw, 1994). Further, in a survey of women who read fashion and beauty magazines, 46.5% said their feelings of self-esteem and confidence were undermined and 68% said they felt worse about their looks after reading these magazines (Then, 1992). Another study demonstrated that endorsement of the thin-ideal stereotype was positively correlated with eating pathology in Western women (Stice, Schupak-Neuberg, Shaw, & Stein, 1994).

This thin-ideal is far from a universal value. In developing countries, there has long been a direct *positive* correlation between body weight and SES (Powers, 1980). Studies among South Asian (Mayer, 1955) and Native American adults (Garb, Garb, & Stunkard, 1975) and children in South China (Chang, Lee, & Low, 1963) and the Philippines (Stunkard, 1977) have demonstrated that an increasing social status is associated with a heavier mean body weight. In some cultures obesity had been and is still considered an appealing secondary sexual characteristic and is admired as a symbol of health and economic security (Furnham & Baguma, 1994; Powers, 1980; Rudofsky, 1972). For example, the Chinese are known to associate fatness with longevity and prosperity, and their gods are usually portrayed as obese. In Sudan female obesity is equated with sexual attractiveness. In this culture a girl about to be married is encouraged by her mother and sisters to indulge in excessive eating (Elsarrag, 1968). Also, a greeting such as "you look fat and fresh today" is regarded as a compliment in certain areas of India (Naipaul, 1965; quoted in Buhrich, 1981).

One study examined how Kenyan Asian (Asian minority residing in East Africa), Kenyan British (native Kenyan Asians now residing in Britain), and British females perceived female body shapes that ranged from very thin to very fat. Although there was an overall preference for the midrange figures in both cultures, Kenyan Asian females tended to perceive thin female shapes slightly more negatively and fat female shapes significantly more positively than the comparable British group. Interestingly, the Kenyan British group's ratings were more similar to the British group than to the Kenyan Asian group (Furnham & Alibhai, 1983). It appeared that this group of native Africans, who had been exposed to Western culture, had adopted the Western preference for thinness, and that their perception and evaluation of body shapes was culturally influenced. Although the sample size was small and unrepresentative of the population, differences in SES and perception of body weight could not account for the results, as these variables were matched in each group. Another study compared the shape evaluations of British subjects with Ugandan subjects. Although both males and females were included, they did not differ from one another within each culture. As expected, there was an overall preference for midrange body shapes. However, Ugandan subjects rated the midrange to obese figures as more attractive than did the British subjects, and, apart from the very fattest figure, the differences became greater as the figures got fatter (Furnham & Baguma, 1994). As the figures increased in size, they were rated as more attractive by the Ugandan subjects and as less attractive by the British subjects. These studies demonstrate that in developing countries there is a greater desirability for fatness, and that the thin-ideal idolized in Western societies is not embraced by all cultures.

DIETING

It is not surprising that many Western men and women engage in dieting behavior in response to their society's obsession with thinness and revulsion toward fatness. American surveys taken between 1950 and 1966 reported that 7% of men and 15% of women were trying to lose weight. By 1978 16% of all adults were dieting, and in 1985 25% of men and 45% of women were dieting to lose weight (Williamson, Serdula, Anda, Levy, & Byers, 1992). Recently, two large American surveys indicated that approximately 24% of men and 40% of women are currently dieting (Horm & Anderson, 1993; Serdula et al., 1993). It appears that young women are particularly susceptible to societal pressures to diet. As early as 1977 it was shown in one survey that three quarters of Western college women had dieted in an attempt to control their weight (Jacobovits, Halstead, Kelley, Roe, & Young, 1977). Serious dieting has been reported by 40% of 18-year-old girls in Sweden (Nylander, 1971) and shown to be well established in British girls as young as 12 years old (Wardle & Beals, 1986). In fact, among young women and adolescent girls, dieting was shown to be more prevalent than not dieting (Polivy, Garner, & Garfinkel, 1986; Polivy & Herman, 1983; Rodin et al.,1985). Polivy and Herman (1987) recognized that "normal" eating for young North American women is now characterized by dieting behaviors.

It is commonly understood that women choose to diet in response to feeling overweight or out of shape. However, not all dieters are objectively overweight, and, for that matter, not all dieters perceive themselves as overweight. In one study, Canadian college women were objectively classified as underweight, normal weight, or overweight. Height and weight were measured in the laboratory and compared to life insurance expectations (Metropolitan Life Insurance Tables, 1983). Dieting status and subjective weight category data were also obtained. Interestingly, 58% of dieting subjects were actually normal weight or underweight. Further, only 66% of these normal weight or underweight dieters reported that they felt overweight. The rest of these dieters were dieting to lose weight, even though they accurately perceived themselves as normal weight or underweight (McFarlane, 1994).

One study examined dieting behavior and attitudes regarding weight among male and female college students in the United States and Australia. Fifty-five percent of all American students reported that they had dieted in the past, compared to only 42% of Australian students. Furthermore, 32% of Americans were currently dieting, whereas only 18% of Australians were presently on a diet.[1] In addition to dieting more frequently, American students reported more body consciousness and concern regarding weight than did Australian students (Tiggemann & Rothblum, 1988). In another study it was demonstrated that Egyptian women were less likely to be classified as dieters than a comparable sample of British women, whereas Egyptian men and British men did not differ with respect to dieting status (Dolan & Ford, 1991). These results suggest that the degree of concern with body weight and shape and the prevalence of dieting in women may be positively related to the extent of Westernization of their particular culture.

Unfortunately for the dieter, research studies have demonstrated that dieting is an ineffective method for producing weight loss (Heatherton, Polivy, & Herman, 1991). Furthermore, it has been proposed that dieting can lead to the onset of eating disorders in some individuals. Although restrained eating does not necessarily lead to an eating disorder, most cases of eating disorders are preceded by dieting (Boskind-Lodahl, 1976; Bruch, 1973; Garfinkel, Moldofsky, & Garner, 1980; Pyle, Mitchell, & Eckert, 1981; Russell, 1979). Many authors have related the increased incidence of anorexia nervosa to the cultural pressures to have a slender body and to the dieting behaviors that are believed to be required to achieve this goal (Garfinkel & Garner, 1982; Garner et al., 1983; Polivy et al., 1986; Silverstein, 1986; Wooley, 1987; Wooley & Wooley, 1979). Similarly, bulimia nervosa has been linked to dieting behavior (Hall & Hay, 1991; Marchi & Cohen, 1990; Polivy & Herman, 1985, 1987; Polivy, Herman, Olmsted, & Jazwinski, 1984; Striegel-Moore et al., 1986; Wardle & Beinart, 1981; Wooley, 1987). According to Polivy and Herman (1985), dieting promotes cognitively regulated eating behavior that renders the dieter more susceptible to disinhibition of restraint and consequent binge eating. It has been demonstrated that vulnerability to bingeing and persistent food preoccupation are common side effects of semistarvation and restrained eating in humans (Baucom & Aiken, 1981; Herman & Mack, 1975; Herman & Polivy, 1975; Keys, Brozek, Henschel, Mickelson, & Taylor, 1950).

To summarize, the obsession to achieve and maintain a thin body has been implicated in the development of eating disorders. This thin-ideal is most revered by upper- and middle-class women of Western society and is intensified by the constant barrage of media images emphasizing a slim physique. The goal of becoming thinner is usually pursued through dieting, which is considered to be an important factor in the etiology of eating disorders. According to all this evidence, then, one would expect eating disorders to be more prevalent in women than in men, in people having higher social status than lower social status, and in subcultures that emphasize a slender body shape than in the general population. Moreover, the prevalence and incidence of eating disorders should be positively related to the Westernization of a culture.

UNIVERSALITY OF SYMPTOMS

There is some discussion about whether there are universal symptoms of eating disorders. Studies employing various research strategies, including case studies, epidemiological surveys, and samples of particular populations in non-Western societies, have found evidence of common eating-disorder symptomatology as described by Western classification systems (Azuma & Henmi, 1982; Buhrich, 1981; Khandelwal & Saxena, 1990; Lee, Chui, & Chen, 1989; Mizushimi & Ishii, 1983; Mumford, Whitehouse, & Choudry, 1992; Nogami & Yabana, 1977, Okasha, Kamel, Sadek, Lotah, & Bishry, 1977; Ong, Tsoi, & Cheng, 1982; Suematsu, Ishikawa, & Kuboki, 1985; Yager & Smith, 1993). The authors of one study commented that during interviews of Pakistani schoolgirls, no other types of eating disorder symptoms other than those recognized by Western nosology were identified (Mumford et al., 1992). Yager and Smith (1993) described a case study of a Muslim girl raised in Pakistan who demonstrated the classic features of anorexia nervosa. In addition to having severe self-induced weight loss, she was preoccupied with weight and appearance and exhibited the personality characteristics typically associated with anorexia nervosa (i.e., perfectionism, interpersonal compliance, and obedience). Her parents and siblings also endorsed concerns with weight. Japanese researchers have identified and coined a term for binge-eating syndrome, *Kiberashi-gui* (Nogami & Yabana, 1977). Furthermore, etiological factors present in Western samples of eating disorder patients, such as examination pressure, loss of a relationship, a physical illness, or being teased about being overweight, were manifest in a sample of Chinese anorexics (Lee, 1991).

However, some researchers have proposed that some eating disorder symptoms do not appear in some non-Western cultures, and there exist additional distinct symptoms that do not appear in Western classification systems. Intense fears of fatness and body image disturbance are reported not to be typical of anorexia nervosa patients in Hong Kong or India (Khandelwal & Saxena, 1990; Lee, 1991). Patients' reasons for refusing food were more likely to be related to somatic complaints, such as abdominal bloating and feelings of fullness. It is interesting to note that in some of the early writings on anorexia nervosa morbid preoccupation with weight was not considered to be central to the diagnosis (Gull, 1868; Lasegue, 1873). Abdominal bloating and lack of appetite were the primary features.

In non-Western countries, weight reduction is often attained purely by dietary restriction rather than by other purging behaviors, such as vomiting or laxative abuse. In a survey of Egyptian students in Cairo, it was found that binge-eating, vomiting, and laxative abuse were absent, whereas dieting and fasting were the common means of achieving weight loss (Nasser, 1986). Similarly, bulimic symptoms are rare in anorexic patients in India or Hong Kong (Chen et al., 1993; Khandelwal & Saxena, 1990; Lee, Hsu, & Wing, 1992). In contrast, Dolan and Ford (1991) found a high prevalence of binge-eating in both female and male university students in Cairo (82% and 76%, respectively). Also, another group of researchers surveyed Japanese universities and revealed that 7.8% of women and 1.1% of men had engaged in binge eating (Nogami, Yamaguchi, Ishiwata, Sakai, & Kusakabe, 1984). It has been suggested that the differences in the degree of Westernization of the students might account for the conflicting findings. Nasser (1986) surveyed students at an Arab-speaking university, while Dolan and Ford (1991) included Arab students attending an English-speaking university. The English-speaking students were likely exposed to a greater degree of Western cultural influences, including pathological eating behaviors. Similarly, the Japanese university students (i.e., Nogami et al., 1984) may have been more exposed to Western cultural values.

Furthermore, some symptoms are not necessarily considered to be problematic. Binges are not always clandestine in Asian cultures; they sometimes replace meals and might even be encouraged by relatives worried about the individual's low weight (Lee, 1991). Fasting in Middle Eastern cultures for religious reasons is also not uncommon (Nasser, 1986).

In summary, the consistent findings of the existence of eating disorders in non-Western societies (albeit often with significantly lower prevalence rates than in the West) suggests that Western diagnostic criteria are valid. The symptoms of emaciation, food refusal, and amenorrhea appear to be universal symptoms of anorexia nervosa. However, there remain some issues regarding the cultural context of diagnosing an eating disorder. The centrality of particular symptoms to the diagnosis is such an issue. It appears that some cultures, such as the Chinese or South Asian, do not find fear of fatness to be primary to the diagnosis of anorexia nervosa (Khandelwal & Saxena, 1990; Lee, 1991). It has been suggested that since obesity is not widespread in these countries, it is not fear-inducing as it is to individuals in the West. Furthermore, historically, obesity has been a symbol of health and prosperity in Asian cultures (e.g., Furnham & Baguma, 1994), whereas being overweight is severely stigmatized in Western cultures.

The presence of bulimic symptomatology appears not to be as widespread in non-Western societies. It is important to evaluate eating disorder symptoms in their cultural context. For example, is fasting a culturally sanctioned expression of religious piety, or is it a symptom of an underlying psychiatric disorder? Finally, criticisms have been directed at psychiatric researchers regarding their bias toward "discovering" cross-cultural similarities and "universals" in mental disorders (Kleinman, 1987). Standardized diagnostic methods will detect those disorders that fit the Western model, but they will ignore those patients who do not fit the model but who may well be exhibiting cultural diversity in the expression of a psychiatric disorder.

METHODOLOGICAL ISSUES

It is important to consider the nature of the existing research studies when evaluating the prevalence and incidence of eating disorders in Western and non-Western societies. There are numerous approaches to studying eating disorders in various cultures, and it is important to evaluate how the studies were conducted, how the samples were surveyed, the type of research tools used in the gathering of the data, and the type of diagnostic criteria applied. Widely varying concepts and procedures for determining eating disorders have led to greatly divergent estimates of their prevalence.

Psychiatric case studies provide detailed descriptions of cases and opportunities to study the disorder within the cultural context of the individual, and they establish that anorexia and bulimia do exist in non-Western women. This is valuable information for better understanding the factors operating in the cross-cultural manifestation of eating disorders. Often this is the only source of information that is available from developing countries, which do not have the resources to allocate to large-scale research studies. However, these types of studies do not provide an estimate of prevalence, because only a very selected sample of individuals come to the attention of the medical and psychiatric community. Cases are also written up based on their uniqueness and rarity and do not provide an accurate picture of the presentation of the disorder.

Epidemiological studies can provide an estimate of prevalence and incidence of eating disorders in the population. Large representative samples of the population are possible. There are some factors to consider when evaluating the reliability and validity of these studies. Often it is students who are surveyed, since they are an easily accessible population. It is probable that students are not representative of the population of the country being studied, thus making generalizations problematic. This is especially relevant for non-Western countries, where individuals at a university may have been exposed to Western values and norms, and, therefore, do not represent a pure sample of the culture. Also, nothing is known about the nonresponders; it is likely that individuals with eating and weight concerns are less willing to answer questions on this subject.

Another issue is the type of instrument used to assess eating disorders. Self-report questionnaires have the advantage of ease of administration and standardization. Large numbers of individuals can be screened in a short period of time. However, there are some concerns, particularly when studying individuals in non-Western societies. All screening instruments for eating disorders have been developed in Europe or North America and are based directly on Western concepts of abnormal eating attitudes or diagnostic criteria for eating disorders. It has been proposed that this poses serious limitations for discovering cross-cultural differences in the presentation of an eating disorder (Kleinman, 1987).

The Eating Attitudes Test (EAT; Garner & Garfinkel, 1979) is a good example of a self-report instrument that has been used extensively to evaluate abnormal eating attitudes and behaviors. It was designed for Western populations and shows good evidence of cross-cultural validity in other Western cultures (Wells, Coope, Gabb, & Pears, 1985). The EAT has been translated into a variety of different languages in order to study the prevalence of eating disorders in other countries. However, several problems have been encountered in using it in non-Western cultures. A factor analysis of results from a survey of South Asian individuals completing a Hindi translation of the EAT revealed a "chaotic pattern" that showed no relation to similar analyses done with Western samples in England, New Zealand, and Canada (King & Bhugra, 1989). The authors concluded that many of the concepts in the questionnaire were not understood in this cultural context. It is difficult to comment on the nature of the prevalence of eating disorders if the instrument is inappropriately applied to a non-Western population. Choudry and Mumford (1992) reported that up to six items of the EAT (translated into Urdu) were invalid in that cultural context. They did finally conclude that enough items passed their evaluation criteria to be confident that the EAT as a whole performed its task adequately. In their survey of English schools in Lahore, Pakistan, Mumford and Whitehouse (1988) found a robust factor structure similar to that of Western samples. However, it should be noted that there were distinct Western features in the prevailing culture that could have contributed to the similarity to Western findings.

Even when the language per se is not a problem, the questionnaire items themselves may contain completely unfamiliar concepts for another culture. It is crucial to consider the linguistic and cultural background of individuals in screening studies

(King, 1993). For example, a survey of Asian students and patients attending a family practice clinic used the Bulimic Investigatory Test (BITE; Henderson & Freeman, 1987) to screen for disordered eating symptoms. The older Asian women had more difficulty understanding the concepts in the questionnaire, whereas younger Asian women were similar to Caucasian women in their weight and shape concerns. Bilingual Chinese students completing English-language questionnaires about eating attitudes and behaviors were unfamiliar with Western terms such as "binge eating" and "laxatives." Furthermore, foods in China are rarely labeled "bad" or "forbidden" and cutting one's food into small pieces is not relevant for the Chinese, since they use chopsticks and their food is often already in small pieces (Lee, 1993). Finally, some eating attitudes and behaviors that are considered abnormal in the questionnaires are viewed as normal in other societies. For example, fasting for religious reasons is common in Middle Eastern cultures (Markantonakis, 1990; Nasser, 1986).

Another useful tool in evaluating eating disorders is the Eating Disorder Inventory (EDI; Garner, Olmsted, & Polivy, 1983b). This self-report questionnaire consists of several subscales that measure psychological aspects of anorexia and bulimia nervosa. In general, women with eating disorders report significantly higher drive for thinness, bulimia, body dissatisfaction, perfectionism, ineffectiveness, interpersonal distrust, maturity fears, and lower interoceptive awareness (awareness of internal signals of hunger and satiety, as well as emotions) than do non-eating-disordered women (e.g., Garner, Olmsted, & Polivy, 1983a). Unfortunately, this measure suffers from the same cultural biases as the EAT and the BITE.

Structured interviews, such as the Eating Disorder Examination (Z. Cooper & Fairburn, 1987), are more reliable in making accurate diagnoses. Self-report questionnaires often overestimate the prevalence of eating disorders as compared to a structured clinical diagnostic interview (King, 1993; Schotte & Stunkard, 1987). On the other hand, it is important that clinical interviews are conducted in a standardized manner. Clinical interviews also require a lot of time and expertise to administer. It is often not feasible to interview large numbers of individuals when screening for psychiatric disorders. Several researchers have employed a combination of methods, first using self-report questionnaires to screen individuals, then following with an interview of those who score in the abnormal range in order to determine the actual presence of an eating disorder.

It is important to have clear diagnostic criteria; otherwise, estimates of prevalence and incidence are unlikely to be accurate. There are several diagnostic classification systems in existence for the diagnosis of eating disorders, and each differs slightly in symptom criteria (e.g., APA, 1980, 1987, 1994; Feighner et al., 1972; Russell, 1970, 1979; World Health Organization, 1992). This makes it difficult to make direct comparisons between studies. Furthermore, some research studies report using modifications of these diagnostic systems but often do not specify how the criteria have been altered.

Even within a particular classification system, the criteria for the diagnosis of an eating disorder changes and evolves over time. For example, the *DSM-III-R* (APA, 1987) has more restrictive criteria for the classification of eating disorders than does the earlier *DSM-III* (APA, 1980). The *DSM-III* criteria for bulimia did not specify the required frequency of binge eating episodes and caused disagreement about what distinguished clinically significant cases from normal and subclinical behavior. Although the problem was remedied with the introduction of *DSM-III-R* (APA, 1987), discrepancies of this type remain and continue to occur in the literature. The *DSM-IV* now specifies particular subtypes of anorexia nervosa and bulimia nervosa that were not present in earlier versions. Different diagnostic criteria are known to produce widely differing figures of eating disorder prevalence (Ben-Tovim, 1988). These methodological issues should be considered during the discussion of the incidence and prevalence of eating disorders in Western and non-Western societies.

THE INCIDENCE AND PREVALENCE OF EATING DISORDERS

Western Caucasian Cultures

According to the *DSM-IV* (APA, 1994), the prevalence of anorexia nervosa among females in late adolescence and early adulthood is 0.5% to 1.0%. The rate for bulimia nervosa is slightly higher, occurring in 1.0% to 3.0% of young females. Although there are limited data concerning the prevalence of eating disorders in males, it is estimated that 90% of the cases occur in females (APA, 1994). It is assumed that males are less likely than females to experience an eating disorder because males do not encounter the undue societal pressure to be thin that females do. Most studies indicate that the incidence of eating disorders within industrialized countries has increased dramatically over the past few decades (APA, 1994; Hall & Hay, 1991; Jones, Fox, Babigan, & Hutton, 1980; Kendell, Hall, Hailey, & Babigan, 1973; Pyle, Halvorson, Neuman, & Mitchell, 1986; Szmukler, 1985; Szmukler, McCance, McCrone, & Hunter, 1986; Theander, 1970; Willi & Grossmann, 1983). The increasing pressure to achieve thinness and the corresponding escalation of eating disorders indicate that there is an important connection between the thin-ideal and pathological eating behavior. However, improved detection and greater community awareness of eating disorders cannot be entirely discounted as being responsible for the recent surge of these disorders.

It has been demonstrated that the prevalence of eating disorders is disproportionately high in student populations (e.g., Gray & Ford, 1985; Pyle et al.,1986; Tamburrino, Franco, Bernal, Carroll, & McSweeny, 1987). In one study done at a private American college, it was found that 12.4% of the women and 2.7% of the men fulfilled *DSM-III* criteria (APA, 1980) for an eating disorder (Hesse-Biber, 1989). Although these higher rates could be a result of overdiagnosis due to lenient criteria, they are consistent with the research on socioeconomic status. The majority of the students in this sample, and students in general, are from upper to middle social status. Because thinness is positively correlated with social status and is a symbol of upward mobility in Western cultures, it is not surprising that the prevalence of eating disorders is elevated in North American college populations. An overrepresentation of eating disorders in the upper social classes has been identified in several past studies (Crisp, Palmer, & Kalucy, 1976; Garfinkel & Garner, 1982; Jones et al.,1980; Kendell et al.,1973; Morgan & Russell, 1975). In contrast, however, researchers conducting recent epidemiological studies have found no relationship between social status and eating disorders (Kendler et al., 1991; Rand & Kuldau, 1992; Whitaker et al., 1990). It may be that the earlier SES bias is becoming less apparent as the thin-ideal is embraced by people of all SES levels (Stice, 1994).

Western Subcultures

The overrepresentation of eating disorders in subcultures where there are intense pressures to maintain a low body weight supports the position that cultural factors are important etiological factors in the development of eating disorders (Garner & Garfinkel, 1980). The eating pathology in students of dance, modeling, and music and in a control group of students in a general arts program was examined in one study. Not surprisingly, eating disorders were overrepresented among dancers and models, for whom the requirement to be thin is especially emphasized. Although none of the music or the control students met the criteria for anorexia, 6.5% of the dance students and 7% of the modeling students were diagnosed as anorexic (Garner & Garfinkel, 1980). In another study, an overrepresentation of disordered eating was discovered in professional ballet dancers who were asked if they had ever had anorexia or bulimia. Thirty-two percent of the dancers reported having an eating disorder (Hamilton, Brooks-Gunn, & Warren, 1985). Although the authors of this study relied on self-reported diagnosis and did not include a control group, the results are consistent with a different study involving ballet students. This prospective study revealed that body dissatisfaction and an intense drive for thinness predicted the emergence of an eating disorder two to four years later (Garner, Garfinkel, Rockert, & Olmsted, 1987).

It has been suggested that athletes who are involved in competitive sports where weight or shape can influence their performance may also be at high risk to develop eating disorders. While there have been anecdotal reports of eating disorders among gymnasts, swimmers, wrestlers, rowers, and skaters, there have been few rigorous investigations in this area. It would seem reasonable to conclude that the increased pressure felt by these groups to achieve and maintain a slim body may directly promote eating disorders. However, an alternative explanation is that people predisposed to develop eating disorders may select careers that emphasize physical appearance (Stice, 1994).

It has been suggested that, in general, men are less interested in their appearance and subjected to less cultural pressures for slimness than are women. This notion has been put forth to support the sex-ratio differentiation with respect to eating disorders (approximately 1 out of 10 individuals with eating disorders are male). However, this unconcern with appearance does not seem to be true for homosexual men. Anecdotal evidence was provided by one author's (I.F.) homosexual male client, who stated, "if you're fat and you're gay you're nobody." In accordance with this statement are the empirical findings that homosexual men report greater concern and dissatisfaction with physical appearance (Kleinberg, 1980; Lakoff & Scherr, 1984) and higher rates of abnormal eating attitudes and behavior than heterosexual men (Silberstein, Mishkind, Striegel-Moore, Timko, & Rodin, 1989; Yager, Kurtzman, Landsverk, & Wiesmeier, 1988). Further, some studies have indicated that a homosexual orientation is more common than expected among men who develop eating disorders than among analogous women patients (Fichter & Daser, 1987; Herzog, Bardburn, & Newman, 1990; Herzog, Norman, Gordon, & Pepose, 1984; P. H. Robinson & Holden, 1986; Schneider & Agras, 1987). In contrast, other studies have failed to confirm higher rates of homosexuality among males with eating disorders (Pope, Hudson, & Jonas 1986; Turnbull, Freeman, Barry, & Annandale, 1987).

Homosexual females may be expected to reject, to some extent, the pursuit of slimness, which is regarded as striving to be attractive to men. By diminishing the importance of the thin-ideal, it is reasonable to predict that homosexual females would be less likely to develop an eating disorder and that they would have a lower prevalence of eating disorders than heterosexual females. However, in a study of 30 lesbian and 52 heterosexual women, in which feminist attitudes were controlled for, no group differences were evident on measures of body esteem or disordered eating (Striegel-Moore, Tucker, & Hsu, 1990). In summary, the preponderance of reported data suggest that homosexuality is associated with a higher-than-normal risk of eating disorders in men. However, there is no evidence that homosexuality is associated with a lower-than-normal risk of disordered eating in women.

Ethnic Groups within the Majority Western Culture

The majority of evidence from surveys and clinical reports indicates that the prevalence of anorexia and bulimia in non-Caucasian groups is lower than in Caucasian populations (Andersen & Hay, 1985; Garfinkel & Garner, 1982; Hedblom, Hubbard, & Andersen, 1981; Hsu, 1987; Jones et al., 1980; Kendell et al., 1973; King, 1989; Mumford, Whitehouse, & Platts, 1991; Pyle et al., 1981; Silber, 1984).

One researcher surveyed 505 Caucasian, 148 Asian, and 25 African American college women (Nevo, 1985). Based on *DSM-III* (APA, 1980) diagnostic criteria, 14% of the Caucasian, 2.7% of the Asian and 4% of the African American women were classified as bulimic. Although the sample size of the African American group was small, a second study supported these findings. Gray, Ford, and Kelly (1987) surveyed 507 African American students and determined that 3% of the subjects met *DSM-III* (APA, 1980) criteria for bulimia nervosa. This percentage was significantly less than a comparable group of Caucasian women, where 13% qualified as eating-disordered.

In another study, 204 Asian and 355 Caucasian schoolgirls in northern England were surveyed. The researchers interviewed the students whose self-report measures indicated a possible eating disorder and found that 3.4% of the Asian girls and only 0.8% of the Caucasian girls met *DSM-III-R* (APA, 1987) criteria for bulimia nervosa. The authors developed a measure of acculturation (degree to which Asian students had adopted the Western culture) based on four questions concerning language, dress, and food. In contrast to what the authors predicted, Asian girls from traditional families were more likely to develop an eating disorder than Asian girls from more Westernized families. The authors suggested that the tensions of living in a traditional Asian family within a Western culture might result in an increased prevalence of disordered eating (Mumford & Whitehouse, 1988; Mumford et al.,1991).

Although the above study suggests that the prevalence of eating disorders among British Asian schoolgirls appears to be higher than for Caucasians, the overall convergence of the data suggests that non-Caucasians are underrepresented among eating-disordered populations in Western cultures (Stice, 1994). The true prevalence figures for anorexia and bulimia in non-Caucasian groups is still unclear, and more research needs to be devoted to investigating the occurrence of eating disorders in these groups.

Non-Western Cultures

The incidence and prevalence of eating disorders are reported to be quite rare in non-Western countries. For example, in epidemiological surveys of Japanese schoolgirls, a range of 0.005%–0.04% met the criteria for anorexia nervosa, with greater prevalence rates occurring in urban centers (Azuma & Henmi, 1982; Mizushimi & Ishii, 1983; Suematsu, Ishikawa, & Kuboki, 1985). One case of anorexia nervosa was identified among 7229 subjects in a large-scale epidemiological study in Hong Kong (Chen et al., 1993). Among Chinese university students in Hong Kong, a prevalence rate of only 0.46% for eating disorders was found in a survey of eating attitudes (Lee, 1993).

Another source of information about eating disorders comes from surveys of cases from medical clinics. A survey of Japanese female students who visited a university health center between 1974 and 1975 found that 1% had received a psychiatric referral for anorexia nervosa (Okasha, et al., 1977). No cases of anorexia nervosa were found in a survey of medical register records in Malaysian hospitals during the period of 1976–1978 (Buhrich, 1981). Thirty cases were seen by psychiatrists in private practice, which gives an indication that there are documented cases of anorexia nervosa in Malaysia. Eating disorders are reported to be very rare in African countries and in India, Singapore, China, Taiwan, and Indonesia (Buchan & Gregory, 1984; Elsarrag, 1968; Khandelwal & Saxena, 1990; Nwaefuna, 1981; Ong, Tsoi, & Chean, 1982; Zheng, 1982).

Several researchers have compared the prevalence of eating disorders in young women living in non-Western cultures to those living in Western countries. One such study compared Arab female university students in Cairo, Egypt, to a matched group of Arab students who had immigrated with their parents to London, England. Six cases of bulimia nervosa were identified in the women in London and none in Cairo (Nasser, 1986). Anorexia nervosa was not diagnosed in either group. Greek adolescents living in Greece were surveyed; 0.4% met criteria for anorexia nervosa, while 1.1% of Greek adolescents whose families had relocated to Germany met those criteria (Fichter, Weyerer, Sourdi, & Sourdi, 1983).

A comparison of anorexic patients in East and West Berlin (when the city was still divided) found less eating-disorder symptomatology (i.e., fewer bulimic symptoms, less desire to be thin, less body dissatisfaction) in the East Berlin sample (Steinhausen, Neumarker, Vollrath, Dudeck, & Neumarker, 1992). A comparison of the prevalence rates for eating disorders in Spain and the United States suggested a higher incidence of bulimia (3.5%) and interest in dieting in the American schoolgirls than in the Spanish girls (0.9%) (Raich, Rosen, Deus, Perez, Requena, & Gross, 1992).

There are instances where the prevalence of eating disorders in non-Western societies is comparable to that of Western countries. For example, researchers who surveyed eating-disorder symptoms in English-speaking schoolgirls in Lahore, Pakistan, found a similar prevalence of bulimia nervosa to that found among Caucasian schoolgirls in England (Mumford, Whitehouse, & Choudry, 1992). The authors noted that the Pakistani girls lived in a dieting milieu, as evidenced by advertisements for slimming clinics and "keep-fit" clubs. These girls were also from the upper social strata and were more likely to have adopted Western styles and habits. In this study their measure of acculturation or degree of "Westernization" was significantly positively associated with eating pathology. These studies suggest that Westernization does have an impact on the prevalence rates of eating disorders, with bulimia and anorexia more prevalent in Western countries (P. J. Cooper & Fairburn, 1982; Halmi, Falk, & Schwartz, 1981).

SOCIOCULTURAL HYPOTHESIS

The convergence of evidence from numerous studies strongly indicates that sociocultural factors play a pivotal role in the development of eating disorders in Western societies (Garner, Garfinkel, & Olmsted, 1983; Streigel-Moore, Silberstein, & Rodin, 1986). In fact it has been proposed (DiNicola, 1990) that anorexia and bulimia are examples of a culture-bound syndrome, as defined as "a collection of signs and symptoms of disease (not including notions of cause) which is restricted to a limited number of cultures primarily by reason of their psychosocial features" (Prince, 1985a, 1985b). Anorexia and bulimia nervosa have been said to have a particular sociocultural "address" which encompasses such variables as sex (i.e., female), social class (i.e., middle and upper classes), occupation (e.g., dancers, models, athletes), and culture (i.e., Western society). But cultural factors are not solely responsible for the development of eating disorders; rather it is a complex interaction of these with predisposing individual, family, and/or biological variables and precipitating factors such as life events and puberty that result in the development of an eating disorder (Garner, Garfinkel, & Olmsted, 1983).

However, the reports of the emergence of eating disorders in developing countries and evidence of eating disorders occurring among immigrants from those countries who relocate to more Western societies call into question this idea of a particular sociocultural address for eating disorders. To explain such phenomena, DiNicola proposes that a culture-change syndrome is emerging (DiNicola, 1990). This syndrome develops under conditions of rapid socioeconomic and sociocultural change. Cultural change occurs in two ways: cultural evolution and human migration (DiNicola, 1985, 1990; Favazza, 1985).

The proposal that the emergence of eating disorders in non-Western populations may be related to cultural change is supported by empirical evidence from comparative studies. Comparisons of young women living in their native non-Western societies with corresponding samples in more Western countries suggest a higher incidence of eating disorders in those individuals living in the Western countries (Fichter et al., 1983; Nasser, 1986; Steinhausen et al., 1992). Both the transition to living away from family, friends, and familiar environment and exposure to Western culture appear to be significant triggers for the development of eating pathology. For example, in the study describing the incidence of bulimia nervosa in Egyptian girls who had moved to London, many of the young women attributed their overeating to loneliness, boredom, or the cold weather (Nasser, 1986). Furthermore, some individuals said that they had contact with other sufferers of bulimia, which suggests the possibility of social transmission (Chiodo & Latimer, 1983). The tension of living in a traditional Asian family within a Western culture was proposed as an explanation for the finding of a greater incidence of eating disorders in Asian schoolgirls living in northern England relative to their English counterparts (Mumford & Whitehouse, 1988).

Case reports of eating disorders among immigrants moving to Western cultures also document acculturation issues as significant. A report of two Russian emigres to the United States, one of whom developed anorexia nervosa and the other who developed bulimia nervosa, cited the pressure to adapt to a new culture and the reorganization of traditional family roles as pathogenic forces that led to an exaggerated identification with that culture; in this case, an overvaluation of slimness as desirable (Bulik, 1987). Similarly, cultural transition has been linked to the development of anorexia nervosa and bulimia nervosa in Southeastern Asian immigrants (Kope & Sack, 1987; Schmidt, 1993).

As developing countries become more industrialized, there is greater exposure to Western attitudes and habits. Some authors suggest that it may only be a matter of time before attitudes toward weight and shape come to mirror those of Western societies (Lee, 1993; Nasser, 1988). Lee (1993) observes that the eating habits of the Chinese in Hong Kong are changing from the traditional low-fat high-fiber foods to an incorporation of more Western fast foods. Obesity is becoming more prevalent among adolescents in Hong Kong, and there are an increasing number of advertisements for weight-loss clinics and fitness clubs. As obesity and attendant weight control become more widespread among the Chinese and ideals of female slimness are incorporated into the Hong Kong culture, eating disorders may increase in frequency. Already it is reported that the incidence of anorexia nervosa, bulimia nervosa, and pathological eating behaviors has increased in Japan, and the influence of American culture on Japanese society is discussed as a significant factor (Nogami et al., 1984; Suematsu et al., 1985).

TREATMENT MODEL

As the incidence and prevalence of eating disorders appears to be on the rise in developing countries and among immigrant populations arriving in the West, the question of treatment becomes an obvious issue. Many steps are involved at various levels of organization when designing appropriate treatment strategies. Issues exist at the national, community, and individual levels.

Epidemiological studies are needed, at both the national and the community levels, in order to evaluate the incidence and prevalence of eating disorders. This is a necessary first step to begin to allocate resources for prevention and treatment programs. An assessment of existing services and an evaluation of patterns of use of health care facilities is also informative. There is a suggestion that non-Caucasian groups are overrepresented in their use of emergency rooms (P. Robinson & Andersen, 1985). Rates of referrals to psychiatric services for non-Caucasian groups, however, are much lower than for equivalent Caucasian populations (Lacey & Dolan, 1988). These findings invite speculation about whether these groups are using community health services appropriately and whether there are barriers to requesting or receiving help. One deterrent could be the ethnically diverse group's attitude toward illness, particularly toward mental illness. There may be cultural differences in labeling behaviors as abnormal. Perhaps only very disturbed individuals are recognized as needing help, and the emergency room is the obvious choice at this point (P. H. Robinson & Andersen, 1985; Holden & P. H. Robinson, 1988). Attitudes of health care providers toward certain ethnic groups may also be a barrier to treatment. Silber (1984) investigated anorexia nervosa in African Americans and Hispanics and found that only one half of the cases had been correctly diagnosed (Silber, 1986). This highlights the ethnocentric assumptions of the Western medical services concerning the likelihood of a non-Caucasian woman presenting with an eating disorder.

The next stage of treatment intervention would depend on the findings of the evaluations of treatment facilities and their use. A fundamental starting point would be to establish some education and information distribution. Education of health care workers about the increasing prevalence of eating disorders in developing countries, in communities of immigrants, and in minority groups is of paramount importance. Equally important is ensuring that information is reaching the targeted population about the type and availability of health care services. This approach may likely have to be tailored in an individual fashion, depending on the cultural context of the community. Established cultural patterns of treatment-seeking may pose barriers to the introduction of Western methods of treatment. For example, some cultures such as the Chinese place great emphasis on internal resources and rely on self-help strategies before seeking help from others (Luk & Bond, 1992). Other cultures seek out traditional healers in preference to Western medical clinics (Buchan & Gregory, 1984; Elsarrag, 1968).

Many types of therapies are currently available for treating eating disorders, including psychoeducation, cognitive-behavioral therapy, psychodynamic/interpersonal, addiction-oriented, single-issue (e.g., body image), and self-help approaches. To date, no particular type of therapeutic approach produces consistently better or worse outcomes than any other (Cox & Merkel, 1989; Garner, Fairburn, & Davis, 1987). Similarly, these therapies, delivered in either individual or group format, appear to be equally effective (Cox & Merkel, 1989; Fairburn, 1988). It is beyond the score of this chapter to describe each type of therapy in detail, so we will limit the discussion to psychoeducation and cognitive-behavioral therapy.

When developing treatment programs within immigrant communities, it is important to be sensitive to the problems young women may have in adjusting to Western society, especially with respect to the prevailing attitudes toward weight and body shape. The first stage in a stepped-care treatment plan is psychoeducation (i.e., the provision of educational information about the disorder). Although psychoeducation is frequently included as one component in multimodal treatment packages, it may also have limited use as an independent intervention (Olmsted & Kaplan, 1995). Information about the ineffectiveness and dangers of dieting and highlighting the incongruity between biology and the thin-ideal would be useful for new immigrants. New immigrants can be informed that there are both adaptive and maladaptive cultural norms that make up Western society. They could be encouraged to adopt and integrate adaptive norms, but be discouraged from embracing Western beliefs and attitudes surrounding weight and shape. Psychoeducation directed at families could also provide essential information about the unique risks and difficulties involved with growing up in a traditional family within Western culture. Efforts could then be directed toward enhancing self-esteem through methods other than decreasing one's body weight. Teaching skills to cope with sociocultural pressures could help young women adjust to their new culture in an adaptive manner (Stice, 1994).

Cognitive-behavioral therapy was the first specific approach for the treatment of bulimia nervosa to be described in detail and supported by clinical data (Fairburn,

1988). Key features of this treatment included helping patients identify circumstances which lead to a loss of control, obtaining specific changes in eating patterns, and reconsidering distorted beliefs associated with eating, weight, and body shape. This approach attempts to change the patient's system of beliefs about herself and her environment through a semistructured, problem-oriented method, focusing directly on the patient's dysfunctional beliefs and values concerning her weight and shape (Fairburn, 1988). Clearly, it is essential to restructure culturally imposed maladaptive beliefs when treating eating-disordered patients.

With reference to treatment interventions on an individual level, few clinicians have specifically addressed the significance of cultural factors in treatment. DiNicola (1990) considers cultural factors to be very important and maintains that they must be addressed directly in treatment. He advocates cultural family therapy when working with immigrants and refugees undergoing rapid intense cultural change. Examining how individuals use language (their native tongue and the acquired second language) in relating to one another—as boundary markers, alliances, coalitions, and exclusions—provides significant information during treatment. For children and adolescents it is important to recognize that there exist two culture gaps, one between the generations (parents and children) and another between the culture at home and that of their new country. Children may often lead a cultural double life. The difficulty of maintaining this dual life takes its toll and, in vulnerable individuals, could be expressed as an eating disorder. Young women, in particular, may be vulnerable to cultural change (Nasser, 1988). Another example of the importance of addressing cultural issues in therapy is a case report of an American Japanese anorexic girl (Koizumi & Luidens, 1984). The successful management of her care involved dealing with issues of cultural conflict for both her and her Japanese mother. Reports such as these highlight the significance of cultural issues in treatment management.

CONCLUSIONS

In summary, the relatively consistent sex and social-class distribution of eating disorders, as well as the apparent elevated rates in culturally vulnerable subgroups and in Western societies, have been offered as support of the contention that cultural factors influence the development of eating disorders. Although any one of these epidemiological observations could have alternative explanations, taken together they are strongly suggestive of cultural influences in the development of eating disorders. Messengers for these sociocultural pressures include the family, peers, and especially the media. There is tremendous pressure on women to meet the current thin standard for physical attractiveness, which often necessitates dieting, and dieting appears to be a factor that may trigger an eating disorder.

Now there is evidence that, as non-Western societies become more industrialized and come into contact with Western societies, there is a cultural transmission of Western values and norms. Traditional attitudes toward food, weight, and body shape appear to be changing to conform to Western ideals. Young immigrant women who move to the West may be particularly vulnerable to embracing and internalizing the value Western culture places on thinness. Investment in weight loss may induce more dieting and possibly increase the incidence of eating disorders.

More research is needed to evaluate the rates of eating disorders in developing countries, especially those which are in contact with Western societies. It is important also to assess the emergence of eating disorders in immigrant communities in the West. The development of treatment resources depends on accurate assessments of the incidence and prevalence of eating disorders. When planning treatment, consideration of such factors as the cultural context, attitudes of help-seekers and health care providers, and other barriers to treatment are vital.

It is necessary to acknowledge that although cultural factors play an important role, they are not sufficient to explain the precise mechanism responsible for the development of an eating disorder in a given individual. The cultural perspective does not explain why some individuals are vulnerable and some are protected. Cultural factors are mediated by the psychology of the individual as well as by familial variables. Prospective studies of eating disorders in high-risk populations will further our understanding of cultural, individual, and family variables. Cross-cultural studies and studies of multicultural groups will aid in elucidating similarities, as well as differences, among cultures in the presentation of eating disorders. This information can add to our understanding of eating pathology and advance the development of a universal theory for eating disorders and of effective intervention and prevention strategies.

Note

1. Although the authors reported that women were significantly more likely to have dieted (59% vs. 24%) and to be currently dieting (32.5% vs. 7.3%) than men, they did not provide data for females and males separately within nationality.

References

American Psychiatric Association. (1980). *Diagnostic and statistical manual of mental disorders* (3rd ed.). Washington, DC: Author.

American Psychiatric Association. (1987). *Diagnostic and statistical manual of mental disorders* (3rd ed., Rev.). Washington, DC: Author.

American Psychiatric Association. (1994). *Diagnostic and statistical manual of mental disorders* (4th ed.). Washington, DC: Author.

Andersen, A. E., & DiDomenico, L. (1992). Diet vs. shape content of popular male and female magazines: A dose-response relationship to the incidence of eating disorders. *International Journal of Eating Disorders, 11,* 283–287.

Andersen, A. E., & Hay, A. (1985). Racial and socio-economic influences in anorexia nervosa and bulimia. *International Journal of Eating Disorders, 4,* 479–487.

Azuma, Y., & Henmi, M. (1982). A study on the incidence of anorexia nervosa in school girls. *Annual Report of Research in Eating Disorders, 30*–34.

Baucom, D. H., & Aiken, P. A. (1981). Effect of depressed mood on eating among obese and nonobese dieting and nondieting persons. *Journal of Personality and Social Psychology, 41,* 577–585.

Ben-Tovim, D. I. (1988). *DSM-III,* draft *DSM-III-R* and the diagnosis and prevalence of bulimia in Australia. *American Journal of Psychiatry, 145,* 1000–1002.

Boskind-Lodahl, M. (1976). Cinderella's stepsisters: A feminist perspective on anorexia nervosa and bulimia. *Signs, 2,* 342–346.

Bruch, H. (1973). *Eating disorders.* New York: Basic Books.

Buchan, T., & Gregory, L. D. (1984). Anorexia nervosa in a Black Zimbabwean. *British Journal of Psychiatry, 145,* 326–330.

Buhrich, N. (1981). Frequency of presentation of anorexia nervosa in Malaysia. *Australian and New Zealand Journal of Psychiatry, 15,* 153–155.

Bulik, C. M. (1987). Eating disorders in immigrants: Two case reports. *International Journal of Eating Disorders, 6,* 133–141.

Chang, K. S., Lee, M. M., & Low, W. D. (1963). Height and weight of Southern Chinese children in Hong Kong. *American Journal of Physiological Anthropology, 21,* 497–509.

Chen, C. N., Wong, J., Lee, N., Chan-Ho, M. W., Lau, J., & Fung, M. (1993). The Shatin community mental health survey in Hong Kong. II. Major findings. *Archives of General Psychiatry, 50,* 125–133.

Chiodo, J., & Latimer, P. R. (1983). Vomiting as a learned weight-control technique in bulimia. *Journal of Behavior Therapy and Experimental Psychiatry, 14,* 131–135.

Choudry, I. Y., & Mumford, D. B. (1992). A pilot study of eating disorders in Mirpur (Pakistan) using an Urdu version of the Eating Attitudes Test. *International Journal of Eating Disorders, 11,* 243–251.

Cooper, P. J., & Fairburn, C. G. (1982). Binge eating and self-induced vomiting in the community: A preliminary study. *British Journal of Psychiatry, 15,* 1955–2025.

Cooper, Z., & Fairburn, C. G. (1987). The Eating Disorders Examination: A semi-structured interview for the assessment of the specific psychopathology of eating disorders. *International Journal of Eating Disorders, 6,* 1–8.

Cox, G. L., & Merkel, W. T. (1989). A qualitative review of psychosocial treatments for bulimia. *The Journal of Nervous and Mental Disease, 177,* 77–84.

Crisp, A. H., Palmer, R. L., & Kalucy, R. S. (1976). How common is anorexia nervosa? A prevalence study. *British Journal of Psychiatry, 128,* 549–554.

DiNicola, V. F. (1985). Anorexia nervosa as a culture-bound syndrome. Symposium on "Eating Disorders," Canadian Psychiatric Association 35th Annual Meeting Abstracts. Quebec, October, 1985, 134–135.

DiNicola, V. F. (1990). Anorexia multiform: Self-starvation in historical and cultural context. *Transcultural Psychiatric Research Review, 27,* 245–286.

Dolan, B., & Ford, K. (1991). Binge eating and dietary restraint: A cross-cultural analysis. *International Journal of Eating Disorders, 10,* 345–353.

Elsarrag, M. E. (1968). Psychiatry in the northern Sudan: A study in comparative psychiatry. *British Journal of Psychiatry, 114,* 945–948.

Fairburn, G. G. (1988). The current status of the psychological treatments for bulimia nervosa. *Journal of Psychosomatic Research, 32,* 635–645.

Fallon, A. F., & Rozin, P. (1985). Sex differences in perceptions of desirable body shape. *Journal of Abnormal Psychology, 94,* 102–105.

Favazza, A. R. (1985). Anthropology and psychiatry. In H. I. Kaplan & B. J. Sadock (Eds.), *Comprehensive Textbook of Psychiatry* (pp. 247–265). Baltimore: Williams & Wilkins.

Feighner, J. P., Robins, E., Guze, S. B., Woodruff, R. A. J.,Winokur, G., & Munoz, R. (1972). Diagnostic criteria for use in psychiatric research. *Archives of General Psychiatry, 26,* 57–63.

Fichter, M. M., & Daser, C. (1987). Symptomatology, psychosexual development and gender identity in 42 anorexic males. *Psychological Medicine, 17,* 409–418.

Fichter, M. M., Weyerer, S., Sourdi, L., & Sourdi, Z. (1983). The epidemiology of anorexia nervosa: A comparison of Greek adolescents living in Germany and Greek adolescents living in Greece. In P. L. Darby, P. E. Garfinkel, D. M. Garner, & D. V. Coscina (Eds.), *Anorexia nervosa: Recent developments in research* (pp. 95–105). New York: Alan R. Liss.

Furnham, A., & Alibhai, N. (1983). Cross-cultural differences in the perception of female body shapes. *Psychological Medicine, 13,* 829–837.

Furnham, A., & Baguma, P. (1994). Cross-cultural differences in the evaluation of male and female body shapes. *International Journal of Eating Disorders, 15,* 81–89.

Garb, J. L., Garb, J. R., & Stunkard, A. J. (1975). Social factors and obesity in Navaho Indian children. In A. Howard (Ed.), *Recent advances in obesity research* (pp. 37–39). London: Newman.

Garfinkel, P. E., & Garner, D. M. (1982). *Anorexia nervosa: A multidimensional perspective.* New York: Brunner/Mazel.

Garfinkel, P. E., Moldofsky, H., & Garner, D. M. (1980). The heterogeneity of anorexia nervosa: Bulimia as a distinct subgroup. *Archives of General Psychiatry, 37,* 1036–1040.

Garner, D. M., Fairburn, C. G., & Davis, R. (1987). Cognitive-behavioral treatment of bulimia nervosa: A critical appraisal. *Behavior Modification, 11,* 398–431.

Garner, D. M., & Garfinkel, P. E. (1979). The Eating Attitudes Test: An index of the symptoms of anorexia nervosa. *Psychological Medicine, 9,* 273–279.

Garner, D. M., & Garfinkel, P. E. (1980). Socio-cultural factors in the development of anorexia nervosa. *Psychological Medicine, 10,* 647–656.

Garner, D. M., Garfinkel, P. E., & Olmsted, M. P. (1983). An overview of sociocultural factors in the development of anorexia nervosa. In P. L. Darby, P. E. Garfinkel, D. M. Garner, & D. V. Coscina (Eds.), *Anorexia nervosa: Recent developments* (pp. 65–82). New York: Alan R. Liss.

Garner, D. M., Garfinkel, P. E., Rockert, W., & Olmsted, M. P. (1987). A prospective study of eating disturbances in ballet. *Psychotherapy Psychosomatic, 48,* 170–175.

Garner, D. M., Garfinkel, P. E., Schwartz, D., & Thompson, M. (1980). Cultural expectations of thinness in women. *Psychological Reports, 47,* 483–491.

Garner, D. M., Olmsted, M. P., & Polivy, J. (1983a). The development and validation of a multi-dimensional eating disorder inventory for anorexia nervosa and bulimia. *International Journal of Eating Disorders, 2,* 15–34.

Garner, D. M., Olmsted, M. P., & Polivy, J. (1983b). The Eating Disorder Inventory: A measure of cognitive behavioral dimensions of anorexia nervosa and bulimia. In P.L. Darby, P. Garfinkel, D. M. Garner, & D. V. Coscina (Eds.), *Anorexia nervosa: Recent developments* (pp. 173–184). New York: Alan R. Liss.

Goldblatt, P. B., Moore, M. E., & Stunkard, A. J. (1965). Social factors in obesity. *Journal of the American Medical Society, 192,* 1039–1044.

Gray, J. J., & Ford, K. (1985). The incidence of bulimia in a college sample. *International Journal of Eating Disorders, 4,* 201–210.

Gray, J. J., Ford, K., & Kelly, L. M. (1987). The prevalence of bulimia in a black college population. *International Journal of Eating Disorders, 6,* 733–749.

Gull, W. (1868). Anorexia nervosa. *Lancet, 17,* 516–517.

Hall, A., & Hay, P. J. (1991). Eating disorder patient referrals from a population region 1977–1986. *Psychological Medicine, 21,* 697–701.

Halmi, K. A., Falk, J. R., & Schwartz, E. (1981). Binge eating and vomiting: A survey of a college population. *Psychological Medicine, 11,* 697–706.

Hamilton, L. H., Brooks-Gunn, J., & Warren, M. P. (1985). Sociocultural influences on eating disorders in professional female ballet dancers. *International Journal of Eating Disorders, 4,* 465–477.

Heatherton, T., Polivy, J., & Herman, C. P. (1991). Restraint, weight loss and variability of body weight. *Journal of Abnormal Psychology, 100,* 78–83.

Hedblom, J., Hubbard, F. A., & Andersen, A. E. (1981). A multidisciplinary treatment program for patient and family. *Journal of Social Work in Health Care, 7,* 67–86.

Henderson, M., & Freeman, C. P. L. (1987). A self-rating scale for bulimia: The BITE. *British Journal of Psychiatry, 150,* 18–24.

Herman, C. P., & Mack, D. (1975). Restrained and unrestrained eating. *Journal of Personality, 43,* 647–660.

Herman, C. P., & Polivy, J. (1975). Anxiety, restraint, and eating behavior. *Journal of Abnormal Psychology, 84,* 666–672.

Herzog, D. B., Bardburn, I. S., & Newman, K. (1990). Sexuality in males with eating disorders. In A. E. Andersen (Ed.), *Males with eating disorders* (pp. 40–53). New York: Brunner/Mazzel.

Herzog, D. B., Norman, D. K., Gordon, C., & Pepose, M. (1984). Sexual conflict and eating disorders in 27 males. *American Journal of Psychiatry, 141,* 989–990.

Hesse-Biber, S. (1989). Eating patterns and disorders in a college population: Are college women's eating problems a new phenomenon? *Sex Roles, 20,* 71–89.

Hesse-Biber, S., Downey, J., & Clayton-Matthews, A. (1987). The differential importance of weight among college men and women. *Genetic, Social and General Psychology Monographs, 113,* 511–528.

Holden, N. L., & Robinson, P. H. (1988). Anorexia nervosa and bulimia nervosa in British blacks. *British Journal of Psychiatry, 132,* 544–549.

Horm, J., & Anderson, K. (1993). Who in America is trying to lose weight? *Annals of Internal Medicine, 119,* 672–676.

Hsu, L. K. G. (1987). Are the eating disorders becoming more common in blacks? *International Journal of Eating Disorders, 6,* 113–125.

Jacobovits, C., Halstead, P., Kelley, L., Roe, D. A., & Young, C. M. (1977). Eating habits and nutrient intakes of college women over a thirty year period. *Journal of the American Dietetic Association, 71,* 405–411.

Johnson, C., Steinberg, S., & Lewis, C. (1988). Bulimia. In R. Clark, R. Farr, & W. Castelli (Eds.), *Evaluation and management of eating disorders: Anorexia, bulimia, & obesity* (pp. 187–225). Champaign, IL: Life Enhancement Publications.

Jones, D. J., Fox, M. M., Babigian, H. M., & Hutton, H. E. (1980). The epidemiology of anorexia nervosa in Munroe County, New York 1960–1976. *Psychosomatic Medicine, 42,* 551–558.

Kendell, R. E., Hall, D. J., Hailey, A., & Babigan, H. M. (1973). The epidemiology of anorexia nervosa. *Psychological Medicine, 3,* 200–203.

Kendler, K. S., MacLean, C., Neale, M., Kessler, R., Heath, A., & Eaves, L. (1991). The genetic epidemiology of bulimia nervosa. *American Journal of Psychiatry, 148,* 1627–1637.

Keys, A., Brozek, J., Henschel, A., Mickelson, O., & Taylor, H. L. (1950). *The biology of human starvation.* Minneapolis, MN: University of Minnesota Press.

Khandelwal, S. K., & Saxena, S. (1990). Correspondence. *British Journal of Psychiatry, 157,* 784.

King, M. B. (1989). Eating disorders in a general practice population: Prevalence, characteristics and follow-up at 12 to 18 months. *Psychological Medicine, 14,* 1–34.

King, M. B. (1993). Cultural aspects of eating disorders. *International Review of Psychiatry, 5,* 205–216.

King, M. B., & Bhugra, D. (1989). Eating disorders: Lessons from a cross-cultural study. *Psychological Medicine, 19,* 955–958.

Kleinberg, S. (1980). *Being gay in America.* New York: St. Martin's Press.

Kleinman, A. (1987). Anthropology and psychiatry: The role of culture in cross-cultural research on illness. *British Journal of Psychiatry, 151,* 447–454.

Koizumi, H., & Luidens, G. (1984). Cross-cultural issues in the treatment of intractable anorexia nervosa. *International Journal of Family Therapy, 6,* 635–642.

Kope, T. M., & Sack, W. H. (1987). Anorexia nervosa in Southeast Asian refugees: A report on three cases. *Journal of the American Academy of Child and Adolescent Psychiatry, 26(5)*, 795–797.

Lacey, J. H., & Dolan, B. (1988). Bulimia in British blacks and Asians. *British Journal of Psychiatry, 152*, 73–79.

Lakoff, R. T., & Scherr, R. L. (1984). *Face value: The politics of beauty.* Boston: Routledge & Kegan Paul.

Lasegue, C. (1873, September). On hysterical anorexia. *Medical Times and Gazette*, 265–266.

Lee, S. (1991). Anorexia nervosa in Hong Kong: A Chinese perspective. *Psychological Medicine, 21*, 703–711.

Lee, S. (1993). How abnormal is the desire for slimness? A survey of eating attitudes and behavior among Chinese undergraduates in Hong Kong. *Psychological Medicine, 23*, 437–451.

Lee, S., Chui, H. F. K., & Chen, C. (1989). Anorexia nervosa in Hong Kong. Why not more in Chinese? *British Journal of Psychiatry, 154*, 683–688.

Lee, S., Hsu, L. K. G., & Wing, Y. K. (1992). Bulimia nervosa in Hong Kong Chinese patients. *British Journal of Psychiatry, 161*, 545–551.

Luk, C. L., & Bond, M. H. (1992). Chinese lay beliefs about the causes and cures of psychological problems. *Journal of Social and Clinical Psychology, 11*, 140–157.

Marchi, M., & Cohen, P. (1990). Early childhood eating behavior and adolescent eating disorders. *Journal of the American Academy of Child and Adolescent Psychiatry, 29*, 112–117.

Markantonakis, A. (1990). Correspondence. *British Journal of Psychiatry, 157*, 783–784.

Mayer, J. (1955). The role of exercise and activity in weight control. In E. S. Eppright, P. Swanson, & C. A. Iverson (Eds.), *Weight control* (pp. 29–48). Ames, IA: Iowa State College Press.

McFarlane, T. (1994). A comparison of objective versus subjective weight classification in restrained and unrestrained eaters. Unpublished raw data.

Metropolitan Life Insurance Company (1983). *Statistical Bulletin, 64*, 2–9.

Mizushima, N., & Ishii, Y. (1983). The epidemiology of anorexia nervosa in Ischikawa prefecture. *Japanese Journal of Psychosomatic Medicine, 23*, 311–319.

Moore, M. E., Stunkard, A. J., & Srole, L. (1962). Obesity, social class and mental illness. *Journal of the American Medical Association, 181*, 962–966.

Morgan, H. G., & Russell, G. F. M. (1975). Value of family backgrounds and clinical features as predictors of long-term outcome in anorexia nervosa: Four year follow-up study of 41 patients. *Psychological Medicine, 5*, 355–371.

Mumford, D. B., & Whitehouse, A. M. (1988). Increased prevalence of bulimia nervosa among Asian schoolgirls. *British Medical Journal, 297*, 718.

Mumford, D. B., Whitehouse, A. M., & Choudry, I. Y. (1992). Survey of eating disorders in English-medium schools in Lahore, Pakistan. *International Journal of Eating Disorders, 11*, 173–184.

Mumford, D. B., Whitehouse, A. M., & Platts, M. (1991). Sociocultural correlates of eating disorders among Asian schoolgirls in Bradford. *British Journal of Psychiatry, 158*, 222–228.

Naipaul, V. S. (1965). *An area of darkness.* London: Andre Deutch.

Nasser, M. (1986). Comparative study of the prevalence of abnormal eating attitudes among Arab female students of both London and Cairo Universities. *Psychological Medicine, 16*, 621–625.

Nasser, M. (1988). Culture and weight consciousness. *Journal of Psychosomatic Research, 32*, 573–577.

Nevo, S. (1985). Bulimic symptoms: Prevalence and ethnic differences among college women. *International Journal of Eating Disorders, 4*, 151–168.

Nogami, Y., & Yabana, F. (1977). On kibarashi-gui binge-eating. *Folia Psychiatrica and Neuro-logica Japonica, 31,* 159–166.

Nogami, Y., Yamaguchi, T., Ishiwata, H., Sakai, T., & Kusakabe, Y. (1984). *The prevalence of binge eating in the Japanese university and high school population.* Paper presented at the International Conference on Anorexia Nervosa and Related Disorders, Swansea, UK.

Nwaefuna, A. (1981). Anorexia nervosa in a developing country. *British Journal of Psychiatry, 138,* 270–271.

Nylander, I. (1971). The feeling of being fat and dieting in a school population. *Acta Socio-Medica Scandinavica, 1,* 17–26.

Okasha, A., Kamel, M., Sadek, A., Lotah, F., & Bishry, Z. (1977). Psychiatric morbidity among university students in Egypt. *British Journal of Psychiatry, 131,* 149–154.

Olmsted, M., & Kaplan, A. (1995). Psychoeducation in the treatment of eating disorders. In K. Brownell & C. Fairburn (Eds.), *Eating disorders and obesity: A comprehensive handbook* (pp. 299–305). New York: Guilford Press.

Ong, Y. L., Tsoi, W. F., & Cheng, J. S. (1982). A clinical and psychosocial study of seven cases of anorexia nervosa in Singapore. *Singapore Medical Journal, 23,* 255–261.

Polivy, J., Garner, D. M., & Garfinkel, P. E. (1986). Causes and consequences of the current preference for thin female physiques. In C. P. Herman, M. P. Zanna, & E. T. Higgins (Eds.), *Physical appearance, stigma, and social behavior: The Third Ontario Symposium in Personality and Social Psychology* (pp. 89–112) . Hillsdale, NJ: Erlbaum.

Polivy, J., & Herman, C. P. (1983). *Breaking the diet habit.* New York: Basic Books.

Polivy, J., & Herman, C. P. (1985). Dieting and binging. *American Psychologist, 40,* 193–210.

Polivy, J., & Herman, C. P. (1987). Diagnosis and treatment of normal eating. *Journal of Consulting and Clinical Psychology, 5,* 635–644.

Polivy, J, Herman, C. P., Olmsted, M. P., & Jazwinski, C. M. (1984). Restraint and binge eating. In C. Hawkins, W. Fremouw, & P. Clement (Eds.), *The binge-purge syndrome* (pp. 104–121). New York: Springer.

Pope, H. G., Hudson, J. I., & Jonas, J. M. (1986). Bulimia in men: A series of fifteen cases. *Journal of Nervous and Mental Disease, 174,* 117–119.

Powers, P. S. (1980). *Obesity: The regulation of weight.* Baltimore: Williams & Wilkins.

Prince, R. (1985a). The concept of culture-bound syndromes: Anorexia nervosa and brain-fag. *Social Science and Medicine, 21,* 197–203.

Prince, R. (1985b). News and views: More on anorexia nervosa. *Transcultural Psychiatric Research Review, 22,* 199–214.

Pyle, R. L., Halvorson, P. A., Neuman, P. A., & Mitchell, J. E. (1986). The increasing preva-lence of bulimia in freshman college students. *International Journal of Eating Disorders, 5,* 632–647.

Pyle, R. L., Mitchell, J. E., & Eckert, E. D. (1981). Bulimia: A report of 34 cases. *Journal of Clinical Psychiatry, 42,* 60–64.

Raich, R., Rosen, J. C., Deus, J., Perez, O., Requena, A., & Gross, J. (1992). Eating disorder symptoms among adolescents in the United States and Spain: A comparative study. *Inter-national Journal of Eating Disorders, 11,* 6–72.

Rand, C. S. W., & Kuldau, J. M. (1992). Epidemiology of bulimia and symptoms in a general population: Sex, age, race, and socioeconomic status. *International Journal of Eating Dis-orders, 11,* 37–44.

Robinson, P., & Andersen, A. E. (1985). Anorexia nervosa in American Blacks. *Journal of Psychiatric Research, 19,* 183–188.

Robinson, P. H., & Holden, N. L. (1986). Bulimia nervosa in the male: A report of nine cases. *Psychological Medicine, 16,* 795–803.

Rodin, J., Silberstein, L. R., & Striegel-Moore, R. H. (1985). Women and weight: A normative discontent. In T. B. Sonderegger (Ed.), *Nebraska symposium on Motivation: Vol. 32. Psychology and gender* (pp. 267–307) . Lincoln: University of Nebraska Press.

Rudofsky, B. (1972). *The unfashionable human body.* New York: Doubleday.

Russell, G. F. M. (1970). Anorexia nervosa: Its identity as an illness and its treatment. In J. H. Price (Ed.), *Modern trends in psychological medicine* (Vol. 2, pp. 131–164). London: Butterworths.

Russell, G. F. M. (1979). Bulimia nervosa: An ominous variant of anorexia nervosa. *Psychological Medicine, 9,* 429–448.

Schmidt, U. (1993). Bulimia nervosa in the Chinese. *International Journal of Eating Disorders, 14,* 505–509.

Schneider, J. A., & Agras, W. S. (1987). Bulimia in males: A matched comparison with females. *International Journal of Eating Disorders, 6,* 235–242.

Schotte, D. E., & Stunkard, A. J. (1987). Bulimia vs bulimic behaviors on a college campus. *Journal of the American Medical Association, 9,* 1213–1215.

Serdula, M. K., Collins, M. E., Williamson, D. F., Anda, R. F., Pamuk, E. R., & Byers, T. E. (1993). Weight control practices of U.S. adolescents and adults. *Annals of Internal Medicine, 119,* 667–671.

Silber, T. (1984). Anorexia nervosa in black adolescents. *Journal of the National Medical Association, 76,* 29–32.

Silberstein, L., Mishkind, M. E., Striegel-Moore, R. H., Timko, C., & Rodin, J. (1989). Men and their bodies: A comparison of homosexual and heterosexual men. *Psychosomatic Medicine, 51,* 337–346.

Silverstein, B. (1986). The role of the mass media in promoting a standard of bodily attractiveness for women. *Sex Roles, 14,* 519–532.

Silverstone, J. T., Gordon, R. A. P., & Stunkard, A. J. (1969). Social factors in obesity in London. *The Practitioner, 202,* 682–688.

Snow, J. T., & Harris, M. B. (1986). An analysis of weight and diet content in five women's interest magazines. *The Journal of Obesity and Weight Regulation, 5,* 194–214.

Steinhausen, H. C., Neumarker, K. J., Vollrath, M., Dudeck, U., & Neumarker, U. (1992). A transcultural comparison of the eating disorder inventory in former East and West Berlin. *International Journal of Eating Disorders, 12,* 407–416.

Stice, E. (1994). Review of the evidence for a sociocultural model of bulimia nervosa and an exploration of the mechanism of action. *Clinical Psychology Review, 17,* 633–661.

Stice, E., Schupak-Neuberg, E., Shaw, H. E., & Stein, R. I. (1994). Relation of media exposure to eating disorder symptomatology: An examination of mediating mechanisms. *Journal of Abnormal Psychology, 103,* 836–840.

Stice, E., & Shaw, H. E. (1994). Adverse effects of the media portrayed thin-ideal on women and linkages to bulimic symptomatology. *Journal of Social and Clinical Psychology, 13,* 288–308.

Striegel-Moore, R. H., Silberstein, L. R., & Rodin, J. (1986). Toward an understanding of risk factors for bulimia. *American Psychologist, 41,* 246–263.

Striegel-Moore, R. H., Tucker, N., & Hsu, J. (1990). Body image dissatisfaction and disordered eating in lesbian college students. *International Journal of Eating Disorders, 9,* 493–500.

Stunkard, A. J. (1977). Obesity and social environment: Current status, future prospects. *Proceedings of the New York Academy of Sciences, 300,* 298–320.

Suematsu, H., Ishikawa, H., & Kuboki, T. (1985). Statistical studies on anorexia nervosa in Japan: Detailed clinical data on 1,011 patients. *Psychotherapy and psychosomatics, 43,* 96–103.

Szmukler, G. I. (1985). The epidemiology of anorexia nervosa and bulimia. *Journal of Psychiatric Research, 19,* 143–153.

Szmukler, G. I., McCance, C., McCrone, L., & Hunter, D. (1986). Anorexia nervosa: A psychiatric case register study from Aberdeen. *Psychological Medicine, 16,* 49–58.

Tamburrino, M., Franco, K., Bernal, G., Carroll, B., & McSweeny, A. J. (1987). Eating attitudes in college students. *Journal of American Medical Womens' Associations, 42,* 42–47.

Theander, S. (1970). Anorexia nervosa: A psychiatric investigation of 94 female patients. *Acta Psychiatrica Scandinavica, Suppl. 214,* 7–194.

Then, D. (1992, August). *Women's magazines: Messages they convey about looks, men and careers.* Paper presented at the Annual Convention of the American Psychological Association, Washington, DC.

Tiggemann, M., & Rothblum, E. D. (1988). Gender differences in social consequences of perceived overweight in the United States and Australia. *Sex Roles, 18,* 75–86.

Turnbull, J. D., Freeman, C. P. L., Barry, F., & Annandale, A. (1987). Physical and psychological characteristics of five male bulimics. *British Journal of Psychiatry, 150,* 25–29.

Venes, A. M., Krupka, L. R., & Gerard, R. J. (1982). Overweight/obese patients: An overview. *The Practitioner, 226,* 1102–1109.

Wardle, J., & Beals, S. (1986). Restraint, body image and food attitudes in children from 12–18 years. *Appetite, 7,* 209–217.

Wardle, J., & Beinart, H. (1981). Binge eating: A theoretical review. *British Journal of Clinical Psychology, 20,* 97–109.

Wells, J. E., Coope, P. A., Gabb, D. C., & Pears, R. K. (1985). The factor structure of the Eating Attitudes Test with adolescent schoolgirls. *Psychological Medicine, 15,* 141–146.

Whitaker, A., Johnson, J., Shaffer, D., Rapoport, J. L., Kalikow, K., Walsh, B. T., Davies, M., Braiman, S., & Dolinsky, A. (1990). Uncommon troubles in young people: Prevalence estimates of selected psychiatric disorders in a nonreferred adolescent population. *Archives of General Psychiatry, 47,* 487–496.

Willi, J., & Grossmann, S. (1983). Epidemiology of anorexia nervosa in a defined region of Switzerland. *American Journal of Psychiatry, 140,* 564–567.

Williamson, D. F., Serdula, M. K., Anda, R. F., Levy, A., & Byers, T. (1992). Weight loss attempts in adults: Goals, duration, and rate of weight loss. *American Journal of Public Health, 82,* 1251–1257.

Wiseman, M. A., Gray, J.J., Mosimann, J. E., & Ahrens, A. H. (1992). Cultural expectations of thinness in women: An update. *International Journal of Eating Disorders, 11,* 85–89.

Wooley, S. C. (1987). Psychological and social aspects of obesity. In A. E. Bender & L. J. Brookes (Eds.), *Body weight control: The physiology, clinical treatment and prevention of obesity* (pp. 177–185). New York: Livingstone.

Wooley, S. C., & Wooley, O. W. (1979). Obesity and women. I. A closer look at the facts. *Women's Studies International Quarterly, 2,* 69–79.

World Health Organization (1992). *The ICD-10 classification of mental and behavioral disorders—Clinical descriptions and diagnostic guidelines.* Geneva: Author.

Yager, J., Kurtzman, F., Landsverk, J., & Wiesmeier, E. (1988). Behaviors and attitudes related to eating disorders in homosexual male college students. *American Journal of Psychiatry, 145,* 495–497.

Yager, J., & Smith, M. (1993). Restricter anorexia nervosa in a thirteen-year-old sheltered Muslim girl raised in Lahore, Pakistan: Developmental similarities to western patients. *International Journal of Eating Disorders, 14,* 383–386.

Zheng, Y. M. (1982). The psychotherapy of child anorexia nervosa—A follow-up study of a case for 23 years. *Chinese Journal of Neurology and Psychiatry, 15,* 46–48.

7

Cultural Issues in the Management of Depression

AMY S. KAISER

RANDY KATZ

BRIAN F. SHAW

Psychology is a culture, an institution, an increasingly socializing agent. Psychology transmits values about health and illness . . . As psychology grows in influence it shapes the goals of behavior for the child, parent, country, and society . . . Psychology has been given the responsibility of defining "healthy" growth and development. Because of this responsibility, psychology needs to become scientifically literate, socially sensitive, culturally aware, and humanely oriented. (Pedersen, 1995, p. 47)

Cultural competence may be as integral to the treatment of depression as knowledge of the condition itself. The process of assessment, diagnosis, and treatment of depression in culturally diverse populations requires the clinical integration of two skill sets. First, it is essential that individuals involved in the management of depression have a comprehensive understanding of the phenomenology of the disorder. In addition, when working across cultures, knowledge of different cultures, skills for intercultural therapeutic interactions, and awareness about the specific cultural groups of the patients are crucial. Both an understanding of the psychopathology of depressive disorders and cultural competence are essential for all therapists. Johnson (1987) describes an ideal clinical situation whereby the therapist does "not overemphasize culture at the expense of recognizing pathology or underemphasize cultural differences at the expense of sensitivity" (p. 327).

The pathological processes of depression have a profound influence on an individual's well-being. Depression involves psychological (e.g., self-criticism, anhedonia), biological (e.g. weight loss, insomnia), and social (e.g., avoidance, passivity) symptoms that impair an individual's ability to function normally. It is important to understand that depression, like other illnesses, may manifest differently depending on the ethnic and cultural norms of the sufferer (Hinton & Kleinman, 1993; Weiss & Kleinman, 1988). The manifestation of depressive symptomatology is often confounded in Western health care settings by the degree of acculturation or assimilation that the patient has experienced. Depression may manifest itself in accordance with the cultural group norms of the patient, in accordance with the typical symptomatic presentation in the host culture, or some combination thereof. To be most effective, any clinical interventions must take this into consideration at assessment, treatment, and follow-up.

Culture has been both narrowly and broadly defined (Pedersen, 1991). In its most narrow form, culture implies the ethnic cultural background of the individual. For instance, a narrow definition would include a person's country of origin and skin color. However, culture as it is defined more broadly includes all aspects of the person, such as demographic affiliations, ethnographic variables, and individual affiliations (Pederson, 1991). Each individual's combination of ethnic, socioeconomic, political, religious, and cultural backgrounds, together with their experiences and distinct personalities, combine to formulate a personal worldview or schema.

A broad understanding of culture requires that the clinician recognize that all group memberships imply a culture but that he or she still distinguish individual differences (Pederson, 1991). Implicit in the broad definition of culture is the notion that all therapeutic experiences are culturally complex despite the fact that the therapist and the patient may share memberships in several groups. It is incumbent on the clinician to assess the weight of each of the cultural components that combine to make up the individual and its impact on the therapeutic process. A clinician may identify a depressed patient as a member of a particular cultural group and conduct the assessment and develop a treatment plan accordingly. The clinician needs to consider not only the ethnic background of the patient, but also all groups of which the patient is a member and the ways in which the patient affiliates with those groups. By including such a wide range of variables in the broad determination of culture, the management of psychopathology in all cases becomes, to some degree, cultural (Speight, Meyers, Cox, & Highlen, 1991).

The therapist and the patient will have different worldviews regardless of whether or not they belong to the same cultural group. To treat depression across worldviews, in the broadest understanding of culture, is therefore to treat across cultures. Multiculturalism, wherein a person is affiliated with two or more groups, may confound the therapeutic treatment across cultures. The nature of all group affiliations has to be considered, because each group membership may have a unique way of impacting on the manifestation of symptoms and therefore on the patient's subjective experience of the depression.

Culture is often defined as a way of life of a people. Jackson and Meadows (1991) caution against defining culture by its surface manifestations alone. For instance, assumptions are often made about people based on their style of dress or dietary preferences. Assumptions based on these criteria will present an incomplete picture that neglects the deeper implications of culture. To effectively understand the degree to which an individual's cultural membership impacts on the clinical process, it is necessary to examine the culture's underlying philosophical assumptions (Jackson & Meadows, 1991).

The focus of this chapter will be upon relevant issues for the clinician as they pertain to the management of depression across cultures. We will discuss issues relevant to diagnosis, assessment, treatment planning, and therapy. In addition, the cultural aspects of depression and the methodological issues which affect prevalence rates will be reviewed.

DIAGNOSIS OF DEPRESSION

The introduction to the fourth edition of the American Psychiatric Association *Diagnostic and Statistical Manual of Mental Disorders* (*DSM-IV*, APA, 1994) has established international uniformity of psychiatric diagnosis and standardized the classification of psychiatric disorders. The authors of *DSM-IV* recognize that culture plays a vital role in the expression and diagnosis of psychiatric disorders. The *DSM-IV* system encourages clinicians to keep cultural considerations in mind in the formulation of each of the five axes of diagnosis. Diagnostic criteria as outlined in the *DSM-IV* should be complemented by knowledge of cultural behavioral norms. The results of a study concerned with the evaluation of mental health across 20 nations suggested that *DSM* applications reported in the absence of specific knowledge about cultural behavior may be "specious" or misleading (Baskin, 1984). Jenkins, Kleinman, and Good (1991) alert clinicians that an essential prerequisite to the effective application of the *DSM* and International Classification of Diseases (ICD-9) (World Health Organization, 1978) categories is the recognition of innuendo and metaphor and that the absence of such appreciation may lead to diagnoses that are not valid across cultures.

A number of culture-bound conditions are also described in *DSM-IV*. Kirmayer (personal communication, 1996) notes that the *DSM-IV* is somewhat contradictory in that the provision of culture-bound syndromes is immediately followed by the recommendation that clinicians make cultural formulations. The premise is that by encouraging clinicians to consider culture as a part of all diagnostic classification, the *DSM-IV* should not then advocate specifically culture-bound syndromes without providing the context from which they emerged. Hinton and Kleinman (1993) note that one of the results emerging from the *DSM* approach to classification has been to trim the contextual meaning from the culture-bound syndrome and to fit what remains into a preexisting *DSM* diagnostic category. Bebbington (1993) contends that culture-bound syndromes are not conditions that are unique to any one culture, but rather that it is the diagnostic categories themselves that are culturally determined. This view is consistent with the observation that conditions that were previously thought to be culture-bound syndromes unrelated to depression tend to be associated with depression (Sartorius, 1986). For example, Kleinman (1977) identifies several culture-bound syndromes that tend to be associated with depression. These include *koro* among the Chinese, and *brain fag* in Africa. In the section of the *DSM-IV* which delineates major depression, cultural aspects of the condition are explored. Conditions which appear most frequently in specific cultures are outlined in this section. In addition, the *DSM-IV* offers cultural variations in symptom manifestation of various illnesses, as is the case for depression.

The diagnosis of a Major Depressive Episode, according to the *DSM-IV,* requires the presence of five significant symptoms, which must include either a predominantly depressed mood and/or loss of interest for at least a 2-week period of time. Other symptoms may be: significant change in weight or appetite; insomnia or hypersomnia; psychomotor retardation or agitation; fatigue or loss of energy; feelings of worthlessness or excessive guilt; diminished concentration, loss of clarity of thought or indecisiveness; and recurrent thoughts of death (*DSM-IV,* 1994).

Diagnostic categories are defined by cutoff points at which an aggregate of symptoms is considered to be a clinical condition. The cutoffs are not arbitrary, but rather have been established in accordance with extensive clinical evidence. It is important to note that the *DSM* is a living document, which is subject to change. Updated versions are adapted to incorporate new findings. The parameters for depression, like several other conditions whose diagnostic criteria have been standardized in the *DSM,* have been modified in every adaptation of the *DSM* (American Psychiatric Association, 1952, 1968, 1980, 1987, 1994). The fluidity regarding the exact qualifying factors which make up depression does not indicate a change in the nature of the condition, but rather reflects an advancement of the current state of knowledge about the condition. For example, in *DSM-III,* one of the characteristics which was indicative of depression was weight loss. In the *DSM-III-R,* this criterion was broadened to include weight gain as well, and this has been extended to the current version, *DSM-IV.* Clearly, weight gain is not a new element of depression but was only recently identified as a significant symptom of the most typical forms of depressive disorder.

In addition to outlining the specific criteria for the classification of depression, the *DSM-IV* provides a brief description outlining the role that culture plays in the presentation of depressive disorder. The experience of depression is somewhat dependent on the cultural group in which it occurs. For instance, in some cultures people tend to present with somatic complaints such as physical aches and pains, while in others people may present with more affective complaints such as sadness.

In the *DSM-IV* (1994, Appendix I, p. 843–844) there is a recommendation that in multicultural environments clinicians devise a cultural formulation as a supplement to the five diagnostic axes. The clinician is offered five categories under which to express a narrative cultural summary. These categories are as follows:

1. *Cultural identity of the individual.* Here, it is suggested that the individual's cultural group be noted. For immigrants, it is advised that the degree of acculturation into the host culture, in addition to the degree of involvement in the culture of origin, also be noted. An assessment of language abilities is recommended. In the case of depression in immigrants, for instance, evaluating the person's involvement in both the host culture and the culture of origin may be particularly pertinent to the assessment. It is possible that a person who has not assimilated into the host culture may appear to have loss of interest, a symptom of depression. In fact, it may only appear that this person has little interest because they have not yet become involved and integrated in their new environment. Enthusiasm may be low due to their feelings of alienation or homesickness.

2. *Cultural explanations of the individual's illness.* This section should address the prominent cultural expressions through which symptoms of illness are presented. This includes: attributions regarding the significance and gravity of the condition in relation to the person's cultural group norms; any illness category by which the group

themselves might classify the illness; the perceived causes and explanatory models used by the individual and their reference group to explain the condition; and preferences for health care. This section helps the clinician to formulate the illness experience of the patient. This may be achieved, for example, by indicating that a person experiencing depression believes that the suffering has been inflicted by Divine retribution and that they are experiencing bodily pain as a punishment for bad deeds. If this is a firmly embedded cultural belief, the depressed person is likely experiencing guilt and may be alienated from their community, which is likely to exacerbate the condition. In addition, it is important to note whether a person's preference for health care is to seek help from the elders in the community, as this may explain potential resistance to traditional Western treatment of depression. This reluctance may translate into a form of social desirability whereby the patient will not present with anything that he or she anticipates to be unacceptable in the esteem of the health care provider.

3. *Cultural factors related to psychosocial environment and levels of functioning.* In this section, availability of social support should be outlined, in addition to culturally relevant interpretations of social stressors and the individual's functional ability. Social support for the depressed patient is most important. Therefore, the extent to which the person is comfortable using their social resources should be noted. In some cultures, people experience shame in connection with their depression and are hesitant to utilize their available resources. L. Kirmayer (personal communication, January 1996) suggests that the concept of the individual is derived from Western culture. In many cultures the individual is deeply embedded in the family structure. This highlights the importance of carefully documenting a family history formulation. A. Kleinman (personal communication, 1995) alerts Western clinicians that social and cultural realities of a non-Western patient may be discounted by focusing interview questions on the individual, rather than including the context of the patient's situation.

4. *Cultural elements of the relationship between the individual and the clinician.* This section calls upon the clinician to note differences in both culture and social status that exist between clinician and patient. It is important to consider the ways in which these discrepancies could affect assessment, diagnosis, and treatment. In the case of depression, the clinician might note behaviors which may be indicative of depression or may be within the realm of the individual's own cultural norms. The social context in which depression is experienced often exacerbates the experience. Wide discrepancies in the cultural or socioeconomic circumstances of the clinician and the patient may create boundaries that may interfere in treatment. Ivey (1995) asserts that failing to help clients understand the influence that social context has on their condition is the major failing of psychotherapy. He advocates helping depressed women understand that familial and cultural issues related to oppressive gender roles impact on their condition. However, within-group differences that exist between patient and clinician may be equally as alienating. In this section, the clinician must examine potential ruptures or misunderstandings due to divergent worldviews or the imbalance of power and authority. The clinician may be valued or discounted; in either case, the information is significant, as it affects treatment (L. Kirmayer, personal communication, January 1996).

5. *Overall assessment for diagnosis and care.* This section should include a discussion concerning the ways in which cultural factors impact upon the diagnosis and

management of the depressed person. Here, culturally relevant treatment considerations should be outlined.

ASSESSMENT OF DEPRESSION IN A CULTURAL CONTEXT

The assessment of depression in a cultural context is confounded by the fact that the symptoms of depression have been reported to manifest differently across cultures (*DSM-IV,* 1994; Kleinman, 1986, 1995; Nikelly, 1988; Spitzer, Williams, Gibbon, & First, 1992). This is further complicated by the fact that "normal" behaviors are conceptualized differently across cultures. For instance, suffering is valued in the tenets of Buddhism (Obeyesekere, 1985), while not in most other cultures. The clinical presentation of a devout Buddhist might therefore be one of exaggerated suffering because it is culturally desirable. Conversely, people from other cultures might attempt to mask their suffering because it is viewed as undesirable or weak. Thus, a therapist who is unaware of the cultural innuendo woven through the presentation of the problem and the expression of the pathology is at risk of misdiagnosing and therefore mismanaging the patient.

Distinct issues of reliability and validity arise in the assessment of depression across cultures. First, in order to design an appropriate intervention strategy, an accurate and applicable descriptive classification or diagnostic system needs to be established. The system of classification must be flexible enough to encompass signs and symptoms of depression as they are manifested across cultures. For instance, depression among Taiwanese people has been reported to present in a somatic form (Krause & Liang, 1992). The clinician who is steeped in Western cultural norms of behavior might overlook the depression by focusing on the physical complaint, expecting that if the diagnosis were to be depression, the patient's primary complaint would be low affect or loss of interest rather than somatization. Nikelly (1988) emphasizes the importance of relevant diagnostic criteria to avoid misdiagnosis or overdiagnosis, because depressed behavior in one culture may not be seen to imply illness in another.

The issue of culture-fair tests has received extensive attention in the literature (Anastasi, 1988; Kinzie & Manson, 1987). The most-studied aspect of culture-fair tests has been intelligence and personality assessment (Helms, 1992; Suzuki & Kugler, 1995). Tests administered to culturally different patients should be considered in terms of cultural fairness and sensitivity. There are a number of specific issues which should be considered when using assessment material with culturally distinct populations. The cultural composition of reference norm groups for all tests administered should be verified. Scoring systems may be based on Western behavioral norms. By subjecting patients from different cultures to tests that do not evaluate their symptoms, behaviors, or traits with an applicable yardstick, we cannot obtain relevant data; furthermore, the effects of the experience may be harmful. For example, the Beck Depression Inventory, when administered to Oriental patients, tends to show an overrepresentation of depressive symptoms in nondepressed groups. Test data that has been skewed by the cultural inapplicability of measures used may start the patient on a trajectory whereby subsequent misdiagnosis is the result of the assessment findings and irrelevant or superfluous treatment is prescribed. Finally, tests that are translated directly for usage with different populations may not be efficient for at least two reasons. First, direct translations may lose their intended meaning in the translation; second, the construct being measured may be unfamiliar in other cultures.

Rogler (1993) recommends a three-stage framework for assessment and diagnosis across cultures. First, he suggests that symptoms and symptom severity must be considered. Next, these symptoms must be considered in terms of their configuration into disorders. Finally, the effects of cultural factors in the interview itself must be considered. This model is based on the premise that a breakdown in any of the stages hinders the other stages in the process of assessment and diagnosis. It is useful to consider a clinical application of the model. For instance, consider a patient who is diagnosed with a somatization disorder, when in fact the patient suffers from depression. A misdiagnosis occurred due to the misconception of symptoms because they were not presented in the more typical Western way. Thus, an assessment of symptoms has taken place and the symptoms have been configured into a diagnostic category; however, the diagnosis is based on a faulty foundation. This will certainly have an impact on subsequent clinical interactions. The point is that adherence to this model simplifies the process of culturally relevant assessment and diagnosis, which are of particular importance. Not only must the assessment tools and interview methods used be culturally sensitive and relevant for the individual, but also the treatment choice must be tailored to accommodate both the cognitive and social-environmental worlds of the patient. Without a culturally sensitive assessment, it becomes very difficult to select appropriate targets for intervention for a given individual's treatment. Some depressed patients, for example, exhibit pervasive anhedonia and require careful planning of daily activities. Others exhibit social-skills deficits and will benefit from skills-acquisition programs. The clinician needs to work in conjunction with the patient to formulate a treatment plan which would consider the social and behavioral norms of the patient's reference group. A treatment plan that encourages the development of what may be considered to be "Westernized" social skills, as they are understood by the clinician, may serve little purpose for a depressed patient whose contextual reality is not Western. Family participation in some aspects of treatment planning is often welcomed by patients in some cultures (Hanson, 1990). In these cases, offering the patient the possibility of familial involvement in treatment planning might serve to reduce anxiety and feelings of isolation. This is consistent with the idea of developing a treatment plan that incorporates all aspects of the person's experience. In addition, in order to evaluate the effectiveness of therapy, some metric of symptom severity is required. If this metric lacks adequate reliability and/or validity within the cultural context, realistic evaluation is impaired, if not prevented. It is important to recall that not all symptoms of depression are present in all cultures. Adequate assessment of depression should not be restricted to a single dimension, such as mood, but should sample the range of relevant factors, including psychological, biological, and social functioning.

There are two general ways of assessing depression: interview techniques and self-report measures (Katz, Shaw, Vallis & Kaiser, 1995). In the following section, these methods will be examined and specific instruments in both categories will be reviewed. Interview methods of assessment allow the greatest flexibility for adaptation to address cultural needs. Interviews allow the clinician the liberty to emphasize issues that are particularly salient in the social-cultural context of the patient. Transla-

tors may be used and interviews may be structured specifically so that they are culturally relevant. On the other hand, self-report measures eliminate the cultural innuendo
of the symptom presentation and reduce the possibility that the patients may present
themselves in a way that they believe will be positively received by a clinician from
the majority culture. We will outline the merits and drawbacks of both interview and
self-report measures and then describe a number of commonly used measures for the
assessment of depression.

Structured and Semi-Structured Interviews

In this section we review several interview methods of assessment. Among the most
frequently used interview methods are the Hamilton Rating Scale for Depression
(HRSD; Hamilton, 1960; Hamilton & White, 1959), the depression subsection of the
Structured Clinical Interview Diagnostic Instrument (SCID; Spitzer, et al., 1992), the
depressive subsection of the Present State Examination (PSE; Wing et al., 1990;
Wing, Birley, Cooper, Graham, & Isaacs, 1967), and the Diagnostic Interview Schedule (DIS; Robins, Helzer, Croughan, & Ratcliff, 1981). More recently, however, instruments have been developed specifically for international use. Examples of such
are the Composite International Diagnostic Instrument (CIDI; Robins et al., 1981)
and the Standardized Assessment of Depressive Disorders (WHO/SADD; Sartorius et
al., 1980). This review is by no means exhaustive, but some of the most common
interview methods of assessment for depression are considered. A more comprehensive list of other popular structured interview schedules and self-report instruments is
presented in Appendix 7.1.

Prior to reviewing some of these interview methods, we consider some of the
more practical issues involved in interviewing a culturally different depressed patient.
These issues include the interviewer's knowledge of the disorder, their knowledge of
the behavioral correlates associated with depression, the interviewer's clinical de-
meanor, and their cultural skills or competence. Cultural skills and competence include the interviewer's knowledge about the cultural behavioral norms for the patient's reference group. These also ideally include the clinician's awareness of his or
her own status of ethnic identity and the way in which these views might affect the
interaction between the interviewer and the patient.

The task of interviewing a depressed patient can be a difficult and frustrating one,
frequently accompanied by irritability and negative affect on the part of the interviewer (Beck, 1967). The difficulty of the task is compounded when the clinician and
the patient encounter cultural barriers such as differences in language, values, and
worldviews. Depressed individuals may experience marked difficulties maintaining
an interpersonal interaction, particularly when they are under pressure to produce
information. This will undoubtedly be exacerbated by frustration if the patient is
facing a linguistic barrier. Patients have been reported to temporarily lose their ability
to communicate in a second language, but not in their mother tongue, when depressed
(Westermeyer, 1987). Should the patient perceive that the clinician is not culturally
competent, the patient will feel misunderstood, and there may be resistance to disclose or to create an alliance with the clinician. As a result, depressed patients may
be unresponsive, have difficulty following questions, or be nondisclosing, all of
which can contribute to the interviewer's frustration.

The interviewer should obtain a relevant and complete history which includes all factors (i.e., ethnic and religious group, social class, gender, history of oppression, and sexual orientation). This history should definitely include information about current and past episodes of depression, significant medical history, and family history. It is often useful to have the patient make a report on a Life History Questionnaire before the initial interview (Lazarus, 1971). Any additional relevant information on known markers or risk factors for depression (e.g., history of bipolar disorder in a first-degree relative) should also be obtained. As a guide to obtaining relevant cultural information and to facilitate the documentation of cultural factors, clinicians should utilize the cultural formulation in the *DSM-IV* as outlined above.

When interviewing a depressed individual, it is important to work toward an understanding of the patient's subjective account of the phenomenology (i.e., the situation *from their perspective*). This has particular significance for the culturally different patient. Kleinman (1987) emphasizes the importance of eliciting the patient's explanatory model of the condition. The explanatory model is the patient's personal subjective understanding of their illness. This includes factors such as the individual's perceived cause of the illness, help-seeking venues that the patient sees as suitable treatment, and their perception of the seriousness or gravity of the illness (Hinton & Kleinman, 1993).

Ying (1990) examined explanatory models of depression among a nonclinical group of immigrant Chinese-American women. She reported a positive correlation between the way in which the women conceptualized their depression and their help-seeking behavior. The women who conceptualized depression in a psychological framework relied on their own resources and their social supports, whereas the women who made biological attributions for their depression were more likely to pursue medical treatment. Despite the discrepancies that existed between groups in terms of help-seeking patterns, attributions did not belong to rigid or discrete categories. People who explained their depression in somatic terms often presented with psychological aspects to the depression, and vice versa, which in turn affected their preference for treatment.

Findings such as these highlight the importance of understanding the depression from the patient's perspective. When the clinician examines the explanatory model of the patient, the clinician is better able to address their unique and individual needs. While a patient's descriptions may seem implausible or exaggerated to the interviewer (e.g., "I am hollow inside," "I think I must be the devil I'm so evil"), they are understandable in that they may be based on a negative view within the cognitive triad of the self, the world, and the future (Beck, 1967; Beck, Rush, Shaw & Emery, 1979). Alternatively, it is important to distinguish these types of statements from cultural forms of expression. For instance, such statements may be normative forms of expression in some cultures or religious groups, such as those that value suffering.

It is commonly believed that discussion of a diagnosis is reassuring to many patients who are confused about their symptomatology. It may not, however, be a relief to some patients, particularly for patients whose cultural group views depression or other psychiatric illness as shameful. Clinicians should also be aware that discussing diagnosis with the patient might increase their sadness as a result of being labeled or because they perceive it to be socially unacceptable for them to divulge that they have depression. For instance, in some cultures the social norm is that males should present themselves as strong, and for them, the admission of depression implies weakness.

Depressed patients may misinterpret an interviewer's comments in a negative way. For example, if an interviewer interrupts the patient in an attempt to structure the interview, the patient may misinterpret this behavior as a lack of respect or an indication that the interviewer is not really interested in what they have to say. The patient may also feel that the interviewer is unfairly exerting cultural dominance. Thus, it is useful from the onset to explain the constraints of the interview with respect to time limitations, necessary information to be gathered, and the importance of structure and direction during the interview. This may help to avoid misunderstandings that could result in the patient's developing negative reactions to the interview process. Patients may be informed that their task is to let the interviewer see the full extent of their current feeling and behavior.

The clinician must always be sensitive to possible suicidal ideation or behavior when interviewing a depressed individual. The myth that questioning about suicide might increase its likelihood has *not* been supported by research or experience. An open, frank discussion of suicide is essential for an accurate assessment of suicidal potential (Linehan, 1981). Several suicide scales may be useful guides to the clinician's questioning: the Suicide Ideation Scale (Beck & Kovacs, 1979) and the Reasons for Living Questionnaire (Linehan & Chiles, 1983).

In addition to the content of the patient's stated reports, nonverbal characteristics may be useful indicators of depression. When using nonverbal cues as indicators of depression, the clinician must be acutely aware that the diversity of body languages across cultures is analogous to the differences in spoken languages; one needs to be fluent in the body language of a culture to accurately decode nonverbal communications. Speech rate and voice quality are often associated with depressed affect. Depressed individuals may often speak in a slowed manner in a voice that is frequently monotone. This must be differentiated from expression, which is less animated than the more familiar style in Western culture. A change in activity level is another nonverbal behavior associated with depression. Depressed individuals may be slowed in their physical movements (psychomotor retardation), as well as their speech rate. Conversely, agitation demonstrated by an increase in activity, such as pacing and wringing of the hands, may be a feature of the depressed individual's presentation. The posture of a depressed individual may also give clues to depression. The depressed patient commonly sits with their head down and shoulders slumped forward, avoids eye contact, and smiles rarely (see work on nonverbal behavior by Ekman & Friesen, 1974; Fisch, Frey, & Hirsbrunner, 1983; Waxer, 1974). For culturally different patients, clinicians would be wise to acquaint themselves with the normative verbal and nonverbal communication of the patient's reference group. This will help to prevent misdiagnosis whereby cultural behavioral norms are mistaken for signs of depression.

It must be stressed that the above verbal and nonverbal signs are not always differentially diagnostic of depression, even in Western culture. These behaviors are frequently observed in psychiatric conditions other than depression (e.g., anxiety disorders and schizophrenia) and are also observed as common behavior in some cultures. In the African culture, for example, direct eye contact may be seen to be impolite. Cultural norms call for downcast eyes during communication, whereas in Western cultures downcast eyes may be perceived to be avoidance. It is important, nonetheless, to be sensitive to the above features, as they are readily observable and are often signs of disordered functioning, and, equally important, may be signs of improvements in the patient's condition.

The Diagnostic Interview Schedule (DIS)   The Diagnostic Interview Schedule (DIS; Robins et al., 1981) is an example of a diagnostic interview that has been developed to be administered by laypersons. The DIS is used to assess a wide variety of psychiatric conditions in addition to depression. In the case of cross-cultural assessments, the advantage of training interviewers who are culturally similar to the interviewee may permit a freer expression of their problems. In addition, the expression of the symptom pattern may be more easily understood by an interviewer who is familiar with normative behavior of the interviewee's cultural group. However, the rigidity of the DIS format may confine the interviewer by not allowing the initiation of a more creative style of probing that might be uniquely pertinent in some cultures.

The DIS has been thought to be a useful instrument for cultural research. Using the structured format helps the clinician to identify relevant issues that might otherwise remain undetected. Rogler (1993) refers to the DIS as one of the tools which "demystifies" assessment and diagnosis across cultures. The DIS has been found to be reliable in assessing depression in various cultures. For instance, Manson, Shore, and Bloom (1985) used the DIS to assess for depression among Hopi Indians. The DIS was modified slightly to accommodate for the conceptualizations of the culture (i.e., the DIS merges the concepts of shame, guilt, and sinfulness, whereas Hopi health workers indicated that each of these concepts is seen to be discernible from the other two, and each needed to be assessed separately).

Another aspect of the DIS that must be heeded with regard to its cross-cultural applicability is that the DIS rule for coding severity of a symptom is contingent on whether the person has sought treatment for the symptom. Rogler (1993) alerts us to the possibility that this may lead to underestimates of the prevalence of mental health problems in some cultures. This is the case because in some cultures help-seeking is not indicative of prevalence but rather is based on cultural norms. In some cultures, consultation with religious leaders or the elders in the community is the most common help-seeking route.

In summary, the DIS may be used for cross-cultural assessments. Some items may need to be adapted for cultural relevance. The interview may be conducted by lay interviewers, allowing for culturally similar or culturally versed interviewers to be trained. Interpreters should note that the DIS rule of severity, which uses help-seeking as a gauge, may not be an appropriate measure of severity in some cultures.

The Present State Examination (PSE)   Another interview method used to assess depression and psychopathology in general is the Present State Examination (PSE; Wing et al., 1967, 1990). This measure is a semistructured interview designed to assess for the presence of a variety of psychopathological conditions over the month preceding assessment.

The PSE was developed by Wing and his colleagues in the United Kingdom and has not been frequently used in North America. Thus, accumulated experience with this scale is limited. Finally, as discussed by Wing et al. (1967), the use of the PSE by a wide variety of interviewers has not been systematically examined. The more recent version, PSE-10, incorporated within the Schedules for Clinical Assessment in Neuropsychiatry system (SCAN), has managed to overcome most of the problems associated with using the PSE in North America. This interview therefore promises to be valuable for the assessment of depression for both clinicians and researchers across cultures.

The Composite International Diagnostic Instrument (CIDI)   The Composite International Diagnostic Interview (CIDI; Robins et al., 1981) is a comprehensive and fully standardized diagnostic instrument for research which uses the International Classification of Diseases (ICD-10) (World Health Organization, 1992) and *DSM-III-R* to establish case criteria. It was designed to bridge the gap between the PSE, which was the instrument of choice in the United Kingdom and Europe, and the DIS, which was primarily used in North America. As such, the CIDI is composed of items from both of these interviews. The aim of the World Health Organization in commissioning the CIDI was the development of a reliable diagnostic criterion and instrument for the assessment of mental disorders across cultures (Janca, Üstün, & Sartorius, 1993).

The CIDI has been subjected to an extensive series of field trials, and findings confirm its value for reliably diagnosing depressive disorders in a number of different settings (Farmer, Katz, McGuffin, & Bebbington, 1987). The CIDI offers an opportunity to determine the distribution, incidence, and prevalence of depression in various settings cross culturally (Essau & Wittchen, 1993).

The Hamilton Rating Scale for Depression (HRSD)   The Hamilton Rating Scale for Depression (HRSD) is historically the most commonly used interview measure of depression (Hamilton, 1960). According to Hamilton, there were a number of major disadvantages with existing measures used to assess depression. The available measures were often developed and normed using a nonclinical population and therefore were not sensitive to qualitative and quantitative differences in clinical depression. Self-report measures had low reliability and were of limited use with semiliterate patients, and general psychopathology measures did not assess depression with sufficient precision. These drawbacks are particularly intrusive in the assessment of depression across cultures. For instance, qualitative details of the illness experience are highly pertinent in formulating a diagnosis across cultures. Although the HRSD was not specifically designed to be culturally sensitive, its flexibility as a clinical scale allows for specific adaptations to different cultural groups.

HRSD interviewers are encouraged to use all sources of information available to them, in addition to the actual interview. This is an ideal directive for clinicians assessing for the symptoms or severity of depression across cultures. Clinicians are not confined by the instrument, but rather they are encouraged to use all available resources to obtain an accurate diagnosis. This might involve the inclusion of the family or the utilization of cultural information from community resources or cultural brokers.

High interrater reliability of the HRSD may be partly a function of the shared background, experience, and attitude that exist when raters from the same setting are used (Sotsky & Glass, 1983). The implications of interrater reliability as a function of shared experience of the interviewers must be considered in a cross-cultural context. Different raters from different settings are less likely to be similar on these factors and may therefore attenuate reliability. There is a heavy loading of somatic items on the HRSD, relative to mood or cognitive items. The heavy loading of somatic symptoms may itself confound reliable detection of depression across cultures. This is due to the tendencies for some groups to express their depressive illness in a somatic form.

In conclusion, the HRSD is an interview measure that appears to be reliable, demonstrates moderate associations with other depression measures, and is sensitive to change. Data suggest that specific steps can be taken to increase reliability and that there is potential for the scale to be used by trained but relatively inexperienced individuals (e.g., undergraduates or lay interviewers). The HRSD may be a valuable instrument for cross-cultural assessment.

The Structured Clinical Interview for DSM-IV (SCID) The Structured Clinical Interview for *DSM-IV* (Spitzer et al., 1992) is an interview technique that assesses Axis I *DSM-IV* disorders in adults. It relies on the clinical judgment of the interviewer and is thought to be a more "clinician-friendly" interview than other structured diagnostic instruments.

Interrater reliability of the SCID was assessed in a Norwegian study, where three raters independently assessed 54 audiotaped interviews that used the SCID for *DSM-III-R* disorders.

The SCID has been translated into a number of different languages and is currently in use worldwide. In a recent study, the SCID was translated into an Indian language (Kannada) for a cultural study of depression (Channabasavana, Raguram, Weiss, & Parvathavardhini, 1993). It was concluded that using the SCID together with other instruments that assess depressive experience provides a good method for cross-cultural research that integrates personal experience and professional concepts of illness. Overall, the SCID promises to be an extremely useful instrument for cross-cultural use.

The Standardized Assessment of Depressive Disorders (SADD-5) The Standardized Assessment of Depressive Disorders (SADD-5) is a structured interview measure (Thornicroft & Sartorius, 1993). Gastpar (1983) describes the development of the SADD and its relationship to the ICD-9. The SADD was developed for the World Health Organization's Collaborative Study on the Assessment of Depressive Disorders to satisfy five requirements: "to be clinically relevant, to have cross-cultural applicability, to have standardized content and rating rules, to be useful to clinicians and researchers and to be acceptable to patients" (Thornicroft & Sartorius, 1993, p. 1024). This study was a multicentered project covering five sites: Basel, Montreal, Nagasaki, Teheran, and Tokyo.

In addition to the five sites of the WHO multicentered project, the SADD has been used to study depression in various cultural settings including India, West Germany, Ethiopia, and Ghana. The reliability of the SADD has been good, and the data collected by clinicians can lead to an ICD-9 diagnosis with sufficient reliability (Gastpar, 1983). The SADD has been extremely useful in cross-cultural research on depression. For instance, in the multicenter project, it was demonstrated that depressed patients throughout the world present with very similar clinical profiles (Jablensky, 1986).

Results with the use of the SADD support the notion that a set of core features of depression is constant across cultures.

SELF-REPORT METHODS OF ASSESSMENT

The use of self-report measures to test for depressive symptoms is another common method of assessing depression. Prior to the discussion of specific self-rating instruments, we will examine some of the pertinent issues integral to using self-report measures in the cross-cultural assessment of depression.

Given the multifaceted nature of depression as it manifests across cultures, consideration of the advantages and disadvantages of self-report versus interviewer rating scales is in order. Interviewer rating scales are thought to have higher validity than self-report measures because of the extent of information available to the interviewer from both the patient and other sources. The interview allows the individual to report on their perceptions of the problem and also permits the clinician to draw conclusions about areas of concern that the individual may not explicitly address (Kazdin, 1981). In cases of assessing for depression across cultures, interview techniques add to the richness of data gathered but require a culturally competent clinician or an interpreter.

When using interview methods for research or clinical purposes, it is important to consider the time and effort required to train interviewers. It is also important to train interviewers for cultural competence whereby they may become sensitive to acquiring culture-specific information regarding symptom presentation and behavioral norms of the group.

Self-report scales, on the other hand, may suffer from problems with validity, despite strong reliability. Most of the scales we will be discussing have high face validity, and, therefore, responses can be easily distorted by individuals who are operating with a social desirability set for reasons other than depression. Individuals who want to mask their depression will have little challenge. For this reason, these tests, like any psychometrics, require careful interpretations. Response variations in self-report measures may represent differences in the symptom manifestation of depression or might be indicative of variations in response patterns such as the tendency of some cultures to answer in a socially desirable manner (Crittenden, Fugita, Bae, Lamug, & Lin, 1992). Also, response patterns, may vary because identical test items may have different meanings across cultures (Weiss & Kleinman, 1988).

There are several drawbacks in the use of self-report measures across cultures (Kinzie & Manson, 1987). One limitation is that they require literacy in the language of the test. This may eliminate the possibility of administering English self-report measures to many people who cannot read and to people from cultures that do not have any written language. This introduces the issue of socioeconomic status, since illiteracy is much more prevalent in the lower classes. Direct translation of measures from one language to another without consideration of content is often insufficient. The direct translation of a measure assumes that pathology manifests itself identically across cultures, when this may not be the case. Depression may not be assessed with ease when using a measure that was developed for a different population (Kinzie & Manson, 1987). Even if a self-report instrument is able to detect depression in patients from different cultural groups, cutoff scores for caseness and formulae for scoring should be modified to incorporate the norms of the cultural group in question. For instance, the General Health Questionnaire (GHQ) (Goldberg, 1972), which was designed for a British population, was calibrated to detect *DSM-III-R* case criteria in a population of Canadian women (Katz et al., 1995).

Finally, as mentioned above, self-report measures introduce the possibility that patients will respond to items in a socially desirable way. There is a risk with self-reporting in general, but in the case of culturally different patients, clinicians must familiarize themselves with response patterns for specific cultures that may be indicative of socially desirable or culture-specific response sets. For instance, there is evidence to suggest that Hispanics have a greater tendency to a positive response bias (i.e., saying "yes") than do other groups (Kinzie & Manson, 1987). Crittenden et al. (1992) have reported significant differences in self-reported symptoms of depression across cultures. It is not clear whether this difference is attributed to methodological factors (in terms of the use of culturally relevant measures), cultural behavioral norms (i.e., patterns of reporting), differences in symptom expression, or to real differences in prevalence of the disorder. Clearly, more research needs to be done to systematically evaluate these factors.

In this section we will describe and evaluate the following self-report tests: the Beck Depression Inventory (BDI; Beck et al., 1979; Beck, Ward, Mendelson, Mock & Erbaugh, 1961), the Zung Self-Rating Depression Scale (SDS; Zung, 1965), the Center for Epidemiologic Studies-Depression Scale (CES-D; Radloff, 1977), and the Vietnamese Depression Scale (VDS; Kinzie, et al., 1982). The VDS is an example of an instrument devised to screen for depression in a specific population. Other such instruments have been developed (see Manson, Shore, & Bloom, 1985, for a description of the American Indian Depression Scale). Note that none of these scales, with the exception of the VSD, were originally designed to diagnose depression, but rather were meant to measure depressive symptomatology or severity. A comprehensive list of other self-report tests that can be used to assess symptoms of depression is provided in Appendix 7.1.

Beck Depression Inventory The Beck Depression Inventory (BDI; Beck, et al., 1961, 1979, 1996) is the most frequently used self-report method of assessing severity of depression.

The BDI has been demonstrated to be applicable across a variety of cultures and has been translated into numerous languages. Cultural applicability has been tested in subjects from Switzerland, France, Finland, and Czechoslovakia, and in Iranian students in the United States (Blaser, Low, & Schaublin, 1968; Delay, Pichot, Lemperiere, & Mirouze, 1963; Stenback, Rimon, & Turunen, 1967; Tashakkori, Barefoot, & Mehryar, 1989). In addition, various forms of the BDI, including an abridged version (13 items, Beck & Beck, 1972) and a modified version, have been used and demonstrated to be adequately reliable and valid (Beck & Beamesderfer, 1974; May, Urquart, & Taran, 1969; Reynolds & Gould, 1981; Scott, Hannum, & Ghrist, 1982). The abridged version has also been shown to be an effective tool for clinicians who require a quickly administered instrument devised to screen for depression (Beck & Beck, 1972). It is not always possible to obtain responses on all BDI items. Tashakkori, Barefoot, and Mehryar (1989) report that responses to an item reflecting change in libido could not be obtained from Iranian students. Iranian students reportedly objected to the question pertaining to shifts in libido due to cultural values and taboos. LaFromboise, Saks, Berman et al., (1995) suggest that the BDI yields unnecessarily false positives for depression among Native Americans. In order to avoid false positives such as these, a calibration of the test for the population should be done.

The assertion that depression is reported in various ways across a variety of cultures supports the notion that the range of depressive experience is broad. This is not to say that depression is a different experience in different cultures, but rather that the different dimensions may be emphasized or reported more (or less) frequently in accordance with cultural group membership. Thus, the broadness of the inquiry of depressive symptomatology in the BDI allows for different emphasis in the reporting of the condition, because it covers a variety of symptoms that are indicative of depression.

Gotlib (1984) contended that in college students high scores on the BDI indicate general psychopathology and are not discriminative of depression. In contrast, Tashakkori, Barefoot, and Mehryar (1989) report findings which refute Gotlib's (1984) point and support the use of the BDI as a measure of depressive symptoms in non-clinical populations across cultures.

In summary, the BDI has proven to be a culturally sound instrument for the assessment of depression across cultures. Some items may need to be omitted or modified in accordance with the cultural norms of specific cultures to ensure applicability and relevance.

Zung Self-Rating Depression Scale (SDS)   Zung (1965) developed a self-rating scale that was intended to be a short, comprehensive, and reliable instrument to measure severity of depression. Raft, Spencer, Toomey, and Brogan (1977) found that general medical outpatients who were diagnosed as having "masked depression" (individuals whose primary complaint was somatic illness) were not identified by the SDS. These authors conclude that the SDS should not be used in a general medical setting due to this possible misclassification. This has significant implications when assessing people across cultures. The cultural presentation of depression for people from various cultures has been reported to be masked with a primary complaint of somatic illness. However, Zung (1967) demonstrated that the SDS is not influenced by a variety of demographic factors, including age, sex, marital status, education, financial status, and intellectual level.

One of the useful features of the SDS is that it has been translated into 10 different languages. Zung (1969) demonstrated that the scale discriminated diagnostic groups (depressed from nondepressed) for most of these translated versions. The availability of translated versions clearly facilitates the use of this scale with a variety of populations. The Zung SDS has been used to study depressive symptoms in a vast range of populations, including Hmong refugees (Westermeyer, Vang, & Neider, 1983). Crittenden and colleagues (1992) described a study which used the SDS to assess symptoms of depression in the United States and in three Asian countries, Korea, the Philippines, and Taiwan. The mean scores on the SDS varied significantly in each of the four countries. They also observed significant differences in symptom manifestation between the sites. The SDS has been instrumental in cross-cultural research in two ways. First, this measure highlights differences in cross-cultural symptoms of depression. In addition, it facilitates the screening for depression in community populations (Draguns, 1973; Marsella, 1980).

The 20 symptoms measured in the SDS are symptoms which have been accepted as indicators of depression in a Western context. Crittenden et al. (1992) alert us to the possibility that symptoms that are more common in non-Western contexts may have been omitted. The effects of these omissions may be felt most intensely by less educated groups in non-Western cultures because of the implication that education leads to the Westernization of symptom manifestation (Marsella, 1980).

Crittenden et al. (1992) identify a distinct characteristic which is relevant for cross-cultural research. The uneven distribution of the items across symptoms could produce higher total scores as a direct result of the cultural patterns of expression of depressive symptoms. For instance, because somatic symptoms are heavily represented on the SDS, a patient whose depression manifests primarily in the form of somatic complaints will appear more depressed than a patient who presents mainly with affective symptoms, because these are scarcely represented. Thus, two people may be experiencing equal severity of symptoms, but due to what is being asked, the patient who manifests fewer somatic symptoms will be deemed by their SDS scores to be experiencing a less severe depression.

In summary, the SDS is an easy-to-administer and widely applicable scale. It has been used extensively for cross-cultural research and appears to be a good instrument to detect depression in different populations. When using this scale for diverse populations, it is important to have knowledge about cultural norms in terms of symptom presentation because of the uneven distribution of somatic and affective items.

Center for Epidemiologic Studies Depression Scale   The Center for Epidemiologic Studies Depression scale (CES-D) was developed to measure depressive symptomatology in the general population (Radloff, 1977). In a cross-cultural validation of the CES-D, Fava (1983) examined symptoms of depression in Northern Italy. Findings suggested that the CES-D is a valid measure which discriminates depressed people from the nondepressed in an Italian population. Fava suggests that this Italian version of the CES-D may also facilitate the assessment of Italian immigrants abroad.

Kinzie and Manson (1987) cite several studies in which some cultural groups score higher on the CES-D than others. In several cases, after controlling for socioeconomic and demographic variables, culture did not prove to be a predictor of depression (see Vernon & Roberts, 1982). There may be a flaw in arriving at the conclusion that culture is not a predictor of depression when one controls for socioeconomic and demographic variables. It can be argued that socioeconomic and demographic barriers are integral to the experience of membership in some cultural groups. Depression is mediated by social realities, such as extreme poverty and homelessness. Krause and Liang (1992) outline the controversy between researchers who advocate statistically controlling for socioeconomic factors prior to the examination of depression in Black American populations and those who believe that controlling for such factors denies that socioeconomics is often integral to the African American experience.

Myers (1993) contends that, in addition to individual factors which precipitate depression, social factors such as extreme poverty and racial and gender oppression may be precipitating factors, as they augment perceptions of lack of control and hopelessness. This notion is supported by Swanson, Linskey, Quintero-Salias, Pumariega, & Holzer (1992), who used the CES-D to study depressive symptoms, drug use, and suicidal ideation among Mexican and Mexican American youth. Rates were lower among Mexican youth in all three areas. These authors attribute high scores to social conditions that correlate with mental health. Ying (1988), who used the CES-D and the SDS to measure depressive symptomatology among Chinese Americans, reports findings that also support this concept. She reported that patients with lower socioeconomic status (SES) had significantly higher scores on the SDS than those with higher SES. Again, this discrepancy points to the relationship between SES, social conditions, and depression, and therefore must be considered when used in cross-cultural research.

The Vietnamese Depression Scale (VDS)   The Vietnamese Depression Scale (Kinzie et al., 1982) is a 15-item self-rating scale that was developed specifically for use with Vietnamese people to overcome the cultural limitations of preexisting scales. Kinzie and colleagues (1982, 1987) describe the development of the scale and the rationale behind it in some detail. The VSD is based on a combination of Vietnamese symptoms that are in accordance with Western symptoms of depression. The authors developed the scale in conjunction with four Vietnamese mental health professionals. Cultural group norms were considered at every stage of development. For instance, the VDS has a 3-point response scale rather than the more typical 5 points because it was determined that Vietnamese people had less awareness of contrasts than do people from Western populations (Kinzie & Manson, 1987).

The scale screens for three classes of symptoms: physical symptoms, psychological symptoms that are typically associated with the Western conception of depression, and symptoms that appeared not to be related to the Western notion of depression. Findings suggest that there are some psychological symptoms that are unique to Vietnamese manifestation of depression but that some biological symptoms of depression may be less culturally specific.

SCOPE OF DEPRESSION AND METHODOLOGY

Depression seems to exist in some form in all cultures (Jenkins et al., 1991). It is, however, noteworthy that in the early 1900s, the incidence of depression in Western countries was high relative to rates in Africa, Asia, and other developing countries, where occurrence was thought to be rare (Weiss & Kleinman, 1988). Currently, there is a broad range of prevalence rates across cultures; however, dysphoria appears to exist in some form in all settings. For instance, Sartorius (1986) notes wide variances in prevalence rates of depression among cultural groups. He reports that Argentinean Indians from Alto Plano experience more depression than those from villages and that native Indonesians have less depression than Chinese living in Indonesia.

Two studies of elderly populations report cross-cultural prevalence rates of depression with different results (Dewey, de la Camera, Copeland, Lobo, & Saz, 1993; Krause & Liang, 1992). Krause and Liang investigated depressive symptomology in four cultural groups using a modified version of the CES-D. Their findings indicated that prevalence rates were highest among older African Americans, followed by White Americans and older adults living in Taiwan. Prevalence rates were lowest for elderly people in Japan. In the second study, Dewey et al. investigated symptoms of depression in elderly people in Spain and in the United Kingdom. Their objective was to identify symptoms that were sensitive to cultural influence and those that were consistent across cultures. They considered both social and historical information in each of the countries. This is deemed pertinent, as social context has been identified as influential to the course and outcome of depression (Weiss & Kleinman, 1988).

In contrast to the findings of Krause and Liang (1992), Dewey et al. (1993) found prevalence rates for older adults in the two countries to be similar. While the latter findings seem to support the idea that there are commonalities in the depressive experience across cultures, the former suggest that there are differences. In order to identify which aspects of the presentation of depression are culturally bound and which are universal to the experience, it is important to examine the potential reasons or explanations for the differences that are not attributable to culture. The attempt to distinguish between universal and culturally distinct symptoms will lead to a more thorough comprehension of the depressive disorder, as it becomes easier to identify core aspects of the condition.

Discrepancies in estimates of prevalence prompt questions regarding the sources and explanations of these differences. Despite the vast variation in manifestation or expression of the condition, the current trend in the field has increasingly highlighted the notion that several core or universal aspects of depression exist. The following questions need to be addressed in order to accurately explain cross-cultural differences in the estimated rates of depression: Are there *actual* differences in the rate at which depression occurs in different cultures? Are reported differences in depression across cultures due to increased susceptibility as a result of differences in social conditions that are conducive to depression? Is the heterogeneity of prevalence rates due to a biological vulnerability inherent in some groups? Might it also be the case that reported differences are exaggerated, because of either methodological differences in the measurement of the construct or variations in the case criteria used across cultures? Or might some of the differences in reported prevalence rates be accounted for by the help-seeking patterns which lead some to seek treatment from traditional or religious healers? These sufferers would be excluded from the pool of the tallied depressed. These questions are debated with fervor within the field. To some extent, each of these possibilities has considerable merit, and it seems that each contributes to the variation in reported prevalence rates of depression across cultures. The question remains: What is the contribution of each of these factors in explaining cross-cultural differences in depressive disorder?

The course of disorders such as depression is deeply influenced by the illness experience as it unfolds within a social context (Hinton & Kleinman, 1993). The social context itself has profound effects on the form that depression takes. For instance, in oppressive environments, patients predisposed to depression may internalize the discriminatory attitudes and come to believe that their oppressors are correct in their views. The internalization of the derogatory views of others has been termed "internalized oppression" (Yamoto, 1992). Coming to believe the negative views of others leads to low self-esteem and feelings of guilt and worthlessness. Thus, the history of oppression or discrimination of the culturally different patient, in addition to the social and historical context, is pertinent data.

Social factors have a profound influence on depressive disorder (Brown & Harris, 1989). Weiss and Kleinman (1988) assert that social context influences the presentation of the depression, as well as its course and outcome. Social circumstances that are the catalysts for depression may be present both on individual and societal levels. Mothers with young children who are unemployed and without a confidant are particularly vulnerable to depressive disorder (Brown & Harris, 1989). Likewise, higher incidence of depression has been reported in the face of political disruption, natural disaster, and war. A. Kleinman (personal communication, January 1995) suggests that the main hypothesis accounting for the significantly higher worldwide prevalence rate of depression among women relates to their powerlessness relative to men. If indeed powerlessness is an impetus for depression, this may explain some of the wide gaps in prevalence rates between groups. For instance, the group most at risk for depression has been reported to be non-Hispanic White women between the ages of 18 and 39 (Karno et al., 1987). In the same vein, the racial group reported to be most vulnerable to mild depression is African Americans (Hacker, 1992).

The lack of methodological uniformity in estimating rates of prevalence of depression in different cultures impedes our knowledge regarding the true differences. This results in the inability to distinguish how much of the reported differences may reflect actual differences and how much are the artifacts of methodological inconsistencies. For instance, Thornicroft and Sartorius (1993), in a 10-year follow-up of the WHO Collaborative Study on the Assessment of Depressive Disorders, examined subtypes of depression across sites. They suggested that differences in the results across sites were statistically explained by location and not by diagnostic subtype. They attribute variations to differences in the services provided across sites, rather than to the subtypes of depression. There may be other explanations for the observed differences, such as cultural differences in the expression of depressive disorder.

Some of the differences in reported prevalence rates of depression across cultures may be partially attributed to variations between sites in research methods such as sampling techniques, assessment and diagnostic methods, investigator training, and theoretical orientation (Sartorius, 1986). Methodological inconsistencies contribute to variable reporting of prevalence rates across cultures. It is possible that the methods of assessment used in some settings are culturally laden and therefore misrepresent the actual prevalence rate. As discussed earlier, measurement instruments may be used inappropriately across cultures. Several of the methodological flaws and measurement inconsistencies discussed in this section that may influence prevalence rates are summarized in Appendix 7.2.

Investigators who report differences in prevalence rates often acknowledge the methodological shortcomings of their studies. For instance, Krause and Liang (1992), who report that elderly African Americans have higher prevalence rates for depression than do elderly Whites, urge caution in the overinterpretation of their results. They suggest two possible explanations for their findings. First, they warn against making generalizations from a small sample size. Second, they believe that by ignoring the social experiential contexts of subjects, attributions regarding differences in prevalence rates may be inappropriate.

Another methodological inconsistency may occur when direct translations of self-report measures are used without consideration of the salience of cultural expression of depressive disorder. Kleinman (1995) suggests that translation of measures is complicated by the use of idioms that do not translate with ease (i.e., "feeling down," or "feeling blue"). Direct translations often lose the intended innuendo of the original version. In some languages, there is a broad lexicon of descriptors that characterize different aspects of depression. In contrast, in other languages the term "depression" covers the whole range of the affective experience (Sartorius, 1986). For example, while depression in North America and other Western cultures is often conceptualized as sadness, in Japan, depression is expressed as "darkness and rain" (Sartorius, 1986). Clearly, to ask a Western patient about their experience with darkness and rain would tell the investigator little about their depressive experience. Thus, translations not only must consider language, but also must translate culturally distinct innuendo. Therefore, accessibility to the same language does not ensure the uniform application of the words (Bebbington, 1993). Evidence from the U.S.-U.K. project indicates that linguistic variations in the expression of depression exist even when the same language is being used in different cultures (Bebbington, 1993). Differences in the expression of depression across cultures may indicate differences in the conceptualization of the disorder. Alternatively, cultures may simply be using different terms to describe a similar experience. Whichever the case, it is clear that for some cultures, linguistic expressions are rich with descriptors, while for others, the term "depression" is an umbrella term to cover all aspects of the experience. This makes it particularly difficult to translate instruments or interviews without the aid of a cultural interpreter. To effectively translate an instrument, the cultural agent not only must be capable of linguistic translation including linguistic connotation, but also must have the knowledge of the various ways in which depression is conceptualized in that culture. Thus, people from different cultures often present differently. This may be due to linguistic restrictions and/or to cultural behavioral norms. Some clinicians might miss the cultural innuendo in the expression of the problem or might overemphasize the importance of culture. In both cases, the results of the assessment would be clouded by the misperceptions of the interviewer.

Differences in prevalence rates across cultures may be due to the fact that investigators throughout the world have not employed uniform case criteria to establish depression. For instance, the Europeans have traditionally used the *ICD* classification system to define cases, whereas the North Americans have used the *DSM* system. Different sites continue to use different classification systems to establish case criteria for depression. Thus, patients may meet case criteria for one classification system while they fail to meet criteria for another. If different systems are used, patients who present with identical symptoms at two sites may be considered to be depressed at one site and not depressed at another. The more recent international acceptance of the *DSM* as a universal classification system may to some degree alleviate this problem.

The methodological issues related to variations in psychiatric disorders across cultures may be examined within the framework of an anthropological model rather than a psychiatric one (Kleinman, 1995). The psychiatric framework assumes that depression is a biological illness that is merely "shaped" or influenced by culture. This model may overemphasize the influence of biology (Kleinman, 1995). The psychiatric model of illness also suggests that patients from non-Western cultures and lower socioeconomic classes mainly present with somatic rather than psychological complaints. Kleinman believes that this polarization serves to mask the real psychiatric condition. His proposed anthropological model focuses on the illness experience (including unique symptom patterns, help-seeking behavior, and responses to treatment), which differs greatly across cultures despite the fact that the disease is the same. The illness (the unique symptom manifestation), according to Kleinman, may take precedence over the disease (the depression) in terms of many aspects of care. The implication of the application of this anthropological model is that despite the fact that depression may be a universal human condition, the approaches to assessment, diagnosis, treatment, and management should differ in accordance with the illness experience of the sufferer. The focus should be upon the illness, which encompasses both the biological and sociocultural aspects of depression, rather than upon the disease, which is limited by biological explanations (Kleinman, 1995).

The current trend toward studying depression from a more comprehensive perspective captures the quality of the experience from the sufferer's perspective. Consider, for example, the Explanatory Model Interview Catalogue (EMIC; Weiss et al., 1992). The EMIC was recently translated and adapted to an Indian language for a cultural study of depression (Channabasavanna, et al., 1993). This holistic approach has led to the view that, despite differences in symptom expression, depression as a disorder has more in common across cultures than was previously thought. Sartorius's (1986) findings indicate that, despite differences in the clinical expression and presentation of depression across cultures, there is more evidence supporting similarities than differences in depression across cultures. Sartorius notes that while clinical presentations do differ, no conclusive evidence exists to prove that cultural factors impact on the form, course, and outcome of depressive disorders.

Numerous studies have accentuated the similarities of depression across cultures. Core features of depression have been acknowledged in the anthropological literature. Nonetheless, these works continue to recognize that presenting features are culture-specific (Weiss & Kleinman, 1988). Similarly, Myers (1993) concluded that the evidence supporting increased vulnerability and higher prevalence rates of depression for African Americans than for Caucasians has been inconsistent. However, he also notes that there is substantial evidence in support of the variation of symptom patterns across cultures.

CULTURAL ASPECTS OF DEPRESSION

Cultural Influence on Symptom Expression

The degree to which culture impacts on the manifestation and experience of depression has been widely debated in the literature. This controversy has been outlined by numerous investigators (Krause & Liang, 1992; Myers, 1993; Paykel, 1982). For instance, Myers (1993) reviewed the differences in depression between African Americans and Caucasians. He presents three competing hypotheses regarding the etiology of intergroup differences. The first hypothesis postulates that, since symptom presentation is similar across groups, comparisons and differences between groups are indicative of actual differences in psychosocial or biological vulnerabilities. The second hypothesis assumes that differences in prevalence estimates are not real, but rather are created by methodological discrepancies or diagnostic inconsistencies. Finally, the third hypothesis suggests that while differences in symptom presentation across ethnic groups do exist, some of the differences are thought to be real, while others are attributed to methodological biases. None of these hypotheses are backed by sufficient evidence (Myers, 1993). Myers adopts the middle-ground perspective, whereby both similarities and differences are recognized in the symptom manifestation of depression among African Americans and Caucasians. This emerges from his biopsychosocial view, which suggests that biological and psychosocial components should be considered both together and in isolation in the study of depression across cultures.

This debate is also highlighted by Krause and Liang (1992), who classify cross-cultural investigators of depression into two groups. One group, the universalists, endorse the view that there are essential qualities of depression which are shared across cultures. The other group, the relativists, contend that depression is manifested and experienced distinctly across cultures. While the strict relativist position has been derived from numerous disciplines, it disregards clinical considerations. On the other hand, extreme universalism may imply too much likeness at the expense of individual differences (Weiss & Kleinman, 1988).

Each of these perspectives, the universal view and the relativist view, has merit. Depression has many similarities across cultural groups, while at the same time it differs in the way the illness is experienced as the result of cultural norms and in response to social conditions. Cultural norms affect the expression and the experience, while difficult social conditions may create vulnerabilities to depression or serve to exacerbate the condition. The experience of depression is unequivocally influenced by the cultural context in which the patient lives. Numerous social factors have been implicated as augmenting vulnerability for depression (Brown & Harris, 1989; Paykel, 1982). In addition to the individual's circumstances, larger social circumstances must be considered as factors which may increase the vulnerability for depression (e.g., extreme poverty, oppression, racism). In line with this thinking, Kleinman (1995) asserts that every disorder has a social basis. It follows logically that the converse to the social causation theory, namely, the social prevention theory, is also plausible. It has been suggested that certain cultural customs, norms, and rituals may serve as protectors against depression. Examples of such are rituals that facilitate mourning (Eisenbruch, 1984) and extended-family systems that provide social support.

While in some cultures, depression may primarily manifest in a somatic form, in others it may present as low affect or guilt. The *DSM-IV* (APA, 1994) identifies various cultural expressions of depression, such as:

> complaints of 'nerves' and headaches (in Latino and Mediterranean cultures), of weakness, tiredness, or 'imbalance' (in Chinese or Asian cultures), of problems of the 'heart' (in Middle Eastern cultures), of being heartbroken (among the Hopi). . . . Cultures may also differ in judgments about the seriousness of dysphoria. Culturally distinctive experiences (e.g., fear of being hexed or bewitched, feelings of 'heat in the head' or

crawling sensations of ants or worms, or vivid feelings of being visited by those who have died) must be distinguished from actual hallucinations or delusions that may be part of a Major Depressive Episode. . . . (*DSM-IV,* 1994 p. 324)

The *DSM-IV* alerts clinicians to be aware of cultural behavioral norms. While the norms of the reference group must be considered, the task of the clinician is to avoid cultural stereotypes.

Numerous cross-cultural researchers have identified specific ways in which cultural groups manifest symptoms of depression. For instance, Pliskin (1987) reported that people of Chinese origin often present with somatic complaints. She reported that Blacks are more apt to exhibit difficulties in the affective domain and Whites most often express cognitive symptoms. People from non-Western societies have been reported to experience fewer of the psychological characteristics of depression, such as guilt and self-effacement (Nikelly, 1988). Black Americans were reported to manifest symptoms of depression in a blend of both intrapsychic and somatic forms (Chang, 1985). Numerous studies have reported that African Americans experiencing depression express more anger and attempt more suicidal gestures than do Caucasians (Myers, 1993).

Krause and Liang (1992) studied differences in depressive symptomology across three cultural populations. They conceptualize depression as a construct divided into three clusters: interpersonal complaints, somatic symptoms, and depressed cognitions. Based on their review of the literature, they expected that Japanese elderly would exhibit depressed symptoms mainly in terms of interpersonal difficulties, that Taiwanese seniors would manifest depressed features in terms of somatic symptoms, whereas American elderly would express depressive symptoms as distressed cognitions. Despite their forecast, the results of the study did not support these hypotheses. They found that elderly Americans more often had higher scores than Orientals on all three clusters of depressive symptoms. Findings such as these are attributed to two things. First, a much higher percentage of Japanese elderly live with their extended families. This serves to diminish the loneliness that is more common among the elderly in North America, who tend to live in more isolated conditions (Hasewega, 1985). Second, Japanese elderly are engaged in a high level of activity, which is commonly thought to be a deterrent to depression (Hasewega, 1985). Krause and Liang conclude that there do not appear to be major differences in cross-cultural manifestations of the symptomology of depression. Their adjustment for age, gender, and educational level had little effect on their conclusions.

Five discrete depressive conditions have been recognized in the Hopi community. These include worry sickness, unhappiness, heartbreak, drunken-like craziness (with or without alcohol), and disappointment pouting (Manson, Shore, & Bloom, 1985). In more Westernized settings, the symptoms which fall into each of these categories would be considered to be symptomatic of depression. For the Hopi, these symptoms are considered to be distinct conditions, with differing causation, and require unique treatment planning (Manson, Shore, & Bloom, 1985).

It is noteworthy that most cases of depression throughout the world have presented in the form of physical ailments, which lead the afflicted to seek treatment from their medical providers (Jenkins, Kleinman, & Good, 1991). Despite the uniqueness of the Western presentation of intrapsychic suffering, the majority of sufferers in the West still somatize (Jenkins, Kleinman, & Good, 1991). Several explanations have been proposed in an attempt to explain the absence of intrapsychic expression of depression: strict codes of etiquette; linguistic deficiencies for psychological descriptors; norms of nonverbal communication; and a physical conceptualization of depression (Jenkins, Kleinman, & Good, 1991).

The different ways in which people experience, express, and cope with perceived distress have been termed "idioms of distress" (Nichter, 1981). Idioms of distress are formulated out of cultural norms and various other values and beliefs. Conceptually, idioms of distress is one way to explain differences in symptom manifestation across cultures. An example of this concept applied to depression in a non-Western patient might be as follows: Rather than expressing intrapsychic difficulties through the idiom of low affect, the depression might be expressed through the idiom of a sore back. Various idioms of distress which express depression have been reported. For instance, the idiom by which people in Afghanistan may express depression is through perceived weakness and the feeling of the heart being squeezed by a hand (Weiss & Kleinman, 1988).

Another example of what is thought to be a culture-specific symptom of depression is excessive guilt. Guilt as a symptom of depression has been less frequently identified in non-Western settings. However, methods of measuring guilt in these settings have been problematic (Weiss & Kleinman, 1988). Excessive guilt as a symptom of depression is an artifact of the Judeo-Christian influence (Murphy, 1982). Guilt as an example of a culturally specific symptom is deliberate. It highlights the fact that some symptoms may be culture-specific and calls attention to the need for flexibility in using the *DSM-IV* for diagnosing depression in culturally different patients. Inclusion of this criteria in the *DSM* does not serve to discredit the criteria. To the contrary, the *DSM-IV* makes extremely clear that symptoms of depression fluctuate across cultures, and cultural formulations on every axis are encouraged. However, it serves to alert diagnosticians to the flexibility required in the cross-cultural application of redefined diagnostic criteria.

The previously accepted notion that Asian people experience depression in somatic terms while Westerners psychologize their symptoms is currently being refuted (M. Beiser, personal communication, January 1995). Somatic symptoms are as integral to the Western experience of depression as they are in non-Western cultures (Kirmayer, 1984). In addition, recent findings suggest that Asians are not experiencing a completely different type of depression than are Westerners. Rather, the notion that Asians somatize is based on the accounts that patients present to their doctors. Asians have been reported to present with psychological aspects to their depression in their personal relationships with their confidants. However, they are less likely to present with their psychological complaints to their doctors (Cheung, 1987). Further evidence that stands in opposition to this polarization is that non-Westerners are unlikely to understand their experience in terms of body dualism, wherein the mind and body are separate entities. The division between mind and body is a Western concept (Hinton & Kleinman, 1993). Most recently, the conceptualization of depression across cultures has seen a thrust towards universalism, whereby the disease is seen to be a universally human condition which is expressed and experienced in diverse ways across cultures.

TREATMENT PLANNING AND THERAPEUTIC ISSUES IN THE TREATMENT OF DEPRESSED PATIENTS ACROSS CULTURES

Treatment Planning: Issues and Concerns

Treatment planning emerges from the process of assessment and diagnosis. In devising a treatment plan, the clinician should consider the aspect of the problem that is subjectively most salient for the patient. It is not uncommon for a patient's primary concern to be inadvertently overlooked in the development of a therapeutic intervention. Level of acculturation and stages of ethnic identity vary widely, and thus both group norms and within-group differences must be considered in the formulation of an intervention. The culturally aware therapist knows that body language, goal setting, decision-making styles, and assessment tools are all culturally laden. An important multicultural skill is the ability to be flexible and "ready to modify, accept, and experiment" (Pedersen, Fukuyama, & Heath, 1989 p. 32). This might include the use of information networks or the recognition of the need for a referral to a more culturally similar therapist (Sue & Sue, 1990).

The decision to work in collaboration with a culturally different patient ethically obligates the therapist to acquire knowledge about the cultural norms, mores, beliefs, practices, history, sex roles, and values of the patient's cultural group. It is important that clinicians become privy to the subtle nuances of various cultural groups. For instance, "saving face" has been identified as an important factor in the interactions of the Asian culture (Wayman, Lynch, and Hanson, 1991). The clinician must understand, for example, that asking questions, in some cultures, may be viewed as a challenge, and therefore is often avoided by the patient. The Spanish American patient cannot be treated in isolation without consideration of the family unit. Men in the Latino culture are often expected to be the providers and women the homemakers. Disability due to depressive disorder impacts upon both genders as an infringement on their culturally expected gender roles (Casas & Vasquez, 1989). It is often not acceptable for Spanish American men to remain in extended rehabilitation because the need for treatment is viewed as disgraceful (Smart & Smart, 1991). Another example of culturally normative behaviors that may affect the therapeutic process is the tendency for Native Americans to depend upon the environment for solutions. This may appear to be passivity or noncompliance in treatment to a clinician who is unaware of this cultural norm. These examples provide evidence in support of the need for therapists to become culturally versed for effective treatment planning.

Linguistic Barriers

When facing a cultural or linguistic barrier, an interpreter or *cultural broker* must be used. A cultural broker is a person who is familiar not only with the patient's language, but also with the cultural norms of the patient's group, and who, optimally, has some clinical knowledge and experience. An interpreter, on the other hand, most often acts solely as a translator. It is clearly preferable to secure the translation services of a person who has knowledge regarding normative behavior for the patient's cultural group.

Introducing a third party into the therapeutic encounter changes the dynamic of the interview. The mere presence of an interpreter or broker introduces a reactive component. Kleinman (1995) provides several directives to facilitate the shift from dyad to triad. First, he warns against the use of family members as interpreters. There is a risk of overinvolvement and perhaps even competing agendas on the part of a familial interpreter. Family members have been noted to distort the patient's account by integrating their own views and censoring information conveyed to the interviewer (Westermeyer, 1987). Also, lay interpreters may be a poor choice for use as translators, as they are often abashed by the personal nature of clinical inquiries (Westermeyer, 1987). Kleinman (1995) suggests that goals and methods of translation be established prior to the interview to avoid misunderstandings. To facilitate an alliance with the patient, Kleinman (1995) advises that chairs be arranged in a triangle and that the interviewer pose short, simple questions and continually watch the patient rather than the translator. In this way, the innuendo of the patient's body language will not be missed. Clinicians should be aware that communication may be difficult when patients are interviewed in their second language. In this case, depression-related concentration difficulties may interfere with the expression of affect.

Cognitive-Behavior Therapy and Culture

Cognitive-Behavior Therapy (CBT; Beck, et al., 1979) is one of the treatments of choice for depressive disorders. It is an adaptable method, requiring a clinician who is aware of culturally normative processes. For instance, the therapist must be able to recognize hopelessness, helplessness, and worthlessness as they manifest in different cultures. They must then shape the course of therapy in accordance with the cultural context of the patient. Cognitive-behavioral techniques can be modified as the clinician becomes familiar with normative cognitive processes of the patient's reference group.

The suitability criteria for CBT (Safran & Segal, 1990) needs modification for culturally different populations. Patients from the minority culture may not *appear* to be suitable candidates, despite the possibility that CBT is a viable and constructive treatment choice for individuals from various cultures. For instance, one of the current indicators of suitability for CBT is willingness to take personal responsibility for one's own emotional change. In several non-Western cultures, the belief in spirits and fate indicate external attributions for illness. There is, however, no reason that this would preclude the effectiveness of a culturally sensitive CBT. Cultural norms and attributions for illness that are different from those in the Western world do not imply that the treatment is inapplicable. Rather, the application of certain concepts must be modified in accordance with cultural group norms. Modification of the suitability criteria for CBT so that they reflect the beliefs and attitudes of different cultural groups would be a stimulating endeavor for future research.

Biological Considerations in Treatment Planning

Biological theories of depression suggest that neurotransmitters play an important role in depressive illness. Several competing biological theories of depression exist (for a decryption of several of these theories, see Golden & Janowsky, 1990). Biological markers are physiological measures that are believed to reflect the presence of depressive disorder. Several biological markers of depression have been identified, although none has yet proven to be a consistently reliable marker for the illness. To some degree they provide a window to the brain. The *DSM-IV* (APA, 1994) identifies a number of different biological markers of major depressive episode. These include: norepinephrine, serotonin, acetylcholine, and gamma-aninobutyric acid. Other tests that may indicate depression are the dexamethasone suppressor test, the clonedine challenge, functional and structural brain imaging, evoked potentials, and waking EEG.

From a cultural perspective, the identification of biological markers for depressive disorder has particular significance. It is not only possible to identify biologically distinct signs that indicate vulnerability to depression, but it is also possible to compare biological signs as they vary across cultures. While cultural distinctions do exist in the manifestation of biological markers, one must not assume that these differences are simply the result of biological differences across groups. Cultural practices and norms have an effect on physiological processes. Some examples of outside factors that impact upon biological factors are nutrition, tropical diseases, the role of the gene pool, and other characteristics of the environment (Weiss & Kleinman, 1988).

One biological variation between cultures is the rate at which medications are metabolized (Poland & Lin, 1993). Silver, Poland, & Lin (1993) present findings which indicate different biological patterns of response to identical doses of tricyclic medications based on cultural group membership. They report clinical evidence which suggests that the response of African Americans to tricyclic antidepressants is more effective than that of Caucasians (also see Strickland et al., 1991). Asians metabolize tricyclics at a less rapid rate than Whites (Silver et al., 1993).

It has not yet been systematically demonstrated whether these differences are entirely the result of metabolic factors or whether they may be attributed to a combination of variables. In addition to the genetic influence on metabolic rates of drug absorption, nonbiological factors have an impact on the response to psychotropic drugs. Reported differences in responses to psychotropic medications seem to be a biological consequence of cultural, socioeconomic, and environmental circumstances, rather than the unique result of genetic determination (Myers, 1993).

Group differences in the rate of metabolizing some antidepressant medications clearly have implications for treatment planning with consideration to prescribed doses. For instance, African Americans were noted to experience more toxic side effects to tricyclic antidepressants than do Caucasians (Silver, Poland, and Lin, 1993). Thus, standard recommended doses may not be applicable to all patients (Jakobsen, 1994). When prescribing this class of antidepressants, in addition to considering individual variability in treatment responses, clinicians should heed the impact of cultural-group membership on response to medication.

The dexamethasone suppression test (DST) is another biological marker of depression that is of particular interest in the discussion of cultural variations in depression. The abnormal response rate for all patients with major depression has been reported to be in the range of 50%. Discrepancies between cultural groups in the percentage of nonsuppression were reported to be 58% for "Anglos", 25% for African Americans, and 0% for Spanish Americans (Escobar et al., 1984). Coppen et al. (1984), in a 13-site WHO study, reported nonsuppression rates ranging from 15% in Moscow to 71% in Copenhagen. Variations in the rate of nonsuppression in the DST may be the result of cross-cultural factors that occur developmentally and may not necessarily be explained by genetic or neurobiological differences (Poland & Lin, 1993).

Psychodynamic Theories of Depression

A psychodynamic perspective on depression is that the ego has lost control over the id and is unable to curtail the superego's hostility. Defense mechanisms and somatic symptoms are seen as ways of shielding the ego and thus protecting against depression. In depressed states, the ego is deemed to be weak and vulnerable to the superego's impulses (Wolman, 1990).

Psychoanalytic psychotherapy for the treatment of depression has its roots in psychodynamic theory. Some therapists have questioned the role that psychoanalysis has in treating depressed individuals. Bemporad (1990) points out that psychoanalytic therapy is not a treatment which focuses on the immediate alleviation of the symptoms of depression. The aim is, however, to help depressed individuals to better defend themselves against the former triggers of depression, in the hopes that recurrences will be less grave. Psychoanalytic treatments for depression aspire to alter the personality structure of the person rather than directly addressing symptoms. This form of therapy may be less conducive to the treatment of depression across cultures because it is heavily dependent on verbal communication. It is essential that the client and therapist share the same linguistic preference. The use of interpreters is not possible for psychoanalytic psychotherapy. In addition, psychoanalytic psychotherapy is both lengthy and costly. Depression often ensues in the case of refugees who encounter difficulties acclimating to their new environments, which may result in feelings of despair, hopelessness, and helplessness. The patient's integration into a new culture ideally will not be a drawn-out process that aims to alter the personality structure of the patient but rather a practical approach that empowers the individual.

Interpersonal Therapy (IPT) for Depression Across Cultures

Interpersonal therapy is based on the premise that depression occurs in an interpersonal context. This orientation does not deny that genetic predisposition and biological symptoms exist. The emphasis of IPT, however, is on the contextual aspects of depression. The goal of IPT is to alleviate symptoms by helping the depressed patient to cope more effectively with interpersonal difficulties that are related to the depressive symptoms. Four main problem areas are identified by IPT as most typically relating to depressive illness: grief, role disputes, role transitions, or interpersonal deficits (Weissman & Klerman, 1990). The experience of coming to a foreign culture could easily precipitate any one of the four problem areas. Moving to a different culture necessarily involves role transitions. The losses which are present in such transitions, even if the changes are perceived to be positive, may exacerbate feelings of depression. Several adaptations have been made to the original IPT that are tailored to specific populations, such as the elderly.

Psychosocial considerations are particularly pertinent in cross-cultural treatment of depression. The difficulties encountered in adjusting to a new cultural context often contribute to depression. The view that IPT takes whereby depression must be seen and treated in an interpersonal context may be highly compatible with the immigrant or refugee experience. The onset of depression in culturally different populations is often accompanied by difficulties in acclimatizing to the new environment, encountering seemingly insurmountable obstacles, and difficulties adjusting to new roles and new interpersonal dynamics with friends, family, and inhabitants of the host culture.

Psychoeducational Approaches to the Cultural Management of Depression

Psychoeducational approaches combine therapeutic techniques with information-giving as therapists adopt the additional role of educator. Psychoeducational programs aim to teach people about depressive illness, thereby enabling or empowering them to better cope with the symptoms and to more fully understand the accompanying biological and cognitive processes. Psychoeducational sessions for depressive illness may include content on etiology, heritability, symptoms, and treatment (Gingerich et al., 1992). Psychoeducation may be offered to the families and caregivers of the patient (Gingerich, et al., 1992). Psychoeducational approaches for both depressed persons and their families in the cultural management of depression may need to be adapted for particular cultural groups. For instance, modules and educational materials should ideally be presented in the mother tongue of the participants. Therapists should consider the ways in which information is conveyed and presented, adjusting psychoeducational materials to accommodate cultural and linguistic barriers.

By acquiring an understanding of the condition, both the patient and family will be better able to cope with the depressive illness. Gingerich et al. (1992) found that families involved in psychoeducational sessions gained support by having their illness -related experiences and emotions validated by other group members. They also supported each other on issues pertaining to communications with health care providers. This may be particularly pertinent for new immigrants who have not yet learned to navigate in the local health care system. In addition, family involvement in psychoeducational programs enables the therapist to comprehend and consider the cultural content in which the depressed person is being treated. Psychoeducational family treatment will enlighten clinicians as to personal, social, and community resources available to the patient, in addition to barriers or obstacles present in the patient's environment which may hinder recovery. Culturally stigmatized behavior may be discussed in connection with the treatment and the illness itself.

CONCLUSIONS

Cultural competence for therapists is no longer a specialty skill but rather is now deemed to be compulsory for all clinicians involved in psychological assessment and treatment of depression. Psychopathology and concomitant presenting problems are expressed through a filter composed of a patient's cultural background and worldview. In order to establish an understanding of the presenting problem, and as a critical aspect of the assessment for psychopathology, the clinician must take the patient's worldview or schematic structure into consideration. It is the responsibility of the clinician to acquire the knowledge, skills, awareness, and sensitivity to address the problems of the culturally different patient in a relevant and ethical way. Where this is not possible, it is the clinician's responsibility to make an appropriate referral to meet the patient's needs.

Clinical psychologists must be equipped to integrate mulicultural counseling theory with the findings of cultural psychology, medical anthropology, and cross-cultural psychiatry. They must merge and adapt these findings to the clinical and research underpinnings of psychology. Clinical psychology's contribution to the body of knowledge regarding mental health and culture will be to apply theoretical knowledge and couple it with rigorous scientific methodology in clinical practice. Outcome studies that examine the differential success of various therapeutic approaches are needed. Process research that focuses on the ways in which culture impacts on therapeutic interactions is also required for the development of effective cross-cultural interventions. It is the role of clinical psychologists to make behavioral and symptomatic observations and to expose culturally different patients to various treatment modalities in order to evaluate their effectiveness in diverse populations.

The wide variance in prevalence rates of depressive disorders across cultures may be a function of social factors that breed higher vulnerabilities in some settings. Some researchers, however, believe that ethnicity has little or no effect on depression once socioeconomic and gender factors are considered. With regard to cross-cultural research, it is imperative that methodological practices be standardized for consistency across settings. This consistency is needed to establish accurate prevalence rates in different settings. It is the role of the clinical psychologist, working within the scientist-practitioner model, to standardize methodology and thus maintain a high standard of scientific rigor.

The controversy in the study of depression across cultures takes place between the cultural relativists and the universalists. Evidence suggests that affective disorders have far more in common across cultures than was previously thought. While there are universal aspects to the condition, there are multiple ways in which it can present. The various manifestations are mediated by the sociocultural circumstances of the individual. Observed differences in the presentation of depressive disorder are likely attributable to differences in cultural norms of expression. However, the culturally competent clinician who is able to sift through the symptom presentation and distinguish the cultural artifacts from the core symptoms will note that the clinical picture of depressive disorder is similar across cultures.

APPENDIX 7.1: SELF-REPORT TESTS THAT ASSESS SYMPTOMS OF DEPRESSION

Inventory of Depressive Symptoms	Weinberg Screening Affective Scale*
Inventory to Diagnose Depression	Childhood Depression Assessment Tool*
Beck Depression Inventory	Costello-Comrey Scale
Geriatric Depression Scale*	QD2 Questionnaire
Zung Self-Rating Depression	Depression Rating Scale for Children*
Wessman-Rick Elation-Depression Scale	Clyde Mood Scale

Center for Epidemiologic Studies Depression Scale
Lee's Self-Rating Scale for Depression
Comprehensive Psychopathological Rating Scale for Depression
Kellner and Sheffield Self-Rating Test
Wittenborn Psychometric Rating Scale
Depression Adjective Checklist
Wakefield Self-Assessment Depression Inventory
Multiscore Depression Inventory
Depression Self-Rating Scale for Children*
Children's Depression Inventory*
Carroll Rating Scale for Depression

Wang Self-Assessing Depression Scale
Institute for Personality and Ability Testing Depression Scale
KAS Hogarty Depression Scale
Rockliff Self-Rating Questionnaire
Plutchik-Van Pragg Self-Report Depression Scale
Depression Questionnaire
Depression Symptom Inventory
Popoff Index of Depression
Rimon's Brief Depression Scale
Hospital Anxiety and Depression Scale
Levine-Pilowsky Questionnaire
The Anxiety and Depression Scale
The Irritability, Anxiety and Depression Scale

*Tests for assessment of depression with special populations

APPENDIX 7.2: METHODOLOGICAL VARIATIONS ACROSS SITES WHICH MAY INFLUENCE ESTIMATED PREVALENCE RATES

a. Sampling methods (Sartorius, 1986) — Sample sizes are often too small to be generalizable

b. Methods of assessment (Sartorius, 1986) — Improper application of instruments. Difficulties with translation of measures. Cutoff scores are often culturally bound. Social desirability influences response patterns differently across cultures.

c. Methods of diagnosis (Sartorius, 1986) — Diagnostic criteria may differ across settings. Misdiagnosis may occur with overemphasis or underemphasis of culture.

d. Investigator training (Sartorius, 1986) — Leads to different emphasis in investigation

e. Orientation of investigator (Sartorius, 1986) — That is, some investigators advocate controlling for socioeconomic factors, while others are opposed. Some are universalists, and others relativists.

f. Differences in presentation shaped by available language to express dysphoria (Bebbington, 1993) — Some languages have greater capacity to express the specifics of the experience.

g. Differences in presentation due to variations in the conceptualizations of depression (Bebbington, 1993)

Patients may emphasize only one aspect of
the experience (due to language constraints, social desirability, or patterns of
symptom manifestation), augmenting
chances of misdiagnosis.

References

American Psychiatric Association. (1952). *Diagnostic and Statistical Manual-DSM I (First edition)*. Washington, DC: Author.

American Psychiatric Association. (1968). *Diagnostic and Statistical Manual-DSM II (Second edition)*. Washington, DC: Author.

American Psychiatric Association. (1980). *Diagnostic and Statistical Manual-DSM III (Third edition)*. Washington, DC: Author.

American Psychiatric Association. (1987). *Diagnostic and Statistical Manual-DSM III-R (Third edition revised)*. Washington, DC: Author.

American Psychiatric Association. (1994). *Diagnostic and Statistical Manual-DSM IV (Fourth edition)*. Washington, DC: Author.

Anastasi, A. (1988). *Psychological testing,* (6th ed.). New York: Macmillan.

Baskin, D. (1984). Cross-cultural conceptions of mental illness. *Psychiatry Quarterly, 56,* 45–53.

Bebbington, P. (1993). Transcultural aspects of affective disorders. *International Review of Psychiatry, 5,* 145–156.

Beck, A. T. (1967). *Depression: Clinical, experimental and therapeutic aspects.* New York: Harper & Row.

Beck, A. T., & Beamesderfer, A. (1974). Assessment of depression: The depression inventory. In P. Pichot (Ed.), *Psychological measurement in psychopharmacology. Modern problems in pharmacopsychiatry* (Vol. 7 pp. 15–16). Basel, Switzerland: Karger.

Beck, A. T., & Beck, R. W. (1972). Screening depressed patients in family practice. A rapid technique. *Postgraduate Medicine, 52,* 81–85.

Beck, A., & Kovacs, M. (1979). Assessment of suicidal intention: The scale for suicide ideation. *Journal of Consulting and Clinical Psychology, 47,* 343–352.

Beck, A., Rush, A., Shaw, B., & Emery, G. (1979). *Cognitive therapy of depression.* New York: Guilford Press.

Beck, A. T., Steer, R. A., & Brown, G. K. (1996). Manual for the Beck Depression Inventory-II. San Antonio, TX: Psychological Corporation.

Beck, A. T., Ward, C. H., Mendelson, M., Mock, J., & Erbaugh, J. (1961). An inventory for measuring depression. *Archives of General Psychiatry, 4,* 561–571.

Bemporad, J. R. (1990). Psychoanalytic therapy of depression. In B. Wolman & G. Stricker (Eds.), *Depressive disorders: facts, theories and treatment* (pp. 296–309). New York: Wiley.

Blaser, R., Low, D., & Schaublin, A. (1968). Die Messung der depressionstiefe mit einmen Fragebogen. *Psychiatric Clinic, 1,* 299–319.

Brown, G. W., & Harris, T. O. (1989). Depression. In G. W. Brown & T. O. Harris (Eds.), Life events and illness (pp. 49–93). New York: Guilford Press.

Casas, J. M., & Vasquez, M. J. T. (1989). Counseling the Hispanic client: A theoretical and applied perspective. In P. B. Pedersen, J. G. Draguns, W. J. Lonner, & J. E. Trimble (Eds.), *Counseling across cultures* (3rd ed., pp. 153–175). Honolulu: University of Hawaii.

Chang, W. (1985). A cross cultural study of depressive symptomatology. *Culture, Medicine and Psychiatry, 9,* 295–317.

Channabasavanna, S. M., Raguram, R., Weiss, M. G., & Parvathavardhini, R., (1993). Ethnography of psychiatric illness: A pilot study. *NIMHANS Journal, 11,* 1–10.

Cheung, F. M. (1987). Conceptualization of psychiatric illness and help-seeking behavior among Chinese. *Culture, Medicine and Psychiatry, 11,* 97–106.

Coppen, A., Harwood, J., & Wood, K. (1984). Depression, weight loss and the Dexamethosone Suppression Test. *British Journal of Psychiatry, 145,* 88–90.

Crittenden, K., Fugita, S., Bae, H., Lamug, C. B., & Lin, C. (1992). A cross-cultural study of self-report depressive symptoms among college students, *Journal of Cross Cultural Psychology, 23,* 163–178.

Delay, J., Pichot, P., Lemperiere, T., & Mirouze, R. (1963). La nosologie des etats depressifs. Rapports entre l'etiologie at la semiologie II. Resultats du questionnaire de Beck. *Encephale, 52,* 497–505.

Dewey, M. E., de la Camera, C., Copeland, J. R. M., Lobo, A., & Saz, P. (1993). Cross cultural comparison of depression and depressive symptoms in older people. *Acta Psychiatrica Scandinavica, 87,* 369–373.

Draguns, J. G. (1973). Comparisons of psychopathology across cultures: Issues, findings, directions. *Journal of Cross Cultural Psychology, 4,* 9–47.

Eisenbuch, M. (1984). Cross-cultural aspects of bereavement: I. A conceptual framework for comparative analysis. *Culture, Medicine, and Psychiatry, 18,* 283–309.

Ekman, P., & Friesen, W. (1974). Nonverbal behavior and psychopathology. In R. Friedman & M. Katz (Eds.), *The psychology of depression: Contemporary theory and research* (pp. 203–224). Washington, DC: Winston.

Escobar, J. I., Mendoza, R., Stimmel, G., Kook, K., Swann, E., & Raiss, C. (1984) The DST in a large outpatient clinic: Its diagnostic and predictive significance. *Psychopharmacology Bulletin, 20,* 89–92.

Essau, C., & Wittchen, H. U. (1993). An overview of the Composite International Diagnostic Interview (CIDI). *International Journal of Methods in Psychiatric Research, 3,* 79–85.

Farmer, A., Katz, R., McGuffin, P., & Bebbington, P. (1987). A comparison between the Composite International Diagnosis Interview and the Present State Examination. *Archives of General Psychiatry, 44,* 1064–1068.

Fava, G. (1983). Assessing depressive symptoms across cultures: Italian validation of the CES-D self-rating scales. *Journal of Clinical Psychology, 39,* 249–251.

Fisch, J., Frey, S., & Hirsbrunner, H. (1983). Analyzing nonverbal behavior in depression. *Journal of Abnormal Psychology, 92,* 307–318.

Gastpar, M. (1983). The ICD-9 and the SADD: Criteria for depression. *Acta Psychiatria Scandinavica,* (Suppl. 310), 31–41.

Gingerich, E., Golden, S., Holley, D., Nemser, J., Nuzzola, P., & Pollen, L. (1992). The therapist as psychoeducator. *Brief Reports, 42,* 928–930.

Goldberg, D. P. (1972). *The detection of psychiatric illness by questionnaire: A technique for the identification and assessment of non-psychotic psychiatric illness.* London: Oxford University Press.

Golden R., & Janowsky, D. (1990). Biological theories of depression. In B. Wolman & G. Stricker (Eds.), *Depressive disorders: Facts, theories and treatment methods* (pp. 3–21). New York: Wiley.

Gotlib, I. H. (1984). Depression and general psychopathology in university students. *Journal of Abnormal Psychology, 93,* 19–30.

Hacker, A. (1992). *Two nations: Black and white, separate, hostile and unequal.* New York: Scribner.

Hamilton, M. (1960). A rating scale for depression. *Journal of Neurology, Neurosurgery and Psychiatry, 12,* 56–62.

Hamilton, M., & White, J. (1959). Clinical syndromes in depressive states. *Journal of Mental Science, 105,* 985–987.

Hanson, M. J. (1990). Honoring the cultural diversity of families when gathering data. *Topics in Early Childhood Special Education, 10,* 112–131.

Hasewega, K. (1985). The epidemiology of depression in later life. *Journal of Affective Disorders,* (Suppl. 1), 3–6.

Helms, J. E. (1992). Why is there no study of cultural equivalence in standardized cognitive ability testing? *American Psychologist, 47,* 1083–1101.

Hinton, L., IV, & Kleinman, A. (1993). Cultural issues and international psychiatric diagnosis. In J. C. Costa-Silva & C. C. Nadelson (Eds.), *International Review of Psychiatry.* Washington, DC: American Psychiatric Association.

Ivey, A. (1995). Psychotherapy as liberation. In J. G. Ponterotto, J. M. Casas, L. A. Suzuki, & C. Alexander (Eds.), *Handbook of Multicultural Counseling* (pp. 53–72). Thousand Oaks, CA: Sage.

Jablensky, A. (1986). Current trends in the methodology of classification. *Acta Psychiatrica Belgica, 86,* 556–567.

Jackson, A. P., & Meadows, F. B. (1991). Getting to the bottom to understand the top. *Journal of Counseling and Development, 40,* 72–76.

Jakobsen, D. M. (1994). Psychopharmacology, women of color. In L. Comas-Diaz & B. Greene (Eds.), *Women of color: Integrating ethnic and gender identities into psychotherapy* (pp. 319–338). London: Guilford Press.

Janca, A., Üstün, T. B., & Sartorius, N. (1993) The ICD-10 symptom checklist. A comparison to the ICD-10 classification of mental and behavioral disorders. *Social Psychiatry and Psychiatric Epidemiology, 28,* 239–249.

Jenkins, J. H., Kleinman, A., & Good, B. J. (1991). Cross-cultural studies in depression. In J. Becker and A. Kleinman (Eds.), *Psychosocial aspects of depression* (pp. 67–99). Hillsdale, NJ: Erlbaum.

Johnson, S. D. (1987). Knowing that versus knowing how: Toward achieving expertise through multicultural training for counseling. *Counseling Psychologist, 15,* 321–331.

Karno, M., Hough, R. L., Burnam, A., Escobar, J. I., Timbers, D. M., Santana, F., & Boyd, J. H. (1987). Lifetime prevalence of specific psychiatric disorders among Mexican American and non-Hispanic whites in Los Angeles. *Archives of General Psychiatry, 44,* 695–701.

Katz, R., Shaw, B. F., Vallis, T. M., & Kaiser, A. S. (1995). The assessment of severity and symptom patterns in depression. In E. E. Beckham & W. R. Leber (Eds.), *Handbook of Depression* (2nd ed.) (pp. 61–85). London: Guilford Press.

Katz, R., Stephen, J., Matthew, A., Newman, F., Shaw, B. F., & Rosenbuth, M. (1995). The East York Health Needs Study I: Prevalence of *DSM-III-R* psychiatric disorder in a sample of Canadian women, *British Journal of Psychiatry, 166,* 100–106.

Kazdin, A. E. (1981). Assessment techniques for childhood depression: A critical appraisal. *Journal of American Academy of Child Psychiatry, 22,* 157–164.

Kinzie, J. D., & Manson, S. M. (1987). The use of self-rating scales in cross-cultural psychiatry. *Psychiatric Hospital & Community Psychiatry, 38,* 190–196.

Kinzie, J. D., Manson, S. M., Vino T. D., Tolan N. T., Anh B., & Pho, T. N. (1982). Development and validation of a Vietnamese language rating scale. *American Journal of Psychiatry, 139,* 1276–1281.

Kirmayer, L. (1984). Culture, affect and somatization. I. *Transcultural Psychiatric Research Review, 21,* 159–188.

Kleinman, A. (1977). Depression, somatization, and the new cross-cultural psychiatry. *Social Science and Medicine, 11,* 3–10.

Kleinman, A. (1986). Illness meanings and illness behavior. In S. McHugh & T. M. Vallis (Eds.), *Illness behavior: A multidisciplinary model* (pp. 149–160). New York: Plenum Press.

Kleinman, A. (1987). Anthropology and psychiatry: The role of culture in cross-cultural research on illness. *British Journal of Psychiatry, 151,* 447–454.

Kleinman, A. (1995). Do psychiatric disorders differ in different cultures? The methodological questions. In N. R. Goldberger & J. B. Veroff (Eds.), *The culture and psychology* (pp. 631–651). New York: New York University Press.

Krause, N., & Liang, J. (1992). Cross-cultural variations in depressive symptoms in later life. *International Psychogeriatrics, 4* (Suppl. 2), 185–202.

Lazarus, A. (1971). *Behavior therapy and beyond.* New York: McGraw-Hill.

Linehan, M. (1981). A social-behavioral analysis of suicide and parasuicide: Implications for clinical assessment and treatment. In J. Clarkin & H. Glazer (Eds.), *Depression, behavioral and directive intervention strategies* (pp. 229–294). New York: Garland.

Linehan, M., & Chiles, J. (1983). Reasons for staying alive when you are thinking of killing yourself: The Reasons for Living Inventory. *Journal of Consulting and Clinical Psychology, 51,* 276–286.

Manson, S. M., Shore, J. H., & Bloom, J. D. (1985). The depressive experience in American Indian communities: A challenge for psychiatric theory and diagnosis. In A. Kleinman & B. Good (Eds.), *Culture and depression* (pp. 331–368). Berkeley, CA: University of California Press.

Marsella, A. (1980). Depressive experience and disorder across cultures. In H. C. Traindis & J. G. Draguns (Eds.), *Handbook of cross-cultural psychology* (Vol. 6, pp. 237–288). Boston: Allyn & Bacon,

May, A. E., Urquart, A., & Taran, J. (1969). Self-evaluation of depression in various diagnostic and therapeutic groups. *Archives of General Psychiatry, 21,* 191–194.

Murphy, H. B. M. (1982). *Comparative psychiatry.* Berlin: Springer-Verlag.

Myers, H. (1993). Biopsychosocial perspective on depression in African Americans. In K. M. Lin, R. E. Poland, & G. Nakasaki, (Eds.), *Psychopharmacology and psychobiology of ethnicity,* (pp. 201–222). Washington, DC: American Psychiatric Press.

Nichter, M. (1981). Idioms of distress: Alternatives in the expression of psychosocial distress: A case study from South India. *Cultural Medical Psychiatry, 5,* 379–408.

Nikelly, A. (1988). Does *DSM-III-R* diagnose depression in non-Western patients? *International Journal of Social Psychiatry, 34,* 316–320.

Obeyesekere, G. (1985). Depression, Buddhism, and the work of culture in Sri Lanka. In A. Kleinman & B. Good (Eds.), *Culture and depression: Studies in anthropology and cross-cultural psychiatry of affect and disorder* (pp. 134–152). Berkeley, CA: University of California Press.

Paykel, E. S. (1982). Life events and early environment. In E. S. Paykel (Ed.), *Handbook of affective disorders* (pp. 71–86). Edinburgh, Scotland: Churchill-Livingstone Press.

Pedersen, P. (1991). Multiculturalism as a generic approach to counseling. *Journal of Counseling and Development, 70,* 8–19.

Pedersen, P. (1995). Culture-centered ethical guidelines for counselors. In J. G. Ponterotto, J. M. Casas, L. A. Suzuki, & C. Alexander (Eds.), *Handbook of multicultural counseling* (pp. 34–49). Thousand Oaks, CA: Sage.

Pedersen, P., Fukuyama M., & Heath A., (1989). Client, counselor, and contextual variables in multicultural counseling. In P. Pedersen, J. G. Draguns, W. J. Lonner, & J. E. Trimble (Eds.), *Counseling across cultures* (3rd ed., pp. 23–52). Honolulu: University of Hawaii Press.

Pliskin, K. L. (1987). *Silent boundaries: Cultural constraints on sickness and diagnosis of Iranians in Israel.* New Haven, CT: Yale University Press.

Poland, R. E. & Lin, K. M. (1993). Ethnicity and biological markers. In K. M. Lin, R. E. Poland, & G. Nakasaki (Eds.) *Psychopharmacology and psychobiology of ethnicity.* (pp. 187–199). Washington, DC: American Psychiatric Press.

Radloff, L. S. (1977) The CES-D scale: A self-report depression scale for research in the general population. *Applied Psychological Measurement, 1,* 385–401.

Raft, D., Spencer, R. F., Toomey, T., & Brogan, D. (1977). Depression in medical outpatients: Use of the Zung scale. *Diseases of the Nervous System, 38,* 99–104.

Reynolds, W. M., & Gould, J. W. (1981). A psychometric investigation of the standard and short form Beck Depression Inventory. *Journal of Consulting and Clinical Psychology, 49,* 306–307.

Robins, L. N., Helzer, J. E., Croughan, J., & Ratcliff, K. S. (1981). National Institute of Mental Health Diagnostic Interview Schedule: Its history, characteristics and validity. *Archives of General Psychiatry, 38,* 381–389.

Rogler, L. H. (1993). Culturally sensitizing psychiatric diagnosis: A framework for research. *Journal of Nervous and Mental Disease, 181,* 401–408.

Safran, J. D., & Segal, Z. V. (1990). *Interpersonal process in cognitive therapy.* New York: Basic Books.

Sartorius, N. (1986). Cross-cultural research on depression. *Psychobiology, 19* (Suppl. 2), 1–11.

Sartorius, N., Jablensky, A., Gulbinat, W., & Ernberg, G. (1980). WHO collaborative study: Assessment of depressive disorders. *Psychological Medicine, 10,* 743–749.

Scott, N. A., Hannum, T. E., & Ghrist, S. L. (1982). Assessment of depression among incarcerated females. *Journal of Personality Assessment, 46,* 372–379.

Silver B., Poland, R. E., & Lin, K. M. (1993). Ethnicity and the pharmacology of tricyclic antidepressants. In K. M. Lin, R. E. Poland, & G. Nakasaki (Eds.), *Psychopharmacology and psychobiology of ethnicity* (pp. 61–89). Washington, DC: American Psychiatric Press.

Smart J. F. & Smart D. W. (1991). Acceptance of disability and the Mexican culture. *Rehabilitation Counseling Bulletin, 34,* 357–367.

Sotsky, S., & Glass, D. (1983, June). *The Hamilton Rating Scale. A critical appraisal and modification for psychotherapy research.* Paper presented at the Annual Convention of the Society for Psychotherapy Research, Sheffield, England.

Speight, S. L., Meyers, L. J., Cox, C. I., & Highlen, P. S. (1991) A redefining of multicultural counseling. *Journal of Counseling and Development, 70,* 29–63.

Spitzer, R. L., Williams, J. B., Gibbon, M., & First, M. B. (1992). The Structured Clinical Interview for *DSM-III-R* (SCID): I. History, rationale, and description. *Archives of General Psychiatry, 49,* 624–629.

Stenbeck, A., Rimon, R., & Turunen, M. (1967). Validitet av Taylor Manifest Anxiety Scale. *Nordica Psykiatrika, 21,* 79–85.

Strickland, T. L., Ranganath, V., Lin, K. M., Poland, R. E., Mendoza, R., & Smith, M. W. (1991). Psychopharmacologic considerations in the treatment of Black American populations. *Psychopharmacology Bulletin, 27,* 441–448.

Sue, D. W. & Sue, D. (1990). *The culturally skilled counselor: Counseling the culturally different, theory and practice.* (2nd ed.). New York: Wiley.

Suzuki, L. A., & Kugler, J. F. (1995). Intelligence and personality assessment: Multicultural perspectives. In J. G. Ponterotto, J. M. Casas, L. A. Suzuki, & C. Alexander (Eds.), *Handbook of multicultural counseling* (pp. 493–515). Thousand Oaks, CA: Sage.

Swanson, J. W., Linskey, A. O., Quintero-Salias R., Pumariega, A. J., & Holzer, C. E., III, (1992). A binational school survey of depressive symptoms, drug use, and suicidal ideation. *Journal of American Academy of Child and Adolescent Psychiatry, 31,* 669–678.

Tashakkori, A., Barefoot, J., & Mehryar, A. H. (1989). What does the BDI measure in college students? Evidence from a non-Western culture. *Journal of Clinical Psychology, 45,* 595–602.

Thornicroft, G., & Sartorius, N. (1993). The course and outcome of depression in different cultures: 10 year follow-up of the WHO collaborative Study on the Assessment of Depressive Disorders. *Psychological Medicine, 23*, 1023–1032.

Vernon, S. W., & Roberts, R. E. (1982). Prevalence of treated and untreated psychiatric disorders in ethnic groups. *Social Science and Medicine, 16*, 1575–1582.

Waxer, P. (1974) Nonverbal cues for depression. *Journal of Abnormal Psychology, 53*, 318–322.

Wayman, K. I., Lynch, E.W., & Hanson, M. J. (1991). Home-based early childhood services: Cultural sensitivity in a family systems approach. *Topics in Early Childhood Speical Education, 10*, 56–75.

Weiss, M. G., Doongaji, D. R., Siddhartha, S., Wypij, D., Bhatawdekar, M., Bhave, A., Sheth, A., & Fernandes, R. (1992, June). The Explanatory Model Interview Catalogue (EMIC): Contribution to cross-cultural research methods from a study of leprosy and mental health. *British Journal of Psychiatry, 160*, 819–830.

Weiss, M. G. & Kleinman, A. (1988). Depression in cross-cultural perspective: Developing a culturally informed model. In P. R. Dasen, J. W. Berry, & N. Sartorius (Eds.), *Cross-cultural psychology and health: Toward applications* (pp. 179–206). Newbury Park, CA: Sage.

Weissman, M., & Klerman, G. (1990). Interpersonal psychotherapy for depression. In B. Wolman and G. Stricker (Eds.), *Depressive disorder: Facts, theories and treatment methods* (pp. 134–148). New York: Wiley.

Westermeyer. J. (1987). Clinical considerations in cross cultural research. *Hospital and Community Psychiatry, 38*, (2) 160–164.

Westermeyer, J., Vang, T. F., & Neider, J. (1983). Migration and mental health among refugees: Association of pre- and postmigration factors with self-rating scales. *Journal of Nervous and Mental Disease, 171*, 92–96.

Wing, J. K., Babor, T., Brugha, T., Burkem, J., Cooper, J. E., Giel, R., Jablenski, A., Regier, D., & Sartorius, N. (1990) SCAN schedules for clinical assessment in neuropsychiatry. *Archives of General Psychiatry, 47*, 589–593.

Wing, J., Birley, J., Cooper, J., Graham, P., & Isaacs, A. (1967). Reliability of a procedure for measuring and classifying "present psychiatric state". *British Journal of Psychiatry, 113*, 499–515.

Wolman, B. B. (1990). Depression: The psychosocial theory. In B. Wolman and G. Stricker (Eds.), *Depressive disorders: Facts, theories, and treatment methods* (pp. 92–124). New York: Wiley.

World Health Organization. (1978). *International classification of diseases (ninth edition).* Geneva, Switzerland: Author.

World Health Organization. (1992). *The ICD-10 classification of mental and behavioral disorders.* Geneva, Switzerland: Author.

Yamoto, G. (1992). Something about the subject makes it hard to name. In M. L. Anderson and P. H. Collins (Eds.), *Race, class, and gender: An anthology* (pp. 65–70). Belmont, CA: Wadsworth.

Ying, Y. -W. (1990). Explanatory models of major depression and implications for help-seeking among immigrant Chinese-American women. *Culture, Medicine and Psychiatry, 14*, 393–408.

Ying, Y. -W, (1988). Depressive symptomology among Chinese-Americans as measured by the CES-D. *Journal of Clinical Psychology, 44*, 739–746.

Zung, W. W. K. (1965). A self-rating depression scale. *Archives of General Psychiatry, 12*, 63–70.

Zung, W. W. K. (1967). Factors influencing the self-rating depression scale. *Archives of General Psychiatry, 16*, 543–547.

Zung, W. W. K. (1969). A cross-cultural survey of symptoms of depression. *American Journal of Psychiatry, 126*, 154–159.

8

Incorporating Culture into the Treatment of Alcohol Abuse and Dependence

BRUCE BAXTER

RILEY E. HINSON

ANNE-MARIE WALL

SHERRY A. MCKEE

Beliefs, values, attitudes, and expectancies that individuals have about drugs and alcohol influence not only their own treatment decisions, but also the potential effectiveness of therapists' decisions regarding the form and goals of treatment. Therapists may not understand, or even be aware of, cultural differences between themselves and their clients and, consequently, may fail to consider how those differences may affect interpretation of drug education messages, decisions regarding treatment entry, and the desirability of different treatment approaches and goals. In this chapter we discuss beliefs and values relevant to drug-related behavior among North American cultural group members that may be useful in improving community and individual prevention and treatment efforts. On a community level, recognition of cultural values should help policymakers formulate more culturally appropriate education and prevention programs, while on an individual level, awareness of cultural values may aid therapists' decisions regarding treatment approaches and goals. The literature available to identify these beliefs and values has typically taken the form of a discussion of differences in variously defined groups. While reading this chapter, the reader should remain aware of the cautions that apply to this literature (for a more extensive discussion, see Trimble, 1991, 1995). Cultural group membership is not precise, and thus attempts to classify individuals into ethnic or cultural groups for research or discussion purposes is problematic. Furthermore, even individuals who identify themselves as members of the same cultural or ethnic group demonstrate heterogeneity in their beliefs, values, attitudes, and expectancies, including those which influence decisions regarding drug use and treatment. We have chosen to limit our discussion almost exclusively to cultural values regarding alcohol, because this is the drug that has received the most research attention. It is quite likely that some of the cultural values identified with alcohol use would not apply to other drugs. If we are successful in showing how cultural variables are relevant to the treatment of alcohol abuse and dependence, this should only serve to highlight the importance of examining culture in regard to treatment and prevention issues with other drugs.

The plan for this chapter is to begin by discussing prevalence rates for alcohol use, definitions of alcohol abuse and dependence, and cultural differences that appear to exist with respect to both problem drinking and utilization of services. In subsequent sections, we outline how differences in cultural values and beliefs influence treatment-seeking, the applicability of contemporary treatment approaches, and the development of specialized treatment programs. We will conclude by offering some suggestions on how attention to cultural values may enhance the prospects for successful treatment.

ALCOHOL USE: PREVALENCE AND DEFINITIONS

Prevalence

The use of alcohol is quite common in North America. A national household survey taken in the United States in 1992 indicated that approximately 83% of respondents reported some lifetime use of alcohol and approximately 65% reported use during the previous year. A 1989 national survey done in Canada found that 82% of men and 70% of women reported having used alcohol in the previous year, while in Ontario approximately 13% of men and 7% of women reported drinking on a daily basis. Despite methodological criticisms of studies examining cultural differences in consumption rates (e.g., see Trimble, 1991, 1995; Tucker, 1985), differences in per capita consumption of alcohol among cultural groups have been found. Native Americans are generally acknowledged to have the highest consumption rate for alcohol, with Whites having higher rates than African Americans or Hispanics (Adlaf, Smart, & Tan, 1989; Beauvais, Oetting, & Edwards, 1985; Brannock, Schandler, & Oncley, 1990; Johnston, O'Malley, & Bachman, 1994; Wallace & Bachman, 1991). It is relevant to note, however, that alcohol consumption among Native Americans varies widely depending on the tribe being considered. For example, May (1982) found that only 30% of Navajo reported drinking during the last year, whereas 84% of the Ojibwa of Canada fell into this category. Interestingly, when asked what percentage of Native Americans drink, both Natives and non-Natives indicated it was greater than 90% (May, 1982). In general, use of most recreational drugs, licit and illicit, tends to be higher among Whites than most other cultural groups, with the exception of alcohol and inhalants in Native Americans and cocaine in Hispanics. It is also well established that men drink more frequently and consume more per occasion than women in all cultural groups. Across cultural groups, however, differences exist with respect to female consumption patterns. The abstention rate among African American and Hispanic women is consistently found to be higher than among White females (Caetano, 1994; Gilbert, 1991; Herd, 1985). In addition, women who belong to the dominant North American culture tend to engage in more binge drinking behavior (i.e., five or more drinks per occasion) (Caetano, 1994).

Definitions

Differing terminology has been used to identify the clinically significant problems that may be associated with alcohol use. The National Council on Alcoholism identifies *alcoholism* as a chronic and progressive disease involving loss of control and resulting in social, legal, psychological, and physical consequences (National Council on Alcoholism, 1972). Other diagnostic classifications eschew use of the term alcoholism. In *DSM-IV* (American Psychiatric Association, 1994), problematic alcohol consumption is denoted as either alcohol abuse or dependence. The essential feature of substance (alcohol or any other drug) abuse is a pattern of use that results in recurrent and significant harmful consequences in at least one of four areas (physical, social, legal, or interpersonal) over a 12-month period. The essential feature of substance dependence is a cluster of cognitive, behavioral, and physiological symptoms (three of seven diagnostic symptoms over a 12-month period) indicating that the individual continues use of the substance despite significant substance-related problems.

Epidemiological research conducted in the United States indicates that alcohol abuse/dependence is the second most prevalent psychiatric condition, with lifetime and 1-year prevalence rates estimated at 13.8% and 8.8%, respectively (Robins & Regier, 1991). Although per capita consumption patterns vary across ethnic groups, very little is known about whether differential prevalence rates for alcohol abuse/dependence similarly exist (Trimble, 1991, 1995). It has been consistently found, however, that cultural minorities, in comparison to members of the dominant cultural group, are overrepresented in drug treatment programs and alcohol-related hospital admissions (Adlaf et al., 1989; Lex, 1987; Weisner, 1986). Female Native Americans, who represent a minority within a minority, are particularly overrepresented in treatment facilities (Weisner, 1986). As noted by several authors (Longshore, Hsieh, Anglin, & Annon, 1992; Trimble, 1995), caution must be exercised in extrapolating data from the population of known drug users, as this group may not be representative of all individuals who suffer from drug abuse/dependence.

In addition, in an examination of patients receiving alcohol treatment in Veterans' Administration hospitals in the United States, Booth, Blow, Cook, Bunn, and Fortney (1992) found that Native Americans, African Americans, and Hispanics tended to be younger than mainstream patients. Similar findings have been reported by other investigators (Lex, 1987; Weisner, 1986). The reasons for minority-group clients in treatment tending to be younger than majority-culture clients are not clear. Some contributing factors could be differential tendencies in diagnosing drug problems, better and earlier delivery of services, differential likelihood of presenting for treatment, increased vulnerability to alcohol, earlier age of onset of use of alcohol, or other factors. Some of these factors are discussed in the section on cultural factors in help-seeking, below.

Cultural Considerations in Defining and Identifying Alcohol Abuse and Dependence

A Role for Culture in Defining Alcohol Abuse.   The Cross-Cultural Applicability Research (CAR) study examined parameters that defined problem drinking in various cultural groups (Bennett, Janca, Grant, & Sartorius, 1993). Results of this study indicate that "normal" drinking is a valid construct across cultures. Six dimensions delineating the presence of problem drinking were found to exist cross-culturally: (1) quantity of consumption, (2) frequency of consumption, (3) context of consumption, (4) negative effects (e.g., health, social, occupational, legal), (5) inability to control drinking, and (6) a developing need to consume greater quantities of alcohol. Although the constructs of normal and problematic drinking were found to be valid across cultures, the defining conditions for these constructs varied. This observation is consistent with the seminal work of MacAndrew and Edgerton (1969) and subsequent research (P. B. Johnson & Gallo-Treacy, 1993; Lex, 1987; Sigelman, Didjurgis, Marshall, Vargas, & Stewart, 1992; Weatherspoon, Danko, & Johnson, 1994), which established that cultural variation in normative drinking practices exists. Thus, in determining whether an individual is suffering from alcohol abuse or dependence, it is critical that drinking and alcohol-related behaviors be considered within the cultural context in which they occur. The notion that problem drinking is culturally defined is explicitly recognized in the World Health Organization's (WHO) definition:

> drug dependence of the alcohol type may be said to exist when the consumption of alcohol by the individual exceeds the limits that are accepted by his culture, if he consumes alcohol at times that are deemed inappropriate within that culture or his intake of alcohol becomes so great so as to injure his health or impair his social relationships. (World Health Organization, 1975, p. 107)

A Role for Culture in the Clinical Recognition of Alcohol Abuse. Despite the recognition that problem drinking is culturally defined, the majority of clinical diagnostic, assessment, and screening instruments currently employed in North American research and treatment facilities are based on ethnocentric conceptualizations of alcohol abuse and dependence. As such, their clinical utility in detecting the full spectrum of alcohol-related problems in culturally diverse populations is uncertain. There is recent evidence that some mainstream clinical instruments, for example, the Structured Clinical Interview for *DSM*-Patient Edition (SCID-P; Spitzer, Williams, Gibbon, & First, 1990) and the Diagnostic Interview Schedule (DIS; Robins, Cottler, & Keating, 1989), are appropriate in assessing some aspects of alcohol abuse and dependence in culturally diverse populations. At the same time, there is reason to believe that clinical instruments might be improved if they were made more culturally sensitive. For example, in determining whether an individual's alcohol consumption warrants clinical intervention, clinicians inevitably inquire about the current pattern of alcohol use. At a minimum, quantity and frequency dimensions are assessed. According to the WHO definition of drug dependence, the interpretation of such quantity and frequency data would require a comparison with normative data from the client's cultural group. Unfortunately, this normative data is not always readily available for different cultural groups. Additionally, it is recognized that quantity and frequency measures are not the only, or even the best, indicators of alcohol abuse and dependence. Importantly, in a collaborative WHO project involving several distinct cultural groups (Saunders, Aasland, Amundsen, & Grant, 1993), the extent to which dimensions of alcohol intake were found to be distinct from alcohol-related problems varied across cultures. Thus, in some cultural groups, the amount of alcohol consumed or frequency of drinking episodes may be less indicative of problem drinking than are negative social or marital consequences (L. V. Johnson & Matre, 1978) or solitary drinking (Bennett et al., 1993). Saunders et al. (1993) concluded that self-perceptions of alcohol-related problems differed across cultures, and thus current clinical instruments may not provide an accurate depiction of the alcohol-related problems of clients from diverse cultures because the full content domain of cultural indications of problem drinking may not be assessed.

Even when a more comprehensive assessment approach is adopted, the use of preexisting structured or semistructured instruments designed to assess alcohol-related problems may be problematic, since the terms and behaviors found in such instruments may not be culture-free. For example, Peele (1984) notes that the work of MacAndrew and Edgerton (1969) demonstrated that "alcohol disinhibition" is interpreted, enacted, and manifested differentially in different cultures. Caetano (1996) has provided evidence that questions assessing "impairment of control" may be endorsed by Hispanics for social reasons and do not actually reflect clinically significant "loss of control." Thus, therapists should take steps to ensure that clients from diverse cultures understand the terms and behavioral descriptions used in clinical instruments, and that they (the therapists) understand clients' use of the same or different terms and behavioral descriptions for alcohol abuse and dependence. Failure to do so may result in a biased and limited understanding of the drug-related problems of clients from diverse cultures. This would bring into question any treatment recommendations and goals that would follow from such an assessment.

There is a similar need to examine the cultural sensitivity of screening instruments used to identify individuals who suffer from preclinical alcohol-related problems or those who are at risk for developing problems due to alcohol consumption. As noted by Cooney, Zweben, and Fleming (1995), the bulk of research on existing screening instruments has been conducted on "alcohol-dependent, white males in treatment programs" (p. 47). To date, there has been little systematic investigation concerning the sensitivity and specificity of various screening instruments across cultural groups (for exceptions, see Cherpitel & Clark, 1995; Lapam et al., 1995). The identification or development of screening instruments for the early detection of alcohol-related problems in culturally diverse populations may have a positive impact on the representation of cultural groups in drug-treatment facilities. Equally important is the need to develop screening instruments that will accurately identify individuals in culturally diverse populations who are in need of, but who do not receive, treatment.

WITHIN-GROUP HETEROGENEITY AND ACCULTURATION

There is considerable variability in the extent to which the members of any cultural group hold any particular belief or value (Brown & Tooley, 1989; Campinha-Bacote, 1991; Rogler, Malgady, Costantino, & Blumenthal, 1987; Weibel-Orlando, 1987; Woodward, Dwinell & Arons, 1992). In fact, members of different cultural groups may be more similar on some values than members of the same cultural group. For example, there are strong geographical differences in value systems, such that an African American woman from a rural area of the southern United States may be more similar in her attitude regarding the moral nature of drinking to a Caucasian woman from the same region than to an African American woman from an urban area in the northeast United States.

In addition, members of the same cultural group may demonstrate variable consumption patterns and attitudes toward drinking as a result of varying degrees of acculturation (Berry, 1980, 1994). It has been consistently found that the level of alcohol consumption among Hispanic women is positively related to their degree of acculturation (Caetano, 1994; Gilbert, 1991; Neff & Hoppe, 1992). To some extent this may be associated with increased income and higher levels of education in more acculturated Hispanic females (Neff & Hoppe, 1992), although other authors have argued that differences in drinking rates remain even when these factors are controlled (Caetano, 1994). Attitudes toward female drinking are more permissive in the dominant culture than in traditional Hispanic culture, and it is likely that the more acculturated Hispanic female has rejected the traditional proscriptive views toward female drinking (Caetano, 1994). In support of this, Cervantes, Gilbert, Salgado de Snyder, & Padilla (1991) found that U.S.-born Mexican American women held higher positive expectancies for alcohol than did immigrant Mexican American women. Such positive expectancies included social pleasure and assertiveness, elevation of mood, reduction of tension, and freedom from inhibition. Importantly, positive expectancies were found to correlate positively with higher levels of drinking. Gilbert (1991) highlights how a difference in attitudes toward drinking between tradition-oriented Hispanic relatives and mainstream-acculturated Hispanic women may stand in the way of constructive communication in Hispanic families. The strong proscriptive stance toward female drinking of tradition-oriented relatives may limit discussion of moderate alcohol use, less dangerous contexts for drinking, and more appropriate ages for drinking. Clarke, Ahmed, Romaniuk, Marjot, and Murray-Lyon (1990) reported a similar finding regarding level of consumption by South Asians (countries of origin: India, Sri Lanka, Pakistan, and Bangladesh) in Britain, such that "exposure to British culture seems an important factor affecting consumption levels since the longer (South Asians) had lived (in Britain) the more they drank" (p. 10). As a general conclusion about the influence of level of acculturation into mainstream North American attitudes toward drug use, Adlaf et al. (1989) found that, among groups ranging from seventh graders to high school seniors in seven different cultural groups (Eastern European, British Isles, African American, Oriental, East and West Indian, Jewish, and Mediterranean), those most at risk for drug use were the more highly acculturated.

Another way in which acculturation may be relevant to alcohol and substance use is whether someone undergoing acculturation is subject to psychological states, such as stress or anomie (L. V. Johnson & Matre, 1978), that lead to drug use (Ja & Aoki, 1993; LaDue, 1994; Takeuchi, Mokuau, & Chun, 1992). Berry (1990, 1994) suggests different end points of the acculturation process that reflect (a) the extent to which the person continues to value and identify with the culture of origin and (b) the extent to which the person values the new culture. Marginalization occurs when someone does not hold values of either the original or the new culture. Marginalization is typically identified as the end point most likely to be associated with problems, one of which may be substance abuse, although other acculturation paths may produce stress and problems. An often-used example of marginalization is that of Native Americans in urban centers who do not receive the support of the traditional Native culture nor acceptance in the mainstream culture (e.g., see Albaugh & Anderson, 1974). Although some have suggested that substance abuse may occur as a result of stress associated with the acculturation process, this has not been unequivocally demonstrated (Oetting, Swaim, Edwards, & Beauvais, 1989).

CULTURAL FACTORS AND HELP-SEEKING FOR ALCOHOL AND DRUG PROBLEMS

Research suggests that help-seeking and treatment for alcohol- and drug-related problems may differ between cultural groups and across gender. Several authors (Booth et al., 1992; Longshore et al., 1992) have reported that African Americans and Hispanics seem to be less likely than Whites to have received any previous treatment for their drug use, whereas Native Americans tend to have fewer treatment experiences than other cultural groups (Weisner, 1986). Weisner (1986) also found that African Americans in treatment had more severe problems than Whites. Similarly, Weisner (1986) reported that Hispanics have higher levels of family, legal, and economic problems due to alcohol but only go to treatment about half as frequently as the rest of the population. The time between the onset of heavy drinking and help-seeking in women has been reported to be shorter than that in men (Weisner, 1986).

Longshore et al. (1992) have indicated that help-seeking is influenced by "predisposing" and "enabling" factors. Enabling factors reflect how help-seeking is influenced by situational variables (e.g., monetary cost, travel time, availability of day care, willingness on the part of an employer to grant time off for treatment). Although enabling factors are often crucial to the decision of whether to seek help or not, they are not the object of discussion in this chapter. Longshore et al. (1992) identify predisposing factors as involving an individual's attitudes toward drinking and treatment, the attitudes of significant others toward drinking and treatment, the perceived need for treatment, and how problematic drinking is defined. What we will call "cultural predisposing factors" for help-seeking will now be discussed (Lex, 1987; Sigelman et al., 1992).

Perception of the Role of Treatment in Society

It is obvious that people are more likely to seek help or be responsive to suggestions that they seek help if they have a positive perception of treatment in general (Weisner, 1986; Westermeyer, 1979). Members of some cultural groups, however, often hold unfavorable views toward treatment. For example, Longshore et al. (1992) found that African Americans were more likely than Whites to cite an unfavorable view of treatment as a reason for not seeking help. Rather than seeing methadone as a means of attaining stability necessary to pursue other treatment avenues, both African Americans and Hispanics viewed methadone as representing oppression and control over minorities by the dominant culture, which they perceived to be more interested in controlling crime than treating addicts (B. S. Brown, 1985). The observation that African Americans nearly always receive methadone treatment rather than a drug-free program (Tucker, 1985), even though race (African American/White) does not predict outcome for clients given methadone maintenance, reinforces this view. Similarly, Weibel-Orlando (1985) has argued that Native Americans often view treatment as a negative resocialization process. The Native American client often enters treatment as a result of engaging in activities (e.g., "partying," "raising a little hell") that are positively valued as part of being a Native in modern, White society (French, 1989; May, 1982; Pedigo, 1983; Sigelman et al., 1992; Weibel-Orlando, 1985). Weibel-Orlando (1985) then describes the treatment experience from the Native American client's viewpoint as involving one in which "considerable time is spent . . . teaching usually a coerced client, first, the concept of alcoholism as an illness, second, convincing him that he is indeed an alcoholic and ultimately that he needs to do something about it" (p. 220). Thus an unfavorable view often reflects the minority client's feeling that either treatment is a form of control or that their beliefs and values are either unknown or unappreciated, particularly when treatment personnel are not minority individuals (Rogan, 1987).

Cultural Conceptualizations of Alcoholism

Caetano (1987, 1989) examined endorsement of components of the disease concept of alcoholism in samples of African Americans, Hispanics, and Whites. He found no differences among these groups in endorsement of the concepts that "alcoholism is an illness" and "to recover, alcoholics have to quit forever." African Americans and Hispanics, however, were more likely than Whites to endorse the ideas that "alcoholics can control their drinking," "most alcoholics drink because they want to," and "alcoholics are morally weak." Endorsement of these items was negatively related to income and education, but the cultural-group differences remained when income and education were statistically controlled. Acknowledging that alcoholism is a disease while at the same time believing that alcoholics are morally weak may seem contradictory to professionals, but Caetano (1989) argues that such a dual classification does not violate cultural definitions of disease and illness for Hispanics. Freund (1985) has reported a similar finding among Polish Americans. Similarly, Rodin (1981) has suggested that alcoholism is classified by most people as a "folk illness" instead of a disease, such that psychosocial and cultural factors are afforded equal explanatory weight with biological factors, even when they may appear to be contradictory. For this reason, Rodin (1981) suggests that professionals may constitute a group whose beliefs about alcoholism are very different from that of their clients, and this may cause drinkers to reject professional care. The "folk illness" nature of alcoholism may also help explain why previous research has found no consistent relationship between endorsement of the disease concept of alcoholism and either the belief that treatment is necessary or useful, the belief that one form of treatment is better than another, or actual help-seeking (Rodin, 1981; Weisner, 1986).

Another predisposing factor with regard to help-seeking is related to the observation that Native Americans subscribe to the view that they are especially vulnerable to alcohol (Sigelman et al., 1992). Bennett et al. (1993) report that Navajo respondents equated normal drinking with binge drinking, and Bennett et al. (1993) and French (1989) found that Native Americans did not believe that they could control their drinking or show normal drinking. Sigelman et al. (1992) found that a sample of Native American youths endorsed the disease concept of alcoholism more strongly than samples of White and Hispanic youths. The impact of this belief in a "special vulnerability" and stronger endorsement of the disease model of alcoholism on help-seeking is, however, unclear. Sigelman et al. (1992) suggested that this pattern of beliefs may make Native Americans more amenable to medical models of treatment as compared to more moralistically based models. It may also make Native Americans less likely to believe that any form of treatment will be useful.

Stigma Associated with Being Labeled "Alcoholic"

Although there is near-unanimous agreement among the public with the concept that alcoholism is a disease (greater than 90% endorsement; Caetano, 1989), there is still considerable stigma associated with identifying oneself as an alcoholic (Caetano, 1987). Caetano (1987) found that about 30% of people who endorsed "alcoholism is a disease" still said they would be ashamed to admit having a problem, and 54% stated they would not seek outside help. Weisner (1986) has argued that avoiding being labeled alcoholic may be one reason why African Americans with less severe problems avoid treatment. In many communities, gossip is a powerful form of social control, and help-seeking may be hindered for fear that others will learn that a family member has an alcohol problem (commonly referred to in the alcoholism treatment field as "keeping the family secret"). Freund (1985), reporting on Polish Americans, and Gaines (1985), reporting on African Americans, state that treatment is less likely to be sought if the only options are located within the community or involve an absence from the community that would be noticed (e.g., long-term inpatient treatment). Freund (1985) found that treatment recommendation varied by generational status among Polish Americans, such that immigrant or first-generation individuals suggested keeping it within the family or among close friends while members of subsequent generations were more likely to suggest AA or medical professionals.

Jordan and Oei (1989) argue that a significant barrier to males' willingness to undergo treatment is that men perceive help-seeking as nonmasculine. The belief that "a real man can hold his liquor," identified with the concept of "machismo" (Neff, Prihoda, & Hoppe, 1991), may hinder acceptance of the fact that problems are being caused by alcohol. Men are more likely than women to identify physical problems upon treatment entry (Rodin, 1981), and this may be because men are less willing to admit being unable to handle alcohol (Jordan & Oei, 1989). This may be related to the observation that men are more likely to be in medically oriented treatment programs and women in psychologically oriented programs (Weisner, 1986).

Cultural Role of Drug Taking and Defining Abuse

As noted earlier, most professional definitions of drug abuse and dependence include a cultural component that typically involves defining drug use as involving abuse or dependence only if patterns of consumption violate culturally sanctioned norms (cf. L. V. Johnson & Matre, 1978) or result in failure to fulfill societal or familial responsibilities (cf. Ja & Aoki, 1993). Although these general criteria may be qualitatively similar in different cultural groups (see Helzer & Canino, 1992), the actual behaviors involved may be dramatically different. For example, one of the most commonly cited indicators of an alcohol problem is "family objects to respondent's drinking." It is not clear, however, whether such objections would be related to the same level of consumption or the same behavioral consequences for different cultural groups. Bennett et al. (1993) highlight this when they note that "specifying the exact amount of alcohol that can be consumed for normal drinking and the social contexts where it is normal is subject to cultural variation" (p. 195).

Several studies have found that Hispanic men drink more heavily than men in the general population and that drinking by Hispanic men often involves heavy binge drinking (Gilbert, 1991; Lex, 1987; Neff & Hoppe, 1992; ; Neff et al., 1991). Despite the fact that the drinking style of Hispanic males would be expected to lead to more problems (Weisner, 1986), Hispanics are less likely than Whites or African Americans to view the consequences associated with heavy drinking as defining a condition in need of treatment (Lex, 1987; Longshore et al., 1992; Weisner, 1986). The concept of machismo, in which the male is expected to drink heavily yet maintain control (Neff et al., 1991), may contribute to this reluctance to define the consequences of drinking as problematic (Eden & Aguilar, 1989; L. V. Johnson & Matre, 1978; Marin, 1990). Although the concept of machismo is typically ascribed to male Hispanic culture, Neff et al. (1991) found attitudes and behaviors that they identified with machismo in African Americans and Whites. For the present discussion, the important point is not that machismo may be associated with heavy drinking but rather that the consequences of such heavy drinking are often what are sought, and, consequently, would not be considered as defining a problem in need of treatment.

Substance use fulfills a variety of roles and social functions in different cultures, and this can result in considerable latitude in determining when substance use has become problematic. For example, several authors (Beauvais & LaBoueff, 1985; Heath, 1987; May, 1982; Sigelman et al., 1992; Weibel-Orlando, 1985) have argued that heavy drinking and binge drinking, with associated acute problems (e.g., violence, driving while intoxicated), are regarded as acceptable recreational activities in many Native communities. Problems arising from acute drunkenness are excused or taken for granted because the person is drunk. In some Native societies, alcohol use fulfills traditional values of generosity, sharing, reciprocity, and compliance with the wishes of relatives and friends (French, 1989; Pedigo, 1983; Savishinsky, 1991). The potential special meaning of sharing drinking, both as a giver and receiver, may help explain the finding that Native Americans are hesitant to label someone alcoholic (Savishinsky, 1991; Weibel-Orlando, 1985) and often express little guilt regarding drinking to excess (Hurlburt & Gade, 1984). Native American children are therefore often exposed to adult models where drinking, and most often binge drinking with acute problems, is, if not condoned, at least not condemned (Sigelman et al., 1992). Witnessing abusive drinking patterns may be particularly influential in determining later drinking behavior in Native children, who are accustomed to modeling as a form of instruction (Brant, 1990). This observation may be related to the finding that Native American youth give lower severity ratings for descriptions of drinking behavior than do White or Hispanic youth (Sigelman et al., 1992).

Herd (1985) has argued that drinking may have dual, and inconsistent, meanings in African American culture. As long ago as the early 1800s, prominent African American leaders argued that the use of alcohol "enslaved" African Americans and impeded advances in social, economic, and political spheres (Herd, 1985). At the same time, a strong temperance, or abstinence, stance toward alcohol was advocated by church leaders. Thus, two very powerful forces reinforced the view that African

Americans should not drink. However, during the era of Prohibition in the United States, one argument used in favor of prohibition was that alcohol had particularly dangerous effects when consumed by African Americans (Herd, 1985). Consequently, prohibition was viewed by many African American leaders as an instrument of racial subjugation, and temperance sentiment was seen as unwittingly supporting the prohibitionists' arguments. Following the repeal of prohibition, drinking assumed a new meaning, whereby it symbolized emancipation, equality, and sophistication (Herd, 1985; there is an unsettling similarity between the view that alcohol consumption by African Americans is a symbol of emancipation and the view promulgated by tobacco companies that cigarette smoking by women is a symbol of female emancipation and equality). The dual meaning of alcohol in African American culture could impact upon help-seeking and treatment in several fashions. An abstinence goal may well be championed by many members of the alcoholic's extended family network who hold religiously oriented temperance sentiments. Conversely, the alcoholic him- or herself, as well as friends, may feel that an abstinence goal reflects racist attitudes and is an attempt at control.

Gaines (1985) has also provided another insight into the meaning of alcohol that could influence help-seeking behavior. In African American culture, different types of alcoholic beverages have different meanings. The term *alcohol* is most often used only to refer to distilled spirits, not beer or wine. Thus, an African American client's statement that they do not use "alcohol" may not be a form of denial which needs to be broken through, but rather an accurate statement from the client's perspective, meaning that they do not drink distilled spirits but may drink beer or wine. Similarly, certain types of alcoholic beverages are considered more potent than others, even though the alcoholic content may be the same. Thus, "dark" distilled spirits (rum, bourbon), red wines, cheap wines, and malt liquors are considered more potent or masculine than "light" distilled spirits (vodka, gin), white wines or ales, which are seen as feminine or refined. (This dichotomy has not been lost on alcohol advertisers, as "dark" beverages, for example, malt liquor, are often targeted to African Americans.) Individuals who assign different meanings to varied types of alcoholic beverages may believe that they have "cut down" drinking by switching from a dark to a light beverage (Gaines, 1985). Volume of intake is often cited as the primary indicator that lay people use to identify problematic drinking (Jordan & Oei, 1989; see also Helzer & Canino, 1992), although professional diagnostic criteria do not state quantity and frequency definitions for dependence or abuse (e.g., *DSM-IV*). Gaines (1985) argues that volume may not be so important in defining problematic drinking in African American culture; instead the quality of the beverage (e.g., dark or light), the place of consumption, and family consequences are more central. For example, Gaines cites the opinion of one African American alcohol counselor that "a (African American) man who has a job and is still with his family wouldn't believe he could have an alcohol problem, no matter how much he drank" (p. 187).

Familial and Social Pressure to Seek Treatment

Research indicates that criticism of the consequences of drinking by family members or relatives is among the most important motivators for someone to seek treatment (Helzer & Canino, 1992). However, cultural values may mitigate the potency of this motivator in some families. Individual autonomy, noninterference, and avoiding embarrassment of others are highly valued in Native American families (Brant, 1990; French, 1989; Sigelman et al., 1992), and family members and relatives often assume a permissive, noninterventionist approach to drinking behavior and its consequences (Savishinsky, 1991; Sigelman et al., 1992). Sigelman et al. (1992) found that this passive "wait and see, leave the problem drinker alone" attitude was evident even among a sample of young (approximate age 12) Native Americans, and more prevalent in these young Native Americans than among comparably aged White and Hispanic youths.

Family pressure to confront problems associated with drug use may also be absent when cultural values place constraints on familial communication. Ja and Aoki (1993) present a summary of how this cultural factor may influence help-seeking in Asian families and communities. Among Asians, communication is not open but rather is often monodirectional, following the hierarchy within the family. Within Asian culture, the topic of substance abuse within the family or community is considered taboo and is not discussed. Acknowledging that a family member has a drug-use problem brings shame and embarrassment to the family, particularly the parents. When problems appear, the response of the family is often to ignore them or deny their existence, hoping they will go away. When forced to confront the problem, the initial response of the family is aimed at reducing family embarrassment. This may involve shaming or chastising the individual, or in extreme cases, rejecting and disowning him or her. Seeking help outside the family is considered only as a last resort because of the shame such an admission brings to the family and to the community (Ja & Aoki, 1993).

Many cultural groups are described as being more strongly "familistic," which typically entails a more extended family network that extends even to nonrelatives, than the dominant culture. Several authors (Gaines, 1985; Marin, 1990) have argued that a strong familistic valuation may make it more difficult for clients from diverse cultures to seek and accept treatment from professionals, who are seen as strangers. Marin (1990) found that Hispanics were twice as likely as Whites to feel that relatives, particularly older relatives, were the best people to help a family member with a drug problem. Furthermore, Hispanics were more convinced than Whites that family members who used drugs would follow their advice to stop.

Factors Affecting Help-seeking in Women

In addition to the values discussed above that may hinder help-seeking, women are subject to additional negative predisposing factors. In general, drinking by women is less acceptable than drinking by men (Gilbert, 1991; Heath, 1985; Higuchi & Kono, 1994; L. V. Johnson & Matre, 1978), and this gender distinction is more culturally validated in some minority groups than in the mainstream culture (Gaines, 1985). Gotoh (1994) reports that in Japan, families of alcoholics are most shamed when the alcoholic is a woman. Hispanic females are traditionally viewed as the center of family life, "a vision that demands chastity, purity, and abstention from alcohol" (Caetano, 1994, p. 240). Similarly, the matriarchal role is often assumed to be of more prominence in African American families than in the majority-culture family structure. The centrality of the matriarchal role has often been cited as one reason why Hispanic and African American females are more often nondrinkers or only light drinkers compared to White females (Brown & Tooley, 1989; Marin, 1990; see Caetano, 1994, for a discussion of the validity of the matriarchal family in relation to drinking).

One consequence of the reduced acceptability of drinking by women is that women may feel more shame about their drinking than men and that they would anticipate and receive a stronger negative reaction; consequently, they would be more likely to hide their drinking and be less willing to acknowledge alcohol as a source of problems, all of which would reduce the likelihood of help-seeking (Jordan & Oei, 1989). Consequently, women are more likely than men to come for treatment due to acute complications, such as suicide attempts or bouts of unconsciousness (Weisner, 1986). Furthermore, women are less likely than men to be supported by family, relatives, and friends in their decisions to seek help. Significant others will often minimize the seriousness of any alcohol-related problems while highlighting the familial and social costs of going into treatment. Other research has shown that husbands often discourage help-seeking and encourage further drinking among women (Jordan & Oei, 1989; Weisner, 1986). In certain cultures, there is a particularly strong value placed on empathic female relationships. It has been suggested (Gilbert, 1991) that including female members of the immediate or extended family would increase the impact of prevention and support groups for female clients from this type of cultural background.

Attitudes of Treatment Professionals

The beliefs and attitudes of staff members of treatment programs may influence who comes to treatment and how they are treated once they do come (Jordan & Oei, 1989; Rodin, 1981). Treatment personnel often hold stereotypical views about appropriate presenting problems and prognoses for different cultural groups or for males and females. As recent as the 1950s, African Americans were still thought to be beyond counseling. Vanicelli (1984) reports that a common belief among treatment personnel is that women have a poorer prognosis than men although there is no evidence to support this notion. Furthermore, staff members view presenting problems as more critical if they conform to preconceived sex-appropriate problems. Vanicelli (1984) concluded that these "negative myths" create significant barriers to women's receiving adequate treatment. Treatment providers need to examine any preconceived beliefs they may have about clients and how these may affect the treatment given.

Although treatment personnel need to guard against the negative impact of stereotypical thinking, awareness of cultural values often identified with minority individuals should serve to sensitize resource personnel and therapists to the possible presence of nonmainstream values that may influence the efficacy of education, assessment, and treatment. This may reduce the tendency to try to fit the client to the therapist's view of substance abuse (Gonzalez, Biever, & Gardner, 1994).

Interest in the effects of cultural values on treatment has led a number of investigators to attempt to assess clients' level of acculturation. In a program described by Campinha-Bacote (1991), each African American client's interpersonal style was assessed as either acculturated, culturally immersed, bicultural, or traditional, in order to identify their appropriateness for mainstream or culturally specific treatment. Stone (1981, 1982; cited in Weibel-Orlando, 1987) attempted to accommodate intracultural heterogeneity in alcoholism treatment by developing a method of identifying Native American clients on a continuum ranging from highly traditional to highly contemporary. Rogler et al. (1987) cite a number of measures of acculturation for Hispanic populations and suggest how these can be used to make a better decision regarding the proper type of treatment.

Considered in isolation, however, acculturation is, at best, only a coarse measure of the cultural variables of interest. A general measure of acculturation implies that a person acculturates on all the cultural variables of interest at the same rate. This is not necessarily true. As noted by Betancourt and Lopez (1993), it is better to directly assess the constructs of interest rather than to use level of acculturation as an indirect indication of what the person's attitudes or beliefs may be. Thus, rather than relying on more gross determinants of values, beliefs, and attitudes, such as ethnic heritage or degree of acculturation, therapists should deal ideally with cultural variables in a manner similar to other individual-difference variables which influence the course of treatment. What seems to be indicated is treatment matching based on an assessment of the individual's values, beliefs, and attitudes relevant to the treatment of substance abuse (Betancourt & Lopez, 1993). This emphasis on individualized treatment for substance abuse reflects suggestions by several researchers for individualized treatment in mental health services in general as the preferred means of dealing with intracultural heterogeneity (e.g., Rogler et al., 1987; Ruiz, 1981).

TREATMENT APPROACHES TO MODIFYING DRINKING BEHAVIOR

In their extensive review of alcohol treatment-outcome studies, Miller et al. (1995) identified 43 distinct therapeutic approaches. These treatment approaches differed across a number of dimensions (e.g., etiology, length, outcome goals, therapeutic strategies) that could be more or less compatible with a client's values and beliefs. It is now acknowledged that the degree of congruency between the therapist's and client's values and beliefs is an important determinant of a client's choice of treatment, engagement in the therapeutic process, and therapeutic outcome (Sue & Zane, 1987). This realization has led to a general trend away from trying to identify the "most effective" treatment approach toward client-treatment matching (Donovan et al., 1994; Donovan & Mattson, 1994; Institute of Medicine, 1990; Mattson & Allen, 1991; Miller & Cooney, 1994; Miller et al., 1995). In the following sections, we will discuss how some of the values and beliefs that have been identified earlier may be more or less compatible with some of the major conceptual approaches to alcoholism. For each conceptual model, the etiological view of alcohol addiction will be discussed. Subsequently, treatment goals, nature of the therapeutic relationship, and details concerning the course of clinical intervention will be provided. Specific aspects of each model that may interact with cultural values will be discussed under each model. In a following section, we will discuss more general aspects of treatment that may be relevant to cultural values.

Disease Model

In keeping with traditional medical views of health and illness, the etiological basis of alcohol addiction is thought to be biological in nature. As a result of an aberrant physiological reaction to alcohol, alcoholics are presumed incapable of controlling their drinking once alcohol is ingested (Jellinek, 1960). This loss of control is the sine qua non of alcohol addiction. This model includes the assumption that alcoholism is an irreversible progressive disease with potentially fatal implications (for a complete discussion, see Gerald, 1981), thus abstinence is the only treatment goal. Treatment is indicated when symptoms suggestive of physical dependence (i.e., withdrawal symptoms, craving, tolerance) and loss of control exist (Gorelick, 1993). The therapist assumes an expert role in imparting information about the nature of the illness and the need to abstain from drinking.

Within this model, treatment is generally prescriptive in nature, consisting typically of medically based interventions (e.g., antidipsotropic medications). Depending on the severity of physical dependence, a two-step treatment approach involving inpatient detoxification followed by outpatient treatment may be warranted. Regular follow-up appointments for purposes of medical monitoring, promoting compliance, and reinforcing sobriety are common (Fuller, 1995). Clinicians often enlist the support of family members (O'Farrell, 1993) and encourage patients to attend Alcoholics Anonymous (AA).

In addition to the usual issues discussed with clients whenever antidipsotropic medication is used, the therapist should be alert to special concerns that some clients from diverse cultures may have when drugs are part of treatment. The use of medication as a part of treatment may be viewed with skepticism by clients from some cultural groups, who may believe that mainstream treatment providers are more interested in controlling or oppressing them than in helping them (B. S. Brown, 1985). The use of drugs as part of treatment may also be in conflict with the machismo value of self-control (Marin, 1990). In fact, the whole concept that the alcoholic has lost control would seem to conflict with this value, which has been identified in males from many cultural groups (De Leon, Melnick, Sckhoket & Jainchill, 1993; Neff et al., 1991). In such a case, the therapist could try to show how treatment would allow the client to be more in control of the harmful effects that drinking may be having on family and friends.

Conceptualizing alcoholism as a disease may be taken by some clients as diminishing the amount of personal responsibility for the addiction. It has been proposed that when this view of diminished responsibility is combined with the view that alcoholism is inevitable among Native Indians, both the individual and the community develop a sense that treatment is futile (Beauvais & LaBoueff, 1985), resulting in a lack of motivation by the individual to seek treatment and by the community to help solve the problem. In addition, one might anticipate that among Native Americans with a traditional acceptance of natural life processes such as disease, presentation of alcoholism as a disease would further lessen motivation for treatment or the belief in treatment efficacy. An alternative conceptualization where substance abuse is presented as the antithesis of living in harmony with nature might be more productive (Beauvais & LaBoueff, 1985).

Spiritual Model

A role for spirituality in recovery is widely endorsed by many practitioners. As noted by McCrady and Delaney (1995), many clinicians refer the majority of their clients to the most well-known spiritual approach to recovery, Alcoholics Anonymous (AA). The emphasis in most spiritual approaches is not on the etiological bases of alcoholism, but rather on how spirituality is important in the recovery process. Consistent with the disease model of alcoholism, proponents of this model view alcoholics as being qualitatively different from nonalcoholics and place a great deal of emphasis on loss of control. Lifetime sobriety is the primary treatment goal of most spiritual approaches.

Typically, most spiritual approaches to recovery are conducted in a group modality, which warrants some special attention with respect to the values and beliefs identified previously in this chapter. Jilek-Aall (1981) indicates that Native Americans like the voluntary and loosely organized nature of AA, where, aside from a few basic rules, members decide how the sessions are conducted and elect individually whether to disclose personal information. However, since Native Americans generally do not like to talk publicly about personal problems or weaknesses, they may balk at the confession-like speeches and the admission that they are powerless over alcohol (Heath, 1987; Hurlburt & Gade, 1984). In contrast, the curative factors inherent in a spiritually oriented group format may make this approach particularly attractive to other cultural groups. The importance of spirituality in African American culture has been discussed previously. The religious aspects of AA may facilitate the acceptance of AA by African American clients (Dembo, Burgos, Babst, Schmeidler, & Le Grand, 1978). According to Caldwell (1983), African Americans' valuation of and attention to interpersonal relationships should make them ideal candidates for AA, since 5 of the 12 steps deal with interpersonal issues. As noted above, many traditional Native Americans reject the notion of lifetime "recovering" from alcoholism and, therefore, would be expected to have difficulty accepting that alcoholics cannot regain control over drinking and must remain abstinent (Heath, 1987). In fact, AA may be viewed by minority clients as an attempt to impose the dominant culture's view of alcohol addiction (Hurlburt & Gade, 1984), and this may result in minority clients being inactive participants (Jilek-Aall, 1981).

AA's emphasis on anonymity may also undermine treatment efforts with individuals who value community or family support. Any hindrance placed on involving the family in the healing process would be at odds with a strong family or community orientation. For these reasons, it is important that the recommendation of AA as part of the treatment package be considered on an individual basis instead of being automatically included for all patients.

Characterological Model

This model views alcohol addiction as a symptom of an underlying personality disturbance (Knight, 1938). While early formulations of alcoholism focused on fixation in the oral stage of psychosexual development (Crowley, 1939; Strecker, 1937), more contemporary approaches emphasize inadequate ego functioning (Berggren, 1984; Forrest, 1984; Wurmser, 1984), difficulties with modulating affect (Khantzian, 1985;

Krystal & Raskin, 1970), or dysfunctional early experiences (Krystal & Raskin, 1970). Most practitioners adopt abstinence as a treatment goal (Berggren, 1984) and recommend a two-stage approach (Yalisove, 1989). The first stage tends to be supportive and didactic in nature (Khantzian, 1985). Once the patient's level of alcohol consumption is reduced, more insight-oriented techniques are employed to uncover the underlying causes of the addiction. In general, therapists tend to be more active and less interpretative with their alcohol-addicted patients (Yalisove, 1989); however, therapy is intensive and lengthy. Often, patients are also encouraged to concurrently attend AA.

Unlike other approaches, therapy tends to focus primarily on intrapsychic functioning. As such, it is best suited to minority clients who believe that alcoholism is predominantly the result of characterological deficits (Watanabe & Ogawa, 1978). In order to be actively engaged in the treatment, however, individuals must also be comfortable exploring their underlying feelings. For certain clients, this may be difficult, as the expression of affect is viewed as a sign of personal weakness (Watanabe & Ogawa, 1978). Also, individuals who place a great deal of emphasis on collectivism and interdependence may interpret this approach as too individualistic (Beauvais & LaBoueff, 1985). Finally, the time commitment involved may be problematic for clients who tend to expect rapid solutions to their difficulties (Watanabe & Ogawa, 1978).

Educational Model

Educational models are based on the assumption that problematic drinking is a result of lack of knowledge concerning the deleterious sequelae of alcohol consumption. Accordingly, once individuals are made cognizant of alcohol's damaging effects, they will presumably be motivated to reduce their alcohol consumption (Heather, 1995). Intervention strategies derived from this framework are typically reserved for individuals who have come to treatment as a result of some specific hazardous alcohol-related behaviors (e.g., DWI), exhibit only low to moderate dependence, or are highly dependent but unwilling to accept alternative treatments. Since alcohol addiction is viewed as volitional behavior, the goal of treatment is not necessarily abstinence. Assuming a didactic and nonconfrontational stance, the therapist assists the client in self-determining the goals of therapy. Unlike other approaches, these interventions are short-term and can be as brief as one session (Heather, 1995).

An approach that attempts to modify, instead of eliminate, drinking may be particularly useful in dealing with Native Americans, who are likely to hold the attitude that binge drinking is a normal pattern of drinking (Beauvais & LaBoueff, 1985; Heath, 1987). By pointing out how the individual's drinking has adversely affected traditional allegiance to the family and community, as well as being inconsistent with the ethos of harmony with nature, an educational approach may provide the Native American alcoholic with the motivation to adopt fewer and less harmful drinking episodes. Moreover, the didactic and nonauthoritarian nature of this approach may be particularly appropriate with clients who are either uncomfortable with self-disclosure or who are likely to question the opinions of "experts." Also, within this approach, information could be disseminated using culture-specific techniques (e.g., storytelling) by "nonexpert" members of an individual's community. Finally, its short-term duration would be appealing to individuals who seek expedient solutions to problems.

An example of how cultural sensitivity could be useful in the application of the educational approach would involve emphasizing different negative aspects of drug use to different clients in order to enhance their motivation for change. For example, Hispanics' beliefs regarding the most important negative consequences of smoking differ from those of Whites. Marin (1990) found that White smokers were mostly concerned about individualistic issues such as withdrawal symptoms, but Hispanic smokers were more concerned about the effects of smoking on the health of other family members, smoking as a bad example to the children, and the bad smell of cigarettes. This suggests that efforts to change drinking in Hispanics should emphasize the effect of drinking on the family, rather than the health of the individual, while the converse may be indicated for Whites.

Systems Model

The basic premise of this model is that, because alcohol addiction does not occur within a vacuum, it is necessary to examine the interpersonal systems in which an individual functions. In this model, the family system is of paramount importance (Gomberg, Nelson, & Hatchett, 1991; McCrady, 1989; O'Farrell, 1995). Treatment may involve components to educate family members about the deleterious effects of alcoholism, as well as how dysfunctional family behaviors constitute coexisting problems of codependency. Behavioral interventions may be used to modify the identified client's drinking, while at the same time attempts are made to alter the behavior of family members that may be reinforcing continued drinking by the identified patient. Treatment of family members is often conducted in the absence of the identified client, and family members are typically referred to self-help groups that complement the 12-step model of AA (e.g., Al-Anon or Adult Children of Alcoholics).

Family therapy may be particularly beneficial when discrepant rates or levels of acculturation exist within a family system. Acculturation stress often occurs when different degrees of acculturation exist either between parents and children or marital partners (Eden & Aguilar, 1989). Children tend to adopt the values of the dominant culture faster than their parents do, and this is often a source of tension when the values of the two cultures conflict. Drug use is one possible outcome of the stress resulting from such acculturation discrepancies. Family therapy, aimed at identifying the sources of conflict within the family system produced by intergenerational differences in acculturation, may be an essential component of substance-abuse treatment programs among clients from diverse cultures where acculturation stress may be occurring.

The amount of emphasis placed on the family system in the treatment of alcoholism should be considered in the context of cultural values. Clients with the cultural value of noninterference may be reluctant to become engaged in family therapy (A. Hill, 1989), whereas for other individuals who place a great deal of importance on the family, this type of treatment may be especially attractive (Marin, 1990).

Behavioral Model

The basic tenet of the behavioral model is that drinking is a learned behavior and lies on a continuum ranging from abstinence to pathological consumption. Within this conceptualization, abstinence is not a required treatment goal. Although individuals addicted to alcohol may strive toward abstinence, controlled drinking may be adopted as a goal of therapy. The therapeutic relationship tends to be collaborative, structured, and short-term in nature. The success of behavioral interventions is thought to be heavily dependent on the patient's willingness to engage in homework activities.

Traditional behavioral explanations of alcohol addiction emphasize how classical and operant conditioning may play a role in the acquisition and maintenance of alcohol consumption. Intervention strategies derived from traditional behavioral models rely heavily on the alteration of external stimuli in an individual's environment. For example, counterconditioning is designed to decrease an individual's desire to drink by pairing aversive agents (e.g., electric shock, emetic drugs, or covert stimuli such as imagined negative events) with the ingestion of alcohol (Rimmele, & Hilfrink, 1995). In an attempt to extinguish craving for alcohol, exposure and response prevention techniques are often employed. Finally, contingency management techniques (either self- or therapist-directed) are utilized to reduce alcohol consumption (Hester, 1995).

More contemporary behavioral approaches embrace the concept of reciprocal determinism (Bandura, 1986) and, as such, view drinking as a product of the interaction between an individual and his/her environment. Purely cognitive models emphasize the role of expectancies about alcohol (S. A. Brown, 1993) or dysfunctional beliefs in the development of problem drinking (Beck, Wright, Newman & Liese, 1993). Practitioners who adhere to this model typically employ cognitive restructuring techniques to modify drinking (Beck et al., 1993). In addition to emphasizing the role of cognitions, social-learning approaches also emphasize the importance of observational learning (i.e., modeling peers and parents) and coping. Consequently, interventions designed specifically to foster the development of effective coping skills (e.g., assertiveness training, systematic desensitization, relaxation therapy), in addition to cognitive restructuring techniques, are also employed. Although these cognitive and social-learning strategies may be used in isolation, they tend to be used extensively in behavioral self-control training (Hester, 1995) and relapse-prevention approaches (Dimeff & Marlatt, 1995).

Cultural differences in expectancies may be important in treatment strategies based on contemporary behavioral approaches. Expectancies about the effects of alcohol are typically assessed using any of several paper-and-pencil self-reports (see S. A. Brown, 1993). Studies have recently been conducted to determine if the expected effects of alcohol vary across cultural groups. Although certain expectancies (global positive, social and physical pleasure, social expressiveness, sexual enhancement, power and aggression, tension reduction, cognitive and physical impairment, careless unconcern) have been found to be valid predictors of drinking in African Americans and Whites (George et al., 1995), cultural variation in the relative importance of these alcohol expectancies have also been found. For example, Gilbert (1991) found that U.S.-born Hispanic women had more positive expectancies about benefits from drinking (e.g., enhanced social pleasure and assertiveness, elevation of mood, reduction of tension, freedom from inhibition) than did immigrant Hispanic women. P. B. Johnson and Gallo-Treacy (1993) reported that drinking behavior among Irish, Italian, and Hispanic females was associated with different expected effects of drinking. For example, the frequency of Italian female drinking was negatively related to expectancies regarding alcohol's disinhibitory effect, but there was little relationship between this expectancy and drinking by Hispanic females. In contrast, Hispanic female drinking was positively related to the expectancy that alcohol would increase assertiveness, and there was little relationship between this expectancy and drinking by Italian females. From a contemporary behavioral viewpoint, it would be important to determine the expected effects of alcohol and then to determine how these expected effects could be achieved by means other than harmful drinking.

CULTURAL VALUES AND GENERAL TREATMENT ISSUES

The literature suggests that clients matched to alcohol treatment programs may have better outcomes that those who are not matched or those who are mismatched (Allen & Kadden, 1995; MacLachlan, 1974). A number of variables, including concurrent psychopathology, alcoholism subtype, severity of dependence, and conceptual level, may influence the effectiveness of various treatment modalities (Project MATCH Research Group, 1993). The set of variables relevant to treatment matching from a cultural perspective is different, involving the client's belief system about alcohol in particular and about other relevant values as described above (Betancourt & Lopez, 1993; Weibel-Orlando, 1987). For example, Weibel-Orlando (1987) advocates combining a program-assessment paradigm with an individual assessment of beliefs and values (e.g., Stone's worldview model for Native Americans). However, little research has been done in this area (Clark, 1987; Wickizer et al., 1994). As a starting point, it may be useful to consider how cultural factors may interact with dimensions that cut across the more specific approaches discussed above.

Abstinence or Some Other Treatment Goal

One component of most interventions for alcohol dependence is instilling the goal of lifelong abstinence. The only model of alcohol addiction, however, which would seem to necessitate such a goal is the disease model. Other models may take abstinence as evidence that the basic cause(s) of the addiction are in remission (e.g., if the client regains spirituality they will not need to drink), but theoretically there appears to be no reason why successful treatment would have to include abstinence.

Some clients may reject abstinence because it conflicts with cultural views of drinking. Support by significant others (e.g., spouse, relatives, friends) for the goal of abstinence is important to acceptance by the client. Individuals whose culture sanctions alcohol consumption as a means of maintaining social relations (Weibel-Orlando, 1989) would have difficulty accepting lifetime sobriety. It may be difficult for a "treated" Native American to reject offers of drinks from other Natives, since this would be seen as rejecting the values of sharing and generosity (Pedigo, 1983; Savishinsky, 1991; Topper, 1985; Weibel-Orlando, 1989). Similarly, alcohol use is an integral part of Hispanic culture and is involved in almost all social functions (Eden & Aguilar,1989). The importance of alcohol in maintaining smooth social relations would be expected to make lifelong abstinence unattractive to many Hispanics. As a consequence of the association of prohibition with racism, African American clients may see insistence on abstinence as a form of racial prejudice and an attempt to prevent full participation in all aspects of society. Minority females acculturated into the dominant cultural values may equate abstinence with gender prejudice based on traditional views that females should not drink. Thus, it would seem advisable to explore the meaning of abstinence with the client in order to determine if it is a culturally acceptable goal.

Alternatives to abstinence would emphasize a harm-reduction approach, perhaps encouraging longer periods between drinking episodes and consumption of less alcoholic beverages, or ensuring that culturally sanctioned drinking episodes minimize the potential for immediate harm (Weibel-Orlando, 1989). The controlled-drinking goal must be supported by significant others in the alcoholic's life (see Heather & Robinson, 1983), and this may come in conflict when the alcoholic is part of an extended-family network in which members are at different levels of acculturation. Savishinsky (1991) has specifically pointed out that Native Americans often drink specifically to get drunk, and thus the concept of drinking without getting drunk is unlikely to be understood or accepted. With this population, then, controlled drinking would perhaps be better defined as longer intervals between binges. French (1989) has also noted that Native Americans seem to be less willing to accept the notion that they can control drinking, which may, in part, be due to the belief that Natives have a special vulnerability to alcohol. The disease model of alcoholism would reinforce the idea of a special vulnerability and may accentuate an already pessimistic view of treatment. Treatment approaches based on educational or behavioral models, which emphasize how drinking behavior is learned and can be modified, would seem to be well suited to integrating such cultural viewpoints.

Nature of the Therapeutic Relationship

The role of the therapist in treatment can vary from that of a sympathetic listener to that of the expert disseminating information. In all treatment models, some variation exists with respect to the role the therapist assumes both within and across sessions. Certain models may, however, accentuate the therapist's role as expert. For example, the disease model, with its medicalization of alcoholism, places the treatment provider in the role of expert analogous to a physician treating an organic disorder. As most disease-oriented approaches are conducted within an institutionalized setting, the status of the therapist as expert is further highlighted. Clients from cultural backgrounds with ethics of noninterference and conflict repression are most comfortable in interactions that deemphasize the expert role of individuals, and they may experience anxiety and embarrassment in interactions where the therapist's role as expert is accentuated (Brant, 1990). Furthermore, these clients may interpret the advice offered by "experts" as an attempt to establish dominance (Brant, 1990). Additionally, clients from cultures that value learned restraint may appear passive or uninterested in situations where others may expect or request more interaction (French, 1989; Hurlburt & Gade, 1984). For these reasons, treatment modalities or practices that emphasize the role of the therapist as expert would likely be rejected by Natives (Brant, 1990; French, 1989; Hurlburt & Gade, 1984). Modeling, where "one is shown rather than told how" (Brant, 1990, p. 537), may be more culturally sensitive. For certain treatment approaches, instruction through modeling is readily obvious (e.g., the behavioral approach), whereas in others (e.g., characterological and disease model) it may be less apparent.

Confrontational counseling is popular in the "Minnesota model" of alcoholism treatment that is dominant in North America (Miller et al., 1995). Confrontational counseling places the counselor in the role of expert (i.e., someone who knows what alcoholism is, what the dangers are, and what the correct solution is), although the expertise of the counselor is often based on their having been an alcoholic. The object of much confrontational counseling is to "break through denial" about having a drinking problem. Hurlburt & Gade (1984) suggested that confrontational techniques may be especially required for Native clients, since these authors found Native female patients to be more denying and less willing to make confessions of weakness than other clients. This apparent excessive denial may reflect a cultural tendency not to talk publicly about personal problems or weaknesses (Jilek-Aall, 1981). As such, confronting denial might only serve to erode the therapeutic relationship. Moreover, for individuals who value empathic and respectful relationships, confrontational strategies may be countertherapeutic (Gilbert, 1991; Longshore et al., 1992; Tucker, 1985; Watanabe & Ogawa, 1978). Tucker (1985) argues that there is a general need for nonconfrontational techniques for the treatment of drug abuse in cultural minorities, since the confrontational method is unsuited to many nondominant North American cultures.

Finally, in treating culturally diverse clients, therapists need to consider boundary issues. In the majority of treatment models discussed (with the exception of AA), therapists typically refrain from interacting with clients outside the therapeutic setting. Members of nondominant cultures, particularly those who value ethics such as mutual obligation, generosity, and reciprocity, may frequently solicit the assistance of therapists in attaining nontreatment goals (Topper, 1985). How therapists negotiate such requests will have a tremendous impact on the therapeutic relationship and, consequently, on client retention and treatment. Clearly, interpretations of such requests devoid of cultural sensitivity would likely endanger any therapeutic alliance that might have existed.

The Impact of Mixed Cultural Treatment Groups

It has been found that the cultural makeup of treatment groups may affect client-completion rates. Wickizer et al. (1994) have commented that in treatment groups of mixed ethnicity, members of the ethnic group in the majority tend to have higher completion rates. French (1989) has noted that Native clients are particularly likely to drop out of mixed cultural treatment groups. These observations suggest that, when possible, more cultural homogeneity in treatment groups should be considered.

Booth et al. (1992) examined completion rates among over 50,000 VA inpatients whom they considered to be roughly socioeconomically homogeneous and found that African Americans and Hispanics were the least likely to complete treatment (a comparison of treatment modalities was not made) or attend detoxification and that Native Americans were the most likely to complete treatment. Wickizer et al. (1994) conducted a comprehensive analysis of completion rates of 5287 clients discharged from all publicly funded drug treatment programs in the state of Washington during the last quarter of 1990. Their conclusion was that "the fit between clients and treatment programs may be an important factor explaining why some clients complete treatment and others drop out" (p. 215). Several variables were associated with completion, including age, first year of addiction, education and assessment center screening (see also Cooney et al., 1995), all of which were positively correlated with completion. Ethnic group also influenced completion rates. Native Americans did worse than any other cultural group (others were African Americans, Hispanics, and Whites) in intensive inpatient alcohol programs. African Americans did worse than any other cultural group in intensive outpatient drug treatment (drug treatment was distinguished from alcohol treatment). Whites did worse than other groups in intensive inpatient drug treatment and did better than other groups in standard outpatient drug treatment.

CREATING NEW PROGRAMS AND USING TRADITIONAL HEALING METHODS

Rather than trying to select a mainstream treatment, some authors have suggested the development of new treatment programs or modification of existing ones to meet the needs of culturally diverse clients (Rogler et al., 1987). Programs that have been used traditionally by minority cultures for centuries, which are only "new" to the mainstream culture, have also been advocated.

Ja and Aoki (1993) describe an approach for treating substance abuse among Asian-Americans that shares some overlap with Western characterological and spiritual models. The program uses psychodrama to help Asians deal with the shame that they experience as a result of alcohol abuse. Residents in the Asian American Residential Recovery Services are asked to create a personal script based on unresolved feelings they harbor towards their parents. The script is then role-played and rehearsed for several months, allowing the client to deal with feelings and issues that arise out of their time spent with counselors and other residents. Finally, the community and the residents' parents are invited to a public performance of the script. Sharing some resemblance to the latter steps of the AA model, clients publicly acknowledge past misdoings and apologize to their community and family. Importantly, there is no reliance on a "higher power," and this public apology is a culturally acceptable method that reduces their shame. This not only allows the addict and his or her family to reenter the community, but also restores a sense of self-respect.

As a culturally sensitive spiritual treatment, Peyotism and the Native American Church has proved effective in reducing substance abuse among a number of Native American tribes (A. Hill, 1993). Participation in Peyote meetings reinforces the drinker's belief that he/she needs to change, provides competition against old drinking behaviors, reduces the social pressure and opportunity to drink, and provides participants with role models who have successfully controlled their drinking. For those who have previously left the Native community, it also educates them about the history and values of the tribe. Members publicly confess their history of substance abuse, as well as other transgressions, which, along with the religious aspects of the treatment, serves to reduce the shame and guilt. While such emotional venting would be culturally inappropriate in most other situations, it is sanctioned within the ceremony. Other culturally tailored drug-use prevention programs for Native Americans are described by Beauvais and LaBoueff (1985) and Bobo, Gilchrist, Cuetkovich, Trimble, and Schinke (1988). For some Native Americans, however, the use of traditional healing methods is often restricted by the availability of the elders needed to conduct the sessions. These activities are not techniques that can be taught to addiction therapists to use in clinics but are sacred ceremonies that can only be conducted by traditional healers (LaDue, 1994).

CONCLUSIONS

The purpose of this chapter was to explore how values and beliefs that may be part of an individual's cultural makeup may affect the treatment of alcohol abuse. One characteristic of the literature reviewed is an emphasis on how cultural values may hinder treatment. This emphasis is itself revealing, since it seems to reflect the view that we should be asking how the client, or at least the client's value system, can be altered to conform to the dominant cultural conception of alcohol abuse (e.g., see Wiebel-Orlando, 1985). One negative outcome of such an emphasis is that it may serve to suggest, at least to some, that some cultural views of drug use are less valid than others. Unfortunately, "cultural sensitivity" is often limited to identifying how others are different from oneself without any intention of trying to understand these differences so as to better appreciate the individual and his/her culture. Researchers and therapists need to ask how the cultural values we have identified above can be used to encourage help-seeking behavior by those people in need of treatment and to increase the probability of treatment success. Ideally, a greater understanding of cultural values can lead to the development of primary prevention programs that respect culturally diverse beliefs.

One way in which the information presented in this chapter may be used is to identify values for purposes of treatment matching. The current enthusiasm for treatment matching centers on psychological variables such as locus of control, conceptual level, and psychiatric functioning. In addition to these potentially important individual-difference variables, research to identify culturally relevant variables for matching may increase treatment utilization and outcome.

Identifying values and beliefs that may affect alcohol treatment in the context of different cultural groups, such as we have done in this chapter, may have been a useful heuristic and may sensitize clinicians to possible areas of concern for particular clients. However, the shortcomings of such a tactic cannot be ignored. Culture is not synonymous with ethnic group. There are "cultural" differences between rich and poor, urban and rural, young and old, Southerners and Northerners, the more or less educated, conservative or liberal, and a host of other categorizations. Many of these differences have been shown to influence some of the values we have described in this chapter (e.g., Rodin, 1981).

What is needed is a more direct assessment, ultimately on an individual level, of the values and beliefs that research indicates are influential in alcohol treatment issues (Betancourt & Lopez, 1993). For example, the therapist could inquire about the client's beliefs concerning etiological factors involved in current alcohol abuse, negative and positive consequences related to current alcohol use, beliefs about treatment efficacy, preferred method of treatment, goals concerning alcohol use, and the motivation toward and attainability of identified goals. This information could be assessed during an intake interview or with a structured instrument (which could be developed to be culturally sensitive). It may then be possible for the therapist to realign the treatment strategy so as to make treatment more acceptable and, just as important, to build on beliefs that naturally motivate the client to participate in therapy. How might this work in practice? Consider a therapist working in a behaviorally oriented short-term treatment setting, assessing a Native client who has been referred for an alcohol abuse problem. During the interview the therapist learns that the client gets into fights when he drinks, but it also becomes clear that the client is not really concerned about his drinking and has no intention of stopping drinking. Instead of trying to convince the client that he is an alcoholic and should commit to lifelong abstinence (what Wiebel-Orlando, 1985, has identified as the typical "negative resocialization" aspect of most treatment for Natives), the therapist could concentrate on the fighting aspect of the behavior. Fighting could be examined in light of how it conflicts with Native values of interdependence and conflict suppression. An emphasis on anger management and identification of high-risk drinking situations, rather than actual drinking behavior, may be more acceptable to the client. This is only one example of how an appreciation of a client's cultural conceptualization of alcohol consumption and alcohol-related behaviors may be capitalized upon to reduce problematic behavior.

Assessing the client's values and beliefs may help the therapist identify better approaches to treatment delivery. There is another potentially important benefit of such a process. This process enhances the therapist/client relationship. By assessing the client's value system, the therapist could be seen as recognizing that the client's value system is important and valid. The client may be more receptive to advice from a therapist whom the client feels is not simply trying to impose their conception of alcohol use. This may be particularly relevant for clients who hold pessimistic views of the sincerity of the methods and motives of treatment personnel.

References

Adlaf, E. M., Smart, R. G., & Tan, S. H. (1989). Ethnicity and drug use: A critical look. *The International Journal of the Addictions, 24,* 1–18.
Albaugh, B. J., & Anderson, P. O. (1974). Peyote in the treatment of alcoholism among American Indians. *American Journal of Psychiatry, 131,* 1247–1250.
Allen, J. P., & Kadden, R. M. (1995). Matching clients to alcohol treatments. In R. K. Hester & W. R. Miller (Eds.), *Handbook of alcoholism treatment approaches: Effective alternatives* (pp. 278–291). Boston: Allyn & Bacon.
American Psychiatric Association. (1994). *Diagnostic and Statistical Manual of Mental Disorders (DSM-IV).* Washington, DC: American Psychiatric Association.
Bandura, A. (1986). *Social foundations of thought and action.* Englewood Cliffs, NJ: Prentice-Hall.
Beauvais, F., & LaBoueff, S. (1985). Drug and alcohol abuse intervention in American Indian communities. *The International Journal of the Addictions, 20,* 139–171.
Beauvais, F., Oetting, E.R., & Edwards, R. W. (1985). Trends in drug use of Indian adolescents living on reservations: 1975–1983. *American Journal of Drug and Alcohol Abuse, 11,* 209–229.
Beck, A. T., Wright, F. D., Newman, C. F., & Liese, B. S. (1993). *Cognitive therapy of substance abuse.* New York: Guilford Press.
Bennett, L. A., Janca, A., Grant, B. F., & Sartorius, N. (1993). Boundaries between normal and

pathological drinking: A cross-cultural comparison. *Alcohol Health and World, 17,* 190–195.

Berggren, B. (1984). Alcohol abuse and super-ego conflicts. *International Journal of Psychoanalytic Therapy, 10,* 215–225.

Berry, J. W. (1980). Social and cultural change. In H. C. Triandis & R. Brislin (Eds.), *Handbook of cross-cultural psychology: Vol. 5. Social psychology* (pp. 211–279). Boston: Allyn & Bacon.

Berry, J. W. (1990). Psychology of acculturation: Understanding individuals moving between cultures. In R. W. Brislin (Ed.). *Applied cross-cultural psychology* (pp. 232–253). Newburg, CA: Sage.

Berry, J. W. (1994). Acculturation and psychological adaptation: An overview. In A. M. Bouvy, F. J. R. van der Vijuer, P. Boski, & P. G. Schmitz (Eds.), *Journeys into cross-cultural psychology* (pp. 129–141). Amsterdam: Swets & Zeitlinger.

Betancourt, H., & Lopez, S. R. (1993). The study of culture, ethnicity, and race in American psychology. *American Psychologist, 48,* 629–637.

Bobo, J. K., Gilchrist, L. D., Cuetkovich, G. T., Trimble, J. E., & Schinke, P. S. (1988). Cross-cultural service delivery to minority communities. *Journal of Community Psychology, 16,* 263–271.

Booth, B. M., Blow, F. C., Cook, C. A. L., Bunn, J. Y., & Fortney, J. C. (1992). Age and ethnicity among hospitalized alcoholics: A nationwide study. *Alcoholism: Clinical and Experimental Research 16,* 1029–1034.

Brannock, J. C., Schandler, S. L., & Oncley, P. R. (1990). Cross-cultural and cognitive factors examined in groups of adolescent drinkers. *The Journal of Drug Issues, 20,* 427–442.

Brant, C. C. (1990). Native ethnics and rules of behavior. *Canadian Journal of Psychiatry, 35,* 534–539.

Brown, B. S. (1985). Federal drug abuse policy and minority groups issues—Reflections of a participant-observer. *The International Journal of the Addictions, 20,* 203–215.

Brown, S. A. (1993). Drug effect expectancies and addictive behavior change. *Experimental Clinical Psychopharmacology, 1,* 55–67.

Brown, F., & Tooley, J. (1989). Alcoholism in the Black community. In G. W. Lawson & A. W. Lawson (Eds.), *Alcoholism and substance abuse in special populations* (pp. 115–130). Rockville, MD: Aspen.

Caetano, R. (1987). Public opinions about alcoholism and its treatment. *Journal of Studies on Alcohol, 48,* 153–160.

Caetano, R. (1989). Concepts of alcoholism among whites, blacks and Hispanics in the United States. *Journal of Studies on Alcohol, 50,* 580–582.

Caetano, R. (1994). Drinking and alcohol-related problems among minority women. *Alcohol Health & Research World, 18,* 233–241.

Caetano, R. (1996, June). *Methodological issues in cross-cultural research.* Paper presented at the meeting of the Research Society on Alcohol, Washington, D.C.

Caldwell, F. J. (1983). Alcoholics Anonymous as a viable treatment resource for Black alcoholics. In T. D. Watts & R. Wright, Jr., *Black alcoholism: Toward a comprehensive understanding* (pp. 85–99). Springfield, IL: Charles C. Thomas.

Campinha-Bacote, J. (1991). Community mental health services for the underserved: A culturally specific model. *Archives of Psychiatric Nursing, 5,* 229–235.

Cervantes, R., Gilbert, M. J., Salgado de Snyder, S. N., & Padilla, A. M. (1991). Psychosocial and cognitive correlates of alcohol use in younger adult immigrant and U.S. born Hispanics. *International Journal of the Addiction, 25,* 687–708.

Cherpitel, C., & Clark, W. B. (1995). Ethnic differences in performance of screening instruments in identifying harmful drinking and alcohol dependence in the emergency room. *Alcoholism: Clinical and Experimental Research, 19,* 628–634.

Clark. L. A. (1987). Mutual relevance of mainstream and cross-cultural psychology. *Journal of Consulting and Clinical Psychology, 55*, 461–470.

Clarke, M., Ahmed, N., Romaniuk, H., Marjot, D. H., & Murray-Lyon, I. M. (1990). Ethnic differences in the consequences of alcohol misuse. *Alcohol and Alcoholism, 25*, 9–11.

Cooney, N. L., Zweben, A., & Fleming, M. F. (1995). Screening for alcohol problems and at-risk drinking in health care settings. In R. K. Hester & W. R. Miller (Eds.), *Handbook of alcoholism treatment approaches: Effective alternatives* (pp. 45–60). Boston: Allyn & Bacon.

Crowley, R. M. (1939). Psychoanalytic literature on drug addiction and alcoholism. *Psychoanalytic Review, 26*, 39–54.

De Leon, G., Melnick, G., Sckhoket, D., & Jainchill, N. (1993). Is the therapeutic community culturally relevant? Findings on race/ethnic differences in retention in treatment. *Journal of Psychoactive Drugs, 25*, 77–86.

Dembo, R., Burgos, W., Babst, D. U., Schmeidler, J., & Le Grand, L. E. (1978). Neighborhood relationships and drug involvement among inner city junior high school youths: Implications for drug education and prevention programming. *Journal of Drug Education, 8*, 231–252.

Dimeff, L. A., & Marlatt, G. A. (1995). Relapse prevention. In R. K. Hester & W. R. Miller (Eds.), *Handbook of alcoholism treatment approaches: Effective alternatives* (pp. 176–194). Boston: Allyn & Bacon.

Donovan, D. M., Kadden, R. M., DiClemente, C. C., Carroll, K. M., Longabaugh, R., Zweben, A., & Rychtarik, R. (1994). Issues in the selection and development of therapies in alcoholism treatment matching research. *Journal of Studies on Alcohol* (Suppl. 12), 138–148.

Donovan, D. M., & Mattson, M. E. (1994). Alcoholism treatment matching research: Methodological and clinical issues. *Journal of Studies on Alcohol* (Supp. 12), 5–14.

Eden, S. L., & Aguilar, R. J. (1989). The Hispanic chemically dependent client: Considerations for diagnosis and treatment. In G. W. Lawson & A. W. Lawson (Eds.), *Alcoholism and substance abuse in special populations* (pp. 205–222). Rockville, MD: Aspen.

Forrest, G. G. (1984). *Intensive psychotherapy of alcoholism.* Springfield, IL: Charles C. Thomas.

French, L. (1989). Native American alcoholism: A transcultural counseling perspective. *Counseling Psychology Quarterly, 2*, 153–166.

Freund, P. J. (1985). Polish-American drinking: Continuity and change. In L. A. Bennett & G. M. Ames (Eds.), *The American experience with alcohol: Contrasting cultural perspectives* (pp. 77–92). New York: Plenum Press.

Fuller, R. K. (1995). Antidipsotropic medications. In R. K. Hester & W. R. Miller (Eds.), *Handbook of alcoholism treatment approaches: Effective alternatives* (pp. 123–133). Boston: Allyn & Bacon.

Gaines, A. D. (1985). Alcohol: Cultural conceptions and social behavior among urban Blacks. In L. A. Bennett & G. M. Ames (Eds.), *The American experience with alcohol: Contrasting cultural perspectives* (pp. 171–197). New York: Plenum Press.

George, W. H., Frone, M. R., Cooper, M. L., Russell, M., Skinner, J. B., & Windle, M. (1995). A revised alcohol expectancy questionnaire: Factor structure confirmation and invariance in a general population sample. *Journal of Studies on Alcohol, 56*, 177–185.

Gerald, M. C. (1981). *Pharmacology: An introduction to drugs* (2nd ed.). Englewood Cliffs, NJ: Prentice-Hall.

Gilbert, M. J. (1991). Acculturation and changes in drinking patterns among Mexican-American women: Implications for prevention. *Alcohol Health and World, 15*, 234–238.

Gomberg, E. S. L., Nelson, B. W., & Hatchett, B. F. (1991). Women, alcoholism, and family therapy. *Family and Community Health, 13*, 61–71.

Gonzalez, R. C., Biever, J. L., & Gardner, G. T. (1994). The multicultural perspective in therapy: A social constructionist approach. *Psychotherapy, 31,* 515–524.

Gorelick, D. A. (1993). Overview of pharmacologic treatment approaches for alcohol and other drug addiction: Intoxication, withdrawal, and relapse prevention. *Psychiatric Clinics of North America: Cultural Psychiatry,* 16, 141–156.

Gotoh, M. (1994). Alcohol dependence of women in Japan. *Addiction, 89,* 941–944.

Heath, D. B. (1985). American experiences with alcohol: Commonalities and contrasts. In L. A. Bennett & G. M. Ames (Eds.), *The American experience with alcohol: Contrasting cultural perspectives* (pp. 461–480). New York: Plenum Press.

Heath, D. B. (1987). Addictive behaviors and minority populations in the U.S. In T. D. Nirenberg & S. A. Maisto (Eds.), *Developments in the assessment and treatment of addictive behaviors* (pp. 339–351). Norwood, NJ: Ablex.

Heather, N. (1995). Brief intervention strategies. In R. K. Hester & W. R. Miller (Eds.), *Handbook of alcoholism treatment approaches: Effective alternatives* (pp. 105–122). Boston: Allyn & Bacon.

Heather, N., & Robinson, R. (1983). *Controlled drinking.* New York: Methuen.

Helzer, J. E., & Canino, G. J. (1992). Comparative analysis of alcoholism in ten cultural regions. In J. E. Helzer & G. J. Canino (Eds.), *Alcoholism in North America, Europe, and Asia* (pp. 289–308). New York: Oxford University Press.

Herd, D. (1985). Ambiguity in black drinking norms: An ethnohistorical interpretation. In L. A. Bennett & G. M. Ames (Eds.), *The American experience with alcohol: Contrasting cultural perspectives* (pp. 149–170). New York: Plenum Press.

Hester, R. K. (1995). Behavioral self-control training. In R. K. Hester & W. R. Miller (Eds.), *Handbook of alcoholism treatment approaches: Effective alternatives* (pp. 148–159). Boston: Allyn & Bacon.

Higuchi, S., & Kono, H. (1994). Early diagnosis and treatment of alcoholism: The Japanese experience. *Alcohol & Alcoholism, 29,* 363–373.

Hill, A. (1989). Treatment and prevention of alcoholism in the Native American family. In G. W. Lawson & A. W. Lawson (Eds.), *Alcoholism and substance abuse in special populations* (pp. 247–272). Rockville, MD: Aspen.

Hill, A. (1993). Cultural considerations for the Native client. In B. M. Howard, S. Harrison, V. Carver, & L. Lightfoot (Eds.), *Alcohol and drug problems: A practical guide for counselors* (pp. 299–303). Toronto, Ontario, Canada: Addiction Research Foundation.

Hurlburt, G., & Gade, E. (1984). Personality differences between Native American and Caucasian women alcoholics: Implications for alcoholism counseling. *White Cloud Journal, 3,* 35–39.

Institute of Medicine, National Academy of Sciences. (1990) *Broadening the base of treatment for alcohol problems.* Washington, DC: National Academy Press.

Ja, D. Y., & Aoki, B. (1993). Substance abuse treatment: Cultural barriers in the Asian-American community. *Journal of Psychoactive Drugs, 25,* 61–71.

Jellinek, E. (1960). *The disease concept of alcoholism.* New Haven, CT: Hillhouse Press.

Jilek-Aall, L. (1981). Acculturation, alcoholism and Indian-style alcoholics anonymous. *Journal of Studies on Alcohol,* (Suppl. 9), 143–158.

Johnson, L. V., & Matre, M. (1978). Anomie and alcohol use: Drinking problems in Mexican American and Anglo neighborhoods. *Journal of Studies on Alcohol, 39,* 894–902.

Johnson, P. B., & Gallo-Treacy, C. (1993). Alcohol expectancies and ethnic drinking differences. *Journal of Alcohol and Drug Education, 38,* 80–88.

Johnston, L. D., O'Malley, P.M., & Bachman, J. G. (1994). *National survey results on drug abuse from the Monitoring the Future study, 1975–1993.* Rockville, MD: National Institute of Drug Abuse.

Jordan, C. M., & Oei, T. P. S. (1989). Help-seeking behavior in problem drinkers: A review. *British Journal of Addiction, 84*, 979–988.

Khantzian, E. J. (1985). The alcoholic patient: An overview and perspective. *American Journal of Psychotherapy, 34*, 4–19.

Knight, R. P. (1938). The psychoanalytic treatment in a sanatorium of chronic addiction to alcohol. *Journal of the American Psychoanalytic Association, 3*, 1443–1448.

Krystal, H., & Raskin, H. A. (1970). *Drug dependence: Aspects of ego function.* Detroit, MI: Wayne State University Press.

LaDue, R. A. (1994). Coyote returns: Twenty sweats does not an Indian expert make. *Women and Therapy, 15*, 93–111.

Lapam, S. C., Skipper, B. J., Owen, J. P., Kleyboecker, K., Teaf, D., Thompson, B., & Simpson, G. (1995). Alcohol use screening instruments: Normative test data collected from a first DWI offender screening program. *Journal of Studies on Alcoholism, 56*, 51–59.

Lex, B. W. (1987). Review of alcohol problems in ethnic minority groups. *Journal of Consulting and Clinical Psychology, 55*, 293–300.

Longshore, D., Hsieh, S.-C., Anglin, M. D., & Annon, T. A. (1992). Ethnic patterns in drug abuse treatment utilization. *The Journal of Mental Health Administration, 19*, 268–277

MacAndrew, C. R., & Edgerton, B. (1969). *Drunken comportment: A social explanation.* Chicago: Aldine.

MacLachlan, J. F. C. (1974). Therapy strategies, personality orientation and recovery from alcoholism. *Canadian Psychiatric Association, 19*, 25–30.

Marin, B. V. (1990). Culturally appropriate prevention and treatment. In R. R. Watson (Ed.), *Drug and alcohol abuse prevention* (pp. 151–165). Clifton, NJ: Humana Press.

Mattson, M. E., & Allen, J. P. (1991). Research on matching alcoholic patients to treatments: Findings, issues, and implications. *Journal of Addictive Diseases, 11*, 33–49.

May, P.A. (1982). Substance abuse and American Indians: Prevalence and susceptibility. *The International Journal of the Addictions, 17*, 1185–1209.

McCrady, B. S. (1989). Outcomes of family-involved alcoholism treatment. In M. Galanter (Ed.), *Recent developments in alcoholism: Vol. 7. Treatment research* (pp. 165–182). New York: Plenum Press.

McCrady, B. S., & Delaney, S. I. (1995). Self-help groups. In R. K. Hester & W. R. Miller (Eds.), *Handbook of alcoholism treatment approaches: Effective alternatives* (pp. 160–175). Boston: Allyn & Bacon.

Miller, W. R., & Cooney, N. L. (1994). Designing studies to investigate client-treatment matching. *Journal of Studies on Alcohol,* (Supp. 12), 38–45.

Miller, W. R., Brown, J. M., Simpson, T. L., Handmaker, N. S., Bien, T. H., Luckie, L. F., Montgomery, H. A., Hester, R. K., & Tonigan, J. S. (1995). What works? A methodological analysis of the alcohol treatment outcome literature. In R. K. Hester & W. R. Miller (Eds.), *Handbook of alcoholism treatment approaches: Effective alternatives* (pp.12–44). Boston: Allyn & Bacon.

National Council on Alcoholism (1972). Criteria for the diagnosis of alcoholism. *American Journal of Psychiatry, 129*, 127–135.

Neff, J. A., & Hoppe, S. K. (1992). Acculturation and drinking patterns among U.S. Anglos, Blacks, and Mexican Americans. *Alcohol and Alcoholism, 27*, 293–308.

Neff, J. A., Prihoda, T. J., & Hoppe, S. K. (1991). "Machismo", self-esteem, education and high maximum drinking among Anglo, Black and Mexican-American male drinkers. *Journal of Studies on Alcohol, 52*, 458–462.

Oetting, E. R., Swaim, R. C., Edwards, R. W., & Beevais, F. (1989). Indian and Anglo adolescent alcohol use and emotional distress: Path models. *American Journal of Drug and Alcohol Use, 15*, 153–172.

O'Farrell, T. J. (1993). A behavioral marital therapy couples group program for alcoholics and their spouses. In T. J. O'Farrell (Ed.), *Treating alcohol problems: Marital and family interventions* (pp. 305–326). New York: Guilford Press.

O'Farrell, T. J. (1995). Marital and family therapy. In R. K. Hester & W. R. Miller (Eds.), *Handbook of alcoholism treatment approaches: Effective alternatives* (pp. 195–220). Boston: Allyn & Bacon.

Pedigo, J. (1983). Finding the "meaning" of Native American substance abuse: Implications for community prevention. *The Personnel and Guidance Journal, 61,* 273–277.

Peele, S. (1984). The cultural context of psychological approaches to alcoholism: Can we control the effects of alcohol? *American Psychologist, 39,* 1337–1351.

Project MATCH Research Group (1993). Project MATCH: Rationale and methods for a multisite clinical trial matching patients to alcoholism treatment. *Alcoholism: Clinical and Experimental Research, 17,* 1130–1145.

Rimmele, C. T., Howard, M. O., & Hilfrink, M. L. (1995). Aversion therapies. In R. K. Hester & W. R. Miller (Eds.), *Handbook of alcoholism treatment approaches: Effective alternatives* (pp. 134–147). Boston: Allyn & Bacon.

Robins, L., & Regier, D. (1991). *Psychiatric disorders in America: The epidemiologic catchment area study.* New York: The Free Press.

Robins, L., Cottler, L., & Keating, S. (1989). *The NIMH Diagnostic Interview Schedule. Version III, revised (DIS-III-R).* Rockville, MD: National Institute on Mental Health.

Rodin, M.B. (1981). Alcoholism as a folk disease: The paradox of beliefs and choice of therapy in an urban American community. *Journal of Studies on Alcohol, 42,* 822–835.

Rogan, A. (1987). Recovery from alcoholism: Issues for Black and Native American alcoholics. *Alcohol Health and Research World, 11,* 42–44.

Rogler, L. H., Malgady, R. G., Costantino, G., & Blumenthal, R. (1987). What do culturally sensitive mental health services mean? The case of Hispanics. *American Psychologist, 42,* 565–570.

Ruiz, R. (1981). Cultural and historical perspectives in counseling Hispanics. In D. Sue (Ed.), *Counseling the culturally different* (pp. 186–215). New York: Wiley.

Saunders, J. B., Aasland, O. G., Amundsen A., & Grant, M. (1993). Alcohol consumption and related problems among primary health care patients: WHO collaborative project on early detection of person with harmful alcohol consumption. *Addiction, 88,* 349–362.

Savishinsky, J. S. (1991). The ambiguities of alcohol: Deviance, drinking and meaning in a Canadian Native community. *Anthropologica, 33,* 81–97.

Sigelman, C., Didjurgis, T., Marshall, B., Vargas, F., & Stewart, A. (1992). Views of problem drinking among Native American, Hispanic and Anglo children. *Child Psychiatry and Human Development, 22,* 265–276.

Spitzer, R. L., Williams, J. B., Gibbon, M., & First, M. B. (1990). *Structured Clinical Interview for DSM-III-R patient edition (SCID-P, Version 1.0).* Washington, DC: American Psychiatric Press.

Strecker, E. A. (1937). Some thoughts concerning the psychology and therapy of alcoholism. *Journal of Nervous and Mental Disorders, 86,* 191–205.

Sue, S., & Zane, N. (1987). The role of culture and cultural techniques in psychotherapy: A critique and reformation. *American Psychologist, 42,* 37–45.

Takeuchi, D. T., Mokuau, N., & Chun, C. (1992). Mental health services for Asian-Americans and Pacific Islanders. *The Journal of Mental Health Administration, 19,* 237–245.

Topper, M. D. (1985). Navajo "alcoholism": Drinking, alcohol abuse, and treatment in a changing cultural environment. In L. A. Bennett & G. M. Ames (Eds.), *The American experience with alcohol: Contrasting cultural perspectives* (pp. 227–251). New York: Plenum Press.

Trimble, J. E. (1991). Ethnic specification, validation prospects, and the future of drug use research. *The International Journal of the Addictions, 25,* 149–170.

Trimble, J. E. (1995). Ethnic minorities. In R. H. Coombs & D. Ziedonis (Eds.), *Handbook on drug abuse prevention: A comprehensive strategy to prevent the abuse of alcohol and other drugs* (pp. 379–410). Needham Heights, MA: Allyn & Bacon.

Tucker, M. B. (1985). U. S. ethnic minorities and drug abuse: An assessment of the science and practice. *The International Journal of the Addictions, 20,* 1021–1047.

Vanicelli, M. (1984). Barriers to the treatment of alcoholic women. *Substance and Alcohol Actions/Misuse, 5,* 29–37.

Wallace, J. M., & Bachman, J. G. (1991). Explaining racial/ethnic differences in adolescent drug use: The impact of background and lifestyle. *Social Problems, 38,* 333–353.

Watanabe, M., & Ogawa, O. (1978). *The therapeutic community modified for the Asian American.* Los Angeles, CA: Asian American Drug Abuse Program.

Weatherspoon, A. J., Danko, G. P., & Johnson, R. C. (1994). Alcohol consumption and use norms in Chinese-Americans and Korean-Americans. *Journal of Studies on Alcohol, 55,* 203–206.

Weibel-Orlando, J. (1985). Indians, ethnicity, and alcohol: Contrasting perceptions of the ethnic self and alcohol use. In L. A. Bennett & G. M. Ames (Eds.), *The American experience with alcohol: Contrasting cultural perspectives* (pp. 201–226). New York: Plenum Press.

Weibel-Orlando, J. (1987). Culture-specific treatment modalities: Assessing client-to-treatment fit in Indian alcoholism programs. In W. M. Cox (Ed.), *Treatment and prevention of alcohol problems: A resource manual* (pp. 261–283). Toronto, Ontario, Canada: Academic Press.

Weibel-Orlando, J. (1989). Hooked on healing: Anthropologists, alcohol and intervention. *Human Organization, 48,* 148–154.

Weisner, C. (1986). The social ecology of alcohol treatment in the United States. In M. Galanter (Ed.), *Recent Developments in Alcoholism, vol. 5,* (pp. 203–243). New York: Plenum Press.

Westermeyer, J. (1979). Research on treatment of drinking problems: Importance of cultural factors. *Journal of Studies on Alcohol,* (Suppl. 9), 44–59.

Wickizer, T., Maynard, C., Atherly, A., Frederick, M., Koepsell, T., Krupski, A., & Stark, K. (1994). Completion rates of clients discharged from drug and alcohol treatment programs in Washington state. *American Journal of Public Health, 84,* 215–221.

Woodward, A. M., Dwinell, A. D., & Arons, B. S. (1992). Barriers to mental health care for Hispanic Americans: A literature review and discussion. *The Journal of Mental Health Administration, 19,* 224–236.

World Health Organization (1975). *A manual on drug dependence.* Geneva: Author.

Wurmser, L. (1984). The role of superego conflicts in substance abuse and their treatment. *International Journal of Psychoanalytic Psychotherapy, 10,* 227–258.

Yalisove, D. L. (1989). Psychoanalytic approaches to alcoholism and addiction: Treatment and research. *Psychology of Addictive Behaviors, 3,* 107–113.

9

Cultural Aspects of Understanding People with Schizophrenic Disorders

JEFFREY R. CARTER
RICHARD W. J. NEUFELD

Schizophrenia is a complex and often misunderstood disorder. In spite of the vast amount of research that this psychiatric condition has generated, many mysteries remain. Debates about the best way to conceptualize schizophrenia that began with Kraepelin and Bleuler in the last century (Davison & Neale, 1990) continue today (e.g., Nicholson & Neufeld, 1993). Although schizophrenia has a strong biological component, culture nevertheless appears to impact on the expression of this disorder. The goal of this chapter is to provide a sample of cultural research regarding schizophrenia[1] and apply this research to specific issues. The latter include diagnostic concerns, such as the interaction of religious beliefs and schizophrenia, and general principles to consider in practice issues, such as the impact of cultural factors on rapport.

The chapter is organized according to the following outline. It begins with a brief attempt to define the disorder. The remainder of the chapter is divided into four sections. The first section is devoted to cultural aspects of phenomenology, including differences in symptoms and course across cultures. The second section concerns the scope of the problem and refers to such issues as incidence, methodological hurdles in research, and possible reasons for the differences in course across cultures. The third section discusses assessment strategies and diagnostic issues. Special attention is given to the interaction of religious beliefs and the diagnostic process. The final section concerns practice issues, including general principles to consider when working with people suffering from schizophrenia. The chapter concludes with a discussion of the role of cultural clinical psychology in the research and treatment of this disorder.

WHAT IS SCHIZOPHRENIA?

General Overview

Schizophrenia appears to fit a diathesis-stress model. Regarding the link between predisposition and schizophrenia, genetic factors and prenatal infection are implicated in certain cases (Kalat, 1988). Other biological markers are less well understood. The link between stress and episodes of active schizophrenia is well established (e.g., Nicholson & Neufeld, 1992; Zubin & Spring, 1977). More specifically, expressed emotion has been linked to relapse (e.g., Karno & Jenkins, 1993; Kazarian & Malla, 1992). Social status is also implicated (Davison & Neale, 1990). In summary, both a predisposition (presumably represented biologically) and stress are considered to be necessary for an individual to develop schizophrenia.

People with schizophrenia appear to differ physiologically from people without the disorder. Typical neurological findings include a reduced size of the frontal lobes of the cerebral cortex and an increased size of cerebral ventricles (Davison & Neale, 1990), as well as fewer neurons in the amygdala and hippocampus (Kalat, 1988). Some evidence suggests a dysfunction in the development of neuronal connections (Feinberg, 1982/83; Hoffman et al., 1995). Finally, a specific neurotransmitter, dopamine, is implicated, particularly regarding symptoms such as hallucinations and delusions (Davison & Neale, 1990; Neufeld & Williamson, in press).

The symptoms of schizophrenia are diverse. They cut across affect, behavior, and cognition. People with schizophrenia often display flat or inappropriate affect. In terms of behavior, they might withdraw socially or they may have increased, manic-like activity. They might also display bizarre gestures or facial expressions. A person with catatonic schizophrenia might take on bizarre postures and hold them for hours. The cognitive symptoms of schizophrenia tend to separate this disorder from other disorders. Perhaps the most distinctive are hallucinations and delusions. Even these symptoms, however, can be found in other disorders, such as organic mental disorders and the manic phase of bipolar depression (American Psychological Association [APA], 1994). Formal thought disturbances, such as overinclusion and paralogic, and attention deficits, such as figure-ground problems, are also common.

Schneider's First Rank Symptoms

A recurring challenge in cultural research is that of reconciling clinicians' use of different diagnostic systems in various countries. Young, Tanner, and Meltzer (1982) indicated that in spite of poor agreement between four diagnostic systems, all systems were measuring the same core concept. These authors concluded that the differences are caused by varying degrees of accuracy across systems and that no system encompasses another. One set of symptoms that was evaluated in that study has influenced most of the common systems. Historically, Kurt Schneider assumed that certain symptoms were related to specific physiological deficits and devised his list of so-called "First Rank Symptoms". The symptoms that he described reliably can be identified by various clinicians, even though Schneider never provided specific definitions: He presented vignettes and these have since been translated from the original German (Chandrasena, 1987). The First Rank Symptoms have intuitive appeal. They have been called the "nuclear symptoms" of schizophrenia. Schneider was not completely justified in assuming that these symptoms reflect purely physiological dysfunction and are free of cultural influence. In any event, Schneider's First Rank Symptoms (see Table 9.1) have found their way into most diagnostic systems.

CULTURAL ASPECTS OF PHENOMENOLOGY

"Nuclear Symptoms"

Schneider originally conceived his First Rank Symptoms as representing purely physiological dysfunction. If so, then it might be construed that First Rank Symptoms should tend to be uniform across cultures. Not only should the prevalence of the First Rank Symptoms be similar as a group, but also the prevalence of individual symptoms should be consistent. A number of studies (Carpenter & Strauss, 1974; Chandrasena, 1987; Coffey, Mackinnon, & Minas, 1993; Malik, Ahmed, Bashir, & Choudhry, 1990) have indicated that neither prediction is accurate. For example, as part of the International Pilot Study of Schizophrenia, Carpenter and Strauss (1974) found that the proportions of people diagnosed with schizophrenia who also had First Rank Symptoms varied greatly across nine different countries. For example, Taiwan and the United Kingdom had rates of 79% and 76%, respectively. The Soviet Union and Czechoslovakia had rates of 31% and 43%, respectively. These researchers used the Present State Examination to tap First Rank Symptoms and the International Classification of Disease (ICD-8) system to make diagnoses.

More recently, Coffey et al. (1993) examined five cultural groups in Australia. They used the ICD-9 system and Present State Examination, and they defined cultural group by country of origin. These researchers found that First Rank Symptoms were most prevalent among the UK immigrant group (73.3%) and least prevalent among the Greek immigrant group (40.8%). First Rank Symptoms were more prevalent among those who had been admitted to the hospital recently, who had been admitted voluntarily, and who had some command of English. Regarding command of English, they discussed two possibilities: first, that command of English reflected acculturation, and second, that using an interpreter may have hidden some symptoms. They concluded that the use of interpreters should not have unduly influenced their capacity to detect First Rank Symptoms. Therefore, acculturation probably accounts for this trend.

In contrast to the International Pilot Study of Schizophrenia, Coffey et al. (1993) concluded that there were no meaningful regional differences in the frequency of individual symptoms. They note that their study was inappropriate for drawing firm conclusions on the prevalence of individual symptoms because of the fairly small sample size. The distribution of individual First Rank Symptoms, however, was not uniform across cultural groups in this study. Coffey et al. (1993) found that thought insertion is greater among migrants from developed countries. They also found that somatic passivity is greater among certain non-Western groups, such as people from Saudi Arabia, Nigeria, and Pakistan. Malik, Ahmed, Bashir, and Choudhry (1990) also found that somatic passivity is higher among people from Pakistan. They relate

Table 9.1. Schneider's First Rank Symptoms

Auditory Hallucinations
    Audible thoughts—hearing voices speaking one's thoughts aloud.
    Voices discussing—hearing voices discussing or arguing about oneself.
    Voices describing—hearing voices describing one's activities.
Delusions
    Delusional percept—a normal perception followed by a delusional interpretation of special significance to that perception.
    Somatic passivity—believing that one is a passive and reluctant recipient of bodily sensations imposed from outside of the self.
    Thought insertion—experiencing one's own thoughts as if they were being imposed from outside of the self.
    Thought withdrawal—believing that one's thoughts are being removed due to something or someone from outside of the self.
    Thought broadcast—believing that one's thoughts are being transmitted to others.
Loss of Agency
    Made affect—believing that one is made to feel certain affects due to imposition or control from outside of the self.
    Made impulses—believing that one is made to have certain impulses due to imposition or control from outside of the self.
    Made volitions—believing that one is made to engage in certain motor activities due to imposition or control from outside of the self.

Source: Descriptions based on Nicholson (1993), Appendix A

this passivity to the Muslim belief in "kismet" (predestination). They note, however, that the "made" items (i.e., made affect, made impulses, and made volitions) were not elevated. Therefore, some other factors must also be operating.

Cultural Manifestations of Symptomatology

The nature of schizophrenic symptoms across cultures has been an issue for many years. In 1968, Al-Issa conducted a literature review and concluded that the incidence of schizophrenia is universal, but the symptoms tend to form different patterns in various cultures. For example, he found that auditory hallucinations are most common in Western culture. Africans tended to display less violence and more blunting of affect, but people from Iran and Italy showed the opposite pattern. Africans also had a high rate of visual hallucinations. Al-Issa also found that religious delusions are rare except among Christians and Muslims. In addition, symptoms change over time within the same culture. For example, in Western culture, ideas of grandeur and aggressive behavior have decreased over the last hundred years. Finally, increased literacy seems to decrease formal thought disorder and flatness of affect. Overall, Al-Issa concluded that schizophrenia seems to affect the area of functioning most stressed by the culture.

One form of schizophrenia that is rare in Western countries but is still common in Asia, Africa, and other developing areas is catatonic schizophrenia (Chandrasena, 1986). Some aspects of this disorder are consistent across cultures: Mutism, stupor, and bizarre mannerisms characterize this disorder, but occasionally posturing and echolalia are present. Chandrasena (1986) conducted a study using the Present State

Examination to determine symptomatology and country of origin to define ethnicity. He found that catatonic schizophrenia was less prevalent among people from the United Kingdom and Canada than among people from Sri Lanka. He attributed this difference primarily to the availability of neuroleptic treatment. Catatonia responds more favorably to medication than some other types of schizophrenia.

Racial Differences

Distinguishing between differences that are cultural and differences that are racial can be difficult, because race and culture often are confounded. Isolating racial differences potentially could be helpful because of the contribution of biological factors to schizophrenia. Finding particular biological mechanisms that account for racial differences in symptomatology would be a major challenge and advance. Along these lines, Cromwell (1993) defines a schizophrenia-related variant as a "measurable variable that has an earlier and relatively closer relationship to specific genes than does clinical schizophrenia itself" (p. 52). Cromwell suggests several correlational questions that researchers can ask regarding schizophrenia-related variants before proceeding with genetic-linkage studies. To date, however, the research focus has simply been that of describing racial differences. The following differences, as compared to White Anglo Westerners, have been noted.

Hispanic   Increased internalization or somatization of symptoms is common among Hispanics. For example, Ruiz (1985) found that Hispanic groups, particularly Puerto Ricans, tended to report physiological complaints in place of anxiety and depression. They reported anger as nervousness. Escobar, Randolf, and Hill (1986) found increased somatization among Hispanic American veterans. They also noted later age of onset (23 years old versus 19 years old).

African Americans   Schizophrenia has traditionally been overdiagnosed in African Americans, usually at the expense of affective disorders. This pattern can be attributed in part to the historic misperception that African Americans lack the sophistication to suffer from affective disorders. Another factor is that clinicians often rely too heavily on protuberant symptoms, such as hallucinations and delusions. These symptoms tend to be found more often among African Americans than among other racial groups (Jones & Gray, 1986; Worthington, 1992). Among African Americans, as opposed to European Americans, these symptoms are also more likely to be found in other disorders, such as affective disorders (Jones & Gray, 1986).

A third factor is the difficulty in establishing rapport between African American patients and, typically, European American professionals. This difficulty is especially prevalent in the United States because of the legacy of slavery. Failure to establish rapport can lead to negativity or to wariness misinterpreted as paranoia (Worthington, 1992). In addition to being more likely to experience hallucinations, African Americans have been found more likely to suffer from memory disturbances, disorientation, and impulsivity than European Americans (Worthington, 1992).

Ruiz (1985) distinguished between people who live in urban and rural communities. He found no meaningful differences between rural and urban European Americans. In contrast, he did find differences between rural and urban African Americans.

Symptomatic rural African Americans tended to be silly, negativistic, aggressive, and hyperactive. They also to a greater degree experienced lability of affect, visual hallucinations, delusions, and confusion. In contrast, symptomatic urban African Americans tended to be autistic and passive.

Course

One of the most counterintuitive findings of international studies of schizophrenia is that people in developing countries tend to have better outcomes than people in developed countries (APA, 1994). In spite of superior treatment facilities and greater community resources in developed countries, people in developing countries have a more optimistic prognosis. This finding has been found across a number of outcome measures after two years (see Table 9.2).

SCOPE OF THE PROBLEM

Incidence

In spite of differences in manifestation and course, the incidence of schizophrenia is essentially the same worldwide (Al-Issa, 1968; Jablensky et al., 1992). Jablensky et al. (1992) recently published the results of an extensive study for the World Health Organization. This study examined incidence and course of schizophrenia in 10 countries. Under a broad definition of schizophrenia, incidence ranged from 1.5 to 4.2 per 100,000 per year. Under a more rigid definition of schizophrenia, incidence was consistent across centers at about 1.0 per 100,000 per year. Participants in the study were all the individuals who made a lifetime first contact in the catchment areas for each of twelve centers. The contact could have been either with the psychiatric facility itself or with any of the traditional healers who cooperated with the study.

Methodological Issues

Defining Schizophrenia   The World Health Organization's research highlights one of the major methodological issues in studying schizophrenia: defining the disorder. The broad definition was simply the clinical diagnosis. The more rigid criterion was derived from a Present State Examination interview.

Ethnicity   Another methodological issue involves the definition of ethnicity. Many studies define ethnicity poorly. Country of residence and country of origin are typical criteria. In large-scale epidemiological studies, such as Jablensky et al. (1992), these definitions may be adequate. For finer work, such as examining differences in symptomatology, more precise definitions are in order. Factors to consider in addition to country of origin might include where the person received their education, languages spoken, length of stay in host country, and degree of acculturation.

Diagnosis   The consistent incidence of schizophrenia across cultures underscores the physiological component in this disease. Unfortunately, conclusive physiological tests

Table 9.2. Course in Developing versus Developed Countries

Condition	Percentage of Time	Percentage of Patients Developing Countries	Developed Countries
Full remission	0	24.1	57.2
	>76	38.3	22.3
Anti-psychotic	0	5.9	2.5
medication	>76	15.9	60.8
In hospital	0	55.5	8.1
	>76	0.3	2.3

Source: Data from Jablensky et al. (1992)

for schizophrenia are not yet available. Therefore, researchers and clinicians alike make diagnoses based on psychological assessments. Although a multitude of scales exist to measure schizophrenia (see Nicholson & Neufeld, 1993), the diagnostic interview still plays a crucial role in diagnosing this disorder.

One common instrument is the Present State Examination, a structured interview designed to assess a person's current mental status. It has survived several editions and is widely used. The manual lists over 500 questions to tap 107 symptoms. Schneider's First Rank Symptoms heavily influenced the content. For example, delusional and hallucinatory experiences are investigated in great detail. The interviewer is free to deviate from the suggested questions to explore interesting responses. The Present State Examination has remarkably good reliability and validity (Neale & Oltmanns, 1981). The two major drawbacks of the Present State Examination are that it requires extensive training and that it measures only the current condition of the patient.

CATEGO is a computer program designed to interpret the Present State Examination. Jablensky et al. (1992) employed this program in their epidemiological study. They are careful to point out that CATEGO scores alone are inappropriate for making diagnoses, because they do not take into account a number of important factors, such as personal and family histories. Their results, which contrast incidence rates based on CATEGO scores and clinical diagnosis, underscore the importance of a thorough diagnostic interview.

Another common device is the Diagnostic Interview Schedule. This structured interview was designed to be administered by nonprofessional interviewers. It takes between an hour and an hour and a half. The results can be applied to several diagnostic systems, and it tends to be both reliable and valid (Groth-Marnat, 1990). One interesting cultural difference exists regarding the Diagnostic Interview Schedule: A subgroup of Anglos denies symptoms on the Diagnostic Interview Schedule but admits to them on a written questionnaire. This pattern was not found among Hispanics (Randolph, Escobar, Paz, & Forsythe, 1985). Information of this kind for other racial groups would be helpful. Research on patterns of self-disclosure across cultures, discussed elsewhere in this volume, would also be informative.

This focus on the interview poses special problems. One major difficulty is that the person making the diagnosis often cannot see psychotic symptoms directly. By definition, only the patient experiences hallucinations. The diagnostician must infer thought disorder and delusions from the verbal productions and actions of the patient. Failure to understand the person's culture or failure to establish rapport can lead to misinterpretations.

Coffey, Mackinnon, and Minas (1993) contended that using interpreters presented some difficulties, but did not interfere with their ability to detect First Rank Symptoms. These symptoms are central to many diagnostic systems. Although working through an interpreter may not mask First Rank Symptoms, this process may interfere with detecting thought disorder. Examining the First Rank Symptoms reveals that these items involve "thought content," for example, hearing voices. In contrast, clinicians tend to detect thought disorder through "thought form," for example, word salad. The duty of the interpreter is to facilitate communication between the two parties. With this goal in mind, the interpreter could very easily try to "clean up" the patient's verbalizations so that they make more sense. This cleaning up could potentially mask formal thought disorder. In addition, interpreters are often friends from the ethnic community or even members of the family. Such untrained interpreters may, intentionally or unintentionally, distort or minimize symptoms. If an interpreter is necessary, then a trained professional is preferred.

In conclusion, many factors must be considered before selecting a diagnosis of schizophrenia. Diagnosticians need to think about racial and cultural influences on symptomatology. The clinical interview plays a crucial role in this diagnosis. Structured interviews are recommended, such as the Present State Examination (when highly trained interviewers are available) and Diagnostic Interview Schedule (when they are not). Ideally, the interviewer and patient share a common language. If not, then a professional interpreter is preferred.

Expressed emotion.   The concept of expressed emotion was developed by sociologist George Brown and his associates and refers to specific attitudes and behaviors (such as hostility, criticism, and overinvolvement) exhibited by the relatives of people who suffer from schizophrenia (Karno & Jenkins, 1993). In general, families with higher expressed emotion are more socially intrusive and tend to avoid silences (Kazarian, 1992). The specific factors of expressed emotion that mediate outcome appear to vary across cultures (Karno & Jenkins, 1993). For example, critical comments and emotional overinvolvement are especially predictive of relapse, but hostility may provide additional predictive power among Natives (Kazarian, 1992).

The standard method of assessing expressed emotion is the Camberwell Family Interview, a semistructured interview of a relative conducted soon after admission (Kazarian & Malla, 1992). The full interview takes three to four hours, but the abbreviated version can be completed in sixty to ninety minutes. Scoring requires up to three times as long as the interview itself, because the rater may have to listen to the audiotape several times before making a final judgment. In addition to factual and historical data, the interviewer attends in a nonjudgmental manner to the feelings and attitudes of the relatives. One difficulty with the Camberwell Family Interview is that its scoring requires specialized training. Raters typically attend a 1- or 2-week workshop and then score practice tapes for several months to reach an interrater reliability of at least $r = .80$. Kazarian (1992) recommends the Five Minute Speech Sample or the Level of Expressed Emotion Scale as screening devices. The more expansive

Camberwell Family Interview should be employed whenever more thorough and accurate information is needed.

Developing Countries A final methodological issue is that schizophrenia may be overdiagnosed in developing countries (Warner, 1992). In particular, other conditions that have better prognosis than schizophrenia, such as nutritional disorders, are confused with schizophrenia. Warner claims this error could lead to the false conclusion that schizophrenia is less problematic in developing countries. Warner points out, however, that this error occurs only when defining schizophrenia in the broad sense.

Course

Cohen (1992; Edgerton & Cohen, 1994) challenges the assertion that people have better prognosis for schizophrenia in developing countries than in developed countries. He also challenges the explanations that others have offered for this assertion.

Cohen (1992) challenged the assertion itself on methodological grounds. He suggested that people who are admitted in Western facilities in developing countries may be different from the people who are not. Subsequent researchers and commentators have discounted this explanation. Several authors (e.g., Jablensky et al., 1992; Sartorius, 1992; Wexler-Morrison, 1992) indicated that most people who suffer from schizophrenia contact all the available resources, including the Western facilities that were involved in the studies. A more potent challenge (Edgerton & Cohen, 1994) is that the attrition rates for follow-up may be higher in developed countries. If the more healthy patients are less likely to remain in contact with the treatment facility, then patients in developed countries may actually have better prognoses.

In any event, the symptoms that lead to treatment appear to be consistent across cultures: The 10 most common symptoms that bring people to a psychiatric facility tend to be the same (Jablensky, et al., 1992; see Table 9.3). In addition, the so-called "negative" symptoms, such as neglect and disturbances in eating, sleeping, and sexual function, are more conspicuous than the dramatic "positive" symptoms, such as talk of persecution and hearing voices. These common symptoms suggest that the experiences that lead people to the psychiatric hospital in both developing and developed countries are essentially the same.

The explanations for the finding that prognosis is more optimistic in developing countries are more problematic than supportive of the finding itself, as will be shown. Understanding variations in the course of schizophrenia across cultures may have to wait for longitudinal, direct observations in natural settings (Edgerton & Cohen, 1994). Some people offer attitudes toward mental illness as a possible explanation. For example, perhaps people in developing countries accept mental illness more than do people in developed countries. This acceptance leads to less stigmatization and encourages recovery. Cohen (1992), however, claims, "Use of confinement, restraint, and exclusion are universal" (Murphy, 1981, as cited by Cohen, 1992, p. 59).

Perhaps people in developing countries do not recognize mental illness. Opposing this point, Cohen (1992) points out that people recognize a common constellation of symptoms as "madness" across cultures. He refers to four isolated East African tribes to illustrate this point. Although their ideas about etiology and prognosis were different, all four agreed with the Western notion of what is "mad." Similarly, White

Table 9.3. Common Reasons for Seeking Psychiatric Care

1. Loss of appetite, sleep dysfunction, or loss of interest in sex.
2. Neglect of usual activities and interests.
3. Behaves as if being persecuted, harmed, or bewitched.
4. Avoiding other people.
5. Frightened or anxious.
6. Behaves as if hearing voices.
7. Claims impossible things.
8. Irritable and angry without reason.
9. Looks sad, mournful, or hopeless.
10. Talks incomprehensibly.

Source: From Jablensky et al. (1992), reprinted by permission.

(1982) argues that Jewish culture identified mental illness as a unique concept as early as the time of David (c. 1,000 B.C.).

Another explanation is that people return to productive work faster in developing countries than in developed countries. Cohen (1992) looks at unemployment rates and incidence of schizophrenia. He assumes that high unemployment means that little work is available. He offers Sri Lanka as an example of a place where unemployment is high and the incidence of schizophrenia is low. The assumption that high unemployment means that there is a slower return to productive work may be invalid, however, because official unemployment rates refer to employment within the capitalist system.

Lin and Kleinman (1988) suggest five explanations that may be more helpful. Empirical evidence supports the first four. First, developing countries tend to be more sociocentric. This tendency is related to decreased isolation. In contrast, Western society tends to be egocentric. Because of the focus on bilaterally defined contractual relationships, isolation increases when individuals are unable to maintain their obligations.

Second, the extended family characteristic of developing countries provides more support for the family members than the nuclear family of Western culture. Living with the family or maintaining strong family ties decreases the risk of relapse (Birchwood, Cochrane, MacMillan, Copestake, Kucharska, & Cariss, 1992). As a result of increased support, frustration is lower for the family members in the developing countries. Lower frustration leads to less expressed emotion.

Expressed emotion is highly related to relapse (Hirsch & Bristow, 1993; Karno & Jenkins, 1993). This association has been shown to be plausible also from a formal analysis of hypothetical symptom sources (Neufeld, 1994; Neufeld, Vollick, & Highgate-Maynard, 1993) coupled with a dynamical system adaptation of the interaction between exogenous stressors and symptomatology (Nicholson & Neufeld, 1992; Neufeld & Nicholson, 1991).

Third, returning to work is an important part of returning to the role of a productive member of society. The officially unemployed have adopted the Western attitude toward labor. The impersonal view that workers are commodities is considered by some as essential to the capitalist system. In contrast, work is "more often assigned than sought" (Lin & Kleinman, 1988, p. 562) in more traditional societies. In Western society, jobs tend to be fixed and people are found to fit them; in traditional societies, people are assigned those jobs that they are capable of performing. This approach is more adaptive for reintegrating the person into society.

Fourth, the stigma of mental illness tends to be lower in developing countries. Many traditional societies ascribe mental illness to medical, physical, or supernatural causes. These causes are external. In contrast, Western thought tends to ascribe mental illness to personality. This relationship is not absolute, however. For example, Chinese culture is non-Western, but it has a strong stigma against the mentally ill.

Finally, Lin and Kleinman (1988) speculate about the effects of natural selection. They point out that they do not have empirical data on this point. They propose that people who have enlarged cerebral ventricles are less likely to survive in developing countries than in developed countries. Because these vulnerable people are less likely to survive, they do not become chronic cases of schizophrenia.

ASSESSMENT STRATEGIES AND ISSUES

Diagnostic Systems

There is a clear need for strict diagnostic criteria for schizophrenia. Fabrega (1994) delineates the assumptions underlying the very possibility of a common international diagnostic system (see also Brody, 1994). Within such a system, racial and cultural differences would need to be taken into consideration to ensure accurate differential diagnoses for schizophrenia. For example, Hispanics tend to somatize emotions such as depression and anxiety, and Blacks are more likely than Whites to manifest hallucinations and delusions in affective disorders. Misdiagnosis could be easy without this kind of information. These warnings are not new: Al-Issa called for the use of culture-fair tests and physiological criteria for diagnosis as early as 1968.

Users of diagnostic systems that are based on the First Rank Symptoms need to consider that they are not purely physiologically based, as previously believed. Landmark, Merskey, Cernovsky, and Helmes (1990) suggest a triad of symptoms that appears to be more promising. They suggest that auditory hallucinations, passivity feelings, and disturbances in affect represent the underlying dimensions for other symptoms. This triad is a better predictor of outcome to fluzphenazine therapy than any of the 13 other diagnostic systems they considered. This finding suggests that these symptoms are tied to physiological factors. In selecting these symptoms, the researchers considered several requirements. Symptoms needed to be both common to the disorder and discriminant for differential diagnosis. They also had to be nonredundant (i.e., the symptoms were independent as well as necessary). Finally, symptoms needed to have high interrater reliability. The triad of auditory hallucinations, passivity feelings, and disturbances in affect meet these criteria.

Ideally, clear physiological signs should indicate the diagnosis of schizophrenia. Unfortunately, brain anomalies are not perfectly, nor in some cases even strongly, correlated with the disorder: Some people with schizophrenia show no detectable physical abnormalities. Furthermore, much information about the brains of people with schizophrenia has been learned through autopsies. With improved scanning techniques, however, progress is being made in the search for physiological signs.

Some researchers (e.g., Magaro & Chamrad, 1983) have found deficits among schizophrenic patients that they claim are identified with one or the other cerebral hemisphere. These deficits, however, cannot be attributed to simple abnormalities in lateralization of function (George & Neufeld, 1987; Mather, Neufeld, Merskey, & Russell, 1990). Gureje (1988) has made some progress, however, with performance measures for handedness and eye (oculomotor) dominance. Although no simple differences exist for dominance, cross-dominance (e.g., right hand and left eye dominant) was more likely among people with schizophrenia (10 out of 70 cases) than among people without schizophrenia (1 out of 40 cases).

Reluctance to Diagnose

Munakata (1989) describes a case in which an airplane pilot responded to an auditory hallucination telling him to "Go somewhere far" and crashed his plane. Twenty-four people died. The pilot had paranoid schizophrenia. His physicians knew, but they reported his diagnosis as "depressive state," "psychosomatic disorder," and "malfunction of the autonomic nervous system" instead.

What led the pilot's physicians to misrepresent his diagnosis? Schizophrenia is a devastating diagnosis in any culture. A number of cultural factors, however, may increase the possibility of misrepresentation. Munakata (1989) notes that disguising schizophrenia as "neurasthenia" is common practice in Japan. The reasons for this practice are embedded in Japanese beliefs about the family and mental illness. In Western society, families are not held responsible for caring for people once they become adults. Many families continue to provide care, but the prevailing attitude in the West is that the state has an obligation to care for people who cannot care for themselves. In contrast, Japan's Mental Health Act obligates guardians (i.e., the family) to arrange treatment for sick family members, to prevent them from injuring themselves, and to manage their finances. It is possible for the family to institutionalize a member without his or her consent. The fact that the family is still responsible for caring for the individual offsets this power. In addition, people with mental disorders are not seen as sick. Instead, mental disorders are seen as the result of heredity or lineage. As a result, one mentally ill person shames the entire family.

Because of these factors, the following pattern of coping arises (Munakata, 1989). First, the family attempts to reduce or eliminate abnormal behavior. Second, the family calls upon trusted outsiders, such as elders, to assist. Third, the family calls on outside helpers such as religious healers and physicians. Fourth, a professional labels the sick family member as mentally ill, and treatment begins. Finally, the family tends to lose hope. Quite possibly, by this point they have exhausted their own resources.

How do these conditions impinge upon a professional who may misrepresent a diagnosis? The answer to this question is tied to the family's attitude toward the professional (Munakata, 1989). The professional is in a position of power. To compensate for this imbalance, the family will attempt to establish emotional ties. In effect, these ties make the professional a member of the family. The professional takes on a patriarchal role. In addition, misdiagnosis is adaptive in several ways. Because schizophrenia carries such a powerful negative stigma, the professional replaces this label with "neurasthenia." In the early stages, the two disorders may be similar. Neurasthenia is seen as a physical disorder. As such, it does no shame to the family. Finally, neurasthenia is "curable." Therefore, the family is motivated to accept treatment. Munakata (1989) describes a number of other intricacies of the working relationships between families and mental health professionals in Japanese culture that are beyond the scope of this chapter.

Religious Beliefs

Another difficulty in diagnosing schizophrenia concerns religious beliefs. A recurring difficulty is that certain religious beliefs, such as "kismet" (predestination) and possession states, meet the criteria for delusions. A conservative rule is, "If it might be true, then do not count it as a delusion." This rule is followed inconsistently in the literature. Many researchers appear to follow it. Most notably, however, people researching the First Rank Symptoms have intentionally followed objective criteria without regard for religious beliefs.

The presence of hyperreligiosity may be informative for differential diagnoses. Brewerton (1994) conducted a retrospective chart analysis of 50 patients at Hawaii State Hospital. He found that religious phenomenology appears to be more strongly related with some disorders than with others. For example, it is less common among patients with psychotic depression than among those with bipolar mania. Among people with schizophrenia, the presence of hyperreligiosity appeared to be related to specific neurological dysfunction. Brewerton (1994) claims, "It is not unreasonable to speculate that psychotic phenomena of a religious nature may involve temporolimbic dysfunction that is related to, yet different from, epilepsy" (p. 303). One difficultly, however, is differentiating religious belief from hyperreligiosity.

The following two scenarios illustrate some of the major differences between what may be viewed as a healthy religious belief and an unhealthy schizophrenic delusion. One involves a Menominee peyotist called Joe, and the other involves a particular Jewish sect, the Bratslav Hasid.

"Joe" the Peyotist   North American Native religion in many instances accommodated Christian ideas fairly easily (C. Brant, Mohawk psychiatrist, personal communication, November 1993). One such case involves a subgroup of Menominee natives called peyotists. These people have a rich and complex religion. One small aspect of this religion involves inducing visions and dreams. Individuals ingest these drugs, and the resulting visions purportedly provide important instruction. Spindler (1987) describes Joe, one member of this group. Other peyotists described Joe as "a little off," attributing his difficulties to exogenous sources, including sorcery or engagement in murder in a previous life.

Important differences exist between Joe and other peyotists, even though the other peyotists also hold atypical beliefs and may hallucinate. First, Joe often excluded himself from the religious ceremonies. He would sit outside by himself and not participate in the drumming and singing. Second, during clinical assessment, Joe and the other peyotists had abnormal Rorschach protocols, but the abnormalities were different. Most peyotists have an unusually strong influence of specific religious themes in their protocols. Not only were these themes absent from Joe's protocol, but he also displayed evidence of poor perceptual processing. Spindler concluded:

Joe is mentally ill because he cannot recognize boundaries in time and social space and therefore cannot find meaning. The peyotists are not mentally ill because they do recognize boundaries in time and space and do find meaning within those boundaries. (Spindler, 1987, p. 13)

The Bratslav Hasid   The Bratslav Hasidic Jews present a slightly different set of challenges (Witztum, Greenberg, & Bauchbinder, 1990). This sect has six times the expected incidence of schizophrenia, in particular paranoid schizophrenia. These people tend to be adult converts, and no genetic factors appear to be implicated. The reason this sect is so attractive for people with schizophrenia may be related to its beliefs. The founder of the sect, Rabbi Nachman, believed, possibly correctly, that he was persecuted. This belief influenced his teaching. In addition, the sect is suspicious of rational thought and avoids conventional medicine. Finally, it is exceptionally tolerant of bizarre behavior.

As with Joe and the peyotists, some important distinctions exist between the people in the sect who have schizophrenia and those who do not. The sect encourages members to study and converse with each other: The people with schizophrenia isolate themselves. The sect encourages people to consider general principles in maintaining a strict routine of prayers and study: The people with schizophrenia focus almost exclusively on specific details, such as reciting Psalms. The sect encourages conservative dress and sanctions specific occasions for self-neglect: The people with schizophrenia are generally unkempt.

Conclusions   Some general principles can help to distinguish religious beliefs from psychopathology. One important consideration is the individual's ability to function. Psychopathology is likely to exist if the person is unable to care for himself or herself on an ongoing basis. Similarly, a person with a pathological condition is more likely to withdraw socially. These generalizations, however, must be tempered with a knowledge of the accepted beliefs of the religious community. Perhaps the most valuable clue to distinguishing the unusual from the pathological is the extent to which the individual adopts the standards of the religious community.

PRACTICE ISSUES

General Principles

The vast complexity of providing suggestions concerning treatment for all cultural groups is beyond the scope of a single chapter. A few basic principles, however, apply to a wide range of situations. Two major concepts to consider are rapport and knowledge of the culture. Knowledge includes such topics as family structure and perceived obligations, beliefs and values, and differences in the use of language. These simple factors may play important roles in the success of treatment. Finally, these factors are not independent: Each interacts with the other treatment factors.

Rapport

Rapport cannot be overemphasized. Worthington (1992) focused on the difficulties Whites could expect in working with Blacks. Racism is widespread and often works both ways. She also warned that as people become more educated, they tend to adopt White attitudes that may make it more difficult to establish rapport. These issues apply to any minority group.

Religious groups present their own issues for the therapist. Witztum et al. (1990) note that they needed to work closely with the client's religious leaders to establish trust. This trust can be vital in gaining compliance. Some religions, including the Bratslav Hasid, are opposed to pharmaceutical treatments. Witztum et al. (1990) were able to get compliance with medications only because they enlisted the aid of the sect's leadership. Finally, they note that the therapist needs to be aware of his or her role. Often, the role of a therapist who is working with a religious client is extremely limited: Treat the mental disorder. In other words, some of the roles that a therapist typically plays may be seen as the domain of the religious leaders.

Knowledge of Family Structure and Perceived Obligations

Rapport is facilitated when the therapist understands the client's culture. An important aspect of culture is the family. The role of the family varies greatly from one culture to another. Several factors can be important. Is the client married? If so, then how is the marriage relationship affected by the disorder? For example, Hispanics tend to get married younger than Anglos and have later age of onset (Escobar et al., 1986; Randolph et al., 1985). Therefore, Hispanics are more likely than Anglos to experience their first psychotic episode after marriage. To what extent is the family blamed for the disorder? Compare Hispanics, who are unlikely to blame the family (Jenkins, 1988), to Japanese, who are very likely to blame the family (Munakata, 1989).

These differences may persist even if members of minority groups are well acculturated. Escobar et al. (1986) indicated that values concerning families and hierarchies survived even among Hispanics who had served in the American military. They also noted that Hispanics with schizophrenia were more likely to live with their families than were Anglos. They are also less likely to be hospitalized. This trend is explained in part by greater family resources accruing to the extended family and by greater tolerance for symptoms.

How involved in treatment does the family want to be? For example, Asian families tend to want to be highly involved. Excluding an Asian family can even lead to treatment failure because of attrition (Lin, Miller, Poland, Nucciao, & Yamaguchi, 1991). This high level of family involvement is a two-edged sword. On the one side, the family provides constant, persistent emotional and material support. On the other side, overinvolvement can lead to resentment, criticism, shame, embarrassment, and inappropriate intrusiveness (Lin et al., 1991).

Intervention Strategies

The combination of prescribing medication and reducing expressed emotion is the foundation of treatment for schizophrenia. Three common factors attend to most successful treatment strategies: psychopharmacological treatment, helping the patient, and reducing family burden (Kazarian & Malla, 1992). Virtually all current approaches to treating schizophrenia include some level of antipsychotic medication. Noncompliance to medication is a significant factor in relapse.

Two strategies for reducing expressed emotion are providing social skills training to the client and family therapy. Hogarty et al. (1991) found that both approaches forestalled relapse in the first year, but that family therapy was required to delay relapse for a second year. In this study, social skills training included instruction, modeling, role play, feedback, and assigned homework. Although Hogarty et al. (1986) found that social skills training failed to reduce expressed emotion, this treatment modality was additive to family therapy in reducing the probability of relapse during the first year.

Empirical evidence supports several approaches to family therapy with this population. A purely psychoeducational approach, however, has not proven effective (Hirsch & Bristow, 1993; Hogarty et al., 1986). Kazarian and Malla (1992) describe several modes of family therapy. All are consistent with the example of Hogarty et al. (1986) in that compliance with medication is emphasized and traditional family therapy attempts to promote insight and resolve underlying issues are eschewed. Instead, training in problem-solving and communication skills, support for the family, and psychoeducation are provided.

Beliefs and Values

Obviously, understanding cultural beliefs and values can help in understanding the client. People with schizophrenia, particularly those who believe in the Judeo-Christian-Muslim tradition, tend to distort these beliefs. Having knowledge of what is actually expected by the cultural or religious group can help the therapist identify what is appropriate or necessary and what is deviant. Knowledge of the culture also helps the therapist to frame interventions in ways that the client will accept.

Differences in the Use of Language

Language is more important in schizophrenia than in many other disorders. Much of our understanding of thought disorder comes from the verbal productions of people with schizophrenia. For this reason, therapists must be familiar with the idioms and jargon of their clients. Any subculture will develop its own jargon and shades of meaning for words. If the therapist and client share no common language, then a professional interpreter should be retained. Preferably, the same interpreter would be present for all sessions with a given client.

Part of the Hispanic tolerance for symptoms stems from linguistic factors. A couple of language differences are important in considering Hispanic populations. One is the perceived difference between the concepts *disease* and *illness*. *Disease* refers to a medical malfunction. In contrast, *illness* refers to the individual's reaction to the disease (Ruiz, 1985). Another linguistic issue involves the English word *nerves* and the Spanish word *nervios* (Jenkins, 1988). For Mexican Americans, *nervios* adequately describes psychoses, but for Anglo Americans, *nerves* does not. In part, socioeconomic status, particularly literacy, explains this difference. This factor, however, fails to account completely for the differences. *Nervios* implies that the difficulty is beyond the control of the individual and does not implicate the family. In addition, *nervios* applies to a broad range of problems, not just schizophrenia. In part, this conceptualization of mental illness enables Hispanic families to think of the patient as, "just like us only more so" (Jenkins, 1988, p. 1241).

ROLE OF CLINICAL PSYCHOLOGY

Perhaps the greatest service the clinical psychologist can perform is to encourage the attitude that people with schizophrenia are, "just like us only more so." This attitude is consistent with certain continuous conceptualizations of schizophrenia (Nicholson, 1993; Nicholson & Neufeld, 1993; Nicholson & Neufeld, 1996). This continuous approach can be applied to individual symptoms, including delusions (Chadwick & Lowe, 1990), negative symptoms (Barnes, 1989), loosening of associations (McConaghy, 1989), and hallucinations (Posey & Losch, 1983). Psychoeducational programs that teach the families of people with schizophrenia about the disease, especially regarding the biological component, are a good start. Public education programs are also helpful.

Developing countries appear to be more effective in this regard than developed countries. As a society, developed countries cannot turn back the clock and become developing countries again. However, those in developed countries can look at the factors that make prognosis better for people in developing countries and emulate them.

One of the greatest barriers for people with schizophrenia is the stigma attached to mental illness. Schizophrenia is especially stigmatized. North Americans may avoid the difficulties the Japanese face with intentional misdiagnosis, but are we really very different? For example, anecdotal observations suggest that the diagnosis of paranoid schizophrenia may be decreasing in relative frequency in some settings (D. Vollick, personal communication, August 1993). This trend may be an attempt to spare the person the stigma that accompanies this diagnosis, at least in the short term. Although the symptomatology of the paranoid subtype may be quite florid, the course of the disorder can be more positive than for other subtypes (Nicholson & Neufeld, 1993). Misdiagnosis, however, is a strategy fraught with pitfalls. Public education is essential to reducing this stigma. In particular, education should emphasize the biological origins of this disease and advances in treatment methods.

Clinical psychologists have made progress in identifying the factors that explain why prognosis is better in developing countries. Although fostering these qualities in society at large may be a laudable goal, it is probably more realistic to focus on fostering them in the community facilities that serve people with schizophrenia. One beneficial factor is group-oriented rather than individual-oriented thinking. That is, a sense of community and connectedness may be especially beneficial for some people who are suffering from schizophrenia. A second factor is the attitude that the family is important and the supportive behaviors that flow from this attitude. A third factor is the attitude that ideally people contribute to their community as they are able, as opposed to concentrating on inflexible job requirements.

Within clinical psychology, cultural issues are important. Graduate-level courses for clinicians who want to work with various cultural groups would be beneficial.

Familiarity with specific cultural groups and knowledge of their beliefs and values is essential. In addition, clinical psychologists should become familiar with working alongside professional cultural interpreters.

Finally, research training tends to differentiate clinical psychologists from other mental health professionals. This area may represent our greatest contribution. One emerging area of research links cognitive-neuropsychological anomalies to specific symptoms (e.g., Neufeld & Williamson, 1996). Implementing in this area provisions for possible racial differences would represent a significant advance. At the level of individual patients, candidate areas for research include specifying the mechanisms by which beliefs moderate symptoms and the effects of acculturation on patterns of symptoms. On a larger scale, research regarding the effects of sociopolitical factors on course of disorder could be elaborated upon. In terms of evolutionary theory, Lin and Kleinman's (1988) hypothesis that natural selection may play a role in observed incidence in developing countries could be investigated.

CONCLUSIONS

As with other areas of research, the more we learn about schizophrenia across cultures, the more we learn that there is to learn. Schizophrenia remains a mystery. Although this disease manifests itself in a myriad of different ways, it is a global phenomenon. Symptoms may vary, but the suffering that drives people to seek help is the same. The work of generations of researchers has brought us to the point where we must now travel beyond mere descriptions to investigate underlying mechanisms. Furthermore, to understand a person with schizophrenia, we must understand his or her culture. Only with increased understanding can we effectively help people who have this terrible disorder.

Notes

1. Schizophrenia has generated much research. We apologize in advance to the many fine researchers whose work is not mentioned here.

References

Al-Issa, I. (1968). Cross-cultural study of symptomatology in schizophrenia. *Canadian Journal of Psychiatry, 13,* 147–156.

American Psychiatric Association (1994). *Diagnostic and statistical manual of mental disorders* (4th ed.). Washington, DC: Author.

Barnes, T. R. (1989). Negative symptoms in schizophrenia. *British Journal of Psychiatry, 155* (Suppl. 7) 1–135.

Birchwood, M., Cochrane, R., MacMillan, F., Copestake, S., Kucharska, J., & Cariss, M. (1992). The influence of ethnicity and family structure on relapse in first episode schizophrenia: A comparison of Asian, Afro-Caribbean, and White patients. *British Journal of Psychiatry, 161,* 783–790.

Brewerton, T. D. (1994). Hyperreligiosity in psychotic disorders. *Journal of Nervous and Mental Disease, 182,* 302–304.

Brody, E. B. (1994). Psychiatric diagnosis in sociocultural context [Editorial]. *Journal of Nervous and Mental Disease, 182,* 253–255.

Carpenter, W. J. & Strauss, J. S. (1974). Cross-cultural evaluation of Schneider's First Rank Symptoms of schizophrenia: A report from the International Pilot Study of Schizophrenia. *American Journal of Psychiatry, 131,* 682–687.

Chadwick, P. D., & Lowe, C. F. (1990). Measurement and modification of delusional beliefs. *Journal of Consulting and Clinical Psychology, 58,* 225–232.

Chandrasena, R. (1986). Catatonic schizophrenia: An international comparative study. *Canadian Journal of Psychiatry, 31,* 249–252.

Chandrasena, R. (1987). Schneider's first-rank symptoms: An international comparative study. *Acta Psychiatrica Scandinavica, 76,* 574–578.

Coffey, G. J., MacKinnon, A., & Minas, I. H. (1993). Interethnic variations in the presence of Schneiderian first rank symptoms. *Australian and New Zealand Journal of Psychiatry, 27,* 219–227.

Cohen, A. (1992). Prognosis for schizophrenia in the Third World. A reevaluation of cross-cultural research. *Culture, Medicine and Psychiatry, 16,* 53–75.

Cromwell, R. L. (1993). Schizophrenia research: Things to do before the geneticist arrives. In R. L. Cromwell & C. R. Snyder (Eds.), *Schizophrenia: Origins, processes, treatment, and outcome* (pp. 51–61). New York: Oxford University Press.

Davison, G. C. & Neale, J. M. (1990). Schizophrenia. In G. C. Davison & I. M. Neale (Eds.), In *Abnormal psychology* (5th ed., pp. 375–408). New York: Wiley.

Edgerton, R. B. & Cohen, A. (1994). Culture and schizophrenia: The DOSMD challenge. *British Journal of Psychiatry, 164,* 222–231.

Escobar, J. I., Randolf, E. T., & Hill, M. (1986). Symptoms of schizophrenia in Hispanic and Anglo veterans. *Culture, Medicine and Psychiatry, 10,* 259–276.

Fabrega, H., Jr. (1994). International systems of diagnosis in psychiatry. *Journal of Nervous and Mental Disease, 182,* 256–263.

Feinberg, I. (1982/83). Schizophrenia: Caused by a fault in programmed synaptic elimination during adolescence? *Journal of Psychiatric Research, 17,* 319–334.

George, L., & Neufeld, R. W. J. (1987). Attentional resources and hemispheric functional asymmetry in schizophrenia. *British Journal of Clinical Psychology, 26,* 35–45.

Groth-Marnat, G. (1990). *Handbook of psychological assessment.* New York: Wiley.

Gureje, O. (1988). Sensorimotor laterality in schizophrenia: Which features transcend cultural influences? *Acta Psychiatrica Scandinavica, 77,* 188–193.

Hirsch, S. R. & Bristow, M. F. (1993). Psychological, family, ethnic, and community factors affecting the course and treatment of schizophrenia. *Current Opinion in Psychiatry, 6,* 53–57.

Hoffman, R. E., Rapaport, J., Ameli, R., McGlashan, T. H., Harcherik, D., & Servan-Schreiber, D. (1995). A neural network simulation of hallucinated "voices" and associated speech perception impairments in schizophrenic patients. *Journal of Cognitive Neuroscience, 7,* 479–496.

Hogarty, G. E., Anderson, C. M., Reiss, D. J., Kornblith, S. J., Greenwald, D. P., Jauna, C. D., & Madonia, M. J. (1986). Family psychoeducation, social skills training, and maintenance chemotherapy in the aftercare treatment of schizophrenia. I. One-year effects of a controlled study on relapse and expressed emotion. *Archives of General Psychiatry, 43,* 633–642.

Hogarty, G. E., Anderson, C. M., Reiss, D. J., Kornblith, S. J., Greenwald, D. P., Ulrich, R. F., & Carter, M. (1991). Family psychoeducation, social skills training, and maintenance chemotherapy in the aftercare treatment of schizophrenia. II. Two-year effects of a controlled study on relapse and adjustment. *Archives of General Psychiatry, 48,* 340–347.

Jablensky, A., Sartorius, N., Ernberg, G, Anker, M, Korten, A., Cooper, J. E., Day, R., & Bertelsen, A. (1992). Schizophrenia: Manifestations, incidence, and course in different cultures: A World Health Organization ten-country study [Monograph]. *Psychological Medicine, Suppl* 20, 1–97.

Jenkins, J. H. (1988). Conceptions of schizophrenia as a problem of nerves: A cross-cultural comparison of Mexican-Americans and Anglo-Americans. *Social Science and Medicine, 26*, 1233–1243.

Jones, B. E., & Gray, B. A. (1986). Problem in diagnosing schizophrenia and affective disorders among Blacks. *Hospital and Community Psychiatry, 37*, 61–65.

Kalat, J. W. (1988). Biology of schizophrenia and related disorders. *Biological psychology* (3rd ed., pp. 433–456). Belmont, CA: Wadsworth.

Karno, M., & Jenkins, J. H. (1993). Cross-cultural issues in the course and treatment of schizophrenia. *Psychiatric Clinics of North America, 16*, 339–350.

Kazarian, S. S. (1992). The measurement of expressed emotion: A review. *Canadian Journal of Psychiatry, 37*, 51–56.

Kazarian, S. S. & Malla, A. K. (1992). Working with the families of long term patients: An expressed emotion perspective. In E. Persad, S. S. Kazarian, & L. W. Joseph (Eds.), *The mental hospital of the 21st century* (pp. 91–106) Toronto, Ontario: Wall & Emerson, Inc.

Landmark, J., Mersky, H., Cernovsky, Z. Z., & Helmes, E. (1990). The positive triad of schizophrenic symptoms: Its statistical properties and its relationship to 13 traditional diagnostic systems. *British Journal of Psychiatry, 156*, 388–394.

Lin, K. M., & Kleinman, A. M. (1988). Psychopathology and clinical course of schizophrenia: A cross-cultural perspective. *Schizophrenia Bulletin, 14*, 555–567.

Lin, K. M., Miller, M. P. H., Poland, R. E., Nucciao, I, & Yamaguchi, M. (1991). Ethnicity and family involvement in the treatment of schizophrenic patients. *Journal of Nervous and Mental Disease, 9*, 631–633.

Magaro, P. A., & Chamrad, D. L. (1983). Hemispheric preference of paranoid and nonparanoid schizophrenics. *Biological Psychiatry, 18*, 1269–1285.

Malik, S. B., Ahmed, M., Bashir, A., & Choudhry, T. M. (1990). Schneider's first-rank symptoms of schizophrenia: Prevalence and diagnostic use: A study from Pakistan. *British Journal of Psychiatry, 156*, 109–111.

Mather, J. A., Neufeld, R. W. J., Merskey, H., & Russell, N. C. (1990). Schizophrenic performance on line bisection: No simple lateralization defects. *Journal of Psychiatric Research, 24*, 185–190.

McConaghy, N. (1989). Thought disorder or allusive thinking in the relatives of schizophrenics? A response to Callahan, Madsen, Saccuzzo, and Romney. *Journal of Nervous and Mental Disease, 177*, 729–734.

Munakata, T. (1989). The socio-cultural significance of the diagnostic label "neurasthenia" in Japan's mental health care system. *Culture, Medicine and Psychiatry, 13*, 203–213.

Neale, J. M., & Oltmanns, T. F. (1981). Assessment of schizophrenia. In D. H. Barlow (Ed.), *Behavioral assessment of adult disorders* (pp. 87–128). New York: Guilford Press.

Neufeld, R. W. J. (1994). *Theoretical stress and stress proneness effects on information processing in light of mathematical models of stochastic processes.* (Research Bulletin No. 720). London, Ontario, Canada: University of Western Ontario, Department of Psychology.

Neufeld, R. W. J., & Nicholson, I. R. (1991). *Differential and other equations essential to a servocybernetic (systems) approach to stress-schizophrenia relations.* (Research Bulletin No. 698). London, Ontario, Canada: University of Western Ontario, Department of Psychology.

Neufeld, R. W. J., Vollick, D., & Highgate-Maynard, S. (1993). Stochastic modeling of stimulus encoding and memory search in paranoid schizophrenia: Clinical and theoretical implications. In R.L. Cromwell (Ed.), *Schizophrenia: Origins, processes, treatment, and outcome: The Second Kansas Series in clinical psychology.* New York: Oxford University Press.

Neufeld, R. W. J., & Williamson, P. C. (1996). Neuropsychological correlates of positive symptoms. In C. Pantelis, H. Nelson, & T. R. E. Barnes (Eds.), *Schizophrenia: A neuropsychological perspective.* (pp. 205–235) London: Wiley.

Nicholson, I. R. (1993). *The classification of the schizophrenias according to symptomatology: A two-factor model.* Unpublished doctoral dissertation, University of Western Ontario, London, Ontario, Canada.

Nicholson, I. R., & Neufeld, R. W. J. (1992). A dynamic vulnerability perspective on stress and schizophrenia. *American Journal of Orthopsychiatry, 62,* 117–130.

Nicholson, I. R., & Neufeld, R. W. J. (1993). A two-dimensional model of paranoid and nonparanoid schizophrenia. *Journal of Abnormal Psychology, 102,* 259–270.

Nicholson, I. R., & Neufeld, R. W. J. (1996). *The problem of dissecting schizophrenia: Evidence against a mixture of disorders.* Manuscript submitted for publication.

Posey, T. B., & Losch, M. E. (1983). Auditory hallucinations of hearing voices in 375 normal subjects. *Imagination, Cognition and Personality, 3,* 99–113.

Randolph, E. T., Escobar, J. I., Paz, D. H., & Forsythe, A. B. (1985). Ethnicity and reporting of schizophrenic symptoms. *Journal of Nervous and Mental Disease, 173,* 332–340.

Ruiz, P. (1985). The minority patient. *Community Mental Health Journal, 21,* 208–216.

Sartorius, N. (1992). Commentary on prognosis for schizophrenia in the Third World. *Culture, Medicine and Psychiatry, 16,* 81–84.

Spindler, G. (1987). Joe Nepah: A "schizophrenic" Menominee peyotist. *Journal of Psychoanalytic Anthropology, 10,* 1–16.

Warner, R. (1992). Commentary on Cohen, prognosis for schizophrenia in the Third World. *Culture, Medicine and Psychiatry, 16,* 85–88.

Wexler-Morrison, N. (1992). Commentary on Cohen, prognosis for schizophrenia in the Third World. *Culture, Medicine and Psychiatry, 16,* 77–80.

White, J. (1982). Christianity and mental illness. In *Masks of melancholy: A Christian physician looks at depression and suicide* (pp. 11–54). Downers Grove, IL: InterVarsity.

Witztum, E., Greenberg, D., & Buchbinder, J. T. (1990). "A very narrow bridge": Diagnosis and management of mental illness among Bratslav Hasidim. *Psychotherapy, 27,* 124–131.

Worthington, C. (1992). An examination of factors influencing the diagnosis and treatment of Black patients in the mental health system. *Archives of Psychiatric Nursing, 6,* 195–204.

Young, M. A., Tanner, M. A., & Meltzer, H. (1982). Operational definitions of schizophrenia: What do they identify? *Journal of Nervous and Mental Disease, 170,* 443–447.

Zubin, J., & Spring, B. (1977). Vulnerability—A new view of schizophrenia. *Journal of Abnormal Psychology, 86,* 103–126.

10

Culture and Pain

GARY B. ROLLMAN

Questions about individual differences are often fascinating, but they are even more so for pain, because pain is a nearly universal experience (congenital insensitivity to pain does exist, but it is exceedingly rare). Still, to say that pain is universal does not suggest that it is to be understood in only physiological or biochemical terms. The human pain experience is composed of sensory, emotional, and cognitive components. In both the expression and management of pain, biological, psychological, and social factors interact in complex ways.

There is an expression to the effect that, "Man endures pain as an undeserved punishment. Women accept it as a natural heritage." While the question of gender differences is best left for another place (Rollman, 1995), related views have been expressed about how different cultural groups have seemed to react to painful events.

Wolff (1985) summarized the prevailing stereotypes:

> Scandinavians are tough and stoic with a high tolerance to pain; the British are more sensitive but, in view of their ingrained 'stiff, upper lip,' do not complain when in pain; Italians and other Mediterranean people are emotional and overreact to pain; and Jews both overreact to pain and are preoccupied with pain and suffering as well as physical health. (p. 23)

The influence of culture on the expression of pain is almost certainly one which begins at birth and extends throughout one's lifetime. The interpretation of pain and the reactions to it are dependent, in large part, upon an individual's past experience—the behavior of his or her family, playmates, and others. Attitudes and anxieties established during the early years are certain to have a permanent impact on pain behavior. This perspective suggests that cultural differences in pain behavior, where they exist, are likely to arise from social rather than genetic differences.

Interest in the link between pain and culture is widespread and, as it mixes science and philosophy, likely to remain controversial. Religious perspectives add further considerations in analyses about the role of pain in our lives,

> In some cultures, pain and the endurance of pain are looked upon as desirable disciplines and worthwhile experiences. Thus, because of the pain and suffering endured by Christ, certain Christians, in an attempt to identify themselves with the "Savior" or "God," or in an attempt to establish an ideal of Christian practice as they view it, embrace pain when it spontaneously occurs with disease (to "bear one's Cross"), or induce it by self-chastisement, i.e., "stigmata in religious zealots" (Hardy, Wolff, & Goodell, 1952, p. 302).

PAIN IN THE LABORATORY

Pain is often studied in two settings: the laboratory and the clinic. The laboratory, where carefully controlled noxious stimuli, such as pressure, temperature, electrical current, or chemicals, can be presented and a host of behavioral reactions can be measured, provides the opportunity to examine stimulus-response relationships with precision. The individual, however, knows that the painful stimuli are controllable and that the pain will not endure beyond the testing session. Clinical pain is more difficult to assess, partly because the stimulus is endogenous and therefore unmeasurable and partly because the affective and cognitive reactions to a pain of uncertain etiology and outcome are inevitably more complex.

The statements made about cultural differences observed in clinical settings are often broad. Sternbach and Tursky (1965) summarized attitudes and expressions observed by Zborowski (1952) and themselves: "Old Americans have a phlegmatic, matter-of-fact, doctor-helping orientation; Jews express a concern for the implication of pain, and they distrust palliatives; Italians express a desire for pain relief, and the Irish inhibit expression of suffering and concern for the implications of the pain" (p. 241).

Sternbach and Tursky (1965) attempted to see whether these differences would be obtained within the laboratory setting. They presented electrical shocks to American-born women who belonged to four different ethnic groups: Yankee (Protestants of British descent whose parents and grandparents were born in the United States), Irish, Italian, and Jewish (the last three born of parents who emigrated to the United States from Europe). In addition, the women were given standardized hour-long interviews regarding their attitudes toward pain. In the laboratory, the groups did not differ in absolute threshold (the level of current required to detect the sensation on the skin), but there were sizable differences in pain tolerance (the level at which participants indicated that the pain had reached the maximum level they wished to experience). The Yankee and Jewish subjects withstood significantly higher values than the Italians, with the Irish at an intermediate level.

Clearly, while interesting, these data ask as many questions as they answer. For one, religion, ethnicity, and national origin are mixed. For another, 15 Massachusetts housewives hardly serve as an adequate sample for making generalizations about either the attitudes or the pain responses of an ethnic or cultural group.

Tursky and Sternbach (1967) addressed some of the limitations of studies such as this, stressing, in particular, the great intragroup variability and the inability to make predictions about an individual's pattern based solely on her ethnic membership. They also began to consider the implications of such findings for biological or psychosocial differences in response to pain. Their selection procedure and some psychophysiological data (differences in skin resistance and skin potential) led them to talk about "ethnic specificity" and "inborn differences," but they saw this as a "tenuous relationship" and felt that the association of attitudinal and autonomic responses "argues for early childhood conditioning in the home rather than a genetic determination" (p. 73).

Others, who used techniques similar to Sternbach and Tursky (1965), were also not restricted by small sample sizes from making broad generalizations about the effects of race or ethnic group. Chapman and Jones (1944) compared 18 African Americans and 18 Americans of North European ancestry on tolerance to radiant heat on the forehead. The lower pain reaction threshold of the African American subjects (who may have differed from the White subjects in myriad ways) led to statements such as "Negroes were able to tolerate much less pain than North Europeans" (Wolff & Langley, 1968, p. 495). The data from 30 Italian subjects also showed lower tolerance values than the North Europeans and led to the observation that "the Negroes did not complain while the subjects of Mediterranean ancestry complained loudly at pain reaction threshold" (Wolff & Langley, 1968, p. 495).

These findings, incidentally, were not supported in a clinical study. Winsberg and Greenlick (1967) evaluated the pain responses of 207 White mothers and 158 African American mothers of similar lower and lower-middle social class admitted to the obstetrical unit of a general hospital in Detroit. While the study is hampered by the fact that typically the physician or nurse rather than the patient reported the degree of pain and how the patients reacted (from "very excitedly" to "very calmly"), the authors found no racial differences in the estimated degree of pain or the nature of the pain response.

Wolff and Langley (1968) observed that "the research investigator is more concerned with the physical nature and somatic basis of pain than with psychosocial and cultural components. The physician, on the other hand . . . realizes that there are ethnic and cultural differences in patients' responses to pain" (p. 495). The cognitive revolution which affected experimental and clinical psychology has changed that state of affairs, although cultural influences on the pain response have received much less attention than other psychosocial variables.

Zatzick and Dimsdale (1990) remarked:

> Differences in pain behaviors have always struck the keen observer, and over the centuries various observers have commented on cultural factors that appear to steer an individual toward pathos or stoicism in response to pain. Many of these observations have been hearsay or mere stereotyping. (p. 544)

The desire to replace anecdotal information with hard data provided the impetus for many experimenters to conduct studies investigating racial, religious, or ethnic factors related to pain, since the laboratory provides a setting in which the relationship between culture and pain can be quantified.

There are, however, problems with many of these studies. As noted earlier, small sample sizes severely limit the generalizability of studies conducted to date. So, too, do samples gathered from a restricted geographical region (say, only from Montreal), investigations of persons from one culture living in another (Italians living in Boston), mixtures of immigrants and later generations, and failure to distinguish between race or religion and culture. Wolff (1985), for example, noted that Blacks residing in New York who have come from West Africa may react more vigorously to experimental pain than those born in the United States, with West Indian Blacks falling in between. While African Americans are often, erroneously, treated as a single group, studies of Caucasians have sampled a variety of ethnic groups and have demonstrated some striking differences (Zatzick & Dimsdale, 1990; however, these have sometimes been ignored or overlooked as Caucasians were lumped together for analysis). Wolff (1985) also observed that "while there are undoubtedly differences in pain reaction between various ethnocultural groups, it is not at all clear if these are due to ethnic or to other cultural and/or psychosocial factors. On the whole, the demonstrated differences are probably more due to learning than they are innate" (p. 27).

PAIN IN THE CLINIC

While the laboratory provides precision, the clinic, as an arena for the study of ethnocultural differences in pain, provides relevancy. There are numerous reasons for studying pain in the real world. For one, clinical pain, with its associated anxiety and despair, adds a heightened level of affect and cognitive involvement to the sensory component of discomfort. For another, the lessons learned from examining how culture shapes the pain response has important implications for the assessment and treatment of painful conditions. Zborowski's (1969) book, *People in Pain,* provided an influential perspective on the role of culture, but its conclusions (Old Americans are stoic, Italians loudly demand pain relief, Jews seek relief but worry about the future implications of their disorder) all came from staff reports at a single Veterans Administration hospital in New York.

Numerous studies have undertaken to examine cultural determinants of pain reactions, examining, in most instances, different cultural groups in the United States and, less often, patients in different countries. Such an epidemiological perspective can add a vital dose of reality to a difficult task. Even here, though, there are some vexing problems. For example, there is no clear agreement as to what constitutes disease or illness (Zola, 1966). There are disorders considered important in some societies that have no counterpart in Western culture. In contrast, disorders like chronic fatigue syndrome, which are widely diagnosed in Western medicine, are not recognized in many other cultures (or, perhaps, are attributed to very different causes; Abbey & Garfinkel, 1992; Ware & Kleinman, 1992).

Moreover, there are many instances of persons who are found to have a painful disorder only when they are surveyed or examined as part of an epidemiological investigation. That is, their symptoms or complaints are no different than those who have been formally diagnosed with an illness, but they never considered them to be severe or important enough to consult a physician.

Zola (1966) suggested that "illness, defined as the presence of clinically serious symptoms, is the statistical norm" (p. 615) and that "signs ordinarily defined as indicating problems in one population may be ignored in others" (p. 617). Back pain, for example, while not considered "good," may be seen by many individuals as "part of expected everyday existence" and, thus, not considered by them as symptomatic of any disorder.

In documenting the influence of culture on symptoms, Zola sampled patients seen in various outpatient clinics at the Massachusetts General Hospital, taking a special interest in the complaints which people of different ethnic background bring to the physician. In particular, he focused on 63 Italians and 81 Irish new-admissions of comparable age, education, and social class. Further analyses were performed on 37 diagnostically matched pairs of the same sex, primary diagnosis, chronicity, and physician-rated seriousness.

Starting with the question, "Where does it hurt?," the study found that the Irish were markedly more inclined to locate their problem in the eye, ear, nose, or throat. The Irish were, however, much more likely to say that the problem was not painful ("It was more a throbbing than a pain. It feels more like sand in my eye," p. 623). Moreover, the Irish described a specific problem; the Italians tended to report a diffuse difficulty. The Italians presented more symptoms, had complaints in more bodily locations, and indicated that they had more kinds of dysfunctions and more diffuse qualities of their condition.

From these findings, Zola speculated that "Italian and Irish ways of communicating illness may reflect major values and preferred ways of handling problems within the culture itself" (p. 626). Rather than being pain- or illness-specific, Zola felt that the number of symptoms and the spread of complaints may be understood in terms of a more generalized expressiveness. So, for the Italians, the complaints may relate to "their expansiveness so often [seen] in sociological, historical, and fictional writing;" a "well seasoned, dramatic emphasis to their lives" (p. 627). Taking a more Freudian tack, Zola suggested that overstatement of symptoms may reflect a defense mechanism of dramatization, a tendency to "cope with anxiety by repeatedly overexpressing it and thereby dissipating it" (p. 627).

The Irish view of life, Zola suggested (1966, p. 627), is more bleak ("long periods of routine followed by episodes of wild adventure"). It was as if "life was black and long-suffering and the less said the better." Consequently, a patient when asked about her reactions to the pain of her illness, stated, "I ignore it like I do most things," and Zola attributed a defense mechanism of denial to explain the Irish illness behavior.

Clearly, the psychodynamic perspective is debatable and dated and other theoretical positions have been proposed to explain related sorts of findings. Fabrega and Tyma (1976), for instance, provided a psycholinguistic basis for cultural differences in pain expression, noting that:

> In English, the process of metaphorization allows the speaker to qualify his experience in a vivid and direct manner ("I have a burning pain") and his overt behavior often reflects this qualification. The native Thai is not provided with this flexible device of metaphorization in describing his pain. It is possible that special qualities of Thai pain which are not rendered verbally are communicated nonverbally. (p. 329)

In Japanese, in contrast, the characterization of pain "is made along several axes, including intense vs. not intense, deep vs. shallow, horizontally-extended vs. horizontally-confined, and temporally-extended vs. temporally-bounded. Pain descriptions often implicate more than one quality" (p. 334). Fabrega and Tyma contrasted sentences roughly translated as "There is a pain deep inside my leg" and "There is a deep pain in my leg," which appear similar in English but have very different connotations to a native speaker of Japanese. "Whereas English pain quality is described through metaphor, Japanese qualities are described more 'naturally' through direct symbolizations of the experience. Elaboration of experiential properties through sound symbolism suggests an emphasis on the fleeting and formless aspects of pain" (p. 336). They concluded with several fascinating questions:

1. Is there a limited set of semantic categories that people and languages draw on to describe pain?
2. Do the pain behaviors of a people bear a relation to the models of pain which the culture imposes on people or to the grammatical rules and conventions which the language system imposes?
3. Which facets of a pain experience are communicated verbally and which ones nonverbally, and how do groups differ in the way they use these channels? Are there cultural invariants in any of these channels?

Mechanic (1972) presented an interesting social-learning perspective on the issue of bodily complaints: "From very young ages, children more or less learn to respond to various symptoms and feelings in terms of reactions of others to their behavior and social expectations in general" (p. 1135). He suggested that the different patterns of response to pain identified by Zborowski (1952) arose from different processes regarding symptom reporting and the search for medical assistance, as well as the willingness to accept psychological interpretations of their complaints. Unresolved then, and still now, is the question of whether the cultural differences noted in the literature are "a result of the fact that children with particular prior experiences and upbringing come to have more symptoms, interpret the same symptoms differently, express their concerns and seek help with greater willingness, or use a different vocabulary for expressing distress?" (p. 1136).

Pilowsky's (1975) Illness Behavior Questionnaire (IBQ) provides a means to quantify differences in some of these factors. The questionnaire has scores for each of seven factors, including general illness behavior, disease conviction and symptom preoccupation, ability to express personal feelings to others, and how illness affects the patient's relationship with family or friends. Although Pilowsky (1975) spoke of the relationship of illness behavior to cross-cultural differences in pain expression, a broad examination of IBQ scores across cultures has yet to be carried out.

Davitz, Sameshima, and Davitz (1976) put the emphasis on the attitudes of caregivers toward pain and suffering rather than those of the patient. They asked nearly 100 nurses in each of the United States, Japan, Taiwan, Thailand, Korea, and Puerto Rico to read descriptions of patients and to judge the amount of physical pain and psychological distress that the patients were experiencing. When faced with the same translations of case descriptions, Japanese and Korean nurses gave moderate ratings of physical pain (3.7 to 3.8 on a 7-point scale) while those from mainland United States and from Puerto Rico assigned low ratings (about 3.0). Likewise, Korean and

Japanese nurses attributed higher degrees of psychological distress to their patients, although, interestingly, so did the Puerto Rican nurses.

Davitz et al. (1976, p. 1297) interpreted these findings in light of "a common American stereotype about the stoicism of Orientals." They found that American nurses believe Asian patients feel far less pain than those from other ethnic backgrounds, whereas Asian nurses believe their patients are especially sensitive to physical pain. The authors suggested that Japanese culture emphasizes control of expressive behavior in spite of the experience of strong feelings, while Americans show greater congruence between internal experience and behavior. If so, they proposed, "American nurses might well reconsider their own beliefs about Oriental patients and make sure that their cultural stereotypes do not interfere with awareness of the pain their Oriental patients may be experiencing."

A somewhat related analysis of nursing assessments, in a very different cultural context, came from Calvillo and Flaskerud (1991). Observing, "cross-cultural studies have demonstrated that white Americans of Northern European origin react to pain stoically and as calmly as possible. This response to pain has become the cultural model or norm in the United States. It is the behavior expected and valued by health caregivers" (p. 16), the authors examined Mexican American pain expression. They began by noting that pain behaviors have to be viewed within a cultural context:

Many Mexican American patients, especially women, moan when uncomfortable. Consequently, they are often identified by the nursing staff as complainers who cannot tolerate pain. In the Mexican culture, crying out with pain is an acceptable expression and not synonymous with an inability to tolerate pain. Crying out with pain does not necessarily indicate that the pain experience is severe or that . . . the patient expects the nurse to intervene." (p. 20)

Calvill and Flaskerud went on to suggest that in the Mexican culture, crying and moaning may help the patient to relieve the pain rather than function as a request for intervention. Health practitioners, operating from the dominant-culture model of response to pain, may, improperly, interpret crying and moaning as an indication that the patients are dramatic, emotional complainers with an inability to manage pain. Accordingly, there is an important need to understand culturally determined attitudes and pain reactions.

Recently, Neill (1993) went back to the main population groupings used in Zborowski's (1969) classic study, looking only at Yankee, Irish, Italian, Jewish, and African American patients who had recently suffered an acute myocardial infarction. Numbers were small, ranging from 7 to 35 per group in a total sample of 89 subjects. Pain was rated on a modified version of the McGill Pain Questionnaire, in which subjects select which, if any, adjectives in 20 categories applied to the pain they suffered during their heart attacks. There were no significant differences. This is not surprising, given the small sample, but perhaps reflects, as well, the changes in American society over the past half-century.

Similar trends toward diminished differences among cultural groups in their attitudes about health and medical care were seen more than 20 years ago by Greenblum (1974). While there had been some reports that suggested that American Jews describe more symptoms and make greater use of medical facilities than others, Greenblum analyzed the data from later studies and concluded that "such distinctiveness is diminishing and may disappear as the relationship of American Jews to other ethnic groups and to the general society changes" (p. 127). He felt that immigrant groups, as they move higher on socioeconomic indices and become less insulated from general society, adopt the dominant medical perspective, and whatever differences existed in medical behavior diminish or disappear.

A number of factors contribute to this pattern of acculturation. Comparison processes are important, as shown in the well-known study by Lambert, Libman, and Poser (1960) in which Jewish and Protestant women at McGill University were tested for pain tolerance. There were no significant differences between them; however, when they were told that their own religious group was less able to withstand pain than other groups, only the Jewish subjects, who came from a cultural minority group, showed a significant elevation in tolerance on subsequent tests of pain responsiveness.

CHRONIC PAIN

Laboratory experiments and many of the studies on clinical pain focus on pain that is relatively brief in duration. The psychological reactions to chronic pain—pain lasting longer than a few months—are very different. Many other aspects of the patient's life are affected: ability to work or enjoy recreational activities, financial status, relationships with family members and friends, self-esteem, degree of depression, and capacity to plan for the future. Often, the pain, while strong and ever-present, becomes a secondary problem to severe psychological distress. Moreover, analgesic drugs, which often function well in attenuating acute or recurrent pain, are typically ineffectual in reducing chronic pain.

Most of the studies that have examined clinical pain reactions in different cultural groups have looked at acute pain—childbirth, postoperative pain, dental pain, and the like. Some recent studies, however, have begun to contrast pain complaints and reactions among individuals from different cultures who suffer from chronic pain.

One problem, of course, is to find diagnostic instruments, whether aimed at eliciting information about pain or illness behavior, that are available for use in different cultures. This is not a trivial problem. Although there are measuring tools such as visual analogue scales, in which patients are asked to mark their degree of pain on a 10- or 15-cm line, perhaps with "no pain" written at the left and "pain as strong as I can imagine" on the right, there has been little research done to examine whether these instructions are interpreted equally across cultures (Aun, Lam, & Collett, 1986) and whether patients understand the distinction between their level of discomfort (a sensory response) and how they feel (which is strongly dependent on affective and cognitive components).

Other pain scales are generally verbal in nature, such as the McGill Pain Questionnaire (MPQ) which asks subjects to indicate which of a large number of adjectives describe their pain. The MPQ has been translated into a number of foreign languages (Arabic, Chinese, Flemish, Finnish, French, German, Italian, Japanese, Norwegian, Polish, Slovak, and Spanish; Melzack & Katz, 1992; Naughton & Wiklund, 1993), but generally it has been used to assess pain within a single cultural setting rather than across several.

Brena, Sanders, and Motoyama (1990) undertook a study of medical, psychological, social, and general behavioral functioning of low-back-pain patients and normal controls in the United States and Japan. The numbers were small (about 10 in each of the four groups), but there were some interesting results, particularly with regard to scores on the Sickness Impact Profile (SIP). This questionnaire contains statements about impairment in 12 categories (such as mobility, social interaction, emotional behavior, sleep, and recreational activities) that can yield scores on three major subscales (Physical, Psychosocial, Other) and an overall score.

While the Japanese and American back-pain patients had similar scores on the Physical subscale, there were differences on the others, with the American patients indicating greater levels of impairment on Psychosocial factors and on work, recreation, sleep, and home management.

The authors considered a number of factors that may account for their results. One possibility is that the questions themselves are interpreted differently across cultures (although the fact that the control groups had similar scores mitigates against this). Brena et al. (1990) suggested that more likely explanations included greater acceptance of a pain problem and enhanced coping skills in a society that values stoicism. Another possibility is that a stoic, ethnically homogeneous society may be less accepting of pain-related impairments. Alternatively, greater family unity, social stability, and "traditional reciprocal loyalty between employers and employees" in Japan may reduce the anxiety associated with a chronic problem and motivate Japanese employees to maintain their vocational and psychosocial function despite physical challenges (p. 123).

This raises a fascinating question for the growing field of medical anthropology (Helman, 1994), addressed by Bates, Rankin-Hill, Sanchez-Ayendez, and Mendez-Bryan (1995), "How do cultural beliefs, values, attitudes, and standards of patients and health care providers influence patients' abilities to cope with their chronic conditions?" (p. 142). Bates et al. looked at numerous aspects of adaptation among chronic pain patients seen at outpatient medical centers in New England and Puerto Rico (100 patients at each), including pain intensity, behavioral responses, attitudinal and emotional responses, and overall adaptation.

Patients in both settings suffered from a variety of chronic disorders such as arthritis, back pain, and nerve damage. Both questionnaire data and in-depth interviews led the investigators to conclude that Yankee Anglo American patients are inexpressive about pain, reluctant to seek psychological explanations for pain (or to accept psychological counseling), likely to endorse a "biomedical world view of the body as a machine-like entity separate from the mind" (p. 150) and have a tendency to hide pain from family and friends by "going off" to be alone.

In contrast, many Puerto Ricans made valiant efforts to continue to work or to keep house (and to suffer extreme distress when that is not possible), to maintain family relationships, and often to express pain openly by wincing, groaning, and describing their pain in emotional terms. Clearly, though, there were sizable degrees of variation within each cultural group.

Analysis of the questionnaire data from low-back-pain patients indicated markedly higher scores for the Puerto Rican patients on the MPQ, on measures of expressiveness, depression, worry, tension, and unhappiness, and perceived disability. Despite this, there were no differences in interference with work, social, or family activities.

The intragroup variation provided some data that deserve consideration for understanding cross-cultural differences. Those who sought pain relief through their own efforts showed less pain than those who relied upon the actions of medical personnel. Those with higher levels of education and income reported less pain. Among Puerto Ricans, those who had greater social support from family and friends were more likely to remain at work. Patients receiving workers' compensation reported greater work stoppage and less confidence in their ability to overcome the pain problem.

These findings indicate that an examination of cross-cultural differences in pain is not simply a matter of looking at pain ratings in a variety of countries or cultural settings. The differences in pain behavior, where they exist, are unlikely to be due to genetics and are not caused by the drinking water. To understand ethnocultural differences, it is necessary to examine the cultures themselves—child-rearing practices, family structure, social support, health care, rate of unemployment, political environment, disability compensation, and opportunities for rehabilitation.

CHILDREN AND PAIN

Given the psychosocial perspective on cultural differences in pain, it would be interesting to look for evidence concerning pain experiences in children. This is an issue made all the more difficult because of the problems in assessing pain in a pediatric population. Recent years have seen numerous advances in developing physiological measures, behavioral observations, and self-reports, including analysis of facial expressions, scales involving faces and colors, and examination of drawings.

Little attention has been paid to the need to validate these scales in different cultural settings. Villarruel and Denyes (1991) found that the demonstration of adequate psychometric properties was still not sufficient for nurses to adopt such scales; they wanted measures which demonstrated cultural relevance or sensitivity.

Consequently, Villarruel and Denyes undertook to develop alternative versions of the "Oucher" scale for Hispanic and African American children. The Oucher comprises a series of six photographs of a 4-year-old White boy showing facial expressions indicating various levels of pain. A pediatric patient is asked to point to the picture which best reflects his or her own level of hurt.

Using photographs of Hispanic and African American children, taken when they were or were not experiencing pain, the authors established an ordering of six photographs that other children could agree represented a progression of pain expression. It remains to be established whether this particular measure will reveal any cross-cultural differences in children's pain levels; whether scales tailored to ethnic origin or race, while culturally sensitive, aid in either pain assessment or in strengthening communication between health practitioners and children of different cultural groups; and whether more neutral measures (such as "happy face" drawings) can achieve both validity and universality in pain assessment.

Abu-Saad (1984) conducted semistructured interviews with Arab American, Asian American, and Latin American school children (24 in each group, aged 9–12 years) to ask about what caused pain for them, what words they used to describe pain ("like a hurt" was the most common descriptor in each group), how they felt when they are in pain, and how they coped with pain. Given that all lived in the same urban environment, the finding that the similarities among the subjects are considerably greater than the differences is not surprising. Nonetheless, studies such as this, if conducted among children residing in different cultural settings and varying in age, may help to identify factors that underlie apparent differences among adults in pain behaviors. They will also advance our understanding of the speed of cultural diffusion or adaptation. Pfefferbaum, Adams, and Aceves (1990) studied pain and anxiety in 37 Hispanic and 35 Anglo children with cancer at a hospital in Texas. The children were very similar in their behavioral responses. It was the parents who differed, with the Hispanic parents reporting significantly higher levels of anxiety than the Anglo ones.

PAIN AND WOMEN

A number of recent studies have focused on cultural aspects of special pain problems related to women. Shye and Jaffe (1991) found sociocultural factors influenced premenstrual symptoms among a sample of 545 Israeli teenagers. Girls of Asian/African ethnic origin reported significantly higher prevalence of backache, bloating, fatigue, breast tenderness, and depression than those of Israeli or Western origin. Likewise, the incidence of dysmenorrhea (painful menstruation) was appreciably higher among the girls of Asian/African cultural origin. Interestingly, the authors looked for other correlates of these pain reports and found that they showed a negative relationship with the mother's educational level. Girls whose mothers had less than 8 years of education had more premenstrual symptoms and more reported pain than those whose mothers had medium or high educational levels. However, when maternal educational level was controlled for, girls whose mothers had immigrated from the Near East or North Africa still had higher reported levels of reported symptoms. Shye and Jaffe felt that the mothers had come from societies which dictated a "traditional, family-oriented role for women" and that their daughters, although born in Israel, "would normally have assimilated many elements of their mothers' orientations" (p. 222).

Beyene (1986) examined cultural differences in the perception and experience of the other end of the fertility cycle, menopause. In an attempt to identify physiological and sociocultural factors related to menopause symptoms (hot flashes are typically associated with this biological transition, while fatigue, irritability, depression, and general emotional problems are much more variable), Beyene sought information from ethnographic sources about the natural history of menopause in "cultures which are significantly unlike those of Western industrialized societies" (p. 49).

The analysis of the literature suggested that "menopause is conditioned by the cultural content which shapes the pattern of a woman's roles" (p. 48). For example, in societies where postmenopausal women are released from some of the taboos and social sanctions associated with female roles (allowing them to go unveiled or able to participate in talking or drinking with men), women experience few of the symptoms which Western women associate with menopause.

Beyene obtained data from rural Mayan Indians in Yucatan, Mexico, and from rural Greek women on the island of Evia, spending 12 months at each site talking to women and to healers and other medical personnel. She was able to conduct life history interviews with about 100 older women in each village, one third of whom were each premenopausal, menopausal, and postmenopausal (more than a year since the cessation of menstruation). Evidence indicated that Mayan women showed almost no symptoms associated with menopause other than irregularity and then cessation of menses. They did not report hot flashes or emotional disturbances.

The rural Greek women, unlike the Mayan women, felt free from taboos and restrictions, but they "associated menopause with growing old, not having energy, and a general downhill life course" (p. 63). For them, more than 70% had hot flashes, and large numbers had headaches, dizziness, and insomnia.

The findings are noteworthy, because they challenge the generally held assumption that hot flashes are inevitable symptoms arising from declining estrogen levels. Before concluding, however, that physiological symptoms are strongly dependent upon social and cultural factors, Beyene (1986) cautioned that it is necessary to conduct further studies to elaborate the role of differences in nutrition, fertility patterns (Mayan women marry early, have repeated pregnancies, and prolonged lactation), and genetics.

A number of studies have been focused on cultural factors associated with childbirth pain. Morse (1989) found that female and male Fijians of native ancestry associate much more pain with childbirth than do Fijians of East Indian ancestry. Weisenberg and Caspi (1989), noting that comparison with others helps to determine what reactions are appropriate to pain and that "the family of origin teaches the person appropriate behaviors" (p. 14), examined the influence of cultural group on the reaction to childbirth pain. They studied 83 Israeli women who came from two groups, one with mothers born in Europe, the United States, or another English-speaking country, and the second whose mothers came from Asia, North Africa, or the Middle East.

Weisenberg and Caspi felt that women of Middle Eastern background, given to greater expression of feelings and emotions, would score higher on Eysenck's extroversion scale and would show greater expressions of pain. However, since an earlier study (Barak & Weisenberg, 1988) found that Middle Eastern women showed a tendency to endorse items more in the direction of denying, wanting to be rid of, and not willing to cope with pain, they predicted a greater use of denial or emotion-reducing strategies rather than active coping.

Women undergoing delivery completed a visual analogue scale to rate their pain at three points during labor. In addition, observers rated various types of behavior, including crying, cursing, twisting in bed, hair pulling, and loss of control. Several days later, the women completed the Eysenck Personality Inventory and a coping scale. The mean pain ratings were high for both groups, but higher for the Middle Eastern women. Those Middle Eastern women with greater levels of education indicated significantly less pain than those with 12 years or less of schooling; there was no effect of education for the Western women.

Likewise, women of Middle Eastern origin showed more observable pain behavior during labor, a measure which was also moderated by educational level. Extroversion and coping scores did not differ between the groups or predict pain behavior. The authors concluded that "educational influences can change the original contribution of family of origin on the reaction to pain" (p. 117). So, too, did participation in a prepared childbirth course. Consequently, factors such as degree of education, training in coping skills, and economic level may be more important than cultural group, at least when women in the same society are considered.

Sometimes, cultural studies have focused in interesting ways on attitudes toward pain as a moderator variable rather than as an outcome measure (Stein, Fox, & Murata, 1991). Studies in the United States have shown that women are reluctant to be screened for breast cancer with mammography, with African Americans and Hispanic women particularly underutilizing the technique. A number of factors may contribute to their behavior, such as economic and educational disadvantages, level of knowledge about cancer, and access to medical insurance, but many women avoid mammograms even when they are readily available at no cost. Stein et al. (1991) identified five possible barriers to the use of mammography: embarrassment, fear of radiation, fear of pain, anxiety about effectiveness, and concern about cost.

They interviewed 1,000 women about their attitudes and concerns. Four of the barriers, embarrassment, radiation, pain, and cost, were significant negative predictors of having a mammogram. African American and Hispanic women were particularly worried about pain during the procedure, giving higher predictions than the White women about the level of pain and giving markedly higher scores on a scale measuring whether pain keeps them from having a mammogram. The authors, understandably, called for "more effort to recognize differences in tolerance for pain and to inform Black and Hispanic women that mammograms usually are not reported to be especially painful and that they take only a few minutes to be performed" (p. 110). Presumably, these recommendations would be echoed by Weller and Hener (1993), who found that Israeli women born in North Africa and Asia reported significantly higher levels of state anxiety than those born in Western countries when awaiting such medical procedures as ultrasound, mammography, or a cervical examination.

The use of good sense is not limited to treating women or to using these medical procedures. Weisenberg, Kriendler, Schachat, and Werboff (1975), after finding that Hispanic dental patients showed higher levels of anxiety than African American or White patients, suggested that tailored anxiety-reduction procedures, implemented by a Spanish-speaking dentist, would help to eliminate their concern. In relation to this, Moore, Miller, Weinstein, & Dworkin (1986) concluded that "pain as a purely physical sensation can no longer serve as the pivotal pain research construct" (p. 332) after showing that dental patients and dentists from various cultural groups differed both in the characteristics of the pain experience that they ranked as important and in the drugs, procedures, and psychological techniques they adopted as useful coping remedies.

EPIDEMIOLOGICAL STUDIES

Many of the studies reported in this chapter are based on measurements, whether psychophysical, clinical, or psychological, obtained from relatively small samples. There have been a number of reports of the incidence of pain across cultural groups for large populations. Ziegler (1990) reviewed the literature concerning the prevalence of headache in various cultures. His report contains numerous interesting anecdotal observations. Although the incidence of headache complaints is relatively high in Western societies, one study from Zimbabwe claimed "headache, a common problem elsewhere, will rarely be complained of" (p. 783). Another said, "Migraine is very uncommon and only one or two cases are seen each year" (p. 783). However, a third study done in Zimbabwe found that it is not the number of people suffering from headaches that is low but the number who have sought help for their problem from either physicians or traditional healers. Epidemiological studies need to be carried out in the community rather than in doctors' offices. Moreover, in Africa, as elsewhere, the incidence of headache complaints differs in rural and urban settings, suggesting that the nature of the population sampled, the characteristics of the interview and questionnaire forms, and local values ("the admission of recurrent pain without obvious cause might carry some social stigma in certain groups" (p. 784) contribute to the incidence of pain complaints and make it difficult to obtain truly accurate cross-cultural information.

CANCER PAIN

International studies of cancer pain have received increasing emphasis in recent years, since the World Health Organization established a cancer pain relief program to improve the care, particularly pain relief, of terminally ill patients. Cleeland, Ladinshi, Serlin, and Thuy (1988) noted that an important issue is the selection of an instrument to measure pain relief that is:

> short enough to be completed by seriously ill cancer patients, samples the severity of the patient's pain and the impact that the pain has upon major dimensions of the patient's life, and is constructed in a manner that allows for comparisons of pain severity and impact across different languages and cultures." (pp. 23–24)

Cleeland et al. (1988) undertook, in the United States and Vietnam, an evaluation of the Brief Pain Inventory (ratings of the past week's pain, using 0–10 scales to indicate "worst," "least," "average," and current pain levels, plus similar ratings of how the pain interferes with activity, walking, mood, sleep, work, and relations with others). In the two countries, there were differences in the analgesic available to treat the patients: 71% of the American sample received codeine, morphine, and related potent compounds, while none of the sample from Hanoi received an analgesic stronger than aspirin (and 64% received none). Not surprisingly, the Vietnamese sample reported high levels of pain. The Vietnamese, however, showed no difference from the Americans in the measures of how pain interfered with their quality of life, a remarkable finding that deserves further attention.

Related data from another Eastern culture were presented by Kodiath and Kodiath (1995). Half a million new cancer cases per year are reported in India, most of which are inadequately treated. The authors observed, for several hours per day, small numbers of cancer-pain patients in the United States and India and interviewed family, friends, and physicians. They concluded that the "patients from the United States felt that they received significant pain relief at all stages. The greatest challenge for them was coping with the reality of a terminal illness, and pain was a minor component of that phenomenon" (p. 193). The Indian patients, often diagnosed only when the pain had become excruciating and faced with a limited number of therapeutic alternatives, suffered badly. They "often mentioned 'wanting to die' because the experience of pain was almost unbearable" (p. 194), but "their emphasis is not on how long but how well one lives" (p. 196) and, in the authors' view, " South Asian patients with cancer emphasize the spiritual aspects of quality of life as being more important than physical functioning" (p. 194).

As part of the developing specialty of "psychooncology," attitudes of physicians and family members in different countries have been compared. In many countries, both groups are reluctant to tell the patient that he or she has cancer, leading Die Trill and Holland (1993) to conclude that there are constraints imposed by cultural norms on the way information about the disease is conveyed. The authors focused on the dilemma faced by patients who are immigrants: "They may bury the past, sometimes under the pressure to accommodate to the new situation" (p. 26). For those who immigrated late in life, "it is not uncommon for younger family members who are usually better adjusted to the new culture to feel burdened with the patient's medical and psychological needs. This attitude may also foster intergenerational conflicts in the context of illness" (p. 26).

Garro (1990) reviewed a number of culturally based dimensions of the response to cancer pain. Many factors play critical influences. As noted earlier, language is one. English has a number of pain terms, some languages have more than a dozen, others have only one. More important, perhaps, are cultural reactions to the patient suffering from cancer. The North American "message of hope" is contrasted with the Japanese tendency to withhold the diagnosis of cancer from the patient ("if the patients know the diagnosis they would give up hope and soon die," p. 42). Pain evaluation and management cannot be separated from its cultural context. Garro concluded that "if caretakers focus exclusively on bodily pain, and ignore the cultural and personal meanings of illness, the inadvertent result of attempts to relieve suffering may be to increase it" (p. 42).

RECONCEPTUALIZATION OF THE ISSUES

To ask whether culture affects pain perception is to ask too simple a question. The complexities of dealing with both culture and pain do not allow such a direct framing of the relationship between the two.

Too often, researchers have made broad generalizations based upon samples of convenience, testing small numbers of persons from some local immigrant community (who have learned the researcher's language, although it is uncertain that they fully understand the often complex experimental instructions or questionnaires), and declaring that persons of culture X are more stoical than those of culture Y. This approach violates rules of sampling. Recruitment issues have received scant attention. We need to look at the factors which inhibit the inclusion of persons from various cultural or language groups in medical and psychological studies.

Moreover, persons of culture X are not all alike. They have many more differences between them than they have similarities. The definition of ethnocultural status requires more attention, particularly in our mobile society. Consider an Ethiopian Jew living in Israel: African, Black, Jewish, and Israeli. Her pain reactions are influenced by many cultures but not circumscribed by any of them. Her daughter will also be Black, Jewish, and Israeli, sharing some cultural characteristics with her, but shaped by other ones as well.

Many problems exist at the pain measurement side of the relationship. Not enough attention has been paid to the differences among laboratory-induced pain, acute pain, recurrent pain, and chronic pain. There are few assessment tools that have been validated across cultural settings. Too much emphasis has been placed on the sensory component of pain, which is not particularly reactive to culture, rather than the more interesting and important affective and cognitive components. We are largely ignorant of the interactive effects of ethnocultural membership of the experimenter and the subject in pain studies; certainly, the great majority of studies on racial or ethnic minorities have been conducted by White investigators.

Too many studies have sought racially or ethnically-based genetic differences in pain expression. There have been some exciting animal studies demonstrating selective breeding of mice with high and low levels of analgesia induced by stress and differential response to morphine (e.g., Mogil et al., 1996), but these findings have implications for understanding individual differences within an ethnocultural group rather than between groups.

Some recent studies of pain responsiveness have been motivated by directives from granting agencies to select diverse populations differing in such characteristics as race. The U.S. National Institutes of Health sought to support research initiatives on health promotion and disease prevention involving African American, Asian American, Native American, Pacific Islander, and Hispanic children. While it is essential to ensure that there are no adverse reactions to drugs among persons of certain ethnic or racial background and to understand the psychosocial factors related to health across ethnocultural (as well as geographic) boundaries, differences in pain behaviors among groups are much more likely due to such factors as education, economic status, and access to medical and social support than to racial or ethnic composition. Moreover, it is folly to lump all persons of Asian extraction together into a single category; there are many cultural, linguistic, and religious differences among persons of Chinese, Vietnamese, Malaysian, and Japanese backgrounds.

A biopsychosocial perspective recognizes that a large number of factors influence individual and group differences in behavior. While biological influences must account for some of the differences between individuals, there is no indication of genetic differences in pain responsiveness across racial or cultural groups.

Such differences that do exist are almost certainly based upon psychological and social characteristics. Further research, using psycholinguistic, social learning, and cognitive perspectives will help to shed light on understanding differences in what people consider to be painful and how they respond.

Future investigations should consider a model such as the following for analyses of group differences in pain responsiveness. Individuals will differ with respect to:

1. Monitoring—the extent to which they pay attention to internal bodily events;
2. Symptom attribution—the extent to which they consider bodily events as indicative of a dysfunction rather than a normal biological process;
3. Coping mechanisms—the manner in which individuals deal with negative events, including their dependence on other individuals (such as health care providers) and agents (such as analgesics) rather than internal psychological processes;
4. Somatization—the extent to which negative psychological events and cognitions contribute to increased reports of physical discomfort.

The nature of the interactions between these processes and the factors which give rise to different patterns of response remain to be determined. Some researchers have begun to examine ethnocultural differences in such psychological variables as locus of control (Bates & Rankin-Hill, 1994) and coping and adaptation (Bates et al., 1995). These lines of investigation are crucial; evidence indicates that some patterns of coping among pain patients, such as praying and hoping, which are certainly influenced by culture, are maladaptive.

Three issues remain. First, are there cultural differences in monitoring, symptom attribution, coping, somatization, and other personality variables? Second, if the answer is yes, how do they influence pain behaviors (and, for that matter, other behaviors; groups that differ in the expression of pain will almost certainly also differ in the expression of anger, joy, depression, and a whole range of human emotions)? Third, what are the psychosocial factors that give rise to these behavior patterns?

Many other questions follow. What is the meaning of cultural differences in emotionality (Lipton & Marbach, 1984)? How important is the link between somatizing behavior and membership in a culture that deemphasizes emotional displays (Ford, 1995)? What should we make of the finding that older and female medical patients may carry on ethnic traditions longer than younger and male ones (Koopman, Eisenthal, & Stoeckle, 1984)? What are the interactions between culture, gender, and age in pain behavior? Given that individual factors are of the greatest importance in accounting for pain, how do cultural factors contribute to the variability (Streltzer & Wade, 1981)? Since immigrant males are often only able to get work which is physically challenging and monotonous, should we be surprised that they are at greater risk for injury, difficult to rehabilitate, and more likely to depend upon compensation (Keel & Calanchini, 1989)? Does heavy physical work lead to a high criterion for reporting pain (as suggested, for example, in a study of Nepalese mountain-climbing porters conducted by Clark & Clark, 1980)?

Will trends toward urbanization and Westernization lead to conformity in pain behaviors across cultures? How quickly will the processes of assimilation and acculturation work to create a form of regression to the mean among immigrant populations? Why has there been so much emphasis on cultural differences in pain when it is likely that equally dramatic differences exist in displays of other behaviors, such as happiness, affection, or grief?

These are not just academic questions. Adequate assessment and management of pain are critical issues. Pain provides an enormous challenge for the patient, his or her family, the medical system, and society (Melzack & Wall, 1988). Moreover, the reduction of pain can influence not only the quality of life but also longevity. Recent animal data indicate that pain inhibits the activity of natural killer cells in the immune system that act against tumor growth (Liebeskind, 1991).

Assessment and management depend upon communication that is free from bias. Among the prime impediments to satisfactory treatment are the assumptions among many practitioners that some cultures are insensitive to pain or that the reports of individuals from other cultures are exaggerated and thus can be discounted. Such stereotypes have no place in medicine or psychology. Pain is experienced by individuals, not by groups. If an individual describes himself or herself as being in pain, there is an obligation to accept that report and to take action to ameliorate the resulting distress.

References

Abbey, S. E., & Garfinkel, P. E. (1992). Neurasthenia and chronic fatigue syndrome: The role of culture in the making of a diagnosis. *American Journal of Psychiatry, 149,* 1638–1646.

Abu-Saad, H. (1984). Cultural group indicators of pain in children. *Maternal Child Nursing Journal, 13,* 187–196.

Aun, C., Lam, Y. M., & Collett, B. (1986). Evaluation of the use of visual analogue scale in Chinese patients. *Pain, 25,* 215–221.

Barak, E., & Weisenberg, M. (1988). Anxiety and attitudes toward pain as a function of ethnic group and socioeconomic status. *Clinical Journal of Pain, 3,* 189–196.

Bates, M. S., & Rankin-Hill, L. (1994). Control, culture and chronic pain. *Social Science and Medicine, 39,* 629–645.

Bates, M. S., Rankin-Hill, L., Sanchez-Ayendez, M., & Mendez-Bryan, R. (1995). A cross-cultural comparison of adaptation to chronic pain among Anglo-Americans and native Puerto Ricans. *Medical Anthropology, 16,* 141–173.

Beyene, Y. (1986). Cultural significance and physiological manifestations of menopause: A biocultural analysis. *Culture, Medicine & Psychiatry, 10,* 47–71.

Brena, S. F., Sanders, S. H., & Motoyama, H. (1990). American and Japanese chronic low back pain patients: Cross-cultural similarities and differences. *Clinical Journal of Pain, 6,* 118–124.

Calvillo, E. R., & Flaskerud, J. H. (1991). Review of literature on culture and pain of adults with focus on Mexican-Americans. *Journal of Transcultural Nursing, 2,* 16–23.

Chapman, W. P., & Jones, C. M. (1944). Variations in cutaneous and visceral pain sensitivity in normal subjects. *Journal of Clinical Investigation, 23,* 81–91.

Clark, W. C., & Clark, S. B. (1980). Pain responses in Nepalese porters. *Science, 209,* 410–411.

Cleeland, C. S., Ladinshi, J. L., Serlin, R. C., & Thuy, N. C. (1988). Multidimensional measurement of cancer pain: Comparisons of US and Vietnamese patients. *Journal of Pain and Symptom Management, 3,* 23–27.

Davitz, L. J., Sameshima, Y., & Davitz, J. (1976). Suffering as viewed in six different cultures. *American Journal of Nursing, 76,* 1296–1297.

Die Trill, M., & Holland, J. C. (1993). Cross-cultural differences in the care of patients with cancer: A review. *General Hospital Psychiatry, 15,* 21–30.

Fabrega, H., & Tyma, S. (1976). Culture, language and the shaping of illness: An illustration based on pain. *Journal of Psychosomatic Medicine, 20,* 323–337.

Ford, C. V. (1995). Dimensions of somatization and hypochondriasis. *Neurologic Clinics, 13,* 241–253.

Garro, L. C. (1990). Culture, pain and cancer. *Journal of Palliative Care, 6,* 34–44.

Greenblum, J. (1974). Medical and health orientations of American Jews: A case of diminishing distinctiveness. *Social Science and Medicine, 8,* 127–134.

Hardy, J. D., Wolff, H. G., & Goodell, H. (1952). *Pain sensations and reactions.* Baltimore: Williams & Wilkins.

Helman, C. G. (1994). *Culture, health and illness.* Oxford, England: Butterworth Heinemann.

Keel, P., & Calanchini, C. (1989). Chronische Ruckenschmerzen bei Gastarbeitern aus Mittelmeerlandern im Vergleich zu Patienten aus Mitteleuropa: demographische und psychosoziale Aspekte. *Schweizerische Medizinische Wochenschrift, 119,* 22–31.

Kodiath, M. F., & Kodiath, A. (1995). A comparative study of patients who experience chronic malignant pain in India and the United States. *Cancer Nursing, 18,* 189–196.

Koopman, C., Eisenthal, S., & Stoeckle, J. D. (1984). Ethnicity in the reported pain, emotional distress and requests of medical outpatients. *Social Science and Medicine, 18,* 487–490.

Lambert, W. E., Libman, E., & Poser, E. G. (1960). The effect of increased salience of a membership group on pain tolerance. *Journal of Personality, 28,* 350–357.

Liebeskind, J. C. (1991). Pain can kill. *Pain, 44,* 3–4.

Lipton, J. A., & Marbach, J. J. (1984). Ethnicity and the pain experience. *Social Science and Medicine, 19,* 1279–1298.

Mechanic, D. (1972). Social psychologic factors affecting the presentation of bodily complaints. *New England Journal of Medicine, 286,* 1132–1139.

Melzack, R., & Katz, J. (1992). The McGill Pain Questionnaire: Appraisal and current status. In D. C. Turk, & R. Melzack (Eds.), *Handbook of pain assessment* (pp. 152–168). New York: Guilford Press.

Melzack, R., & Wall, P. D. (1988). *The challenge of pain* (2nd Ed.). London: Penguin.

Mogil, J. S., Sternberg, W. F., Marek, P., Sadowski, B., Belknap, J. K., & Liebeskind, J. C. (1996). The genetics of pain and pain inhibition. *Proceedings of the National Academy of Sciences of the United States of America, 93,* 3048–3055.

Moore, R. A., Miller, M. L., Weinstein, P., & Dworkin, S. F. (1986). Cultural perceptions of pain and pain coping among patients and dentists. *Community Dentistry and Oral Epidemiology, 14,* 327–333.

Morse, J. M. (1989). Cultural variation in behavioral response to parturition: Childbirth in Fiji. *Medical Anthropology, 12,* 35–54.

Naughton, M. J., & Wiklund, I. (1993). A critical review of dimension-specific measures of health-related quality of life in cross-cultural research. *Quality of Life Research: An International Journal of Quality of Life Aspects of Treatment, Care and Rehabilitation, 2,* 397–432.

Neill, K. M. (1993). Ethnic pain styles in acute myocardial infarction [Response]. *Western Journal of Nursing Research, 15,* 531–543.

Pfefferbaum, B., Adams, J., & Aceves, J. (1990). The influence of culture on pain in Anglo and Hispanic children with cancer. *Journal of the American Academy of Child and Adolescent Psychiatry, 29,* 642–647.

Pilowsky, I. (1975). Dimensions of abnormal illness behavior. *Australian and New Zealand Journal of Psychiatry, 9,* 141–147.

Rollman, G. B. (1995). Gender differences in pain: The role of anxiety. *Pain Forum, 4,* 331–334.

Shye, D., & Jaffe, B. (1991). Prevalence and correlates of perimenstrual symptoms: A study of Israeli teenage girls. *Journal of Adolescent Health, 12,* 217–224.

Stein, J. A., Fox, S. A., & Murata, P. J. (1991). The influence of ethnicity, socioeconomic status, and psychological barriers on use of mammography. *Journal of Health and Social Behavior, 32,* 101–113.

Sternbach, R. A., & Tursky, B. (1965). Ethnic differences among housewives in psychophysical and skin potential responses to electric shock. *Psychophysiology, 1,* 241–246.

Streltzer, J., & Wade, T. C. (1981). The influence of cultural group on the undertreatment of postoperative pain. *Psychosomatic Medicine, 43,* 397–403.

Tursky, B., & Sternbach, R. A. (1967). Further physiological correlates of ethnic differences in responses to shock. *Psychophysiology, 4,* 67–74.

Villarruel, A. M., & Denyes, M. J. (1991). Pain assessment in children: Theoretical and empirical validity. *Advances in Nursing Science, 14,* 32–41.

Ware, N. C., & Kleinman, A. (1992). Culture and somatic experience: The social course of illness in neurasthenia and chronic fatigue syndrome. *Psychosomatic Medicine, 54,* 546–560.

Weisenberg, M., & Caspi, Z. (1989). Cultural and educational influences on pain of childbirth. *Journal of Pain and Symptom Management, 4,* 13–19.

Weisenberg, M., Kriendler, M. L., Schachat, R., & Werboff, J. (1975). Pain, anxiety and attitudes in Black, white and Puerto Rican patients. *Psychosomatic Medicine, 37,* 123–135.

Weller, A., & Hener, T. (1993). Invasiveness of medical procedures and state anxiety in women. *Behavioral Medicine, 19,* 60–65.

Winsberg, B., & Greenlick, M. (1967). Pain response in Negro and white obstetrical patients. *Journal of Health and Social Behavior, 8,* 222–228.

Wolff, B. B. (1985). Ethnocultural factors influencing pain and illness behavior. *Clinical Journal of Pain, 1,* 23–30.

Wolff, B. B., & Langley, S. (1968). Cultural factors and the response to pain: A review. *American Anthropologist, 70,* 494–501.

Zatzick, D. F., & Dimsdale, J. E. (1990). Cultural variations in response to painful stimuli. *Psychosomatic Medicine, 52,* 544–557.

Zborowski, M. (1952). Cultural components in responses to pain. *Journal of Social Issues, 8,* 16–30.

Zborowski, M. (1969). *People in pain.* San Francisco: Jossey-Bass.

Ziegler, D. K. (1990). Headache: Public health problem. *Neurologic Clinics, 8,* 781–791.

Zola, I. K. (1966). Culture and symptoms—An analysis of patients' presenting complaints. *American Sociological Review, 31,* 615–630.

PART IV

GROUPS OF SPECIAL INTEREST

11

Culture and Child Psychopathology

BARRIE EVANS

BETTY KAMAN LEE

Although cultural factors have received some attention from clinicians, counselors, therapists, and educators over the past 15 years in the United States and Canada (Chodzinski, 1985; Christmas, 1982; Foster & Ferman, 1982; Pedersen, 1985; Solomon, 1982), most relevant research on culture and psychopathology has been focused on adults (Al-Issa, 1982; Draguns, 1982). Also many of the findings are contradictory and are lacking an organizing theoretical framework (Beiser, Dion, Gotowiec, Hyman, & Vu, 1995). The *Handbook of Child Psychopathology* (2nd ed., Ollendick & Hersen, 1989), a frequently used advanced textbook on the subject, devotes little over a half page to a discussion of factors related to "ethnic derivation and socioeconomic status." In the recent *Handbook of Child Behavior Therapy in the Psychiatric Setting* (Ammerman & Hersen, 1995), there are no references in the subject index either to "culture" or "ethnicity." Also, Vargas and Willis (1994) had planned a special issue of the *Journal of Clinical Child Psychology* devoted entirely to the treatment and assessment of ethnic minority children and adolescents. Because of a lack of submissions, they were able to produce only a special section and not an entire issue. As these authors point out, mental health services to culturally diverse children, youth, and families are increasing and will be provided largely by practitioners who are not members of these cultural groups. It is therefore vitally important that researchers and practitioners gain the knowledge to equip themselves to develop and implement culturally sensitive and appropriate services. They also comment that, because of secular trends and political and social pressures, professional practice has had to forge ahead to develop culturally appropriate services despite the paucity of theory, conceptualization, or research that can serve to inform it. For example, in Ontario,

Canada, provincial licensing and accreditation standards for children's mental health centers set requirements for culturally sensitive and culturally appropriate care and treatment for individual clients (Ontario Association of Children's Mental Health Centers [OCMHC], 1996).

Although interest has been increasing recently, research is still sparse. It would, however, be misleading to leave the impression that there is no mental health literature (some of it touching on childhood disorders) pertaining to culture. The field of family therapy, for example, has been quite sophisticated in its understanding and application of cultural factors in family work by mental health professionals. An early but still valuable resource for clinicians with a wealth of descriptive information about families in different cultures is *Ethnicity and Family Therapy* (McGoldrick, Pearce, & Giordano, 1982). Case reports and nonexperimental clinical studies of the influence of cultural factors continue to dot the landscape of the family therapy literature. These case studies and descriptive reports give testimony to the importance of taking into account culturally specific factors in understanding family functioning. In many cases, these reports suggest that the key to successful treatment outcomes in otherwise unfathomable cases can be found in a culturally specific approach to therapy (e.g., Koizumi & Luidens, 1984).

Another area of practice in which cultural factors have been considered is the area of psychometric assessment. Psychologists have made a unique contribution to the field of childhood psychopathology in the development and application of standardized assessment measures and tools. Culture-fair intelligence and ability tools have had a fairly lengthy history. The prototypic instrument to assess learning potential in culturally diverse children is the System of Multicultural Pluralistic Assessment (SOMPA) (Mercer & Lewis, 1978). This and similar instruments were designed in response to legal challenges to the validity of the use of instruments standardized on White populations in the classification of culturally diverse children for educational purposes. Unfortunately, the SOMPA has been met with mixed reaction over the years. Sattler (1988) does not recommend its use because of inadequate validity. In the authoritative text, *Assessment of Children* (Sattler, 1988), there is a very informative chapter on the assessment of ethnic minority children; this should be required reading for all clinical child psychologists. An encouraging sign is the recent development of clinical tools specifically designed for use with culturally diverse populations as opposed to translations and adaptations of tools designed originally for children from Western cultures. An example of this is the TEMAS (Tell Me a Story) projective technique (Constantino, 1986), which was constructed as a projective test for culturally diverse children and adolescents. The projective stimuli depict Hispanic and African American characters in common inner-city and familial settings. Psychometric studies have validated its discriminative capacity to identify clinical groups in populations of African American and Hispanic children (Constantino, Malgady, Rogler & Tsui, 1988).

This chapter, divided into two sections, attempts to review culture and child psychopathology. In the first section, cultural factors in relation to diagnostic categories and child clinical symptomatology are examined. The section includes some epidemiological findings, as well as other information related to specific types of childhood psychopathology. There are two different types of epidemiological study: cross-cultural studies that compare samples drawn from different nations and cultural group studies that use samples drawn from within a single country. The latter type can also be subdivided into both studies of established cultural groups and studies of immigrants and refugees. Simple comparative studies between cultural groups or studies that attempt to identify culturally specific characteristics may be useful in generating hypotheses regarding the mechanisms and determinants of psychopathological development in the cultural context. They frequently, however, do not address these determinants or mechanisms directly nor present an overall theoretical framework. The second section attempts to address this concern and reflects a developmental psychopathology approach (Sroufe & Rutter, 1984). This approach follows the proposition that psychopathology develops through continuously interacting biological, psychological, and broader social influences and through a balancing of risk factors and protective mechanisms that alter the probability of successful or unsuccessful adaptation. In this section, the focus is not only on cultural risk factors, which increase the probability of disorder and dysfunction, but also on culturally mediated protective mechanisms that can guard against psychological maladaptation.

It is quite apparent that many of the risk factors in negative psychological outcomes are not necessarily inherent in cultural membership but come with the associated conditions of poverty, oppression, racial discrimination, and stereotyping. It is an impossible task in this chapter to do justice to these important issues, which are common to the experiences of cultural groups. It is also impossible to avoid completely any reference to these factors, as they are inextricably bound to the identities of many cultural groups. The coverage of these complex issues is, by necessity, somewhat selective. There is an extensive literature on inner-city poverty and disadvantage in the United States, and no attempt will be made to summarize this here. In Canada, the demographics of poverty are somewhat different, and it is the relative poverty and disadvantage of the Aboriginal peoples which presents a major social problem. For information on the social and health status of Aboriginal peoples in Canada, the reader is directed to the Canadian Institute of Child Health (CICH) report *The Health of Canada's Children* (2nd ed., CICH, 1994).

The perspective of this chapter is to some extent Canadian, although not exclusively, and reflects some of the concerns and issues facing the country. Canada is currently receiving approximately 215,000 immigrants and refugees a year. Beiser et al. (1995) allude to the paucity of research on health patterns and development of children in immigrant and refugee communities and the need for research to inform policy development and service planning in Canada. Refugees, because of the violent break with their homeland and preimmigration trauma frequently followed by a particularly difficult immigration process, are viewed as a group at risk for mental health problems (Williams & Berry, 1991). A recent Canadian study by Rousseau, Drapeau, and Corin (1996) of Southeast Asian and Central American refugee children whose families have been in Quebec about 5 years found that 22% of Southest Asian children and 35.7% of Central American children were experiencing significant school problems and that the presence of school problems coexisted with significant emotional problems.

CHILD PSYCHOPATHOLOGY IN A CULTURAL CONTEXT

Conduct and Behavior Disorders

The highest numbers of referrals to mental health services for youth in North America involve problems of aggression, acting out, and disruptive behavior. There has been a detectable increase in the rates of these problems over the last 20 years and a secular increase in the incidence of various types of antisocial behavior in the United States and probably also in Canada, although Canadian longitudinal data are not available (Achenbach, 1993; Achenbach & Howell, 1993; Loeber, 1990). Child behavior problems of this nature are classified in the American Psychiatric Association's (1994) *Diagnostic and Statistical Manual of Mental Disorders* (4th ed.) under the diagnostic categories of oppositional defiant disorder and conduct disorder. Oppositional defiant disorder is characterized by the display of age-inappropriate and persistent angry, defiant, irritable, and oppositional behavior. Conduct disorder is a more severe expression of behavior disorder often involving criminal acts, aggression, antisocial behavior, inflicting pain, and denying the rights of others.

DSM-IV (1994) attempts to set a "gold standard" for the definition of childhood disorders of a psychological nature, and the use of their criteria has become ubiquitous in the United States and Canada, especially for research purposes. The definition of behavior problems presents a considerable challenge from a cultural perspective, since definitions of acceptable and unacceptable behavior vary considerably across different cultures and also within a culture. There are many differing standards as to what constitutes normal childhood behavior at different stages in development. At one level, there may be some general agreement about what constitutes unacceptable forms of severely antisocial behavior, because these behaviors contravene universal mores (e.g., assault, stealing). Even in examples such as these, the meaning given to deviant behavior (e.g., attributions of an internal or external locus of control), the age at which criminal responsibility is imputed, and the types of sanctions applied to these behaviors (harsh physical discipline, such as beatings, corrective incarceration, or rehabilitative counseling), may vary widely across cultures.

There continues to be considerable debate even in mainstream child clinical psychology and child psychiatry as to whether behavior disorders should rightly be considered as "mental disorders" (implying that the locus of the problem is within the individual). An earlier version of the *Diagnostic and Statistical Manual* (*DSM-III*, American Psychiatric Association, 1980), recognized a distinction between "socialized" and "unsocialized" types of conduct disorder. The first type is presumed to develop through association with a delinquent subculture; it is thus implied that it is not so much a mental disorder as social deviance. DSM-IV (1994) acknowledges the importance of social context and states that a diagnosis of conduct disorder should be applied only when the behavior reflects an underlying intraindividual pathology rather than a reaction to the social context. A specific "cultural" caution is given regarding the case of immigrant youth who have fled from war-torn countries. Their aggression may not be symptomatic of disorder; rather it may be viewed as being necessary for survival. In clinical situations, it is of obvious value in developing the treatment plan to acknowledge and understand the social and experiential factors that underlie the development of aggressive behavior.

Understanding the social and experiential factors associated with any cultural group is necessary in order to avoid leaping to any biogenetic explanations of ethnic or racial differences. A number of studies have found an association between conduct disorders and race. This has been shown with children of African origin (in both the United Kingdom and the United States) and Aboriginal children in the United States, both having a higher prevalence rate of conduct problems than either Caucasian or Asian groups (Offord, 1989). Offord (1989) cited methodological problems with a number of these studies and considered that the results could be accounted for by factors such as location of residence, living conditions, and family and school circumstances. After taking into account the conditions of disadvantage and psychosocial adversity that give rise to the development of antisocial behavior, Rutter (1979) considered that there is no evidence that culture makes a differential contribution to the prevalence of conduct problems.

Guerra, Tolan, Hoesmann, Van Acker and Eron (1995) reported an important study of the relative contributions of economic disadvantage, stressful events, and individual beliefs to aggressive behavior in inner-city African American, Hispanic, and White children. They found that within this disadvantaged population, individual levels of relative poverty are associated with higher aggression scores early in development. They also found that poorer children are more likely to experience greater life-stress events and more neighborhood violence and are more likely to adopt beliefs condoning aggression. They were unable to completely disentangle cultural factors, as those who were relatively more disadvantaged were likely to be African Americans. These authors, however, considered culture an important mediating factor, and they proposed that the mechanisms of influence are different for different cultural groups. For example, stress appeared to be a more important mediator for the African American and White groups, whereas for Hispanic children, beliefs seemed to be the more important mediator. The authors considered that sensitivity to these cultural differences in the etiology of aggression is necessary in the design of appropriate interventions (Guerra et al., 1995).

The mediating impact of other variables correlated with culture was also shown in a study by Chavez, Oetting, and Swaim (1994). They reported that the high prevalence rate of delinquent acts by youth of Hispanic background can be understood in terms of the high school dropout rate in this group. They cited figures from the U.S. Department of Education (1992) giving a conservative school dropout rate of 35.3% for Hispanics compared to 8.9% for Caucasian non-Hispanics and 13.6% for African Americans. These authors found that Mexican American youths were no more likely to engage in delinquent acts than other school dropouts. Dropping out of school per se confers a higher risk for delinquency than does cultural group membership alone. Zigler and Stevenson (1993) reported that the characteristics associated with dropping out of school include underdeveloped reading and academic skills, negative self-concepts, stressful family situations, personal dissatisfaction with other students or teachers, intense personal problems unrelated to school, and feelings of anxiety due to economic need.

Cross-national studies present another perspective from which cultural influences on behavior disorders can be examined. A number of studies using behavior rating scales such as the Achenbach Scales (Child Behavior Checklist; Achenbach & Edelbrock, 1983; Teacher Report Form; Achenbach & Edelbrock, 1986) have been reported comparing children and youth from various countries with a U.S. sample. The scales have been translated into various languages and tested for validity. For example, a Spanish version of the Achenbach Child Behavior Checklist has been validated on a large community sample of Puerto Rican children (Rubio-Stipec, Bird, Canino, & Gould, 1990). The Achenbach scales yield a number of scores, including individual problem item scores, narrow-band category scores (e.g., aggression), broad-band scores for externalizing (undercontrolled, behavior or conduct) and internalizing (overcontrolled, emotional or "neurotic") problems and total problem scores. Weisz, Suwanlert, Chaiyasit, and Walter (1987) and Weisz, Suwanlert, Chaiyasit, Weiss, Achenbach, and Trevathan (1989) used these scales to study children from Thailand, a Buddhist nation in which conduct and behavior problems such as aggression are disapproved of and discouraged. Consistent with their expectations, Weisz et al. (1987) found that more undercontrolled (behavior) problems (disobedience, fighting, arguing) were reported for U.S. youth than for Thai youth, who showed more overcontrolled problems. These findings support their contention that the form that psychopathology is likely to take is shaped by normative cultural patterns (values, beliefs, expectancies, and child-rearing practices) and reflects an exaggeration of these patterns in what they refer to as a "problem-suppression-facilitation model." Contrary to their expectations, however, Thai teachers rated their youth to have more undercontrolled as well as more overcontrolled problems than U.S. youth (Weisz et al., 1989). The authors consider the possibility that Thai children find certain aspects of school particularly stressful or that Thai teachers are particularly sensitive to problem behaviors and have a low tolerance threshold. The authors comment that Thai teachers apply rigorous standards of conduct to their pupils. This finding supports a different interpretation of the mechanism of cultural influences, which they refer to as the "adult distress threshold model." This model suggests that culture influences adults' attitudes toward children's behavior, determining how distressing it is. The authors conclude, given the collateral finding that overcontrolled problems are more prevalent than undercontrolled problems within the Thai sample, that the problem-suppression-facilitation model is more compelling (Weisz et al., 1989).

Three recent cross-national studies with these scales, comparing children of Jamaica and the United States, present some mixed findings. In the first, M. C. Lambert, Weisz, and Knight (1989) found no significant differences between total problem scores on the Achenbach Child Behavior Checklist (Achenbach & Edelbrock, 1983) for Jamaican children versus U.S. children. Parents in both countries reported significantly more externalizing or conduct problems (e.g., fighting, stealing) than internalizing problems (e.g., anxiety, withdrawal). This study was followed by two epidemiological studies of samples drawn from normal populations, one using parent reports and the other using teacher reports. Parents reported few significant differences (M. C. Lambert, Knight, Taylor, & Achenbach, 1994), with no overall differences in total problem scores. Jamaican teachers reported higher overall problem scores (attributed to rating problems more severely on the 3-point scale as opposed to rating more problems; M. C. Lambert, Knight, Taylor, & Achenbach, 1996). In all their comparisons, the variable of nationality accounted only for a very small amount of the variance. It should be pointed out that nationality did not equate to ethnic origin, as 90% of the Jamaican sample were of African descent and 10% Chinese and East Indian; the U.S. sample were 77% White, 15% African, and 8% other.

Attention-Deficit Hyperactivity Disorder

Attention-deficit hyperactivity disorder is one of the most common childhood psychiatric conditions. It is characterized by age-inappropriate levels of hyperactivity, impulsivity, and inattentiveness. *DSM-IV* (1994) identifies three subtypes: primarily inattentive, primarily hyperactive, and combined type. The condition arises at an early stage in development and is persistent in varying manifestations across the lifespan. Prevalence rates tend to be higher for children rather than adolescents, and a number of studies place the overall prevalence to be in the range of 4%–6% (Szatmari, 1992). Attention-deficit hyperactivity disorder occurs frequently with other behavioral and emotional problems (Barkley, 1990).

Differences in rates of attention-deficit hyperactivity disorder among cultural groups in the United States have been reported. N. M. Lambert, Sancoval, and Sassone (1978) found higher teacher-reported rates of hyperactivity among African American children than among White children. A higher prevalence rate in African American children was also found by Langsdorf, Anderson, Walchter, Madrigal, and Juarez (1979), who reported that almost 25% met a cutoff score on a teacher rating scale commonly used to define hyperactivity. Bauermeister (1995) reported, in a study of Puerto Rican children, that over 25% of an island-wide sample of children were rated by teachers as showing classic symptoms of the disorder.

The increased prevalence rates in African American children are most likely attributable to socioeconomic factors. Support for this comes from Szatmari (1992). He noted that socioeconomic factors are strongly correlated with aggression and conduct problems, which frequently show comorbidity with attention-deficit hyperactivity disorder. When comorbidity for other disorders is controlled, cultural factors no longer make a significant contribution to the prevalence of attention-deficit hyperactivity disorder. It should also be noted that teacher ratings tend to be overinclusive and cannot be used alone to make a diagnosis of attention-deficit hyperactivity disorder using *DSM-IV* (1994) criteria.

Zigler and Stevenson (1993) stated that many Hispanic children are at risk for unwarranted referral because they are often suspected of presenting symptoms of attention-deficit hyperactivity disorder, when in fact symptoms arise from cultural differences in body language. Bauermeister, Berrios, Jiminez, Acevedo, and Gordon (1990) noted that Puerto Rican children are more animated in their body movements and gestures, show more eye movement, and focus less on the listener's face than White Americans. Furthermore, Hispanic children more often react as a group than as individuals (Bauermeister et al., 1990). Therefore, it is quite customary for them to answer a question together rather than taking turns. Such styles of interaction may be interpreted by Western educators and clinicians as apparent inattentiveness, impulsivity, and overactivity. Achenbach et al. (1990) clearly demonstrated this possibility. In their study, White American and Puerto Rican teachers were asked to rate two demographically matched groups of children from the general U.S. population and from Puerto Rico. White American teachers, but not Puerto Rican teachers, rated the behaviors of the Puerto Rican children as distressing and in need of intervention.

Luk, Leung, and Lee (1988) report a cross-national study of Chinese children in Hong Kong using a standard measure for the assessment of attention-deficit hyperactivity disorder, the Connors' Teacher Rating Scale (Connors, 1973). Questionnaire measures are particularly susceptible to cultural and linguistic variations in shades of meaning that can affect the overall validity of a scale. A common practice, which was followed in this case, is forward and backward translation to ensure that the meanings in one language are satisfactorily reflected in the other. The results showed, contrary to common beliefs and cultural stereotyping, not only that hyperactivity and inattention problems were prevalent in the Chinese population but also that the scores were higher than in either a U.S. or a U.K. sample. Explanations given for this finding were similar to those put forward by Weisz et al. (1987,1989): results showed either a lower threshold related to intolerance of disruptive behavior in the crowded Hong Kong classrooms or a genuine reflection of a higher level of hyperactive/inattentive behavior. There was no way of distinguishing between these alternative explanations with the data that they presented.

Childhood Depression and Suicide

The same *DSM-IV* (1994) criteria are used for identifying the clinical syndrome of depression in children as in adults; the only formal modification recognizes that young children may not express subjective feelings of dysphoria and are more likely to show irritability. Both major depressive episodes and chronic dysthymia are recognized in children and adolescents. Kovacs, Feinberg, Crouse-Novak, Paulauskas, and Finkelstein (1984) considered that dysthymia in children differs from major depression in an emphasis on gloomy thoughts and other negative affect, with fewer symptoms such as anhedonia, social withdrawal, fatigue, reduced sleep, and poor appetite.

Some epidemiological studies have identified differences in prevalence rates of depression across cultures, whereas others have not. Kandel and Davies (1982) found no differences in symptom levels between African and White American children. Costello et al. (1988) found no differences in depression rates comparing African American and White American children. Garrison, Jackson, Marsteller, McKeown, and Addy (1990) found some differences using the Center for Epidemiological Studies—Depression Scales (Radloff, 1977) in seventh-grade children. African American children had higher scores, but by the ninth grade these differences were apparent only for females. Yates (1987) reported that between 20%–25% of Native American children suffer some form of emotional disorder, which is substantially higher than estimates for non-Native children. The high suicide rate among Aboriginal youth is a major concern in both the United States and Canada. The Canadian Institute of Child Health reports that during the 5-year period from 1986 to 1990 the average suicide rate among Canadian Indian youth between 10 and 19 years of age was 37 per 100,000, compared to the total Canadian rate of 7 per 100,000 (CICH, 1994). Inouye (1988) noted that the highest rates of adolescent suicide are found on Indian reservations in the United States. Gotowiec and Beiser (1993) reported that Aboriginal youths in Canada are two to three times more likely to commit suicide than any other racial/ethnic group, a trend that has held true for at least the last 3 decades.

The meaning attributed to emotions, including depression, appears to be very culture-specific (Russell, 1991). This is particularly apparent in comparing Western and Eastern cultures. Western mind-body dualistic thinking draws a distinction between physical and psychological symptoms, whereas this is not the case in many Eastern cultures. Manson (1995) cited two cases of non-Western (adult) patients that illustrate the overlap between the somatic and affective dimensions of depression. In both cases, the patients were brought to attention because of their complaints about "whole-body sickness" or daily headaches; both patients were depressed about their interpersonal problems. Western diagnostic criteria may be inappropriate for diagnosing depression in non-Western clients, as the criteria tend to depend exclusively on self-referring statements of dysphoria (e.g., "I feel blue" or "I am bothered by things that usually do not bother me"); the non-Western client is more likely to perceive the self in relation to others and to show concerns about disappointing people or about conflict in the roles of wife and daughter in the family.

It is also generally characteristic of Asian cultures that complaints about emotional problems do not get special attention; in contrast, complaints about physical illness receive immediate attention, concern, and care. In these cultures, to admit to emotional problems brings shame to the entire family (Yee & Hennesy, 1982). Therefore, members of these cultures who have internalized such shame may not disclose their emotions. Without having a knowledge of these different cultural practices and values, Western clinicians may have difficulties identifying the underlying problems, especially among children, who are not able to express themselves well.

Fears and Anxieties

Anxiety disorders are the most common class of psychopathology affecting children and adolescents (Anderson, Williams, McGee, & Silva, 1987; Bernstein & Borchardt, 1991). Types of anxiety disorders in children include separation anxiety disorder, avoidant disorder of childhood, and overanxious disorder. In addition, children can be diagnosed with "adult" anxiety disorders such as phobic disorder, panic disorder, obsessive-compulsive disorder, and post-traumatic stress disorder.

Two of the most commonly used scales for the assessment of children's fears, the Fear Survey Schedule for Children—Revised (Ollendick, 1983) and the State-Trait Anxiety Inventory for Children (Speilberger, 1973), have been translated into a variety of languages and administered to children and adolescents in a number of countries. Fonesca, Yule, and Erol (1994) reviewed studies of the Fear Survey Schedule (Children's Version) and found that, with only some relatively minor exceptions (e.g., a tendency for Latin cultures to be more expressive of emotions than Nordic cultures), relatively similar scores were obtained across a variety of North American, European, Asian, and Eastern countries. Furthermore, the types of fears that were endorsed the most frequently were very consistent: fear of being hit by a car, of a parent's death, of not being able to breathe, of a bomb attack, of fire, of a burglar, of falling from a height, and of death. Research on the State-Trait Anxiety Inventory is also yielding consistent findings across cultures. For example, Ahlawat (1986) found similar factor structures between an Arabic version and the American version of the scale. One exception to the consistency of cross-cultural findings is found in a study by Tikalsky and Wallace (1988), who reported that Navajo children had more fears than rural non-Native U.S. children as measured on the Louisville Fear Survey for Children. They interpret their findings in terms of the value placed on fears among the Navajo as a sign of perceptivity rather than weakness.

In adults, it has been found that African Americans have higher rates of panic and phobias than Whites, even when sociodemographic factors were controlled; this has been attributed to the experience of more stressful life events, including separation from parents and other traumatic childhood events (Friedman & Paradis, 1991; Kirmayer, Young, & Hayton, 1995). There do not appear to be any comparable data for children.

Post-traumatic stress disorder is important in relation to cultural factors. Symptoms of post-traumatic stress disorder are particularly common in refugees who leave their war-torn motherland and manage to survive (Mollica, Wyshak, & Lavelle, 1987). Semeniuk (1995), in an article written to inform the public about the impact of war on children, graphically described how children who survive a war are especially afflicted with post-traumatic stress disorder, which can be expressed in different ways. He illustrated this by describing a seven-year-old Arab boy who was suddenly attacked by Israeli soldiers on his way home. In the weeks following his encounter with the soldiers, his mother noticed several behaviors unusual for him, like beating up his sisters, burning himself with fire, wetting his bed, and acting aggressively and disobediently. Children who suffer from post-traumatic stress also frequently engage in repetitive symbolic play behavior, for example, playing an "Arabs and Jews" war game. Play and art therapy are particularly useful clinical approaches for such children, and these approaches can easily be adapted for use with children from different cultural backgrounds.

Sleep disturbance is one of the possible consequences of psychological trauma. Dollinger, Molina, and Monteiro (1996) reported a study of poor urban Brazilian children that investigated the hypothesis that children's sleep disorders are environmentally and culturally determined. Brazilian children who live in poverty in the large cities are exposed to the specter of death squads who kill street children. Dollinger et al. found support for their hypothesis in the fact that Brazilian youth with disturbed sleep were more likely to experience anxiety in their lives (death squads), fears of death and dying, and fears about environmental conditions. These correlates of sleep disturbances were compared to correlates of sleep disturbance in other samples, such as learning-disabled adolescents and children who were victims of a weather disaster. The constellation of fears and anxieties differed considerably from sample to sample, reflecting the specific concerns of the group of children, and was therefore assumed to be culturally and environmentally mediated.

Asian children may be misdiagnosed as having social phobia, as they present with some culturally normative behaviors which may be considered socially deviant in a North American environment, namely, shyness-withdrawal. X. Chen, Rubin, and Sun (1992) showed that shyness-sensitivity was significantly negatively correlated with peer acceptance among Canadian children. Among Chinese children, however, shyness-sensitivity was positively associated with sociability-leadership and with peer acceptance. Asian children are taught to be cautious, behaviorally inhibited, self-restrained, reticent, and sensitive as early as the age of four (Ho, 1986). These qualities are considered indices of mastery, maturity, and accomplishment (Ho, 1986).

Another interesting finding from the X. Chen et al. (1992) study is that a good sense of humor, which is highly regarded in the Western culture, was considered as an "aggressive-disruptive" behavior among the Chinese sample. As these examples illustrate, before a clinician labels a child from a different culture as maladaptive or deviant, it is essential to have a thorough understanding of the child's cultural values and background.

Elective mutism (also referred to as selective mutism since the mutism is displayed selectively—usually with nonfamily members) is a form of childhood psychopathology disorder that fits into the broader category of social phobias. It is a behavior pattern in which children who possess age-appropriate speech choose to remain silent or speak only to self-selected persons (DiNicola, 1995). A marked increase in the prevalence of this disorder among immigrant children has been noted. Bradley and Sloman (1975) reported a tenfold increase in the prevalence of elective mutism among immigrants as compared to English-speaking families in Toronto. Based on a review of the literature which shows that the largest single risk factor for elective mutism is migration, DiNicola (1995, p. 33) proposed that this disorder can be best understood as "culture-change syndrome."

Eating Disorders

Anorexia nervosa and bulimia nervosa are two major eating disorders which afflict adolescents. Anorexia nervosa involves a failure to maintain body weight, whereas bulimia nervosa includes a cycle of binge eating and purging without life-threatening weight loss. Characteristics of anorexia nervosa include self-induced starvation, bizarre attitudes toward food, and a distorted body image (Zigler & Stevenson, 1993). Anorexia nervosa is described as a Western culture-bound syndrome that reflects the value Western cultures place on body image: slimness equals physical attraction (DiNicola, 1995; Levine & Gaw, 1995). Some immigrant adolescents, from cultures with very low risk for eating disorder, display anorexia nervosa after migrating to Western countries. This may reflect their adoption of Western values, where the drive for thinness and the social modeling of dieting are widespread. There is some evidence that the incidence may be increasing among the groups who were thought to have very low rates, such as African Americans and non-Western immigrants (Hsu, 1990). Hsu (1990) reports that eating disorders do occur in Japan and Malaysia with the same patterns (female, upper-income levels), but prevalence rates are not known.

Autism and Childhood Psychosis

Autism is found in *DSM-IV* (1994) in the pervasive developmental disorders category, which also includes Asperger's syndrome; Rett's syndrome; childhood-onset disintegrative disorder; and pervasive developmental disorder, not otherwise specified. Space does not permit a full description of these disorders here. Briefly, autism is of unknown but presumably biological origin and is characterized by often severe deficits in social interaction, language and communication, and other cognitive functions, coexisting with bizarre and unusual behaviors and manifesting from an early age. Because of its presumed biological origins, one would expect to find evidence of autism in all cultures. A number of studies from various countries confirm that autism is likely a universal phenomenon (Bryson, Clark, & Smith, 1988 [Canada]; Steffen-burg & Gillberg,1986 [Scandinavia]; Sugiyama & Abe, 1989 [Japan]). Diagnostic criteria appear to be consistent across Western and Eastern cultures, as shown by the discriminative validity of a Japanese translation of Schopler's Childhood Autism Rating Scale (Kurita, Miyake, & Katsuno, 1989).

The same diagnostic criteria as used for adults (delusions, hallucinations, thought disorder, disorganized behavior, and negative symptoms) define childhood-onset schizophrenia in *DSM-IV* (1994). Although confirmatory studies are lacking, childhood-onset schizophrenia is also likely a universal phenomenon. The meaning attributed to markedly unusual and bizarre behaviors differs across cultures, and this determines the way in which psychosis is viewed and the kind of response the parents and family have to the child who is exhibiting the problem. In one case, familiar to one of the authors, a Vietnamese adolescent boy presented with psychotic thought disorder and bipolar affective disorder symptoms. There appeared to be no adequate means of conveying our Western diagnosis to the family in a way that appeared to be meaningful to them, even though we utilized a cultural interpretation service. This may be surprising since Sue (1982) reports that Asians tended to have a higher proportion of individuals diagnosed as psychotic than other cultural groups. He concluded that, compared to other cultural groups, Chinese Americans and other Asian Americans showed lower utilization rates of mental health facilities but greater severity of emotional disturbance when first brought to the attention of mental health services. The reluctance of Asian groups to use mainstream children's mental health services was shown in a study by Yeh, Takeuchi, and Sue (1994), who found that Asian American children who received services at culture-specific centers were less likely to drop out after the first session, utilized more services, and had better outcomes than those who attended mainstream services.

RISK FACTORS AND PROTECTIVE MECHANISMS

This section examines some of the mechanisms that increase or decrease the probability of psychopathological development, viewed from a cultural context.

Language and Communication Differences as Potential Risk Factors

The inability to function in the language of the majority obviously impairs academic functioning in the mainstream unless compensatory programs are in place. What is not so obvious is the potential impact on children's overall mental health if they are unable to function in the language of the majority. According to Wyspianski and Fournier-Ruggles (1985), lack of vocabulary and knowledge of the syntax of the majority language contributes to feelings of inadequacy and inferiority. In one observational study, Sarda (1990) reports that Francophones in a predominantly English environment felt ashamed because they could not adequately express themselves in English and because the quality of their language was not what they thought it should be. Even African American children, whose first language is English, are at risk of feeling a sense of inferiority. For a long time, African American children have been labeled as having deficient language skills by researchers and educators because they speak a nonstandard dialect of English (Zigler & Stevenson, 1993). The dialect may go beyond the use of particular idiomatic words or expressions and may involve fundamentally different styles of communicating. For example, African American parents ask their offspring fewer questions at home than White families do, and the questions African American families ask are typically open-ended prompts that allow their children to recount their knowledge or experiences through long and elaborate verbal responses. As a result, these children may display hesitation in school in answering what, for them, are unusual questions that require them to provide brief, factually correct answers.

Culture goes beyond verbal language; the messages conveyed by nonverbal behaviors are as important as those conveyed verbally (Waxer, 1985). Gaze behavior, for example, has been found to be culturally specific (Waxer, 1985). Beebee (1974) reports that in Western culture one's credibility increases with increased eye contact. In contrast, Waxer (1985) reported that avoidance of direct eye contact in relation to authority figures has been reported in many West African cultures and practiced by people from diverse cultures. Consequently, Western educators or counselors may interpret the gaze behavior displayed by non-Western children as shy, inattentive, rude, or even hostile.

A child's apparent ease in speaking the host country language is a double-edged sword. There is no doubt that a good vocabulary and accent-free speech is reassuring to teachers and others that a child has mastered the new language. Beiser et al. (1995) noted that this may occur when true language fluency has not yet been attained. This may lead teachers and others to make false assumptions about children's competencies.

Culture Change and Intergenerational Family Conflict as Potential Risk Factors

A source of stress for children who either emigrate at a young age to or are born in a host country is the conflict between traditional values of the old country as manifested by their parents and the values of the new country most influentially demonstrated by their peers (Rosenthal, 1984; Baptiste, 1990; Eppink, 1979). Older children who emigrate have a dual conflict: not only have they been brought up according to their indigenous cultural values, but they also may have been well established within their peer groups (Baptiste, 1990). It has been found that many new immigrant youngsters feel angry and depressed because of their resentment at leaving their home country and peer support networks, as well as losing their status in their peer hierarchy (Baptiste, 1990). In the new environment, immigrant children may experience significant difficulties in coping with their demoted status in the new social settings of the host country. Furthermore, they need to overcome the difficulties of language and schooling (Aronowitz, 1984). They also need to learn the norms and expectations for appropriate behaviors in the new culture. The behaviors that once were appropriate in the country of origin may be unacceptable in the new culture. For example, Asian immigrant children may discover that shy, dependent, self-restrained, and inhibited behaviors that were highly valued in the home country are no longer considered positive in their new school setting or peer group (X. Chen, Rubin, & Sun,

1992). Instead, these traits are often regarded as maladaptive and may lead to peer rejection in North America (French, 1990; Rubin & Mills, 1988). With such a considerable gap between the old and new cultures, immigrant children are typically found to present inhibition, dejection, sleeplessness, poor appetite, subacute symptoms of anxiety and depression, or even behavioral disorders (Aronowitz, 1984; Ashworth, 1975; Eppink, 1979; Horowitz & Frenkel, 1976).

Children who were born and raised in the majority culture, as well as those immigrant children who have been living in the dominant country for a considerable time, also experience cultural conflicts. In their case, the traditional culture is usually and most strongly represented by parents and family, and the majority culture is typified by peers, school, and mass media. These conflicts often appear to come to a head around the time of adolescence. This is a time when youth in Western societies are encouraged to become self-reliant (Feldman & Rosenthal, 1990). The increasing independence and individuation of adolescents and young adults from the family of origin is viewed positively and supported as a sign of independence in Western culture (Baptiste, 1990; Feldman & Rosenthal, 1990). Huang (1994) states that in most Asian cultures there is no developmental stage comparable to that of adolescence in Western cultures and that the issues of individual identity formation and self-differentiation are minimized. Among many non-Western families, independence and self-assertiveness are often perceived as a sign of giving up the family, and this may lead to familial disappointment (Baptiste, 1990; LeVine & Padilla, 1980; Ponterotto & Casas, 1991). As a result, many children from diverse cultures are overwhelmed by the mixed and conflicting messages they receive (Feldman & Rosenthal, 1990).

Increasing numbers of families with adolescent children from diverse cultures are seeking therapy because of intergenerational conflicts between parents and children (Baptiste, 1990; Chiu, Feldman, & Rosenthal, 1992). Although generational conflict is common in all societies (Baptiste, 1990), generational conflict in immigrant families tends to be manifested in terms of a cultural clash between parents and children.

Many children from diverse cultures feel pressured to make a choice between the values of their indigenous culture and of the Western culture (Aronowitz, 1984). On the one hand, they want to be part of the Western culture (Baptiste, 1990; Nguyen & Williams, 1989). On the other hand, they may fear that their desires and attempts to become Westernized will be viewed as an act of disloyalty or betrayal by their families. Aronowitz (1984) commented also on the fear that if they abandon traditional cultural values they may be rejected by their subculture without being assured of membership in the dominant culture. One study conducted by Charron and Ness (1981) clearly presented the dilemma of ethnic children. They found that Vietnamese adolescents who were not forming friendships with their American peers were at risk for emotional distress. On the other hand, the result of successful school-based relationships with Americans was often in conflict with their Vietnamese parents.

Many immigrant parents and children experience role conflicts, which can lead to problems and stresses in the parent-child relationship (Baptiste, 1990; Naditch & Morrissey, 1976). Immigrant children tend to be faster and more flexible than their parents or grandparents in acculturating to dominant culture (usually Western) behaviors, attitudes, values, and habits. This is so-called "asymmetric acculturation" (Beiser et al., 1995; Chiu, Feldman, & Rosenthal, 1992). The different rates of acculturation of parents and children often polarize the family. Inadvertently, parents may increase the stress in the family by their use of their children as translators and cultural inter- preters. Although this may appear to be a solution to the family's communication difficulties, it results in a risk of role-reversal and destabilizes the normal patterns of community and authority (Beiser et al., 1995).

In Asian cultures, children's roles are highly structured and explicitly defined within the hierarchical structure of the family. These roles may not correspond to roles prescribed for their Western friends. Baptiste (1990) reports that immigrant working mothers often ask their children to assume some domestic responsibilities like preparing meals, washing dishes, and taking care of their younger siblings (Bap- tiste, 1990). Beiser et al. (1995) note that age of arrival in the host country is an important variable. Children who arrive in a resettlement country as preadolescents or who are born in their parents' adopted country are more likely than older children to adopt majority-culture values and experience more intergenerational conflict.

According to Baptiste (1990), family communication problems arise when English has become the children's first and often their only language. Consequently, difficul- ties in communicating with grandparents and parents, who often remain monolingual in their mother tongue, gradually intensify. Some children are reluctant to talk to their grandparents and parents because they feel ashamed of their parents' and grand- parents' speech. Eppink (1979) stated that some ethnic children look down on their parents because they speak the new language badly (often with accents). Frequently, they label their parents' or grandparents' speech as "funny talk" or "weird" (Baptiste, 1990). Some immigrant parents will speak selectively in their native language to their children, and in these circumstances language often becomes a political tool in the family. For example, a mother addresses her adolescent daughter in her native tongue, and although the daughter understands, she responds in English. There may be subtle- ties of meaning contained in this simple interchange. For example, the daughter wants to show her independence and acceptance of the majority culture; the mother experi- ences this as defiance and loss of closeness in the relationship. In one family familiar to one of the authors, the mother spoke in English to the daughter except when reprimanding her, which she did in Polish.

Many immigrant and refugee parents feel that they must preserve the traditional family values (Nguyen & Williams, 1989). In most cases, however, what they dis- cover is that their children do not have the same goal as they do. When the child displays the norms and values of the dominant culture, which the parents have been deliberately avoiding, intercultural conflict, which manifests as intergenerational con- flict of values, strikes to the core of the family (Sluzki, 1979). In a study conducted by W. E. Lambert (1987), immigrant parents were asked whether immigrants to the United States should give up their traditional ways and take on the American way of life or whether they should maintain their traditional ways of life as much as possible when they come to America. The results indicated that the vast majority of parents took an extreme maintenance position with respect to culture-maintenance as well as language-maintenance. In some cases, parents may attempt to make some adjustments to the Western values while still keeping the traditional family values and their au- thority. For example, in one study conducted by Nguyen and Williams (1989), Viet- namese parents were found to approve certain adolescent privileges regarding dating, marriage, and career, while at the same time still endorsing traditional values such as absolute obedience to parental authority. The results suggested that Vietnamese adolescents felt confused and conflicted by such ambivalence, and numerous instances of disagreement and lack of compromises remained between the adolescents and their families. From the children's perspective, the conflict arose not because of having to deal simultaneously with two different normative systems of behavior but because they perceived that their Western behaviors were being thwarted and condemned by their parents. From the parents' perspective, they saw these behaviors as signs of disobedience and disloyalty (Baptiste, 1990).

Acculturation Stress and Cultural Identity Crisis as Potential Risk Factors

The process whereby an ethnic individual minimizes the differences with, and adjusts to, the majority culture following immigration is referred to as acculturation (Berry, 1980, 1985). Problems that arise during the process of acculturation may include difficulties resulting from differences in language, physical appearance, environment, and cultural values and expectations (Chataway & Berry, 1989). Acculturation experiences can be very stressful for young people, especially teens. Berry (1985) found that, compared to the nonethnic population, ethnic high school youths scored significantly higher in inadequacy, depression, anxiety, sensitivity, anger, and tension. There appear to be different ways in which acculturation takes place. Pawliuk, Grizenko, Chan-Yip, Gantous, Mathew, and Nguyen (1996) described four different possible styles that can evolve. The first is *assimilation,* in which the culture of origin is rejected in favor of the culture of the host country. The second is *integration,* in which the cultural origins are retained in participating in the larger culture. The third is *separation,* in which the original culture is maintained without participating in the larger culture. The fourth is *marginalization,* which results from rejecting both the culture of origin and that of the host country.

Pawliuk et al. (1996) reported one of the few systematic studies of psychological functioning and acculturation style in children. They recruited a multiethnic sample of children from a pediatric clinic in Montreal, Canada. An acculturation questionnaire was administered to 48 children aged 6 to 17. Using the classification scheme as described above, 54% had adopted an integrative style, 40% an assimilative style, 6% a marginalized style, and none a separation style. A similar questionnaire was given to their parents, which revealed that 41% had adopted an integrative style, 47% a separation style, 9% an assimilated style, and 3% a marginalized style. Twenty-three percent of this nonrandom sample scored at or above the 98th percentile on total behavior problems on the Achenbach Child Behavior Checklist (Achenbach & Edelbrock, 1983). Children who adopted an assimilation style were found to be overrepresented in this high-scoring group. The authors speculate that the parents of assimilated children view their child's assimilation as rebelliousness and thus report more behavior problems. A small association was found between parental assimilation variables (father's ability to speak the host language and the number of mother's Canadian friends) and lowered level of internalizing problems and higher social-competence scores. Otherwise, the authors report that the acculturation style (of either the child or the parents) was not greatly associated with child psychopathology. The lack of significant findings may be related to the small number of those showing a marginalized style, the style which these authors consider to present the highest risk.

One of the inevitable issues that ethnic children in adolescence must face is their perception of their own cultural identity (LeVine & Padilla, 1980). This issue of cultural identification may particularly encumber ethnic adolescents who are already at a crucial developmental stage, namely, dealing with an identity crisis in which youth commonly struggle with issues of autonomy and separation from parents and peer influence (Chiu, Feldman, & Rosenthal, 1992; Erikson, 1968; Shaffer, 1994). Several researchers have reported acute identity crisis among ethnic youths (Ashworth, 1975; Naditch & Morrissey, 1976). Yates (1987) partly attributes the high rate of depression, intergenerational conflict, and behavioral problems among ethnic children to what he terms "maladaptive acculturation"; that is, these children have rejected either the dominant culture or their parents' original culture. P. W. Chen (1977) suggests that ethnic individuals who assimilate the majority culture and reject the indigenous culture may become over-Westernized. Hostility towards and denial of their own cultural orientation may cause them to turn the hostility inward and to develop a form of "racial self-hatred." Eppink (1977) suggests that if ethnic children acquire a negative image of their parents or their mother tongue, they are likely to develop a negative self-image and feelings of loss of identity.

Clearly the relationship between acculturation and adolescent adjustment is complex and more empirical research is needed. Lee (1996) has completed a study of the relationship between acculturation and socio-emotional adjustment among Chinese-Canadian adolescents attending a Chinese language school in the Toronto area in Canada. One hundred and twenty-four young adolescents (7th and 8th grade) were given a battery of questionnaires measuring acculturation and adjustment. Adolescent adaptation to Western culture was significantly and negatively correlated with self-reported loneliness ($r = -.62$, $p < .001$), depression ($r = -.47$, $p < .001$), as well as mother-reported internalizing problems ($r = -.47$, $p < .001$). Also, adolescents' and parents' levels of acculturation were found to be positively correlated. It can be assumed that the parents of these children valued maintenance of Chinese cultural values by enrolling their children in this school. Although causal directionality cannot be inferred from this correlational study, the parents who also embraced Western culture, thus representing an integrational mode of acculturation, appeared to have better adjusted adolescent children.

The Protective Mechanisms of Familial/Social Support and Personal Competencies

Many immigrant and ethnic children are exposed to multiple risks because risks tend to be interrelated (e.g., role conflicts, family discord, acculturation stress). The more risk factors to which children are subjected, the greater the probability that they will develop psychopathology (Rutter, 1979). Clinical professionals should be sensitive to the double, triple, or multiple jeopardy in which these children are placed. Given this potential, it is surprising that the rate of disorders is not higher than it actually is. One has to assume that protective mechanisms are operating that enhance the resistance to risk factors and decrease the probability of poor psychological outcomes (Rutter & Rutter, 1992). One such mechanism is the stress-buffering role of social support (Dean & Lin, 1977; Sandler, Miller, Short & Wolchik, 1989). Zigler and Stevenson (1993) suggest that the presence of a caring adult, a parent, some other relative, a teacher, or a neighbor may help offset the negative effects of stress. This was borne out in one study of marital conflict and its impact on children. In the presence of marital conflict, a close relationship between a child and an adult outside the family reduced the likelihood that the child would develop psychopathological symptoms (Jenkins & Smith, 1990).

Is there evidence of the protective value of social support for children from diverse cultures or refugee and immigrant children? Some years ago, Rogler (1978) described the social, psychological, and physical survival of immigrant Puerto Ricans in the South Bronx and found that the successful adaptation among these immigrants was due to the help-giving familial and cultural systems they brought with them, the supportive systems they created in the host society, and the supportive systems that were already there in the cultural community. More recently, Knight, Virdin, and Roosa (1994), in a study of social and family correlates of mental health among Hispanic and White American children, emphasized the importance of extended familial support. They found that Hispanic individuals may be protected against poor psychological outcomes by the great number of social supports provided by the extended families and the levels of religious belief in the Hispanic circle.

Although, as mentioned earlier, adherence to traditional family values can result in stressed parent-child relationships (Nguyen & Williams, 1989), there is also evidence that maintaining values from the old country can exert a protective influence. One study of Mexican-born and U.S.-born Mexican youth in a California school district found that alcohol and drug use rates were lower in the Mexican-born group, whereas the rates for the U.S.-born were similar to non-Mexican U.S. youth (Boles, Casas, Furlong, Gonzalez, & Morrison,1994). These authors commented that traditional Mexican values do not condone alcohol and drugs. They also consider the possibility that increased in-home and work responsibilities in this group might act as protective mechanisms.

Along with social supports, there are personal factors that are considered to protect children in circumstances of risk. These include well-developed skills and talents, personal competencies, and opportunities to engage in compensatory experiences (see Offord, 1989). LaFromboise, Coleman, and Gerton (1993) theorized that bicultural competence is related to good psychological health; bicultural competence may act therefore as a protective mechanism. According to Ramirez (1991), some ethnic individuals are able to perceive multicultural diversity as a precious opportunity to stimulate their personal development. They recognize that there can be positive aspects of being bicultural. Individuals who adopt such attitudes are generally culturally flexible people, who are willing to learn by observation, by listening, and by exposure to different worldviews and different life philosophies. It has been suggested that there is a Western "field-independent" cognitive style (preference for independent and task-oriented work, as well as discovery or trial-and-error learning, competing, and gaining individual recognition, seeking nonsocial rewards, focusing on details and parts of things) and a non-Western "field-sensitive" cognitive style (preference for working with others to achieve common goals, assisting others, openly expressing positive feelings for teacher, seeking guidance and demonstration from teacher, dealing with concepts that are relevant to personal interests and experiences, and working with concepts in humanized or story format) (Ramirez, 1991). If an ethnic child is able to integrate both the field-independent and field-sensitive cognitive styles in academic settings, one might predict success. Although this remains a hypothesis without any direct evidence in support of it, Ramirez (1983) found that successful children and college students tended to be more flexible, with an ability to shuttle between different cognitive and cultural styles, compared to their less successful peers.

Bilingualism and biculturalism are positive assets to cognitive growth (Bhatnagar, 1985), as evidenced by the observation that bilingual/bicultural children appear to develop certain cognitive abilities earlier than their monolingual peers (Zigler & Stevenson, 1993). Bhatnagar (1985) stated that bilingualism and biculturalism provide a kind of mental and cultural flexibility that is very conducive to intellectual development. As with a bicognitive style, bilingual competency may very well act as a protective mechanism. Further studies are needed to investigate the complex relationships between risk factors, protective mechanisms, psychological health, and the development of pathology in a cultural context.

CONCLUDING REMARKS AND FUTURE DIRECTIONS

One of the objectives of this chapter is to inform the clinical practitioner who operates at the individual case level. Clinical work usually involves formulating questions or hypotheses while in the process of gathering information from tests, observations, and interviews which are then tested empirically by recommending a particular course of action. A culturally sensitive clinician will bring forward questions and hypotheses about the contribution of the cultural context to the presenting problem and will avoid bringing superficial answers and preformed opinions. Our understanding is moving beyond simplistic linear formulations of the relationship between cultural factors and child disorders toward a deeper understanding of the culturally determined processes and contextual and systemic factors that determine the health and adjustment of any individual child. Linear thinking leads to overly simplistic formulations. For example, African American children are more likely to have behavior disorders than White children; Hispanic children are prone to increased prevalence rates of attention-deficit disorder; resettlement or acculturation stress causes psychological distress and disorder; failure to assimilate is a cause of poor mental health among refugees and immigrants. On close examination, these formulations stem from stereotyping; failure to take into account culturally determined learning style differences; failure to recognize that resettlement stress, like other stressors, can increase the risk of maladaptation but may also create opportunities and possibilities for growth (Beiser et al., 1995); and ignorance of the benefits of biculturalism.

One contribution of a developmental psychopathology perspective is to emphasize the complex systemic interplay between risk factors and protective mechanisms in the development of an individual and their relationship to psychological health and dysfunction. Rutter and Rutter (1992) have articulated the ways in which protective mechanisms operate. They can reduce the impact of risks either by altering the meaning of the risks, reducing the exposure to the risks, reducing negative chain reactions, establishing and maintaining self-efficacy and self-esteem, and opening up opportunities for growth. To date, little recognition has been given to culturally determined protective mechanisms that can act as a buffer against the forces that produce negative psychological outcomes. It is essential for a clinician to recognize and acknowledge an ethnic child's protective mechanisms that guard against psychological malad-adaptation. Children often need help and support from an understanding adult to discover and maintain their strengths (Zigler & Stevenson, 1993). The role of a clinical practitioner is thus very crucial in the identification and mobilization of personal strengths and resources.

Cultural sensitivity involves an understanding of differing beliefs and value systems of different cultures. It goes beyond this, however, to recognize these as strengths and to build on them as an effective clinical tool in working with children and families from different cultures. Clinical practice has in the past often focused on cultural differences as negative forces; indeed, the term "cultural deprivation" was coined to reflect the belief that children from diverse cultural groups were in some ways lacking. This view proposed that individuals from diverse cultural groups were more likely than Whites to grow up in disadvantaged cultural environments, such as poor neighborhoods with poor living conditions where they were deprived of proper cognitive stimulation and positive role models (Ponterotto & Casas, 1991). It presumed that as a result of such culturally deprived environments, children from diverse cultural groups tended to succeed less frequently in school, in the home (in terms of marital and family stability), and at work than their White counterparts (Ponterotto & Casas, 1991). There are three problems with this model. The first is that it overlooks the functionally effective determinants of psychological disorder (poverty, lack of opportunity, exposure to violence). The second is that it emphasizes deficits and neglects strengths, competencies, and skills found in ethnic families, communities, and cultures (Sue, 1982). The third is that this model led practitioners to view the minority cultures as possessing some deviant characteristics and to attempt to discover what it might take to fix them according to Western-based judgments (Sue, 1982; Ponterotto & Casas, 1991). As Gotowiec and Beiser (1993) stated, a deficit-model orientation defines differences as aspects of the dominant culture that are missing in minority cultures and does not foster understanding or enhancement of the strengths of minority cultures.

Another objective of this chapter is to determine the ways in which research knowledge can inform us about how we organize clinical services to children. What are the "best practices" on which to base the organization of clinical services? Although there is nothing definitive that can be offered at this time, there are a number of potentially sound recommendations that can be considered. They are as follows:

1. Agencies and services should have policies that address the accessibility of services to culturally diverse populations—including availability of materials published in the languages of the community and the presence of barriers, physical and psychological, which inhibit certain groups from even asking for help.

2. Clinicians must receive cultural sensitivity training. Such training must go beyond offering overly simplistic, descriptive information in an effort to make the clinician aware of different cultural practices. This only feeds into an "expert" stance and may lead to overgeneralization and stereotyping. It is believed that clinicians must be encouraged to cultivate an inquiring attitude and a genuine interest in cultural diversity, allowing themselves to be taught by each one of their clients.

3. Consideration has to be given to developing culturally specific services provided by representatives of the culture in cases where they are shown to be more effective than traditional services. It is recognized that this is also a political and economic

issue and that some groups may demand their own services, claiming an entitlement to them.

4. The tools of our trade must be appropriate for the populations with which we work. Testing instruments designed for, or at least adapted for, use with minorities must be used. Where no such tools are available, more harm than good might come out of using tools that have not been validated with cultural groups.

5. Clinical services alone are not sufficient. Offord (1995) considered that interventions must go beyond those who seek service and who have clinically identified problems. Seeing problem cases on a one-by-one basis is expensive and time-consuming and can never play a major role in reducing the burden of suffering of immigrant and refugee children with mental health problems (Offord, 1995). As important as clinical practice is, it is only one point on the continuum of intervention in the relief of human suffering and improvement of the quality of life. The continuum also includes preventing problems before they have become clinically significant. Offord (1995) called for a cost-effective blend of clinical, targeted (for those at high risk), and universal interventions. Universal interventions must include broad social and political changes that counteract racism and the resulting oppression and marginalization of selected groups of humanity.

References

Achenbach, T. M., & Edelbrock, C. S. (1986). *Manual for the Teacher's Report Form and Teacher Version of the Child Behavior Profile.* Burlington: University of Vermont, Department of Psychiatry.

Achenbach, T. M. (1993). Taxonomy and comorbidity of conduct problems: Evidence from empirically based approaches. *Development and Psychopathology, 5,* 51–64.

Achenbach, T. M., Bird, H. R., Canino, G., Phares, V., Gould, M. S., & Rubio-Stipec, M. (1990). Epidemiological comparisons of Puerto Rican and U.S. mainland children: Parent, teacher, and self-reports. *Journal of the American Academy of Child and Adolescent Psychiatry, 29,* 84–93.

Achenbach, T. M., & Edelbrock, C. (1983). *Manual for the Child Behavior Checklist and Revised Child Behavior Profile.* Burlington, VT: University of Vermont, Department of Psychiatry.

Achenbach, T. M., & Howell, C. T. (1993). Are American children's problems getting worse? A 13-year comparison. *Journal of the American Academy of Child and Adolescent Psychiatry, 32,* 1145–1154.

Ahlawat, K.S. (1986). Cross-cultural comparison of anxiety for Jordanian and U.S. high school students. In C. D. Spielberger and R. Diaz-Guerrero (Eds.), *Cross cultural anxiety* (Vol. 3, pp. 93–112). Washington, DC: Hemisphere/Harper & Row.

Al-Issa, I. S. (1982). *Culture and psychopathology.* Baltimore, MD: University Park Press.

American Psychiatric Association. (1980). *Diagnostic and statistical manual of mental disorders* (3rd ed.). Washington, DC: Author.

American Psychiatric Association. (1994). *Diagnostic and statistical manual of mental disorders* (4th ed.). Washington, DC: Author.

Ammerman, R. T., & Hersen, M. (1995). *Handbook of child behavior therapy in the psychiatric setting.* New York: Wiley.

Anderson, D. J., WIlliams, S., McGee, R., & Silva, P. A. (1987). *DSM-III* disorders in preadolescent children: Prevalence in a large sample from the general population. *Archives of General Psychiatry, 44,* 69–76.

Aronowitz, M. (1984). The social and emotional adjustment of immigrant children: A review of the literature. *International Migration Review, 28,* 237–257.

Ashworth, N. M. (1975). *Immigration children and Canadian schools.* Toronto, Ontario, Canada: McClelland & Stewart.

Baptiste, D. A., Jr. (1990). The treatment of adolescents and their families in cultural transition: Issues and recommendations. *Contemporary Family Therapy 12,* 3–22.

Barkley, R.A. (1990). *Attention deficit hyperactivity disorder: A handbook for diagnosis and treatment.* New York: Guilford Press.

Bauermeister, J. (1995). ADD and Hispanic (Puerto Rican) children: Some thoughts and research findings. *Attention, 2,* 16–19.

Bauermeister, J., Berrios, B., Jiminez, A., Acevedo, L., & Gordon, M. (1990). Some issues and instruments for the assessment of attention deficit hyperactivity disorder in Puerto Rican children. *Journal of Clinical Child Psychology, 19,* 9–16.

Beebee, S. A. (1974). Eye contact: A nonverbal determinant of speaker credibility. *Speech Teacher, 23,* 21–25.

Beiser, M., Dion, R., Gotowiec, A., Hyman, I., & Vu, N. (1995) Immigrants and refugees in Canada. *Canadian Journal of Psychiatry, 40,* 67–72.

Bernstein, G. A., & Borchardt, C.M. (1991). Anxiety disorders of childhood and adolescence: A critical review. *Journal of the American Academy of Child Psychiatry, 30,* 519–532.

Berry, J. W. (1980). Acculturation as varieties of adaptation. In A. M. Padilla (Ed.), *Acculturation: Theory, models, and some new findings* (pp. 9–25). Boulder, CO: Westview.

Berry, J. W. (1985). Psychological adaptation of foreign students. In R. J. Samuda & A. Wolfgang (Eds.), *Intercultural counseling and assessment: Global perspectives* (pp. 235–248). Toronto, Ontario, Canada: Hogrefe.

Bhatnagar, J. (1985). Counseling South Asian immigrants. In R. J. Samuda & A. Wolfgang (Eds.), *Intercultural counseling and assessment: Global perspectives* (pp. 191–202). Toronto, Ontario, Canada: Hogrefe.

Boles, S., Casas, J. M., Furlong, M., Gonzalez, G., & Morrison, G. (1994). Alcohol and other drug use patterns among Mexican American, Mexican and Caucasian adolescents: New directions for assessment and research. *Journal of Clinical Child Psychology, 23,* 39–46.

Bradley, S., & Sloman, L. (1975). Elective mutism in immigrant families. *Journal of the American Academy of Child Psychiatry, 14,* 510–514.

Bryson, S. E., Clark, B. S., & Smith, I. M. (1988). First report of a Canadian epidemiological study of autistic syndromes. *Journal of Child Psychology and Psychiatry, 29,* 433–445.

Canadian Institute of Child Health. (1994). *The health of Canada's children: A CICH profile.* (2nd ed.). Ottawa, Ontario, Canada: Author.

Charron, D. W., & Ness, R. C. (1981). Emotional distress among Vietnamese adolescents. *Journal of Refugee Settlement, 1,* 7–15.

Chataway, C. J., & Berry, J. W. (1989). Acculturation experience, appraisal, coping, and adaptation: A comparison of Hong Kong Chinese, French, and English students in Canada. *Canadian Journal of Behavioral Science, 21,* 295–309.

Chavez, E. L., Oetting, E. R., & Swaim, R. C.(1994). Dropout and delinquency: Mexican American and Caucasian non-Hispanic youth. *Journal of Clinical Child Psychology, 23,* 47–55.

Chen, P. W. (1977). *Chinese Americans view their mental health.* San Francisco: R & E Research Associates.

Chen, X., Rubin, K. H., & Sun, Y. (1992). Social reputation and peer relationships in Chinese and Canadian children: A cross-cultural study. *Child Development, 63,* 1336–1343.

Chiu, M. L., Feldman, S. S., & Rosenthal, D. A. (1992). The influence of immigration on parental behavior and adolescent distress in Chinese families residing in two Western nations. *Journal of Research on Adolescence, 2,* 205–237.

Chodzinski, R. T. (1985). Increasing the effectiveness of school counseling: A multicultural perspective. In R. J. Samuda & A. Wolfgang (Eds.), *Intercultural counseling and assessment: Global perspectives* (pp. 355–365). Toronto, Ontario, Canada: Hogrefe.

Christmas, J. J. (1982). Trying to make it real: Issues and concerns in the provision of services for minorities. In F. U. Munoz & R. Endo (Eds.), *Perspectives on minority group mental health* (pp. 109–131). Washington, DC: University Press of America.

Connors, C.K. (1973). Rating scales for use in drug studies in children. *Psychopharmacology Bulletin,* 24–42.

Constantino, G. (1986). *TEMAS (Tell Me a Story).* Los Angeles: Western Psychological Services.

Constantino, G., Malgady, R. G., Rogler, L. H., & Tsui, E. (1988) Discriminant analysis of clinical outpatients and public school children by TEMAS: A thematic apperception test for Hispanics and Blacks. *Journal of Personality Assessment, 52,* 670–678.

Costello, E. J., Costello, A. J., Edelbrock, C., Burns, B. J., Dulcan, M. K., Brent, D., & Janiszewski, S. (1988). Psychiatric disorders in pediatric primary care. *Archives of General Psychiatry, 45,* 1107–1116.

Dean, A., & Lin, N. (1977). The stress-buffering role of social support. *Journal of Nervous and Mental Disease, 165,* 403–417.

DiNicola, V. F. (1995). A prospectus for transcultural child psychiatry. In N. Grizenko, L. Sayegh & P. Migneault (Eds.), *Transcultural issues in child psychiatry* (pp. 7–53). Verdun, Quebec: Editions Douglas.

Dollinger, S. J., Molina, B. S., & Monteiro, J. M. C. (1996). Sleep and anxieties in Brazilian children: The role of cultural and environmental factors in child sleep disturbance. *American Journal of Orthopsychiatry, 66,* 252–261.

Draguns, J. G. (1982). Methodology in cross-cultural psychology. In I. Al-Issa (Ed.), *Culture and psychopathology* (pp. 33–70). Baltimore, MD: University Park Press.

Eppink, A. (1979). Social psychological problems of migrant child and cultural conflicts. *International Migration, 17,* 87–119.

Erikson, E. H. (1968). *Identity: Youth and crisis.* New York: Norton.

Feldman, S. S., & Rosenthal, D. A. (1990). The acculturation of autonomy expectations in Chinese high schoolers residing in two Western nations. *International Journal of Psychology, 25,* 259–281.

Fonesca, A. C. , Yule, W., & Erol, N. (1994). Cross-cultural issues. In T. H. Ollendick, N. J. King, & W. Yule (Eds.). *International handbook of phobic and anxiety disorders in children and adolescents* (pp. 67–84). New York: Plenum Press.

Foster, M., & Ferman, L. A. (1982). Minority populations and mental health manpower development: Some facts of life. In F. U. Munoz & R. Endo (Eds.), *Perspectives on minority group mental health* (pp. 143–155). Washington, DC: University Press of America.

French, D. C. (1990). Heterogeneity of peer-rejected girls. *Child Development, 61,* 2028–2031.

Friedman, S., & Paradis, C. (1991). African American patients with panic disorder and agoraphobia. *Journal of Anxiety Disorders, 5,* 35.

Garrison, C. Z., Jackson, K. L., Marsteller, F., McKeown, R., & Addy, C. (1990). A longitudinal study of depressive symptomatology in young adolescents. *Journal of the American Academy of Child and Adolescent Psychiatry, 29,* 581–585.

Gotowiec, A., & Beiser, M. (1993, Winter). Aboriginal children's mental health: Unique challenges. *Canada's Mental Health,* 7–11.

Guerra, N., Tolan, P., Hoesmann, L., Van Acker, R., & Eron, L. (1995). Stressful events and individual beliefs as correlates of economic disadvantage and aggression among urban children. *Journal of Consulting and Clinical Psychology, 63,* 518–528.

Ho, D. Y. F. (1986). Chinese pattern of socialization: A critical view. In M. H. Bond (Ed.), *The psychology of the Chinese people.* Oxford, England: Oxford University Press.

Horowitz, T. R., & Frenkel, E. (1976). *The adjustment of immigrant children to the school system in Israel.* Jerusalem: The Szold Institute.

Hsu, L. K. G. (1990). *Eating disorders.* New York: Guilford Press.

Huang, L. N. (1994). An integrative approach to clinical assessment and intervention with Asian American adolescents. *Journal of Clinical Child Psychology, 23,* 21–31.

Inouye, D. (1988). Children's mental health issues. *American Psychologist, 43,* 813–816.

Jenkins, J. M., & Smith, M. A. (1990). Factors protecting children living in disharmonious homes: Maternal reports. *Journal of the American Academy of Child and Adolescent Psychiatry, 29,* 60–69.

Kandel, J. H., & Davies, M. (1982). Epidemiology of depressive mood in adolescents. *Archives of General Psychiatry, 39,* 1205–1212.

Kirmayer, L. J., Young, A., & Hayton, B. C. (1995). The cultural context of anxiety disorders. *The Psychiatric Clinics of North America: Cultural Psychiatry, 18,* 503–522.

Knight, G. P., Virdin, L. M., & Roosa, M. (1994). Socialization and family correlates of mental health outcomes among Hispanic and Anglo American children: Consideration of cross-ethnic scalar equivalence. *Child Development, 65,* 212–224.

Koizumi, H., & Luidens, G. (1984). Cross-cultural issues in the treatment of intractable anorexia nervosa. *International Journal of Family Therapy, 6,* 156–164.

Kovacs, M., Feinberg, T. L., Crouse-Novak, M. A., Paulauskas, S. L., & Finkelstein, R. (1984). Depressive disorders in childhood. I. A longitudinal prospective study of characteristics and recovery. *Archives of General Psychiatry, 41,* 229–237.

Kurita, H., Miyake, Y., & Katsuno, K. (1989). Reliability and validity of the Childhood Autism Rating Scale—Tokyo Version (CARS-TV). *Journal of Autism and Developmental Disorders, 19,* 389–396.

LaFromboise, T., Coleman, H. L. K., & Gerton, J. (1993). Psychological impact of biculturalism: Evidence and theory. *Psychological Bulletin, 114,* 395–412.

Lambert, M. C., Knight, F. H., Taylor, R., & Achenbach, T. M. (1994). Epidemiology of behavioral and emotional problems among children of Jamaica and the United States: Parent reports for ages 6–11. *Journal of Abnormal Child Psychology, 22,* 113–129.

Lambert, M. C., Knight, F. H., Taylor, R., & Achenbach, T. M. (1996). Comparisons of behavioral and emotional problems among children of Jamaica and the United States: Teacher reports for ages 6–11. *Journal of Cross Cultural Psychology, 27,* 82–97.

Lambert, M. C., Weisz, J. R., & Knight, F. (1989). Over- and undercontrolled clinic referral problems of Jamaican and American children and adolescents: The culture general and culture specific. *Journal of Consulting and Clinical Psychology, 57,* 467–472.

Lambert, N. M., Sancoval, J., & Sassone, D. (1978). Prevalence of hyperactivity in elementary school children as a function of social system definers. *American Journal of Orthopsychiatry, 48,* 446–463.

Lambert, W. E. (1987). The fate of old-country values in a new land: A cross-national study of child rearing. *Canadian Psychology, 28,* 9–20.

Langsdorf, R., Anderson, R. F., Walchter, D., Madrigal, J. F., & Juarez, L. J. (1979). Ethnicity, social class and perception of hyperactivity. *Psychology in the Schools, 16,* 293–298.

Lee, B. K. (1996). Acculturation and socio-emotional adjustment in Canadian-Chinese adolescents. Unpublished M.A. thesis. London, Ontario, Canada: Department of Psychology, The University of Western Ontario.

LeVine, E. S., & Padilla, A. M. (1980). *Crossing cultures in therapy: Pluralistic counseling for the Hispanic.* Pacific Grove, CA: Brooks/Cole.

Levine, R. E., & Gaw, A. C. (1995). Culture-bound syndromes. *The Psychiatric Clinics of North America: Cultural Psychiatry, 18,* 523–536.

Loeber, R. (1990). Development and risk factors of juvenile antisocial behavior and delinquency. *Clinical Psychology Review, 10,* 1–41.

Luk, S. L., Leung, P. W. L., & Lee, P. L. M. (1988). Connors' Teacher Rating Scale in Chinese children in Hong Kong. *Journal of Child Psychology and Psychiatry, 29,* 165–174.

Manson, S. M. (1995). Culture and major depression. *The Psychiatric Clinics of North America: Cultural Psychiatry, 18,* 487–502.

McGoldrick, M., Pearce, J. K., & Giordano, J. (1982). *Ethnicity and family therapy.* New York: Guilford Press.

Mercer, J. R., & Lewis, J. F. (1978). *System of multicultural pluralistic assessment.* San Antonio, TX: The Psychological Corporation.

Mollica, R. F., Wyshak, G., & Lavelle, J. (1987). The psychosocial impact of war trauma and torture on Southeast Asia refugees. *American Journal of Psychiatry, 144,* 1567.

Naditch, M. P., & Morrissey, R. F. (1976). Role stress, personality, and psychopathology in a group of immigrant adolescents. *Journal of Abnormal Psychology, 85,* 113–116.

Nguyen, N. A., & Williams, H. L. (1989). Transition from East to West: Vietnamese adolescents and their parents. *Journal of American Academy of Child and Adolescent Psychiatry, 28,* 505–515.

Offord, D. R. (1995). The mental health of immigrant and refugee children. *Canadian Journal of Psychiatry, 40,* 57–58.

Offord, D. R. (1989). Conduct disorder: Risk factors and prevention. In D. Shaffer, I. Phillips, & N. B. Enzer (Eds.), *Prevention of mental disorders, alcohol and other drug use* (pp. 273–307). Rockville, MD: U.S. Department of Health and Human Services.

Ollendick, T. H. (1983). Reliability and validity of the Revised Fear Survey Schedule for Children (FSSC-R). *Behavior Research and Therapy, 21,* 685–692.

Ollendick, T. H., & Hersen, M. (1989). *Handbook of child psychopathology* (2nd Ed.). New York: Plenum Press.

Ontario Association of Children's Mental Health Centers (1996, March). *O.A.C.M.H.C. Accreditation Standards, Revised.* Toronto, Ontario, Canada: Author.

Pawliuk, N., Grizenko, N., Chan-Yip, A., Gantous, P., Mathew, J., & Nguyen, D. (1996). Acculturation style and psychological functioning in children of immigrants. *American Journal of Orthopsychiatry, 66,* 111–121.

Pedersen, P. B. (1985). Intercultural counseling: U.S. perspectives. In R. J. Samuda & A. Wolfgang (Eds.), *Intercultural counseling* (pp. 71–82). Toronto, Ontario, Canada: Hogrefe.

Ponterotto, J. G., & Casas, J. M. (1991). *Handbook of racial/ethnic minority counseling research.* Springfield, IL: Charles C. Thomas.

Radloff, L. S. (1977). The CES-D scale: A self-report depression scale for research in the general population. *Applied Psychological Measurement, 1,* 385–401.

Ramirez, M., III. (1983). *Psychology of the Americas: Mestiza perspectives on personality and mental health.* Elmsford, NY: Pergamon Press.

Ramirez, M., III. (1991). *Psychotherapy and counseling with minorities: A cognitive approach to individual and cultural differences.* Elmsford, NY: Pergamon Press.

Rogler, L. H. (1978). Help patterns, the family, and mental health: Puerto Rican in the United States. *International Migration Review, 12,* 248–259.

Rosenthal, D. A. (1984). Intergenerational conflict and culture: A study of immigrant and nonimmigrant adolescents and their parents. *Genetic Psychology Monographs, 109,* 53–75.

Rousseau, C., Drapeau, A, & Corin, E. (1996). School performance and emotional problems in refugee children. *American Journal of Orthopsychiatry, 66,* 239–251.

Rubin, K. H., & Mills, R. S. L. (1988). The many faces of social isolation in childhood. *Journal of Consulting and Clinical Psychology, 6,* 916–924.

Rubino-Stipec, M., Bird, H., Canino, G., & Gould, M. (1990). The internal consistency and concurrent validity of a Spanish translation of the Child Behavior Checklist. *Journal of Abnormal Child Psychology, 18,* 393–406.

Russell, J. A. (1991). Culture and the categorization of emotions. *Psychology Bulletin, 110,* 426.

Rutter, M. (1979). Protective factors in children's responses to stress and disadvantages. In M. W. Kent & J. E. Rolf (Eds.), *Primary prevention of psychopathology: Vol. 3. Promoting social competence and coping in children* (pp. 49–74). Hanover, NH: University Press of New England.

Rutter, M., & Rutter, M. (1992). *Developing minds.* London: Penguin.

Sandler, I. N., Miller, P., Short, J., & Wolchik, S. A. (1989). Social support as a protective factor for children in stress. In D. Belle (Ed.), *Children's social networks and social supports* (pp. 277–307). New York: John Wiley.

Sarda, M. (1990). Beyond bilingualism: Providing mental health services to Franco-Ontarian children. *Children's Mental Health, 3,* 2–6.

Sattler, J. M. (1988). *Assessment of children* (3rd ed.). San Diego, CA: Author.

Semeniuk, R. (1995). War babies. *Equinox, 79,* 36–49.

Sluzki, C. E. (1979). Migration and family conflict. *Family Process, 18,* 379–390.

Solomon, B. B. (1982). A theoretical perspective for delivery of mental health services to minority communities. In F. U. Munoz & R. Endo (Eds.), *Perspectives on minority group mental health* (pp. 85–92). Washington, DC: University Press of America.

Spielberger, C. D. (1973). *Manual for the State-Trait Anxiety Inventory for Children.* Palo Alto, CA: Consulting Psychologists Press.

Sroufe, L. A., & Rutter, M. (1984). The domain of developmental psychopathology. *Child Development, 55,* 17–29.

Steffenburg, S., & Gillberg, C. (1986). Autism and autistic-like conditions in Swedish rural and urban areas: A population study. *British Journal of Psychiatry, 149,* 81–87.

Sue, S. (1982). Ethnic minority research: Trends and directions. In F. U. Munoz & R. Endo (Eds.), *Perspectives on minority group mental health* (pp. 171–183). Washington, DC: University Press of America.

Sugiyama, T., & Abe, T. (1989). The prevalence of autism in Nagoya, Japan: A total population study. *Journal of Autism and Developmental Disorders, 19,* 87–96.

Szatmari, P. (1992). The epidemiology of attention-deficit hyperactivity disorders. In G. Weiss (Ed.), *Child and adolescent psychiatric clinics of North America: Attention-deficit hyperactivity disorder* (pp. 361–372). Philadelphia: Saunders.

Tikalsky, F. D., & Wallace, S. D. (1988). Culture and the structure of children's fears. *Journal of Cross-Cultural Psychology, 19,* 481–492.

Vargas, L. A., & Willis, D. J. (1994). Introduction to the special section: New directions in the treatment and assessment of ethnic minority children and adolescents. *Journal of Clinical Child Psychology, 23,* 2–4.

Waxer, P. H. (1985). Nonverbal aspects of intercultural counseling. In R. J. Samuda & A. Wolfgang (Eds.), *Intercultural counseling and assessment: Global perspectives* (pp. 49–66). Toronto, Ontario, Canada: Hogrefe.

Weisz, J. R., Suwanlert, S., Chaiyasit, W., & Walter, B. R. (1987). Over- and undercontrolled referral problems among children and adolescents from Thailand and the United States: The wat and wai of cultural differences. *Journal of Consulting and Clinical Psychology, 55,* 719–726.

Weisz, J. R., Suwanlert, S., Chaiyasit, W., Weiss, B., Achenbach, T. M., & Trevathan, D. (1989). Epidemiology of behavioral and emotional problems among Thai and American children: Teacher reports for ages 6–11. *Journal of Child Psychology and Psychiatry, 30,* 471–484.

Williams, C. L., & Berry, J. W. (1991). Primary prevention of acculturative stress among refugees: Application of psychological theory and practice. *American Psychologist, 46,* 632–641.

Wyspianski, J. O., & Fournier-Ruggles, L. A. (1985). Counseling European immigrants: Issues and answers. In R. J. Samuda & A. Wolfgang (Eds.), *Intercultural counseling and assessment* (pp. 225–234). Toronto, Ontario, Canada: Hogrefe.

Yates, A. (1987). Current status and future direction of research on American Indian children. *American Journal of Psychiatry, 144,* 1135–1142.

Yee, B. W. K., & Hennesy, S. T. (1982). Pacific/Asian American families and mental health. In F. U. Munoz & R. Endo (Eds.), *Perspectives on minority group mental health* (pp. 53–70). Washington, DC: University Press of America.

Yeh, M., Takeuchi, D. T., & Sue, S. (1994). Asian American children treated in the mental health system: A comparison of parallel and mainstream outpatient service centers. *Journal of Clinical Child Psychology, 23,* 5–12.

Zigler, E. F., & Stevenson, M. F. (1993). *Children in a changing world: Development and social issues* (2nd ed.). Pacific Grove, CA: Brooks/Cole.

12

Cultural Aspects of Family Violence

SHAHÉ S. KAZARIAN

LEVONTY Z. KAZARIAN

The past two decades have witnessed a growing awareness worldwide of the reality of family violence. Acts of physical abuse, and neglect, sexual abuse, and emotional abuse against children and acts of violence and psychological maltreatment in intimate relationships and against the elderly are occurring on a daily basis in the homes of many people around the world, independent of culture, economic status, and sexual orientation. Family violence has manifested itself in different cultures and across the life span and has taken a variety of forms, including infanticide, physical abuse, painful initiation ceremonies, physical neglect, sexual molestation, prostitution, rape, pornography, emotional and psychological abuse, and spiritual abuse (Canadian Panel on Violence Against Women, 1993; Finkelhor & Korbin, 1988; Levinson, 1989; Ntiri, 1993; Podnieks & Pillemer, 1991; U.S. Advisory Board on Child Abuse and Neglect, 1990; U.S. Congress House Select Committee on Aging, 1991). It has been estimated that violence against women alone costs Canadians at least $4.2 billion (Egan, 1995). Interpersonal abuse has also been shown to have deleterious effects on physical health, psychological adjustment and well-being, and quality of life (Arbesman, Kahler, & Buck, 1993; Kendall-Tackett, Williams, & Finkelhor, 1993; Weaver & Clum, 1995).

In North America, violence as a major health priority has been recognized by the U.S. Surgeon General (Koop, 1985), the American Medical Association (1992), the Canadian Panel on Violence Against Women (1993), and the American Psychological Association (Koss et al., 1994). The clinical and public health significance of violence has also been recognized by inclusion of a new diagnostic category, Problems Related to Abuse and Neglect, in the fourth edition of the *Diagnostic and Statistical Manual of Mental Disorders* (*DSM-IV;* American Psychiatric Association, 1994); and by the inclusion of the topic as a separate chapter in a recent abnormal psychology textbook (Wilson, Nathan, O'Leary, & Clark, 1996).

Considering the developmental nature of family violence and the psychological, social, and economic costs associated with violence, there has also been increased societal recognition of effective intervention and prevention approaches. Health Canada received a report of a special advisor in which 74 recommendations were listed for eliminating child sexual abuse in Canada (Rogers, 1990). In 1989, a National Panel was established by the Canadian government to provide a comprehensive study of violence against women (Canadian Panel on Violence Against Women, 1993). The American Psychological Association's (APA) Committee on Women in Psychology also established the Task Force on Male Violence Against Women to assist in addressing problems associated with one aspect of family violence, male violence against women. In addition to reviewing current psychological research on the prevalence, causes, and effects of different types of abuse toward women, the Task Force was mandated to describe existing interventions and to make recommendations regarding interventions, legal changes, and policy initiatives (Koss et al., 1994). Each of the final reports of the Canadian Panel on Violence Against Women and the Task Force on Male Violence Against Women provides both a comprehensive and scholarly treatise on the topic of violence against women and an excellent resource to those interested in the area of family violence. In the present chapter, we examine the cultural aspects of family violence in general, and wife abuse in particular, with a view to providing a more expanded and integrated approach to family violence theory, research, and practice.

DEFINITION OF FAMILY VIOLENCE

Terminology is critical not only from the perspectives of theory and research, but also from the perspective of validating and understanding the subjective experiences associated with family violence (Koss et al., 1994). The study of family violence has been compromised by various terminologies and definitions, providing for conceptual inconsistencies and difficulties in comparisons across studies nationally or internationally. For example, a variety of terms have been used in relation to violence in intimate relationships, including spousal abuse, wife abuse, partner abuse, wife assault, and wife battering. Wife abuse is an exclusionary term in that it refers to violence perpetrated by a husband against a wife. Spousal abuse, on the other hand, is inclusionary in that it does not preclude husband beating as an aspect of intimate relationships. Partner abuse is even more inclusionary than spouse abuse in that it considers abuse in homosexual and lesbian relationships, in addition to those that are heterosexual, and in nonmarital relationships (i.e., dating or cohabiting couples).

Similarly, the use of the terms *abuse* and *violence* in studies of family violence has been inconsistent. Gelles and Cornell (1983a) have cautioned against the conceptual equivalence of the terms violence and abuse. In their review of the international literature on family violence, they have referred to violence as all forms of physical aggression and have defined abuse in broader terms that are inclusive of violence (i.e., acts of violence or injurious physical aggression, mistreatment, malnourishment, violent and nonviolent sexual abuse, and medical neglect).

Koss et al. (1994), on the other hand, adapted their working definition of violence toward women from Kelly (1988). They defined violence broadly to include psychological abuse. According to Koss et al. (1994), male violence toward women encompasses "physical, visual, verbal, or sexual acts that are experienced by a woman or girl as a threat, invasion, or assault and that have the effect of hurting her or degrading her and/ or taking away her ability to control contact (intimate and otherwise) with another individual" (p. xvi). The Canadian Panel on Violence Against Women also included the spiritual domain in their definition of violence against women (Canadian Panel on Violence Against Women, 1993). Finally, the *DSM-IV* listed severe mistreatment (physical abuse, sexual abuse, and child neglect) as a problem that may warrant clinical attention from the perspectives of both victims and perpetrators. While no specific definitions were provided for abuse or neglect, five categories of abuse and neglect were identified in the *DSM-IV:* physical abuse of a child, sexual abuse of a child, neglect of a child, physical abuse of an adult, and sexual abuse of an adult.

Child abuse is a generic term and represents different forms of maltreatment, including physical abuse or neglect, emotional abuse or neglect, and sexual abuse. Efforts have been made to provide consensus definitions of child maltreatment (Finkelhor & Korbin, 1988; Korbin, 1991), psychological abuse (Brassard, Germain, & Hart, 1987; O'Hagan, 1995) and child sexual abuse (Schecter & Roberge, 1976). Finkelhor & Korbin (1988) argued that not all harm experienced by children should be construed as maltreatment. Consequently, they defined child abuse as "the portion of harm to children that results from human action that is proscribed, proximate, and preventable" (p. 4). Schecter and Roberge (1976) defined child sexual abuse as sexual exploitation in which dependent and developmentally immature children and adolescents are involved in "sexual activities they do not fully comprehend, are unable to give informed consent to, and that violate the social taboos of family roles." Finally, Brassard, Germain, and Hart (1987) defined psychological maltreatment of children and youth as acts of omission and commission (e.g., rejection, isolation, exploitation, and missocialization) that are deemed to be emotionally damaging by psychological criteria and expert professional opinion.

The definition of family in family violence research and comparisons across family structures on rates of family violence have rarely been considered. Family violence studies in Western cultures have been conducted on nuclear families (i.e., a family composed of a wife, a husband, and their children) to the exclusion of other forms of family structure. While the nuclear-family type has been implicated as a risk factor for family violence (e.g., Straus, Gelles, & Steinmetz, 1980), comparisons of rates of family violence for different family structures is instructive. Levinson (1989) conducted a cross-cultural study and examined the relationship between social structure and family violence in 90 societies throughout the world. In this anthropological study, wife beating and child physical punishment were found to be the two most common types of family violence. While family structure and wife beating were independent, a lower rate of child punishment was found for the extended-family type, followed by the nuclear-family type and the mother-child family type. The potential mitigating effects of embeddedness of child rearing in social networks have been described by Korbin (1991). Protective functions listed include reduced social isolation, increased scrutiny, and greater consensus and enforcement of socially acceptable child-rearing practices and standards.

DEFINITION OF CULTURE

Culture has been neglected in the study of family violence. Its neglect has been evidenced by the paucity of literature on family violence in immigrant, refugee, and racial minority groups in host countries and by the lack of consideration of psychological adaptation processes in family-violence theory, research, and practice. The neglect of culture in the study of family violence is paradoxical in view of the widespread rejection of the biomedical model, which tends to pathologize victims of abuse, and the almost zealous embracement of systemic and psychosocial underpinnings of family violence.

The inappropriate definition of culture in family-violence studies has been manifested in a variety of ways. The few studies that have been conducted on cultural groups have entangled culture with socioeconomic status and poverty and have defined cultural groups in terms of ethnicity or race (e.g., Melton & Flood, 1994). Use of these terms as conceptual equivalents to culture in family-violence research has failed to take into consideration important acculturation processes and has obscured the heterogeneity of people within the broad categories of race and ethnicity.

Segal (1992) cautioned against the ethnocentric transfer of child-abuse concepts to non-Western cultures and argued in favor of theoretical and empirical evaluation of the phenomenon within culture-specific constructs. Haj-Yahia and Shor (1995) indicated that understanding of perceptions of child maltreatment and intervention approaches in family life are unlikely without consideration of the political and ecological context of cultural communities. For example, Haj-Yehia and Shor (1995) found that students from the West Bank in helping professions rated the degree of maltreatment associated with child abuse equal to that associated with neglect. This finding is in contrast to the Western view, in which situations of abuse are considered to be more serious than those involving neglect. The different perception of maltreatment in the two cultures was attributed to the greater emphasis in Arab culture on parental sacrificial behavior in favor of children's needs.

Consideration of culture in the context of family violence within and across national boundaries is appropriate and warranted. Inclusion of the cultural perspective in the definition of family violence has the advantage of balancing ethnocentric or cultural relativistic views and providing a coherent framework for family-violence theory and research within host communities or the international community. The application of the cultural perspective to the definition of family violence has been most evident in the area of child maltreatment. Korbin (1991) has recommended the use of three levels for formulating a culturally appropriate definition of child maltreatment. The first level pertains to cultural practices and beliefs in child rearing. Korbin (1991) indicates that cultural conflict in defining child maltreatment is most likely at this level, as what might be viewed as acceptable belief or practice in one culture may be construed as abusive or neglectful by outsiders. A contemporary issue that exemplifies cultural conflict at this level is the practice of female circumcision (see Brant, 1995; Brant, Wyatt, & Martin, 1995; Martin, 1995).

The second level of formulating a culturally appropriate definition of child maltreatment pertains to idiosyncratic deviations from a continuum of acceptable behaviors within a culture. Korbin (1991) indicates that it is at this level that child maltreatment is most legitimately identified across cultural boundaries, as all communities have criteria for identifying practices and beliefs that exceed their acceptable standards. The third level refers to the degree that such societal conditions as familial poverty, unemployment, and hunger are tolerated culturally. Korbin (1991) indicates that these societal conditions are beyond the control of individual caregivers, even though they tend to be associated with child maltreatment.

The relevance of Korbin's (1991) analysis of child maltreatment to family violence in general is self-evident. The implication of this cultural perspective to family violence study is that cultural variations in social environments (i.e., beliefs, values, and behaviors) and physical environments (i.e., natural and man-made physical structures), as well as acculturative processes and stresses (Berry, 1990, 1994), are essential factors to be considered in developing universal definitions, theories, and practices. Acculturation refers to group or individual changes in individuals from a culture of origin due to contact with other cultures (including host culture), provided the individuals are involved in the process of change within the culture of origin. Group-level changes include changes in social structure and economic base, whereas individual level changes include those pertaining to attitudes and behaviors, as well as identity and values (Berry, 1990). Acculturation attitudes (Berry & Kim, 1988) refer to the four acculturation outcomes of assimilation (rejection of culture of origin and adoption of host culture), integration (acceptance of both culture of origin and host culture), separation (acceptance of culture of origin and rejection of host culture), and marginalization (rejection of both culture of origin and host culture). Finally, acculturative stress refers to stressors and psychological distress associated with the process of acculturation. For example, immigrant families may become isolated from their traditional kin and social networks. Their children may also develop noncompliant behavior and disobedience as they adopt Western values and beliefs and ways of interacting with their parents (e.g., calling the police to govern their conflicts with their parents). Acculturation factors have been implicated in health and mental health (e.g., Rogler, Cortes, & Malgady, 1991) and are relevant to the understanding of family violence.

SCOPE OF THE PROBLEM OF FAMILY VIOLENCE

Family violence affects children, youth, adults, and older people from every culture, including the mainstream culture, and from every economic, religious, and educational background. Children may experience physical abuse and neglect, sexual abuse, emotional maltreatment, and ritual abuse and may also witness interpartner violence. In adults, physical, sexual, psychological, and spiritual abuse may occur in heterosexual and homosexual relationships irrespective of culture, and victims of the abuse in these relationships may be either male or female. Finally, abuse and neglect in the elderly occur in the form of psychological, physical, sexual, and financial mistreatment,

Accurate incidence and prevalence rates on family violence are compromised by the private nature of abuse and neglect, by the lack of definitional consensus on the different types of abuse, and by the methodological limitations inherent in the studies reported (Ammerman & Hersen, 1992; Gelles & Cornell, 1983b; Health Canada,

1995; Korbin, 1993). Nevertheless, the available data on mainstream culture supports the pervasiveness of child abuse (American Humane Association, 1984; Hansen, Conaway, & Christopher, 1990; National Center on Child Abuse and Neglect, 1988; Straus, 1994; Straus & Gelles, 1986; U.S. Advisory Board on Child Abuse and Neglect, 1990; Van Biema, 1994; D. A. Wolfe, 1987), elder abuse (Straus & Gelles, 1986), and partner abuse (Straus, Gelles, & Steinmetz, 1980).

Incidence and prevalence studies on child abuse have shown that every year approximately 3 to 4 million American households (Gelles & Straus, 1988; National Center on Child Abuse and Neglect, 1988) and 500,000 Canadian households (Carlson, 1984; MacLeod, 1987) experience a significant degree of violence. According to the National Center on Child Abuse and Neglect, 2 million reports on child abuse are received annually in the United States, 1 million of which are followed up by child protective service agencies. In addition, a telephone survey has revealed that 10.7% of caregivers use a severe violent act as a means of child control. Child abuse and child sexual abuse represent problems of an international nature. For example, Finkelhor (1994) reviewed epidemiological data from 19 countries, in addition to those from North America. While the studies varied in scope, definition of the problem, and methodological sophistication, the findings were such that the rates of child sexual abuse from the different countries were comparable to those from the United States and Canada, ranging from 7% to 36% for females and 3% to 29% for males. The wide range in prevalence rates seen in child maltreatment studies is likely due to cultural differences in child abuse practices and perceptions of child maltreatment. For example, Kouno and Johnson (1994) provided a historical account of child abuse in Japan and suggested that the coin-operated-locker baby is a type of child maltreatment that may be unique to that culture. Similarly, Mejiuni (1991) classified types of child maltreatment in Nigeria and described the practice of childhood marriage as a form of abuse. Mejiuni (1991) reported the case of a 12-year-old girl who refused to obey her father's command to marry the man to whom she was betrothed when she was a child. Evidently, the girl went on a hunger strike and died after her irate father chopped off her leg for consistently running away from the home of her betrothed.

Studies on physical and sexual violence against women have been conducted using national and city samples. A variety of methodologies has also been used, including face-to-face interviews (Randall & Haskell, 1993; Straus et al., 1980) and telephone interviews (Straus & Gelles, 1992). Straus and Gelles (1992) reported that each year about 4% of women in conjugal or cohabiting relationships experience physical aggression involving the use of beating, a knife, or a gun. Randall and Haskell (1993) interviewed a random sample of 420 women between the ages of 18 and 64 living in a Canadian multicultural metropolis. Their preliminary findings indicated that 56% of the women had experienced some form of unwanted or intrusive sexual act before reaching the age of 16, that two out of three women 16 years and older had experienced the criminal act of sexual assault (including sexual touching), and that 27% of the women had experienced a physical assault in an intimate relationship. Koss et al. (1994) reviewed prevalence studies on physical aggression in the United States and pointed out that experts estimate, on the basis of 17 years of empirical research, that one in every three women will be physically assaulted at least once by an intimate partner during adulthood.

Epidemiologic studies carried out in North America and Europe on elder maltreatment have shown comparable rates of elder abuse and neglect: 2.2% for physical abuse, 1.1% for habitual verbal aggression, and 0.4% for neglect (Lachs & Pillemer, 1995). Higher rates of elder mistreatment have been reported for institutionalized elderly (Health Canada, 1995; Pillemer & Moore, 1989) and those with Alzheimer's disease (Paveza et al., 1992). The U.S. Congress House Select Committee on Aging (1991) has estimated that between 1 million and 2 million older Americans experience maltreatment each year. The international nature of the elder abuse problem has been affirmed recently (Sykes, 1996).

EMPIRICAL RESEARCH ON FAMILY VIOLENCE
WITHIN HOST CULTURES

Prevalence studies on family violence have been based on the mainstream culture. Studies involving diverse cultural groups in host countries have been few and limited methodologically in that they have confounded social class with culture; have included the terms *ethnicity, race,* and *women of color* as conceptual equivalents to culture; have ignored within-group heterogeneity; and have failed to consider the level of acculturation of participants. To illustrate the methodological practice of such "lumping", it is instructive to examine the term *women of color.* This term refers to women with diverse cultural, linguistic, economic, social, and sexual orientations (Canadian Panel on Violence Against Women, 1993). Women of color may have been born in a host country, and their families may have been in the host country for generations. Alternatively, women of color may have come from different countries of origin to a host country under one of five categories of immigration: independent, family class, assisted relatives, refugees, and temporary work permit. Finally, they may speak different languages, may represent different castes and racial groups, and their identifications with their culture of origin and the host culture may be different. In view of these complex conceptual issues, understanding the effect of culture on family violence is likely to be enhanced with the practice of methodological "splitting" rather than "lumping."

In comparison to family violence studies on mainstream culture in Western societies, there is very little literature on family violence in relation to the various cultural groups within these communities. The limited research on the role of culture in family violence is instructive. Family violence is an international phenomenon and occurs in cultural groups in host countries. Family violence in the form of child physical abuse and neglect, child sexual abuse, partner abuse, and elder maltreatment have been reported for Indigenous people, immigrant, refugee, and racial minority groups (Haffejee, 1991; Huston, Parra, Prihoda, & Foulds, 1995; Korbin, 1993; Koss et al., 1994; McKelvey & Webb, 1995; Mennen, 1994; National Organization of Immigrant and Visible Minority Women of Canada, 1993, 1995; Smallwood, 1995). While family violence in diverse cultures in host countries exists, it is important to realize that these findings do not provide evidence that such practices are condoned in Indigenous, immigrant, refugee, and racial minority communities (Ho, 1990; Korbin, 1993), in much the same way that evidence on family violence in North America does not indicate that family violence is an accepted practice in mainstream cultures. This is an important assertion, as individuals from mainstream cultures have the disturbing belief that immigrants, refugees, and racial minority groups sanction violence in their countries of origin or that these groups import such practices to the host country. "Maybe it's okay to beat your wife or child in Turkey, but it is not okay to beat your wife or child here in Canada," is a common expression directed by mainstream culture to immigrant, refugee and racial minority groups or individuals. The truth of the matter is that family violence is not okay in Mexico, or Spain, or Armenia, or Israel, or Lebanon, or any other culture.

Korbin (1993) reviewed cultural diversity and child maltreatment research in the United States and concluded that there was no empirical basis to support the assertion that rates of child abuse are higher among cultural, ethnic, or racial groups. Similar conclusions were drawn by Vida (1994) in relation to elder abuse and neglect. Mennen (1994) reviewed studies on ethnic/racial differences in sexual-abuse trauma and concluded that the results were conflicting and inconclusive. Mennen (1994) also reported a trend of longer duration of sexual abuse for mainstream girls than for Spanish American or African American girls.

O'Keefe (1994) studied a sample of racially/ethnically diverse battered women and their children and found few significant racial/ethnic differences on measures of marital satisfaction, partner abuse, and child abuse. Kantor, Jasinski, & Aldarondo (1994) found that the incidence of marital violence in Hispanic American subgroups was comparable to those in Anglo American families. Contrary to earlier reports of higher partner abuse for African American women (Hampton & Gelles, 1994; Straus et al., 1980), these women showed comparable rates to mainstream women (Cazenave & Straus, 1992; Hampton & Gelles, 1994), even though the lethality of violence in their case was considerably higher. Similarly, Mexican American men showed comparable abuse rates to African American men and mainstream men (Gondolf, Fisher & McFerron, 1988; Sorenson & Telles, 1991). However, Mexican American women born in Mexico showed lower risk of being abused than Mexican American women born in the United States or mainstream women. Similar findings were shown for a Puerto Rican–American group (Kantor et al.,1994).

Comparative studies are important for establishing culture-specificity or universality. A study by Scarf (1988) suggests caution in generalizing findings on family violence from mainstream culture to other cultures. In this study, the characteristics of 200 battered Jewish wives were compared to reported characteristics of mainstream battered wives. A summary of these comparisons is provided in Table 12.1

In contrast to non-Jewish battered women, Scarf (1988) reported that Jewish battered wives in her study were not exposed to familial violence in their developmental years, had been engaged for a relatively long period of time prior to marriage, and had support for their marriages from their parents. In addition to perceived warnings of violence prior to marriage, the partners of the Jewish women had shown sexual dysfunctions (e.g., premature ejaculation) on an ongoing basis, beginning during their honeymoons. Similarly, and in contrast to three stages of battering (tension building, acute battering, and contrition) described by Walker (1979) that are seen in mainstream wife battering, Scarf (1988) reported that attacks on Jewish women in her sample had been unprovoked and not preceded by arguments or fighting and that the Jewish husbands failed to try to make up after the battering episodes. The Jewish women had also invariably felt responsible for precipitating the battering episode,

Table 12.1. Profiles of Non-Jewish and Jewish Battered Women

Characteristics	Non-Jewish Women	Jewish Women
History of family violence	yes	no
Duration of engagement	short	long
Parental approval of marriage	no	yes
Perceived premarital warnings	no	yes
Honeymoon disappointment	no	yes
Partner sexual dysfunction	no	yes
First beating attack	first pregnancy	first pregnancy
Stages of battering		
Fighting	yes	no
Beating	yes	yes
Making up (e.g., sex)	yes	no
Acceptance of violence over time	increase	decrease
Immediate reaction to a beating		
Feeling guilty	yes	yes
Begging forgiveness	no	yes
Screaming	yes	never

Source: Extracted from Scarf (1988).

and their immediate reactions had been to ask for forgiveness. Finally, the Jewish battered women had made every effort to ensure that the attention of children and neighbors was not drawn to the fact that abuse was occurring in the sanctity of the house.

The finding of differential profiles for Jewish and non-Jewish women by Scarf (1988) suggests the cultural specificity of some aspects of wife abuse. The finding also supports the importance of considering culture in studies on family violence. It is interesting to note that the study by Scarf (1988) was not referenced in the final report of the Task Force on Male Violence Against Women (Koss et al., 1994). As discussed by the author, her findings, if replicated, have important theoretical and practical implications for the study of wife battering. Theoretically, the absence of both familial violence and stages of battering in the Jewish sample are problematic to social-learning theory and to Walker's (1979) stage model of wife battering. Practically, the findings suggest intervention approaches that require more specificity to cultural beliefs and practices.

Taken together, empirical findings on culture and family violence provide the following important conclusions. First, there has been academic inattention to family violence and culture in general and to specific cultural groups (e.g., Indigenous people) in particular (Chester et al., 1994). Second, comparative studies do not support the stereotype that the diverse cultural groups in host cultures are more violent or accepting of violence than their Western counterparts. This assertion is consistent with conclusions reached by the Canadian Panel on Violence Against Women. In their final report, the panel indicated categorically that they were "aware of no statistics that support" the notion that "violence is more prevalent and/or accepted in non-Western immigrant communities" (Canadian Panel on Violence Against Women, 1993, p. 89). Third, the finding of a lower rate of abuse for Spanish American women born in Mexico or Puerto Rico than for those born in the United States and of the longer duration of child sexual abuse in mainstream culture support the importance of considering acculturation factors and cultural factors that mitigate against such practices. The comparable rate of family violence is particularly revealing considering that immigrant, refugee, and racial-minority individuals have the added vulnerability for acculturative adjustments and stresses in host cultures. While the majority of them cope extremely well with the psychosocial stressors they encounter and succeed in their economic and psychological adaptation efforts, a small minority do fail, and a certain percentage, comparable to majority-culture individuals, respond to their situation in the form of family violence. While their abusive reactions cannot be excused or condoned, neither can their failure be attributed to their culture.

THEORETICAL PERSPECTIVES ON FAMILY VIOLENCE

Single-factor theories on the genesis of family violence have focused on victim characteristics, perpetrator profiles, and contextual factors (see Table 12.2). For example, such child characteristics as poor health, handicap and deformity, gender, developmental age, and maladaptive behavior have been implicated in child maltreatment (see Korbin, 1991). Perpetrator characteristics associated with child maltreatment include those relating to alcohol abuse, drug abuse, psychiatric problems, and parental incompetence. Contextual factors that have been associated with child maltreatment and child sexual abuse have included poverty, social isolation, parental absence, and marital discord. More recently such factors as oppression, racism, discrimination, acculturation, and acculturative stress are also implicated. Haffejee (1991) has observed an association between interreligious marriage and child sexual abuse. This author has postulated that the erosion of traditional values and norms associated with interreligious relations contributes to irresponsible caregiver behavior, which manifests itself in child sexual abuse.

In addition to single-factor theories, integrative, transactional, transitional, social-information processing, and stress and coping models have been advanced (Belsky, 1980; Birns, Cascardi, & Meyer, 1994; Campbell, Harris, & Lee, 1995; Carden, 1994; Cicchetti & Rizley, 1981; D. G. Dutton, 1995b; Feldman & Ridley, 1995; Gelles & Cornell, 1983b; Hillson & Kuiper, 1994; Lenton, 1995; Levinson, 1989; Maxwell & Maxwell, 1992; Milner, 1993; Spaccarelli, 1994; Wolf, 1992; D. A. Wolfe, 1987). While detailed discussion of all of these models is beyond the scope of this chapter, brief descriptions of few of the models are provided in Table 12.2. Several conclusions can be drawn from the brief review of the theories on the genesis of family violence. First, the etiology of family violence is likely multifactorial rather than singular. Second, the level of empirical support for the various theories seems variable, with least support for single-factor explanations (D. G. Dutton, 1995b; Perilla, Bakerman, & Norris, 1994). Third, the etiological theories reviewed are incomplete in that they tend to pay lip service to the role of culture in family violence (Hine, 1989, Ucko, 1994). In a recent strategic document on Violence Against Immigrant, Refugee and Racial Minority Women, it was asserted that "immigrant and visible minority women are critical of mainstream and middle class, white, feminist ap-

Table 12.2. Etiological Theories of Family Violence

Perpetrator Theory: Family violence is produced by physical or psychological pathology in the perpetrator or the victim.

Personality Theory: Borderline personality organization is the basis for repetitive and cyclical abusiveness in intimate relationships.

Resource Theory: Control of economic resources in the family is associated with male dominance and family violence.

Status Inconsistency Theory: Erosion of a man's traditional power in the family and the concomitant increase in a woman's power contributes to family violence.

Exchange Theory: Family violence is based on high benefits and low costs to the perpetrator. Male aggressiveness, family isolation, and economic inequality provide social context for abuse.

Culture of Violence Theory: Occurrence of family violence is related to level of societal violence, i.e., high in violent societies and low in peaceful societies.

Patriarchal Theory: Societal endorsement of the values of aggressiveness, male dominance, and female subordination cause the use of physical force to endorse dominance and control.

Social Learning Theory: A combination of contextual factors (violence in family of origin, stress, and aggressive personality style) and situational factors (marital discord and substance use) cause family violence.

Ecological Theory: Societal legitimization of aggression against family members, socioeconomic disadvantage, and familial isolation from social support networks are significant precursors of family violence.

General Systems Theory: Family violence is seen as the product of a positive feedback loop involving individual, familial, and societal factors. Factors specifically identified in the model include sexist societal and familial organization, societal legitimization of violence, intergenerational transmission of violence, resource control, and isolation of the nuclear family.

Social Information Processing Model: Perpetrator cognitions in the form of perceptions, interpretations, evaluations, expectations, information integration, and response selection are operative in child abuse.

Stress and Coping Model: Perpetrator cognitive appraisals of stress, both primary and secondary, and coping dispositions are implicated in child abuse and neglect.

---

proaches to wife abuse and violence against women, which marginalize the needs and realities of immigrant, refugee, and racial minority women" (National Organization of Immigrant and Visible Minority Women of Canada, 1993, p. 2). Finally, only more recently have process-oriented explanations been considered in the etiology of family violence (Hillson & Kuiper, 1994; Milner, 1993; Spaccarelli, 1994). For example, and consistent with Hillson and Kuiper's (1994) theoretical formulations, cultural beliefs and values have been found to moderate cognitive appraisals and coping with family violence issues. More specifically, comparison between Mexican American women and mainstream women has shown that the former have a more tolerant attitude toward partner abuse and that they minimize the seriousness of physically assaultive incidents (Torres, 1991). While mainstream women considered being constrained against their will, slapping, having things thrown on them, and being pushed, shoved or grabbed as abusive acts, Mexican American women did not consider these acts as constituting abuse (Torres, 1991). Similarly, Moon and Williams (1993) found that elderly Korean American women in their study were less likely to perceive situations as abusive than African American women and mainstream culture women. Consideration of cultural factors and process-oriented factors are likely to enhance our theoretical understanding of family violence and contribute to more effective intervention and prevention strategies.

FAMILY VIOLENCE: SERVICE UTILIZATION AND DELIVERY

Community Practice Considerations

A historical perspective on social system interventions in North America and the effectiveness of community intervention projects (CIP) is provided by Edleson and Tolman (1992). In addition to the Minnesota and other models of CIPs (Brygger & Edleson, 1987; Gamache, Edleson, & Schock, 1988; Pence, 1983; Pence and Paymar, 1993; Pence & Shepard, 1988), a model community approach to family violence in general and woman abuse in mainstream and culturally diverse groups in particular has been developed in London, Ontario, Canada. Also known as the Forest City, London has, at present, a population of 326,000 people, 20% of whom were born outside the country. From 1986 to 1991, the city has received 20,600 newcomers for settlement, representing a variety of cultures and languages.

There have been several problems associated with past approaches to family violence in mainstream culture and in cultural groups in a variety of communities: individualistic responses, inadequate resources, fragmentation in service delivery, absence of advocacy, lack of support for research, insensitivity to needs of culturally diverse communities, neglect of health promotion, and little emphasis on accountability. Koss et al. (1994) have also concluded that community support systems have been inadequate in serving the needs of battered women from diverse cultures.

Over the past two decades, the London, Ontario, community has been recognized as a forerunner in the development of an integrated, coordinated, and academically based approach to family violence, including abused women, their children, and perpetrators of woman abuse. An important aspect of the London approach has been adoption of the following principles to family violence: systemic, community-focused, client-centered, coordinated, advocacy, outreach, inreach, education, and accountability.

Current services available for abused women, their children, and violent partners from diverse cultures including mainstream culture are listed in Table 12.3. The list is not exhaustive, and except for Family Service London, Rotholme, and Second Stage Housing, where fees are based on income or ability to pay, there are no fees associated with the services listed.

The direct and indirect services to abused women have been developed in the community over the past two decades. Emergency services in the form of hospital-based emergency departments, calls to police or to an Abused Woman's Help-Line, and temporary housing services are provided. It is worth noting that police are mandated under the Criminal Code of Canada to press charges in all cases of physical and sexual assault against women, provided there are reasonable and probable grounds that such assault has occurred. Short-term and long-term counseling and legal services are available. The latter include legal advice on matters pertaining to custody and access, restraining orders, separation and divorce, and immigration. As important, services to assist women and their children with court and legal procedures are provided through the Child and Access program of the Family Court Clinic. Advocacy in the form of helping women understand the service systems and assisting them in accessing the needed services is provided.

Table 12.3. Services for Abused Women in the London, Ontario, Community

---

Family Consultant Service, London Police: provides crisis intervention in conjunction with London Police; makes referrals to community agencies for victims of family abuse; operates 7 days a week and up to 20 hours per day.

Women's Community House: provides crisis intervention, temporary housing for women and children, and counseling.

Atenlos Native Family Violence Services: operates Zhaawanong (a shelter for Native women and their children), provides counseling, referral, and advocacy as well as family violence control and prevention.

London Second Stage Housing: provides support services and 25 self-contained apartments as secure, affordable, and temporary housing for women and children (2 apartments for those with disabilities).

Family Service London: Offers individual, couple, and family counseling for men, women, and children.

Rotholme: provides women and family temporary housing, crisis counseling, referrals, and advocacy.

Sexual Assault Center London: operates a 24-hour crisis and support line and provides counseling (individual and group), advocacy, and a resource room to the public.

London Family Court Clinic: provides clinical assessment of families and children prior to their appearance in court; supports research and training on children witnessing abuse and women and children in shelters.

Changing Ways: provides a three-tiered program model of intervention for male perpetrators of woman abuse; accepts voluntary or court-directed clients.

Womenpower Inc.: provides vocational and career counseling (individual and group) for women, as well as resource for resume writing, job search, and interview techniques and education information.

London Cultural Interpretation Service: provides qualified interpreters in a variety of languages to assist service agencies and professionals in communication and culture interpretation. Interpretation services are fully subsidized for abused women and for emergency services.

Kerry Reade Newcomer Centre: provides information, orientation, resource materials, referrals, and counseling (settlement and employment) to government-sponsored newcomers.

Women Immigrants of London: provides counseling (individual and group) to assist refugee women in community integration, English-language development, and career preparation, including paid job placements.

London InterCommunity Health Centre: Offers holistic health care, services for children and seniors, counseling community programs, English as a Second Language classes, and self-esteem, support and discussion groups for women from diverse cultures; prevention of wife abuse.

Much of the impetus for the development of the family-violence model in the London community came from the service and research activities of the Family Consultant Service of the London Police. In 1978, the community witnessed the genesis of the Women's Community House. To ensure coordination of community efforts in dealing with family violence, the London Coordinating Committee on Family Violence, later renamed the London Coordinating Committee to End Woman Abuse (LCCEWA), was also established. At present, the London Coordinating Committee to End Woman Abuse is a network of social, health, education, and justice services (The London Coordinating Committee to End Woman Abuse, 1992; Women's Community House, 1993). The London Coordinating Committee to End Woman Abuse represents over 30 agencies, and its mandate is to provide an integrated community response to end violence against women in intimate relationships. Its objectives include promoting coordination between the service systems, including providing resource material on woman abuse, ensuring consistency in approach to woman abuse among member organizations, and promotion of community education on the issue of woman abuse. To ensure that the special needs of cultural groups for service delivery and advocacy within the community are addressed proactively, the London Coordinating Committee to End Woman Abuse has established an active Multicultural Subcommittee. More recently, the Multicultural Subcommittee evolved into the London Multicultural Committee to End Woman Abuse and is represented as an independent member on the London Coordinating Committee to End Woman Abuse.

A second important aspect of the London approach to family violence has been its commitment to academic excellence. The Center for Research on Violence Against Women and Children (CRVAWC) has assumed a leadership role in this respect. The Center for Research on Violence Against Women and Children is one of five Research Centers funded by the Social Sciences and Humanities Research Council of Canada and Health and Welfare Canada. It represents a collaborative venture between Fanshawe College, The University of Western Ontario, and the London Coordinating Committee to End Woman Abuse. The purpose of the Center is promotion and development of action-oriented and community-centered research, based on a feminist conceptualization of violence against women and children. The following constitute the four areas of research in the Center's mandate to end violence against women and children: evaluation of intervention approaches, civil and criminal remedies, education and training, and prevention. Current research projects include examination of the effectiveness of treatment programs for male perpetrators of abuse and the perceptions of women who have used the Integrated Model of Woman Abuse Services in the London Community. Of particular importance has been the commitment of the Center for Research on Violence Against Women and Children to test all projects against the standards of racial, cultural, and sexual sensitivity.

A third important aspect of the London approach to family violence has been its strong focus on cultural health promotion for the purposes of prevention of illness and psychological distress in immigrant, refugee, and racial-minority women. In partnership with the London Coordinating Committee to End Woman Abuse and diverse cultural groups, the London InterCommunity Health Center (LIHC) program of the Multicultural Women's Community Development Project (MWCDP), has assumed a leadership role in cultural health promotion endeavors in the London community (L. Z. Kazarian, 1993). The Multicultural Women's Community Development Project is funded by Canadian Heritage, the Ministry of Citizenship, and United Way. The London InterCommunity Health Center and the Multicultural Women's Community Development Project have served as model programs nationally and provincially. For example, the Multicultural Women's Community Development Project has served as a model program to similar initiatives in several other culturally diverse communities (Toronto, Kitchener, and Guelph) in the Province of Ontario.

The main goal of the Multicultural Women's Community Development Project has been promotion of health in women from diverse cultures in the community by consideration of four health determinants: individual competence, empowerment, social support, and community support systems. The program comprises three components: Volunteer Facilitators Training Group, Social Support Groups, and Culture-Specific Resource Development . The Volunteer Facilitators Training Group provides training for women from various cultures in developing and facilitating social support groups for women in their respective cultural communities. Training is provided in a group format with emphasis on process, empowerment, and knowledge of women's health issues. It is of interest to note that women graduates of the Volunteer Facilitators Training Group are known in the community as the Women of the World (WOW!).

After their graduation, the Women of the World are empowered to organize Social Support Groups (SSG) to help other women in their respective cultural communities to deal with issues specific to their communities. Consistent with the principle of empowerment, the development and facilitation of these groups, as well as the specific group activities, are determined by leaders and group members. Popular social support activities include cooking sessions, outings, and discussion topics on Family Law, Communications Skills, Assertiveness, Stress and Health, Starting Your Own Business, and Family Violence. Financial and administrative support for the groups and their activities are coordinated by a Project Coordinator. The third component of the Multicultural Women's Community Development Project involves the development of informational resources for the cultural groups in the community. The resources are developed in consultation with women from the local community and in as many languages as required.

Needless to say, support staff and service providers of the London InterCommunity Health Center are all available to the Multicultural Women's Community Development Project participants. Service providers include physicians, nursing staff, social workers, a psychologist, mental health workers, community workers, and an art therapist. Participants are also referred to other community services when these are not available at London Intercommunity Health Center. Since the inception of the Multicultural Women's Community Development Project in 1990, extensive contacts and partnerships have been established with mainstream community agencies and those serving immigrant, refugee, and racial minority groups.

The structure and process of the Multicultural Women's Community Development Project has been invariant over the past five years in view of its effectiveness in assisting women from diverse cultures in dealing with issues of marginalization, social, economic, and cultural isolation and vulnerabilities to violence. The mandate to assist women at high risk for family violence originated from the initial Social Support Groups of the Multicultural Women's Community Development Project. The discussion topic on family violence in the Social Support Groups facilitated by the Battered Women's Advocacy Center invariably resulted in disclosure of abuse by multicultural women participants, either in the group meetings themselves or afterward. This serendipitous observation culminated in the establishment of the first phase of the Wife Abuse Program of the Multicultural Women's Community Development Project. In this phase an effort was made to validate in more detail the need for a Wife Abuse program for immigrant, refugee, and racial-minority groups in the London community. Discussions and liaisons with a variety of agencies in the community supported the need for a systematic and systemic approach to address the problem. Although London had community services and supports for victims of wife abuse, follow-up needs assessments and discussions indicated that many immigrant, refugee, and racial-minority women were staying in or returning to abusive situations because of barriers and gaps in services specific to their cultural groups.

Due to the sensitive nature of the issue of family violence in cultural groups, including mainstream culture, and due to its continued denial in the majority of the ethnocultural communities, consideration was given to an approach that provided for outreach to multiple cultural groups and a methodology that was deemed nonthreatening, culturally sensitive, preventative, and collaborative. The initial programmatic initiative involved the group of women facilitators who spoke the following languages: Arabic, English, Eretrian, Persian, Polish, Somali, Spanish, and Urdu. Multiple community agencies were also secured for program involvement to provide for partnership relationships, to desensitize multicultural women and service providers to each other, and to ensure bidirectional interaction and learning.

The first phase of the approach involved the Wife Assault Prevention Training Program. This program consisted of a series of workshops involving immigrant, refugee, and racial-minority women, service providers, and the general community. The goal of the program was to increase access to preventive and treatment services for immigrant, refugee, and racial-minority women in London and the region by raising awareness of issues related to violence in the home, familiarizing participants with community services, and considering the development of culture-specific resources.

As part of the Wife Assault Prevention Training Program, Women of the World received special training in the areas of personal sensitivity, family violence, and services for abused women in the community. To enable Women of the World to educate and to assist abused women in their respective communities in using appropriate and needed services, they were provided with training workshops. The Battered Women's Advocacy Center, Women's Community House, Sexual Assault Center, Family Court Clinic, and Changing Ways were all participants in the "people resource" training program.

The outcome of the Wife Assault Prevention Training Program was positive from the perspectives of increasing the understanding and competence of the trained facilitators in the area of wife abuse and of resource development. In relation to the latter, two booklets, *Wife Abuse: Resource Package* and *Wife Abuse: Discussion Guide* were developed for use as guides by Women of the World in their respective Social Support Groups. The program also provided a medium for the establishment of a working relationship between the trained facilitators and service providers, interagency collaboration, improved understanding of the barriers to service utilization and delivery and of gaps in services, improved coordination of service delivery, and opportunity to build positive intercommunity relationships. It is worth mentioning that 4 of the 12 women in the initial "people resource" training program identified themselves as victims of wife abuse!

The second phase of the Wife Abuse Program of the Multicultural Women's Community Development Project was implemented in collaboration with the Multicultural Subcommittee of London Coordinating Committee to End Woman Abuse (L. Z. Kazarian, 1994). The goal of the Wife Assault Prevention Education module was to increase the accessibility of community services for abused women to immigrant, refugee, and racial-minority women. The objectives of the program were achieved by: (a) planning and implementing cultural sensitivity and antiracism training workshops to service providers; and (b) developing and implementing a training program for immigrant and racial-minority women on cultural sensitivity and antiracism in the context of wife abuse, so that these women (Cross-Cultural Education Team) were better prepared to advise and train community service providers and members of ethno-specific community groups.

The first component of the module provided for a one-day workshop attended by 105 service providers who represented about 30 organizations. Eleven workshop leaders constituted the Cross-Cultural Education Team and represented a range of cultural and racial minority groups. Four major areas were covered during the workshop: the experience of immigrating, working toward eliminating racism in organizations, working towards culturally sensitive practices, and cultural concepts of wife abuse. Needless to say, this component of the Wife Assault Prevention Education program was successful in achieving its short-term objective.

The second component of the module involved 12 weekly sessions of 3 hours each and included the following topics: strategies for identifying needs of service providers for training in cultural sensitivity and antiracism, the role of culture in behavior and communication, the role of women and the family in the cultural context, knowledge of service providers, cultural concepts of woman abuse, and the impact of racism on access to general and abuse-specific services for women from diverse cultures. Eleven of a pool of 25 women from diverse cultural and racial minority groups participated in this training component.

The third phase of the Wife Abuse Program of the Multicultural Women's Community Development Project involved efforts to support the Cross-Cultural Education Team to evolve into a private consultant service such that services on cultural sensitivity training to agencies could be provided on a fee-for-service basis (L. Z. Kazarian, 1995). To this end, the Cross-Cultural Education Team was provided the following training: conference organization, assertiveness, antiracist organizational change strategies, public-speaking skills, group-facilitation skills, marketing strategies, knowledge of service providers, conflict resolution, and team building. Following this in-depth training, the Cross-Cultural Education Team provided cultural sensitivity training to six major service providers in the community. The common theme in all these presentations was Working Towards Culturally Sensitive Practice. Specific topics for presentations included Feminism and Homosexuality within Multicultural Community, Genital Mutilation, Men's Cultural Roles and Expectations and How the Experience of Immigrating Challenges These Assumptions, and Problems of Adolescents Trapped Between Parent Culture and Canadian Culture: The Role of Women and Children.

The three phases of the Wife Abuse Program associated with the Multicultural Women's Community Development Project have provided known short-term gains. The program has impacted positively on the quality of life of the women participants and has provided for effective community partnerships and collaboration. The fourth phase of the Wife Abuse Program of the Multicultural Women's Community Development Project is currently underway, the focus of which is assessing the effects of funding cuts on the community and the challenge of procuring alternative funding or approaches to responding to the needs of abused women, their children, and perpetrator partners.

While the approach taken in London and other communities has increased understanding of family-violence issues in diverse cultures within host cultures and helped in identifying gaps and barriers to service utilization and delivery practices, the need for continued initiatives in the area of cultural family violence remains apparent. Service providers in different communities tend to be frustrated when they provide victims of family violence with information about resources in the community and find out that the clients have failed to adhere to their prescriptions. Future efforts to address the issues surrounding the provision of culturally appropriate and effective community interventions require two considerations. The first involves an in-depth knowledge of acculturation processes and the individual, familial, and societal factors associated with service utilization practices. A summary list of known factors that affect the daily lives of women from diverse cultures and those that contribute to their vulnerability for violence, as well as moderate their service utilization practices, is provided in Table 12.4. While the factors that are listed are based on personal observations and qualitative research on immigrant, refugee, and racial-minority women in Canada (Battered Women's Advocacy Center, 1994; Canadian Panel on Violence Against Women, 1993; MacLeod et al., 1993; National Organization of Immigrant and Visible Minority Women of Canada, 1993, 1995), the relevance of many of the issues to women in mainstream culture is self-evident. Despite this commonality, a fundamental value difference which influences the service utilization patterns of cultural groups is their collectivistic, as opposed to the individualistic mainstream, orientation. The conflict with regard to this and other value dimensions (Triandis, 1990) is supported by research on abused women from diverse cultures (MacLeod et al., 1994). The abused women in this study were mainly critical of the emphasis of mainstream services on individual rights rather than community rights, individual counseling rather than family building, and individual support rather than support to family and partner support.

The second consideration in future efforts to address service utilization and delivery issues involves exploration of alternative methods to short-term shelters and crisis management of family violence. Such approaches include establishment of ethnospecific shelters and more use of natural support systems, such as friends and relatives. The comparative effectiveness of these approaches is an additional challenge that deserves consideration.

Table 12.4. Cultural Factors Associated with Vulnerability to Violence and Service Utilization Practices

---

Feelings of shame, disgrace, and guilt
Economic and social dependence on spouse or partner
Concern for the welfare of children and family unity
Ostracism by community and family
Lack of language skills
Social isolation
Worry over immigration status, work permit status, and deportation
Economic role reversal (wife employed, husband unemployed)
Poverty
Differential rates of acculturation (wife more readily accepting host-culture values than partner)
Reexperience of trauma (e.g., shelter as a reminder of refugee camp)
Discrimination
Incompatibility of culture-of-origin practices with host-culture practice
Dependence on public transportation
Lack of child-care services in programs
Lack of knowledge and familiarity with community support systems
Absence of culture-specific services including staff conversant in client's language
Concern over confidentiality
Racism and cultural insensitivity in mainstream programs
Need for family-oriented rather than individual-oriented services
Mainstream service emphasis on short-term dependency on the state (welfare)

A final important aspect of the London approach to family violence is its focus on prevention. One such program has involved the promotion of health relationships in high-risk youth with a view to prevention of violence in future relationships. In this program, young adolescents with a history of family violence and child abuse are provided with weekly small-group meetings for competence enhancement (D. A. Wolfe, Wekerle, & Scott, 1997).

Clinical Practice Considerations

In view of the high likelihood of encountering individuals with past and current expernience of abuse in clinical and community practice, psychologists require scientific and technical competence, professional competence, and knowledge of services, agencies, legislation, regulations, and ethical issues pertaining to family violence (American Psychological Association Committee on Professional Practice and Standards, 1995; S. S. Kazarian, in press). Psychologists also require consideration of the role of culture in family violence and empathic and nonjudgmental attitudes. Cultural factors that require specific consideration are psychologists' exploration of their own values and beliefs and an understanding of the cultural values, norms, and practices of clients, their acculturation experiences, service utilization patterns, and community support system requirements.

A variety of clinical resources for conceptualizing and assessing family violence that are of relevance to mainstream, immigrant, refugee, and racial-minority groups are available (Ammerman & Hersen, 1992; Berry, Kim, Power, Young, & Bujaki, 1989; Butcher, 1995; M. A. Dutton, 1992; Edleson & Tolman, 1992; Foy, 1992; Hillson & Kuiper, 1994; Koss et al., 1994; Spaccarelli, 1994; Walker, 1994; Weaver & Clum, 1995; V. V. Wolfe, Gentile, & Wolfe, 1989). A multimodal assessment approach for victims and perpetrators involves interviews, traditional assessment tools, and specific psychometric instruments. Areas for assessment include premorbid personality and adjustment, clinical diagnosis, medical examination, negative life style (e.g., substance use), neuropsychological functions, stress appraisals and coping, impact of abuse, including psychological trauma and shame, physical safety, custody and access, social support, community support systems, and acculturative attitudes and stress. Use of reliable and valid measures and inclusion of measures of acculturation are critical for culturally appropriate evaluation and intervention.

There are a number of specific measures that are useful for the assessment of family violence. An illustrative, rather than an exhaustive, list of these measures is provided in Appendix 12.1. In general, these measures have been developed mainly for Western culture, they are available primarily in English, and their utility for individuals from diverse cultures requires determination.

Clinical measures for child sexual abuse and trauma have been described by Miller and Veltkamp (1995). Measurement instruments include those pertaining to post-traumatic stress disorder, depression, self-esteem, behavioral problems, and adaptive competencies. Assessment approaches for maltreating caregivers and their children include the Parent Interview and Assessment Guide (D. A. Wolfe, 1988), the Child Abuse and Neglect Interview Schedule (Ammerman, Hersen, & Van Hasselt, 1988), the Home Observation for Measurement of the Environment (Bradley & Caldwell, 1984) instrument, the COPE scale (Carver, Scheier, & Weintraub, 1989), the Child

Behavior Checklist (Achenbach & Edelbrock, 1983), and the Eyberg Child Behavior Inventory (Eyberg & Ross, 1978).

A comprehensive approach to the assessment of elder abuse and neglect has been provided by Breckman & Adelman (1992). Diagnostic and psychological distress measures for adult victims of abuse include structured interviews for symptom assessment in general and for post-traumatic stress disorder (PTSD) in particular. These include the Structured Clinical Interview (SCID; Spitzer & Williams, 1986), the Impact of Event Scale (IES; Horowitz, Wilner, & Alvarez, 1979), the Minnesota Multiphasic Personality Inventory—Derived PTSD Subscale (Keane, Malloy, & Fairbank, 1984), and the Beck Depression Inventory (BDI; Beck, Ward, Mendelson, Mock, & Erbaugh, 1961). The SCID is available in Dutch (Arntz, van Beijsterveldt, Hoekstra, Hofman, Eussen, & Sallaerts, 1992; Koster Van Groos GAS, 1987) and the BDI in Chinese (Chan & Tsoi, 1984; Shek, 1990), French (Bourque & Beaudette, 1982), and Spanish (Murphy, Conoley, & Impara, 1994). In view of the importance of PTSD for treatment of family violence (M. A. Dutton, 1992) and considering that members of refugee families currently in abusive relationships may have been victims of torture, evaluation of the utility of recently developed PTSD scales is required. The Harvard Trauma Questionnaire (Mollica, Caspi-Yavin, Bollini, Truong, Tor, & Lavelle, 1992), which is available in different languages (Cambodian, Laotian, Vietnamese), is an example of such a measure.

Two personality measures that have been used in the area of wife abuse are the Minnesota Multiphasic Personality Inventory-2 (Butcher, Graham, Williams, & Ben-Porath, 1990) and the Millon Clinical Multiaxial Inventory (MCMI-II; Millon, 1987). These two personality assessment measures should be used with caution in family violence assessment to minimize misdiagnosis (Rosewater & Walker, 1985). In addition, the influence of acculturation factors on profiles derived from these two and other similar instruments needs consideration.

Significant progress has been made in the measurement of acculturation in North America in the past three decades, providing for the availability of a variety of acculturation scales for a variety of cultural groups (Dana, 1993; S. S. Kazarian, 1993). These measures have been used in the areas of health and mental health (Rogler et al., 1991), but are of relevance to family violence assessment. Acculturation scales developed on the conceptual framework proposed by Berry (1980, 1990) include those for Indigenous people and for French Canadian, Portuguese Canadian, Korean Canadian, Hungarian Canadian, and Latin Canadian cultures (Berry et al., 1989; Dona & Berry, 1994).

A fundamental consideration in family-violence assessment and intervention is validation of the abuse experience. Pathologizing of family violence on the part of mental health professionals provides for victimization of the abused, condonement of systemic practices of sexism, racism, classism, and aggression, and alienation of victims and survivors of abuse and the grass-roots workers who are assisting them and advocating on their behalf. Clinical interventions focus on the victims and the perpetrators of abuse and assume different theoretical models including feminist, cognitive behavioral, family systems, and integrative perspectives (Caesar & Hamburger, 1989; Feldman & Ridley, 1995). Identification of the active ingredients of intervention packages are required both for treatment effectiveness and efficiency (e.g., Hyde, Bentovim, & Monck, 1995).

Consideration of the perspective of culture in the assessment and treatment of child sexual abuse is crucial. According to Heras (1992), this includes understanding the context of child sexual abuse, the influence of family structure on the clinical assessment process of child sexual abuse, and the distinction between cultural values, beliefs and practices, and dysfunctional behaviors. In view of the known short-term and long-term effects of sexual abuse and considering the value of intervention for positive outcome, efforts to ensure child and family entry into therapy are necessary. There is suggestive evidence to indicate that sexually abused children from diverse cultures are less likely to enter into the mental health service system. Haskett, Nowlan, Hutcheson, and Whitworth (1991) have found that African American children who have experienced sexual abuse are significantly less likely to sustain involvement in treatment after the first therapeutic contact than their Caucasian counterparts. Tingus, Heger, Foy, and Leskin (1995) have found a similar pattern for African American and Spanish American children in their study. An important cultural factor that requires specific consideration in evaluation and treatment of child sexual abuse is the value of purity and virginity. The social and psychological consequences of penetration abuse and the meaning of virginity to the child, the family, and the cultural community are important therapeutic themes.

D. A. Wolfe and Wekerle (1993) have identified three domains for interventions with abusive and/or neglectful caregivers of children: child-focused interventions, parent-focused interventions, and comprehensive/multiservice programs. Child-based interventions focus on improvements in cognitive, social, and moral development, self-control, and safety and protection from harm. Parent-based interventions focus on caregiver skill development in areas of child management, anger control, stress management, and cognitive restructuring, as well as improvements in social networks and supports. Comprehensive/multiservice programs focus on abusive or neglectful families in efforts to address the multiplicity of their needs within their naturally occurring context. On the basis of their review of 21 child-abuse studies of treatment outcome, Wolfe and Wekerle (1993) suggested increased treatment focus on parental competence and stress reduction. They also observed the absence of the cultural perspective in child-abuse intervention and prevention studies, a conclusion also supported by Melton and Flood (1994). An important cultural factor that requires specific consideration in evaluation and treatment of child abuse is the value of family privacy. For example, family privacy is sacred in Arab culture, such that only relatives and close friends are trusted with intervention in family life (Haj-Yahia & Shor, 1995). This approach to resolving relations within the family contrasts with the typical Western secular method, in which the nature of interactions within the family are governed by formal institutions. Culturally sensitive approaches are required to attend to issues surrounding legitimacy of intrusion upon family privacy in efforts to protect the welfare of children and to respect the privacy of families. Haj-Yahia and Shor (1995) propose initial communication with the father rather than interaction with the mother or child without the father's knowledge. The latter approach to intervention is likely to jeopardize the therapeutic relationship with the family.

The most detailed clinical approach to intervention with battered women is provided by M. A. Dutton (1992), while a comprehensive review of clinical intervention approaches with perpetrators of woman abuse and of risk factors associated with battering are provided by Edleson and Tolman (1992), Gelles, Lackner and Wolfner (1994), Pressman and Sheps (1994), and Feldman and Ridley (1995).

The cognitive-behavioral treatment approach for battered women as described by M. A. Dutton (1992) is based on a core set of 13 general assumptions adapted from a variety of sources. These include nonjudgmental acceptance and validation of the experience of abuse, preparedness to provide support, alliance and advocacy for safety and building options, therapeutic skills in dealing with recounting of trauma and its sequelae, the therapeutic value of education, attention to use of drugs and alcohol as agents to deal with the experience of trauma, and the right for self-determination. In a cultural context, historical experiences of physical torture, sexual torture, and political detention are important issues in the therapeutic process.

Treatments directed at perpetrators include group interventions, individual counseling, and conjoint therapies. Clinical issues addressed in these varied individual or group interventions include attitudes toward violence and personal responsibility, planning for safety, acquisition of skills incompatible with aggression, and interpersonal communication (Edleson & Tolman, 1992; Margolin & Burman, 1993; Pressman & Sheps, 1994; Russell & Frohberg, 1995). A significant and much-needed recent development has been the recognition that treatment standards for abuser programs are required to address issues pertaining to quality of abuser programs and therapist and counselor qualifications (Adams, Rosenbaum, & Stewart, 1994). An additional positive development has been greater recognition of the need for programming for the children of battered women (Crockford, Kent & Stewart, 1993; Edleson & Peled, 1994; Jaffe, Hurley & Wolfe, 1990; Jaffe, Suderman, & Reitzel, 1992; Jaffe, Wolfe, & Wilson, 1990; Saunders, 1994).

Studies on psychological interventions for elder abuse have also been described but not systematically evaluated. Huckle (1994) discussed caregiver burden and recommended the psychological interventions of psychoeducation, group therapy, behavioral strategies, family therapy, and telephone help lines to assist individuals who are caring for the elderly with dementia to cope with the burden of caring. Similarly, Green and Soniat (1991) advocated a family-systems perspective for examining caregiver roles and responsibilities and dealing with family burden.

An important limitation of the assessment and treatment approaches to family violence is their failure to operationalize the level of readiness of victims and/or perpetrators for behavioral change. The Stages of Change model (DiClemente & Prochaska, 1985; Prochaska & DiClemente, 1983) for maladaptive behaviors provides a conceptual framework for consideration of clinical issues pertaining to level of victim readiness to leave any abusive relationship and to level of readiness of perpetrators to end their pattern of abusive behaviors. In the Stages of Change model, five phases, each with a corresponding process of change, are postulated. The five stages are precontemplation, contemplation, preparation, action, and maintenance. The Stages of Change model has been supported in a variety of health-related behaviors (Fernando & Kazarian, 1995) and has relevance to clinical practice in the area of cultural family violence.

Despite the significant developments in clinical assessments and interventions for battered women, their children, and perpetrators of violence, cultural issues associated with clinical service delivery have not assumed prime consideration. Edleson and Tolman (1992) have supported the importance of cultural factors in assessment and treatment of family violence. Similarly, Koss et al. (1994) have recognized the challenge of integrating mainstream family-violence interventions with the cultural values of those from nondominant cultures. Culturally appropriate assessments and interventions are likely to be enhanced by incorporation of culture in family-violence theory, research, and practice.

CONCLUSIONS

A major obstacle to the embracement of the role of culture in family violence is the "melting-pot" ideology of Western psychology. In such a model, variance associated with culture is absent or, if it does exist, it is attributed to the extreme minority of those immigrants who have failed their test of assimilation because of inherent defects in their personalities. The unforeseen consequence of the melting-pot ideology is that people in mainstream communities are rendered cultureless while those in diverse cultures are pathologized. The cultural family-violence perspective discussed in this chapter is based on the perspective of social pluralism and is inclusive of Western and non-Western cultures. The advantage of this model is that it acknowledges variance in values, norms, and practices among Western and non-Western communities. It also allows individual exploration of values and beliefs as they affect people's roles as citizens, clients, or service providers. An added advantage of this model is that it promotes the pursuit of universality in the definition of family violence and its theories rather than presuming universality, as does Western psychology. Finally, the inclusive nature of the model is conducive to integration of human experiences, rather than taking a divisive "us and them" outlook, for the benefit of addressing the universal problem of family violence and producing change in an ugly landscape.

APPENDIX 12.1 FAMILY VIOLENCE MEASURES

Child Abuse Potential Inventory (Milner, 1986, 1994)

Childhood Level of Living Scale (Hally, Polansky, & Polansky, 1980)

Children's Impact of Traumatic Events Scale—Revised (V. V. Wolfe, Gentile, Michienzi, Sas, & Wolfe, 1991)

Child Abuse and Trauma Scale (Sanders & Becker-Lausen, 1995)

The Children's Attributions and Perceptions Scale (Elliott & Briere, 1992)

History of Victimization Form (V. V. Wolfe, Gentile, & Bourdeau, 1987)

Sexual Abuse Fear Evaluation Subscale (V. V. Wolfe & Wolfe, 1986)

Conflict Tactics Scales (Straus, 1979)

Psychological Maltreatment Scale (Taylor, Underwood, Thomas, & Franklin, 1988)

Psychological Maltreatment of Women Inventory (D. G. Dutton & Starzomski, 1993; Tolman, 1989)

Propensity for Abuse Scale (D. G. Dutton, 1995a)

Abusive Behavior Index (Shepard & Campbell, 1992)

Severity of Violence Against Women/Men Scale (Marshall, 1992a, 1992b)

Partner Abuse Scale (Hudson, 1992)
Measure of Wife Abuse (Rodenburg & Fantuzzo, 1993)
Wife Abuse Inventory (see Poteat, Grossnickle, Cope, & Wynne, 1990)
Attitudes Toward Christian Women Scale (Postovoit, 1990)
Index of Spouse Abuse (Hudson & McIntosh, 1981; see Aldarondo & Straus, 1994; Feldman & Ridley, 1995)
Relationship Conflict Inventory (see Aldarondo & Straus, 1994; Feldman & Ridley, 1995).

References

Achenbach, T. M., & Edelbrock, C. (1983). *Manual for the Child Behavior Checklist and Revised Child Behavior Profile.* Burlington, VT: Author.
Adams, D., Rosenbaum, A., & Stewart, T. P. (1994). Treatment standards for abuser programs. *Violence Update, 5,* 5–9.
Aldarondo, E., & Straus, M. A. (1994). Screening for physical violence in couple therapy: Methodological, practical, and ethical considerations. *Family Process, 33,* 425–439.
American Humane Association. (1984). *Trends in child abuse and neglect: A national perspective.* Denver, CO: Author.
American Medical Association. (1992). *Violence: A compendium for JAMA, American Medical News, and specialty journals of the American Medical Association.* Chicago, IL: Author.
American Psychiatric Association. (1994). *Diagnostic and statistical manual of mental disorders* (4th ed.). Washington, DC: Author.
American Psychological Association Committee on Professional Practice and Standards. (1995). Twenty-four questions (and answers) about professional practice in the area of child abuse. *Professional Psychology: Research and Practice, 26,* 377–385.
Ammerman, R. T., & Hersen, M. (Eds.). (1992). *Assessment of family violence: A clinical and legal source book.* New York: Wiley.
Ammerman, R. T., Hersen, M., & Van Hasselt, V. B. (1988). *The Child Abuse and Neglect Interview Schedule (CANIS).* Unpublished instrument, Western Pennsylvania School for Blind Children, Pittsburgh.
Arbesman, M., Kahler, L., & Buck, G. M. (1993). Assessment of the impact of female circumcision on the gynaecological, genitourinary and obstetrical health problems of women from Somalia: Literature review and case series. *Women & Health, 20,* 27–39.
Arntz, A., van Beijsterveldt, B., Hoekstra, R., Hofman, A., Eussen, M., & Sallaerts, S. (1992). The interrater reliability of a Dutch version of the Structured Clinical Interview for *DSM-III-R* personality disorders. *Acta Psychiatrica Scandinavica, 85,* 394–400.
Battered Women's Advocacy Center. (1994). *Outreach to women in London: An assessment of the needs and obstacles experienced by doubly disadvantaged women.* London, Ontario, Canada: Author.
Beck, A. T., Ward, C. H., Mendelson, M., Mock, J., & Erbaugh, J. (1961). An inventory for measuring depression. *Archives of General Psychiatry, 12,* 57–62.
Belsky, J. (1980). Child maltreatment: An ecological integration. *American Psychologist, 35,* 320–335.
Berry, J. W. (1980). Acculturation as varieties of adaptation. In A.M. Padilla (Ed.), *Acculturation: Theory, models and some new findings* (pp. 9–25). Boulder, CO: Westview.
Berry, J. W. (1990). Psychology of acculturation: Understanding individuals moving between cultures. In R. W. Brislin (Ed.), *Applied cross-cultural psychology* (pp. 232–253). Newbury Park, CA: Sage.
Berry, J. W. (1994, July). Disability attitudes, beliefs and behaviors: Overview of an interna-

tional project in community based rehabilitation. In P. Cook (chair), *Culture, Health and Disability*. Symposium conducted at the 12th International Congress of Cross-Cultural Psychology, Pamplona, Spain.

Berry, J. W., & Kim, U. (1988). Acculturation and mental health. In P. Dasen, J. W. Berry, & N. Sartorius (Eds.), *Health and cross-cultural psychology* (pp. 207–236). London: Sage.

Berry, J. W., Kim, U., Power, S., Young, M., & Bujaki, M. (1989). Acculturation attitudes in plural societies. *Applied Psychology: An International Review, 38,* 185–206.

Birns, B., Cascardi, M., & Meyer, S. L. (1994). Sex-role socialization: Developmental influences on wife abuse. *American Journal of Orthopsychiatry, 64,* 5–59.

Bourque, P., & Beaudette, D. (1982). Etude psychometrique du questionnaire de depression de Beck aupres d'un echatillon d'etudients universitaires francophones. *Canadian Journal of Behavioral Science, 14,* 211–218.

Bradley, R. H., & Caldwell, B. M. (1984). 174 children: A study of the relationship between home environment and cognitive development during the first 5 years. In A. W. Gottfried (Ed.), *Home environment and early cognitive development: Longitudinal research* (pp. 5–56). New York: Academic Press.

Brant, R. (1995). Case vignette: Child abuse or acceptable norms [Response]. *Ethics and Behavior, 5,* 284–287.

Brant, R., Wyatt, G. E., & Martin, T. (1995). Case vignette: Child abuse or acceptable cultural norms. *Ethics and Behavior, 5,* 283–293.

Brassard, M. R., Germain, R., & Hart, S. N. (1987). *Psychological maltreatment of children and youth*. New York: Pergamon Press.

Breckman, R. S., & Adelman, R. D. (1992). Elder abuse and neglect. In R. T. Ammerman & M. Hersen (Eds.), *Assessment of family violence: A clinical and legal sourcebook* (pp. 236–252). New York: Wiley.

Brygger, M. P., & Edleson, J. L. (1987). The Domestic Abuse Project: A multisystems intervention in women battering. *Journal of Interpersonal Violence, 2,* 324–336.

Butcher, J. N. (Ed.). (1995). *Clinical personality assessment: Practical approaches*. New York: Oxford University Press.

Butcher, J. N., Graham, J. R., Williams, C. L., & Ben-Porath, Y. S. (1990). *Development and use of the MMPI-2 content scales*. Minneapolis, MN: University of Minnesota Press.

Caesar, P. L., & Hamburger, L. K. (Eds.). (1989). *Treating men who batter: Theory, practice and programs*. New York: Springer.

Campbell, J. C., Harris, M. J., & Lee, R. K. (1995). Violence research: An overview. *Scholarly Inquiry for Nursing Practice, 9,* 105–126.

Canadian Panel on Violence Against Women (1993). *Changing the landscape: Ending violence—achieving equality*. Ottawa, Canada: The Minister Responsible for the Status of Women.

Carden, A. D. (1994). Wife abuse and the wife abuser: Review and recommendations. *Counseling Psychologist, 22,* 539–582.

Carlson, B. E. (1984). Children's observations of interpersonal violence. In A. R. Roberts (Ed.), *Battered women and their families* (pp. 147–167). New York: Springer.

Carver, C. S., Scheier, M. F., & Weintraub, J. K. (1989). Assessing coping strategies: A theoretically based approach. *Journal of Personality and Social Psychology, 56,* 267–283.

Cazenave, N. A., & Straus, M. A. (1992). Race, class, network embeddedness, and family violence: A search for potent support systems. In M. A. Straus & R. J. Gelles (Eds.), *Physical violence in American families: Risk factors and adaptation to violence in 8,145 families* (pp. 321–339). New Brunswick, NJ: Transaction.

Chan, C. M., & Tsoi, M. M. (1984). The BDI and stimulus determinants of cognitive-related depression among Chinese college students. *Cognitive Therapy and Research, 8,* 501–508.

Chester, B., Robin, R. W., Koss, M. P., Lopez, J., et al. (1994). Grandmother dishonored: Violence against women by male partners in American Indian communities. *Violence and Victims, 9,* 249–258.

Cicchetti, D., & Rizley, R. (1981). Developmental perspectives on the etiology, intergenerational transmission, and sequelae of child maltreatment. *New Directions for Child Development, 11,* 31–55.

Crockford, M., Kent, G., & Stewart, N. (1993). Play friendly and safe: A therapeutic group model for young children (5–8 years old) who have witnessed wife assault. *Journal of Child and Youth Care, 8,* 77–86.

Dana, R. H. (1993). *Multicultural assessment perspectives for professional psychology.* Needham Heights, MA: Allyn & Bacon.

DiClemente, C. C., & Prochaska, J. O. (1985). Processes and stages of self-change: Coping and competence in smoking behavior change. In S. Shiffman & T. A. Wills (Eds.), *Coping with substance use* (pp. 319–363). New York: Academic Press.

Dona, G., & Berry, J. W. (1994). Acculturation attitudes and acculturation stress of Central American refugees. *International Journal of Psychology, 29,* 57–70.

Dutton, D. G. (1995a). A scale for measuring the propensity of abusiveness. *Journal of Family Violence, 10,* 203–221.

Dutton, D. G. (1995b). Male abusiveness in intimate relationships. *Clinical Psychology Review, 15,* 567–581.

Dutton, D. G., & Starzomski, A. J. (1993). Borderline personality in perpetrators of psychological and physical abuse. *Violence and Victims, 8,* 327–337.

Dutton, M. A. (1992). Assessment and treatment of post-traumatic stress disorder among battered women. In D. W. Foy (Ed.), *Treating PTSD: Cognitive-behavioral strategies* (pp. 69–98). New York: Guilford Press.

Edleson, J. L., & Peled, E. (1994). Small group interventionwith children of battered women. *Violence Update, 4,* 1–2.

Edleson, J. L., & Tolman, R. M. (1992). *Intervention for men who batter: An ecological approach.* Newbury Park, CA: Sage.

Egan, M. J. (1995). *Violence against women costs $4.2 billion, study says.* London Free Press, pp. A1–A2 Wednesday, December 6.

Elliott, D. M., & Briere, J. M. (1992). Sexual abuse trauma: Validating the Trauma Symptom Checklist (TSC-40). *Child Abuse and Neglect, 16,* 391–398.

Eyberg, S. M., & Ross, A. W. (1978). Assessment of child behavior problems: The validation of a new inventory. *Journal of Clinical Child Psychology, 7,* 113–116.

Feldman, C. M., & Ridley, C. A. (1995). The etiology and treatment of domestic violence between adult partners. *Clinical Psychology: Science and Practice, 2,* 317–348.

Fernando, M. L. D., & Kazarian, S. S. (1995). Patient education in the drug treatment of psychiatric disorders: Effects on compliance and outcome. *CNS Drugs, 3,* 291–304.

Finkelhor, D. (1994). The international epidemiology of child sexual abuse. *Child Abuse and Neglect, 18,* 409–417.

Finkelhor, D., & Korbin, J. (1988). Child abuse as an international issue. *Child Abuse and Neglect, 12,* 3–24.

Foy, D. W. (Ed.). (1992). *Treating PTSD: Cognitive-behavioral strategies.* New York: Guilford Press.

Gamache, D. J., Edleson, J. L., & Schock, M. D. (1988). Coordinated police, judicial and social service response to woman battering: A multisystem evaluation across three communities. In G. T. Hotaling, D. Finkelhor, J. T. Kirkpatick, & M. Straus (Eds.), *Coping with family violence: Research and policy perspectives* (pp. 193–209). Newbury Park, CA: Sage.

Gelles, R. J., & Straus, M. A. (1988). *Intimate violence.* New York: Simon & Schuster.

Gelles, R. J. & Cornell, C. P. (1983a). *International perspectives on family violence.* Lexington, MA: Heath.

Gelles, R. J., & Cornell, C. P. (1983b). International perspectives on child abuse. *Child Abuse and Neglect, 7,* 375–386.

Gelles, R. J., Lackner, R., & Wolfner, G. D. (1994). Men who batter: The risk markers. *Violence Update, 4,* 1–10.

Gondolf, E. W., Fisher, E., & McFerron, J. R. (1988). Racial differences among shelter residents: A comparison of Anglo, Black, and Hispanic battered women. *Journal of Family Violence, 3,* 39–52.

Green, R. R., & Soniat, B. (1991). Clinical interventions with older adults in need of protection: A family systems perspective. *Journal of Family Psychotherapy, 2,* 1–15.

Haffejee, I. E. (1991). Sexual abuse of Indian (Asian) children in South Africa: First report in a community undergoing cultural change. *Child Abuse and Neglect, 15,* 147–151.

Haj-Yahia, M. M., & Shor, R. (1995). Child maltreatment as perceived by Arab students of social science in the West Bank. *Child Abuse and Neglect, 19,* 1209–1219.

Hally, C., Polansky, N. F., & Polansky, N. A. (1980). *Child neglect: Mobilizing services* (DHHS Publication No. OHDS 80-30257). Washington, DC: U.S. Government Printing Office.

Hampton, R. L., & Gelles, R. J. (1994). Violence toward black women in a nationally representative sample of black families. *Journal of Comparative Family Studies, 25,* 105–119.

Hansen, D. J., Conaway, L. P., & Christopher, J. S. (1990). Victims of child abuse. In R. T. Ammerman & M. Hersen (Eds.), *Treatment of family violence* (pp.17–49). New York: Wiley.

Haskett, M. E., Nowlan, N. P., Hutcheson, J. S., & Whitworth, J. M. (1991). Factors associated with successful entry in child sexual abuse cases. *Child Abuse and Neglect, 15,* 467–476.

Health Canada (1995). *Abuse and neglect of older adults in institutional settings: Discussion paper.* Ottawa, Ontario, Canada: Minister of Supply and Services.

Heras, P. (1992). Cultural considerations in the assessment of child sexual abuse. *Journal of Child Sexual Abuse, 1,* 119–124.

Hillson, J. M., & Kuiper, N. A. (1994). A stress and coping model of child maltreatment. *Clinical Psychological Review, 14,* 261–285.

Hine, D. C. (1989). Rape and the inner lives of Black women in the Middle West: Preliminary thoughts on the culture of dissemblance. *Signs, 14,* 912–920.

Ho, C. K. (1990). An analysis of domestic violence in Asian American communities: A multicultural approach to counseling. *Women and Therapy, 9,* 129–150.

Horowitz, M. J., Wilner, N., & Alvarez, W. (1979). Impact of Event Scale: A measure of subjective stress. *Psychosomatic Medicine, 41,* 209–218.

Huckle, P. L. (1994). Families and dementia. *International Journal of Geriatric Psychiatry, 9,* 735–741.

Hudson, W. W. (1992). *The WALMYR assessment scales scoring manual.* Tempe, AZ: Walmyr.

Hudson, W. W., & McIntosh, S. R. (1981). The assessment of spouse abuse: Two quantifiable dimensions. *Journal of Marriage and the Family, 43,* 873–885.

Huston, R. L., Parra, J. M., Prihoda, T. J., & Foulds, D. M. (1995). Characteristics of childhood sexual abuse in a predominantly Mexican American population. *Child Abuse and Neglect, 19,* 165–176.

Hyde, C., Bentovim, A., & Monck, E. (1995). Some clinical and methodological implications of a treatment outcome study of sexually abused children. *Child Abuse and Neglect, 19,* 138–150.

Jaffe, P. G., Hurley, D. J., & Wolfe, D. (1990). Children's observations of violence. I. Critical issues in child development and intervention planning. *Canadian Journal of Psychiatry, 35,* 466–470.

Jaffe, P. G., Suderman, M., & Reitzel, D. (1992). Child witnesses of marital violence. In R. T. Ammerman & M. Hersen (Eds.), *Assessment of family violence: A clinical and legal handbook* (pp. 313–331). New York: Wiley.

Jaffe, P. G., Wolfe, D. A., & Wilson, S. K. (1990). *Children of battered women.* Newbury Park, CA: Sage.

Kantor, G. K., Jasinski, J. L., & Aldarondo, E. (1994). Sociocultural status and incidence of marital violence in Hispanic families. *Violence and Victims, 9,* 207–222.

Kazarian, L. Z. (1993, September). *Multicultural Women's Community Development Project: Service delivery model and outcome.* In S. Radcliffe (chair), *Immigrant-refugee settlement: Implementing a healthy coordinated approach.* Workshop conducted at the Multicultural Health Coalition Provincial Conference, Kingston, Ontario, Canada.

Kazarian, L. Z. (1994). *Wife assault prevention education program: Final report for the Ministry of Citizenship.* London, Ontario, Canada.

Kazarian, L. Z. (1995). *Wife assault prevention program: Final report for the Ministry of Citizenship.* London, Ontario, Canada.

Kazarian, S. S. (1993). *Measurement of acculturation: A review.* Unpublished manuscript, The University of Western Ontario.

Kazarian, S. S. (in press). Assessment and treatment of children and adults: Legal, professional standards and ethical considerations. In D. R. Evans (Ed.), *The law, standards of practice and ethics in the practice of psychology.* Toronto, Ontario, Canada: Emond Montgomery.

Keane, T. M., Malloy, P. F., & Fairbank, J. A. (1984). Empirical development of an MMPI subscale for the assessment of combat-related post-traumatic stress disorder. *Journal of Consulting and Clinical Psychology, 52,* 881–891.

Kelly, L. (1988). *Surviving sexual violence.* Minneapolis, MN: University of Minnesota Press.

Kendall-Tackett, K. A., Williams, L. M., & Finkelhor, D. (1993). Impact of sexual abuse on children: A review and synthesis of recent empirical studies. *Psychological Bulletin, 113,* 164–180.

Koop, C. E. (1985). *The Surgeon General's workshop on violence and public health, source book.* Leesburg, VA: U.S. Public Health Service/Department of Health and Human Services.

Korbin, J. E. (1993, July). Culture diversity and child maltreatment. *Violence Update,* 3–9.

Korbin, J. E. (1991). Cross-cultural perspectives and research directions for the 21st century. *Child Abuse and Neglect, 15,* 67–77.

Koss, M. P., Goodman, L. A., Browne, A., Fitzgerald, L. F., Keita, G. W., & Russo, N. F. (1994). *No safe haven: Male violence against women at home, at work, and in the community.* Washington, DC: American Psychological Association.

Koster van Groos, G. A. S. (1987). Gestructureerd klinisch interview voor *DSM-III-R* persoonlijkheidsstoornnisse. Heeswijk-Dinther, Netherlands: Author.

Kouno, A., & Johnson, C.F. (1994). Child abuse and neglect in Japan: Coin-operated-locker babies. *Child Abuse and Neglect, 19,* 25–31.

Lachs, M. S., & Pillemer, K. (1995). Abuse and neglect of elderly persons. *The New England Journal of Medicine, 332,* 437–443.

Lenton, R. L (1995). Power versus feminist theories of wife abuse. *Canadian Journal of Criminology, 37,* 305–330.

Levinson, D. (1989). *Family violence in cross-cultural perspective.* Newbury Park, CA: Sage.

London Coordinating Committee to End Woman Abuse. (1992). *An integrated community response to prevent violence against women in intimate relationships.* London, Ontario, Canada: Author.

MacLeod, L. (1987). *Battered but not beaten: Preventing wife battering in Canada.* Ottawa, Ontario, Canada: Canadian Advisory Council on the Status of Women.

MacLeod, L., Shin, M. Y., Hum, Q., Samra-Jawanda, J., Rai, S., Minna, M., & Wasilenka, E. (1993). *Like a wingless bird: A tribute to the survival and courage of women who are abused and who speak neither English nor French*. Ottawa, Ontario, Canada: Health Canada.

Margolin, G., & Burman, B. (1993). Wife abuse versus marital violence: Different terminologies, explanations, and solutions. *Clinical Psychology Review, 13*, 59–73.

Marshall, L. L. (1992a). Development of the Severity of Violence Against Women Scales. *Journal of Family Violence, 7*, 103–121.

Marshall, L. L. (1992b). The Severity of Violence Against Men Scales. *Journal of Family Violence, 7*, 189–203.

Martin, T. (1995). Case vignette: Child abuse or acceptable cultural norms [Response]. *Ethics and Behavior, 5*, 290–292.

Maxwell, E. K., & Maxwell, R. J. (1992). Insults to the body civil: Mistreatment of elderly in two Plains Indian tribes. *Journal of Cross-Cultural Gerontology, 7*, 3–33.

McKelvey, R. S., & Webb, J. A. (1995). A pilot study of abuse among Vietnamese Amerasians. *Child Abuse and Neglect, 19*, 545–553.

Mejiuni, C. O. (1991). Educating adults against socioculturally induced abuse and neglect of children in Nigeria. *Child Abuse and Neglect, 15*, 139–145.

Melton, G. B., & Flood, M. F. (1994). Research policy and child maltreatment: Developing the scientific foundation for effective protection of children. *Child Abuse and Neglect, 18*, 1–28.

Mennen, F. E. (1994). The relationship of race/ethnicity to symptoms in childhood sexual abuse. *Child Abuse and Neglect, 19*, 115–124.

Miller, T. W., & Veltkamp, L. J. (1995). Assessment of sexual abuse and trauma: Clinical measures. *Child Psychiatry and Human Development, 26*, 3–10.

Millon, T. (1987). *Manual for the Millon Clinical Multiaxial Inventory-II*. Minneapolis, MN: National Computer Systems.

Milner, J. S. (1986). *The Child Abuse Potential Inventory: Manual* (2nd ed.). Webster, NC: Psytec.

Milner, J. S. (1993). Social information processing and physical child abuse. *Clinical Psychology Review, 13*, 275–294.

Milner, J. S. (1994). Assessing physical child abuse risk: The Child Abuse Potential Inventory. *Clinical Psychology Review, 14*, 547–583.

Mollica, R. F., Caspi-Yavin, Y., Bollini, M. P. H., Truong, T., Tor, S., & Lavelle, J. (1992). The Harvard Trauma Questionnaire: Validating a cross-cultural instrument for measuring torture, trauma, and posttraumatic stress disorder in Indochinese refugees. *The Journal of Nervous and Mental Disease, 180*, 111–116.

Moon, A., & Williams, O. (1993). Perceptions of elder abuse and help-seeking patterns among African American, Caucasian American and Korean American elderly women. *Gerontologist, 33*, 386–395.

Murphy, L. L., Conoley, J. C., & Impara, J. C. (Eds.). (1994). *Tests in print IV* (Vol. 1). Lincoln, NE: The University of Nebraska Press.

National Center on Child Abuse and Neglect. (1988). *Study of national incidence and prevalence of child abuse and neglect: 1986*. Washington, DC: U.S. Department of Health and Human Services.

National Organization of Immigrant and Visible Minority Women of Canada. (1993). *Violence against immigrant, refugee and racial minority women, Phase I, Strategic response: Towards the development of a national strategy to eradicate violence against immigrant, refugee and racial minority women in Canada*. Ottawa, Ontario, Canada: Author.

National Organization of Immigrant and Visible Minority Women of Canada. (1995). *Violence against immigrant, refugee and visible minority women, Phase II, A manual for promoting awareness and understanding, networking and linking, organizing activities for breaking down barriers.* Ottawa, Ontario, Canada: Health Canada.

Ntiri, D. W. (1993). Circumcision and health among rural women of Southern Somalia as part of a family life survey. *Health Care for Women International, 14,* 215–226.

O'Hagan, K. P. (1995). Emotional and psychological abuse: Problems of definition. *Child Abuse and Neglect, 19,* 449–461.

O'Keefe, M. (1994). Racial/ethnic differences among battered women and their children. *Journal of Child and Family Studies, 3,* 283–305.

Paveza, G. J., Cohen, D., Eisendorfer, C., Freels, S., Sempa, T., Ashford, J. W., Gorelick, P., Hirschman, R., Luchins, D., & Levy, P. (1992). Severe family violence and Alzheimer's disease: Prevalence and risk factors. *Gerontologist, 32,* 493–497.

Pence, E. (1983). The Duluth Domestic Abuse Intervention Project. *Hamline Law Review, 6,* 247–275.

Pence, E., & Paymar, M. (1993). *Education groups for men who batter: The Duluth model.* New York: Springer.

Pence, E., & Shepard, M. (1988). Integrating feminist theory and practice. In K. Yllo & M. Bograd (Eds.), *Feminist perspectives on wife abuse* (pp. 282–298). Newbury Park, CA: Sage.

Perilla, J. L., Bakerman, R., Norris, F. H. (1994). Culture and domestic violence: The ecology of abused Latinas. *Violence and Victims, 9,* 325–339.

Pillemer, K., & Moore, R. W. (1989). Abuse of patients in nursing homes: Findings from a survey of staff. *Gerontologist, 29,* 314–320.

Podnieks, E., & Pillemer, K. (1991). *National survey on abuse of the elderly in Canada.* Toronto, Ontario, Canada: Ryerson.

Postovoit, L. E. (1990). The Attitudes Toward Christian Women Scale (ACWS): Initial efforts towards the development of an instrument measuring patriarchal beliefs. *Journal of Psychology and Christianity, 9,* 65–72.

Poteat, G. M., Grossnickle, W. F., Cope, J. G., & Wynne, D. C. (1990). Psychometric properties of the Wife Abuse Inventory. *Journal of Clinical Psychology, 46,* 828–834.

Pressman, B., & Sheps, A. (1994). Treating wife abuse: An integrated model. *International Journal of Group Psychotherapy, 44,* 477–498.

Prochaska, J. O., & DiClemente, C. C. (1983). Stages and processes of self-change in smoking: Towards and integrative model of change. *Journal of Consulting and Clinical Psychology, 51,* 390–395.

Randall, M. & Haskell, L. (1993) Women's Safety Project. In Canadian Panel on Violence Against Women, Changing the Landscape: Ending Violence—Achieving Equality. Ottawa, Ontario, Canada: The Minister Responsible for the Status of Women.

Rodenberg, F. A., & Fantuzzo, J. W. (1993). The measure of wife abuse: Steps toward the development of a comprehensive assessment technique. *Journal of Family Violence, 8,* 203–228.

Rogers, R. (1990). *Report of the Special Advisor to the Minister of National Health and Welfare on child sexual abuse in Canada.* Ottawa: Health and Welfare Canada.

Rogler, L. H., Cortes, D. E., & Malgady, R. G. (1991). Acculturation and mental health status among Hispanics: Convergence and new directions for research. *American Psychologist, 46,* 585–597.

Rosewater, L. B. , & Walker, L. E. (1985). *Handbook of feminist therapy: Women's issues in psychotherapy.* New York: Springer.

Russell, M. N, & Frohberg, J. (1995). *Confronting abusive beliefs: Group treatment for abusive men.* Thousand Oaks, CA: Sage.

Sanders, B., & Becker-Lausen, E. (1995). The measurement of psychological maltreatment: Early data on the Child Abuse and Trauma Scale. *Child Abuse and Neglect, 19,* 315–323.

Saunders, D. G. (1994). Helping battered women in child custody disputes. *Violence Update, 5*, 1–2.

Scarf, M. (1988). *Battered Jewish wives: Case studies in the response to rage.* Lewiston, NY: The Edwin Mellen Press.

Schecter, M. D., & Roberge, L. (1976). Sexual exploitation. In R. E. Helfer & C. H. Kempe (Eds.), *Child abuse and neglect: The family and the community* (pp.127–142). Cambridge, MA: Ballinger.

Segal, V. A. (1992). Child abuse in India: An empirical report on perceptions. *Child Abuse and Neglect, 16*, 887–908.

Shek, D. T. L. (1990). Reliability and factorial structure of the Chinese version of the Beck Depression Inventory. *Journal of Clinical Psychology, 46*, 35–43.

Shepard, M., & Campbell, J.A. (1992). The abusive behavior inventory: A measure of psychological and physical abuse. *Journal of Interpersonal Violence, 7*, 291–305.

Smallwood, G. (1995). Child abuse and neglect from an Indigenous Australian's perspective. *Child Abuse and Neglect, 19*, 281–289.

Sorenson, S. B., & Telles, C. A. (1991). Self-reports of spousal violence in a Mexican-American and non-Hispanic White population. *Violence and Victims, 6*, 3–15.

Spaccarelli, S. (1994). Stress, appraisal, and coping in child sexual abuse: A theoretical and empirical review. *Psychological Bulletin, 116*, 340–362.

Spitzer, R. L., & Williams, J. B. W. (1986). *Structured clinical interview for DSM-III-R.* New York: New York State Psychiatric Institute.

Straus, M. A. (1979). Measuring family conflict and violence: The conflict tactics scale. *Journal of Marriage and Family, 41*, 75–88.

Straus, M. A. (1994). *Beating the devil out of them: Corporal punishment in American families and its effects on children.* New York: Free Press.

Straus, M. A., & Gelles, R. J. (1986). Societal change and change in family violence from 1975–1985. *Journal of Marriage and the Family, 48*, 465–479.

Straus, M. A., & Gelles, R. J. (1992). *Physical violence in American families: Risk factors and adaptation to violence in 8145 families.* New Brunswick, NJ: Transaction.

Straus, M. A., Gelles, R. J., & Steinmetz, S. (1980). *Behind closed doors: Violence in the American family.* New York: Anchor Press.

Sykes, J. T. (1996). Elder abuse plagues aging societies. *Psychology International, 7*, 1–3.

Taylor, J., Underwood, C., Thomas, L., & Franklin, A. (1988). Measuring psychological maltreatment of infants and toddlers. In R. L. Jones (Ed.), *Tests and measures for black populations.* Berkeley, CA: Cobb & Henry.

Tingus, K. D., Heger, A. H., Foy, D. W., & Leskin, G. A. (1995). Factors associated with entry into therapy in children evaluated for sexual abuse. *Child Abuse and Neglect, 20*, 63–68.

Tolman, R. M. (1989). The development of a measure of psychological maltreatment of women by their male partners. *Violence and Victims, 4*, 159–177.

Torres, S. (1991). A comparison of wife abuse between two cultures: Perception, attitudes, nature, and extent. *Issues in Mental Health Nursing: Psychiatric Nursing for the 90's: New concepts, new therapies, 12*, 113–131.

Triandis, H. C. (1990). Theoretical concepts that are applicable to the analysis of ethnocentrism. In R. W. Brislin (Ed.), *Applied cross-cultural psychology* (pp. 34–55). Newbury Park, CA: Sage.

Ucko, L. G. (1994). Culture and violence: The interaction of Africa and America. *Sex Roles, 31*, 185–204.

U.S. Advisory Board on Child Abuse and Neglect (1990). *First report of the U.S. Advisory Board on child abuse and neglect.* Washington, DC: HHS/NCCAN.

U.S. Congress House Select Committee on Aging (1991). *Elder abuse: What can be done?* Washington, DC: Government Printing Office.

Van Biema, D. (1994, November 14). Parents who kill. *Time, 144,* 50–51.

Vida, S. (1994). An update on elder abuse and neglect. *Canadian Journal of Psychiatry, 39,* S34–S40.

Walker, L. (1979). *The battered woman.* New York: Harper Colophon Books

Weaver, T. L., & Clum, G. A. (1995). Psychological distress associated with interpersonal violence: A meta-analysis. *Clinical Psychology Review, 15,* 115–140.

Wilson, G. T., Nathan, P. E., O'Leary, K. D., & Clark, L. A. (1996). *Abnormal psychology: Integrating perspectives.* Needham Heights, MA: Allyn & Bacon.

Wolf, R. S. (1992). Victimization of the elderly: Elder abuse and neglect. *Reviews in Clinical Gerontology, 2,* 269–276.

Wolfe, D. A. (1987). *Child abuse: Implications for child development and psychopathology.* Newbury Park, CA: Sage.

Wolfe, D. A. (1988). Child abuse and neglect. In E. J. Mash & L. G. Terdal (Eds.), *Behavioral assessment of childhood disorders* (2nd ed., pp. 627–669). New York: Guilford Press.

Wolfe, D. A., Wekerle, C. & Scott, K. (1997). *Alternatives to violence: Empowering youth to develop healthy relationships.* Thousand Oaks, CA: Sage.

Wolfe, D. A., & Wekerle, C. (1993). Treatment strategies for child physical abuse and neglect: A critical progress report. *Clinical Psychology Review, 13,* 473–500.

Wolfe, V. V., Gentile, G., & Bourdeau, P. (1987). *History of Victimization Form.* Unpublished instrument. Children's Hospital of Western Ontario, London, Ontario, Canada.

Wolfe, V. V., Gentile, C., Michienzi, T., Sas, L., & Wolfe, D. A. (1991). The Children's Impact of Traumatic Events Scale: A measure of post-sexual-abuse PTSD symptoms. *Behavioral Assessment, 13,* 359–383.

Wolfe, V. V., Gentile, C. & Wolfe, D. A., (1989). The impact of sexual abuse on children: A PTSD formulation. *Behavior Therapy, 20,* 215–228.

Wolfe, V. V. & Wolfe, D. A. (1986). *The Sexual Abuse Fear Evaluation.* Unpublished instrument, Children's Hospital of Western Ontario, London, Ontario, Canada.

Women's Community House. (1993). *Outreach package.* London, Ontario, Canada: Author.

13

Biopsychosocial Considerations
in Refugee Mental Health

KATHY A. WINTER
MARTA Y. YOUNG

The continuing influx of refugees to Western countries, such as Canada and the United States, presents important challenges to social service and mental health delivery programs (Nicassio, 1985). In particular, clinical psychologists are increasingly faced with the difficult task of developing and implementing psychological services that meet the diverse needs of refugee populations in a culturally sensitive manner (Westermeyer, 1986). This chapter highlights the contributions of researchers and clinicians to issues related to refugee mental health. Specifically, sections that follow provide an overview of migration-related stressors, psychiatric and psychological difficulties manifested by many refugees, and current approaches to assessment and intervention, as well as primary prevention and service utilization. Although the majority of available research pertaining to these issues is concentrated on individuals of Southeast Asian descent, an attempt will be made to detail facts central to other refugee groups, whenever possible. Prior to examining these topics, however, terminological issues and refugee movement trends will be described.

The 1951 United Nations Convention and Protocol Relating to the Status of Refugees (United Nations 1983) defined a refugee as any person who:

> owing to a well-founded fear of being persecuted for reasons of race, religion, nationality, membership of a particular social group or political opinion, is outside the country of nationality and is unable, or owing to such fear, is unwilling to avail himself [herself] of the protection of that country; or who, not having a nationality and being outside the country of his [her] former habitual residence as a result of such event, is unable, or owing to such fear, is unwilling to return to it. (p. 150)

Social scientists have pointed out, however, that this definition is rather limiting, as it does not include displaced persons who have not crossed an international boundary or individuals who are forced to flee from their homes due to war or famine (Stein, 1981; Williams & Berry, 1991). From a psychological viewpoint, a more meaningful and broader definition of the refugee category would include "the trauma and stresses, persecution and danger, losses and isolation, uprooting and change of the refugee experience" (Stein, 1986, p. 6).

An essential element of being a refugee is the involuntary nature of such a decision. Whereas immigrants and sojourners (e.g., foreign students) are voluntary migrants who typically migrate to better themselves economically or educationally or to reunite with their families, refugees are forced to leave their country, often out of fear rather than from a desire to resettle elsewhere (Nicassio, 1985). As described by Kunz (1971, 1973) in his model of flight, immigrants are pulled to the new country by opportunity while refugees are pushed out by war and persecution (Stein, 1986).

Recent figures reveal that there are over 23 million official refugees in the world, that is, individuals who are registered with the United Nations as having fled persecution and who are under the protection of the United Nations High Commissioner for Refugees (UNHCR; Kane, 1995). In addition, it is estimated that there are a further 27 million internal refugees who have fled their homes and communities but cannot be counted as official refugees, as they have not crossed any international borders (Kane, 1995). While the majority of these refugees remain in developing countries (in refugee camps), an increasing proportion of them are seeking and obtaining asylum in Europe and North America.

During the past 4 decades, refugee movements have shifted from a predominantly East-West pattern to a South-North flow (Nef & da Silva, 1991). Thus, post–World War II refugees predominantly came from Eastern Europe, whereas refugees currently originate from countries such as Afghanistan, Somalia, Cambodia, Vietnam, and Guatemala (Adelman, 1991). These trends are important in that they reveal that refugees are increasingly coming from cultures, races, and religions that are significantly different from the resettlement countries that accept them, and this in turn has implications for refugees' adaptation to the host country.

MIGRATION-RELATED STRESSORS FACED BY REFUGEES

While adjusting to a new culture is a challenge for most migrants, refugees in particular tend to confront culture change from a vulnerable position compared to other migrant groups (Nicassio, 1985; Uba, 1994). That is, the many stressors faced during the premigration, migration, and postmigration phases of resettlement impact heavily upon the lives of refugees. Specifically, many refugees have endured premigration traumata, such as war, repression, and torture, before leaving their homelands. Migration or flight itself is often fraught with dangers and threats, such as spending many days without food or water on small unseaworthy vessels or trekking through jungles, being vulnerable to physical attack or rape, or fearing being caught by guards or pirates. Those who are successful in fleeing often spend years in refugee camps in third world countries, such as Thailand, Philippines, or Rwanda, where life is extremely stressful and uncertain both physically and mentally (e.g., shortages of food and water, unsanitary and overcrowded conditions, separation or loss of family members, threats of physical and sexual violence).

Once refugees are accepted in a host country, a process that often takes years, they are faced with a number of daunting postmigration or resettlement issues. After an initial period of elation and relief, refugees often find themselves going through culture shock (Oberg, 1960). This phase is characterized by confusion regarding cultural norms, values, and roles, changes in living environment (e.g., housing, diet, climate), and language difficulties (Uba, 1994). In addition, refugees have to learn quickly how to navigate largely foreign government agencies such as the social and legal services or the educational system. Securing employment can also be particularly stressful for refugees who have to deal with discriminatory hiring practices and who often do not have the necessary language skills or appropriate job experience in the host country. It is therefore not uncommon for refugees to find themselves either unemployed or severely underemployed given their previous education and work experience (Stein, 1986; Westermeyer, 1986; Wiseman, 1985), resulting in significant job dissatisfaction, financial difficulties, and loss of social status (Ajduković & Ajduković, 1993; Uba, 1994).

Unfortunately, migration has tremendous impact upon the lives of children, as well. In addition to having to deal with the trials and tribulations faced by adults, refugee children are faced with several further sources of stress. Common additional sources of stress experienced during migration include premature separation from family members, decreased parental support, living with distressed adults, and loss of educational opportunities (Ajduković & Ajduković, 1993). Furthermore, upon arriving in the resettlement country, refugee children are bombarded with a host of new pressures. Among others, children are more than likely faced with the inability to speak or comprehend the language, difficulties at school, peer rejection, pressure to accommodate to a new culture, and natural developmental challenges (Ajduković & Ajduković, 1993; Lee, 1988). Another source of stress during the postmigration period is intergenerational conflict. Since children acculturate more quickly, great disparity between parents' and childrens' values and expectations results. Moreover, because children quickly become accustomed to the new way of life, they are often expected to bridge the gap between the different language and culture for their parents (Lee, 1988).

CLINICAL ISSUES: PROBLEMS MANIFESTED BY REFUGEES

In view of the traumatic migration events experienced by refugees and the stresses of adjusting to a new culture, it is not surprising that many refugees manifest mental health difficulties during resettlement. Depending on the particular constellation of symptoms experienced (e.g., psychosomatic complaints, hallucinations, suicidal ideation, violent outbursts, etc.), psychiatric disorders typically range from posttraumatic stress disorder (PTSD), adjustment disorder, chronic depression, and anxiety to paranoid schizophrenia and psychosis. Other related clinical difficulties include trauma, substance abuse, and family violence. In the text that follows, psychiatric disorders and related clinical problems experienced by refugees of all ages will be examined, highlighting in particular PTSD, trauma, substance abuse, and family violence. Prior to examining clinical issues pertinent to refugees, however, variations in the type and prevalence of mental disorders across diverse refugee groups are surveyed.

Psychiatric Disorders as a Function of Refugee Group

A review of the literature depicting the type and prevalence of psychiatric problems manifested by various refugee groups suggests that while the rates of psychiatric disorders vary across culture, only slight differences exist in the types of *DSM-IV* diagnoses received. For example, although the prevalence of clinical disorders varied across patient samples of Eastern European (Buchwald, Klacsanzky, & Manson, 1993), Iranian (Bagheri, 1992), East German (Bauer, Priebe, Kurten, Graf, & Baumgartner, 1994) and Southeast Asian refugees (Kinzie, Fredrickson, Ben, Fleck, & Karls, 1984; Kinzie, Tran, Breckenridge, & Bloom, 1980; Kroll et al., 1989; Meinhardt, Tom, Tse, & Yu, 1986; Mollica, Wyshak, & Lavelle, 1987), the most common diagnoses included adjustment disorder (39–60%), schizophrenia (9–11%), PTSD (10–14%), depression (8–33%), anxiety disorder (13%), personality disorder (8%), and paranoia (5%). Analysis of the literature with respect to psychiatric symptoms in nonpatient groups revealed results analogous with the above. That is, although the rates of psychiatric disorders were again found to be highly varied, the same types of psychiatric disorders were found among clinically diverse nonpatient refugee groups (Carlson & Rosser-Hogan, 1991; Cheung, 1994; Gong-Guy, 1986; Hinton et al., 1993).

With regard to the highly varied prevalence rates of psychiatric disorders across cultural groups, some researchers have suggested that inconsistencies are merely artifacts of the studies themselves. That is, variations in prevalence rates across studies can be attributed to issues such as sample size, duration of resettlement, nature of stressors endured during migration processes, and diagnostic criteria used (Cheung, 1994; Hauf & Vaglum, 1994). Cambodians, for example, have been identified as the Southeast Asian population at highest risk for stress-related problems, as they have experienced more severe trauma and have been found to be more depressed and less well-educated than any other refugee group collectively (Meinhardt et al., 1986; Mollica et al., 1987).

Common Psychiatric Disorders and Related Clinical Problems

Post-traumatic Stress Disorder (PTSD)   According to the *Diagnostic and Statistical Manual of Mental Disorders-Fourth Edition* (*DSM-IV;* American Psychiatric Association, 1994), the essential feature of PTSD is "the development of characteristic symptoms following exposure to an extreme traumatic stressor," either through direct experience or witnessing events "that involved actual or threatened death or serious injury, or a threat to the physical integrity of self or others" (p. 427). The person must respond to the event with intense "fear, helplessness, or horror" (p. 428). Common symptoms resulting from exposure to the traumata include persistent reexperiencing of the traumatic event (e.g., distressing dreams, hallucinations, flashbacks, physiological reactivity on exposure to stimuli resembling the traumatic event), persistent avoidance of stimuli associated with the trauma and numbing of general responsiveness (e.g., avoidance of thoughts, feelings, activities, and people that arouse recollections of or are associated with the trauma, restricted affect, feelings of detachment), and persistent increased arousal (e.g., irritability, sleep and concentration difficulty, exaggerated startle response). In order to receive a *DSM-IV* diagnosis of PTSD, the symptoms must be present for at least one month and cause clinically significant distress in social, occupational, or other areas of functioning.

The most frequently identified symptoms of PTSD in refugees include depressed mood, preoccupation with past events, recurrent dreams, distress when exposed to reminders of previous life, reexperiencing the traumatic event, sleep disturbance, diminished interest, difficulty concentrating, autonomic arousal, anger, irritability, and feelings of guilt and remorse (Bagheri, 1992; Cheung, 1994). In view of these symptoms, PTSD in refugee populations is often associated with at least one other psychiatric diagnosis, usually major affective disorder (Garcia-Peltoniemi & Jaranson, 1989; Goldfeld, Mollica, Pesavento, & Farone, 1988; Kinzie et al., 1984; Ramsay, Gorst-Unsworth, & Turner, 1993). Several researchers have found, for example, that 80% of those diagnosed with PTSD were also diagnosed as having a mood disorder (Mollica et al., 1992; Veer, 1992). A comorbidity of 50% has also been observed between PTSD and anxiety disorders, particularly panic disorder and generalized anxiety disorder (Veer, 1992). Other common diagnoses include pain disorders, organic brain syndromes (Westermeyer, 1989), and adjustment disorders (Mollica et al., 1990). Finally, common symptoms of PTSD (e.g., avoidance of close personal relationships, emotional numbing) may also mimic features of personality disorders.

In refugees, several possible precipitants of PTSD have been advanced. Cheung (1994), for example, found that number of traumas experienced, coping style, and postmigration stress were the best predictors of PTSD in Cambodian refugees. In a similar fashion, Carlson and Rosser-Hogan (1991) found a significant relation between severity of trauma endured prior to migration and the extent of psychiatric symptoms reported.

While trauma endured prior to, during, and following migration (i.e., torture, witnessing the harm or death of family/friends, severe food shortage, ill health, and loss of property and livelihood) is considered to play a central role in the etiology of PTSD (Carlson & Rosser-Hogan, 1991; Cheung, 1994; Hauf & Vaglum, 1994; Mollica et al., 1987), premorbid factors, including psychiatric history, age, and gender, have also been considered to be important predictors of PTSD (Bagheri, 1992; Cheung, 1994; Hauf & Vaglum, 1994). Despite the fact that Carlson and Rosser-Hogan (1991) and Cheung (1994) did not find a significant relation between onset of PTSD and gender, both Bagheri (1992) and Hauf and Vaglum (1994) found gender to be a significant predictor of PTSD in refugees. In both cases, men were at least twice as likely to receive a diagnosis of PTSD. It has been suggested that men manifest symptoms of PTSD more often than women, as their heavy involvement in war and politics increases their tendency to become victims of torture (Bagheri, 1992). Finally, Cheung (1994) found that, although marital status and duration of time in the new country did not influence the onset of PTSD, age was a significant predictor, with individuals greater than 65 years of age having a higher rate of PTSD.

Torture   It is estimated that between 30 and 60 percent of the world's refugees have been tortured. Torture is typically defined as "state-induced pain and suffering, whether physical or mental, which constitutes an aggravated and deliberate form of cruel, inhuman or degrading treatment or punishment" (Amnesty International, 1984). Ninety-eight countries are known to practice torture on their citizens, and thirty are engaged in systematic violations of human rights (e.g., Iran, Cambodia, China, Turkey, Guatemala, and Bosnia-Herzegovina). While it is traditionally thought that the majority of torture victims are young men (Rasmussen & Lunde, 1980), recent studies indicate that women are detained and tortured as frequently as men (Fornazzari, 1989) and that they are often subjected to sexual torture (Amnesty International, 1990; Cole, Espin, & Rothblum, 1992; Mollica & Son, 1989).

The major aim of torture is to destroy the psychic integrity of the individual (Becker, Lira, Castillo, Gomez, & Kovalskys, 1990; Reid & Strong, 1988; Silove, 1988; Silove, Tam, Bowles, & Reid, 1991). From a clinical viewpoint, the aims of torture can be likened to a "twisted, up-side version" of what is typically accomplished in psychotherapy (Ritterman, 1987, p. 43). As stated by Silove et al. (1991),

the sophisticated techniques used are often perversions of the principles which underlie psychotherapy, namely the heightening of the person's level of arousal, altering his or her level of awareness, loosening previously held beliefs and assumptions, and fostering an emotionally charged relationship with the perpetrators. The broader goal of this process, which is too often aided and abetted by medical practitioners, is to render political leaders and social militants powerless, so as to prevent further political opposition to the ruling régime and to act as a strong deterrent to other political opponents in the community (p. 482).

Thus, torture is not only aimed at the individual but also at the family and at the community in that it seeks to destroy families and to terrorize entire communities.

The observed sequelae of torture can be organized in three major themes, namely, incomplete emotional and cognitive processing, losses and concomitant depressive reactions, and somatic/physical symptoms (Ramsay et al., 1993; Turner & Gorst-Unsworth, 1990). Symptoms related to the incomplete processing of emotions and cognitions include recurrent and intrusive recollections of the event; intense distress when exposed to internal or external cues reminiscent of the torture; associated hyperarousal (e.g., sleep difficulties, angry outbursts, memory and concentration difficulties); and persistent avoidance of stimuli associated with the traumatic torture experience (Allodi & Stiasny, 1990; Fornazzari & Freire, 1990; Larsen & Pagaduan-Lopez, 1987; Mollica et al., 1987; Ramsay et al., 1993). These symptoms describe essential elements of post-traumatic stress disorder as outlined in the preceding section.

The experience of torture is also linked with a number of significant losses. Many survivors have to deal with the loss of bodily parts (e.g., limbs, eyes) and loss of general health. In addition, survivors frequently deal with the effects of having lost family members through disappearances and summary executions (Fornazzari & Freire, 1990). In addition, women who were tortured while pregnant often lose their babies either through miscarriage, lack of adequate medical attention, or removal at birth. For asylum-seekers, these losses are further compounded by loss of country and culture, downward mobility, and rejection from host nationals (Turner & Gorst-Unsworth, 1990). Not surprisingly, survivors often exhibit a constellation of depressive symptoms that are linked to the many losses they have experienced (Becker et al., 1990).

Typical somatic and physical sequelae of torture include headaches, stomach pains, scarring from lacerations and burns, fractures, tuberculosis, deafness and blindness, weight loss, broken teeth, skin rashes, chronic pain syndromes, head injuries, and difficulty walking due to being beaten on the soles of the feet (Agger, 1986; Allodi & Cowgill, 1982; Allodi & Stiasny, 1990; Fornazzari & Freire, 1990; Larsen & Pagaduan-Lopez, 1987). Sexual dysfunction is not uncommon in survivors who were sexually tortured (Bustos, 1988; Goldfeld et al., 1988; Lira & Weinstein, 1986).

The most common diagnosis given to refugees who present with a history of incarceration and torture is post-traumatic stress disorder (Allodi & Stiasny, 1990; Mollica & Caspi-Yavin, 1991; Pope & Garcia-Peltoniemi, 1991). More specifically, PTSD has been found to afflict over 50% of refugees who come from countries where torture is prevalent (Mollica, Wyshak, de Marneffe, Khuon, & Lavelle, 1987) and has been found with rates greater than 70% in survivors of torture (Garcia-Peltoniemi & Jaranson, 1989). In cases where it seems appropriate to give a diagnosis of post-traumatic stress disorder, it may be useful to specify its relation to experiences of torture and detention, in an attempt to differentiate it from other subcategories of PTSD (e.g., rape trauma, childhood sexual abuse, therapist-patient sex syndrome).

Survivors of torture can also manifest transient symptoms characteristic of personality disorders (Sack, Angell, Kinzie, & Roth, 1986). Being passive-dependent or passive-aggressive, for example, may be "adaptive" personality styles that were acquired in order to survive the torture experience and living in a repressive régime. In addition, clients may exhibit personality changes due to brain damage secondary to torture. Personality disorder diagnoses should therefore be made with extreme caution with this population to avoid misdiagnosis (Veer, 1992).

While the physical and psychological consequences of torture are widespread, the deleterious effects of traumatic experiences are prevalent in other areas of life. In a sample of Cambodian refugees living in the United States, for example, Uba and Chung discovered that trauma was a significant predictor of employment status and income. Specifically, after controlling for current psychological functioning, Uba and Chung found that individuals who had experienced a trauma that still disturbed them, had experienced more traumas, or spent more years in refugee camps were more likely to be unemployed. Moreover, despite the fact that number of years in refugee camps was not a significant predictor, individuals who had experienced a greater number of traumas were more likely to have lower incomes.

Substance abuse   Given the stresses of the migration process, it is not surprising that, regardless of age, some individuals turn to drugs and alcohol in an attempt to cope with their problems (Lin, 1986). While certain refugee groups (e.g., European, Latin American, Asian) have been found to have high levels of drug and alcohol consumption (Bagheri, 1992; Lin, 1986), the extent and nature of substance abuse is difficult to ascertain, as refugee groups typically deny problems in this area (D'Avanzo, Frye, & Froman, 1994). Studies have shown, however, that although the majority of problem drinkers are men, women and children also report using alcohol and prescription drugs for the self-treatment of stress, pain, insomnia, emotional difficulties, and nervousness (D'Avanzo et al., 1994; Frye & D'Avanzo, 1994).

In addition to alcohol and prescription drugs, there has also been some evidence to suggest that refugees use more "hard core" drugs in an attempt to alleviate their physical and emotional pain and suffering. As one illustration, Westermeyer, Lyfoung, Westermeyer, and Neider (1991), in a sample of 50 Hmong refugees seeking treatment for opium addiction, discovered that opium was purportedly used to relieve painful physical and psychological symptoms.

Family violence   Although wife beating has recently begun to be formally recognized as a problem warranting consideration (Crites, 1991), the age-old patriarchal belief that a wife is the property of her husband and the belief in the imbalance of power between men and women remains. Specifically, in collectivist countries, individual rights and freedoms are subordinated to family and community expectations and traditions (Crites, 1991). As such, a substantial number of immigrant and refugee women who have been victims of abuse in their countries of origin are being trapped in violent homes upon arrival in resettlement countries (see Jang, Lee & Morello-Frosch, 1991, for a review). Moreover, adjustment to life in a new country makes already isolated families even more vulnerable to domestic violence (Jang et al., 1991). Frequently, economic pressures force wives to seek employment outside the home, often making them the sole breadwinners for the family. It is not surprising that in such circumstances some men resort to violence in an attempt to maintain the dominant role within the family (Crites, 1991).

In addition to physical harm, wife beating causes severe psychological damage. According to one researcher, common symptoms experienced by victims of wife beating are depression and psychosomatic illness (Crites, 1991). Despite horrific conditions at home and the terrible consequences of abuse, many immigrant and refugee women do not seek assistance. As one illustration, Frye & D'Avanzo (1994) learned that 72% of Cambodian women react to spousal abuse by either talking softly to the perpetrator or doing nothing in order to keep the problem in the family. For some, it is the lack of knowledge pertaining to legal rights and availability of social services that keeps these women from reaching out, while for others it is the fear of discovery and deportation. Finally, for others it is the fear that shame and humiliation will be cast on their family, parents, and ancestors that keeps these women from sharing the details of their abuse (Crites, 1991; Jang et al., 1991).

Problems Manifested by Refugee Children

Tremendous psychological effects of war and trauma exist for children as well as for adults. Studies examining the type and prevalence of psychological distress in refugee children and adolescents suggest that this group is at exceptionally high risk for a number of mental health difficulties, including PTSD, adjustment disorder, anxiety, depression (Arroyo & Eth, 1985; Felsman, Leong, Johnson, & Felsman, 1990; Hjern, Angel, & Höjer, 1991; Kinzie, Sack, Angell, & Manson, 1986; Masser, 1992; Sack et al., 1986), eating disorders, general somatization (Ajduković & Ajduković, 1993), and acting-out behaviors (e.g., alcohol abuse, drug addiction, aggression, defiance, strained parent-child relationships, etc.) (Arroyo & Eth, 1985; Hjern et al., 1991; Morgan, Wingard, & Felice, 1984).

Similar to adult refugees, much of the current research pertaining to problems experienced by refugee children focuses on PTSD. The prevalence of this disorder has been found to reach as high as 50% (Kinzie et al., 1986; Masser, 1992; Sack et al., 1986). Typically, PTSD has been found to exist in children who have endured severe traumatic stress, including personal violence, natural disasters, physical abuse, kidnapping, and incest (Masser, 1992).

Although the concept of PTSD has been extended to younger people, its manifestations are different in children than in adults. Specifically, as compared to adults, children and adolescents with PTSD have fewer flashbacks, less psychogenic amnesia, and more pessimistic expectations with regard to the future and survival. They also tend to engage in thematic play, reenact initial trauma suffered, and imitate violent behavior (see Arroyo & Eth, 1985). In addition to the differences in PTSD symptomatology experienced by adults and children, variations of symptoms resulting from exposure to violence and extreme trauma have been found between children of different ages. PTSD in infants and toddlers, for example, is characterized by high anxiety, social withdrawal, and regressive behavior. School-aged children, on the other hand, tend to have flashbacks, exaggerated startle responses, poor concentration, sleep disturbance, somatic complaints, and conduct problems (Arroyo & Eth, 1985). Finally, adolescents often have nightmares and intrusive recollections of violence and trauma, engage in aggressive behavior and delinquency, and experience guilt related to their own survival (Arroyo & Eth, 1985; Kinzie et al., 1986).

A number of risk factors associated with the onset of psychopathology in children have been identified for the different phases of migration. Among others, risk factors such as parental psychopathology, poverty, malnutrition, lack of shelter, physical abuse, war trauma, exposure to violence in country of origin, and separation from parents have been identified for premigration and migration phases (Arroyo & Eth, 1985; Edwards & Beiser, 1994; Hjern, et al., 1991; Masser, 1992; McKelvey, Mao, & Webb, 1992). In contrast, risk factors identified for the postmigration period include the social situation in the resettlement country, isolation from mainstream community, knowledge of hostlanguage, and mother's poor ability to cope (Ajduković & Ajduković, 1993; Edwards & Beiser, 1994; Hjern et al., 1991). Additional general risk factors include age at arrival, interruption of schooling, and lack of exposure to the teaching language (Hjern et al., 1991).

Despite the setbacks and obstacles that many refugee children face before, during, and after flight to freedom, many children have been found to prosper in resettlement countries. While the lack of risk factors makes children less vulnerable to psychopathology, the presence of protective factors, including positive personality disposition and a supportive family and community, help to guard children against the effects of stress and trauma (Edwards & Beiser, 1994). As one illustration, there is some evidence to suggest that children are better able to survive traumatic migration experiences when accompanied by loving parents and families (Ajduković & Ajduković, 1993; Melville & Lykes, 1992).

ASSESSMENT

Having examined various psychiatric disorders and related clinical difficulties commonly experienced by refugees, attention will now be focused on assessment of these problems. First, consideration will be given to several issues that impact upon the efficacy of assessment procedures with refugees. Second, specific devices used to assess PTSD, depression, anxiety, and torture will be examined, highlighting where possible the general assets and shortcomings of these instruments. Consideration will also be given to assessment tools frequently used with refugee children.

General Assessment Issues

Adequate assessment of psychopathology in refugees is a multifaceted task. In addition to having a working knowledge of cultural beliefs and values, the clinician must ensure that he or she has an adequate understanding of the factors impacting on the lives of refugees. More importantly, however, the efficacy of assessment procedures is contingent upon the clinician's ability to deal with these issues as potential barriers to diagnosis. At least six difficulties relating to assessment have been identified in the literature: recognition and understanding of one's own cultural beliefs and biases; failure to consider the entire refugee experience; patient disclosure; cultural differences in communication styles; language barriers; and diagnostic instruments.

Recognition and Understanding of One's Own Cultural Beliefs and Biases   The clinician must have an awareness of self that includes cultural beliefs, values, stereotypes, and biases. Such an understanding will enable the health care practitioner to realize that personal identity is unique to each and every person. Furthermore, this open-mindedness will help the clinician to begin to comprehend the existential dimensions that characterize refugees' experiences (Boehnlein & Kinzie, 1992), as well as the similarities and differences that exist between cultures (Pernice, 1994). In this vein, appropriate assessment and treatment can be negotiated that reflect a combination of the therapist's intellectual integrity and the patient's cultural beliefs.

Failure to Consider the Entire Refugee Experience   A common oversight in the assessment of refugees is the clinician's failure to consider all the phases of the resettlement process and the factors implicated at each stage (cf. the previous section on migration-related stressors). Such an understanding will serve to guide the appropriate treatment and services required during premigration, migration, and postmigration phases (Kinzie et al., 1990; Lee, 1988).

Patient Disclosure   The years of trauma faced by refugees engender fear and distrust, which extends to Western clinicians and researchers (Pernice, 1994). Typically, refugees believe that disclosure of personal information will have a negative impact on relatives living in their countries of origin and may even jeopardize personal safety and affect their status in resettlement countries. Consequently, refugees often tend to refuse participation in assessment procedures or fail to sign informed consent forms, for fear of being held legally responsible for their responses (Pernice, 1994).

Cultural Differences in Communication Styles   Typically, individuals from non-Western cultures have their own unique communication styles that are far different from their Anglo American counterparts. Indochinese refugees, for example, are less expressive and direct in their communication styles than Westerners, making assessment of this population a difficult venture. Due to the traditional Southeast Asian value of suppression of emotion, these refugees often conceal their distressing psychological difficulties, citing instead somatic complaints, unemployment, limited funds, and so forth as their most pressing problems (Gong-Guy, Cravens, & Patterson, 1991). Assessment is further complicated by Southeast Asians' respect for authority. Specifically, when confronted with authority figures, refugee clients often appear to be readily agreeable and furnish responses that reflect politeness and the desire to please others (Lin & Shen, 1991). This may result in conflicting messages being sent to the clinician with respect to the nature and extent of the presenting problems (N. A. Nguyen & Williams, 1989; Pernice, 1994).

Language Barriers   Difficulty in assessment is perpetuated by the lack of a common vehicle of communication between the refugee patient and the practitioner. Each language is characterized by its own form, style, vocabulary, and metaphors; even nonverbal communication differs across cultures (Lin & Shen, 1991; Pernice, 1994). In Indochinese languages, for example, a distinctive system of personal pronouns and classifiers denotes social hierarchies. Failure to address the refugee patient/client using the appropriate terms may result in a breach of etiquette, which subsequently may lead to refusal to participate in assessment procedures (Pernice, 1994). Even working through an interpreter does not always circumvent difficulties. In addition to threatening confidentiality, the presence of an interpreter increases the likelihood that biased or socially desirable responses will be given, especially if the interpreter is a well-known and respected member of the refugee's community (Pernice, 1994).

Diagnostic Instruments   Finally, assessment is impeded by the lack of adequately translated, standardized, and normed psychological tests. For the most part, clinicians rely on assessment instruments that have been standardized for English-speaking Anglo Americans (Gong-Guy et al., 1991; Mollica et al., 1992). As a result, translated versions of Western assessment devices are often not clearly understood, as they are plagued by cross-cultural variation in wording, meaning, and differences in expressions pertaining to various psychiatric difficulties. Some terms, for example, are difficult to translate because comparable words may not even exist in non-Western cultures (Pernice, 1994). One must also consider that different experiences may engender different manifestations of distress (Kinzie & Manson, 1985). Clearly, there is a need to develop psychometrically sound and culturally sensitive assessment methods (Mouanoutoua, Brown, Cappelletty, & Levine, 1991; Reese & Joseph, 1995).

Common Assessment Devices

Assessment of PTSD   A number of different instruments have been used to assess PTSD in refugees. Whereas some instruments focus on types of traumatic experiences encountered during migration, others directly measure symptoms associated with a

DSM diagnosis of PTSD. The Post-Traumatic Inventory (Meinhardt et al., 1986) and an adapted version of the Life Events and Social History Interview Schedule (Mollica et al., 1987) are examples of the former. Examples of the latter include the PTSD section of the Diagnostic Interview Schedule (DIS; Robins, Helzer, Croughan, & Ratcliff, 1981), the Anxiety Disorder Interview Schedule for PTSD (Blanchard, Gerardi, Kolb, & Barlow, 1986), and the PTSD checklist (Carlson & Rosser-Hogan, 1991). The Harvard Trauma Questionnaire (HTQ; Mollica et al., 1992) is a checklist that measures both traumatic experiences and symptoms directly pertaining to a *DSM* diagnosis of PTSD.

Despite the fact that several measures of PTSD exist, the majority were designed or adapted for use with Indochinese refugee samples. Moreover, of the available instruments, only a few are valid and reliable cross-culturally. The Anxiety Disorder Interview Schedule for PTSD (Blanchard et al., 1986) and the Diagnostic Interview Schedule (Robins et al., 1981), for example, have been used in Indochinese samples, yet these instruments have only been shown to be reliable and valid within English-speaking populations. The Harvard Trauma Questionnaire (HTQ; Mollica et al., 1992), in contrast, is one measure of PTSD that was developed specifically for use with Indochinese refugees, and it has been shown to be both reliable and valid.

The HTQ is a cross-cultural self-report instrument that is composed of three sections. The first section consists of 17 trauma events (e.g., lack of food or water, murder of family or friend, torture). Respondents are asked to report whether they have experienced, witnessed, or heard about any of the listed events. The second section includes a series of open-ended questions that require respondents to describe the most terrifying or traumatic situations they encountered in their country of origin or during resettlement. The third part lists thirty symptoms that are related to trauma and to torture. Sixteen of these symptoms are related to *DSM-III-R* (American Psychiatric Association, 1987) criteria for PTSD, and fourteen are symptoms commonly seen by the authors in their clinical experience with survivors of trauma and torture (e.g., "feeling ashamed of the traumatic or hurtful things that have happened to you", "feeling as if you are going crazy"). Although the questionnaire was not originally written in any Indochinese language, forward-back translation procedures produced a final version of the HTQ in the Khmer, Lao, and Vietnamese languages. The HTQ has an internal consistency of .93, a test-retest reliability of .90 with a 1-week interval between administrations, and an interrater reliability of .96 (Mollica et al., 1992). The convergent validity of the HTQ has also been shown to be quite good in that it correctly classified PTSD patients 93% of the time and non-PTSD patients 84% of the time.

While not originally designed for use with refugees, another measure of PTSD worth mentioning is the Self-Rating Inventory for Post-traumatic Stress Disorder (SIP; Hovens et al., 1994). This newly developed Dutch-language self-rating questionnaire consists of 47 items that correspond to *DSM-III-R* and *DSM-IV* criteria for PTSD. All items are written without specific reference to trauma and are scored for intensity using a 4-point Likert scale. Validated on a sample of war trauma victims and psychiatric outpatients, the SIP has been found to be an effective instrument for diagnosing PTSD. For example, the SIP has an internal consistency of .96, a test-retest reliability of .90 with at least a 1-week interval between administrations, and has been found to correlate highly with several external measures of PTSD. Moreover, the SIP has adequate sensitivity and specificity, as it has been shown to adequately differentiate between PTSD and non-PTSD individuals, as well as traumatized non-PTSD individuals and nontraumatized psychiatric patients.

Assessment of Depression and Anxiety   Several different measures are used to assess depression and anxiety in refugee populations. Examples of some of these measures include the Vietnamese Depression Scale (Kinzie et al., 1982), the Zung Scale for Depression (Westermeyer, 1986), the Depression scale of the 90-item Symptom Checklist (SCL-D; Derogatis, Lipman, & Covi, 1973), the Structured Clinical Interview for *DSM-III-R* (Spitzer, Williams, Gibbon, & First, 1988), the Hmong Adaptation of the Beck Depression Inventory (HABDI; Mouanoutoua et al., 1991), and the Cambodian version of the Hopkins Symptom Checklist-25 (HSC-25; Mollica et al., 1987). Similar to measures of PTSD, the above-named devices have generally been designed or adapted for use with Indochinese refugees, and only a few have been restandardized in languages other than English. One example of such an instrument is the Cambodian version of the HSC-25 (Mollica et al., 1987). The HSC-25, which is frequently used to assess anxiety and depression in refugees (see Carlson & Rosser-Hogan, 1991; Hauf & Vaglum, 1994; McKelvey et al., 1992), consists of 10 symptoms of anxiety and 15 symptoms of depression. For each item, respondents are required to rate the frequency of occurrence in one of four categories, ranging from "not at all" to "extremely." Not surprisingly, the HSC has been found to be a reliable and valid instrument in the assessment of anxiety and depression in Southeast Asian refugees. The Cambodian version of the HSC-25 has been validated with Khmer populations and has been found to correctly classify anxious and depressed individuals 88% of the time and nonanxious and nondepressed 73% of the time (Mollica et al., 1987). The HSC-25 has also been found to have an interrater reliability of .98 and a test-retest reliability of .84 (for the anxiety component only) (Mollica et al., 1986). Another instrument that has been standardized on Southeast Asian refugee samples and has been shown to be a highly reliable and useful instrument is the Hmong Adaptation of the Beck Depression Inventory (HABDI; Mouanoutoua et al., 1991). Unlike many other assessment tools, the translation of this instrument from English into Hmong was sensitive to cultural-specific content and format. Using a 3-point Likert scale, respondents are required to indicate the frequency of occurrence of each of 21 symptoms of depression. The HABDI has an internal consistency of .93 and a test-retest reliability of .92 with a 2-week interval between administrations. With respect to convergent validity, the HABDI correctly identified 94% of depressed and 78% of nondepressed in two Hmong samples (Mouanoutoua et al., 1991).

Assessment of Torture   A comprehensive assessment of torture includes not only a standard evaluation of psychological functioning, but also an assessment of trauma history (e.g., torture, pre- and post-trauma stressors), family history, pre-trauma functioning, as well as current problems in adjustment and functioning (e.g., occupational, financial, housing).

In many cases it is also essential that survivors of torture undergo a complete medical examination by a physician familiar with the consequences of torture. Many have suffered from the effects of starvation and frequently have untreated physical illnesses. Given the sexual torture inflicted on many refugees, it may be important to screen for venereal diseases, pregnancy, and damage to the sexual organs. In addition, while symptoms such as headaches and memory and concentration difficulties may be stress-related, many survivors of torture have suffered from severe blows to the head. As a consequence, neurological and neuropsychological assessments may be warranted to rule out brain damage. Similarly, many survivors suffer from debilitation pain syndromes due to the extreme physical torture they have experienced. A referral to a physiatrist or rehabilitation psychologist for an in-depth chronic pain assessment may therefore be warranted (cf. Turk & Melzack, 1992).

Self-rating scales are useful aids in the diagnostic process (Cienfuegos & Monelli, 1983; Mollica & Caspi-Yavin, 1991; Mollica & Lavelle, 1988; Westermeyer, 1989). A number of currently used self-rating scales have been translated in many languages. Examples include the General Health Questionnaire (Pan & Goldberg, 1990), the Zung Depression Scale (Westermeyer, 1986), the Symptom Checklist-90 (SCL-90; Derogatis et al., 1973), and the Minnesota Multiphasic Personality Inventory-2 (MMPI-2; Butcher, Dahlstrom, Graham, Tellegen, & Kaemmer, 1989).

In addition to the self-rating scales mentioned above, several semistructured interview schedules have recently been developed to document specifically trauma-related events and symptomatology (cf. Allodi Trauma Scale, Allodi, 1985; Harvard Trauma Questionnaire, Mollica et al., 1992). Although many of these clinical measures have not been tested psychometrically (e.g., Allodi Trauma Scale), as described earlier, the Harvard Trauma Questionnaire (HTQ) is a reliable, valid, and sensitive instrument for measuring torture, trauma, and PTSD in Cambodian, Laotian, and Vietnamese samples (Mollica & Caspi-Yavin, 1991; Mollica et al., 1992). Clinical experience with the Harvard Trauma Questionnaire demonstrates that survivors of torture respond more positively to trauma-related questions when they are presented in a neutral, more impersonal approach (i.e., in a questionnaire format) than when similar questions are posed during a traditional open-ended intake interview. For example, Indochinese patients reportedly stated that it helped to "put words around" or describe the trauma events (Mollica & Caspi-Yavin, 1991).

Assessment Tools for Children   Scales used to measure PTSD in children include the Diagnostic Interview for Children and Adolescents (DICA; Welner, Reich, Herjanic, Jung, & Amado, 1987), the 42-item War Trauma Scale (Sack et al., 1993), the 56-item Stressful Life Events Scale for Youth (Sandler & Block, 1979; see Sack et al., 1993), and the Youth Adaptation Rating Scale (Beall & Schmidt, 1984; see Muecke & Sassi, 1992).

Anxiety and depression in children have been measured by the HSCL-25 (Mollica et al., 1987; see Felsman et al., 1990; Muecke & Sassi, 1992; McKelvey et al., 1992), the Vietnamese Depression Scale (Kinzie et al., 1982; see Felsman et al., 1990), and the Kiddie Schedule for Affective Disorders and Schizophrenia (KSADS; Puig-Antich, Orvaschel, Tabrinzi, & Chambers, 1980).

SERVICE DELIVERY AND UTILIZATION

Although exact figures detailing the number of services available to refugees are largely unavailable, there is agreement that serious limitations exist in the delivery of mental health services to refugees throughout the resettlement process (Gong-Guy et al., 1991; Robinson, 1980). In overseas camps, for example, the mental health services available to refugees are typically characterized by fragmentation, instability, lack of trained professional mental health care workers, lack of leadership, and language barriers (Gong-Guy et al., 1991). Similarly, in the host country, psychiatric hospitals and clinics, as well as community health centers specializing in refugee care, are plagued by numerous barriers to service delivery, including severe shortages of trained bilingual and bicultural staff, misdiagnosis, reliance on culturally inappropriate assessment and therapy approaches, and limited accessibility of services (Gong-Guy et al., 1991; Kazarian & Joseph, 1994; Robinson, 1980). Despite apparent dissatisfaction with service delivery to refugees, several programs are providing culturally congruent psychiatric care while at the same time effectively meeting the rapid rise in demand for these services (Jaranson & Bamford, 1987; Kinzie et al., 1980; Mollica et al., 1987). Moreover, a review of the literature revealed that a number of promising intervention and primary prevention strategies have been developed and incorporated for use with refugees.

In the following section, four successful and culturally sensitive mental health service delivery models will be reported. Next, common intervention and primary prevention programs for refugees will be examined. Finally, factors that influence refugees' patterns of service utilization will be considered. This section will conclude with a few comments regarding means of increasing service utilization in this population.

Models of Service Delivery

After having launched a large-scale investigation of refugee mental health programs across the continental United States, members of the Refugee Assistance Program—Mental Health Technical Assistance Center, located at the University of Minnesota, identified four culturally sensitive and widely representative mental health service delivery models: the psychiatric model, the community mental health model, the primary health care clinic model, and the multiservices or social services model (Jaranson & Bamford, 1987). Among other factors, each of the models was found to vary as a function of number of refugees served, severity of illnesses treated, and service approach.

Programs within the psychiatric model, for example, serve the least number and generally only attend to the more severely ill refugees. Located in large medical centers or in university teaching hospitals, psychiatric programs are guided by the medical model and are characterized by a diversity of services (Jaranson & Bamford, 1987). Programs within the community mental health model, in contrast, target the needs of various refugee groups (children, elderly, chemically dependent) at all levels of functioning. While inpatient services are relatively limited and difficult to access, community mental health programs provide a continuum of services, including screening, emergency, outpatient, partial hospitalization, transitional halfway-house services, and education, on a case-management basis (Jaranson & Bamford, 1987). As compared to the first two models, programs within the primary health care model serve a greater number of refugees and are based on a consultation-liaison approach. Although the range of mental health services is generally less, programs within the primary health care model are better integrated. As one illustration, there is more communication and a greater sense of connectedness between the physical and mental health services offered (Jaranson & Bamford, 1987). Finally, programs within the multiservices/social services model serve the greatest number of refugees as compared to the other models. Based on a psychosocial prevention approach, these programs offer a variety of services in addition to mental health (e.g., English as a second language classes, health and nutrition classes, employment counseling, recreation and social programs, etc.). Moreover, similar to programs within the primary health model, the stigma of mental illness is less of a barrier to receiving assistance within the multiservices/social services model (Jaranson & Bamford, 1987).

Intervention

Treatment of PTSD and Depression   Psychotherapy (individual, group, family), and pharmacotherapy are common Western-style therapeutic techniques used to treat PTSD and depression in refugee populations. Regardless of which therapeutic technique is chosen, however, there is considerable debate regarding the effectiveness of the strategy.

The question of applicability of psychotherapy to individuals socially and culturally distant from that of Westerners has been an issue for debate for many decades (Dahl, 1989). It has been argued that traditional Western verbal therapies are neither suitable nor readily accepted by non-Westerners because of fundamental differences in communication styles, values, and beliefs (Cheung, 1993; Kinzie et al., 1988). In the case of Indochinese refugees, for example, the basic principles of psychotherapy, which center around expressing emotion and talking about one's past experiences in relation to current difficulties, are often foreign to these individuals, who have been taught to suppress affect, tolerate suffering, and hold a fatalistic attitude toward their existence (Cheung, 1993). It has also been suggested that lack of psychological-mindedness, lack of interest in introspection, feelings of shame resulting from the acknowledgment of psychological difficulties, reluctance to speak about personal problems beyond the confines of the family, and cultural beliefs about the causes of psychiatric disorders make psychotherapy a difficult endeavor with Indochinese populations (McQuaide, 1989).

Whereas some researchers have reported success with psychotherapy (e.g., Kinzie et al., 1988; Lee, 1988; S. Nguyen, 1982), others have found short-lived and/or limited reductions in symptoms and even magnification of symptoms (e.g., Kinzie et al., 1984; Mollica & Lavelle, 1988). However, despite the fact that psychotherapy sometimes does not appear to be efficacious with certain refugee groups, some forms of psychotherapy (i.e., group, family) have been found to be more effective than others.

The main difficulty with individual psychotherapy derives from the development of the therapeutic relationship (Dahl, 1989). Specifically, due to traditional values and beliefs, it is often very difficult to establish a working alliance with individuals from non-Western cultures. Indochinese refugees, for example, typically regard the therapist as a teacher or a healer and themselves as the student or the one to be healed. Moreover, these individuals tend to believe that to disagree with or show skepticism toward the clinician is a sign of disrespect. Therapeutic neutrality is another basic component of psychotherapy that is often compromised in individual therapy with

Indochinese refugees. That is, in addition to requesting reassurance that they will get better, these patients expect to be told exactly how to go about returning to an optimal state of health (see Dahl, 1989).

Group therapy is an effective and feasible treatment modality used with refugee populations. This intervention provides a supportive atmosphere in which refugees who share common experiences, culture, language, and values and beliefs can meet to discuss similar problems (Kinzie et al., 1988). In addition to discussing areas of difficulty, group therapy provides a forum in which to discuss the origins of psychiatric illness and to elucidate the role of medicine. Group therapy also provides refugees with the opportunity to increase verbal interaction with others in their own language, reconstruct social networks, and revive lost cultural identity (see Kinzie et al., 1988; S. Nguyen, 1982). Group therapy is not without its share of difficulties, however. In a 1-year program of group therapy involving four cultural groups, Kinzie and his colleagues (1988) discovered that communication style, respect for authority, and traditional social relationships greatly influenced group dynamics. That is, frequent breakdowns in communication were attributed to the unfamiliarity and suspiciousness of the disclosure required, concerns over confidentiality, and fear of being confrontational or disrespectful to elders.

Family therapy is another well-accepted and effective treatment available for use with refugees (Lee, 1988). This therapy emphasizes the importance of the family unit and, when successful, engenders feelings of cohesion among all family members in a structured, problem-focused, education-oriented manner (Lee, 1988).

In addition to psychotherapeutic techniques, pharmacologic intervention is commonly used to alleviate the symptoms of PTSD and depression in refugees. The appropriateness of these techniques, however, has been widely challenged, as there is little research to support the efficacy of psychopharmacological interventions in the treatment of refugees. Further, appropriate dose ranges and possible side effects, including toxicity, have not yet been fully determined (Fernando & Kazarian, 1995). Evidence collected to date suggests that large cross-cultural variations in physiological responses to various psychotropics exist (Fernando & Kazarian, 1995; Lin & Shen, 1991). For example, compared with Caucasians, Asians are particularly sensitive to antipsychotics, especially haloperidol and benzodiazepines (Lin, Poland, Smith, Strickland, & Mendoza, 1991). As another illustration, although a number of antidepressant drugs have been found to have unacceptable psychopharmacological effects on Mien refugees (Kinzie, Leung, Boehnlein, & Fleck, 1987; Moore & Boehnlein,1991b), these same drugs were associated with significant clinical improvement in groups of Hmong, Lao, Vietnamese, and Cambodians (Moore & Boehnlein, 1991b). Despite the fact that some drugs are possibly less effective for use with certain refugee populations, it is widely believed that psychopharmacology is essential for the treatment of refugee patients with PTSD and depression (Kinzie, 1985; Lin, 1986; Tung, 1985).

Several explanations for nonadherence to pharmacologic régimes have been advanced in the literature. Physiological incompatibility with antidepressant medications, due to differences in drug metabolism and genetic composition, has been cited as a major factor related to compliance in Indochinese refugees (Cheung, 1993; Lin & Shen, 1991; Moore & Boehnlein, 1991a). Lack of knowledge pertaining to pharmacological mechanisms of action is another factor influencing drug compliance in refugee populations. Indochinese refugees, for example, expect that Western medications will exert their therapeutic effects almost instantaneously, and therefore these individuals often do not take their medications continuously for extended periods of time (Lin & Shen, 1991; Moore & Boehnlein, 1991a, 1991b). Refugees' indigenous health beliefs and practices also affect medication compliance. In addition to their belief that drugs are only to be used to alleviate physical symptomatology, disapproval over having to take either multiple drugs or drugs that make them feel over-medicated reduces medication compliance in refugees (Lin & Shen, 1991; Moore & Boehnlein, 1991a, 1991b; Van Boemel & Rozée, 1992).

Treatment of Torture Survivors   While there is growing awareness of the need for specialized treatment services for survivors of torture in the past decade (cf. centers for victims of torture, Chester, 1990), the development of treatment approaches for highly traumatized and tortured refugees remains in its infancy (Goldfeld et al., 1988; Mollica & Lavelle, 1988). Current approaches to work with survivors of torture distinguish between time-limited or short-term techniques aimed at stabilizing clients and longer term therapeutic techniques aimed at helping survivors emotionally integrate their traumatic experiences (Veer, 1992).

1. *Short-term techniques.* Survivors of torture are often significantly distressed and overwhelmed when first seen in therapy. Primary aims include helping clients regain adequate functioning with respect to everyday behavior and reducing symptoms (Veer, 1992). One supportive technique is to give survivors the opportunity to tell their stories so that overwhelming and distressing feelings can be expressed. In addition, providing explanations for and furnishing information regarding the cause of their symptomatology can decrease any fears that clients may have about "going mad," thereby alleviating anxiety.

At times, concrete assistance may be most beneficial for clients' immediate well-being. Survivors in exile are not only trying to deal with the trauma, but also suffer from a "concatenation of subsequent stressors which disempower them in the social, cultural and political spheres" (Silove et al., 1991, p. 482). In particular, refugees have to overcome a number of obstacles, including language, housing, employment, public transportation, acculturation, and discrimination (cf. the previous section on migration-related stressors). These obstacles can impede the successful resolution of many immediate and concrete needs (such as finding a home or a job, applying for welfare, etc.). Often, refugees will expect those with whom they have current contact, including their therapists, to solve these needs. While the therapist may not be able to address all of their concerns due to time or resource constraints, it is essential that appropriate referrals be made as a means of establishing trust in the therapeutic relationship, meeting a wider array of refugees' needs, and improving well-being.

In a recent study, Van Boemel and Rozée (1992) discovered that, although group therapy may have been slightly more effective, skills training successfully reduced psychological distress and improved well-being and visual acuity in a sample of psychosomatically blind Cambodian women. After having participated in ten 1-hour group sessions designed to teach minimal skills (e.g., basic communication in English, telephone usage, public transportation, currency), these victims of torture reported increased feelings of happiness, decreased feelings of sadness, reduction in frequency of crying, and improved visual acuity.

2. *Longer-term therapeutic techniques.* Many survivors try to cope with their torture-related trauma by attempting to forget and by pretending that it never happened. In many cases, however, the trauma continues to live in the form of psychological distress and psychosomatic symptoms. Recounting the trauma is often seen as cathartic, and is an important component of therapy with survivors of torture. Several authors, however, have suggested that simply recounting and reliving the trauma is not, in and of itself, therapeutic and can lead to an increase in intrusive and painful thoughts with a concomitant increase in distress and symptomatology (cf. Mollica & Lavelle, 1988). It is equally important that the trauma be seen in a new context. Therefore, the clinician's main goal is to help clients "reframe" what has happened to them. This reframing allows survivors to experience the pain in a more meaningful way (Agger, 1989).

One reframing method is the *testimonio,* or oral history, developed by Chilean psychologists Lira and Weinstein under the repressive régime of Pinochet and initially published under pseudonyms (cf. Cienfuegos & Monelli, 1983; Dominguez & Weinstein, 1987). This method consists of essentially helping the survivor record in detail the painful and traumatic experiences they have endured. In essence, the therapist encourages them to bear witness to their abuse by encouraging them to express experiences that had been relegated to the private domain. While they are providing their detailed accounts, one of the therapist's roles is to help survivors express their emotional reactions to the torture. The testimony therefore moves continually between the cognitive and emotional levels, seeking to integrate the affect with the traumatic experiences. While doing this work, it is important to respect survivors' defenses by encouraging and allowing them to work at their own pace. If survivors are pressured to open up too quickly, they risk being overwhelmed and revictimized (Cienfuegos & Monelli, 1983; Dominguez & Weinstein, 1987).

Another important function of the testimony method is to help survivors reframe their experience. One way in which this reframing is achieved is by normalizing and validating clients' reactions and experiences. Therapists can provide reassurance to survivors that their symptoms are indeed common to individuals who have undergone similar experiences and not a defect in the individual. Through normalization of the torture experience and its aftereffects and the examination of coping skills, survivors come to understand that their reactions were appropriate to the situation and allowed them to survive. Thus, survivors learn that their symptoms are not "crazy" in the psychopathological sense of the term and that they have the option to change or to modify the coping strategies that are no longer adaptive in their current life.

Furthermore, it is essential to help survivors deindividualize the blame and reattribute the responsibility for what happened to them to their torturers and to the repressive and violent tactics of the régime. In this way, each survivor can see their "private symptoms as part of an attempt at ideological destruction" (Agger, 1989, p. 314). In other words, it is important to reconceptualize the abuse by countering the denial and stressing its reality. Survivors need to understand that they are not responsible for their torture, nor did they cause the torture to occur because of something inherent in their personality or character.

Once the testimony is completed, the therapist and survivor read through it, rework it, and edit it. Thus, by repeatedly working through the trauma, cognitions and feelings can be processed until the traumatic events are objectified (Agger, 1989, p.

315). In essence, "the testimonio, by retracing the thread of a life course until it was broken by the repression, and the survival skills that promoted life after the traumatic events, facilitates a recovery of personal and social identity, a mending of the lifeline" (Aron, 1992, p. 184).

Reactions of Therapists Dealing with refugee-related trauma is not only difficult for survivors, but also for the professionals who witness their pain. This has been referred to as "burnout," "vicarious trauma" (UNHCR, 1993), "secondary post-traumatic stress disorder" (Dolan, 1991), and more recently as "compassion fatigue" (Figley, 1995). Symptoms experienced by health care providers are similar to those seen in survivors of torture and include insomnia, lack of interest in relationships and sex, sadness and depression, feeling overwhelmed and incompetent, recurrent intrusive thoughts of the trauma, nightmares or dreams about torture, generalized anxiety, withdrawal, cynicism, and discouragement (Bustos, 1990; Dolan, 1991; UNHCR, 1993). While therapists may differ with respect to their vulnerability to these symptoms, these symptoms have been observed in many highly trained and experienced clinicians.

Compassion fatigue can be prevented or alleviated by engaging in physical activity, taking time off, using relaxation techniques, joining a support group for professionals involved with survivors of torture, seeking individual or group supervision, and managing one's caseload by ensuring an adequate balance of presenting problems (Dolan, 1991; UNHCR, 1993). The recognition of physical and psychological limits will ensure that all professionals working with this highly traumatized population will provide continued effective and ethical interventions.

Primary Prevention

Due to increased levels of psychopathology and high rates of mental disorder in refugees compared to the general population, the need for public health interventions is apparent. A review of the literature revealed primary prevention programs for refugees aimed at three levels: community, national, and international ranks. At the community level, programs designed to address difficulties experienced by groups as opposed to individual refugees are emphasized. In contrast, at the national and international levels, primary prevention programs are designed to ameliorate premigration, migration, and postmigration experiences and to promote widespread multicultural and multiracial understanding and tolerance through public education (see Williams & Berry, 1991).

According to Williams and Berry (1991), primary prevention programs, whether they be at the community, national, or international level, should follow several structural requirements. In addition to advocating that primary prevention programs should be based on stress and acculturation research (see Williams & Berry, 1991), those researchers emphasized the importance of the guidelines proposed originally by Cowen (1982) and Bloom (1982) for the development of primary prevention programs. Cowen (1982), for example, suggested that primary prevention must be (a) group or population based, (b) targeted toward at-risk groups, and (c) developed from previous research or theory about improving psychological health or preventing maladaptation. Bloom's (1982) model of primary prevention, in comparison, included (a) the selection and identification of a particularly stressful life event and who has experienced that event, (b) an epidemiological study indicating the outcomes of these events, (c) the development of hypotheses about how to reduce the negative outcomes of the stressors, and (d) the development and evaluation of experimental prevention interventions based upon the hypotheses.

Consistent with the requirements advocated by Williams and Berry, Ajduković and Ajduković (1993) recently described the development of a model for the prevention of mental health risks among displaced persons and refugees. This model takes into consideration three sets of factors: (a) past and current stressors, (b) factors that moderate successful coping with stressors (i.e., coping style, personality, and available resources), and (c) manifestations of stress and difficulties in psychosocial adaptation (i.e., behavioral, psychological, social, and physical). The goal in designing this model was to develop intervention programs that are specially tailored to meet the psychological needs of different refugee groups (see Ajduković & Ajduković, 1993).

Service Utilization

Regardless of the number of mental health services available for refugees, a question remains as to the extent of service utilization. Research has indicated that, although refugees have come to rely increasingly on human services in the past 15 years, in total only a small percentage of refugees use mental health services (e.g., Robinson, 1980).

Factors Influencing Extent and Type of Involvement in Services   Although many refugees suffer from psychiatric and psychological difficulties, several factors contribute to the underutilization of the much-needed mental health services (Van Boemel & Rozée, 1992). For example, unfamiliarity with the self-referral process, unawareness of the type and location of mental health services offered, limited access to services due to lack of proficiency in English, fear, lack of services that have an awareness and respect for the culture and traditions, and refugees' beliefs, have been suggested as barriers that directly influence refugees' extent and type of involvement in mental health services (Gong-Guy et al., 1991; Van Boemel & Rozée, 1992).

In addition to barriers that influence whether or not services are used, factors that predict refugees' service utilization have also been identified. In a study of two Caribbean refugee minorities, Portes, Kyle and Eaton (1992) discovered that the most important predictors of service utilization were differential exposure to health care facilities in the country of origin; facilitative role of the receiving cultural community; facilities staffed by people who understand refugees' language and culture; need for care; and several predisposing factors including age, sex, and marital status.

Improving Service Utilization   In order to increase service utilization in refugee populations, the specific religious, linguistic, psychological, and social organizational characteristics of the target population must be considered (Canda & Phaobtong, 1992). Instead of merely adapting Western interventions and primary prevention strategies to fit the needs of refugees, we must attempt to design strategies that are specifically tailored to those who are culturally different from ourselves. Prilleltensky (1993), for example, set about designing a social-action project, whose aim was to reduce the stressors associated with immigration and to facilitate adaptation and integration of family members into a small Latin American community in southern Ontario, by soliciting the specific needs of his target group. Through a series of interviews and focus-group discussions, Prilleltensky (1993) was able to elicit the unique experiences associated with adaptation to a new culture, which he then translated into objectives for a primary prevention program.

CONCLUSIONS

Since the early 1980s, the number of refugee landings in Canada and the United States has dramatically increased. With this influx comes a number of people with different cultural and historical backgrounds, all attempting to become integrated into a new way of life. While not all refugees suffer from mental health problems that require formal assistance, the growing cultural diversity in North America has, nevertheless, underscored the need for clinical psychologists and other health care practitioners to develop culturally sensitive attitudes and practices. Accordingly, the aim of this chapter was to elucidate the role that clinical psychology plays in the delivery of health care to refugees by examining the contributions of various researchers and clinicians to issues pertaining to refugee mental health.

In addition to providing an overview of terminological issues and refugee movement trends, we examined migration-related stressors faced by refugees. Next, the scope of refugees' psychiatric and psychological difficulties was discussed. Generally, the research has shown that, although slight variations in prevalence rates have been found, regardless of age and culture, many refugees experience a number of mental health difficulties and related clinical problems, including among others PTSD, anxiety and depression, torture trauma, substance abuse, and family violence. Attention was then turned to assessment issues. In addition to presenting six potential barriers to diagnosis, we discussed common instruments used to assess PTSD, anxiety, and depression in both adult and child refugees. Issues pertaining to the assessment of torture trauma were then described, highlighting in particular the physical and psychological regimens that constitute a thorough evaluation. The final section of the chapter examined patterns of refugee service delivery and utilization. In this section, current approaches to treatment of PTSD, depression, and torture trauma were reviewed. In addition, primary prevention programs for refugees aimed at three levels were examined. Finally, the availability of refugee services was considered, along with factors that influence extent and type of involvement in and methods for improving service utilization.

Despite the seemingly comprehensive and complete state of present knowledge pertaining to refugee mental health, several limitations exist. Given the disproportionate research available on Indochinese refugees, for example, it is clear that future research must begin to carefully explore and document the needs of other refugee groups, including those from countries such as Afghanistan, Somalia, and Guatemala. In particular, efforts should be concentrated on establishing effective assessment and treatment procedures that span culturally diverse refugee populations. Another limitation is that the literature, including this chapter, is highly sensitive to cultural distinctions and oftentimes ignores intracultural variations and similarities that exist between cultures. Accordingly, future research should attempt to emphasize that individual differences exist within cultures, as well as to delineate the common threads that unify mankind.

In conclusion, the effective delivery of mental health care to refugees is a multi-faceted endeavor. Through acquiring an adequate knowledge of migration-related stressors, common mental health difficulties experienced by refugees, and current approaches to assessment and intervention, as well as primary prevention and service utilization, clinicians will not only be better able to meet the needs of this population, but will engender a widespread cross-cultural way of thinking.

References

Adelman, H. (1991). *Refugee policy: Canada and the United States.* North York, Ontario, Canada: York Lanes Press.
Agger, I. (1986). Seksuel torture af kvindelige politiske fanger. *Nord Sexol, 4,* 147–161.
Agger, I. (1989). Sexual torture of political prisoners: An overview. *Journal of Traumatic Stress, 2,* 305–318.
Ajduković, M., & Ajduković, D. (1993). Psychological well-being of refugee children. *Child Abuse and Neglect, 17,* 843–854.
Allodi, F. (1985). Physical and psychiatric effects of torture: A Canadian study. In E. Stover & E. O. Nightingale (Eds.), *The breaking of bodies and minds: Torture, psychiatric abuses and the health professions* (pp. 58–78). New York: Freeman.
Allodi, F., & Cowgill, G. (1982). Ethical and psychiatric aspects of torture: A Canadian study. *Canadian Journal of Psychiatry, 27,* 98–102.
Allodi, F., & Stiasny, S. (1990). Women as torture victims. *Canadian Journal of Psychiatry, 35,* 144–148.
American Psychiatric Association (1987). *Diagnostic and statistical manual of mental disorders* (3rd ed., rev.). Washington, DC: Author.
American Psychiatric Association (1994). *Diagnostic and statistical manual of mental disorders* (4th ed.). Washington, DC: Author.
Amnesty International. (1984). *Torture in the eighties.* New York: Author.
Amnesty International. (1990). *Women in the front line.* New York: Author.
Aron, A. (1992). Testimonio, a bridge between psychotherapy and sociotherapy. In E. Cole, O. Espin, & E. Rothblum (Eds.), *Refugee women and their mental health: Shattered societies, shattered lives.* Binghamton, NY: Harrington Park Press.
Arroyo, W., & Eth, S. (1985). Children traumatized by Central American warfare. In S. Eth & R. S. Pynoos (Eds.), *Posttraumatic stress disorder in children* (pp. 101–117). Washington, DC: American Psychiatric Press.
Bagheri, A. (1992). Psychiatric problems among Iranian immigrants in Canada. *Canadian Journal of Psychiatry, 37,* 7–11.
Bauer, M., Priebe, S., Kurten, I., Graf, K., & Baumgartner, A. (1994). Psychological and endocrine abnormalities in refugees from East Germany. Part 1. Prolonged stress, psychopathology, and hypothalamic-pituitary-thyroid axis activity. *Psychiatry Research, 51,* 61–73.
Beall, S., & Schmidt, G. (1984). Development of a Youth Adaptation Rating Scale. *Journal of School Health, 54,* 197–200.
Becker, D., Lira, E., Castillo, M. I., Gomez, E., & Kovalskys, J. (1990). Therapy with victims of political repression: The challenge of social reparation. *Journal of Social Issues, 46,* 133–149.
Blanchard, E. B., Gerardi, R. J., Kolb, L. C., & Barlow, D. H. (1986). The utility of the

Anxiety Disorder Interview Schedule (ADIS) in the diagnosis of posttraumatic stress disorder (PTSD) in Vietnam veterans. *Behavior Research and Therapy, 24,* 577–580.

Bloom, B. L. (1982). Epilogue. In S. M. Manson (Ed.), *New directions in prevention among American Indian and Alaska native communities* (pp. 337–394). Portland, OR: Oregon Health Sciences University.

Boehnlein, J. K., & Kinzie, J. D. (1992). *DSM* diagnosis of posttraumatic stress disorder and cultural sensitivity: A response. *Journal of Nervous and Mental Disease, 180,* 597–599.

Buchwald, D., Klacsanzsky, G., & Manson, S. M. (1993). Psychiatric disorders among recently arrived Eastern Europeans seen through a U. S. refugee counseling service. *International Journal of Social Psychiatry, 39,* 221–227.

Bustos, E. (1988). Sexuality and exile in traumatized refugees: A psychodynamic understanding. *Nordisk Sexologi, 6,* 25–30.

Bustos, E. (1990). Dealing with the unbearable: Reactions of therapists and therapeutic institutions to survivors of torture. In P. Suedfeld (Ed.), *Psychology and torture* (pp. 143–163). New York: Hemisphere.

Butcher, J. N., Dahlstrom, W. G., Graham, J. R., Tellegen, A., & Kaemmer, B. (1989). *Minnesota Multiphasic Personality Inventory (MMPI-2). Manual for administration and scoring.* Minneapolis MN: University of Minnesota Press.

Canda, E. R., & Phaobtong, T. (1992). Buddhism as a support system for Southeast Asian refugees. *Social Work, 37,* 61–67.

Carlson, E. B., & Rosser-Hogan, R. (1991). Trauma experiences, posttraumatic stress, dissociation, and depression in Cambodian refugees. *American Journal of Psychiatry, 148,* 1548–1551.

Chester, B. (1990). Because mercy has a human heart: Centers for victims of torture. In P. Suedfeld (Ed.), *Psychology and torture* (pp. 165–184). New York: Hemisphere.

Cheung, P. (1993). Somatisation as a presentation in depression and post-traumatic stress disorder among Cambodian refugees. *Australian and New Zealand Journal of Psychiatry, 27,* 422–428.

Cheung, P. (1994). Posttraumatic stress disorder among Cambodian refugees in New Zealand. *International Journal of Social Psychiatry, 40,* 17–26.

Cienfuegos, A., & Monelli, C. (1983). The testimony of political repression as a therapeutic instrument. *American Journal of Orthopsychiatry, 53,* 43–51.

Cole, E., Espin, O., & Rothblum, E. (1992). *Refugee women and their mental health: Shattered societies, shattered lives.* Binghamton, NY: Harrington Park Press.

Cowen, E. L. (1982). Primary prevention research: Barriers, needs, and opportunities. *Journal of Primary Prevention, 2,* 131–137.

Crites, L. (1991). Cross-cultural counseling in wife beating cases. *Response to the Victimization of Women and Children, 13,* 8–12.

Dahl, C. I. (1989). Some problems of cross-cultural psychotherapy with refugees seeking treatment. *American Journal of Psychoanalysis, 49,* 19–32.

D'Avanzo, C. E., Frye, B., & Froman, R. (1994). Culture, stress and substance use in Cambodian refugee women. *Journal of Studies on Alcohol, 55,* 420–426.

Derogatis, L. R., Lipman, R. S., & Covi, L. (1973). The SCL-90: An outpatient psychiatric rating scale—Preliminary report. *Psychopharmacological Bulletin, 9,* 13–27.

Dolan, Y. (1991). *Resolving sexual abuse: Solution-focused therapy and Ericksonian hypnosis for adult survivors.* New York: Norton.

Dominguez, R., & Weinstein, E. (1987). Aiding victims of political repression in Chile: A psychological and psychotherapeutic approach. *Tidsskrift for Norsk Psykologforening, 24,* 75–81.

Edwards, R. G., & Beiser, M. (1994). Southeast Asian refugee youth in Canada: The determinants of competence and successful coping. *Canada's Mental Health, 42,* 1–5.

Felsman, J. K., Leong, F. T. L., Johnson, M. C., & Felsman, I. C. (1990). Estimates of psychological distress among Vietnamese refugees: Adolescents, unaccompanied minors, and young adults. *Social Science and Medicine, 31,* 1251–1256.

Fernando, M. L., & Kazarian, S. S. (1995). Patient education in the drug treatment of psychiatric disorders: Effects on compliance outcome. *CNS Drugs, 3,* 291–304.

Figley, C. (1995). *Compassion fatigue: Coping with secondary traumatic stress in those who treat the traumatized.* New York: Brunner/Mazel.

Fornazzari, X. (1989, November). *Psychiatric care of Latin American immigrants and refugees: A comparative study.* Paper presented at the Conference on Health, Political Repression and Human Rights, San José, Costa Rica.

Fornazzari, X., & Freire, M. (1990). Women as victims of torture. *Acta Psychiatrica Scandinavica, 82,* 257–260.

Frye, B. A., & D'Avanzo, C. D. (1994). Cultural themes in family stress and violence among Cambodian refugee women in the inner city. *Advances in Nursing Science, 16,* 64–77.

Garcia-Peltoniemi, R., & Jaranson, J. (1989, November). *A multidisciplinary approach to the treatment of torture victims.* Paper presented at the Second International Conference of Centers, Institutions, and Individuals Concerned with the Care of Victims of Organized Violence, San José, Costa Rica.

Goldfeld, A. E., Mollica, R. F., Pesavento, B. H., & Farone, S. V. (1988). The physical and psychological sequelae of torture: Symptomatology and diagnosis. *Journal of American Medical Association, 259,* 2725–2729.

Gong-Guy, E. (1986). *California Southeast Asian mental health needs assessment.* Oakland, CA: Asian Community Mental Health Services.

Gong-Guy, E., Cravens, R. B., & Patterson, T. E. (1991). Clinical issues in mental health service delivery to refugees. *American Psychologist, 45,* 642–648.

Hauf, E., & Vaglum, P. (1994). Chronic posttraumatic stress disorder in Vietnamese refugees: A prospective community study of prevalence, course, psychopathology, and stressors. *Journal of Nervous and Mental Disease, 182,* 85–90.

Hinton, W. L., Chen, Y. J., Du, N., Tran, C. G., Lu, F. G., Miranda, J., & Faust, S. (1993). *DSM-III-R* disorders in Vietnamese refugees: Prevalence and correlates. *Journal of Nervous and Mental Disease, 181,* 113–122.

Hjern, A., Angel, B., & Höjer, B. (1991). Persecution and behavior: A report of refugee children from Chile. *Child Abuse and Neglect, 15,* 239–248.

Hovens, J. E., van der Ploeg, H. M., Bramsen, I., Klaarenbeek, M. T. A., Schreuder, J. N., & Rivero, V. V. (1994). The development of the Self-Rating Inventory for Posttraumatic Stress Disorder. *Acta Psychiatrica Scandinavica, 90,* 172–183.

Jang, D., Lee, D., & Morello-Frosch, R. (1991). Domestic violence in the immigrant and refugee community: Responding to the needs of immigrant women. *Response to the Victimization of Women and Children, 13,* 2–7.

Jaranson, J. J., & Bamford, P. (1987). *Program models for mental health treatment of refugees* (NIMH Contract No. 278–85–0024). St. Paul, MN: University of Minnesota, Refugee Assistance Program—Mental Health Technical Assistance Center.

Kane, H. (1995). *The hour of departure: Forces that create refugees and migrants.* Washington, DC: Worldwatch Institute.

Kazarian, S. S., & Joseph, L. W. (1994). Caring for refugees in a mental hospital. *Canadian Journal of Psychiatry, 39,* 189.

Kinzie, J. D. (1985). Overview of clinical issues in the treatment of Southeast Asian refugees. In T. Owan, B. Bliatout, K. M. Lin, W. Liu, T. D. Nguyen & H. Z. Wong (Eds.), *Southeast Asian mental health: Treatment, prevention, training, and research* (pp. 113–136). Rockville, MD: National Institute of Mental Health.

Kinzie, J. D., Boehnlein, J. K., Leung, P. K., Moore, L. J., Riley, C., & Smith, D. (1990). The prevalence of posttraumatic stress disorder and its clinical significance among Southeast Asian refugees. *American Journal of Psychiatry, 147,* 913–917.

Kinzie, J. D., Fredrickson, R. H., Ben, R., Fleck, J., & Karls, W. (1984). Posttraumatic stress disorder among survivors of Cambodian concentration camps. *American Journal of Psychiatry, 141,* 645–650.

Kinzie, J. D., Leung, P., Boehnlein, J. K., & Fleck, J. (1987). Antidepressant blood levels in Southeast Asians: Clinical and cultural implications. *Journal of Nervous and Mental Disease, 175,* 480–485.

Kinzie, J. D., Leung, P., Bui, A., Ben, R., Keopraseuth, K. O., Riley, C., Fleck, J., & Ades, M. (1988). Group therapy with Southeast Asian refugees. *Community Mental Health Journal, 24,* 157–166.

Kinzie, J. D., & Manson, S. M. (1985). Five years' experience with Indochinese refugee psychiatric patients. *Journal of Operational Psychiatry, 14,* 105–111.

Kinzie, J. D., Manson, S. M., Vinh, D. T., Tolan, N. T., Anh, B., & Pho, T. N. (1982). Development of validation of a Vietnamese-language depression rating scale. *American Journal of Psychiatry, 193,* 1276–1281.

Kinzie, J. D., Sack, W. H., Angell, R., & Manson, S. (1986). The psychiatric effects of massive trauma on Cambodian children. Part 1. The children. *Journal of the American Academy of Child Psychiatry, 25,* 370–376.

Kinzie, J. D., Tran, K. A., Breckenridge, A., & Bloom, D. (1980). An Indochinese refugee psychiatric clinic: Culturally accepted treatment approaches. *American Journal of Psychiatry, 137,* 1429–1432.

Kroll, J., Habenicht, M., Mackenzie, T., Yang, M., Chan, M. Y. S., Vang, T., Nguyen, T., Ly, M., Phommasouvanh, B., Nguyen, H., Vang, Y., Souvannasoth, L., & Cabugao, R. (1989). Depression and posttraumatic stress disorder in Southeast Asian refugees. *American Journal of Psychiatry, 146,* 1592–1597.

Kunz, E. F. (1971). Exile and resettlement: Refugee theory. *International Migration Review, 15,* 42–51.

Kunz, E. F. (1973). The refugee in flight: Kinetic models and forms of displacement. *International Migration Review, 7,* 125–146.

Larsen, H., & Pagaduan-Lopez, J. (1987). Stress-tension reduction in the treatment of sexually tortured women: An exploratory study. *Journal of Sex and Marital Therapy, 13,* 210–218.

Lee, E. (1988). Cultural factors in working with Southeast Asian refugee adolescents. *Journal of Adolescence, 11,* 167–179.

Lin, K. M. (1986). Psychopathology and social disruption in refugees. In C. L. Williams & J. Westermeyer (Eds.), *Refugees and mental health* (pp. 61–73). Washington, DC: Hemisphere.

Lin, K. M., Poland, R. E., Smith, M. W., Strickland, T. L., & Mendoza, R. (1991). Pharmokinetics and other related factors affecting psychotropic responses in Asians. *Pharmacology Bulletin, 27,* 427–439.

Lin, K. M., & Shen, W. W. (1991). Pharmacotherapy for Southeast Asian psychiatric patients. *Journal of Nervous and Mental Disease, 179,* 346–350.

Lira, E., & Weinstein, E. (1986, May). *La tortura sexual.* Paper presented at the Seminario Internacional: Consecuencias de la represion en el Cono Sur. Sus efectos medicos, psicologicos y sociales, Montevideo, Uruguay.

Masser, D. S. (1992). Psychological functioning of Central American refugee children. *Child Welfare, 71,* 439–456.

McKelvey, R. S., Mao, A. R., & Webb, J. A. (1992). A risk profile predicting psychological distress in Vietnamese Amerasian youth. *Journal of the American Academy of Child and Adolescent Psychiatry, 31,* 911–915.

McQuaide, S. (1989). Working with Southeast Asian refugees. *Clinical Social Work Journal,* *17,* 165–176.

Meinhardt, K., Tom, S., Tse, T., & Yu, C. (1986). Southeast Asian refugees in the "Silicon Valley": The Asian health assessment project. *Amerasia, 12,* 43–65.

Melville, M. B., & Lykes, M. B. (1992). Guatemalan Indian children and the sociocultural effects of government-sponsored terrorism. *Social Science and Medicine, 34,* 533–548.

Mollica, R. F., & Caspi-Yavin, Y. (1991). Measuring torture and torture-related symptoms. *Psychological Assessment: A Journal of Consulting and Clinical Psychology, 3,* 581–587.

Mollica, R. F., Caspi-Yavin, Y., Bollini, P., Truong, T., Tor, S., & Lavelle, J. (1992). The Harvard Trauma Questionnaire: Validating a cross-cultural instrument for measuring torture, trauma, and post-traumatic stress disorder in Indochinese refugees. *The Journal of Nervous and Mental Disease, 180,* 111–116.

Mollica, R. F., & Lavelle, J. (1988). Southeast Asian refugees. In L. Comasdiaz and E. E. H. Griffiths (Eds.), *Clinical guidelines in cross cultural mental health* (pp. 262–302). New York: Wiley.

Mollica, R. F., & Son, L. (1989). Cultural dimensions in the evaluation and treatment of sexual trauma. *Psychiatric Clinics of North America, 12,* 363–379.

Mollica, R. F., Wyshak, G., de Marneffe, D., Khuon, F., & Lavelle, J. (1987). Indochinese versions of the Hopkins Symptom Checklist-25: A screening instrument for the psychiatric care of refugees. *American Journal of Psychiatry, 144,* 497–500.

Mollica, R. F., Wyshak, G., de Marneffe, D., Tu, B., Yang, T., Khown, F., Cuelho, R., & Lavelle, J. (1986). *Hopkins Symptom Checklist-25 Manual: Cambodian version.* Brighton, MA: St. Elizabeth's Hospital, Indochinese Psychiatry Clinic.

Mollica, R. F., Wyshak, G., & Lavelle, J. (1987). The psychosocial impact of war trauma and torture on Southeast Asian refugees. *American Journal of Psychiatry, 144,* 1567–1572.

Mollica, R. F., Wyshak, G., Lavelle, J., Truong, T., Tor, S., & Yang, T. (1990). Assessing symptom change in Southeast Asian refugee survivors of mass violence and torture. *American Journal of Psychiatry, 147,* 83–88.

Moore, L. J., & Boehnlein, J. K. (1991a). Treating psychiatric disorders among Mien refugees from highland Laos. *Social Science and Medicine, 32,* 1029–1036.

Moore, L. J., & Boehnlein, J. K. (1991b). Posttraumatic stress disorder, depression, and somatic symptoms in U.S. Mien patients. *Journal of Nervous and Mental Disease, 179,* 728–733.

Morgan, M. C., Wingard, D. L., & Felice, M. E. (1984). Subcultural differences in alcohol use among youth. *Journal of Adolescent Health Care, 5,* 191–195.

Mouanoutoua, V. L., Brown, L. G., Cappelletty, G. G., & Levine, R. V. (1991). A Hmong adaptation of the Beck Depression Inventory. *Journal of Personality Assessment, 57,* 309–322.

Muecke, M. A., & Sassi, L. (1992). Anxiety among Cambodian refugee adolescents in transit and resettlement. *Western Journal of Nursing Research, 14,* 267–291.

Nef, J., & da Silva, R. (1991). The politics of refugee generation in Latin America. In H. Adelman (Ed.), *Refugee policy: Canada and the United States* (pp. 52–80). North York, Ontario, Canada: York Lanes Press.

Nguyen, N. A., & Williams, H. L. (1989). Transition from east to west: Vietnamese adolescents and their parents. *Journal of the American Academy of Child and Adolescent Psychiatry, 28,* 505–515.

Nguyen, S. (1982). Psychiatric and psychosomatic problems among Southeast Asian refugees. *Psychiatric Journal of Ottawa, 7,* 163–172.

Nicassio, P. (1985). The psychosocial adjustment of the South East Asian refugee: An overview of empirical findings and theoretical models. *Journal of Cross-Cultural Psychology, 16,* 153–173.

Oberg, K. (1960). Cultural shock: Adjustment to new cultural environments. *Practical Anthropology, 7,* 177–182.

Pan, P.-C., & Goldberg, D. P. (1990). A comparison of the validity of GHQ-12 and CHQ-12 in Chinese primary care patients in Manchester. *Psychological Medicine, 20,* 931–940.

Pernice, R. (1994). Methodological issues in research with refugees and immigrants. *Professional Psychology: Research and Practice, 25,* 207–213.

Pope, K., & Garcia-Peltoniemi, R. (1991). Responding to victims of torture: Clinical issues, professional responsibilities, and useful resources. *Professional Psychology: Research and Practice, 22,* 269–276.

Portes, A., Kyle, D., & Eaton, W. W. (1992). Mental illness and help-seeking behavior among Mariel Cuban and Haitian refugees in South Florida. *Journal of Health and Social Behavior, 33,* 283–298.

Prilleltensky, I. (1993). The immigration experience of Latin American families: Research and action on perceived risk and protective factors. *Canadian Journal of Community Mental Health, 12,* 101–116.

Puig-Antich, J., Orvaschel, H., Tabrinzi, M. A., & Chambers, W. (1980). *The Schedule of Affective Disorders and Schizophrenia for School Age Children—Epidemiologic version: KIDDIE-SADS-E.* New York: New York State Psychiatric Institute and Yale University School of Medicine.

Ramsay, R., Gorst-Unsworth, C., & Turner, S. (1993). Psychiatric morbidity in survivors of organised state violence including torture: A retrospective series. *British Journal of Psychiatry, 162,* 55–59.

Rasmussen, O. V., & Lunde, J. (1980). Evaluation and investigation of 200 torture victims. *Danish Medical Bulletin, 27,* 23–240.

Reese, P. R., & Joseph, A. (1995). Quality translations—no substitution for psychometric evaluation. *Quality of Life Research, 4,* 573–574.

Reid, J., & Strong, T. (1988). Rehabilitation of refugee victims of torture and trauma: Principles and service provision in New South Wales. *Medical Journal of Australia, 148,* 340–346.

Ritterman, M. (1987). Torture: The counter-therapy of the state. *Family Therapy Networker, 11,* 43–47.

Robins, L. N., Helzer, J. E., Croughan, J., & Ratcliff, K. (1981). The National Institute of Mental Health Diagnostic Interview Schedule: Its history, characteristics, and validity. *Archives of General Psychiatry, 38,* 381–389.

Robinson, C. (1980). *Special report: Physical and emotional health care needs of Indochinese refugees.* Washington, DC: Indochina Resource Action Center.

Sack, W. H., Angell, R., Kinzie, J. D., & Roth, B. (1986). The psychiatric effects of massive trauma on Cambodian children. Part 2. The family, the home, and the school. *Journal of the American Academy of Child Psychiatry, 25,* 377–383.

Sack, W. H., Clarke, G. N., Chanrithy, H., Dickason, D., Goff, B., Lanham, K., & Kinzie, J. D. (1993). A 6-year follow-up study of Cambodian refugee adolescents traumatized as children. *Journal of the American Academy of Child and Adolescent Psychiatry, 32,* 431–437.

Sandler, I. N., & Block, M. (1979). Life stress and maladaptation of children. *American Journal of Community Psychology, 1,* 425–440.

Silove, D. (1988). Children of apartheid: A generation at risk. *Medical Journal of Australia, 148,* 346–353.

Silove, D., Tam, R., Bowles, R., & Reid, J. (1991). Psychosocial needs of torture survivors. *Australian and New Zealand Journal of Psychiatry, 25,* 481–490.

Spitzer, R. L., Williams, J. B. W., Gibbon, M., & First, M. B. (1988). *Structured Clinical Interview for DSM-III-R (SCID).* New York: New York State Psychiatric Institute, Biometrics Research.

Stein, B. (1981). The refugee experience: Defining the parameters of a field study. *International Migration Review, 15*, 1–2.

Stein, B. (1986). The experience of being a refugee: Insights from the research literature. In C. L. Williams & J. Westermeyer (Eds.). *Refugee mental health in resettlement countries* (pp. 5–23). Washington, DC: Hemisphere.

Tung, T. M. (1985). Psychiatric care for Southeast Asians: How different is different? In T. Owan, B. Bliatout, K. M. Lin, W. Liu, T. D. Nguyen, & H. Z. Wong (Eds.), *Southeast Asian mental health: Treatment, prevention, training, and research* (pp. 5–40). Rockville, MD: National Institute of Mental Health.

Turk, D. C., & Melzack, R. (Eds.). (1992). *Handbook of pain assessment*. New York: Guilford

Turner, S., & Gorst-Unsworth, C. (1990). Psychological sequelae of torture: A descriptive model. *British Journal of Psychiatry, 157*, 475–480.

Uba, L. (1994). *Asian Americans: Personality patterns, identity and mental health*. New York: Guilford Press.

Uba, L., & Chung, R. C. (1991). The relationship between trauma and financial and physical well-being among Cambodians in the United States. *The Journal of General Psychology, 118*, 215–225.

United Nations (1983). *Convention and Protocol Relating to the Status of Refugees Final Act of the United Nations Conference of Plenipotentiaries on the Status of Refugees and Stateless Persons and the Text of the 1951 Convention Relating to Refugees. Resolution 2198 adopted by the General Assembly and the Text of the 1967 Protocol Relating to the Status of Refugees*, Article 1 A(2): 12 and 39. New York: Author.

United Nations High Commissioner for Refugees. (1993). *Draft guidelines: Evaluation and care of victims of trauma and violence*. Geneva, Switzerland: Author.

Van Boemel, G. B., & Rozée, P. D. (1992). Treatment for psychosomatic blindness among Cambodian refugee women. *Women and Therapy, 13*, 239–266.

Veer, G. van der. (1992). *Counseling and therapy with refugees: Psychological problems of victims of war, torture and repression*. New York: Wiley.

Welner, Z., Reich, W., Herjanic, B., Jung, K. G., & Amado, H. (1987). Reliability, validity, and parent-child agreement studies of the diagnostic interview for children and adolescents (DICA). *Journal of the American Academy of Child and Adolescent Psychiatry, 26*, 649–653.

Westermeyer, J. (1986). Migration and psychopathology. In C. L. Williams & J. Westermeyer (Eds.), *Refugee mental health in resettlement countries* (pp. 5–23). Washington, DC: Hemisphere.

Westermeyer, J. (1989). *Psychiatric care of migrants: A clinical guide*. Washington, DC: American Psychiatric Press.

Westermeyer, J., Lyfoung, T., Westermeyer, M., & Neider, J. (1991). Opium addiction among Indochinese refugees in the United States: Characteristics of addicts and their opium use. *American Journal of Drug and Alcohol Abuse, 17*, 267–277.

Williams, C. L., & Berry, J. W. (1991). Primary prevention of acculturative stress among refugees: Application of psychological theory and practice. *American Psychologist, 46*, 632–641.

Wiseman, J. (1985). Individual adjustments and kin relationships in the "new migration": An approach to research. *International Migration Review, 23*, 349–367.

14

Cultural Aspects of Deafness

CATHY J. CHOVAZ

There are as many ways of defining deafness as there are ways to experience it. A person may be born deaf, be deafened prelingually at a very young age, or be deafened postlingually during childhood or adulthood. In addition, people may experience a mild to moderate loss and be classified as hard of hearing. These people usually benefit from use of a hearing aid to improve speech discrimination and to function more like a hearing person. Persons who have a severe to profound loss (usually sensorineural) are considered deaf and may function using a variety of communication methods such as sign language, lipreading, writing, and speech.

From the medical perspective deafness is defined in terms of decibel loss and loss of auditory discrimination ability. This medical view is often a pathological perspective in the sense that deafness is the lack of something, rather than the presence of anything (Lane, 1992). The criterion for being deaf from a medical perspective is solely related to the results of an audiogram measuring the ability to hear and discriminate speech. In much of the early research, deafness was discussed from a hearing-centered, medical, and somewhat paternalistic model. This perspective tends to operate from the "broken ear with a child attached" model. Many of the disciplines, such as communicative disorders, audiology, or even neuropsychology, often function from a pathological orientation, and it is within this framework that deafness was examined as an "illness" (Tavormina, Boll, Dunn, Luscomb, & Taylor, 1981) or as a "wrong to be made right" (Gregory, 1976).

In contrast to the medical view, many members of the Deaf community operate within an entirely different worldview and perceive themselves as members of a smaller linguistic minority with a rich cultural identity. The decibel loss or discriminative ability is not a criterion for membership. Their language is a visual one (American Sign Language), their identity rooted in people with similar life orientations, and their heritage is as rich and meaningful as that of a hearing person. This chapter will focus on the culturally Deaf individual and will follow the notation of deaf with a capital "D" as representative of cultural implications, and the lowercase "d" as it refers to deafness as determined solely through audiological criteria (Woodward, 1972).

It has long been the tendency for mental health professionals to frame their understanding of Deaf people on the physiological condition of not hearing. Psychologists have historically interpreted all aspects of the lives of Deaf people as a consequence of this fact. It has only been over the past few decades that the rich heritage of Deaf people has begun to be acknowledged by mental health professionals. Part of this reluctance has most likely been due to the fact that the written expression of Deaf culture is still in its infancy as compared to the wealth of written records of many other cultures. However, the recent growing awareness of the lives of these people as something other than medical cases "to be fixed" has awoken a sense of pride in the Deaf people. This sense of empowerment has resulted in a proliferation of written and media expressions; in addition, it has fostered a general desire by many of the majority hearing culture to genuinely appreciate and learn about the multidimensional nature of Deaf culture.

The awakening of knowledge and attitudes toward a Deaf culture also resulted in psychologists' having to reframe deeply entrenched perceptions regarding the personality and intellectual characteristics of the Deaf individual. Psychological test results began to be challenged by a handful of clinical psychologists in the field who recognized the dangers inherent in administering verbal tests to a nonverbal population. Characteristics previously denoted as pathological were beginning to be recognized as appropriate behaviors within a cultural context. It is being recognized more and more that psychologists in general and clinical psychologists specifically must approach a large number of the population who are deaf from a cultural perspective rather than an audiological perspective. Only from a cultural clinical perspective will psychologists be able to effectively address the needs of this special group.

CULTURAL ASPECTS OF DEAFNESS

To best understand Deaf culture, it is helpful to reflect back in time regarding society's view toward deafness. Tom Humphries (1977), an American Deaf educator and author, first coined the term "audism" as the name for the paternalistic, hearing-centered endeavor that often professed to serve deaf people. Lane (1992) further defined audism as the strategies used by the hearing majority to control and oppress the deaf minority. Wixtrom (1988) paralleled the two views of deafness with the first view as a pathology and the second view as a difference. With the first perspective, a person might define deafness as a pathological condition or a defect, labeling the deaf person as abnormal. With the second perspective, a person might define deafness as a difference or characteristic which distinguishes Deaf people as a linguistic and cultural minority. For example, with the first perspective, people might seek a *cure* for deafness, whereas with the second perspective people might emphasize the *abilities* of Deaf people.

Radical events, such as the organized "Deaf President Now" protest (March 1988) that effectively shut down Gallaudet University in Washington, D.C., for a week and resulted in the appointment of a Deaf university president, as well as the passage of Bill 4 (an amendment to the Education Act) in Ontario, Canada in 1993 which is the first of its kind to recognize and authorize the use of American Sign Language (ASL) and Langue Des Signes Quebecois (LSQ) as languages for educational instruction, have contributed to the present cracks in audism. These cracks in audism have served to remind mental health professionals that access to these people from an effective clinical psychological perspective will only happen through a thoughtful effort to further understand their cultural identity. It is through exploration, understanding, and acceptance of this cultural identity that psychologists will be able to effectively partake in clinical interventions with Deaf people.

Deafness is unlike a culture which is bound to a particular ethnicity. The criterion for membership in the Deaf culture is whether an individual identifies with other Deaf people and behaves as a Deaf person. Woodward (1972) proposed the convention of lower- and upper-case letters to distinguish this group of people from those who may be losing their hearing due to illness, trauma, or age from the group of people who share a common language and a culture. These people have inherited their sign language and hold a well-defined set of beliefs, values, and traditions separate from the larger hearing society.

Although Woodward's convention is useful, it is not entirely comprehensive. For example, the majority of deaf children are born to hearing parents. In order then for the culture to survive, there must be a time of enculturation in which the deaf child has adopted the conventions of the culture and has become Deaf. This is clearly in contrast to the majority of cultures where membership is irrevocably given with birthright. It is difficult to understand the complete logistics of this enculturation process as to the conscious and unconscious processes involved, yet clearly there exists a group of Deaf people as there exists a group of deaf people. The majority of this cultural transmission appears to occur at the Deaf residential schools.

Deafness presents an interesting cultural phenomenon. The idea of a plurality of cultures within a family is not an entirely foreign concept. There is a similar parallel in an adoption across racial lines. The acquisition of a cultural identity from one's peers rather than from the family is similar to the experience of homosexual people (Dolnick, 1993), yet most homosexuals are able to share meaningful communication among family members. For the majority of Deaf people, the luxury of open and meaningful family communication is very rare.

Despite some of these difficulties in terminology, Woodward's convention remains useful for establishing a framework that clearly distinguishes Deaf culture from merely a camaraderie with others who have a similar physical condition (Woodward, 1982). The actual decibel loss is not the criterion for membership but is only a characteristic of the culture. Theoretically it is quite possible for a person with no hearing loss to be an accepted member of the Deaf culture if the person's behavior, identification, and general lifestyle is that of a Deaf person. This has been referred to as attitudinal deafness, which is distinct from audiometric deafness (Furth, 1973; Meadow, 1972; Woodward & Markowicz, 1975), and is a clear illustration of the criterion for membership. However, more commonly group members all do experience some level of hearing loss, yet the actual decibel loss in terms of severity is not generally known or discussed by individual members.

Padden (1988), herself a Deaf linguist and scholar, has described Deaf culture within a definition involving five separate and distinct aspects: language, values, traditions, rules of behavior, and identity.

Language

Deaf people consider American Sign Language (ASL) to be their native language. ASL is a visual-gestural language with a full set of rules of grammar and syntax. It is not a new language, and, in fact, some linguists will argue that signed languages preceded spoken languages, as the vocal apparatus developed much later in the human evolutionary process. However, it has only been in the last few decades that ASL has been given the status of a true language, largely as a result of the work of William Stokoe, who, with his colleagues, published *A Dictionary of American Sign Language* (1965/1976). This publication was a watershed event in both the field of deafness and in the lives of Deaf people, as it resulted in a resurgence of studies from the disciplines of psychology, linguistics, and deaf education. The beginning of the shift in attitudes toward deafness resulted in the establishment of several research labs in the United States, such as at Gallaudet University, Northeastern University, and the Salk Institute for Biological Studies, devoted to the linguistic study of this language.

Prior to this recognition and status, ASL was often considered to be a Deaf person's poor excuse for English and was usually ridiculed and banned in educational systems. The fact that ASL has survived this oppression speaks to its tenacity as a language, as well as that of the people who use it. One linguist, Woodward (1978), has suggested three reasons for the survival of ASL. First, the oppression confronting the Deaf community may have actually caused its members to unite somewhat more strongly in defense of their language. Second, due to the physiological barrier imposed by hearing loss, it is natural for Deaf people to continue to gravitate toward a language designed for visual rather than auditory processing. The third and most fascinating reason relates to the fact that Deaf people rarely use ASL with a hearing person, preferring to code-switch to a variety of signing called Pidgin Signed English (a gestural form of communication loosely following English, although not a true language). The end result of this has been that few hearing persons have truly mastered ASL. It has been postulated that the reasons for this relate to the centrality and importance of ASL to the Deaf culture (Woodward, 1982). The restricting of hearing people to the use of a bastardized version of ASL protects the Deaf community from outside influence, which, in turn, will protect the status of ASL within the Deaf culture.

There is a general disassociation from speech in the Deaf culture. This does not imply that there is an antagonism toward speech, for the majority of Deaf people will attempt to use speech to some degree in their dealings with hearing people. Padden (1980) writes, "Since speech has traditionally been forced on Deaf people as a substitute for their language, it has come to represent confinement and denial of the most fundamental need of Deaf people: to communicate deeply and comfortably in their own language" (p. 97). On a cultural level, then, speaking is not considered appropriate behavior.

Before the 1960s and the advent of simultaneous communication (*Simcom* refers to the simultaneous use of a spoken and signed language with definite threats to the integrity of both), many Deaf people preferred to sign with their mouths completely shut and motionless (Padden & Humphries, 1988). This was considered to be proper and aesthetically pleasing. Today, if one was to attend a Deaf cultural event, it would only be the elderly Deaf people who continue to sign in this manner. The younger Deaf people have relaxed this attitude toward mouth movements while signing, although exaggerated movements are still not acceptable.

It is probable that some of these cultural mores toward speech have resulted from the oppression felt by the Deaf people of their language. It was only ten to twenty years ago that Deaf children were forced to use speech in school and punished for the use of sign language. It was in these school residences, behind the teachers' backs in school, and in the playground that the Deaf children truly experienced the joys of communication with their peers.

The importance of language to people has been well documented (Fishman, 1972; Kelman, 1972; Sacks, 1989). Language has been described as being one of the absolutely essential defining characteristics of a group that is trying to achieve recognition as a legitimate entity (Fishman, 1972). The suppression, denial, or eradication of a people's language has been demonstrated to have disastrous long-term effects on those people. Davies (1945), writing originally in 1845, said, "To impose another language on . . . a people is to send their history adrift . . . to tear their identity from all places . . . it is the chain on the soul." It is small wonder, then, that the memories held by the Deaf people of the denial of their language have resulted in a general cultural nonacceptance of speech.

The majority of Deaf people lip-read to some degree at varying levels of ability (Berger, 1972). Lipreading, or speechreading, is not considered to be directly related to intelligence (Berger, 1972) and tends to be of greatest value to those persons who have enough residual hearing to hear and understand some speech sounds (O'Neill & Oyer, 1981). Lipreading is a difficult skill made more difficult by the fact that many of the sounds made (e.g., "p" and "b," or words spoken by a person with facial hair) are indistinguishable on the lips. Only 33% of English speech sounds are visible on the lips (Hardy, 1970), and the best lipreaders get only 25% of what is said even with good lighting and clear speakers (Vernon & Andrews, 1990). This results in lipreading becoming largely a guessing game, made somewhat easier when one is knowledgeable of the context of the conversation and familiar with the speakers, but with marked limited effectiveness as a mode of communication. Contrary to what many people believe, lipreading is best done in a three-dimensional context, which means lipreading TV or movie screens is impossible.

Values

Deaf people place a high priority on their language. Due to the nature of the language, their hands and eyes are also highly valued. It is through their eyes that Deaf people communicate, establish and maintain relationships, and generally function. The eyes of Deaf people are literally their windows to the world. Like their eyes, Deaf people place high value on the hands. Padden (1980) writes:

> Because Sign Language uses the hands there is a "sacredness" attached to how the
> hands can be used to communicate. . . . Deaf people believe firmly that all hand ges-
> tures must convey some kind of visual meaning and have strongly resisted what appear
> to be "nonsense" use of hands—one such example is Cued Speech. (p. 96)

Due to the great value placed on communication by Deaf people, qualified sign language interpreters are often also highly esteemed in the Deaf community. In the past,
the hearing children of Deaf parents assumed the interpreting roles at an extremely
young age for their parents and often continued on in adult life as sign language
interpreters. In recent years, with the advent of programs to formally train interpreters, as well as the knowledge of the detrimental effect this early responsibility may
have on a young child, the members of the Deaf culture are utilizing the services of
highly trained professionals to a much greater degree.

The Deaf culture in both the United States and Canada highly values the provincial or state deaf residential schools. These residential schools for deaf children provide a vital link in the transmission of Deaf culture and ASL from one generation to
the next (Lane, 1992). There has been considerable controversy in the mid-1990s
over potential closure of the residential schools in favor of the mainstreaming of all
children. The Deaf community has reacted violently, with organized movements and
protests to the government to show their extreme disapproval of this possibility. Similarly, the disability lobby group has been active in their disapproval of the segregation
of deaf children into residential schools. It is somewhat ironic that both factions
appear to be struggling for much the same issue but from different perspectives. The
mainstream activists and the disability lobby group are fighting for the equal treatment of all children. The Deaf activists are fighting for the same equality but feel
that the deaf residential schools are the most appropriate place to provide a strong
cultural identity equal to that of the mainstream cultural identity afforded the hearing
child. The difference is that members of the Deaf culture do not view their children
as disabled, and their struggle to provide equal but appropriate cultural education
through the residential schools is not viewed as involuntary segregation (Lane, 1992).

The last highly valued component of the Deaf culture is the Deaf clubs. Most cities
have a Deaf club, which is the meeting place where all social events take place. Deaf
people place a high priority on social gatherings among other Deaf people. It is likely
that this directly relates to the sense of isolation experienced by most Deaf adults who
live and work within the larger hearing community. The chance to be among those who
use the same language at a social gathering is welcomed and greatly valued. It is quite
common for Deaf people to remain in groups, talking very late, long after the restaurant
has emptied of people or the bars have closed. The reason appears to be that Deaf people
gain support and trusting companionship from other Deaf people who share the same
cultural beliefs and attitudes (Padden, 1980). These opportunities for fellowship are
maximized, especially if there is limited opportunity for clear communication in other
areas of their lives (i.e., work situations). The Deaf have established an extensive network of sports tournaments on a national basis. These sports tournaments are often one-
or two-day events and provide an opportunity for Deaf people from a distance to renew
friendships, maintain close ties, and share in a mutual heritage. It is common for entire
families to travel to these events, and they provide a rich environment for Deaf children
to be exposed to Deaf adult role models.

Rules of Behavior

There are definite ethics and rules of behavior that exist among the Deaf culture. On a collective level, there tends to be a penchant for group decision making, and mutual aid and reciprocity are important in the Deaf culture (Lane, 1992). There is a strong group loyalty, and it has been observed that this may extend to the exclusion of hearing outsiders from cultural knowledge and information. When one reflects back upon the long history of the oppression of deaf individuals in terms of their language, their identity, and their very right to a culture, this exclusion of hearing outsiders appears to be clearly a reflexive and protective measure.

On an individual basis, eye contact is regarded as a very powerful regulator of ASL and hence dictates many of the behavioral codes (Padden, 1986). It is considered rude to break eye contact during a conversation and indicates disinterest or rejection of the conversation. Eye contact may be used as a referent in space (Baker & Cokely, 1980), and thus plays a vital role in the meaning of the signs.

Facial expressions serve special linguistic functions and may mark syntactic constructions such as topics, relative clauses, and questions or function as adverbs and qualifiers (Corina, 1989). The facial expressions of a Deaf individual may parallel somewhat the vocal intonations of a hearing individual.

Touching another person's arm to gain their attention before signing is an acceptable rule of behavior within the Deaf culture. It is vital that eye contact be made before any meaningful conversation can transpire. Introductions among Deaf people typically involve the sharing of much more information than in hearing introductions. The Deaf person will usually identify themselves with their full first and last names, their sign names, the city they are from, and typically the residential school they attended. In addition, extra information, such as having Deaf parents or other Deaf family members, is usually included. This type of complex introduction is important to Deaf people, since the cultural group tends to be fairly small, and maintaining ties with all members is a means of preserving group cohesiveness (Padden, 1980).

Greetings and farewells among members of the Deaf culture are accompanied by hugging. It is not uncommon upon entering a room to greet each person with a hug before commencing any conversation. Leave-takings among members of the Deaf culture are usually very prolonged departures (Hopper & Mowl, 1987). It has been suggested that these lengthy farewells are related to the reluctance to leave an environment where communication has been effortless, perhaps unlike what the Deaf person experiences in the work situation. In addition, before the ease of telecommunications now available with TTYs (Teletypes) and the Bell Relay Service (an operator-assisted call between Deaf and hearing people), it was necessary to plan in advance the details of the next meeting date or time. Even now, with the technological opportunities available for contact between two Deaf people using TTYs, there is a cultural tendency to prefer face-to-face conversations. The reasons for this are inherently related to the nature of the language. As ASL is so dependent on facial cues and expressions, the type of dialogue permitted on a TTY monitor screen is flat and greatly devoid of important linguistic markers.

It is considered culturally appropriate for Deaf people to be very forthright in their conversation. Descriptions of events, people, and places become vibrant in the hands of a Deaf signer. It is common for descriptions to be both concrete and candid. For example, if a Deaf person was describing someone to another Deaf person, specific physical markers such as a limp or a prominent birthmark may be used as identifiers. This is in direct contrast to hearing people, who tend to be highly sensitive about drawing attention to any sort of physical characteristic. The Deaf attitude is not one of insensitivity, but it is one of frankness. The perceptions of Deaf people tend to be emphatically visually based, and as such their worldviews tend to be likewise.

Traditions

The cultural values of Deaf people are not explicitly written in books. Most cultures have treasured books containing a record of their traditions. These books are often passed from one generation to another as a method of cultural transmission. There is no written form of ASL, and therefore Deaf people have developed different routes of preserving and passing on their traditions.

The folklore of the culture includes storytelling, local legends and traditions, jokes, and humorous stories based on the Deaf experience (Hafer & Richmond, 1987). Storytelling holds great importance, and entire events may be organized around the invitation to an ASL storyteller. These stories are much more than just capsules of Deaf history; they are active ways of affirming basic beliefs of the group and instructions on how to live one's life (Padden, 1988). Technological advances have been embraced by Deaf people, and many ASL storytellers have now committed their stories to videotape.

Identity

The most important premise of the Deaf culture is an identification with Deaf people through shared experiences and active participation in group activities (Higgins, 1980). The label that a person gives him- or herself is an important indicator to the Deaf person of their identification with the Deaf. Padden (1988) points out that in hearing culture it tends to be desirable to distinguish between degrees of hearing loss; that is, hard of hearing, hearing impaired, deaf, and so forth. In the Deaf culture, these distinctions are not considered to be important in terms of the group functioning. The label "Deaf" is not so much a label of deafness as a label of identity with other Deaf persons. Undue attention is not given to actual levels of hearing loss. This concept of identification is beautifully illustrated by the fact that the sign for *Deaf* may be used in an ASL sentence to mean *my friends,* which in turn conveys the cultural meaning of *Deaf* (Padden, 1988).

SCOPE OF THE PROBLEM AND METHODOLOGY

The demographics of deafness depend on the number of people considered deaf, hearing impaired, or hard of hearing and how each of these terms is defined. Given that there is no legal definition of deafness comparable to the legal definition of blindness, terms such as "deaf" and "deafness" can have a variety of meanings. The National Center for Health Statistics (NCHS, 1991) of the U.S. Department of Health and Human Services estimates that 8.6% of the total American population 3 years old and older have hearing problems. This translates into an estimated 20 million persons in the United States with some degree of hearing loss. It has proven difficult to estimate how many of that number consider themselves to be culturally Deaf. The Center for Assessment and Demographic Studies at Gallaudet University in Washington, D.C., estimates that there are 550,000 Deaf persons in the United States (Holt & Hotto, 1994).

The 1991 Health and Activities Limitations Survey (HALS) estimated that 1 out of every 25 Canadians had some degree of hearing loss, a total of 1,022,220 persons (Canadian Association of the Deaf, 1994). The Canadian Association of the Deaf pointed out that these people were solely those identified through self-report and that the ratio of hearing loss in Canada is closer to 1 out of every 10, making it the largest chronic disability in North America. By the measurements of the Canadian Association of the Deaf in 1994, there were approximately 260,000 profoundly deaf and deafened Canadians (78,000 of them living in Ontario), and possibly 2.5 million hard-of-hearing Canadians (Canadian Association of the Deaf, 1994). It is not known from these statistics how many Canadians consider themselves to be culturally Deaf. One might speculate that the framing of deafness as a "chronic disability" would discourage culturally Deaf people from identifying themselves on self-report surveys used for the gathering of national statistics.

It is evident that the significant incidence of deafness increases the likelihood that a clinical psychologist may work with a client who is Deaf at some point in his or her career. However, given the tendency for culturally Deaf people to live in fairly close proximity to each other to facilitate fellowship, contact, and support, the opportunities for working with Deaf people are significantly increased in communities where there is a residential school for the Deaf, established clubs for the Deaf, and a network of Deaf adults in the workforce.

The first step when working with a Deaf client is to truthfully acknowledge the limitations of one's experience and knowledge. Although it is hoped that chapters such as these aid and abet the clinical psychologist in such situations, it is recognized that no textbook is a substitute for actual experience. If it is at all possible, clinical psychologists are strongly encouraged to network with colleagues who may have experience in this area and who are able to provide some helpful counsel. It is far more dangerous to assume that meaningful communication and/or therapy is taking place than to request some time to properly prepare oneself. To be an effective therapist, the psychologist must divorce him- or herself from the "disease" model of deafness and attempt to view the Deaf person as an individual with a specific, conscious linguistic, cultural, and political identity with the Deaf community. The following are offered as specific areas where the psychologist can examine the efficacy of the relationship dynamics.

Communication

Effective communication between the psychologist and the client is the basis for therapeutic gains. The language of a culturally Deaf client is usually ASL; the therapist is thus also required to have fluency in the language. Fluency will enable the psychologist to understand the client's use of personal space, turn-taking, eye gaze, and other linguistic and paralinguistic indicators. For example, the tone of one's voice is equivalent to the spatial and temporal patterning of signs (Bellugi, 1980). Specific movements of the eyes, face, head, and shoulders may indicate inflection or intensity of meaning. Just as sarcasm may be a telling defense mechanism in a hearing client, so may specific body movements serve similar functions in a Deaf client. Similarly, gaze shifting and body shifting of the Deaf individual hold great importance. Gaze shifting and body shifting do not represent a meaningful break in eye contact but rather have the effect of putting what was said "in quotes", indicating *what* was said and *who* said it (Baker & Cokely, 1980). It can be devastating to the treatment or therapy if this kind of information is either misinterpreted or completely missed.

Facial expressions are also critical components of ASL. Whereas in a spoken language the lack of facial expression may indicate a flattened affect, the same does not necessarily hold true in ASL. Withholding expression may be likened to withholding every other word in spoken discourse, and, as such, even a depressed patient may sign vibrantly in order to convey a message. In contrast, it may be the mistake of therapists to suspect a manic reaction in an enthusiastic signer, even though this again may only be a cultural nuance of the language. In a therapy session, a single facial expression may convey a wealth of meaning to the astute psychologist familiar with ASL.

Eye contact is one of the more dominant regulators of ASL. In a therapy session (especially when the purpose is for information gathering), it is common for a hearing psychologist to take notes. This creates a cultural conflict, for the discontinuity of eye contact may be interpreted by the Deaf individual as lack of respect or interest in them as a client. Similarly, if a Deaf client avoids eye contact, it is probably a clinical marker related to the underlying issue rather than a sign of shyness, as commonly expressed by hearing persons.

The actual content of the communication may also be strongly regulated by the linguistic parameters of ASL. Deaf people typically do not engage in prolonged niceties of conversation but prefer to engage in frank and direct communication. In terms of treatment or therapy, this characteristic of Deaf people can be very beneficial. It is common for Deaf clients to get to the heart of the issue immediately and attend to the peripheral details later. This is advantageous for early identification of issues of concern. This does not imply that resolution of issues occurs any quicker in a Deaf client, but that the process may be somewhat different than with a hearing client.

Interpreters

Hearing psychologists who are not fluent in the language of the Deaf may utilize a certified sign-language interpreter to facilitate communication. Although there is clearly a valued and effective role for interpreters, there remains some concern about their use in a mental health setting. Initially, there is often the tendency for both the psychologist and the client to direct their communications toward the interpreter rather than to each other (i.e., "tell him that I feel . . ."). The introduction of the interpreter changes the relationship between therapist and client into a triadic rather than dyadic one. Stansfield and Veltri (1987) explain the differences created by the triadic relationship: each person acts as an intermediary between the other two, making the whole process much more complicated and perhaps less meaningful therapeutically. Interpreters work by a strict code of ethics, whereby they are to remain external to the situation and only function as a communicative facilitator; however, they often become part of the process by default (Stansfield, 1981).

Although qualified ASL interpreters can be extremely effective cultural and linguistic bridges, there also tends to be a dimension of hostile-dependence inherent in this type of relationship. Hostile-dependency feelings may emerge when the Deaf person genuinely is in need of the interpreter's services to access a particular situation, yet feels some degree of anger toward that same person for that perceived dependency need (Vernon & Andrews, 1990). In turn, there have been many situations where this has led to an abuse of power and manipulation by the interpreter, who has misperceived a genuine need for services as a sign of dependency. It can be an extremely delicate and difficult situation for both the Deaf person and the interpreter to manage successfully.

Due to the lack of qualified Deaf mental health professionals, in addition to the lack of qualified mental health hearing professionals fluent in ASL, the only options for treatment open to Deaf people have been with the use of an interpreter. The high esteem in which the community holds the interpreter may place certain perceived restrictions and limitations on what the Deaf person feels free to share with the practitioner. This has been noted more in interpersonal or psychodynamic situations than in behavioral or educational paradigms. There may be some degree of embarrassment or mistrust that the information is being interpreted correctly to the mental health professional, especially if it is of a highly volatile, emotional, and personal nature. There may be a tendency for the interpreter to want to become emotionally involved or to feel the need to edit or explain to the therapist what the Deaf individual "really means." Finally, the impact on the interpreter as a person can be immense and overwhelming (especially as they do not usually have any formal training themselves in this area) and tends to contribute to the high degree of burnout experienced by the profession.

Interactional Dynamics

As in any client-therapist relationship, the practitioner must be attuned to issues of transference and countertransference with a Deaf client. A culturally aware and linguistically competent practitioner will be at a greater advantage in creating a milieu to be "with" the client. However, it also may be that the fluent and supportive practitioner may become metaphorically the parent figure the Deaf person wishes they had.

To fully understand transference of this nature, it is important to remember that many parents are thrust into the world of deafness by virtue of giving birth to their child. Epidemiological studies suggest (Vernon & Andrews, 1990) that 90% of deaf children are born to hearing parents, and most research suggests that these children are at higher risk in terms of lower self-esteem (Yachnik, 1986) and academic achievement (Kampfe & Turecheck, 1987) than those born to Deaf parents. The reaction of hearing parents to the discovery of their child's deafness has been similarly compared to the reactions of all human beings to the psychological trauma of a serious disease or life tragedy. The difference in this particular situation, though, is that often parents never seem to progress through the stages leading to the healthy resolution of grief (Vernon & Andrews, 1990). It has been the observation of this author that many parents seem to become immobilized in the initial stages of denial and anger and remain there for the rest of their lives. Although clearly recognized as an immense challenge for parents to face, Vernon and Andrews (1990) write "Some never get past the stage of 'How could this happen to me?' to the realization that it did not happen to them, but to their child" (p. 131). Basic parenting issues related to raising a hearing or a deaf child may be fundamentally the same; however, deafness tends to impose an enormous complexity on the process (Luterman, 1987).

The hearing parents are often first confronted with the traditional attitude of the medical profession, which has been to view deafness from a pathological perspective. The birth of their child has often been equated with a horrendous physical tragedy and immediately labeled as deviant. This is in great contrast to the baby born to Deaf parents who are thankful and rejoice upon learning that their child has been born deaf. All too often, the hearing parents of a deaf baby are bombarded with audiologists, otologists, pediatricians, special educators, speech-language therapists, and psychologists who assess, measure, diagnose, and generally serve to greatly confuse the parents with their differing opinions as to the identity and course of development of their deaf child. It is certainly understandable that the bewildered hearing parents who have never before encountered deafness may cling desperately to the opinions offered to them by the hearing professionals. What is not as clearly understandable is how or why deafness has continued to be viewed from this negative, pathological model when there are so many Deaf successful adults who are living legacies to their culture and who furthermore have succeeded despite the hearing professionals' fateful prophecies. Nonetheless, the reality is that the majority of these families have very little familiarity with deaf individuals or the Deaf community in their area (Liben, 1978). The result of all these dynamics is that a great number of Deaf adults come from families who have never learned to sign, often resulting in difficult or distant family relationships. Clearly the hope for the future will include education of hearing parents with respect to the cultural needs of their Deaf children.

It may well be that during therapy all these family dynamics culminate in attitudes toward the hearing psychologist. The Deaf client may align him- or herself with the psychologist by virtue of their hearing status and fantasize about what parental attitudes and signing skills might have been. Alternatively, the Deaf clients may project toward the therapist many years of anger related to intense feelings of loneliness within and alienation from their families.

All clients clearly bring their past histories with them into therapy. Depending on past experiences with hearing culture, the Deaf client may view hearing persons as superior to all deaf persons. This may be seen in the Deaf client who chooses to see only a hearing psychologist, as they "know more than Deaf people." The opposite may be the Deaf person who is untrusting or suspicious of a hearing professional because of minority-group dynamics and oppression (Vernon & Makowsky, 1969). Deaf clients may consciously or unconsciously attempt to control the therapist through the communication mode; they have been observed to deliberately increase speed of signing and to choose signs unfamiliar to the therapist (Schlesinger & Meadow, 1972).

The hearing psychologist must also be aware of countertransference patterns. Even the most culturally aware person may still unconsciously seek to maintain a Deaf client in a helpless position, thereby validating their own merit as helper. In addition, it may prove painful for hearing psychologists to examine their own role in the oppression of the Deaf or even to acknowledge that they are part of the larger majority responsible for many years of educational and emotional oppression.

Likewise, a Deaf therapist must also guard against countertransference. With the culturally Deaf client comes a long and often painful history of oppression and discrimination. Countertransference involves the overidentification of people and/or themes in one's own life and may consciously or unconsciously surface in the mind of the therapist who has also experienced similar oppression.

ASSESSMENT STRATEGIES AND ISSUES

Historically, assessment practices with Deaf individuals have been fraught with errors. In the early 1900s, the American system of educating students with hearing loss was strictly an oral approach. Children were forbidden to sign, and the goal of education seemed to be to make deaf children as equal to hearing children as possible. Around the same time psychologists were becoming interested in deafness and, more specifically, in the area of language acquisition. Given that it was not deemed necessary for psychologists to have to sign with these children, research studies that investigated intelligence, achievement, and personality of the deaf child flourished.

It is with some uneasiness that one reads the history of psychology and deafness (for a comprehensive review, see Pollard, 1993) and realizes the injustices done to Deaf individuals in the name of research. Rudolf Pintner is widely regarded as the first psychologist to formally take an interest in the area of deafness. He rightly observed that many of the popular tests of the day, developed and normed for hearing children, were very limited in their use with deaf children. His first published paper, coauthored with Donald Paterson in 1915 (cited in Pollard, 1993), described the limitations of using the Binet scale with deaf children because of the verbal linguistic requirements. Some 25 years later, in 1941, Pintner published a paper summarizing his findings of the general intelligence of the deaf child (cited in Pollard, 1993). Perhaps in response to the political views of the era toward deafness and disabilities in general, his view that the deaf child was basically intellectually comparable to the hearing child was strongly tempered with caution. The caution expressed by Pinter, a leading researcher in the field, resulted in the perception that the deaf child was intellectually inferior. This perception has only recently been challenged by comprehensive reviews that identify significant methodological flaws and limitations inherent in many research studies (Braden, 1994).

Cognitive testing of deaf children has proven to be a challenge for many practitioners. Historically, since deaf children did not speak, they were automatically classed with the mentally retarded (Bender, 1970). As a result, many deaf children were placed in institutions for the retarded and were forgotten. Psychologists then became interested in the variance between the cognitive abilities of hearing and deaf children, and there was a flourish of studies documenting the mental deficits of deaf children as compared to hearing children (Pintner, Eisensen, & Stanton, 1946; Pintner & Reamer, 1920). These deficits were later requalified as qualitative rather than quantitative differences in intelligence quotients and abilities (Myklebust, 1960), although unfortunately this mind-set of deficit rather than difference often became the stereotypical description of the deaf child. A great deal of effort has been made by relatively few psychologists in the last few decades to challenge these erroneous assumptions through the design of more appropriate standardized tests and administration methods (Moores, 1978; Vernon & Andrews, 1990). Braden (1994) conducted a meta-analysis that showed a remarkable similarity between the nonverbal intelligence of deaf and normal hearing people and intriguing trends regarding the differences on verbal IQ scores, achievement tests, and parental-hearing status.

There are three tests of intelligence that have been specifically normed on deaf children (Ontario Ministry of Education, 1988). The Hiskey-Nebraska Test of Learning Aptitude (Hiskey, 1966) is a nonverbal test of learning ability specifically designed for deaf and hard-of-hearing children between the ages of 3 and 17. The prime benefit of this test is that it examines a child's short-term visual memory and short-term memory for visual sequences. The weakness of this test is that it is complex and very time-consuming to administer. The Leiter International Performance Scale (Leiter, 1948, 1979) is a test of nonverbal intelligence for children between the ages of 2 and 18. The Leiter is a highly visual task-oriented test appropriate for use with deaf children, although some research studies suggest that it overestimates a child's IQ (Boyd & Shapiro, 1986; Lindsay, Shapiro, Musselman, & Wilson, 1988). In addition, it is not clear how the information yielded from the Leiter is useful in terms of academic strengths and weaknesses.

The most widely used tests of general intelligence are the Wechsler scales (Wechsler, 1974, 1981, 1989, 1991). The Wechsler tests are all composed of verbal and performance scales, and the composite scores yield an IQ score. Historically, only the performance (nonverbal) scales have been administered to deaf children, and norms were developed for the Wechsler Intelligence Scale for Children-Revised (WISC-R; Wechsler, 1974). Currently the Wechsler Intelligence Scale for Children-III (WISC-III; Wechsler. 1991) does not have norms developed for deaf children. It is becoming the practice for practitioners fluent in ASL to administer both the Performance and Verbal scales to a deaf child. Although the test is not standardized in this language and there are no developed norms, the results of carefully administered tests in ASL yield significant information regarding the child's learning strengths and weaknesses. It is hoped that in the future norms for deaf individuals will be developed for all three of the Wechsler scales—the Wechsler Preschool and Primary Scale of Intelligence-Revised (WPPSI-R; Wechsler, 1989); the Wechsler Intelligence Scale for Children-III (WISC-III; Wechsler, 1991); and the Wechsler Adult Intelligence Scale-Revised (WAIS-R; Wechsler, 1981).

Parallel to the interest in cognitive testing, mainstream psychology began a fervent search for the "deaf personality." Psychologists, although perhaps well intentioned, enthusiastically administered personality and intelligence tests developed and normed for hearing people (i.e., the MMPI, Rorschach, WAIS, etc.) to Deaf people. Unfortunately, these tests were routinely administered using a language which was not the language of the Deaf—spoken English. A trend was started whereby a precedent had been set to judge Deaf people against hearing standards, and the Deaf person was clearly inferior (Pollard, 1993). Studies began to emerge depicting the Deaf individual as egocentric, impulsive, concrete, and intellectually deficient.

It has only been in the past few decades that psychologists have begun to reexamine psychometric testing of Deaf individuals. Clearly, some intelligence and personality tests are culturally biased. For example, most personality tests are written at a tenth-grade English level, although only 1 Deaf student in 10 reads at an eighth-grade level or better and the average Deaf student graduating from high school has only a third-grade reading level (Lane, 1992). These results are not surprising, given that ASL is usually their first language; the acquisition of written English is a second language and was not well addressed in the school systems until the early to mid-1990s.

Other examples of cultural bias may be seen in the content of the questions themselves. For example, the Minnesota Multiphasic Personality Inventory-2 (MMPI-2; Butcher, Dahlstrom, Graham, Tellegen & Kaemmer, 1989) consists of 567 true-or-false questions that elicit a wide range of self-descriptions scored to indicate a level of emotional adjustment. Consider just a few of the questions such as #5, having to do with being awakened by noise, #22, with being understood, #25, with wanting to be a singer, and, finally, #307, with feeling that hearing well is bothersome.

Lane (1992) feels that the MMPI-2 suffers from many of the invalidating weaknesses that have been pervasive in psychometric testing of Deaf people: it is difficult to administer and to interpret and has inappropriate content and norms. Nonetheless, there are studies in the literature that continue to utilize inappropriate measures for testing Deaf individuals. These studies seem to further contribute to the paternalistic errors made by psychologists in the past. It is encouraging to note that greater effort has been made recently to develop and standardize personality tests for deaf individuals. For example, Shafqat (1986) reports that the Sixteen Personality Factor Questionnaire (16PF) was translated onto a videotape for use with Deaf individuals. Although efforts such as these should be applauded, the researchers felt it impossible to translate the written English form of the test into ASL and still preserve the integrity of the test. They chose to use instead Pidgin Signed English, which is a manually coded form of signed English and not a language unto itself or of the Deaf people. It is hoped that in the future such personality measures will be videotaped in the rich language of ASL, becoming a much more powerful and valid assessment measure of Deaf individuals.

The most poignant and dramatic illustration of the need for sound clinical assessment measures was revealed in the case of Junius Wilson, a deaf individual from Goldsboro, North Carolina. In 1925, when he was 17 years of age, Mr. Wilson was accused of rape. Although he was never formally convicted, the state castrated him and locked him up in a state mental hospital for 69 years. The rape charges were dropped in 1970, but Mr. Wilson remained imprisoned. Tragically, it was not until the early 1990s that officials realized that Mr. Wilson was not retarded or mentally ill and had been wrongfully institutionalized all of his life.

It would appear that Mr. Wilson's only "crime" was being deaf. Inadequate assessment measures, coupled with insurmountable language barriers, resulted in his assumed guilt. At the age of 87 years, Mr. Wilson is now a free man, although a lifetime of imprisonment has taken its toll. The State's restitution to this victim of society has been to provide him with a comfortably furnished three-bedroom brick house on the grounds of the state hospital. Mr. Wilson has begun to socialize on a very limited basis, utilizing a basic form of a Raleigh sign language which had been commonly used by deaf Black people in the 1920s in the southern states. It is chilling to realize what a difference a meaningful psychological assessment would have made in the life of this man.

CLINICAL PSYCHOPATHOLOGIES

The literature is sparse concerning the psychopathology of Deaf people. Much of the research that is present seems somewhat contradictory in nature, and some of this is undoubtedly related to the many methodological problems inherent in these studies (Vernon & Andrews, 1990). The assessment of a patient in a mental health setting is a crucial beginning to effective therapy. Unfortunately, diagnoses have often been either missed due to linguistic or cultural misunderstandings or conducted using methods which have yielded false results. Commonly, deafness has been misdiagnosed as an intellectual disability, psychiatric illness has been missed completely, or psychiatric illness has been diagnosed where none exists (Chapman, 1994). The lack of qualified psychologists fluent in ASL and cognizant of Deaf culture has contributed to the use of inappropriate and culturally insensitive tests that tend to penalize the Deaf patient for being deaf or for differences in cultural attitudes rather than revealing true psychopathology. At this point in time, there is no empirical evidence indicating that Deaf people need mental health services in any greater number than the hearing population (Myers & Danek, 1989).

Schizophrenia

It is generally accepted from the current research that schizophrenia is triggered by a biochemical component coupled with a particular stressor (J. Carter, personal communication, May 1993). Most of the research studies indicate that the prevalence of schizophrenia among Deaf people is about the same as among hearing people (Altshuler, 1978; Grinker, 1969; Robinson, 1978; Vernon, 1978, 1980) and that when it does occur, visual and auditory hallucinations seem to occur with the same frequency as for hearing patients (Altshuler, 1978).

Many studies, however, indicate that there tends to be a greater chronicity component in terms of number of hospital admissions among Deaf people than among hearing people (Basilier, 1964; Denmark & Eldridge, 1969; Remvig, 1969, 1972). Vernon and Andrews (1990), however, concluded that most of this chronicity is due to errors in diagnosis and lack of treatment available for Deaf patients. The difficulties in communication have resulted in longer and more frequent hospital stays for Deaf patients, despite the fact that the rate of schizophrenia appears to be essentially the same in both populations.

These same difficulties in communication have also often contributed to errors in diagnosis. Evans and Elliot (1981) point out that Deaf persons are often viewed as having poor insight, poverty of content, lability of affect, poor rapport, vagueness, and an inability to complete a course of action. The written communication of Deaf people may look disjointed and psychotic as a function of ASL grammar or English deficits, and "may simulate strikingly a severe thought disorder" (p. 789). The authors conclude, however, that many of these "symptoms" may be more a product of the less-than-adequate relationship between the Deaf patient and practitioner than a reflection of the patient's personality. Evans and Elliot suggest that the diagnosis of schizophrenia in Deaf persons be restricted to the core symptoms of delusional perceptions, abnormal or illogical explanations, hallucinations, loss of ego boundaries, inappropriate or restricted affect, and remoteness from reality.

Paranoid Disorders

Deaf people are often characterized as being paranoid or overly suspicious. This belief has been so strong that the *Diagnostic and Statistical Manual of Mental Disorders (DSM-III)* indicated that deaf people are at prime risk for paranoid disorders (American Psychiatric Association, 1980). Likewise, *DSM-IV* (American Psychiatric Association, 1994) differentiates that "paranoid personality disorder must be distinguished from . . . paranoid traits associated with the development of physical handicaps (e.g., a hearing impairment)" (p. 637). This would appear to be one of the greatest myths in the psychological and psychiatric literature (Vernon & Andrews, 1990) in that research has consistently shown no greater proportion of paranoia or paranoid schizophrenia among Deaf than among hearing psychotics (Basilier, 1964; Grinker, 1969; Remvig, 1969, 1972; Robinson, 1978). However, the literature on hard-of-hearing people does imply that partial hearing may predispose persons to suspiciousness in that they can only catch parts of conversations.

Affective Disorders

There is much controversy in the literature regarding the rate of depression among Deaf people. Some studies indicate no qualitative or quantitative difference in depression rates among Deaf and hearing populations (Grinker, 1969; Remvig, 1969, 1972; Robinson, 1978). Other studies report a lower rate of depression among the Deaf than hearing populations (Altshuler, 1978; Knapp, 1948, 1953). Interestingly enough, this has been linked to the psychoanalytic notion that less chance of superego formation exists among the Deaf, because their deafness affords them less exposure to societal and parental admonitions. This in turn would lead to less opportunity to develop feelings of guilt, self-hate, and other forms of self-deprecation that are basic to depression (Vernon & Andrews, 1990).

Autism

Autism has not been reported to exist disproportionately among Deaf people whose etiology is other than prenatal maternal rubella (Vernon & Andrews, 1990).

Organic Factors

Many of the leading causes of deafness are also the major etiologies of brain damage (Vernon, 1980). Some of the organic factors associated with deafness may also lead directly to chronic brain syndromes that cause psychosis. In this sense, there is a higher proportion of mental disturbance among those Deaf individuals whose etiology of deafness is associated with an organic psychosis (Vernon & Andrews, 1990).

TREATMENT ISSUES

Appropriate treatment strategies with Deaf persons are grounded in the practitioner's sensitivity to and awareness of cultural and linguistic differences. For example, relaxation therapy for an anxious Deaf client may be very appropriate but may need to be done differently than with a hearing client. Music as a form of relaxation is not helpful, and the need for visual contact to maintain communication precludes the practitioner leading the client in deep relaxation with closed eyes. However, alternative strategies, such as a videotaped progression of deep relaxation, the repetitive signing of a phrase (almost like a mantra familiar to hearing people) following an ASL description of the relaxation process, or the use of art as a relaxation medium may be very effective.

Behavioral therapy (Ouellette & Ford, 1983) may be an effective treatment when specific problem behaviors and objectives can be identified. Behavioral therapy has been implemented most often in educational settings with children. Success has been reported with both Deaf children and adults, using behavioral strategies such as positive reinforcement, modified token economy, shaping, overcorrection restitution, time-out, and negative practice.

Given the developmental sequelae of growing up Deaf within a hearing family, therapy involving the entire family may be appropriate. Within systems theory, deafness is not the sole domain of the child but instead affects all of the family members. Family therapy may be extremely useful in assisting the parents and siblings to see the Deaf child as a capable and autonomous individual requiring equal status in the family. Long (1983) suggests that, if the parents and the siblings are not fluent in sign, the sessions be conducted with a skilled interpreter in addition to a knowledgeable practitioner.

The process of individual psychotherapy with a Deaf client may "feel" somewhat different to the therapist, although the goal of expressing thoughts and behaviors within a supportive environment is the same as with a hearing client. Specific theoretical approaches to individual therapy may be just as successful with Deaf clients, as long as they are implemented from within an appropriate sociocultural context. For example, Farrugia (1985) reports that Adlerian or individual therapy with Deaf individuals has been utilized as an effective treatment strategy when the language of therapy is ASL and the practitioner is knowledgeable in Deaf culture.

SERVICE UTILIZATION/DELIVERY

A culturally Deaf client requires appropriate prevention, intervention, and postintervention strategies as does any hearing client. Clinical psychologists in clinical settings would do well to familiarize themselves with this "silent" culture in preparation for the possibility of working with a Deaf person in the future. There is a serious dearth of mental health resources available in Canada for the Deaf individual. Psychology departments are usually less than prepared to provide services to these people, largely due to the linguistic barrier and unfamiliarity with deafness. There are unfortunate stories of Deaf patients such as Mr. Junius Wilson being admitted to psychiatric hospitals where they have been "forgotten." These cases most likely are related to staff members' inability and frustration with therapy, as well as a lack of persons to advocate for Deaf patients. Very few hospitals or agencies are equipped with teletype devices (TTYs) that permit the Deaf person to phone directly when in need or crisis. The advent of the Bell Relay Service in Ontario, Canada, is a start in improving accessibility, but there is a long way to go before mental health care is truly within reach for the Deaf. Technological advances such as electronic mail and computer word-processing programs are proving helpful for scheduling appointments and requesting help in an emergency, thereby improving the accessibility of mental health facilties. It is a mistake, though, to believe that these technological devices can substitute for a practitioner skilled in ASL, and to rely on these measures in a therapy session is not an acceptable altnerative to fluency in ASL.

There are several innovative centers in the United States which have established psychiatric inpatient programs for Deaf people. One such program was initiated in 1986 at a state hospital in Massachusetts and was the first of its kind in the state. This program is based on four cultural values, which are:

1. The least restrictive environment for serving deaf people is a Deaf environment;
2. Communication needs to be appropriate, as well as affirming of the Deaf community;
3. Staff have to be recruited, hired, and developed with the necessary cultural and clinical skills; and
4. Therapeutic approaches have to be specifically designed for Deaf psychiatric patients (Glickman & Zitter, 1989, p. 46).

Glickman and Zitter (1989) describe the benefits and challenges of implementing such a culturally affirmative program. The concept that Deaf people should be served separately from hearing people often tends to echo the inequality problems of segregation. However, the directors of this program feel that, for specialized deaf services, integration becomes "problematic when it demands of minority communities that they yield up cultural differences that are a source of collective identity and pride and forces them to communicate in a language that is not their own" (p. 48). Conversely, a culturally affirmative program creates a more positive milieu in which to address mental health. One of the distinct features of this program is the critical need for culturally sensitive staff of which a significant percentage are themselves culturally Deaf.

Another useful strategy in the United States has been the publication of a national directory of mental health services and supportive rehabilitative programs for Deaf persons by the American Deafness and Rehabilitation Association. The directory appears in the April issue of the journal *American Annals of the Deaf* each year. It lists federal programs for people who are Deaf under the Office of Special Education and Rehabilitation Services, state vocational rehabilitation offices, state departments of education and health, independent programs for Deaf people, state associations of Deaf people, social/recreational programs and agencies, and national professional organizations and centers. As well, Long, High, & Shaw (1989) have published a comprehensive national directory of mental health services for deaf persons in which appropriate and available mental health services are listed for the United States. Although there are not currently any inpatient psychiatric programs specifically designed for Deaf persons in Canada, there are several community mental health services. The Canadian Hearing Society, which has chapters in most urban cities, does offer vocational counseling, usually by a trained Deaf counselor. The national office in Toronto established a community counseling program in 1986, named Connect Counseling Services. It is a community-based mental health service, funded by the Ministry of Health, that offers assistance to deaf, deafened, and hard-of-hearing adults (16 years and older) and their families. Connect provides consultation, education, and direct client services free of charge. The staff, some of whom are hearing and some of whom are Deaf, include a psychologist, social workers, mental health clinicians, intake counselors, and mental health interpreters.

ROLE OF CULTURAL CLINICAL PSYCHOLOGY

A chapter on Deaf culture may be expected to include a description of the psychology of the Deaf individual. However, this author is not convinced that there truly exists a psychology of the Deaf, any more than there exists a psychology of the Caucasian or a psychology of the African American. It is clear each cultural group defines itself differently according to what is valued and accepted and according to the language of expression, yet it is not as clear that this constitutes a psychology of each particular group. It is an error to assume the culture defines the psychological well-being of its members.

It is evident that the reality of a Deaf individual is very different from the reality of a hearing individual, and as such this cultural context may exert influences over intellectual, emotional, and behavioral functioning. Deaf people constitute a linguistic and cultural minority and, as a result, have experienced many of the discriminations and prejudices often imposed by larger majority groups. Internalization of these feelings can certainly diminish the self-worth of Deaf individuals, who may resign themselves to the fact that "deaf equals dumb." The unfortunate separation from family members, both geographical separations to attend residential schools, and emotional separations due to linguistic barriers, undoubtedly contributes to profound feelings of loneliness and isolation for many Deaf persons during the formative years. It may be that this serves as a precursor to various psychopathologies rooted in an extreme sense of angst and general feeling of not belonging. It is difficult to belong when your world is not accessible.

A study of the Deaf culture reveals a powerful legacy of group solidarity through a shared language, set of values and traditions, and rules of behavior. The strengths and weaknesses evident in this culture share a common bond with all humanity. It is the responsibility of the educated psychologist to fully understand the framework within which the mental health of the Deaf culture is expressed. Working from within a cultural clinical metamodel enables the psychologist to assess, diagnose, and treat clients within their natural context. It is only with this understanding and awareness that the profession will be able to fully provide comprehensive psychological services to special interest groups such as Deaf individuals.

References

Altshuler, K. Z. (1978). Toward a psychology of deafness. *Journal of Communication Disorders, 11,* 159–169.

American Deafness and Rehabilitation Association (1996, April) *Directory of mental health services for Deaf persons.* Little Rock, AR: Author.

American Psychiatric Association. (1980). *Diagnostic and statistical manual of mental disorders.* (3rd ed.). Washington, DC: Author.

American Psychiatric Association. (1994). *Diagnostic and Statistical Manual for Mental Disorders,* Fourth Edition. Washington, DC: Author.

Baker, C., & Cokely, D. (1980). *American Sign Language: A teacher's resource text on grammar and culture.* Silver Spring, MD: TJ.

Basilier, R. (1964). Surdophrenia: The psychic consequences of congenital or early acquired deafness. Some theoretical and clinical considerations. *Acta Psychiatrics Scandinavia, 40* (Suppl. 180), 362–374.

Bellugi, U. (1980). How signs express meaning. In C. Baker & R. Battison (Eds.), *Sign language and the Deaf community: Essays in honor of William Stokoe* (pp. 53–74). Silver Springs, MD: National Association of the Deaf.

Bender, R. (1970). *The conquest of deafness.* Cleveland, OH: Case Western Reserve.

Berger, K. W. (1972). *Speechreading: Principles and methods.* Baltimore, MD: National Education Press.

Boyd, J., & Shapiro, A. H. (1986). A comparison of the Leiter International Performance Scale to WPPSI performance with preschool deaf and hearing impaired children. *Journal of Rehabilitation of the Deaf, 20,* 23–26.

Braden, J. P. (1994). *Deafness, deprivation, and IQ.* New York: Plenum Press.

Butcher, J. N., Dahlstrom, W. G., Graham, J. R., Tellegen, A. M., & Kaemmer, B. (1989). *MMPI-2: Manual for administration and scoring.* Minneapolis, MN: University of Minnesota Press.

Canadian Association of the Deaf (1994). *Statistics on Deaf Canadians.* Ottawa, Ontario, Canada: Author.

Chapman, K. (1994). Psychiatric disability and deafness. *New Paradigm, 6,* 1– 4.

Corina, D. P. (1989). Recognition of affective and noncanonical linguistic facial expressions in hearing and deaf subjects. *Brain and Cognition, 9,* 227–237.

Davies, T. (1945). *Essays and poems with a centenary memoir: 1845.* Dublin: Ireland: Gill.

Denmark, J. C., & Eldridge, R. W. (1969). Psychiatric services for the deaf. *Lancet, 14,* 259–262.

Dolnick, E. (1993). Deafness as a culture. *Deaf Life, 6,* 12–17.

Evans, J., & Elliot, H. (1981). Screening criteria for the diagnosis of schizophrenia in deaf patients. *Archives of General Psychiatry, 38,* 787–790.

Farrugia, D. (1985). Adlerian counseling and the deaf client. In G. B. Anderson & D. Watson (Eds.), *Counseling deaf people: Research and practice* (pp. 145–166). Little Rock, AR: Arkansas Research and Training Center on Deafness and Hearing Impairment, University of Arkansas.

Fishman, J. (1972). *Language and nationalism: Two integrative essays.* Rowley, MA: Newbury House.

Furth, H. (1973). *Deafness and learning: A psychosocial approach.* Belmont, CA: Wadsworth.

Glickman, N. S., & Zitter, S. M. (1989). *On establishing a culturally affirmative psychiatric inpatient program for deaf people.* Unpublished manuscript, Westborough State Hospital, Westborough, MA.

Gregory, S. (1976). *The Deaf child and his family.* New York: Halsted Press.

Grinker, R. R. (Ed.). (1969). *Psychiatric diagnosis, therapy, and research on the psychotic deaf.* (Final report, Grant No. R.D. 2407) Chicago: Department of Health, Education, and Welfare, Social and Rehabilitation Service.

Hafer, J. C., & Richmond, E. D. (1987, June). *What hearing parents should learn about Deaf culture.* Paper presented at the 53rd Biennial Meeting of the Convention of American Instructors of the Deaf and the 59th Annual Meeting of the Conference of Educational Administrators Serving the Deaf, Santa Fe, NM.

Hardy, M. (1970). Speechreading. In H. Davis & S. R. Silverman (Eds.), *Hearing and deafness* (pp. 335–345). New York: Holt, Rinehart, & Winston.

Higgins, P. C. (1980). *Outsiders in a hearing world: A sociology of deafness.* Beverly Hills, CA: Sage.

Hiskey, M. (1966). *Hiskey-Nebraska Test of Learning Aptitude.* Lincoln, NE: Author.

Holt, J., & Hotto, S. (1994) *Demographic aspects of hearing impairment: Questions and answers.* Washington, DC: Center for Assessment and Demographic Studies, Gallaudet University.

Hopper, M., & Mowl, G. (1987, August). *United States of America Deaf culture: A culturegram.* Paper presented at the Rochester Institute for the Deaf National Conference, St. Paul, MN.

Humphries, T. (1977). *Communicating across cultures (deaf/hearing) and language learning.* Unpublished doctoral dissertation, Union Graduate School, Cincinnati, OH.

Kampfe, C. M., & Turecheck, A. G. (1987). Reading achievement of prelingually deaf students and its relationship to parental method of communication: A review of the literature. *American Annals of the Deaf, 132,* 11–15.

Kelman, M. (1972). Introduction. In J. Fishman, *Language and nationalism: Two integrative essays.* Rowley, MA: Newbury House.

Knapp, P. H. (1948). Emotional aspects of hearing loss. *Psychosomatic Medicine, 10,* 203–222.

Knapp, P. H. (1953). The ear listening and hearing. *Journal of American Psychoanalytic Association, 1,* 672–689.

Lane, H. (1992). *The mask of benevolence.* New York: Knopf.

Leiter, R. (1979). *Leiter International Performance Scale.* (Rev. ed.), Chicago: Stoelting.

Liben, L. S. (1978). *Deaf children: Developmental perspectives.* New York: Academic Press.

Lindsay, P. H., Shapiro, A. H., Musselman, C., & Wilson, A. (1988). Predicting language development in deaf children using subscales of the Leiter International Performance Scale. *Canadian Journal of Psychology, 42,* 144–162.

Long, G. A. (1983). Deafness and family therapy. In B. Heller & D. Watson (Eds.), *Mental health and Deafness: Strategic perspectives* (pp. 132–146) Little Rock, AR: American Deafness and Rehabilitation Association.

Long, G. A., High, C., & Shaw, J. (1989). *Directory of mental health services for deaf persons* (2nd ed.). Little Rock, AK: American Deafness and Rehabilitation Association.

Luterman, D. (1987). *Deafness in the family.* Boston, MA: College-Hill Press.

Meadow, K. (1972). Name signs as identity symbols in the Deaf community. *Sign Language Studies, 17,* 237–246.

Moores, D. F. (1978). *Educating the deaf: Psychology, principles, and practices.* Boston: Houghton Mifflin.

Myers, P. C., & Danek, M. M. (1989). Deafness mental health needs assessment. *Journal of the American Deafness and Rehabilitation Association, 22,* 72–78.

Myklebust, H. R., Neyhus, A., & Mulholland, A. (1962). Guidance and counseling of the deaf. *American Annals of the Deaf, 197,* 383–408.

National Center for Health Statistics (NCHS). (1991). Health interview survey. Washington, DC: U.S. Department of Health and Human Services.

O'Neill, J. J. , & Oyer, H. J. (1981). *Visual communication for the hard of hearing.* Englewood Cliffs, NJ: Prentice-Hall.

Ontario Ministry of Education (1988). *A manual of assessment instruments suitable for hearing impaired students.* Toronto, Ontario, Canada: Author.

Ouellette, S. E., & Ford, N. M. (1983). The use of behavioral techniques with hearing-impaired persons: Introduction and overview. In B. Heller & D. Watson (Eds.), *Mental health and Deafness: Strategic perspectives* (pp. 80–85) Little Rock, AR: American Deafness and Rehabilitation Association.

Padden, C. (1980). The Deaf community and the culture of Deaf people. In C. Baker & R. Pattison (Eds.), *Sign language and the Deaf community* (pp. 89–103). Silver Spring, MD: National Association of the Deaf.

Padden, C. (1986). American Sign Language. In J. Van Cleve (Ed.), *Encyclopedia of Deaf people and deafness* (pp. 93–102) New York: McGraw-Hill.

Padden, C. (1988). The interaction of morphology and syntax in American Sign Language. *Outstanding dissertations in linguistics, Series IV.* New York: Garland Press.

Padden, C., & Humphries, T. (1988). *Deaf in America: Voices from a culture.* Cambridge, MA: Harvard University Press.

Pintner, R., Eisensen, J., & Stanton, M. (1946). *The psychology of the physically handicapped.* New York: Crofts.

Pintner, R., & Reamer, J. F. (1920). A mental and educational survey of schools of the Deaf. *American Annals of the Deaf, 65,* 451.

Pollard, R. Q. (1993). 100 years in psychology and deafness: A centennial retrospective. *Journal of the American Deafness and Rehabilitation Association, 26,* 32–46.

Remvig, J. (1969). Deaf-mutism and psychiatry. *Acta Scandinavica, Supplementum,* 210.

Remvig, J. (1972). Psychic deviations of the prelingual deaf. *Scandinavian Audiology, 1,* 35–42.

Robinson, L. D. (1978). *Sound minds in a soundless world.* (HEW Publication No. ADM 77–560). Washington, DC: U.S. Government Printing Office.

Sacks, O. (1989). *Seeing voices: A journey into the world of the Deaf.* Berkeley, CA: University of California Press.

Schlesinger, H. S., & Meadow, K. P. (1972). *Sound and sign: Childhood deafness and mental health.* Berkeley, CA: University of California Press.

Shafqat, C. (1986). Unpublished manuscript, Golden West College, Huntingdon Beach, California.

Stansfield, M. (1981). Psychological issues in mental health interpreting. *R.I.D. Interpreting Journal, 1,* 18–32.

Stansfield, M., & Veltri, D. (1987). Assessment from the perspective of the sign language interpreter. In H. Elliot, L. Glass, & J. W. Evans. (Eds.). *Mental health assessment of deaf clients* (153–164). Boston: Little, Brown.

Stokoe, W. C., Casterline, D., & Croneberg, C. G. (1976). *A dictionary of American Sign Language.* Silver Spring, MD: Linstok Press. (Original work published 1965).

Tavormina, J. B., Boll, T. J., Dunn, N. J., Luscomb, R. L., & Taylor, J. R. (1981). Psychosocial effects on parents raising a physically handicapped child. *Journal of Abnormal Child Psychology, 9,* 121–131.

Vernon, M. (1978). Deafness and mental health: Some theoretical views. *Gallaudet Today, 9,* 9–13.

Vernon, M. (1980). Perspectives on deafness and mental health. *Journal of Rehabilitation of the Deaf, 13,* 9–14.

Vernon, M., & Andrews, J. (1990). *The psychology of deafness: Understanding Deaf and hard of hearing people.* New York: Longman.

Vernon, M., & Makowsky, B. (1969). Deafness and minority group dynamics. *Deaf American, 21,* 3–6.

Wechsler, D. (1991). *Manual for the Wechsler Intelligence Scale for Children-III.* San Antonio, TX: The Psychological Corporation.

Wechsler, D. (1989). *Manual for the Preschol and Primary Scale of Intelligence-Revised.* San Antonio, TX: The Psychological Corporation.

Wechsler, D. (1981). *Manual for the Wechsler Adult Intelligence Scale-Revised.* San Antonio, TX: The Psychological Corporation.

Wechsler, D. (1974). *Manual for the Wechsler Intelligence Scale for Children-Revised.* San Antonio, TX: The Psychological Corporation.

Wixtrom, C. (1988). Two views of deafness. *The Deaf American, 38,* 21.

Woodward, J. (1972). Implications for sociolinguistic research among the deaf. *Sign Language Studies, 1,* 1–7.

Woodward, J. (1982). *How you gonna get to heaven if you can't talk to Jesus? On depathologizing deafness.* Silver Spring, MD: TJ.

Woodward, J., & Markowicz, C. (1975). Synchronic variation and historical change in American Sign Language. *Language Sciences, 37,* 9–12.

Yachnik, M. (1986). Self-esteem in deaf adolescents. *American Annals of the Deaf, 131,* 305–310.

Index

AA. *See* Alcoholics Anonymous
Abel, T. M., 68, 77, 96
Acculturation, 18, 25, 28, 39, 40, 42–47, 53
  and alcohol abuse, 219–221
  and cancer, 48
  and coronary heart disease, 48
  and depression, 49–50, 178
  and refugees, 51–52
  and schizophrenia, 50
Achenbach, T. M., 292, 294–295, 304, 309, 335, 339
Acocella, J. 22
Advanced Progressive Matrices, 77
Akhtar, S., 134, 145
Al-Issa, I. 144, 145, 249, 251, 256, 263, 289, 309
Albee, G. W., 4, 6, 16, 30
Alcohol Abuse, 215
  assessment, 218–219
  behavioral model, 232
  definitions, 217–219, 223
  disease model, 229
  educational model, 231
  help seeking, 221–228
  prevalence, 216
  spiritual model, 230

  systems model, 231
  therapeutic relationship, 235
  traditional healing, 237
  treatment groups, 236
  treatment goals, 234
Alcoholics Anonymous, 223, 229–232
Allison, K. W., 9, 15, 30
Allodi, F., 353–354, 361, 370
Allodi Trauma Scale, 361
Alloy, L. B., 22, 30
Allport, G. W., 62, 95, 96
Altmaier, E. M., 23, 30
American Psychiatric Association, 128, 132, 152, 160, 163, 247, 251, 292, 393
American Psychological Association, 3, 5, 12, 15, 19–25, 29
American Sign Language, 379–380, 383– 384, 386–387, 391–392, 394–395
Ammerman, R. T., 334, 339
Anastasi, A., 77, 96, 182, 209
Andrews, J., 381, 387–388, 390, 392–394
Anxiety, 127
  agoraphobia, 129, 130, 136
  Atague de nervios, 136
  behavioral treatment, 141–142
  brain-fag syndrome, 134, 179

Anxiety, (*continued*)
  drug therapy, 144
  generalized anxiety disorder, 129
  isolated sleep paralysis, 142
  Kayak-angst, 136
  Koro, 136, 179
  linguistic factors, 130
  obsessive-compulsive disorder, 132–134
  panic disorder, 128–129
  phobias, 129–130
  prevalence, 28–134
  purity mania, 133
  Shinkeishitsu, 135
  Shuk yang, 136
  situational factors, 130
  social phobia, 129
  test, 138
Anxiety Disorder Interview Schedule, 359
APA. *See* American Psychiatric Association
  or American Psychological Association
APM. *See* Advanced Progressive Matrices
ASL. *See* American Sign Language

Bandura, A., 25, 30, 233, 239
Baptiste, D. A., Jr., 301–304, 310
Bayton, J. A., 19, 31
BDI. *See* Beck Depression Inventory
Bebbington, P. E., 107, 188, 197, 208–209
Beck, A. T., 111, 121, 184–185, 191, 203,
  209, 233, 335, 239, 339
Beck Depression Inventory, 49, 191–192,
  335
Beck, S. J., 68, 96
Beiser, M., 29, 31, 51–53, 54, 141, 145, 201,
  289, 296, 301, 303, 307–308, 310, 356
Belar, C. D., 6, 31
Bellack, A. S., 14
BEMA. *See* Board of Ethnic Minority
  Affairs
Ben-Porath, Y. S., 66–67, 96, 335
Ben-Tovim, D. I., 161, 169
Bennett, L. A., 218–219, 222, 239
Bernal, M. E., 9, 11–13, 15, 20, 22, 31
Bernhardt, K. S., 6, 8, 31
Bernstein, D. A., 14
Berry, J. W., 8, 18–19, 25, 28, 29, 31, 39–
  40, 42–47, 49–50, 54–55, 74–76, 78,
  96, 110, 120, 121, 130, 220, 240, 291,
  304, 310, 320, 334–335, 339, 349, 367–
  368
Betancourt, H., 9, 19, 21, 31, 228, 238, 240

Bickman, L., 6, 12, 15, 31
Binet, A., 72, 97
Birchwood, M., 255, 263
BITE. *See* Bulimic Investigatory Test
Blanchard, E. B., 359, 370
Bleuler, E., 68, 97, 246
Bleuler, M., 68, 97
Board of Ethnic Minority Affairs, 23
Bond, M., 14, 31, 55
Bootzin, R. R., 22
Bornemann, T., 51
Boulder Model, 4–5
Brant, C. C., 226, 235, 240, 258
Bridges, J. W., 8
Brislin, R. W., 18, 25, 27, 31, 46, 55, 65–66,
  97
Brouwers, M. C., 108–109, 121
Brown, G. W., 196, 199, 209
Bulimic Investigatory Test, 160
Burnam, M. A., 18, 31, 50, 55
Burvill, P. W., 50, 55
Butcher, J. N., 22, 29, 31, 63–66, 83, 97,
  334–335, 340, 361, 371, 391, 397

Caetano, R., 216, 219–220, 222, 226, 240
California School of Professional
  Psychology, 20, 22
Camberwell Family Interview, 253
Canadian Psychological Association, 5, 8,
  23, 29
CAR. *See* Cross-cultural Applicability
  Research
Carpenter, W. J., 248, 264
Carson, R. C., 22, 32
Carstairs, G. M., 141
Carter, J., 392
Cattell, R. B., 137, 146
Centre for Epidemiological Studies
  Depression Scale, 193–194
CES-D. *See* Centre for Epidemiological
  Studies Depression Scale
Chandrasena, R., 248, 264
Cheung, F. M., 67, 97, 201, 210
Child Abuse and Neglect Interview
  Schedule, 334
Child Behavior Checklist, 294, 335
Child Institute of Child Health, 291
Child Psychopathology, 289
  attention-deficit hyperactivity disorder,
    295–296
  autism and childhood psychosis, 299

biculturalism and, 307–309
conduct and behavior disorders, 292–295
depression and suicide, 296–297
eating disorders, 299
fears and anxieties, 297–299
prevalence, 290–291
protective factors, 305–307
risk factors, 300–305
Chinese Values Survey, 48
Chung, R., 51, 55
CICH. *See* Child Institute of Child Health
CIDI. *See* Composite International
Diagnostic Instrument
Clark, K., 5
Clark, L. A., 9, 17, 19, 22, 32, 67, 97, 241,
317
Clements, C. B., 23, 32
Coffey, G. J., 248–249, 253, 264
Cohen, A., 254, 255, 264
Colored Progressive Matrices, 77
Comas-Diaz, L., 29, 32
Composite International Diagnostic
Instrument, 184, 188
Conners, C. K., 296, 311
Conners Teacher Rating Scale, 296
Constantino, A., 13, 18, 29, 219, 290, 311
Costello, E. J., 296, 311
CPA. *See* Canadian Psychological
Association
CPM. *See* Colored Progressive Matrices
Crisp, A. H., 161, 170
Cross-cultural Applicability Research, 217
CSPP. *See* California School of Professional
Psychology
Cultural assessment
emic perspective, 62
etic perspective, 62
Cultural psychology
collectivism, 17–18
cultural pluralism, 17–18
emic approach, 17–18
Culture Fair Intelligence Scale, 77

Dahlquist, L. M., 11, 14–15, 32, 115–116, 121
Dahlstrom, W. A., 67, 361, 391
Dana, R. H., 18, 23, 29, 32, 335, 341
Dasen, P. R., 39–40, 55, 74, 76, 120
Davison, G. C., 246–247, 264
De Vos, G. A., 68, 98
Deafness, 377
affective disorders, 393

assessment strategies, 389–392
autism, 393
cultural perspective, 377–380
identity, 384
interpreters, 386–387
language, 380
medical perspective, 377–380
organic factors, 393
paranoid disorders, 393
prevalence, 384–385
role of psychology, 396–397
rules of behavior, 383
schizophrenia, 392
service issues, 394–396
traditions, 384
treatment strategies, 394
values, 381–382
Depression, 128–129, 177
assessment of, 182–184
biological treatment, 203–205
cognitive-behavior therapy, 203
cultural formulation, 180–182
diagnosis, 179
interpersonal therapy, 205
linguistic barriers, 202–203
prevalence, 194–198
psychoanalytic therapy, 205
psychoeducational approach, 206
relativist perspective, 199
self-report measures, 190–194
structured interviews, 184–190
treatment planning, 202
universalist perspective, 199
Derogatis, L. R., 360–361, 371
Dexamethasone Suppression Test, 204
Diagnostic and Statistical Manual of the
American Psychiatric Association
I, 128, 180
II, 180
III, 128–129, 132–133, 160–161, 163, 180,
292, 393
III-R, 160, 163, 180, 189, 359–360
IV, 127, 136, 142, 152, 179–180, 199–
200, 217, 292, 295–296, 299–300, 351–
352, 359, 393
Diagnostic Interview Schedule, 129, 184,
187, 218, 252, 359
Diagnostic Schedule for Children and
Adolescents, 361
DICA. *See* Diagnostic Schedule for Children
and Adolescents

DiClemente, C. C., 337, 341
DiNicola, V. F., 165, 170, 299, 311
DIS. *See* Diagnostic Interview Schedule
Dobson, D. J. G., 3, 15, 32
Dobson, K. S., 3, 6, 15, 32
Draguns, J. A., 65, 98, 193, 289, 311
DSM. *See* Diagnostic and Statistical Manual
    of the American Psychiatric Association
DST. *See* Dexamethasone Suppression Test
Dutton, D. G., 325, 338, 341
Dutton, M. A., 334–335, 336, 337, 341

EAT. *See* Eating Attitudes Test
Eating Attitudes Test, 159–160
Eating Disorders, 152
    addiction oriented therapy, 167
    amenorrhea, 158
    anorexia nervosa, 157
    binge eating, 157
    body size, 153–155
    bulimia nervosa, 152, 167
    cognitive behavioral therapy, 167
    dieting, 155–157
    Kiberashi-gui, 157
    prevalence, 161–165
    psychodynamic/interpersonal therapy, 167
    psychoeducation, 167
    self help approach, 167
    single issue therapy, 167
    sociocultural hypothesis, 165–166
ECA. *See* Epidemiological Catchment Area
    Study
Egli, E., 63, 98
EIWA. *See* Escala de Intelligencia Wechsler
    para Adoltos
Ekman, P., 186, 210
Ellis, A., 111, 121
EMAS. *See* Endler Multidimensional
    Anxiety Scales
EMIC. *See* Explanatory Model Interview
    Catalogue
Endler, N. S., 130, 137–138, 146
Endler Multidimensional Anxiety Scales, 138
Epidemiological Catchment Area Study,
    129–130, 132
Erikson, E., 111, 121, 311
Escala de Intelligencia Wechsler para
    Adoltos, 75
Escobar, J. I., 18, 50, 204, 210, 250, 252,
    260, 264
Exner, J. E., 68–71, 98

Explanatory Model Interview Catalogue, 198
Eyberg, S. M., 335, 341
Eyberg Child Behavior Inventory, 335
Eysenck, H. J., 74, 98

Fabrega, H., Jr., 256, 264, 271–272, 284
Family violence, 316
    clinical approach, 334–338
    community approach, 327–334
    definition, 317–320
    prevalence, 320–325
    theoretical perspectives, 325–327
Fear Survey Schedule for Children, 297
Feighner, J. P., 160, 170
Fernando, M. L. D., 29, 337, 341, 364,
    372
Finkelhor, D., 316, 318, 321, 341
Five Minute Speech Sample, 253
Folkman, S., 47, 56
Fox, R. E., 7, 32
Fried, R., 68, 70, 98
Friedman, M., 51, 55
Friedman, S., 141–143, 146, 311
Furnham, A., 46, 50, 55, 154–155

Gardner, H., 72–73, 98
Garfield, S. L., 7, 32
Garfinkel, P. E., 152–153, 155–156, 159–
    163, 165, 171
Garner, D. M., 152–156, 159–163, 165, 167,
    171
Garro, L. C., 281
Gelles, R. J., 317–318, 321 323, 325, 337,
    341–342
General Health Questionnaire, 361
George, L., 257, 264
Gladwin, T., 62, 98
Goldstein, A. P., 16, 32
Goodenough-Harris Drawing Test, 77
Gotlib, I. H., 192, 210
Graham, J. R., 67, 335, 361, 391
Graves, T., 42, 56
Gray-Little, B., 62, 98
Griffith, E. E. H., 29, 56
Groth-Marnat, G. 252, 264

HABDI. *See* Hmong Adaptation of the Beck
    Depression Inventory
Haj-Yahia, M. M., 319, 336, 342
Hallowell, A. I., 68, 99, 131, 147
Halmi, K. A., 165, 171

HALS. *See* Health and Activities Limitations
   Survey
Hamilton, M., 184, 211
Hamilton Rating Scale for Depression, 184,
   188–189
Hartman, H., 111, 122
Hathaway, S. R., 4, 6, 33
Harvard Trauma Questionnaire, 335, 359,
   361
Hays, P. A., 13, 29, 33
Health and Activities Limitations Survey,
   385
Health Psychology
   derived etic approach, 40–41
   emic approach, 40
   imposed etic approach, 40
Helman, C., 41, 56, 284
Herman, C. P., 155–156, 172
Hersch, C., 4–6, 33
Hersen, M., 14, 289, 334, 33
Hills, H. I., 15, 33
Hirsch, S. R., 255, 261, 264
Hiskey-Nebraska Test of Learning Aptitude,
   390
Hmong Adaptation of the Beck Depression
   Inventory, 360
Ho, D. Y. F., 17–18, 33, 113–115, 298, 311,
   322
Hofstede, G., 109, 122
Hogarty, G. E., 261, 264
Holzman, W., 51, 56
Home Observation for Measurement of the
   Environment, 334
Hopkins Symptom Checklist-25, 360–361
Hough, R. L., 18, 50
HRSD. *See* Hamilton Rating Scale for
   Depression
HSC-25. *See* Hopkins Symptom Checklist-25
Hsu, L. K. G., 163, 172, 299, 312
Humphries, T., 378, 398

ICD. *See* International Classification of
   Disease
Isaac, P. D., 19, 33
Ibrahim, F. A., 113, 117, 122
Impact of Event Scale, 335
Inouye, D., 296, 312
Intelligence
   emic perspective, 74
   etic perspective, 74
Intercultural training, 27

International Classification of Disease-8, 248
International Classification of Disease-9,
   179, 189
International Classification of Disease-10,
   127
Interpersonal Therapy, 205
IPT. *See* Interpersonal Therapy

Jablensky, A., 127, 147, 189, 211, 251–252,
   254–255, 265
Jaffe, P. G., 337, 342–343
Jahoda, G., 19, 33
Jaranson, J. M., 29, 33, 372
Jayasuriya, L., 46, 56
Jones, J. M., 10, 20–21, 33
Joseph, L. W., 29, 362

Kagitcibasi, G., 18, 75, 99
Kaiser, A. S., 183
Karno, M., 10, 18, 33, 50, 147, 196, 211,
   247, 253, 255, 265
Katz, R., 183, 188, 191, 211
Kazarian, L. Z., 329, 331, 332, 343
Kazarian, S. S., 23, 28, 29, 33, 247, 253,
   261, 265, 334, 335, 337, 343, 362, 364,
   372
Kazdin, A. E., 14, 190, 211
Kessler, R. C., 129, 147
Khantzian, E. J., 230–231, 243
Kiddie Schedule for Affective Disorders and
   Schizophrenia, 361
Kiesler, C. A., 7, 34
Kim, U., 18, 26, 28, 34, 46–47, 56, 110,
   122, 320, 334
Kimble, G. A., 6, 34
Kinzic, J. D., 352–358, 360–364
Kinzie, J. D., 182, 190–191, 193–194, 211,
   372–373
Kirmayer, L., 41, 56, 181, 201, 211, 298,
   312
Kleinman, A., 41, 56, 131, 139, 141, 159,
   172, 178–179, 182, 185, 190, 194–198,
   200–201, 203–204, 211–212, 255–256,
   263, 270
Klerman, G., 205
Klonoff, E., 40
Klopfer, B., 68, 99
Kluckhon, C., 113, 122
Kohut, H., 111, 122
Korbin, J., 316, 318–323, 325, 343
Korchin, S. J., 9, 10, 34

Korman, M. 6, 15, 34
Koss, M. P., 316–318, 321–322, 327, 334, 338, 343
Kraeplin, E., 246
KSADS. *See* Kiddie Schedule for Affective Disorders and Schizophrenia
Kuiper, N. A., 325–326, 334, 342
Kurtz, R., 7

Lader, M., 128–129
LaFromboise, T., 11, 25, 28, 34, 192, 306, 312
Lambert, W. E., 274, 285, 312
Landmark, J., 256
Landrine, H., 40, 56
Lane, H., 382–383, 391
Langue Des Signes Quebecois, 379
Larsen, R. M., 64
Lazarus, R. S., 47, 56
Lee, E., 46–47, 50, 122, 373
Lee, S., 157–158, 160, 164, 166, 173
Leighton, D. C., 132, 147
Leitner International Performance Scale, 77, 390
Level of Expressed Emotions Scale, 253
Lewis, A., 127, 148
Lonner, W. J., 65, 99
Lopez, S. R., 9, 19, 21, 99, 228, 238
LSQ. *See* Langue Des Signes Quebecois
Lubin, B., 64, 99

Mahgoub, O. M., 132, 134, 148
Mainstream psychology
  etic approach, 17–18
  individualism, 17–18
  monoculture, 17–18
Major Depressive Episode, 180
Malgady, R. G., 13, 18, 29, 34, 219, 290, 320
Malik, S. B., 248, 265
Malla, A. K., 247, 253, 261
Malzberg, B., 46–47, 50, 56
Mann, J. W., 49, 56
Manos, N., 67, 99–100
Marin, G., 13–14, 34, 224, 226, 229, 232
Marks, I. M., 128–129, 148
Marlatt, G. A., 233
Marsella, A. J., 63, 65, 100, 212
Matarazzo, J., 64
Mather, J. A., 257, 265
Mavreas, V. G., 107, 123, 148

May, R., 112, 127, 148
Mayne, T. J., 15,
Mazmanian, D., 12
McGill Pain Questionnaire, 274–275
McHolland, J., 11, 17, 19–20, 22, 34
MCMI-II. see Millon Clinical Multiaxial Inventory
McNeil, E. B., 17, 34
Meller, P. J., 29
Melzack, R., 274, 283, 285, 361
Merskey, H., 256–257
Michenbaum, D., 111, 123
Milich, R., 14
Miller, W. R., 228, 236, 243
Millon, T., 335, 344
Millon Clinical Multiaxial Inventory, 335
Mineka, S., 22
Minnesota Multiphasic Personality Inventory, 64–67, 76, 78–79, 96, 335, 361, 390–391
  basic and supplementary scales profile, 81
  content scales profile, 82
  interpretive report, 83–85, 93–94
  validity pattern, 80
Minority Relations Practices Survey, 11
MMPI-2. *See* Minnesota Multiphasic Personality Inventory
Mollica, R. F., 107, 123, 298, 313, 335, 344, 351–354, 360–363, 374
MPQ. *See* McGill Pain Questionnaire
MRPS. *See* Minority Relations Practices Survey
Munakata, T., 257–258, 260, 265
Murphy, H. B. M., 41, 46, 50, 56–57, 131, 144, 148, 201, 212, 254
Myers, C. R., 3
Myers, H., 193, 198–200, 204, 212

Nasser, M., 157–158, 160, 164–165, 168, 173
Nathan, P. E., 22, 317
National Centre for Health Statistics, 384
National Council of Schools of Professional Psychology, 20
NCHS. *See* National Centre for Health Statistics
NCSPP. *See* National Council of Schools of Professional Psychology
Neale, J. M., 246–247, 252, 265
Nemiah, J. C., 132, 148
Netzel, M. T., 14, 35

Neufeld, R. W. J., 246–247, 252, 255, 257, 262–263, 265–266
Nicholson, I. R., 246–247, 249, 252, 255, 262, 266
Nogami, Y., 157, 166, 174
Norcross, J. C., 7–8, 35

Oberg, K., 46, 57
Odegaard, O. 50, 57
Offord, D. R., 293, 306, 309, 313
Okasha, A., 132, 134, 141, 148, 157, 174
Okazaki, S. 62, 100
Olmedo, E. L., 10, 19, 35, 45
Olmstead, M. P., 152, 156, 160, 162, 165, 167, 174
O'Leary, K. D., 22, 317

Padden, C., 380–384
Padilla, A. M., 9, 12–13, 15–16, 22, 25, 29, 35, 130, 148, 220, 302
Pain, 267
    biopsychosocial perspective, 282
    cancer, 280
    children, 276
    chronic, 274
    in the clinic, 270–274
    in the laboratory, 268–270
    prevalence, 279–280
    women, 277
Pancheri, P., 65
Paykel, E. S., 198–199, 212
Payton, C. R., 23, 35
Pedersen, P. B., 113, 115–118, 123, 177–178, 212, 313
Perls, F., 112, 123
Pernice, R., 29, 35, 375
Persad, E., 12, 34
Petersen, D. R., 5, 6, 35
Pfeiffer, W., 136, 149
Phares, E. J., 14, 35
Pilowsky, I., 272, 285
Polgar, S., 41, 57
Polivy, J., 155–156, 160, 174
Ponterotto, J. G., 9–11, 19, 21, 29, 35, 302, 308, 313
Poortinga, U. H., 39, 74, 76, , 100, 120
Post Traumatic Inventory, 359
Post Traumatic Stress Disorder, 51, 335
Present State Examination, 133, 141, 184, 187, 248, 252–253
Prince, R., 134–135, 149, 165, 174

Prochaska, J. O., 7–8, 337, 345
PSE. *See* Present State Examination
Psychotherapy, 8, 106, 110
    behavioral, 8
    cognitive-behavioral, 106, 111, 113–114
    eclectic, 8
    existential/humanistic, 8, 106, 112–114
    Gestalt, 8
    interpersonal relations, 8
    practice, 115–117
    Psychoanalytic, 8
    psychodynamic, 106, 111, 113–114
    rational-emotive, 8
    Reality, 8
    Rogerian, 8
    social learning, 8
    systems, 8
    training, 118–121
    value-orientations model, 113–115
PTSD. *See* Post Traumatic Stress Disorder

Rachman, S. J., 128
Radloff, L. S., 191, 193, 213, 296, 313
Raimey, V., 4, 35
Ramirez, M., III, 29, 35, 306–307, 313
Rangaraj, A., 52, 57
Rappaport, H., 29, 35
Rappaport, M., 29, 35
Rasmussen, S. A., 132, 149
Raven, J. C., 77, 100
Raven Progressive Matrices, 77–78, 88, 92, 96
Redfield, R., 42, 57
Refugees, 348
    assessment of, 357–358
    assessment tools, 358–361
    children, 355–356
    community mental health model, 362
    definition, 348
    family violence, 355
    post traumatic stress disorder, 351–352
    primary health care clinic model, 362
    primary prevention, 367–368
    psychiatric model, 362
    service utilization, 368–369
    stressors, 349
    substance abuse, 354
    torture, 353–353
    treatment, 363–367
Richard, H. C.,23
Ritchie, P., 6, 36

Robins, L. N., 129, 149, 184, 187–188, 213, 217–218, 244, 359, 375
Rogers, C., 112, 119, 123
Rogler, L. H., 13, 18, 29, 36, 45, 57, 183, 187, 213, 219, 228, 237, 244, 290, 306, 313, 320, 335, 345
Rollman, G. B., 267, 285
Rorschach, 67, 76, 78, 96, 390
   Beck system, 68–69
   Comprehensive system, 69–71
   interpretive report, 79–88, 93–94
   Kataguchi system, 68–69
   Klopfer system, 68–69
   Piotrowski system, 68, 70
   protocol, 102–105
   Rappaport system, 68–69
Rouse, S., 64
RPM. See Raven Progressive Matrices
Rumbaut, R., 51, 57
Russell, J. G., 135, 149
Russo, N. F., 10–11, 36
Rutter, M., 291, 293, 305, 307, 314

SADD-5. See Standardized Assessment of Depressive Disorders-5
SAD-L. See Schedule for Affective Disorders and Schizophrenia-Lifetime Version
Santiego-Negron, S., 15, 36
Sarason, B. R., 22, 36
Sarason, I. A., 22, 36
Sartorius, N., 40, 179, 184, 188–189, 196–197, 208, 213, 218, 254, 266
Sattler, J. M., 29, 36, 72, 77, 101, 290, 314
Sayette, M. A., 15, 36
Scarf, M., 323–324, 346
Schedule for Affective Disorders and Schizophrenia-Lifetime Version, 129
Schizophrenia, 246
   assessment of, 256–257
   course, 251, 254–256
   diagnosis, 257–258
   expressed emotion, 253–255, 261
   family structure, 260
   family therapy, 261
   first rank symptoms, 247–248, 252–253
   individual therapy, 261
   language, 261
   phenomenology, 248–251
   prevalence, 251

   psychoeducational approach, 261
   psychopharmacological treatment, 261
   rapport, 260
   religious beliefs, 258–259
   role of psychology, 262
Schmidt, F. L., 29, 36
Schneider, K., 247
Schofield, W., 16, 36
SCID. See Structured Clinical Interview Diagnostic Instrument
SCL-D. See Symptom Check List-Depression
Segall, M. H., 23, 36, 39, 62, 74, 76, 101, 120
Self Disclosure, 106
   collectivism, 109
   Eastern culture, 107–109, 117
   individualism, 109
   Western Culture, 107–109, 117
Self Rating Inventory for Post Traumatic Stress Disorder, 359–360
Seligman, M., 52, 57, 128, 149
Sendin, C., 68, 71, 101
Shakow, D., 4, 6, 8, 36
Shaw, B. F., 183, 185
Shoham, S. G., 26, 36
Sigelman, C., 222–224, 226, 244
SIP. See Self Rating Inventory for Post Traumatic Stress Disorder
Sixteen Personality Factor Questionnaire (16 PF), 391
SOMP. See System of Multicultural Pluralistic Assessment
Sorentino, R. M., 108, 123–124
Spearman, C. E., 72, 101
Spielberger, C. D., 137–140, 149–150, 297, 314
Spitzer, R. L., 182, 184, 189, 213, 218, 244, 335, 360, 375
SPM. See Standard Progressive Matrices
Sroufe, L. A., 291, 314
STAI. See State Trait Anxiety Inventory
STAIC. See State Trait Anxiety Inventory for Children
Standard Progressive Matrices, 77
Standardized Assessment of Depressive Disorders-5, 184, 189
State Trait Anxiety Inventory, 137–138, 140
State Trait Anxiety Inventory for Children, 137, 297

Steinmetz, S., 318, 321
Sternbach, R. A., 268–269, 285
Sternberg, R. J., 72–74, 101
Straus, M. A., 318, 321, 323, 339, 346
Strauss, J. S., 248
Stressful Life Events Scale for Youth, 361
Stricker, G., 17, 36–37
Strickland, B. R., 4, 37
Strozier, A. L., 15
Structured Clinical Interview Diagnostic
    Instrument, 184, 189, 218, 335, 360
Stunkard, A. J., 153–154, 160, 175
Suarez-Balcazar, Y., 9, 37
Sue, S., 9, 12, 16–17, 19, 29, 37, 62, 107,
    110, 113–116, 118, 124, 150, 228, 244,
    300, 314
Sue, D. W., 15, 29, 37, 107–110, 113–116,
    118, 124, 130, 150, 202, 213
Sussman, S. I., 12, 34
Suzuki, L. A., 29, 37, 182, 213
Symptom Check List-Depression, 360–361
System of Multicultural Pluralistic
    Assessment, 290
Szapocznik, J., 116, 124
Szatmari, P., 295, 314
Szmukler, G. I., 161, 175–176

TAI. See Test Anxiety Inventory
Taijinkyofusho, 135
TASK. See Test Anxiety Scale for Children
Tell Me a Story, 290
Telles, C. E., 18, 50
TEMAS. See Tell Me a Story
Test Anxiety Inventory, 139–140
Test Anxiety Scale for Children, 139
Thorndike, R., 65, 72–73, 101
Toukmanian, S., 119–120, 124
Triandis, H. C., 18, 25–26, 37, 109–110,
    113, 124, 333, 346
Trimble, J. E., 215–217, 244–245
TSK. Taijinkyofusho
Tursky, B., 268–269, 285
Tyler, F. B., 18, 37

UNESCO. See United Nations Educational,
    Scientific and Cultural Organization
UNHCR. See United Nations High
    Commission for Refugees
United Nations Educational, Scientific and
    Cultural Organization, 43

United Nations High Commission for
    Refugees, 51, 349

VandenBos, G. R., 12, 37
VDS. See Vietnamese Depression Scale
Velasquez, R., 62, 101
Vernon, M., 381, 387–388, 390, 392–394,
    399–400
Vietnamese Depression Scale, 194, 360–361
Vives, M., 71, 101
Vollick, D., 255, 262

WAIS-R. See Wechsler Adult Intelligence
    Scale-Revised
Walker, C. E., 14, 37
Walker, L., 323–324, 334, 347
War Trauma Scale, 361
Ward, C., 45, 57
Watts, R. J., 9, 37
Waxer, P. H., 124, 214, 301, 314
Webster, E. C., 6, 37
Wechsler, D., 73–74, 101, 390, 400
Wechsler Adult Intelligence Scale-Revised,
    74–75, 390
Wechsler Intelligence Scale for Children-III,
    74, 76, 390
Wechsler Intelligence Scale for Children-
    Revised, 390
Wechsler Preschool and Primary Scale of
    Intelligence, 74
Wechsler Preschool and Primary Scale of
    Intelligence-Revised, 390
Weil, R., 17, 38
Weissman, M. M., 128–129, 133–134, 150,
    205, 214
Westermeyer, J., 29, 38, 46, 51, 57, 184,
    192, 203, 214, 221, 245, 348, 352, 355,
    360–361, 376
WHO. See World Health Organization
Wiggins, J., 3, 38
Williams, C. L, 29, 38, 51, 57, 67, 291, 302–
    303, 306, 314, 335, 349–350, 358, 367–
    368, 376
Williams, K. E., 141–143, 150, 218
Williamson, P. C., 247, 263
Wilson, G. T., 22, 38, 347
Wing, J. K., 184, 187, 214
Winnicott, D., 111, 124
WISC-III. See Wechsler Intelligence Scale
    for Children-III

Witmer, L., 4
Wolfe, D. A., 321, 325, 334, 336–337, 347
Wolfe, V. V., 334, 338, 347
Wolff, B. B., 267–270, 286
Woodward, J., 378–380, 400
World Health Organization, 41, 127, 184, 189, 218
WPPSI. *See* Wechsler Preschool and Primary Scale of Intelligence
Wright, M. J., 3, 38
Wundt, W., 3

Yashida, T., 25, 27
Yates, A., 296, 315
Ying, Y. -W., 185, 194, 214

Young, M., 28, 266
Youth Adaptation Rating Scale, 361
Yutrzenka, B. A., 9, 21, 38

Zatzick, D. F., 269, 286
Zayas, L. H., 13, 38
Zborowski, M., 268, 270, 272–273, 286
ZDS. *See* Zung Self Rating Scale for Depression
Ziegler, D. K., 279, 286
Zola, I. K., 270–271, 286
Zubin, J., 247, 266
Zung, W. W. K., 191–192, 214
Zung Self Rating Scale for Depression, 49, 192–193, 360–361